A HISTORY OF SWEDISH LITERATURE

The American-Scandinavian Foundation and the University of Minnesota Press gratefully acknowledge the generous supplementary financial support toward publication of this volume of the Swedish Institute (Stockholm), the Anglo-Swedish Literary Foundation (London), and the Graduate School of the University of Minnesota

A HISTORY OF SWEDISH LITERATURE

BY Alrik Gustafson

Published for the American-Scandinavian Foundation
by the University of Minnesota Press   Minneapolis

PRINTED IN THE UNITED STATES OF AMERICA AT THE LUND PRESS, INC., MINNEAPOLIS

Library of Congress Catalog Card Number: 61-7722

PUBLISHED IN GREAT BRITAIN, INDIA, AND PAKISTAN BY THE OXFORD UNIVERSITY PRESS,
LONDON, BOMBAY, AND KARACHI, AND IN CANADA BY THOMAS ALLEN, LTD., TORONTO

Acknowledgments for permission to reproduce copyrighted material are herewith gratefully recorded: to George Allen & Unwin Ltd., London, for quotations from *A Selection from Modern Swedish Poetry*, tr. by C. D. Locock (London, 1929, 1936); to The New American Library of World Literature, Inc., for Richard B. Vowles's translation of Karl Vennberg's "Chronometry" in the eleventh issue of *New World Writing*, copyright 1957 by The New American Library of World Literature, Inc.; to Simon and Schuster, Inc. and Max Reinhardt, Ltd., for two passages from Gustaf Lannestock's translation of Vilhelm Moberg's *The Emigrants* (New York and London, 1951); to Caroline Schleef, for her translation from Dan Andersson's "The Prisoner" in *Charcoal-Burner's Ballad & Other Poems* (New York, 1943); and to Richard B. Vowles, for a number of his translations of modern Swedish verse.

TO MY FRIEND
Pär Lagerkvist

Preface

IT IS an enormously precarious task to write the history of a whole national literature, and more precarious to compress it within the covers of a single volume. How precarious the task is, perhaps only those few venturesome souls who have attempted it can know. The task bristles with problems of all kinds — problems of organization, of proper apportionment of space, of decisions involving the inclusion or exclusion of authors, of evaluations and judgments which engage one ultimately in such diverse conceptual complexes as aesthetic theory and philosophical speculation, political conflict and the intricacies of religious experience and thought. The task in the present instance is further complicated by the circumstance that the particular national literature under consideration has been written in a tongue foreign to the English-speaking audience for whom this book has been prepared. Add to this the fact that the chief glory of Swedish literature is its lyric poetry (the genre which most stubbornly yields its secrets to the labors of translator or interpreter), and it should be clear that the present writer can hardly pretend that he has done much more than brought his readers into the anterooms of that extensive edifice which harbors the treasures of Swedish literature. If he has succeeded at times in doing more, if he has at points penetrated farther than the anterooms and opened his readers' way into something like a genuine understanding of and feeling for the literature of Sweden at its best, he can but attribute whatever success he may have had to the spell which this literature has for many years cast over him.

Insuperable as certain of the difficulties of the literary historian may be, these difficulties are to some extent eased in the present instance by two considerations: first, that Swedish literature has maintained down through its thousand-year existence a sense of continuity which enables one to grasp it as a whole, as an organically developing cultural unit, and secondly, that this quality of continuity identifies itself more or less intimately with the general drift of a Western European culture familiar to all educated Englishmen and Americans. Though Swedish literature may seem at times to the "outsider" somewhat strange, possibly even a bit exotic, he will much more often recognize in this literature qualities and trends that appear in one way or other everywhere in the literature of Europe. Sweden has had, as we shall see, her Period of the Enlightenment under the aegis of French rationalism and English empiricism, her Romanticism under the spell of German philosophical idealism and English historicism, her late-nineteenth-century "realistic breakthrough" under the impact of French naturalism and English utilitarianism; and Swedish authors of our century have drunk deep from such seductive springs of literary "modernism" as the surrealism of France and the primitivism of America and of England's D. H. Lawrence. So closely, indeed, has the course of Swedish culture been tied in at one time or other with that of France or Germany or England — and in late years with certain literary trends in the United States — that an English-speaking reader of Swedish literature might be led to assume that Swedish culture is an essentially derivative, imitative culture, a culture incapable of asserting itself in its own terms, of creating its own idiom, its own peculiarly Swedish set of moods and values.

Actually, of course, this assumption is true only in a limited sense — in the sense that any highly civilized small nation such as Sweden is inevitably fated to follow in the main the cultural leads of her larger neighbors. But in following cultural leads from without, Sweden has not become so absorbed by them that she has lost a sense of her own national cultural destiny. The course of Sweden's literary history, especially in the later centuries of its development, provides sufficient evidence that Swedish genius is capable both of assimilating foreign cultural material for its own purposes and pursuing its own creative bent in distinctly fresh and original ways. The very *continuity* of Sweden's cultural development suggests that it has managed to preserve its own identity even while willingly — at times, indeed, eagerly — exposing itself to cultural currents originating outside its own borders.

Many of those Swedish authors who have been most profoundly attracted to foreign cultures have simultaneously identified themselves in one way or other with Sweden's own cultural traditions. "It is useful," the brilliant poet-critic Oscar Levertin once wrote with reference to his country's long-established literary tradition, "for a national culture to feel that it is 'not from yesterday' and that a nation's spiritual vitality is strengthened by a sense of living solidarity with the past." These are the words of a literary traditionalist, but not, it should be observed, of a narrow cultural nationalist, for though Levertin's poetic motifs and themes are not infrequently Swedish his thought is largely French-oriented. Levertin's poetry and criticism combine foreign and native elements, as does the work of many of his countrymen. Even Strindberg's restless modern genius, which fed so headily on foreign fare and reacted so violently against certain forms of Swedish traditionalism, was scarcely capable of freeing itself from the spell of his nation's past. Though Strindberg's recurrent (one might say persistent) preoccupation with this past can hardly be equated with a conventional traditionalism, and scarcely reflects what Levertin meant by "a sense of living *solidarity* with the past," it suggests in certain ways nevertheless some vital points of contact with the Swedish past. And among Swedish authors generally a sense of more or less living contact with the past persists despite their simultaneous willingness to open their arms to all manner of new, often revolutionary ideas.

In fact, the creative vitality of Swedish poetry and prose, particularly in the last century or two, may perhaps largely be accounted for in terms of a constantly maintained interplay between the old and the new, the traditional and the revolutionary or the potentially revolutionary. Generally the give and take of this interplay is neither sharp nor strident, and happy compromise rather than the clash of dogmas has determined the paths which Swedish literary developments were to take. But at times the interplay takes on the form of sharp conflict, the demand for change becomes insistent, with a consequent acceleration of literary developments attuned to the realistic exigencies of modern life. When, for instance, economic developments of the second half of the nineteenth century began to transform the face of Sweden and force social and political changes, literature met the challenge of the times by discarding the splendid poetic trappings of Romanticism and clothing itself for the most part in a sober, realistic, workaday prose. And even when, in the 1890's, a semi-romantic reaction against the realistic breakthrough of the 1880's took place, the reaction was in essence partial and temporary, serving in the main but to check the tradition-defying excesses of the 1880's and bring into a finer balance than hitherto the competing cultural demands of the past and the present. Swedish literature in our century has in consequence been able to go a kind of "middle way," joining the extremes of tradition and revolt in something of the same spirit as that which characterizes Sweden's social and political developments in our day.

But Sweden's literary development has not, as we shall see, achieved the relative maturity and balance of today without a struggle. Her literary growth has had its lapses, its periods of frustrations and sterility, its moments of petty squabbling, its abortive experiments of one kind or other. And yet her cultural resources have in the long run been sufficient to sustain down to our day a literary discipline of marked intelligence and sensitivity. Today, as in earlier centuries, Swedish literary talent struggles with the problems of form and idea which challenge to the utmost the skill and perceptive capacities of the creative artist. And though some may question whether the Sweden of our century has produced a genius of, say, the stature of a Bellman or a Strindberg, the number of Swedish authors of real distinction in the last fifty years is considerably greater than in any earlier period, and not a few of them are worthy of taking their places on the Swedish Parnassus alongside the greatest figures of an earlier day. Learning from the past while acutely aware of the urgent claims of the present and future, Swedish literary talent continues in our day to create with vigor and imagination, adding its measure of beauty and truth to the permanent treasures of Swedish culture. At times, even — as in the case of Pär Lagerkvist — Swedish literature today has provided an arresting voice in the cultural forum of the world.

In the chapters which follow I have not written a literary history in the limited sense, that is to say concerned myself all but exclusively with purely literary matters. Rather I have attempted to trace literary developments and throw light on literary figures in their relation to a dynamic, ever-changing Swedish society, its institutions, its traditions, its way of life. I have done so not only because literary *history* must concern itself with such matters but also because not many of my English-speaking readers are apt to be familiar with the political developments and social and economic conditions out of which Swedish literature has immediately grown. I may be permitted to add in this connection that I have at every point attempted to be as objective in my judgments as a literary historian is supposed to be. I am not, however, laboring under the illusion that absolute objectivity is possible — or for that matter in all cases desirable. At least not when one is dealing with the arts. Swedish literature has been to me down through the years of my concern with it something *more* than merely an object of study. It has provided me with pleasurable as well as painful sensations in the measure that it has aroused my unqualified admiration or given me cause to protest or at least to pause and wonder. I have therefore at times had to "take sides" — even on occasion to find myself in disagreement with literary judgments more or less universally accepted among Swedish readers and critics. It will, for instance, become apparent in my chapter on the Swedish Romantics that I am not *quite* as impressed by *some* of the poetry of Esaias Tegnér as are most of my Swedish colleagues.

I have taken every precaution, however, to guard against overhasty or prejudiced judgments and to insure accuracy in statements of fact. In my preparatory studies for the present book I have reread most of the works upon which I pass judgment, I have examined carefully much of the extensive, often brilliant Swedish criticism and scholarship on the authors concerned, and I have prevailed upon my colleagues both in Sweden and America to read portions of my manuscript and offer frank appraisal and criticism of it. Among the scholars and critics who have given generously of their time in the reading of those parts of my manuscript which cover the periods of their special competence are Professor Dag Strömbäck of the University of Uppsala, Professor Henry Olsson, Docent Örjan Lindberger, Docent Carl Reinhold Smedmark, and fil. lic. Inge Jonsson, all of the University of Stockholm, Docent Harald Elovsson of the University of Lund, Professor Gösta Franzén of the University of Chicago, and Professor Assar Janzén of the University of California at Berkeley. Docent Lindberger's readiness to examine with great care my three last chapters at a time when he himself was readying a manuscript for the press places me under a special debt of gratitude to him. Whatever success I may have had in avoiding factual errors and interpretative blunders may in no small measure be attributed to the rigorous examination to which my manuscript has been subjected at the hands of my colleagues, but whatever errors may still have passed unnoticed are, of course, my own responsibility.

The chapters of this book which have given me the greatest trouble are the first and the three last, the first because we know so little about the period with which it deals, the last three because we know so much. If the origins of Swedish literature leave the historian with a feeling of uneasiness because they are veiled in the almost impenetrable mists of an at best semi-historical past, the literature of our own day leaves one equally uneasy because in its clamorous, many-voiced immediacy it so mercilessly taxes our powers of discrimination and judgment. When the historian must grope desperately for the few facts which a distant past stubbornly yields, he is often forced to the expediency of speculation. When he is overwhelmed by the multiplicity of detail of the contemporary scene, he may be tempted to oversimplify in his effort to get some kind of order out of apparent chaos. To what extent I have managed to avoid these pitfalls I must leave to the experts among my readers to judge. Where honest differences of opinion among scholars exist, as is often the case in learned studies on the earlier periods, it has been my usual practice merely to note the existence of scholarly disagreement, and then go on to present the view which in a given instance seems to me most acceptable. It would seem clear that in a single-volume work aimed at the general reader an airing of the details of scholarly controversy hardly has a place.

Some of my more initiated readers may be disturbed by my failure to mention certain authors or works or by my relatively full treatment of certain figures at what might be considered the expense of others. I can but say in my own defense that I have done what I could within the covers of a single volume to include as many representative figures as possible and to distribute space among them as judiciously as I know how. In the matter of omissions I may add that I myself am as much disturbed as anyone is likely to be that I have not had the space at my disposal to deal in more detail than I have in the present book with Swedo-Finnish literature and with Swedish literary criticism generally as distinguished from purely creative literature. Interesting and worthy of attention as is that part of the literature of Finland written in the Swedish tongue, I have unhappily been compelled to ignore it except where, in two instances particularly — those of Runeberg and the "poetic moderns" of the 1920's — it has made its impact felt sharply across the Baltic to the West and contributed significantly to Swedish literature proper. The poetry of Runeberg has become as thoroughly assimilated into the literary bloodstream of both Sweden and Finland as, for instance, the comedies of Holberg have become the joint literary property of Denmark and Norway; and such arresting Swedo-Finnish poetic modernists as Edith Södergran and Elmer Diktonius have had a definitive influence in determining one of the principal directions which Swedish verse on both sides of the Baltic has taken in the last quarter century. To Runeberg I have given in consequence the full attention that he deserves in any history of Swedish literature, and as for the Swedo-Finnish modernists I have provided, I trust, sufficient space to clarify in general their role in guiding into new poetic paths a number of their distinguished contemporaries and successors in Sweden.

With regard to the rather extensive body of Swedish literary criticism, I have restricted myself largely, in the first place, to noting wherever appropriate the part taken by critics in the literary debates of their day, and secondly, to commenting briefly on the critical contributions of such author-critics as Atterbom, Levertin, and Anders Österling, Erik Blomberg, Artur Lundkvist, and Thorsten Jonsson. Much more could be (and possibly should have been) done with literary criticism as such, especially as it has been practiced in the last generation or two by, among others, such critics as Fredrik Böök and Olle Holmberg, Sven Stolpe and Knut Jaensson, Ivar Harrie, Margit Abenius, and Elisabeth Tykesson. But this would lead us, I feel, too far astray from our primary concern with literature itself, with the creative products of Swedish genius and near-genius as they appear in their manifold forms from generation to generation.

Occasionally I have in the present book stolen from myself, used with the permission of my publishers certain paragraphs or more extended passages which have previously appeared under my name in other books or journals that are out of print or no longer easily available.

It remains for me to say a word about verse translations as employed in these pages, to explain my practice in citing titles, and to express my appreciation to those (aside from the scholars mentioned above) who have contributed in one way or other to lightening my burden in the writing and seeing through the press of the present book.

Because the difficulties of the verse translator are innumerable, and he is in consequence only rarely equal to his task, I have taken care, when quoting Swedish verse in an English version, to employ the English version in question only if in my judgment it is on the whole a satisfactory approximation of the original. When no English (or no satisfactory English) version exists, I have provided an English version of my own. Finally, the point cannot be too often made — and emphasized sharply — that verse translations at best are only more or less satisfactory approximations of the original, and that only the reader who has mastered

Swedish can hope to experience the rare magic of really great Swedish poetry.

My usual practice in citing titles has been to give the original Swedish title when a work of book-length (a novel, a play, a longer poem) is first referred to in these pages, followed immediately within parentheses by an English translation of the title and the date of publication of the Swedish original. If the work has appeared in an English translation, the title of the translation is given *in italics* preceded by the abbreviation "tr." It should be noted that the date after the title of a given translation is that of the Swedish original, *not* the date of publication of the translation in question. After the first citation of the Swedish title it has usually been my practice to use only the English version of the title, italicized whether or not an English translation of the work in question has appeared. In a very few cases, such as that of Strindberg, where it might seem pedantic to provide both the Swedish titles of his most widely known works and their English equivalents, it has seemed best to employ only the English titles when referring to works with which an English-speaking reader may be expected to be familiar. For shorter works generally (lyric poems, short stories, essays), it has not been found practicable to indicate whether a given work exists in translation, but the List of Translations at the close of this volume provides the reader with considerable guidance in locating available English versions of the shorter literary genres.

Among the more satisfying pleasures which come to an author on the completion of a book is the opportunity to acknowledge his indebtedness to those who have assisted him along the way. Of the institutions to which I am particularly indebted, the American-Scandinavian Foundation was responsible for launching me on the project; the Swedish Institute at Stockholm and the Anglo-Swedish Literary Foundation of London have provided financial assistance which has enabled us to keep the price of the book within reason; two Stockholm publishers, Natur och Kultur and Bonniers, and the Swedish Institute have generously contributed illustrative material; the University of Minnesota, aside from providing ideal working conditions in the magnificent Scandinavian collections of the University Library, has facilitated my work by allowing me research grants and leaves of absence from teaching duties; and the University of Minnesota Press, as co-publisher with the American-Scandinavian Foundation of my book, has taken on the numerous responsibilities connected with its actual production. Of the individuals to whom I am most grateful I can mention here only a few, those who have been closest to my work at every stage in its development: Dr. Henry Goddard Leach of the American-Scandinavian Foundation, who originally suggested the project and has followed it with warm interest from its inception to its completion; Mr. Denzell Smith, my assistant, who has eased my task in innumerable ways; Miss Esther Peterson, Principal Librarian, whose promptness in making available to me current Swedish accessions to the University Library has been of great value, especially in the preparation of the last chapters of my book; and my wife, Cleyonne, who has never failed me in loyalty and sensitive understanding of my work. What, finally, I owe to the numerous company of Swedish critics and scholars who have preceded me in the challenging task of interpreting the treasures of Swedish poetry and prose only those who are familiar with the work of these critics and scholars can appreciate.

A. G.

Minneapolis
August 1960

Table of Contents

List of Illustrations

The early Germanic runic alphabet, 4. The two Scandinavian runic alphabets, 5. The Ramsundsberg rock carving, 9. Woodcut from Olaus Magnus's *Historia*, 1555, 64. Engraving from first edition of Stiernhielm's *Hercules*, 88. Title page of the first number of *Then svänska Argus*, 114. Vignettes from Bellman's *Fredmans Epistlar*, 132. Masthead of the first number of *Aftonbladet*, 200. Playbill for Strindberg's Intimate Theater, 272. Scene sketch by Strindberg for *A Dream Play*, 274. Drawing for *The Wonderful Adventures of Nils*, 313. Old country fiddler, 326. Vignette for *Word Art and Pictorial Art*, 395. Vignette by Harriet von Löwenhjelm for her *Poems*, 456.

BETWEEN PAGES 28 AND 29

Burial mounds, Old Uppsala, and rune stone, Litslena. Detail from *Äldre Västgötalagen*. Statue in wood of Saint Birgitta in Vadstena church. Medieval bride stealing, from *Der Renner*, ca. 1400.

BETWEEN PAGES 92 AND 93

Georg Stiernhielm. Title page from *Atland, eller Manheim*, 1679. Emanuel Swedenborg. Carl von Linné.

BETWEEN PAGES 156 AND 157

Carl Michael Bellman. Scene from modern revival of a sketch by Bellman. Johan Henric Kellgren. Anna Maria Lenngren. Erik Gustaf Geijer. Esaias Tegnér. Erik Johan Stagnelius.

A HISTORY OF SWEDISH LITERATURE

The Origins

THOUGH IT IS PROBABLE that there existed in Sweden a reasonably rich native literature before the introduction of Christianity into the country in the eleventh century, the actual survivals of such a literature are exceedingly few in number and scarcely of a high literary quality. Aside from some rock carvings reflecting well-known literary themes and a few runic inscriptions containing short poetic fragments of some distinction, it is only in the provincial laws (of ancient origin though not committed to writing until the thirteenth and fourteenth centuries) that we can discern indubitable evidences of an early Swedish literature. Unlike Denmark with its *Gesta Danorum*, and Norway, much of whose early literature has survived in a rich Icelandic literary tradition, Sweden must in the main resort to the precarious scholarly game of "literary reconstruction" in order to gain some notion of that largely hypothetical "lost" literature which — only in all *probability* — existed within her boundaries during pre-Christian times. Fortunately, the archaeologist's artifacts and historical remains for the early periods, together with the more or less direct testimony of certain Germanic sources outside Sweden (chiefly those of Norway-Iceland and England), enable us to more than merely "guess at" a one-time existent oral Swedish literature which has now all but entirely disappeared.

It is necessary, therefore, for one who proposes to sketch the first chapter in a history of Swedish literature to indulge to some extent in certain speculative, hypothetical considerations in order to suggest in broad outline something of what may have been the total picture of a primitive Swedish literature, only fragments of which have come down to us. But before attempting such a reconstruction, we should examine

3

the few evidences of actual literary survivals preserved in certain rock carvings and runic inscriptions.

This is scarcely the place in which to enter into the intricate complex of learned controversy which for a century has sought to solve the difficult problems connected with the origins of the runes — whether they derive from the Greek or the Latin alphabets or from a combination of both, and whether their geographical origins are to be traced to the northern shores of the Black Sea, which is probable, or to the regions immediately north of Italy. Suffice it to say in general here that the runes (from whatever earlier language they derive and wherever their geographical cradle may have been) provided the primitive Scandinavian with a basis for his first written language, that they appeared in Scandinavia as early as the close of the second century A.D., that their usage in the North spread rapidly during the following centuries, and that they were not substantially supplanted by the Latin alphabet until well down into the Middle Ages. In the Germanic world of the great folk migrations the runic alphabet consisted of twenty-four runes, which later in the Scandinavian countries was reduced to sixteen both in the Swedish-Norwegian and in the Danish versions, each of which seems to have developed relatively independent of the other though the Danish version came finally to be used in Sweden and Norway as well as in Denmark.

If Sweden by contrast with her Scandinavian neighbors is largely lacking in early literary survivals of a more impressive kind, she does have the distinction of having within her borders an incomparably large number of rune stones. Of the somewhat more than 3000 Scandinavian runic inscriptions which have survived, some 2500 lie within the present boundaries of Sweden, while the majority of the remainder are about equally divided between Denmark and Norway, with a scattering of them in ancient Scandinavian colonies dispersed over such a wide geographical area as Ireland, Cumberland, and the Isle of Man in the South to Greenland in the North. Even in Greece there once was to be found a Scandinavian runic inscription carved on the famous Piraeus Lion, which in 1687 was carried off as war booty to Venice, where it remains to our day. Within the specifically Swedish area of runic distribution, the loosely defined administrative district which later became the province

The early Germanic runic alphabet

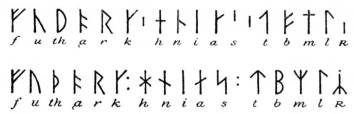

The two Scandinavian runic alphabets, the lower, employed first in Denmark, came finally also to be used in Norway and Sweden

of Uppland has by far the greatest number, some 1100, while the neighboring district of Sörmland to the south has about 300, and Östergötland and Gotland each has about 200. Elsewhere, runic inscriptions have been found in all the older Swedish districts from Skåne in the far south to Ångermanland in the north.

The overwhelming majority of runic inscriptions that we now have are inscribed on stones commemorating the dead, though some of the oldest have come down to us on spearheads, amulets, and other small metal or bone objects. The very earliest Scandinavian runes are those inscribed on a spearhead from Stabu in Norway, from the end of the second century, and on diverse burial objects from Denmark dating not more than a century later. From the Swedish Baltic island of Gotland we have rune-inscribed spearheads and rune stones from a period only slightly later, and it may be assumed despite the lack of conclusive evidence that the use of runes had penetrated into Sweden approximately as early as into Denmark and Norway.

Though it is possible that the runic alphabet originally came into being in order to serve the immediate practical purposes of everyday communication, we know from the testimony of the Poetic (or Elder) Edda as well as from many of the runic inscriptions themselves that the runes were often felt to have certain magic powers, thought of as deriving from their supposedly divine origins. According to one ancient Scandinavian tradition Odin had been initiated into the mysteries of runic magic by the Giants against whom the Gods were in constant strife; and in the ornamental detail characteristic of so many of the later rune stones the figures of either Odin or Thor are not uncommon. In fact, Thor's famous hammer at times supplants the Christian cross as a form of protection against evil on rune stones which can be dated far down into Christian times.

5

It would seem, however, that most of the runic inscriptions whose purposes are primarily magical (the so-called *trollrunor*) are from pre-
Christian times. These early runes were sometimes inscribed on spearheads, apparently to importune the assistance of the gods in battle, or
on amulets to protect the bearer, or on objects placed within graves to
call down curses on any who might seek to desecrate the resting place
of the dead. The earliest known Swedish runic inscription (found on a
spearhead on the island of Gotland) includes the following curious series
of letters, s i o a g, and from the indecipherable piling-up of vowels it
is assumed that the letters have a grimly disguised magical rather than
any intelligible communicative purpose. A much more clear-cut example of runic witchcraft is found, however, on a stone dating from around
700 near Björketorp in the southeastern Swedish province of Blekinge,
on one side of which is inscribed the single portentous word u þ A r A b
A S b A (meaning: curse, malediction), and on the other, six lines of
runes threatening evil — in measured, elevated, maledictory language —
to any who desecrate the stone. Among the more fascinating Norwegian
monuments from roughly the same period, and containing similar runic
sorcery to discourage irreverence for the dead, is the famous Eggjum
stone.

Such semantic sorcery is not common, however, among the runic inscriptions which have survived, whatever may have been the case with
a still earlier runic tradition. Most of the runes are simple, straightforward
memorial inscriptions, usually containing, in a terse, quite unadorned
language, three pieces of information: the name of the person commem-
orated, the names of the survivors responsible for raising the memorial,
and, on stones of relatively late date, the name of the carver. Many of
these runic inscriptions — short, factual, containing but a bare private
record — are of interest primarily to the philologist in pursuit of the
origins of the Scandinavian languages. Others attract the historian in
search of records of early Viking activities. Among the more interesting of the latter are the twenty-four so-called Ingvar stones, which
provide a contemporary record of a famous but ill-fated Swedish ma-
rauding expedition deep into Gardarike (Russia), and the even more
numerous stones raised in honor of Swedes who, as henchmen of Knut
the Great, harried England in the first decades of the eleventh century
and assisted in the collection of the notorious Danegeld.

Some — not many — of the rune stones come to fascinate even the
student of literature, who, unlike the philologist and the historian, is

constantly on the lookout for the kind of written document which is *in itself* interesting — a document which in some aspect of form or some facet of feeling or vision reflects at least the beginnings of a more or less conscious artistic intent in the handling of the runes. Here and there the sensitive ear can discern something of a personal note momentarily breaking through the conventional memorial tone of the runic inscription — a note of genuine feeling, as in a mother's laconic lament, "mother had them inscribed after her son, hers, her only," on a stone from Uppland; or the expression of warm gratitude toward a certain Torsten of Södermanland, who had "treated his house karls well"; or the special praise for bravery in battle shown by one "who did not flee at Uppsala, but fought as long as weapons he had." At least one example of humor has been recorded in Swedish runes, where the rune carver plying his trade on a pillar in the parish church at Löt, in Öland, wryly vents his dissatisfaction at the miserly payment he is to receive, with the tart lines:

> If me more they had given
> I better would have written!

A more impressive evidence of literary qualities in runic inscriptions is, however, the quite frequent occurrence of a rhythmic language — even of verse patterns — breaking through the otherwise matter-of-fact prose record. Most of the verse is of a very elementary kind, and might have been composed by almost any reasonably gifted person of the time. But not infrequently the verse becomes more complex, more skillful — occasionally taking on the classic Old Norse poetic form known as the *fornyrdislag*, as in a central passage on the Rök stone, the most famous of all rune stones. The Rök stone (found imbedded in the wall of the parish church of Rök in Östergötland) owes its fame especially to two circumstances: the runes, more than seven hundred and sixty of them, completely covering all sides of the huge stone, are of nearly every known variety (the early twenty-four-figure runes, the later sixteen-rune type with practically all its variants, and mixed, frequently indecipherable forms); and after more than a hundred years of ingenious interpretative labors there is little agreement among scholars as to the precise meaning of large portions of the inscription.

The poetic fragment, however, which is found among the strange congeries of runes on the Rök stone, and which in its alliterative pattern of eight short lines (or four longer lines broken by caesura) is easily identifiable as the *fornyrdislag* verse form, may be translated with some certainty as follows:

7

Ruled Tjodrek
the valiant warrior,
warriors' chief,
o'er shore of Reidhavet;
sits now accoutred
on saddle-horse his,
shield with strap fastened,
prince of the Märings.

The question as to who the Tjodrek of this verse was is somewhat obscure, but he is usually identified with Teodorik, king of the East Goths in Italy, 471–525 A.D.

If this is so, it has been reasoned, the verse appearing on the Rök stone *might* be a fragment of a larger poetic work now lost. And this theory in turn has led some scholars to suggest that there *may* have existed within the boundaries of Sweden as early as the middle of the ninth century a more widespread verse-epic tradition than can be demonstrated with any certainty. Tantalizing as this theory may be, it is somewhat nebulous in the absence of more conclusive evidence.

But in support of the theory that Sweden had a reasonably rich pre-Christian literary tradition despite the lack of substantial survivals, it should be noted that several records, and particularly one – the elaborate Ramsundsberg rock carving with its short runic text – provide indubitable evidence that not more than two centuries after the Rök stone was carved there existed in Sweden a thorough familiarity with the most famous of all Germanic heroic traditions, the group of tales centering upon Sigurd Fafnesbane and gathered up finally in the *Volsungasaga*. The Ramsundsberg rock carving – a marvelously well-preserved late example of a primitive Scandinavian rock-carving art form (*hällristningar*) practiced most diligently in the Bronze Age (from around 1500 to 500 B.C.), long before the introduction of runes – is called the "Sigurd carving" because within its boldly designed serpentine scroll is depicted a series of figures easily identifiable as representing certain of the central episodes in the life of the hero Sigurd. The short runic inscription on the scroll itself reads: "Sigrid made this bridge, [she was] Alrik's mother [and] Orm's daughter, for Holmger's, her husband's soul, [he was] Sigröd's father." What connection there may be between the inscription and the Sigurd carvings to which it is attached is obscure. Among other Swedish rune stones containing pictorial material from the Sigurd tradition the most interesting is the Gök stone, located but a dozen miles

8

The Ramsundsberg rock carving, frequently called the Sigurd rock
carving because of its pictorial record of details included
in the *Volsungasaga*

from the Ramsundsberg carving in Södermanland and vying with it in
elaboration of detail and design.

It has often been maintained that Sweden, unlike Iceland and Norway,
can boast of no survivals from that final, highly self-conscious, sundown
development of a native Scandinavian poetic tradition called skaldic
poetry. In the past those who reasoned that skaldic verse may have been
a part of an early Swedish literary tradition have pointed to the late tenth-
century Karlevi stone, which records a fine example of the typical skaldic
verse known as *dróttkvaett*, with its intricate interplay of alliteration
and assonance and its complicated use of kennings. But it has been noted
that the only thing undeniably Swedish about this carving is that it
stands on Swedish soil. It was in all probability composed by a Norwegian or Icelandic skald, and its subject is a Danish chieftain. All we *know*
about skaldic activities in Sweden is that those skalds who on occasion
performed at Swedish courts were either Icelandic or Norwegian in
origin. Whether there were any native Swedish skalds is difficult to
establish with any finality, though the distinguished runologist Sven B. F.
Jansson has recently made an impressive case (based primarily on the
runic inscription on a small copper box found at Sigtuna in 1911) for
the existence of a native Swedish skaldic tradition.

Few as the immediately Swedish literary survivals before the Middle
Ages may be, and relatively unimpressive as most of them admittedly
are, particularly when compared with the Icelandic-Norwegian survivals from the same period, one might well wonder if it is not somewhat fatuous to assume that these runic inscriptions and rock carvings

9

really reflect much by way of a larger, lost Swedish literary tradition. And our conclusion would perhaps have to be negative were it not for the fact that certain broadly inclusive Germanic sources provide some fascinating glimpses into a pre-Christian world of Swedish life and manners which in certain ways fill out the fragmentary and sketchy picture with which we otherwise would have to be satisfied.

Among the earliest non-Scandinavian references to Sweden that are of some interest are those to be found in Tacitus's *Germania* (c. 100 A.D.) and in the Gothic chronicler Jordanes's *De origine actibusque Getarum* (On the Origins and History of the Goths, c. 550 A.D.), but neither yields much detail about the early Swedes nor is either concerned specifically with literary matters. Much more interesting to the literary historian is Adam of Bremen's *Gesta Hammaburgensis ecclesiae pontificum* (tr. *History of the Archbishops of Hamburg-Bremen*, c. 1070), in which is contained the famous description of worship at Old Uppsala, the cradle of ancient Scandinavian myth and the center of primitive Scandinavian religious ritual. What especially interests the student of literature in Adam of Bremen's lurid account of the bloody immolations practiced at Old Uppsala ("Everyday [during the sacrificial rites] they sacrifice one human being along with other living creatures, so that in nine days there are seventy-two victims . . .") is the reference to "incantations . . . usually sung in the performance of a libation" — incantations which, Adam notes with due ecclesiastical caution, are "numerous and indecent, and it is better not to speak of them." A Swedish scholar has conjectured that these may well have been songs to the god of fertility Frö, in a vein similar to those celebrating Phallus found in Aristophanes. However this may be, it is quite clear from the testimony of Adam of Bremen that ancient Swedish ritualistic practices included song as a central element, and here we undoubtedly come upon one of the basic points of origin for Swedish poetry. From the standpoint of the literary historian working in a period so niggardly in literary survivals, it is regrettable that the good monk Adam felt constrained in the name of decency to omit the texts of songs which apparently were an organic part of the Uppsala ritual.

The central place which Old Uppsala occupied in ancient Scandinavia, not only in religious but also in political matters, can easily be established by the frequent references to the district in the Icelandic-Norwegian eddic and saga tradition. The document which in the greatest detail reflects Uppsala's primacy in these matters is the *Ynglinga Saga*, first of the sagas included in Snorre Sturlason's celebrated history of the Norwegian kings, called *Heimskringla* from the opening words of the book, "the earth's ring." In keeping with the custom among authors of the sagas, Snorre quotes liberally from skaldic poems. It may be said that the very basis for his *Ynglinga Saga* is a skaldic poem, *Ynglingatal* (now lost except for Snorre's generous citations from it), composed, according to Snorre, by one Tjodolf of Hvin. Though the evidence is hardly conclusive, Tjodolf seems to have been one of those several skalds whom King Harald the Fairhaired (860–930 A.D.) gathered around him to provide an elevated form of entertainment at his court and, even more important, to enhance his royal reputation both in his day and for posterity.

Tjodolf, it seems, had in *Ynglingatal* taken upon himself the tricky responsibility of providing an appropriately impressive genealogical tree for the "small king" Ragnvald, a relative of King Harald. By indirection – whether consciously or not is unclear – Ragnvald's genealogical tree as traced by Tjodolf could serve as well Harald's family pretensions. Going manfully to his task, Tjodolf demonstrates to his own satisfaction (and doubtless to his master's) that the royal Norwegian line he serves can be traced back through no less than twenty-one generations of kings and gods – to Odin himself.

Though this rather overwhelming genealogical succession is pursued by Tjodolf in order to provide a proper lineage for a Norwegian royal family, almost all of the more than a score of generations of alleged forebears are Swedish gods and kings, the ancient Uppsala royal succession which went under the name Ynglings. This circumstance accounts for the fact that Tjodolf's *Ynglingatal* may be said to have a much greater importance for the Swedish historian and literary historian than for the Norwegian. In addition to providing accounts of religious practices at Old Uppsala – strikingly similar to those recorded by Adam of Bremen – Tjodolf sketches the whole political history (with generous doses of myth for the early periods) of those Swedes whose administrative district was centered at Old Uppsala. And it may even be, as some have speculated, that Tjodolf's poem is to be considered simply a relatively late Norwegian adaptation of several earlier Swedish heroic poems or sagas. Whether Tjodolf actually had at hand old Swedish eddic or saga material in a reasonably finished oral or written literary form cannot be proved, but it seems likely; and if he did we may in *Ynglingatal* find ourselves but one step removed from a significant body of pre-Christian Swedish literature which unfortunately has not been preserved.

Precarious as such speculations may be when unsupported by other evidence, they can be bolstered by some details from another non-Swedish source — the Old English epic *Beowulf*, composed probably about 700 A.D., nearly two centuries before *Ynglingatal*. Though *Beowulf* came to be written down in England, its hero is a Geat (Swedish Goth) and nearly all its action takes place in Denmark and Sweden. Consequently one must assume Scandinavian origins for most of the mythological and historical materials upon which *Beowulf* is based. To what extent these origins are Danish or Swedish has been the subject of a lively and prolonged debate among scholars, which has not yet led to any definitive conclusions — if it ever will. Nonetheless, much can be said for a Swedish provenance for large parts of the material in *Beowulf*: the hero himself, the poem tells us, is a prince (later a king) of the Geats, who inhabited what is now southern Sweden; Hygelac, Beowulf's uncle, and a historical figure mentioned by Gregory of Tours among others, figures rather prominently, late in the poem, as king of the Geats; the word "Svéorice" (modern Swedish *Svearike*, "kingdom of Sweden") appears in *Beowulf* for the first time in any known document; and large portions of the later action in *Beowulf* are concerned with internal Swedish political and military affairs, especially the bloody wars between the Svear, from the Uppsala regions, and the Geats, which led finally to a unification of Sweden under the victorious Svear. These wars of the sixth century occupy the attention of the Tjodolf who wrote *Ynglingatal* as much as they do the unknown poet of *Beowulf*, and it seems likely that the authors of both poems used a common source. That this source existed in Sweden in a fairly stable oral form is implied by the fact that the historical figures and episodes treated in both *Beowulf* and *Ynglingatal* appear in both poems in substantially the same order.

Only this close, and no closer, however, can one get to a probable Swedish heroic literature of a skaldic type from Viking or pre-Viking times. And this is necessarily a scholarly reconstruction, not an examination of actual literary remains. The unhappy fact is that, aside from the fragmentary testimony of certain runic inscriptions, no pre-Christian Swedish literature has been preserved, unless one includes parts of the Swedish provincial laws — which, however, did not come to be written down until the Middle Ages. Latter-day Swedes may find comfort in the fact, noted above, that Sweden's runic inscriptions at any rate far outnumber those of her Scandinavian neighbors and, possibly more important, that these Swedish runic inscriptions are *strictly contemporary* written records — which is not the case with the eddic, skaldic, and saga material from Iceland and Norway nor the ancient lore contained in the *Gesta Danorum* of Saxo Grammaticus.

In a chapter dealing with Swedish literary origins it should perhaps finally be noted that the often repeated phrases "The Heroic Age" and "The Viking Age," as applied broadly to Scandinavian culture of pre-medieval times, are in certain respects misleading. Recent scholars — place-name investigators among others — have shown that the later phases of this period were relatively peaceful on the domestic front, characterized by rapid agricultural expansion and significant social developments. Though Viking forays to foreign shores may offer the most dramatic evidence of Scandinavian activities in pre-medieval times, they by no means provide us with the full picture of early Scandinavian life. "The Heroic Age" was not as exclusively "heroic" as popular tradition would have it. The "Viking" who indulged in adventure and sought plunder in foreign lands also found time to plow the home fields and organize at least the rudiments of a stable society within his home borders. In fact, the extent to which the Swedish Viking stayed at home may in part have been responsible for his failure to develop and preserve a rich heroic tradition in poetry. He may have been too busy with immediate practical tasks to indulge more than casually in the arts, at least in their more sophisticated forms.

The Middle Ages

THE CHRONOLOGICAL DEMARCATION of the Swedish Middle Ages commonly accepted by historians is a period of something more than four and a half centuries, from about 1060 to 1521. Though these dates are to be identified most immediately with the Christianization of Sweden, they include more broadly the whole complex of political and cultural developments within the country that broke down the ancient barriers of Swedish isolation within a limited Scandinavian orbit and brought Sweden finally, for the first time, into the wider European community of nations. The first of these dates may be said to mark the triumph of Christianity over Scandinavian paganism in Sweden; the last marks the political and religious upheaval which brought an end to Roman Catholic power in the country and established Swedish Lutheranism.

It should be stressed, however, that the date 1060 is somewhat arbitrary — a date historians have found loosely convenient to mark the displacement of a rapidly disintegrating paganism by the new religion from the South. Pagan resistance to the new religion was considerably more stubborn and long-drawn-out in Sweden than in the other Scandinavian countries. The reasons for this are in part geographical and in part religious-political. Denmark geographically was actually a part of Continental Europe, and both Iceland and Norway were fairly accessible to Europe by way of the seas, while what may be called the ancient Swedish state, centered relatively inland in the north Mälar region, was considerably less accessible to Christian missionary activities originating on the Continent. Besides, by the end of the tenth century, Denmark, Norway, and Iceland had become politically unified national entities; and it was therefore less difficult in these countries to have

Christianity officially *pronounced* as the new religion of the state. In Denmark and Norway this was done by royal decree, in Iceland by an act of parliament.

In Sweden circumstances did not permit such a simple solution. Politically Sweden was anything but stable during the first half and more of the eleventh century, and in religious matters conditions seem to have been quite fluid, particularly in the Mälar lake regions of Uppland where pagan religious life maintained itself with an apparently increasing intensity well beyond the middle of the century. Olof Skötkonung, first of the Christian kings in Sweden, was, indeed, baptized as early as 1000 A.D., but he seems to have been early forced to transfer his base of operations from Uppland to Västergötland, an indication of the precarious hold of a newly baptized Christian monarch over his pagan subjects. Historians have long been intrigued and at times baffled by the welter of documents, literary and historical, which provide only more or less adequate glimpses into late phases of the conflict between paganism and Christianity in the key area around Old Uppsala; and only recently have these historians, with the assistance of archaeology, succeeded in establishing with reasonable certainty the broad outlines of development within the conflict.

For more than two centuries before the issue of paganism versus Christianity was really sharply drawn in Sweden, the ancient religion of the country had been gradually undermined by the new religion from the South. Broadly speaking, the penetration of Christianity into the country took place in two ways, as an incidental by-product of Viking forays to the Christian South and West, roughly 800 to 1000 A.D., and as a deliberate Christian missionary activity in Sweden, first, during the ninth century from northern Germany, and later, in the eleventh century, largely from England. Though the effect of early Viking forays upon the Christianization of Sweden is difficult to trace in detail, it is undoubtedly of fundamental importance, serving to create in the North a state of mind which by degrees relaxed its early antagonism to the new religion and finally came to accept it. Missionary activity in Sweden is somewhat more easy to follow, chiefly because of the testimony of two important historical documents, bolstered by a rather rich dossier of archaeological and runological evidence. The historical documents of primary importance are the previously referred to Adam of Bremen's *Gesta Hammaburgensis ecclesiae pontificum* (c. 1070) and Rimbert's *Vita Ansgarii* (completed not later than 876), which concern themselves at many points with the missionary activities in Sweden originating from the north German archbishopric of Hamburg-Bremen. The archaeological evidence is found in the story of burial practices, especially in the ninth century at Birka. The runological evidence, very rich in the Uppland area, dates chiefly from the eleventh century.

Act I in the dramatic conflict between the old and the new religions as reflected in these documents is localized at the famous trading center of Birka, established about 800 A.D. on the island of Björkö on Lake Mälar. To this place — not many miles to the south of Old Uppsala, the ancient religious and political gathering place of the Svear — comes Ansgar, the "Apostle to the North," for the first time, c. 830. Though not received with any great enthusiasm by the reigning king at Birka, he is allowed to preach the new doctrine, and he gains a number of converts, among them Hergeir, counsellor to the king. After Ansgar's return to the Continent, and upon his elevation to Archbishop of the Hamburg-Bremen diocese, under which Scandinavia at this time is listed, he sends a certain Gautbert (first and only Bishop of Birka) to establish a permanent base of missionary operations among the Uppland Swedes. Gautbert, however, is soon driven away from Birka, probably because of ill-timed missionary zeal on his part, and an assistant, Nithard, suffers martyrdom. Later, in 854, Ansgar himself returns to Birka, seems to have been favorably received, re-establishes the local church, and leaves behind him on his departure another religious leader for the Christians at Birka. Rimbert, the author of *Vita Ansgarii*, who in 865 succeeds Ansgar as head of the Hamburg-Bremen diocese, continues his predecessor's interest in the missionary activity centered at Birka; but upon Rimbert's death, in 888, this missionary work seems to have ceased altogether, for what reason it is impossible to say. That a reasonably large Christian group existed in Birka during these years is, however, clear from archaeological research into burial customs at Birka. The several hundred graves examined reveal that the dead were buried without cremation rites, the custom otherwise characteristic of pagan burials at the time.

Act II in the drama of religious conflict shifts the scene of action to Sigtuna, somewhat to the north of Birka and much nearer to Old Uppsala. Though obscure in matters of detail, the general picture at Sigtuna is sufficiently clear. The protagonists now are more numerous, the conflict more complex and sharp, and the stakes are higher — which of the two religions is finally to be the official faith of the region? No longer does it seem possible for the two religions to exist side by side; no longer can a native polytheistic paganism solve its problem by the evasive expedient of simply *adding to* its usual multiplicity of gods another god — the White Christ.

According to a persistent but recently challenged tradition, Sigtuna was founded quite deliberately by Olof Skötkonung, the first Christian Swedish king, as a new and more daring outpost of Christianity — an outpost poised advantageously on the very threshold of Old Uppsala, where at the time an eruptive and defiant paganism is gathering its previously somewhat scattered forces around the central symbol of its faith, the far-famed sacrificial temple. Olof himself, as we have seen, is soon forced to depart from the area on his refusal to serve in a king's traditional priestly capacity at the blood sacrifice at Old Uppsala. His immediate successors, Anund Jacob and Emund, both Christians, seem to have managed to avoid becoming sharply involved in the tense religious situation. Emund, in fact, counsels against plans hatched by one Adalvard, Bishop of Sigtuna in the 1060's, to make a frontal attack on Old Uppsala by an act of violence — the destruction of the old Uppsala temple. So embittered are the natives of Uppland on their discovery of this proposed act of desecration that Adalvard is driven away from Sigtuna.

Act III — and the last — shifts the scene to Old Uppsala itself. Here occurs in rapid succession a series of violent and lurid religious upheavals which mark the death throes of the old religion. The most dramatic of these episodes, and possibly the most crucial, is the one — from the 1080's — in which Inge, who with his brother Hallsten reigns over Uppland, is driven from Old Uppsala in a hail of stones by an incensed peasantry when he refuses to function as the priest-king of sacrifice at the ancient Uppsala ritual. He is replaced on the throne by his brother-in-law, Blot-Sven, who is prepared to fulfill the required priestly functions. But three years later Inge returns, wreaks murderous vengeance on Blot-Sven and his followers, and apparently (scholars are in disagreement on the point) burns the pagan temple.

Though Inge's bloody deed of vengeance may in a sense be said to symbolize the final defeat of a defiant Swedish paganism in Uppland, it should be emphasized that the triumphant Christianity whose task it now is to consolidate its gains in the country could only slowly carry through its broad religious program. Many are the evidences that the ancient religion of the land died slowly, piecemeal as it were, yielding the last vestiges of its primitive vitality only when overcome by force. It is not unusual at this time, for instance, to come upon cases where both Christ and Thor were worshipped — or either, depending upon which seemed to the worshipper, at the moment, to be the stronger. And in relatively isolated parts of the country, such as Dalarna and Småland, the older religion held sway almost as if no new religion had been established. It is interesting to note that the Norwegian king Sigurd Jorsalfar (the Crusader) feels constrained, as late as 1123, to embark on "a crusade" to Småland in order "to Christianize the people, because the inhabitants did not maintain the Christian faith, even though some of them had partaken of baptism."

Such "crusades," which proposed to Christianize by force, if necessary, those Swedish districts that were less than enthusiastic in accepting the new faith, came with the years to be expanded, with the encouragement and blessing of the Church at Rome, to the eastern shores of the Baltic, where particularly Finland was repeatedly visited by Swedish expeditions bent on expressing their religious zeal by heroic military exploits. Aside from the alleged humanitarian values which such expeditions were supposed to bring to barbaric heathen populations, they served to provide a perhaps necessary outlet for those primitive elements in Swedish character, only lately become "Christian," which before had found expression in the Viking expeditions to the east and south. The Church naturally looked with disfavor on the older type of Viking foray, which had been so destructive of Christian values, while it cannily channeled the restless energies of the North under a new banner and in a new form — the Christian crusade.

In the Swedish Church itself, whose problem it was to consolidate its gains and assume leadership in the task of civilizing a frequently refractory population, conditions were such for more than a century after the fall of Old Uppsala that one might well wonder whether Christianity *had* really triumphed in the land. Many local churches were built, but for a long time no effective general organization of these churches was established, and the clergy seems on the whole to have been ill-equipped for its task, in many cases uneducated, frequently lacking in spiritual vision, often even mercenary, and at times crudely immoral. Though the clergy were supposed to obey the rule of chastity, it was not unusual for them to marry or live in concubinage, especially before the Skänninge Meeting (1248), which formally forbade marriage for the Swedish clergy. The grasping mercenary vices of the clergy are sufficiently reflected in the provincial laws, which find it necessary to protect the peasant against clerical avarice by stating with unequivocal exactitude the fees allowed for such services as baptism, extreme unction, and masses for the dead. The peasant himself, it may be observed in passing, was quite equal to the situation. He insisted on his religious rights, but, as one Swedish scholar has said, "he did not want to pay a penny more than was required in the extremely detailed contract, and he purchased exemption from purgatory with the same thrifty care that he used in buying a team of oxen"!

That conditions within the young Church were less than ideal for some time after the official acceptance of Christianity in Sweden is natural. That such conditions should persist as long as they did is somewhat less easy to understand — unless one assumes, as one must, that the country as a whole was still, for at least a century after the temple at Uppsala had fallen, a vast and essentially primitive missionary field rather than a firmly knit religious community. It is true that permanent bishoprics had been established at various places in the country: at Skara in Västergötland, indeed, as early as 1013; and by the early twelfth century at Linköping, Eskilstuna, Strängnäs, Sigtuna, and Old Uppsala. The first Swedish archbishop, Stefan, was installed at Uppsala in 1164. He served, however, under the jurisdiction of the Archbishop at Lund, at this time a Danish city. It can be said, indeed, that not until 1248, at the church congress at Skänninge, did Sweden attain a firm general church organization and church discipline. It was at this meeting that the papal legate, Vilhelm of Sabina, forced the law of celibacy for the first time on the Swedish clergy and otherwise was instrumental in bringing the Swedish Church firmly within the discipline of the Church of Rome.

The relative ease with which in 1248 the new church organization was effected suggests that general developments in the country were now highly favorable to those trends which for some time had sought a closer identification with the life of the Continent. In matters religious, aside from church-building and church organization, several monastic orders were by this time solidly established in the land, the Cistercians having come early as 1143, and the Franciscans and Dominicans somewhat later, in 1218 and 1233 respectively. In politics the Folkung dynasty was busily at work moulding the loose federation of provinces which had been the Swedish nation into a new and powerful national entity. Out of the older yeoman peasant class — the only class of the earlier society — a new political aristocracy and a powerful ecclesiastical aristocracy were springing into being, serving alternately to bolster and to challenge the new royal might. And with all this a flood-tide of Continental culture spread rapidly over the land, displacing at almost every point those vestiges of an older pagan culture which had managed to survive during the earlier period of Christian infiltration. The new culture brought with it a new art, a new language, Latin, and new literary ideals.

In fact, even before the period with which we are now dealing – the Middle Ages proper in Sweden, beginning around 1250 – the older native Scandinavian literary traditions were either dead or dying. The appearance of skalds at Swedish courts was not uncommon right down to the rise to power of the Folkungs; but they seem to have been without exception visiting Icelandic or Norwegian skalds, and it is apparent that their day was drawing to a close. Viking chieftains and their henchmen, in whose crude courts the skald had found a perfect audience, no longer existed in the North; and the world of Scandinavian mythology, on which the skaldic tradition had fed for centuries, had little validity in a society turning gradually but persistently Christian. Little wonder is it therefore that the art of the Scandinavian skald decayed, spinning out dull and endless genealogies or inventing lifeless actions in place of the splendid visions of things that may well never have been "on land or sea."

The prose saga, a more flexible form than skaldic verse, continued for a time to flourish in the new Christian world of Icelandic-Norwegian West Scandinavia, adapting itself with greater ease to the new literary ways of a larger world, and it lived on, albeit in rather strange garments, well down into the Middle Ages proper. This last – decadent – stage in the history of the saga is illustrated particularly in the so-called *fornaldarsaga*, characterized by an excess of romantic themes and utterly incredible complications of action. "Its fantastic elements," writes the Danish scholar Axel Olrik, in contrasting it with the earlier saga tradition, "become stronger and stronger, and digress farther and farther from reality." The literal translation of *fornaldarsaga* is "saga of antiquity," but so fantastic were many of them, that in their heyday they were often called "lying sagas," and modern scholars refer to them as "fiction sagas."

It is clear from the *fornaldarsaga* that non-Scandinavian ingredients are creeping into the traditional West Scandinavian saga form – strange and fabulous ingredients from the Orient and from Greece as well as from medieval saints' legends and the world of chivalric romance. Scholars have at times speculated on a possible Swedish oral origin of some of these late-born sagas, suggesting that they may derive in part from Swedish contacts with the East via Russia. However this may be, no written forms of such sagas have survived in the East Scandinavian area, with the exception of the short *Gutasaga*, which has come down to us as a kind of "introduction" to *Gutalagen* (the provincial law of Gotland). All that otherwise can be demonstrated by way of identifying the *fornaldarsaga* tradition with Sweden is that some of the action in these sagas is localized in Sweden (*Rolf Götrikssons saga*, *Hervararsagan*, and others) and some of the characters are Swedish (such as Ingeborg, Hjalmar, and Orvar Odd in *Hervararsagan* and the fabulous Starkad in the *Gesta Danorum* and elsewhere).

If only a tenuous case can be made for the existence of either a late skaldic or a saga tradition in Sweden during the early Middle Ages, the Swedish *landskapslagar* (provincial laws) provide splendid evidence of a kind of native literary tradition during these years, deeply rooted in the pagan past. Though these laws did not come to be recorded for the first time until the thirteenth century, and consequently contain a considerable overlay of Christian ideas, they represent in most respects a pre-Christian Scandinavian world of idea and form. Aside from their literary-historical significance, these laws are of the greatest interest to the student of law, for they represent primitive Germanic conceptions of law and justice in a remarkably pure form, relatively little affected by the traditions of Roman law which had elsewhere, in the Germanic regions to the south, left a much stronger imprint on legal ideas and formulations.

That the Swedish provincial laws, whose origins lie so far back in the pagan past, came to be written down for the first time in the thirteenth century can be explained in terms of certain rapid changes in the Swedish social and political developments of the time. In the earlier, more primitive, exclusively peasant society, an able provincial *lagman* (law man) could master the laws of his district, repeat them orally at the annual meetings of the *ting* (a provincial legislature and court of justice in one), and interpret the law in cases of particular difficulty. Now, however, a new, much more complex, medieval society was springing into being, with new privileged classes and new institutions, political and religious, with rapidly expanding commercial activities, and with a new, ambitious royal hegemony deliberately pursuing a political and military policy which was to spell out the end of that earlier loose federation of districts or provinces which was the older Swedish state. All of this meant that the old institution of the *lagman* was doomed, if for no other reason because no one individual could bear the enormous legal burden posed by the new conditions. And the new circumstances meant also that it was obviously in the interests of the Folkung dynasty to encourage a systematic codification of the old provincial laws (*landskaplagar*) which would tend ultimately to issue into a law for the whole land (*landslag*). This, in fact, is precisely what happened: *Västgötalagen* (for the province of Västergötland) came first, in its earliest form from the second or third decade of the thirteenth century; and then in rapid succession followed *Upplandslagen, Västmannalagen, Dalalagen, Östgötalagen, Hälsingelagen, Värmlandslagen* (which has not survived), and *Smålandslagen*, of which only one section has come down to us. Finally — in the middle of the fourteenth century — a royal commission appointed by King Magnus Eriksson, the last of the Folkungs, proposed after long and systematic labors a broadly inclusive *landslag* (Law of the Realm), which gradually displaced the earlier separate *landskapslagar*.

Significant as these developments are from a legal point of view, the laws are at least as interesting as literature. It may be said, indeed, that the codification of the provincial laws is in many ways the most important single literary contribution of the Swedish Middle Ages. What came afterward — political chronicles, saints' legends, even the visions of Saint Birgitta and the ballads — are by comparison with the provincial laws relatively pale and imitative, somewhat tardy Swedish efforts to follow, only more or less happily, voguish literary leads from the Continent. Though the verbal finesses of scholasticism and the systematizing rigidities of canon law left at times their mark on the final codification of the Swedish provincial laws, they retain on the whole much of the primitive flavor of their pagan origins. They are native to the core. "By contrast with other written documents of the time," writes a Swedish scholar recently, "these laws have an archaic flavor. . . . They represent in our medieval literature a very characteristic style, the most popular, the most traditional and primitive, and incomparably the most artistic in formulation." The judgment on these laws is certainly not exaggerated.

Their freshness and spontaneity of utterance, their concrete, down-to-earth, factual quality, and their direct, clipped, rugged phrasing are to be accounted for chiefly, it would seem, by their origins in the actual world of the annual *ting* assembly, with its pressing legal and legislative business and its motley hurly-burly of general activities. It has been observed that the opening words of *Smålandslagen* and the closing words of *Östgötalagen* are addressed directly to an imagined audience, the kind of audience gathered at an actual meeting of the *ting*. And it may be added that the language of the laws throughout points back to the *ting*: it is pre-eminently a spoken language close to the immediate sources of life in conflict. The pattern of discourse is frequently narrative, episodic, with a keen sense of dramatic situation and sharp economy of dialogue. The prose — on the surface disarmingly simple, apparently relaxed — is essentially quite disciplined and controlled, reflecting by turn the concrete epigrammatic quality of the folk proverb and the strong rhythmic patterns of primitive Scandinavian poetry. At times, in fact, portions of these laws take on actual verse form. Two reasons have been suggested for the verse patterns of the provincial laws: that they add a certain dignity to legal utterance, and that they provide necessary props for the memory. Never does the prose of the provincial laws reduce itself to abstractions, a common sin of legal jargon, nor does it yield to soft and romantic phrasing, a more common human failing. Even where the humanitarian idealism of Christian teaching and practice shines through the cold, factual, pagan fabric of these laws — and this is fairly frequent — the mode of utterance remains restrained, dignified, impartial. In fact, these laws are a miracle of legal clarity and judicial balance — literary documents of a high order. It is fitting that the earliest Swedish manuscripts which have survived are those recording some of these provincial laws.

The ancient provincial laws were finally codified and recorded, as we have seen, during a period of political and religious consolidation that radically changed the whole cultural character of Sweden. The Church, as a civilizing agency, was most immediately responsible for the new cultural ideals which were largely to shape the new literature, though secular elements were not entirely lacking in this literature. Most of the authors of the new literature are unknown; but they are almost certainly in the great majority of cases, if not always, from the upper social strata created by the new religious and political conditions in the country — clerics, prominent political functionaries, and the like. The clerical members of this group were almost without exception educated abroad, in such newly established universities as those at Bologna, Prague, and especially Paris. It has been estimated that at least fifty Swedish students — a very considerable number for the time — were studying in Paris in 1329, a year from which we have a relatively complete list of resident Scandinavian students. One of the more famous teachers in Paris in the second half of the thirteenth century was the Aristotelian Boetius de Dacia, suspected of Averroistic heresy, who seems to have died about 1284 in Italy, presumably called there to be interrogated by the papacy. Despite his Swedish origin (Swedish or Danish, we cannot be sure which), Boetius de Dacia had his whole career abroad. Though he exercised no clearly demonstrable influence in Sweden, his lectures, with their radical application of Aristotelian thought to the religious ideas of his time, almost certainly were heard by Swedish students resident in Paris during his time there.

Though Sweden has the distinction of having the first university in the North — Uppsala, founded in 1477 — this university exerted little cultural influence during its early history. In fact, the new Swedish university maintained only a most precarious existence for scarcely more than a generation after its founding, and then ceased to exist, not being re-established until 1593. If, however, this first experiment in university education in Sweden languished and soon died, lower schools flourished and exercised a considerable influence on the cultural life of the nation, especially its religious side. These schools, first founded by the highly educational-minded mendicant orders, and later established as church or cathedral schools (*katedralskolor*), were organized primarily for pre-theological training; but not uncommonly sons of prominent members of the secular community were also admitted, to acquire at least a modicum of such learning as might fit them for public life.

Even more important in some ways for the new medieval culture than these lower schools was the pursuit of higher learning within many of the more flourishing monastic institutions, where the more intellectually gifted monks assiduously copied manuscripts, collected documents of all kinds which in some cases resulted in the building up of impressive monastic libraries, and in other ways pursued scholarly — and in certain cases even literary — careers. Especially the Dominicans and the Franciscans were "book conscious" from their very beginnings on the Continent, and this tradition was ardently followed in Sweden, where cloisters of both orders were established less than a generation after the rise of these orders abroad. What has survived of the library of Sigtuna cloister, one of the first two Dominican cloisters in Sweden (founded c. 1227), reveals a theological collection of considerable range; and even more impressive is the library of about 1400 titles owned at the close of the fifteenth century by Vadstena cloister, the mother cloister of the Birgittine order which operated as an independent division under the order of Saint Augustine.

One of the less fortunate aspects of the educational and learned monopoly maintained by the Church in Sweden was its intolerance toward the residual folk literature (largely if not entirely oral) of the nation's past, a perhaps inevitable consequence of the long and bitter opposition to the Church by Swedish defenders of an earlier pagan faith. This meant that the new literature had practically no points of continuity with the past, the only important exception (a magnificent one, to be sure) being, as we have seen, the provincial laws. The language of the great majority of the religious documents recorded in the cloisters was Latin, and when Swedish was used, the material dealt with is almost without exception foreign in origin. In matters of content these documents consisted almost exclusively of translations or adaptations of current saints' legends, theological treatises, biblical paraphrases, sermons and popular sermon materials (collections of the so-called *exempla*), and liturgical literature of all kinds, especially the Offices composed particularly to celebrate special religious holidays and saints' days. Among the more notable of these otherwise imitative and derivative works are a few original liturgical offices and hymns in Latin, a translation into Swedish of the first five books of the Old Testament, and a Swedish version of one of the more famous collections of saints' legends from the Continent. The liturgical offices and hymns particularly worthy of note were composed by four of the more eminent Swedish ecclesiastics of the time, the learned and able Brynolf Algotsson, Bishop of Skara (d. 1317), and three churchmen who were in one way or another close to Birgitta — Nikolaus Hermansson, Bishop of Linköping (d. 1391), magister Petrus Olovsson from Skänninge, the first Confessor General of the Birgittine cloister of Vadstena (d. 1378), and Archbishop Birger Gregersson (d. 1383). There has been some difference of opinion among Latinists as to the literary level attained by Bishop Brynolf in his offices in honor of two Swedish local saints (Helena of Skövde and the Södermanland apostle Eskil) and in the *Historia de spinea corona* (On Christ's Crown of Thorns); but at least some of the Latin hymns of the other Swedish churchmen here mentioned are of a reasonably high order of literary excellence, especially the first stanza of the *Rosa, rorans* by Bishop Nikolaus:

> Rosa, rorans bonitatem,
> stella, stillans claritatem,

Birgitta, vas gracie,
rora celi pietatem,
stilla vite puritatem
in vallem miserie!

Medieval Swedish poetry at its best seldom approaches such excellence of utterance, and usually it falls considerably below this level.

Much closer to popular medieval religious taste than such formal liturgical literature in Latin were the prose legends of the saints, a literary form which appealed to the learned and the unlearned alike. The saints' legends reflect a naïve delight in every variety of narrative excess, pursue with rapt attention the most fantastic of actions, glory unabashedly in the sharpest conceivable of conflicts, and never question the fabulous, the unbelievable, the miraculous. At times, the prose of the saints' legends takes on the sheer visionary quality of great poetry (Dante, it should be remembered, derives in part from the tradition of the saints' legends); but for the most part the strenuous moralizing quality of the legends precludes the intrusion of genuine poetic qualities. The conflict in these tales between the world of darkness and the world of light, between the flesh and the spirit is constant and unyielding; and only through the most heroic resistance to evil, and with the final assistance of God's ineffable grace, do the saints in these legends triumph at the last and enter into the glory of God. The moral was one that needed no learned interpretation, no subtle scholastic insights or applications. All who read, or heard, these legends grasped their meaning directly, immediately.

Though the native Swedish production of saints' legends was a rather modest one, there was readily available for Swedish consumption a more than sufficient supply of these tales in innumerable Continental collections, one of which — the famous *Legenda aurea* by the Italian Dominican monk Jacobus de Voragine — became the basis for the so-called *Fornsvenska legendariet,* the oldest collection of saints' legends in Swedish, and, except for the provincial laws, the longest extant medieval prose text in Old Swedish. Jacobus de Voragine's work seems to have been rendered into the Swedish of the *Fornsvenska legendariet* by a Swedish Dominican monk for the practical purpose of making these legends available to a Swedish society of Dominican nuns, whose level of learning was not sufficiently high to permit an adequate response to the original Latin text.

It has been suggested with some reason that the Swedish monk in question *may* have been one Petrus de Dacia (d. 1289), who was at the probable time of the composition of *Fornsvenska legendariet* a cloister brother at Skänninge, later prior of the Dominican cloister at Visby on Gotland. However this may be, Petrus de Dacia had from his earliest years become deeply engrossed in the mystical world of the saints' legends, and during his later years he came to write a biography about a saintly West German woman of his own time which represents the saint's legend on the highest level of literary accomplishment. So fascinating is the spell which Petrus de Dacia's biographical work has exercised in the tradition of hagiography down through the centuries that no less a person than the late nineteenth-century skeptic Ernest Renan devoted a study to him in the *Revue des deux mondes* as late as 1880.

In the Swedish literary tradition Petrus de Dacia has quite properly been called Sweden's "first author." This distinction is his because he is the first literary figure in Sweden whose personality shines clearly and intimately through his work. Though the literary tradition of the saint's legend had stiffened into the most rigid conventions of mood and form by the time Petrus de Dacia turned to the genre, he managed to breathe into it a warmth of feeling and a sharp simplicity of vision found only in the genre at its best. Despite his considerable learning, based on extensive studies on the Continent in Dominican centers of advanced learning such as Cologne and Paris, he retained always an extraordinary sensitivity to the more ecstatic, mystical sides of medieval religious culture. It was during his first period abroad, while pursuing studies at the Dominican *studium générale* at Cologne, that he met at Stumbelen, a village to the north of Cologne, the Beguine sister Kristina, who became the great experience in his life and the subject of his famous saint's legend, the *Vita Christinae Stumbelensis*. After his departure from Cologne, Petrus de Dacia met Kristina only once, and then briefly, late in life; but they maintained an intimate correspondence until his death in 1289, and his story of her life (unfinished because he preceded her in death) was written under the profoundest of convictions that she was a creature especially chosen by God to do His errands and reveal His will among mankind.

From some points of view the *Vita Christinae Stumbelensis* is just another saint's legend, a religious tale full of miraculous phenomena, conventional situations, and a naïve delight in the everyday minutiae of its subject's life and labors. What distinguishes Petrus's work sharply, however, from the run-of-the-mill saints' legends of the day is its profoundly *personal* quality, its way of reflecting its author's character and temperament, his innermost feelings. Most literary works of the Middle Ages seem coldly impersonal beside the warmth of this Swedish monk's feeling for his subject, a warmth at times veering close to passion, without, however — at least consciously — breaking into mere eroticism. That this warmth of feeling bordering upon human love derives primarily from Petrus de Dacia's actual meetings with Kristina is apparent both from the *Vita* and from the extensive correspondence between the two which has survived. As a man of substantial learning for his day, Petrus may very well have derived, in some measure, the particular formulation of his concept of love as a spiritual union with the beloved from a well-established religious-literary tradition, a tradition whose most immediate source may have been Bernard of Clairvaux but which may be traced back to Dionysius Areopagita and Augustine and finally to Plato. It was perhaps no accident that Dante was formulating a similar view of love contemporaneously with Petrus de Dacia, though almost certainly the Swedish monk was unaware of the fact.

If Petrus de Dacia is Sweden's first author, Birgitta (c. 1302–73) is Sweden's first seer. Born a decade and a half after Petrus de Dacia's death, Birgitta is in almost every respect a religious personality of a diametrically opposite kind from the sensitive Dominican monk whose retiring other-worldly spirit found the end of existence in a passive mystical adoration of one whom he considered a saint. In contrast with Petrus de Dacia, Birgitta is a person of action. Much as she may in theory have recognized that humility is a central Christian virtue, she seems in fact to have been strong-willed, aggressive, at times even arrogant. Her famous visions were only rarely, if ever, purely contemplative mystical ends in themselves. They tended rather to have a strong moralizing bent, in many cases passing severe judgments on her contemporaries — especially people in high places, dukes and kings, cardinals and popes.

She came quite naturally by her critical preoccupations with contemporaries of wealth and station, for she was born into and married within the highest Swedish artistocracy of her day, and the first four and a half decades of her life were years of more or less direct contact with Swedish court and near-court life. Her father, Birger Persson, as Lawman of Uppland and chief of the royal commission which first formulated a Law of the Realm, was one of the most wealthy and powerful men of his time in Sweden, while on her mother's side she was related to the Folkungs,

Burial mounds at Old Uppsala, sixth century, and rune stone from Lits-lena, Uppland (photos: ATA)

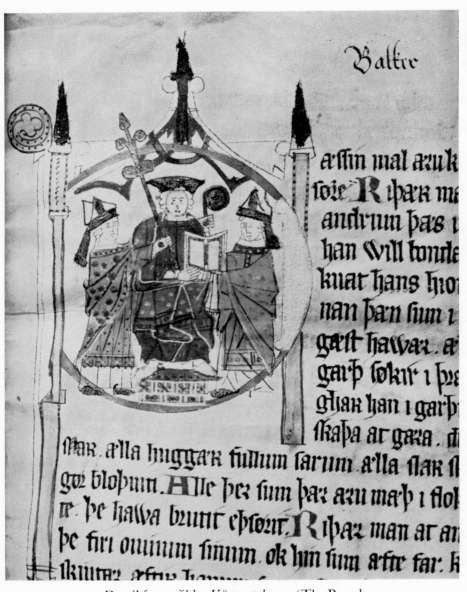

Detail from *Äldre Västgotalagen* (The Royal
Library, Stockholm)

Statue in wood of Saint Birgitta at Vadstena cloister church,
late fifteenth century (photo: ATA)

Medieval bride stealing, from Hugo von Trimberg's *Der Renner*, ca. 1400 (The Royal Library, Stockholm)

who had occupied the Swedish throne for two generations before her birth. And she had been married — at the tender age of thirteen — into one of the most powerful families of Östergötland.

Although Birgitta bore eight children and seems to have been an able, practical, and enterprising mistress over the family's vast properties, she maintained during these years (with the understanding and encouragement of her husband) a half-ascetic religious regimen unusual for a member of her class. Upon her husband's death in 1344 she devoted herself exclusively to the religious life. In 1349 she departed from Sweden for Rome, her headquarters until her death in 1373. Eleven years later Vadstena cloister, the mother cloister of the Birgittine order which she founded, was consecrated, and in 1391 Birgitta was canonized.

Though she triumphed after her death, Birgitta's years of widowhood were strenuous and heavy, filled with religious labors which had their share of frustrations and disappointments. The immediate occasion for her going to Rome in 1349 was the celebration of 1350 as a jubilee year by the Church, during which pilgrims converged on the Eternal City from all over Europe. For reasons not entirely clear she remained in Rome the remainder of her life, except for occasional excursions to immediately outlying regions and a pilgrimage to Jerusalem shortly before her death. Her life in Rome settled down to a strict regimen of religious observances, to charitable activities of all kinds, to attempts to prevail on the Pope to return to Rome from his "Babylonian captivity" at Avignon, and finally — and most important — to efforts to obtain papal sanction for her monastic rule as the first step in the establishment of a new religious order.

It was through one of her visions that the new monastic rule had come to Birgitta. These visions dealt, however, with a great variety of other matters, religious and political; and they reflect an imaginative flight and a visionary intensity which has no parallel in the literature, religious or profane, of the Swedish Middle Ages. The task of editing the visions was entrusted to Birgitta's confessors, particularly toward the end of her life to her Spanish father confessor, Alfons of Jaen, who was responsible for selecting which of the visions were to be included in the papers presented for the consideration of the Church when Birgitta was proposed for sainthood. The visions included in these papers, together with some others, ultimately became the official canon of her revelations, which existed only in manuscript until their publication in book form, in 1492, under the title *Revelationes celeste*.

Already in childhood Birgitta had experienced moments of religious ecstasy which took on a tentative visionary quality, but not until after her husband's death did her visionary gifts come to provide the dominant element in her religious experience. According to her own testimony Christ and the Virgin Mary appeared to her in these visions, and she recorded their words (nearly always by dictation to her confessors) directly after the divine personages appeared to her. Unfortunately for the accuracy of the record, Birgitta had no very great knowledge of Latin; and the record of her words which we now have consists almost exclusively of her confessors' Latin versions of her original Swedish, the only exception being a couple of manuscript fragments in Old Swedish, almost certainly in Birgitta's own hand. The linguistic gap between Birgitta's actual words and the Latin transcript (even when she checked the transcript, as she often did) poses certain obvious difficulties to one who seeks to ascertain the exact literary quality of the visions, but thanks to Birgitta's marked verbal talents these difficulties are not quite as serious as they might seem to be. One has the feeling, in many passages at any rate, that one is very close to the original, that the Latin form of Birgitta's learned confessors has not substantially watered down the strong pulse-beat, the homely, coarse-grained figures of speech, and the imaginative intensity of her original Swedish. Even the necessarily circumspect Latin of churchmen has not destroyed the impression of a highly personal style. It is a style with few literary finesses, with little refinement of phrase or image, with no subtle development of idea, but rather a style of remarkable concreteness and vividness, of a restless, at times explosive drive, instinct at almost every point with that quality of strong moral indignation which is the central mark of Birgitta's personality.

This moral indignation, as we have noted, was no respecter of persons. In fact, one sometimes has the impression that Birgitta was never more happy than when she was swinging the scourge of judgment over men most highly placed in the religious and political life of the time. Dukes and cardinals who had strayed into sin are frequent subjects of her visions and objects of her condemnation, while kings and popes who have not done God's will as she sees it are mercilessly flayed by her avenging spirit. At times her judgments have a kind of magnificent pretentiousness, as when she all but orders the Pope to return to Rome or when she attempts, unasked (and, at the time, unknown), to mediate a peaceful settlement between the kings of England and France. At other times she assumes the august mantle of a judge under circumstances and in terms suggesting other than elevated motives, as in the several instances in which she seeks directly to determine the course of Swedish politics. The conclusion seems inescapable that the numerous attacks upon Magnus Eriksson in the *Revelationes* are inspired less by a sense of justice than by a motive of personal vindictiveness engendered largely by King Magnus's unwillingness to yield to Birgitta's imperious will. The fact that she secretly incited a group of Swedish noblemen to attempt to depose the King reveals how far she was prepared to actively interfere in the unstable political life of the time. This amounted to treason by devious and underhanded means, a somewhat dubious activity for a future saint no matter how weak she felt the reigning king might be. And it is reasonably clear today that King Magnus, despite his faults, was scarcely the puerile personality which certain of Birgitta's visions had led Swedes for centuries to assume. But it should perhaps be added that the apparent vindictiveness of Birgitta does not weaken the literary quality of those passages devoted to the reigning Folkung monarch. On the contrary, some of these passages are among the most memorable of Birgitta's visions. The ways of imaginative genius are various and strange. Vindictiveness inspired by intense suspicion or hatred has more than once in the annals of literature hatched a vision of dark and mysterious splendor.

There can be little doubt that despite her not inconsiderable human limitations Birgitta was one of the really outstanding personalities of her day, an amazing aggregate of saintly virtues, worldly pretensions, and striking visionary genius. Never for a moment after the first central vision of her life, in which, as she puts it, she became "the bride of Christ" and his spokesman (*språkrör*) in the world, did she falter in obeying the divine will as she came to experience it through repeated confrontations with the Son and the Mother Virgin. And though she had to bow to the will of the Church when her monastic rule was in certain ways made subordinate to the rule of Augustine, her dream of becoming the founder of a new monastic order was finally realized. This did not come, however, until after her death, when her devoted daughter Katarina succeeded in establishing the Birgittine order, which spread rapidly beyond its Swedish origins in the mother cloister at Vadstena to the other Scandinavian countries and then to Italy, Spain, Germany, the Netherlands, and England. Aside from its religious importance, Vadstena also came to be of the greatest cultural significance in Sweden in the late Middle Ages. Its monks and nuns (Birgitta's rule called for monastic institutions including both sexes) were exceedingly diligent in collecting and transcribing manuscripts, and its library became with the years a most impressive repository for religious books of all kinds. Many, if not most, of the medieval Swedish documents which have survived have done so probably chiefly because of the diligence of the Vadstena scribes, whose special pride was the library of their cloister. A Swedish medievalist has said "that practically all of our religious literature from the Middle Ages has been produced in Vadstena cloister."

Though religious and political exigencies in later centuries occasioned the elimination of most of the Birgittine cloisters, only a handful of them having survived to our day, Saint Birgitta is still held in honored memory among the company of the saints. In Sweden her star was of course eclipsed sharply during the Reformation and after, but in our century her life and work have become the objects of an increasing number of distinguished scholarly investigations and her complex personality has attracted the attention of poets, dramatists, and novelists. Strindberg, in the historical drama *Folkungasagan* (tr. *The Saga of the Folkungs*), has paid his rather irreverent woman-hating respects to her. Verner von Heidenstam, in *Heliga Birgittas pilgrimsfärd* (The Pilgrimage of Saint Birgitta), has devoted an entire novel to her. And, most recently, the famous Danish convert to Catholicism Johannes Jørgensen has added to his series of brilliant saints' lives a monumental study of Saint Birgitta. A fascinating and controversial figure during her lifetime, Birgitta has remained down through the centuries an object of strong attraction or irritation among those who have concerned themselves with her. Perhaps there is no more valid evidence of the essential vitality of her person and her work.

Though much of the literature of the Swedish Middle Ages concerned itself with religious matters, a not inconsiderable amount of secular literature was also produced. Except for the folk ballads, however, this literature only rarely reflects literary qualities of any distinction; and in only one case (that of Bishop Thomas and the so-called Frihetsvisan) does one come upon an identifiable literary personality of some originality and power. Otherwise this literature is in the main one of translation or adaptation or imitation, largely foreign in origin and usually not especially impressive in its Swedish raiment.

The reason most frequently offered for this rather unimpressive body of Swedish secular literature in the Middle Ages is that the more literate Swedes of the time were with few exceptions churchmen, who quite naturally concerned themselves with a literary activity of an almost exclusively religious kind. Another possible reason is that the bitterness which characterized the long-drawn-out conflict in Sweden between paganism and Christianity engendered a more than usually harsh reaction against whatever earlier native secular literary traditions may have existed. The scant Swedish production of specifically chivalric literature in the Continental manner may also be attributed in part to the attitude of the Church, though a more immediate and tangible reason is probably the fact that Sweden never had a highly developed feudal society in the Continental sense, a condition necessary for the spontaneous and full flowering of a chivalric literary tradition. Magnus Ladulås, the second of the Folkungs to occupy the throne, sought in the late years of the thirteenth century to reduce the barbaric elements in Swedish society by emulating chivalric practices at court and introducing on a limited scale the institution of knighthood. But neither in economic resources nor in cultural sophistication was Sweden prepared to emulate the chivalric practices and ideals of her distant feudal neighbors to the South. Not much more than the outward trappings of knighthood ever existed in Sweden. The Swedish medieval state at its best was a rather primitive social and political entity, in some respects not radically removed from the simple patterns of a relatively crude Viking civilization, and therefore adapted itself rather awkwardly and only partially to the Continental code of chivalric tradition. Under the circumstances, no significant body of chivalric literature could be produced in the country. No vital new literary tradition could be built on superficial observances of courtly jousts and sundry external chivalric practices, inasmuch as the profession of knighthood came so late to Sweden, largely *after* the period of its flowering on the Continent.

But if chivalric literature did not flourish in Sweden, scattered evidences of its impact have survived, most interestingly from the first half of the fourteenth century in the so-called *Eufemiavisor* and in certain portions of *Erikskrönikan*, the earliest of the "rhymed chronicles" and the most important from a literary point of view. Also extant from the fifteenth century is a sizable number of romances in the chivalric manner, but these late-born tales of knightly adventure are of little importance except that they bear witness to the persistence of the genre in Sweden down to the very threshold of the Reformation. In fact, at least one of these romances, a Swedish translation of a Latin version of the destruction of Troy, appears as late as 1529.

The three tales that make up the *Eufemiavisor*, like all the other chivalric romances which have survived in Old Swedish texts, are Swedish only in the most round-about and tenuous way: a Norwegian queen was responsible for having them recorded; the subject matter is non-Scandinavian in origin; only the language and the royal personage to whom the tales were addressed are Swedish. It was quite natural that these tales came to Sweden via Norway, where a more highly developed chivalric literary tradition had been established, a country in which both the French romance tales centering upon Charlemagne and the British Arthurian materials had come to be highly cultivated under Håkon Håkonsson (1217–63) and his successors. In Norway the knightly tales came to supplant the earlier *fornaldarsagor* and, like these romantic sagas, were written down in prose form. The collective title *Eufemiavisor* is derived from the name of the Norwegian queen who had the three tales turned into Swedish verse by a more than usually literate retainer in the service of Duke Erik Magnusson of Sweden as a gracious courtesy to the Duke when Queen Eufemia was seeking to arrange a marriage between Erik and her only daughter, Ingeborg. The queenly matrimonial machinations were for a time frustrated by a number of complications beyond her control (therefore the *three* tales, following each other in the order of their Swedish composition by fairly substantial time intervals); but "love finally won out" — as in "Flores and Blanzeflor," one of the three tales here turned into Swedish — and the persistence of the queen resulted at last in the royal wedlock.

Besides the well-known romance "Flores and Blanzeflor," which in origin can be traced back to a late Greek love story, the *Eufemiavisor* included "Hertig Fredrik" (Duke Frederick) and "Ivan Lejonriddaren" (John the Knight of the Lion), both of which derive ultimately from French romances, the latter from a celebrated tale by Chrétien de Troyes, the most distinguished practitioner of the art of the chivalric romance. The Swedish versions are free adaptations of their originals rather than exact translations, but in content they reflect closely the whole feudal world of romance on the Continent. Their pages contain effusive apostrophes to the knightly way of life and elaborate descriptions of chivalric court practices, the narrative sequences are infinitely involved and liberally invested with a multitude of miraculous phenomena, and the cult of love — so dear to the hearts of those who cultivated the chivalric romance — is given due attention. In "Flores and Blanzeflor," a tender tale of love between two very young people, the cult of love is reflected in its more innocent and naïve forms, while in "Duke Frederick" and "John the Knight of the Lion" the love theme is pursued in a much more sophisticated manner, a practice characteristic of the chivalric romance in its more advanced and decadent manifestations. Pure as the love of the knight for his lady was supposed to be in the world of chivalry, those who practiced the art of the chivalric tale were not always averse to conceiving the relationship between the sexes in at least obliquely sensual forms; and the popular appeal of these tales was certainly in no small measure due to the titillating manner in which they maintained — more or less deliberately — a coy balance between the frankly erotic and the apparently ideal love. The more frankly erotic picture of love is most clearly reflected in the *Eufemiavisor* in "Duke Frederick," especially in certain scenes in a maiden's boudoir, to which the Duke gains access by means of a "wishing ring." The good knight, invisible to the maiden, beholds at his leisure, with evident sensuous (if not actually sensual) pleasure, the physical charms of the lady whose privacy he has violated. Such slightly disguised lascivious scenes are not employed in "John the Knight of the Lion," which manages to retain the reader's interest in the love theme in ways less characteristic of the chivalric romance, chiefly by means of ingeniously handled comic complications in certain later phases of the relationship between the knight and his lady love. In these episodes the knight is something less than heroic and loyal, the lady something more than lovely and gentle.

With reference to poetic form the *Eufemiavisor* has the distinction of being the first relatively lengthy Swedish document in *knittelvers*, a kind of doggerel verse rhyming in couplets, the line containing usually four accented syllables with a varying number of unaccented ones. This most common of medieval verse forms, used extensively wherever the metrical romance was cultivated, displaced in the North the earlier alliterative Scandinavian verse patterns. Considering the paucity of Swedish predecessors in the new form, one must be impressed by the unusual control of the form in the hands of the unknown personage (or personages) who put the Eufemia tales into Swedish verse early in the fourteenth century. Couplet rhyming occurs occasionally in runic inscriptions of a considerably earlier date, and recognizable *knittelvers* forms are used in a portion on Christ's Suffering in *Fornsvenska legendariet*, composed around 1300; but it was not until the new end-rhyming form, with its line-structure of regularly distributed accents, became used extensively in the knightly tales included in the *Eufemiavisor* that this verse pattern broke definitely through in Sweden and became the point of departure for a poetic form which — with many variations down through the centuries — dominated the practice of Swedish verse practically to our own day. In the late Middle Ages *knittelvers* had to compete with the somewhat more complex verse patterns of the folk ballad, and later both of these had to give way successively to a considerable variety of more elegant and sophisticated verse forms, primarily to the Classical hexameter and to the French classical alexandrine in the seventeenth century and to English blank verse in the late eighteenth century.

If the metrical romance was a literary import, little practiced in Sweden, a related form — the historical chronicle in verse — was by contrast quite extensively cultivated. The first of these, *Erikskrönikan* (The Chronicle of Erik, sometimes called The Elder Chronicle), roughly contemporaneous with the *Eufemiavisor*, deals with Swedish historical events occurring shortly before its composition. The others — the most important of which are *Nya eller Karlskrönikan* (The New or Karl Chronicle) and *Sturekrönikorna* (The Sture Chronicles) — together cover without any appreciable gaps the entire sequence of historical events in Sweden after those dealt with in *Erikskrönikan*, i.e., from the early fourteenth down to the end of the fifteenth century. Except for *Erikskrönikan*, however, these historical chronicles have little literary significance beyond the merely formal fact that they are composed in rhymed verse. From the standpoint of the political historian, on the other hand, they are of much greater importance, dealing as they do with contemporary and near-contemporary political developments in Sweden; but their strong propagandistic bias (they are all written to justify the actions of those who commissioned their composition) forces the historian to use them with considerable circumspection.

The literary superiority of *Erikskrönikan* over the other verse chronicles is evident in many ways: in the skill with which the verse itself is handled, in its author's flair for vivid descriptive realism (as reflected especially in such oft-quoted passages as the one describing preparations for the departure of Birger Jarl and his "Crusaders" for Finland), and in the enthusiasm and elegance with which the author at many points communicates to the reader his awareness of the vital inner relationship between the contemporary Swedish political scene, in its relatively modest confines, and the larger, more spacious, more colorful world of feudal practices and chivalric romance of other lands. *Erikskrönikan* may without too much exaggeration be called a historical romance, employing as it does actual historical material which is treated with a poetic freedom and invested with a certain "coloring of the imagination" not entirely unworthy of historical romance at its best. A distinguished Swedish medievalist suggests that Sir Walter Scott himself would have been delighted had he read certain of the vivid descriptive passages in *Erikskrönikan*. Scott might also have appreciated the chronicler's imaginative fusion of a sense of political realities with a warm poetic enthusiasm for all that is encompassed in the chivalric view of life. Scott could no doubt have improved upon the materials in *Erikskrönikan* had he come upon them and been moved to recast them in the unique cauldron of his own historical magic; but one feels sure that he would have enjoyed the Swedish original for what it is, even while demonstrating how the tales may have been more skillfully handled. The unknown author of *Erikskrönikan* is not, it may be admitted, to be counted in the company of the really gifted poets; but he certainly occupies a high place — possibly the highest — in the more modest company of those who attempted the art of verse in the Swedish Middle Ages. Among those who used verse in the historical chronicle he stands quite alone.

A prose document of considerable historical and some literary importance appearing in Sweden at about the same time as *Erikskrönikan*, and in its political-historical subject matter loosely related to this chronicle, is the work entitled *Um styrilsi konunga ok höfthinga* (commonly called *Konungastyrelsen*, "The Royal Rule"). Though this work is partly a translation of, and otherwise in considerable part based upon, Egidius de Columnas's *De regimine principum* (c. 1280), it uses this source, together with a considerable variety of other medieval and classical sources, with such freedom that the Swedish work is by no means lacking in originality in the pursuit of its theme, the rights and responsibilities of a royal ruler. Stylistically the prose is of a very high order, interesting particularly because it is sharply reminiscent of the pithy, vigorous Swedish of the provincial laws. It was obviously composed by a man of unusual learning and talents as a book of precepts to guide the career of a prince — the young Magnus Eriksson, destined to occupy the Swedish throne as the last of the Folkungs. Scholars have for many years been intrigued by the mystery of authorship of *Konungastyrelsen*, some having attempted to establish that a chancellor in the Folkung court, one Phillipus Ragvaldi, was the author *both* of this work and *Erikskrönikan*; but neither this fascinating hypothesis nor any other efforts to identify the

37

author (or authors) of either *Erikskrönikan* or *Konungastyrelsen* can be said to have been proved.

The late Middle Ages in Sweden was a period of definite literary decline, explained chiefly, it would seem, by political conditions unfavorable to literary activity. The fall of the Folkung dynasty shortly after the middle of the fourteenth century created a state of political confusion in the country, mitigated in part by the elevation to the Swedish throne of Albrecht of Mecklenburg in 1371. His brief reign was followed by Sweden's not too willingly joining (in 1397) the so-called Kalmar Union of Scandinavian states, under the rising star of Danish political leadership. Sweden was almost from the beginning a highly refractory member of the Union, and the political scene in Sweden during the whole of the fifteenth century consisted of an almost unbroken series of confused conflicts for power between those of the Swedish nobility who favored Danish political domination and a group of "national-minded" Swedish noblemen who were allied at times with an aroused Swedish peasantry.

Under the circumstances it is natural that literary production in the waning years of the Swedish Middle Ages should lack almost entirely that sense of youthful vitality and imaginative drive characteristic of documents from the Folkung period: the provincial laws, *Erikskrönikan*, and the religious works of Petrus de Dacia and Saint Birgitta. Although in part primitive and barbaric, the period of the Folkungs had been nonetheless an era of positive cultural attainments and no little idealistic fervor. Although crude and fragmentary, the early Folkung efforts to establish a new chivalric society and a new religious community were genuine enough, and at least tentatively successful. In contrast the period which followed was on the whole a dreary waste of narrow, cold-blooded political maneuvering, largely bereft of the drive and lift and sense of political and religious vision found in the annals of the Folkungs despite the many bloody pages in the Folkung record. Only in the Engelbrekt-led uprising of the 1430's and in the struggle of the Stures toward national rehabilitation in the last decades of the fifteenth century can we descry clearly, in the confused political patterns of the times, any high levels of national vision. But neither Engelbrekt's efforts nor the Sture activities had any decisive results. They served merely to keep the vision of national independence alive in a political climate otherwise characterized by petty, scheming small-mindedness.

The difference between the Early and Late Middle Ages in Sweden is reflected sharply in the contrasts everywhere apparent between *Eriks-krönikan*, a product of an early semi-chivalric Folkung tradition, and the two later, fifteenth-century verse chronicles, *Karlskönikan* and *Sture-krönikorna*. And the falling off in literary vitality in the waning years of the Swedish Middle Ages is even more apparent in two historical prose works from late in the fifteenth century — one, the so-called *Prosaiska Krönikan* (The Prose Chronicle), by an unknown Franciscan monk; the other, a work entitled *Chronica regni Gothorum*, by Ericus Olai, who held a professorship in his last years (he died in 1484) at the recently established University at Uppsala. In contrast with the verse chronicles, these prose works are entirely devoid of literary qualities. And despite, or probably because of, their historical pretensions (they propose, unlike the verse chronicles, to deal with the *whole* of Swedish history) we find them of interest chiefly as historical curiosities. Both employ quite uncritically the most fantastic of sources, especially in their eager search for Swedish "origins," which they trace with unabashed naïveté back to the least reliable of traditions. According to *Prosaiska Krönikan* (fatuously following a "lead" from Isidore of Seville), the racial and political genealogy of the Swedes can be traced back to Magog's son Gog; and from such "beginnings" the national lineage of Sweden is pursued through a maze of curious foreign sources into the Uppsala Ynglingatal family tree and down to historical times. Ericus Olai's *Chronica* is almost as mad as *Prosakrönikan* in its use of questionable sources and its insistent desire to establish a sufficiently ancient and impressive lineage for the Swedish nation; but unlike *Prosaiska Krönikan* it does seek manfully, if not successfully, to break through the heavy underbrush of sources, to distinguish personal motivations in the drift of historical events, and to provide some sense of historical contexts in explaining these events.

Because Ericus Olai at least attempted something more than an uncritical listing of historical events, he has been called "the father of Swedish historical writing." Possibly, however, his chief distinction for Swedish historical writing is the much more dubious one of having provided the point of departure for the trend — in later centuries developing into a mania — to bolster Swedish patriotic self-assurance by making wildly exaggerated claims as to the pre-eminence of Sweden's ancient origins. His use of the word "Gothorum" (with its quite unhistorical *identification* of the Goths and the Geats) suggests, as we shall see in later chapters, a line which Swedish historians, with only one or two exceptions, followed quite blindly down to the end of the seventeenth century. Not

39

until the political catastrophe signalized by the death of Charles XII in 1718, and the subsequent "age of reason," was this illusory line of historical interpretation silenced — and even then not finally, for a hundred years later the Swedish Romantics of the "Gothic School" disinterred the idea, bringing the ghost tentatively to life again in magnificently sustained poetic measures. When the sober modern historian clashes with the romantic mythmaker the historian triumphs slowly — if, indeed, he triumphs at all except within the limited circle of his profession.

If the last century or so of the Swedish Middle Ages was in the main a period of limited, uninspired, often pettily motivated political conflicts and of definite literary decline, it did produce one document — the poem known as "Frihetsvisan" (The Song of Liberty) — which in certain ways represents the high point of medieval literature in Sweden. This poem, and another, "Trohetsvisan" (The Song of Loyalty), are the only ones in Swedish from this time whose author is with some certainty identifiable — a Bishop Thomas Simonsson of Strängnäs. Aside from his probable authorship of these two poems, what we know about Bishop Thomas (d. 1443) has to do exclusively with his religious-political activities. And we are acquainted with these activities only sketchily despite the assiduous efforts of recent scholars to define more precisely the political role which he played and out of which "The Song of Liberty" issued.

According to a centuries-old Swedish tradition Bishop Thomas was a Swedish nationalist, strongly opposed to the Scandinavian Union, and his poem was the classical articulation of the Swedish national cause in its heroic opposition to the foreign oppression of the day. Modern scholarship has challenged this view and has demonstrated rather convincingly that the Bishop was something of a political opportunist, not above shifting his political position from time to time when he felt that such maneuvering might bring advantages to the Church. But however tarnished in part the Bishop's escutcheon may have become under the anti-myth-making propensities of modern scholarship, the literary-historical fact remains that in "The Song of Liberty," and only to a lesser extent in "The Song of Loyalty," Bishop Thomas gave eloquent and moving poetic expression to his countrymen's desire for freedom at a time when this freedom was all but a myth in the land. Though other poets of the time tried their hand at political poems of a similar kind (mention may be made of the so-called "Visbyvisa" and "Brunkebergsvisan," both of which were apparently popular in the late fifteenth century), only "The Song of Liberty" has had the poetic vitality to live on in the popular patriotic traditions of the Swedes.

The pre-eminence of "The Song of Liberty" among poems of its kind is to be explained in part by Bishop Thomas's unusual poetic gifts and in part by the immediate circumstances out of which the poem sprang, the Engelbrekt Rebellion of the 1430's. Uninspiring on the whole as were the political conflicts in Sweden in the first half of the fifteenth century, the movement organized and directed by the popular folk hero Engelbrekt Engelbrektsson impresses us both for the skill of its leadership and the unselfish idealism of its purposes. For once at least in the dull, selfishly motivated succession of minor conflicts characteristic of the period, the whole land was aroused under the leadership of a born folk leader in effective *national* protest against the oppressor. The fact that Engelbrekt died at the hand of a personal enemy just when he seemed to have triumphed in his war for liberty in no way dimmed the glory of his deeds, nor did his death suggest to his people that they should be less jealous in the future of the measure of freedom which they had gained under his leadership.

In fact, it is this last point — that a people must continue to be aware of the necessity of maintaining its hard-won freedom — which becomes the central theme of "The Song of Liberty." In its general structure the poem falls into two parts: the first a narrative-descriptive account of conditions in the land before the rise of Engelbrekt, and the changes effected by Engelbrekt's work; the second a superb hymn to freedom, a hymn which in the simple majesty of its utterance lifts the reader far above the immediate political circumstances out of which the poem sprang, singing finally the praise of freedom as the fundamental condition of the good life in all times and all climes. Central in this hymn is the oft-quoted stanza:

> The finest thing is liberty
> Which you may seek the world around
> Wherever good men can be found.
> And if your honor dear you hold
> You'll value freedom more than gold,
> For honor comes when men are free.
>
> *Translated by Marianne Schultz*

A recent scholar has traced a few of the details in this stanza back to some obscure Latin distichs, but the Swedish verse rises so high above the Latin distichs in poetic power that it can scarcely be said to be an imitation. In "The Song of Liberty" are combined as never earlier in a Swedish poem essentially all of the ingredients of great poetry: a figurative language of appropriate concreteness and vitality, a central idea of immediate emotional urgency which has at the same time universal implications for man, and a free-swinging rhythmic pattern which gives a magnificent singing quality to the verse. Little wonder is it that certain stanzas of "The Song of Liberty" have lived on for centuries down to our day in the Swedish national consciousness. "The Song of Liberty" is, indeed, the first in time, and not the least in power, of that small handful of Swedish poems which are "classical" in the sense that they have an actuality far beyond their times. So impressed have some Swedes been by the elevated simplicity with which "The Song of Liberty" develops its patriotic theme that they have sought to have it adopted as the Swedish national anthem.

It might be assumed from what we have hitherto examined of Swedish medieval literature that this literature, whether religious or secular, was invariably practical or didactic in purpose. We have seen in instance after instance how medieval authors in Sweden have employed prose or poetry, as the case may be, more or less directly in the immediate service of the Church or the State. Birgitta demands repentance and invokes God's judgment on the sinner. Those who codified the provincial laws serve the practical disciplinary purposes of the State. In the verse chronicles and in the two poems by Bishop Thomas we become involved in contemporary political polemics and inspired urgings to patriotic feeling and action. In all of these cases whatever purely *literary* qualities the works contain may be said to be a by-product, a happy accident of temperament or circumstance or tradition. Only in one instance in this literature, in *Erikskrönikan*, do we come more than occasionally upon passages which seem less deliberately motivated by a desire to teach or preach than by a wish to entertain or give pleasure. And that this was the author's intention in *Erikskrönikan* is clear from the opening lines of the poem, in which he explicitly invites us to seek pleasure "in lovely words and pleasantries before we go to dine." We have seen however, that even in this work the author has additional purposes — more serious purposes — than merely to provide lively literary pleasantries for the delectation of the Court; and it must be admitted that these more serious intentions tend to dominate the poem, giving to it in no small measure those practical, didactic qualities which mark so much of Swedish medieval literature.

Erikskrönikan is, in the last analysis, a poem in which bloody political realities and sharp polemic partisanship are only intermittently obscured by the elegant graces of a gallant chivalric literary tradition as practiced and perfected on the Continent.

It remained for another literary genre, the ballad, to introduce into Sweden a literature which — in its purest early forms at least — was quite devoid of immediate didactic purposes, a literature which found its very *raison d'être* in the sheer joy simply to bring pleasure to those who heard it. The identification of the ballad with music and the dance and with popular folk festivals accounts largely for its lack of didacticism, its spontaneity, its naïve delight in a tale well told, its instinctive rejection of the ready moral formula.

To one who wishes to provide even a brief account of the Swedish medieval ballad two serious difficulties present themselves: first, it is often exceedingly difficult to distinguish between Swedish ballads and those of Denmark and Norway, so inextricably intertwined are the ballad traditions of these countries; and second, except for a single fragment none of the Swedish ballad texts which have come down to us is in the strict sense of the term a genuine medieval text. The earliest ballad texts which we have were not recorded until the years 1570 to 1660, and the majority date from the nineteenth century. What happened to the original medieval texts in the centuries which intervened before their late recording is impossible to say with any precision, though significant attempts to solve this problem have been made by a number of Scandinavian scholars, most brilliantly perhaps in a work first published in 1891 by the Danish medievalist Johannes C. H. R. Steenstrup and which later appeared in an English translation under the title *The Medieval Popular Ballad*. Though this work largely uses Danish ballad texts for purposes of illustration, its conclusions are in general equally applicable to an understanding of the Swedish ballad.

It was appropriate, if not inevitable, that the most important pioneer work on the ballad should be done by a great group of Danish scholars, Svend Grundtvig, Steenstrup, and Axel Olrik; for it was via Denmark that the ballad tradition reached Norway and Sweden in its movement northward from its Continental cradle in France, and many more Danish ballads have been preserved than is the case either in Norway or Sweden. From the labors of these Danish scholars, joined among others by Knut Liestøl in Norway and Sverker Ek in Sweden, we now know a great deal about the circumstances under which the ballad arose in Scandinavia and we can be reasonably sure what the genuine medieval ballad in the Scandinavian countries was like.

It came to Scandinavia first from France, later from Britain; and it spread rapidly — in part because of the role it played in the enormously popular group dance of the time, in part because its oral nature made it readily accessible to the widest possible audience, and in part because it released repressed energies in a folk psyche too long submissive to the heroic idealism of a primitive Scandinavian world view. "The pre-Christian Scandinavian world," writes Olrik,

regarded the dance as a foreign and distasteful custom. Its flexibility, its susceptibility to mood, its vague longing, its smoldering eroticism — these were entirely opposed to the ideal of fortitude that underlay the heroic song of the ancient period. Hence we find the skalds mocking the hopping and skipping of the dancers. Saxo at times scourges the power which the dance has over his contemporaries, but for the most part he passes it over in silence.

The Catholic Church, though it had its own heroic ideal, was on the whole more tolerant of the dance; and it was not unheard of that ballads were sung to the rhythms of the dance in fields within earshot of the parish church, no incongruity apparently being sensed when dance rhythms blended with priestly chants across the countryside. At times even the churchyard itself, with its community of the dead, provided the locale for the lively dance beat of the ballad!

The Swedish ballad tradition seems to have reached its high water mark rapidly in the hundred years or so after the middle of the thirteenth century, after which it continued to maintain itself in a somewhat modified form down into the early years of the sixteenth century. At this point the Lutheran Reformation, with its heavy-handed morality, succeeded for a time in weakening the hold which the ballad had maintained on the folk imagination, though it continued for centuries to maintain a certain stubborn vitality in the oral tradition of the Swedish peasantry — a circumstance which accounts in part for the treasury of ballad texts which have come down to us. The recorded form of these texts has survided in three ways: through the ten so-called *visböcker* (song books) written down in the main by women of the higher nobility in the late sixteenth and seventeenth centuries, through the first printed collections of ballads resulting from the early nineteenth-century Romantic interest in folk literature (E. G. Geijer and A. A. Afzelius, *Svenska folkvisor från forntiden*, I–III, 1814–16, and A. I. Arwidsson, *Svenska fornsånger*,

I–III, 1834–42), and finally through the enthusiastic work of various amateur and semi-amateur folklorists who, over the last hundred years, have scoured the Swedish countryside for evidences of a still living literary tradition among the folk. Though a great deal of scholarly attention has been paid to this rather rich body of ballad material, it is unfortunate that no inclusive critical edition of these Swedish ballads matching the magnificent Grundtvig-Olrik edition of the Danish ballads has as yet appeared.

In its form the Swedish ballad, like that of Denmark and Norway, differed in no essential respects from the ballad tradition of the Continent, out of which it originally grew. Its aim was to tell in verse a story, lively or melancholy or harsh as the case might be, often in dialogue form, the whole being held together in terms of theme or mood or both by a refrain repeated at the close of each stanza. The stanza itself consisted of either two or four lines, the latter being a relatively late development in Scandinavia. The two-line stanza employed the couplet rhyme, while only the second and fourth lines rhymed in the four-line stanza. In the so-called chain dance (*kedjedans*) the leader of the dance would sing the entire text as he took part in the dance, while in the ring dance (*ringdans*) the leader stood in the center of the closed circle of dancers who joined in the refrain of the ballad whose full text the leader alone sang. The dance itself in its original form as deriving out of a chivalric tradition was relatively stately and dignified, though there is plenty of evidence to suggest that it later got more or less out of hand, developing in its late less happy stages rather crude madcap characteristics as it departed from its early courtly environs and became a more simple and unsophisticated form of entertainment among peasants and burghers.

Aside from its stanzaic structure and its use of the refrain, the central characteristic of the ballad is its narrative concentration. The tale it has to tell is told rapidly, with an absolute minimum of descriptive detail, with a highly sparing use of the lyrical element, with no pretense at psychological subtleties, and with no commentary on the part of the author. The action, related with a laconic swiftness in the form of dialogue, resembles a miniature, highly telescoped drama, abrupt, vivid, intense. Descriptive detail is limited to stereotypes — ladies almost invariably being delicate of build, with "fingrar små" (fingers small) and "gula lockar" (golden locks), and they are attired more often than not in "sabel och mård" (sable and marten capes), while their knights ride on "gångare

grå" (trotters gray), attired in "skarlakan röd" (scarlet red), and in moments of conflict they draw the "brune brand" (red-gleaming sword).
The lyrical element, when it occurs, is restricted to the refrain or, on
occasion, to a phrase or two of the opening stanza, providing but a bare
hint of the mood implicit in the action of the tale, as when in the melancholy "Svennens sorg" (The Squire's Sorrow), a soft autumnal note
of tragedy is suggested:

Moder sporde hon sonen god
— medan lövet faller ned —

Mother questioned her good son
— while the leaf descends —

or in the gentle midsummer mood of "Duvans sång på liljekvist" (The
Dove's Song on a Lily Sprig):

Det sitter en duva på liljekvist
— i midsommartider —

A dove it sits on a lily sprig
— at midsummertide —

or the lovely "driver dagg, faller rim" (driving dew, hoarfrost falling)
in "Herr Olov och älvorna" (Sir Olov and the Elves), one of the most
beautiful of the ballads dealing with the supernatural creatures of the
woods and countryside.

The subject matter of the Scandinavian ballad is various. In its most
distinguished forms it is concerned with knightly deeds and reflects the
patterns of life typical of the chivalric tradition (the so-called *riddar-
visor*); otherwise it treats of legendary matter and supernatural phenomena (*legendariska och natur-mytiska visor*), or tells tall tales based on ancient heroic traditions (*kämpavisor*), or reflects in a variety of ways the
life of burgher and peasant (*borgare- och bondevisor*). The knightly ballads together with the legendary and supernatural ballads maintain on the
whole a dignified tone and are frequently tragic in outcome, while the
kämpavisor and the ballads deriving from the world of burgher and peasant are more realistic and often contain broad humorous elements which
frequently break over into crude and grotesque effects. Mention may
also be made of that variation of the chivalric ballad which celebrates
important historical events, represented in Sweden most impressively in
"Kung Sverker och slaget vid Lena, 1208" (King Sverker and the Battle
of Lena) and in the much later "Gustav Vasa och dalkarlarna" (Gustav
Vasa and the Men from Dalarna).

Of these four basic subject matters of the Scandinavian ballad, the *kämpavisa* was developed originally, and most extensively, in Norway, while the other types are on the whole more characteristic of Denmark and Sweden. Judging from the ballads which have survived, Denmark is pre-eminent among the Scandinavian countries in the chivalric ballad with its world of knights and ladies and their loyal squires, though many such ballads have come down to us also in Sweden. In most respects the Danish and Swedish ballads of this kind are similar in subject matter and form if not in quality; but Sweden has the distinction — whether dubious or not may be left to the taste of the reader — of having an unusually large number of *brudrovsvisor*, ballads which concern themselves with the theme of the stolen bride.

Though the playfully serious practice of stealing brides was not exactly uncommon in the relatively brutal society of the Scandinavian Middle Ages, the unusual frequency of its occurrence in the Swedish ballad tradition is perhaps to be attributed less to the actual frequency of the phenomenon in the life of the time than to its lively narrative possibilities, particularly when the stolen bride was a person of high social standing. And in Sweden a number of ballads concern themselves with a most remarkable series of bride stealings, involving female personages of no less station than a proud daughter of a Swedish king, and, in turn, her daughter and her daughter's daughter. The most notable of these ballads are "Vreta klosterrov" (The Vreta Cloister Bride Stealing), "Falken Albrektssons brudrov" (Falken Albrektsson's Bride Stealing), and "Palle Bossons brudrov" (Palle Bosson's Bride Stealing). In the latter two a special piquancy enhances each of the tales because the bride dislikes the intended bridegroom and is gaily stolen away at the last moment by the good knight whom the lady "truly loves." The gay impertinence of the act in the case of Falken Albrektsson must have been an especially choice morsel for the Swedish public of the day, for the ballad is based on an actual historical event from 1288, and the act of Falken Albrektsson was considered so serious a breach of the law by the king, Magnus Ladulås, that he intervened, imprisoned Falken's father, a *lagman* in Västergötland, and one of Falken's brothers. Other members of the family, together with Falken and his lady, escaped to Norway.

In sharp contrast to the bride-stealing ballads about Falken Albrektsson and Palle Bosson is "Vreta klosterrov," one of the most impressive of Swedish ballads. In this case the stealing of the bride was especially notable not only because the lady was a princess but also because the act

47

involved a bloody violation of the sanctity of the celebrated Cistercian cloister at Vreta, where the princess Elin was in temporary residence. Besides, the princess, according to the ballad, resisted the act of violence and was carried away by force to become the bitterly unwilling bride of her abductor, Sune Folkvarsson. The most memorable part of the ballad is the final scene of reckoning between the imperiously proud woman and the man who had taken her against her will. The scene occurs fifteen years after the abduction, when Elin is about to die. Sune, somewhat chastened by the years and the imminence of Elin's death, pleads forgiveness for all his "guilt and offense," offering to do penance by making a pilgrimage on "bare feet" to Rome. But Elin is unimpressed, and breaks out in wildly bitter and passionate denunciation of the man who had wronged her. And she dies, fiercely proud and unforgiving in spirit, with words of caustic denunciation on her lips. There is something of the savage agony of Medea in the character and the tragic fate of this proud northern princess Elin.

For a century and more after Herder's theory of ballad authorship was first promulgated in the late eighteenth century, the answer to the question "who *composed* the ballads?" has been fraught with much speculation and controversy. The early nineteenth-century Romantics, following Herder, assumed a collective "folk" authorship of the ballads, and contrasted such authorship sharply with the individual authorship of more conscious and sophisticated literary genres. It seems clear now, however, that though no names of individual authors of ballads have come down to us, individuals were responsible for ballads in their original form. From what class these individuals came, whether from the highest social strata or from the loyal squires of the knightly class or from itinerant entertainers of one kind or another is not clear, though the internal evidence of the ballads points most sharply to the latter two classes. That the "folk" as a group had, however, much to do with the form of many of the ballads which have come down to us is undeniable, for it was on the lips of the folk that the ballad lived down through the centuries, constantly subject to the modifying influences of folk life and folk traditions. In this sense, but only in this sense, can we still employ the Swedish term *folkvisa* (folk ballad) — taken from Herder's term *Volklied* — to the poems with which we have been concerned.

If it is definitely misleading to use the term "folk ballad" in the strict sense of folk authorship of the ballad, it is probably less misleading to assume folk authorship in the case of another body of popular literature which has its origins in a folk tradition in most cases much older than the ballad. I refer to that miscellany of folk material in prose ranging from the folk tale and folk legend to the short, pithy folk sayings ordinarily taking on the form of the proverb and the riddle. To sum up briefly the origins and nature of these primitive literary forms is even more difficult than in the case of the ballad, partly because scholarship has been more assiduous than effective in dealing with these forms and partly because these forms derive out of conditions of life and chronological contexts far less capable of definition and dating than in the case of the ballad.

Though some recent scholars make a good case for "learned" origins of Swedish proverbs and riddles, it would seem probable that these two forms, together with the folk tale and the folk legend, are closer to a purely *folk* tradition than is the ballad, and that they represent on the whole a considerably more indigenous phenomenon than does the ballad. In any case the Scandinavian proverb and the riddle, the folk tale and the legend, needed no relatively sophisticated literary tradition from France or England to point the way to a literary form. They existed in the Scandinavian countries from the most ancient times, as is sufficiently clear from material of this kind in the Eddic poems, the sagas, and the provincial laws. That this popular literature in Scandinavia ultimately took on accretions from abroad is incontestable, but the point is that it existed in a long-established native tradition long before extensive contact with a larger outside world brought new elements into the stream of the older Scandinavian tradition, and it managed even in a later day to maintain in the main an essentially independent and original form and flavor. The ballad, by contrast, was in the North what Olrik calls a "naturalized" form, although it flourished in Scandinavia and came to establish a vital Scandinavian tradition of its own.

In the Swedish forms of the popular prose narrative from the Middle Ages and earlier it is customary to distinguish between two types, the *folksägen* and the *folksaga*, though it is often difficult to classify any particular tale as clearly either the one or the other. In the actual practice of primitive story telling the two types tend frequently to lose their separate identities and blend into each other. At any rate what critical parlance means by *folksägen* is a tale based, at least in origin, upon a real action in an actual world, while the *folksaga* is a tale of a more fantastic kind, deriving its materials ultimately from an essentially imagined, usually supernatural world. The *folksägen* differs from the *folksaga* also in that it tends to teach or point a practical moral and is frequently local in character, while the *folksaga* usually aims simply to entertain and amuse and is international in flavor.

Generally speaking this distinction applies also to the difference between two types of Swedish folk sayings, the *ordspråk* (the proverb, more strictly speaking) and the *ordstäv* (wise-saw). Though both of these are similar in the vivid concentration with which they give utterance to a practical folk philosophy, the *ordspråk* does this usually in a relatively dignified, serious tone: "He who evades the hangman will not escape the devil." "One must stand on a high mountain if one is to see one's destiny." "Money opens all doors except Heaven's." The *ordstäv*, on the other hand, is much more apt to coin its thought in broadly humorous, sharply satirical forms: " 'He has learned his art from me,' said the devil of the politician." " 'You are like my rooster, cocky about your tail,' said the cottager to the Master of the Royal Household who arrived in uniform." " 'It will be accordingly,' said the priest [as he] baptized the child for a penny." Of all the short folk forms, the riddle (*gåtan*) is certainly the oldest; and though it often concerns itself with practical, everyday matters and has its moments of grotesque folk humor, it probably derives from — and frequently gives expression to — that sense of mystery in life so characteristic of the primitive mind. It therefore approaches genuine poetic utterance more frequently than does the *ordspråk* or the *ordstäv*. The most elevated form in which we know the riddle in the Scandinavian tradition is in some of the songs of the *Poetic Edda*.

Religious Reformation and Cultural Decline

IN THE ANNALS of Swedish literature no period is on the whole more sterile than the hundred years or so following the breakthrough of the Lutheran Reformation in Sweden in the 1520's. Except for the work of Olaus Petri, "the Swedish Martin Luther," the translations by various hands of the Old and New Testaments, and the letters and speeches of the Reformation King, Gustav Vasa, very little of literary value appears in the generation immediately following the break with the Catholic Church; and the generation which followed the death of Gustav Vasa (1560) was characterized chiefly by a fanatical, often sharply personal religious controversy which produced almost exclusively partisan historical works of dubious importance and a flurry of scurrilous religious pamphlets on the lowest level of verbal utterance. Only at the close of the century and immediately after, when a rigid religious orthodoxy had become firmly established, were conditions somewhat more favorable for literary production; but even then only two figures rise much above the level of literary mediocrity. The two are Johannes Messenius, whose historical writings are of considerable value and whose dramas represent the first fumbling steps in the direction of a national drama, and Lars Wivallius, who may be considered the first really important lyric poet in Sweden.

This is a paltry literary harvest, indeed, at a time when abroad the fresh, seminal forces of the Renaissance were successfully challenging medieval scholasticism and asceticism, when the national literatures of France and England were experiencing the creative vitality of La Pléiade and the Elizabethan drama, and other countries were experiencing literary renewal in various significant ways. Even Denmark, where a religious reformation developed contemporaneously with that of Sweden, managed to avoid more successfully than Sweden the cultural blight which so long prevailed in Gustav Vasa's kingdom and that of his immediate successors.

Various reasons can be given for the cultural sterility of these years in Sweden, nearly all of them deriving more or less directly out of the immediate political and economic conditions in the country in the first decades of the sixteenth century. The Reformation itself, in fact, derives primarily from these conditions rather than from any popular, broadly based religious motivations. It was, in its origins at least, a religious transformation dictated from above, by the able and crafty Gustav Vasa himself, who found it politically convenient to encourage the work of those religious personalities who at the beginning of his reign were prepared to challenge the authority of the Roman Catholic Church and launch a new set of religious ideas and a new ecclesiastical organization. When the newly crowned King in 1523 called the young Olaus Petri from the relative obscurity of Strängnäs to Stockholm, appointing him secretary to the city's council and permitting him to preach in Storkyrkan, the chief church in the capital, the King did so deliberately, cannily sensing the advantages which might accrue to his kingdom by reducing the authority hitherto maintained by the hierarchy of the Catholic Church. Besides, the King was in desperate need of large financial resources, a need which could most conveniently and quickly be supplied by the great wealth of the Church in Sweden. Successful though he had been in destroying Danish political power over his land, he managed to carry through his struggle for independence only by becoming almost hopelessly indebted to Lübeck, one of the chief merchant cities of the Hanseatic League. Economic dependence under Lübeck might be preferable to political dependence under Denmark, but neither was desirable; and Gustav Vasa, a political realist of the first order, had few if any qualms in carrying out a series of radical reductions of Church property in order to fill the nation's (and incidentally his own) coffers and thereby see his way clear to eliminating his subservience to Lübeck and consolidate his power in the country. And the royal rapaciousness as exhibited in Gustav Vasa's reduction of the vast Church properties had a rather ironic counterpart in the miserliness with which the King doled out economic advantages to the new Lutheran Church. He insisted at all points upon retaining complete power, political and religious, in his own hands, finding a new Lutheran Church more obeisant to his political intentions than the old Catholic Church, whose hierarchy had for centuries wielded a very considerable economic and political power in the land.

Justifiable as these measures may have seemed from a political point of view, they were often carried out with such ruthless disregard for humane values that Swedish culture during the reign of Gustav Vasa suffered a severe setback. The Catholic Church had been the chief cultural bulwark of Sweden in the Middle Ages. This bulwark was now destroyed, and the King, busy with a formidable accumulation of practical political problems, made no serious efforts to establish new cultural institutions or refurbish the older cultural traditions of his kingdom. In fact, he himself ordained or permitted a long series of brutal cultural vandalisms. The cathedral schools languished and Uppsala University was allowed to disintegrate completely. But this cultural barbarism — the term is not too strong — is perhaps most shockingly reflected in the fate of the cloister libraries, several of which as we have seen were among the more distinguished in Europe. The cloisters were one after another closed, their religious objects containing silver or gold or precious stones were confiscated, and the treasures of their libraries were in many instances used by the King's bailiffs as wrappings for the bailiffs' records. Not until after Gustav Vasa's death, when his two sons Erik and Johan occupied successively the throne, did the royal house of Vasa show any concern for cultural values; but then it was too late to recover priceless manuscripts and such objects of religious art as had been melted down and otherwise used in order to pay the national debt and stabilize the economy. And though educational institutions could be and were in part re-established, they hardly recovered for a century or more the cultural status which they had formerly occupied in Sweden.

In the light of all this the reader of Gustav Vasa's letters is at first nonplused when he comes upon passages in which the King laments bitterly the decay particularly of the lower schools — until one notes that the King's displeasure derives exclusively from the fact that the prevailing illiteracy has a serious effect on the recruiting of citizens for the immediate and practical exigencies of governmental administration. Gustav Vasa had no eye for the broad, civilizing function of education; he needed clerks and secretaries and a host of minor administrative personages in the day-to-day work of his chancellory with its vast administrative ramifications throughout the country, and the functionaries necessary to proper administrative efficiency were in need of at least a minimal level of literacy to perform their work.

It is a rather queer quirk of history that the practical political opportunist Gustav Vasa, who was so blind to higher cultural values, should himself become by an accident of circumstance and temperament one of the two important literary figures of his day in Sweden. The accident of circumstance which made of him an author of a kind despite his lack of literary interests was the constant necessity under which he labored to communicate directly by speech and letter with his subjects, who did not always respond with enthusiasm to his official proposals and actions. What gave to these communications that special flavor which raised them above the usual impersonal level of governmental communications was the King's remarkable temperament — earthy, intense, imaginative, with a striking flair for the apropos illustration, the concrete, homely phrase, the telling formulation of argument.

We have no definitive texts of any of the King's speeches, but the testimony of contemporaries bears adequate witness to their popularity and effectiveness. Of the letters we have a great many, and they provide plenty of evidence of the natural gift for words which the King commanded. These letters, though official communications of a monarch to his subjects, are couched in simple, direct, highly personal terms, like those of a father to his children. And their range of expression is considerable, from direct utterance to devastating irony, from cajolery to thunderous threats, from the merely pathetic to the near tragic. Perhaps their most striking characteristic, however, is their complete lack of evasiveness, their readiness to avoid circumlocutions and meet issues head on, as when the King writes to the people of Lödöse (who had appealed to early letters of privilege) that he "paid no more attention to a lot of old letters than to a blueberry," or when he writes to the most distinguished of the Catholic bishops Hans Brask, who had protested the use of cloisters as military bivouacs — "where you write that this took place in violation of the freedom of the Church and against the law which we have sworn to uphold, I know well enough that necessity breaks the law, not only the law of man but at times even God's law." Much as the worthy Hans Brask may have had to complain about the manner in which Gustav Vasa handled Church property and the whole problem of the Church in Sweden, he could hardly complain that the King justified his actions by a devious logic. It is little wonder that Bishop Hans left the kingdom shortly after receiving this letter from the King. He was sufficiently intelligent to understand the implications of the letter for the whole future of Swedish Catholicism while Gustav Vasa occupied the throne.

For more than half of his long reign of nearly forty years Gustav Vasa's place on the throne was a somewhat precarious one. Not only was his right to the throne challenged by some at home and threatened by powerful religious and political forces abroad, but his subjects were frequently restless under his severe rule and given to rebellious acts. In consequence, crisis followed upon crisis during the early years of the reign; and it is characteristic of Gustav Vasa's methods in dealing with these crises that they were met as often — and as effectively — by the word as by the sword. In fact, it may be said that to Gustav Vasa the word was almost in the literal sense of the term a sword, an instrument of active propaganda by which the wills of a refractory folk were bent to his own will and to his vision of the nation's welfare. He was his own propaganda minister, by far the most able propagandist who has occupied the Swedish throne. Many were the strings in his instrument of propaganda, but the one which he used most skillfully was the appeal to self-interest and the identification of the self-interest of the folk with his own. In speech and letter he marshaled the evidence for his case with extraordinary skill, it may even be said with cunning, reminding a stubborn peasantry of what they owed him in terms of peaceful conditions which permitted them to sow and reap without fear of interruption or pre-emptive taxation. "Your hired men and maids," the King writes to the grumbling peasantry of Uppland in a typical letter dated December 8, 1539, "go out into the fields without sorrow and gladly to their work; likewise in the evening happily and in peace they return home again; all the hills and vales and fields stand now pleasantly and are well-adorned." Otherwise was it, he reminds them, in the days when they had to suffer all manner of evil at the hands of "the horrible Danish bloodhound monarch Kristiern . . . so that you had no peace or calm in your lives nor on your property, but your wives, children, relatives, and friends and everything in the land was stupefied and without consolation; your hired help, maids and farm laborers, as well as your cattle and beasts of burden, wandered about early and late on the land in search of sustenance . . . your farms, houses, fields, and meadows became an uncultivated wasteland . . ." And after describing in great detail more of these miseries under an earlier foreign rule, the moral — that the peasantry should attend to its duties and the King to his — is finally applied with the ring of unmistakable royal authority: "Tend Ye to your houses, fields, meadows, wives, children, beasts of burden and cattle, and desist from mouthing your opinions on Our political and religious rule!" After which follows a sharp reminder of the King's absolute power, based on divine right, in all final decisions regarding the administration of the kingdom.

Anxious as Gustav Vasa was in speeches and letters to justify his actions in the eyes of his contemporaries, he was equally anxious to justify himself in the judgment of future generations, the final judgment of history. Already in the middle of the 1530's, therefore, he began casting about for a likely person to write a history of his reign. His choice first fell upon Olaus Petri. Though Olaus Petri was not averse, as we shall see, to historical research, he managed to evade the delicate task of writing an official history about a suspicious and testy king with whose policies he did not always agree. The King's choice then fell on Peder Swart, Bishop of Vesterås, who, apparently with the direct assistance of the King, composed an inoffensive history of Gustav Vasa's reign down to 1533. Afterward Per Brahe, the King's nephew, continued this history down to the end of his uncle's reign.

If a king on the throne by an accident of circumstance and temperament became a master of effective Swedish prose in the daily pursuit of his manifold and arduous political duties, a preacher in a pulpit came during the same years to ply the literary trade equally effectively in matters religious. The preacher, Olaus Petri (c. 1493–1552), was in his way as remarkable a personality as was Gustav Vasa. Together, the king, who built firmly the foundations of the modern Swedish state, and the preacher-reformer, who was chiefly responsible for the establishment of its new religion, dominated the Swedish scene during their day.

Aside from the fact that Olaus Petri was the son of an apparently well-to-do blacksmith in Örebro, we know practically nothing about his early years. That he studied as a youth in Sweden can be taken for granted, though in what type of school is uncertain, and whether he attended the newly established University of Uppsala cannot be established. Our first clear record of his advanced studies are from Germany, where he first came to the University of Leipzig in the late spring of 1516, but a few months later he matriculated at Wittenberg, where we can assume that he was attracted by Luther as well as by the liberal humanistic spirit prevailing there in contrast to the reactionary scholasticism of Leipzig. He remained at Wittenberg two years, before his departure having taken the Master's degree. Upon his return to Sweden he became attached in a pedagogical capacity to the cathedral school at Strängnäs, from whence, as we have seen, he was called into the King's service in 1523, serving first, from 1524 to 1531, as secretary to the city council of Stockholm, and later, from 1531 to 1533, as the King's chancellor.

His studies at Wittenberg and his early contact with Gustav Vasa were decisive in determining his career. At Wittenberg he came under the spell of Martin Luther in the early, vitally eruptive years of the Reformation, before Lutheranism stiffened into a dogmatic system scarcely less arid than the scholasticism it sought to displace. And Olaus Petri managed to maintain many of the fresh impulses of the early years of the Reformation which he had experienced under the spell of the embattled Luther of the early years. The call into Gustav Vasa's service a few years after Olaus Petri's return to Sweden precipitated him rapidly into the political and religious hurly-burly at the beginning of the King's reign. The fact that the young religious reformer was called to the chancellorship in 1531, after his years of service in the Stockholm city government, suggests that as a public servant he had done well. But to serve the King directly in the day-to-day activities of the royal chancellory was another matter, and soon the clash of temperament and idea between the King and his chancellor resulted in the latter's dismissal. The King's discontent on this occasion is reflected in the characteristically picturesque judgment that, as a chancellor, Olaus Petri was scarcely more capable than "a Holstein-Friesian cow at spinning silk and a jackass as a lute player [*luteslagare*]"!

Upon his first entering the public service, almost ten years before his abrupt departure from the chancellory, it is clear that the young and idealistic reformer was not aware that the King intended to use him for his own political purposes. But it was not long before he began to sense the disparity between his own religious idealism and the King's religious opportunism, and this led gradually not only to his departure from the King's service but also to occasional direct criticism of the King's policies and actions, particularly in matters affecting religion and the new Lutheran Church. Late in 1539 the strained relations between Gustav Vasa and his former chancellor erupted in a charge of treason and a sentence of death against the latter; and though the sentence was rescinded, Olaus Petri's public career suffered a permanent eclipse and he lived on in relative obscurity until his death in 1552. This decade of political retirement was not, however, one of religious and literary inactivity. It was a period which included much labor of revision on many of his earlier religious works, and during which he wrote his famous history of Sweden (*En swensk cröneka*), the most important work of a long and prolific literary career which had begun about a generation earlier in the first years of the Lutheran breakthrough in Sweden.

Though Olaus Petri was not ordained to the ministry officially until late in his career, he was active from the beginning in the pulpit and with a many-sided religious authorship. So busy was his pen, indeed, that in the early years of the Reformation in Sweden his domination of the book market amounted almost to an exclusive access to the recently introduced Swedish printing press. In order to fill the needs of the new religion he worked feverishly on translations and original works of all kinds, catechisms, collections of homilies, church manuals, psalms, an occasional polemic work, sermons on special occasions (including one on the unhappy prevalence of swearing, addressed among others at the King, whose violent temper often sought an outlet in earthy oaths), and — most important — in biblical translations and his Swedish history. The frequency of translations from the German, especially from the works of Luther, in the earliest phase of Olaus Petri's literary activity is to be explained in part by the close contact between the German and Swedish reformers and in part by the urgent need for a new religious literature in a Sweden so recently detached from the Roman Church. As this need became less urgent Olaus Petri's own religious genius asserted itself with a freshness and originality not unworthy in its modest way of the example of Luther and Melancthon and other leading Continental religious figures.

Except for the courage with which he expressed his opinions, however, Olaus Petri was in most ways an author of quite another kind than Luther. His writing has none of the gusty outspokenness, the overwhelming vitality of Luther's. Rather he impresses by the simple clarity of his style, a style which employs no rhetorical tricks to attain its ends and which seldom if ever spills over into crudities of utterance or the sharp personal polemic that mars so much of the prose of the time. But above all one must admire Olaus Petri's prose for the purity of its Swedish in a period in which the language otherwise had almost lost its national character through the influence particularly of Low German, which had begun to infiltrate the Swedish language far back in the Middle Ages. Later the commercial domination of Scandinavia by the Hanseatic League had flooded Sweden with a North German vocabulary and orthography. Though the work of Olaus Petri and other Swedish reformers reflects some High German forms, most clearly in the biblical translations, Olaus Petri sought his way back primarily to the spoken language of his country, to the dialects, and in this way his work becomes the point of departure for what the philologists call *äldre nysvenska* (Early New Swedish), which marks the first major departure from *fornsvenska* (Old Swedish) in the direction of *yngre nysvenska* (Modern New Swedish), the language of our day.

Aside from Olaus Petri's central significance in the matter of language, however, most of his work is of little purely literary interest. With some relatively minor exceptions (including particularly the noble humanistic formulation of judicial rules called *Domareregler*), it may be said that the only works of his which today can move our literary sense as distinguished from any religious-pedagogical predilections are his work on the translation of the Bible and his Swedish chronicle.

This is not the place in which to enter in detail into the vexed question of Olaus Petri's exact part in the translations into Swedish of the New Testament (published 1526) and the complete Bible (1541). Suffice it to note that scholars, by means of philological and stylistic studies, seem to have seriously challenged, if not actually exploded, the theory that Olaus Petri was alone, or even essentially alone, responsible for the translation of the New Testament of 1526. That he had a part in this work, if not a major part, seems evident, though there is little agreement as to which portions are his and who the other translators may have been. Still more confused is the question as to the distribution of the burden of translating the first complete Swedish Bible, the so-called Gustav Vasa Bible of 1541; but it is clear that the task was organized by Laurentius Petri, Olaus Petri's younger brother and the first Protestant Archbishop of Sweden, and that the project was distributed among a number of translators, including Olaus Petri. It is therefore convenient to consider these two monumental biblical translations in the general context of Olaus Petri's work.

The word "monumental" is by no means too strong in describing these translations, for they are of the very first importance both in the quality of the translations and the influence which they have wielded in the religious and cultural history of Sweden. No Swedish book before or since has had anything like the impact of these translations on the folk mind, or has tended over so many generations to shape — if somewhat less significantly — the ways of thinking and turns of phrase of the more sophisticated Swede. Though it is a romantic notion that these translations made the Bible immediately available to the masses, it is true that with a gradually developing folk literacy the Bible came in time to take its place alongside the almanac as the only printed matter known to the great masses of the people. How well the early reformer-translators did their work is evident from the fact that later editions of the Swedish Bible, such as those of 1618 and 1703, were essentially merely slight revisions of the first Swedish Bible rather than really new versions. It was not, in fact, until 1917 that a completely new version appeared.

The sense of triumph felt in the fact that the whole of the Bible had finally become available in the nation's own language is reflected in the full titles of the two basic translations — *Thet nyia Testamentit på Swensko* and *Biblia, thet är, all then Helgha Scrifft på Swensko*. Of the two works the translation of the New Testament seeks on the whole to maintain the closest possible contact with a homely everyday language while the later translation of the entire Bible maintains a somewhat more elegant and elevated style without losing a sense of contact with the everyday world. In both cases the translators were aware of their responsibility to use as pure a Swedish as was possible at that time, eschewing both the Scylla of ecclesiastical Latinized turns of phrase and the Charybdis of Low German and Danish vocabulary and orthography which had interpenetrated the Swedish at so many points in the two or three preceding centuries. These translations were in consequence a kind of declaration of independence for the native tongue, a more or less conscious effort to assert a *national ideal* in the use of the written and printed word even while the more ostensible purpose may have been to bring a people to the worship of God. Never before had the Swedish language resounded with such resonant authority, ranging freely in its scale of utterance from the pithy homeliness — at times the raciness — of a proverbial folk language to the simple majesty of phrasing characteristic of the ancient provincial laws, and maintaining everywhere a sense of spare and noble dignity worthy of the high subject which the words sought to bring alive in an age when barbaric dissension rather than the serene authority of an established faith tended to absorb the spirit and dissipate the energies of man. If — as seems clear — these translations were the collective work of a great number rather than of two or three devoted scholars, it is the more remarkable that this company of translators seem moved by such a single-minded and noble literary ideal.

In the Reformation literature of Sweden nearly everything else is ordinary and ephemeral by comparison, necessary for the day as may have been the miscellany of catechisms, church manuals, collections of psalms, and sundry other printed materials which served their practical purposes in matters of church organization and religious worship. When Olaus Petri put his hand to such work, as he so often did, the results were worthy enough, but there was little of literary flight, of real inspiration here. Only in one work of a more ambitious kind – in *En swensk cröneka* (A Swedish Chronicle) – does Olaus Petri measure up to, and in some ways excel, the standard of literary excellence attained by the biblical translators of that time, among whom he had his honored place.

Olaus Petri's Swedish Chronicle is an original work of historical scholarship, and as such it represents a level of creative work above that of the translator, no matter how inspired. Besides, it is a work which in its use of sources, its independence of judgment, and its critical acumen is far in advance of its time, while its style makes it pleasurable reading even in our day.

This work had a long period of gestation, beginning apparently with the young Olaus Petri's contact with ecclesiastical and secular archives at Strängnäs and Stockholm in the 1520's. But so pressing were the official demands upon him during these early years, that he could scarcely find time for sifting his materials and writing his history until well into the 1530's, when the King himself, desirous of having recorded for posterity a good report on his reign, sought to enlist the facile pen of Olaus Petri for this service despite the not too happy relations between the two men after Olaus Petri's dismissal some years before as the King's chancellor. If the crafty King wanted in this instance to trap his former chancellor into a kind of literary submission, he did not succeed, for Olaus Petri found some excuse for a refusal of the King's suggestion even as he busied himself on the side with a chronicle which he conceived and finally executed as anything but an obsequious official history of the reigning monarch's work.

It became, rather, a general, critical history of Sweden from the earliest discernible beginnings down through the succession of events which led to Stockholm's Bloodbath in 1520. With its aftermath – the successful revolt against the perpetrator of the Bloodbath, Christian II, and the rise three years later of Gustav Vasa to the Swedish throne – Olaus Petri's Chronicle does not deal. Nor does it concern itself with the delicate subject of Gustav Vasa's reign. Thus on the surface it might seem that Olaus Petri avoided the dilemma of dealing with a king whose rule he could not always approve; but in fact his treatment of the immediately preceding period, the last decades of the Union with Denmark, was so lacking in national partisanship and so objective in its judgment of both the religious and political conditions of the time that Gustav Vasa, who had become aware of the existence of Olaus Petri's Chronicle in manuscript, sent out a general alarm against the work, going so far as to demand in a long and bitter letter the direct assistance of the Archbishop Laurentius Petri, Olaus's brother, in impounding copies of the manuscript. Under the circumstances it is no wonder that Olaus Petri's Chronicle did not appear in print during his or the King's lifetime and that passages from copies of the manuscript which the King had succeeded in ferreting out were used as evidence in the charges of treason leveled against Olaus Petri in the celebrated trial beginning in December 1539.

That the Chronicle could be used as supporting evidence in a treason trial was possible only because of a choleric, over-suspicious King, whose conception of history was neither more nor less critical and objective than that of other kings and princes of the time, or, for that matter, political leaders of our day. What surprises us more is that Olaus Petri could be so objective at a time when few of even the better historians entertained the idea of critical objectivity in the writing of history. In this respect, as in certain others, Olaus Petri is far in advance of his time. In Sweden, as elsewhere, we must wait until late in the nineteenth century before it is generally taken for granted that history should be written with disinterested objectivity. Only in Olaus Petri's strong tendency to interpret history essentially in moral terms does he differ sharply from the modern historian. Otherwise, both in his judgment of events close to his own day and in his handling of events actual or imagined of the far past, Olaus Petri is remarkably objective and discerning. In his treatment of ancient times in Scandinavia he seeks always to distinguish between fact and legend and to eliminate completely great masses of the latter from serious historical consideration. In this connection he discusses the nature of historical sources in a manner which in spirit and general critical intelligence, if not in refinements of definition, reminds one of the most modern historical scholarship.

That Olaus Petri did not succeed in leading Swedish historical scholarship of his day and the immediately following generations into less patriotic and partisan paths than this scholarship took is to be attributed partly to a common human weakness which Swedes share with other national groups and partly to a magniloquent theory of Swedish national origins which, in Ericus Olai's *Chronica regni Gothorum*, antedates Olaus Petri by more than a half century and which persisted for some three hundred years after, with varying degrees of emotional ardor and uncritical enthusiasm. We shall have occasion later to examine in some detail this phenomenon as it affects Swedish literature most profoundly, first in the seventeenth century, and later, at the beginning of the nineteenth century.

Meantime it should be recorded here as something more than a literary curiosity that Ericus Olai's fatuous theory of Swedish national origins, which the sober historical intelligence of Olaus Petri sought to counteract among his countrymen, was being given its first really definitive and influential formulation at the very time when the Swedish reformer was composing his Chronicle. Far off in Rome at this time sat a homesick former Swedish archbishop, Johannes Magnus (1488–1544), the last of the active Catholic primates of Sweden, who found some recompense for his unhappy exile abroad by allowing his fertile, highly charged patriotic brain to spin fantastic accounts of the all but unique nature of Sweden's national origins and historical development. Accepting Isidore of Seville's notion that the Swedes descended directly from Gog and Magog of Old Testament antiquity, Johannes Magnus sought to trace through innumerable classical and medieval sources the whole historical chronology from early biblical times down to his own day. Read widely and admired by others than the Swedes (Tasso took from it the subject of his tragedy *Il rè Torrismondo*), Johannes Magnus's work was published in 1554 by his brother Olaus Magnus (1490–1557), under the title *Historia de omnibus gothorum sueonumque regibus*. Olaus Magnus himself, also resident in Rome as a refugee from the Swedish Reformation, wrote a fascinating geo-ethnographical work on the Northern countries at about the same time as his primate brother composed his famous "history." Olaus Magnus's work, *Historia de gentibus septentrionalibus* (1555), has become a frequently used source for our knowledge of Swedish folk life and folk culture in the late Middle Ages. Its vivid eyewitness description of the circumstances under which the ballads were sung as an accompaniment to the dance is the classic contemporary account of ballad practices on the Swedish countryside in the late Middle Ages. Though inspired by the same strenuous patriotism as his brother Johannes's history, Olaus Magnus's book is on the whole considerably more reliable and served for many years as the standard work on Scandinavia in learned circles everywhere in Europe. An English edition appeared in 1658. Olaus Magnus was also responsible for issuing in 1539 at Venice one of the most famous maps of the time, the *Carta marina*, an ethnographical

Woodcut from Olaus Magnus's *Historia de gentibus septentrionalibus* (1555)

map of Scandinavia. His *Historia* was, in fact, designed in part to interpret details of his famous map.

For a time after the death of Gustav Vasa in 1560 it looked as if the cultural sterility of a reign which had produced few works of literary value might give way to a new cultural and literary blossoming. Like so many hard-handed self-made men Gustav Vasa seemed to have something of a sneaking admiration for things of the mind, if we are to judge by the quality of education he insisted his sons should have. They were brought up — the three of them who in rapid succession occupied the throne in the late decades of the sixteenth century — as Renaissance princes, highly educated, interested in the arts, and profoundly aware of their privileges and powers. Unlike their father, whose intellectual horizons came to be limited largely by a German Reformation culture, his sons found many of their cultural ideals in the more spacious and exciting world of the French Renaissance, introduced to them by their tutors who had been brought to the Swedish court from abroad. Whether in their political thinking they later came under the spell of that most radical of Renaissance political theorists, Machiavelli (the point has been raised in the case of Erik XIV), they at times operated on the political scene in a manner which certainly reminds one of a Machiavellian prince.

The new cultural interest at court under the sons of Gustav Vasa can best be studied in the architecture and related arts and crafts of the time. Gustav Vasa himself had begun a kind of architectural renaissance in the land, but his taste ran toward heavy monumental public buildings not far removed from the utilitarian ideal of the fortress-castle of the Middle Ages. His sons had more refined Renaissance tastes, which took more account of the comforts and conveniences of daily living within the castle confines and reflected a special fondness for the graces of living and for luxurious, highly ornate decorative detail. Artists were brought to the country from abroad to brighten the royal apartments with a lavish variety of color and form quite foreign to the simpler, semi-barbaric tastes of Gustav Vasa. Along with this went certain intellectual and literary interests aroused by the early training of the young princes and fed by their later cultural pretensions and political ambitions. Erik, the most gifted and least stable of the sons, was a considerable mathematician and something of an artist and literary amateur. Johan, the second son, considered himself a liberal humanistic religious thinker, whose desire to bring more of grace and beauty into the severe form of the new Lutheran ritual foundered on the treacherous religious and political shoals of the day. Charles, who seems to have lived pretty well without ideals, at least of an artistic or cultural kind, was the son of Gustav Vasa who most resembled the father.

Given such representatives of a Renaissance training and culture on the throne as Erik and Johan, why was it that the aftermath of the Swedish Reformation did not develop in directions more favorable to the arts than did the earlier years of the Reformation proper? A part of the answer to this question is to be found in the fact that the new Renaissance culture in Sweden in the late decades of the sixteenth century was a relatively superficial phenomenon, given to excesses and represented primarily by two royal personalities who were peculiarly ineffectual in projecting their ideas and ideals into the larger collective consciousness of the nation. But an even more important explanation of the low cultural ebb at the close of the sixteenth century in Sweden is the tragic tangle of religious controversy and political conflict which dissipated the energies of the people and created a bitterness of feeling seldom equaled in the history of the nation. The conflict, concerned with questions of religious orthodoxy and their political implications, reached its climax in the years around 1590 — less crucially in Johan III's struggle with a conservative and powerful Lutheran clergy over liturgical forms, more seriously, after Johan III's death in 1592, in the struggle over Sigismund's effort to establish his right to the Swedish throne. Though Sigismund as the eldest son of Johan III was within his legal rights in claiming the Swedish throne, as a Catholic and elected King of Poland he was looked upon with undisguised horror by a powerful Lutheran clerical tradition in Sweden. Duke Charles, the ambitious younger brother of the deceased monarch, saw his opportunity of access to the throne by allying himself with this Lutheran orthodoxy and with an equally conservative peasant traditionalism. The combined opposition of the Duke and these two groups was too much for Sigismund, who finally saw the hopelessness of his cause and retired permanently to Poland where the political situation required his undivided attention. After the collapse of Sigismund's cause, Duke Charles moved swiftly and harshly to consolidate his power, indulging in bloody reprisals against the remaining remnants of the Sigismund party and crushing everywhere the opposition to his power among a nobility not especially ready to concur in his absolutist designs.

Bloody as certain phases of the religious-political conflict at the close of the sixteenth century had been, Charles's weapons, as well as those of his enemies, were more frequently the word and the pen than the sword and the gallows. What "literature" came in consequence to be written during the years of the conflict was almost exclusively a polemic pamphlet literature, distinguished only by the extreme virulence of its invective. Even the rather considerable body of historical writings of these years suffers more than usually from the ugly partisanship of the time.

After the conflict itself had subsided a formidable pall of religious orthodoxy settled down upon the land, disciplining in a dozen petty ways the daily life of the people and choking the free play of man's spirit without which a living literature could scarcely exist, let alone flourish. Sweden had become politically unified under the iron hand of an absolute monarch and religiously consolidated under the harsh surveillance of an all-powerful Established Church. Not until the middle of the seventeenth century did the rigid façade of religious orthodoxy show signs of breaking under the pressures of new ideas pouring into the country in consequence of Sweden's political expansion in the Thirty Years' War, but even this period of bold political expansion did not deliberately challenge the authority of the new orthodoxy. Not until the eighteenth century is there a serious challenge to this authority; then, as we shall see, under the double impact of certain pietistic religious trends and the general secularization of culture which followed upon the influx of the Enlightenment.

In the years which followed immediately upon the triumph of Lutheran orthodoxy only two literary figures of some stature break the deadly monotony of the Swedish cultural scene. One of these — Johannes Messenius — provides us with an interesting lesson in the ways of a gifted personality who can manage his pen with such facile adaptability as to shift his loyalties from the Catholics to the Protestants and back again to the Catholics without any apparent disturbance of conscience, while the other — Lars Wivallius — brings to Swedish literature the first indubitably rich lyric gift and otherwise amuses us with a life story which in some ways is as ingratiatingly irresponsible as the career of that prince among literary rascals, François Villon. Strange are the vicissitudes of the pen: in a period of stern morality and rigid orthodoxy in Sweden, the only literature of importance is created by an unscrupulous careerist and an irrepressible rascal! By a perhaps not so strange literary coincidence both the careerist and the rascal spent considerable time in Kajaneborg, the gloomy Swedish deportation prison of the day, in northern Finland.

The brilliant but unscrupulous Johannes Messenius was born around 1579. After an early education at the Birgittine cloister of Vadstena, near his birthplace, he was trained at the famous Jesuit seminary at Braunsberg, where missionaries were prepared as a part of the program of the Counter Reformation for the re-conversion of the North. Upon the completion of his training at Braunsberg he cast about for a likely prince whom his learning and talents might serve and bring to him in recompense the desirable preferments and emoluments. Being a Swede by birth and a Catholic by conversion and training, he first sought to sell his pen to Sigismund, who for some unknown reason ignored his approaches. The discomfiture suffered in this instance drove him into the hands of Sigismund's most implacable enemy, King Charles IX of Sweden, and the King knew how to use his man. He was first assigned to write a series of pamphlets against Sigismund and the Papists, pamphlets in which he reveals himself as a master of devastating invective. Almost immediately upon becoming attached to the King's service Messenius moved rapidly up the ladder of preferment, in 1609 as professor of law and government at the University of Uppsala, from which post he was removed because of his arrogant and quarrelsome temperament and appointed a judge of the newly established Supreme Court and Keeper of the Royal Archives. Unfortunately for his Swedish career it was discovered that he had entered into contacts with the Polish Jesuits. Cast into prison, he spent nearly twenty years at Kajaneborg, not being freed until the year before his death in 1636. During the long Kajaneborg years he busied himself with scholarly and literary matters, chiefly his most important historical work, *Scondia illustrata.*

There was something of the Renaissance mind's nervous energy and restless diversity of interests in Messenius, though his primary enthusiasm seems to have been history. This enthusiasm first becomes apparent during the hectic days of pamphleteering and political intrigue in the court of Charles IX, at which time he wrote a number of rather fantastic and now forgotten shorter historical studies of diverse contents, with such presumably deliberate eye-catching titles as *Amphitheatrum, Sveopenta-protopolis, Tumbae, Specula,* and *Theatrum nobilitatis.* The many later claims upon his time as a professor and as a government official did not permit a more serious pursuit of his historical studies. Under the enforced leisure at Kajaneborg he turned finally to the ambitious task of writing a history of the whole of Scandinavia, including Iceland and Greenland, a work which he considered quite properly his *magnum opus* and the work by which he hoped to be remembered.

Together with Olaus Petri's Chronicle, Messenius's *Scondia illustrata* represents on the whole the best of Swedish historical writing for generations to come. In its mere bulk the work is impressive, filling nine large tomes, the last of which has been lost. For the earlier periods Messenius is satisfied with a rather pedestrian account based uncritically on Johannes Magnus's fatuous historical fantasies, but when Messenius's history comes down to his own time, the sixteenth and early seventeenth centuries, its pace quickens and one feels the living pulse of historical actuality beating restively under the solid and intelligent progression of his analysis and his interpretation. Like Olaus Petri, his historical interpretation of his own and the immediately preceding periods is remarkably free from partisanship and bias, religious or political. This seems especially remarkable in the light of Messenius's literary apprenticeship as a partisan pamphleteer in the early years of the seventeenth century. One should not, however, attribute this freedom from bias to the operation of any higher historical principles on Messenius's part. As a political prisoner in what may have seemed to him a fluid political situation, it might be safest to take no sides. Whether the triumph of Vasa absolutism and Lutheran orthodoxy was a permanent triumph might very well at the time be difficult to foresee.

Messenius's historical interests are reflected also in a phase of his literary proclivities related only loosely to his political activities and historical writing. I refer to the six pseudo-historical dramas which he threw hastily together during his short sojourn at Uppsala, apparently in order to attract attention to his person and consolidate his growing popularity as a teacher. Unimportant as these plays are in themselves, they have some importance in the history of Swedish literature as the first considerable body of original plays in Swedish on secular subjects.

Before Messenius composed his plays the drama in Sweden had carried on a distinctly limited existence, first as a rather clumsy instrument of religious and moral teaching during the Middle Ages (a late example is the *Tobie comedia*, often attributed to Olaus Petri, from 1550), and later, under the impact of humanism, as a pedagogical device whereby school-boy Latinists learned through performances of Plautus and Terence to perfect their oral fluency in Latin. Obviously neither of these purposes was calculated to encourage the rise of a native Swedish drama, despite the fact that developments in the theater abroad, especially the popularity of the English players on the Continent, beckoned people concerned with the theater in new and exciting directions. That these developments to the South had some importance for the appearance in Swedish drama in the early seventeenth century of certain sporadic and partial departures from the earlier didactic drama of the Middle Ages and the Reformation is probable, though difficult of demonstration. In any case plays of a new kind were written in Sweden at this time, plays which in a rather clumsy but spirited manner breathe a new dramatic spirit.

Besides Messenius, the figures who should especially be mentioned in this context are two provincial headmasters with ponderous Latinized names — Magnus Olai Asteropherus, whose *En lustig comedia vid namn Tisbe* (Thisbe, A Merry Comedy, performed 1610) departs completely from the didactic academic drama and in its form is distinctly superior to other Swedish dramas of the day, and Jacobus Petri Rondeletius, who in his "tragi-comedy" *Judas redivivus* (performed 1614) employs biblical material with a freedom unheard-of before. In *Thisbe* the author's intention is less to teach than to entertain, and in *Judas redivivus* grotesque entr'actes serve to lighten the chief dramatic preoccupation with crime and moral degeneration. And both of these plays, together with others of the time such as Samuel Petri Brask's *Filius prodigus* (1645), employ broad comic effects (called "folk scenes") in which realistic details of costume and stage properties are often matched by a racy quality of dialogue.

In comparison with these plays Messenius's six dramas have little new to offer except their exclusive concentration on national themes and their more serious cultural pretensions. In the Introduction to one of his plays Messenius proposes nothing less than "to write the whole history of Sweden in 50 comedies and tragedies, and publicly produce them." The plan was as gigantic as the dramatist's failure to realize it was for us fortunate — considering the paucity of real dramatic gifts exhibited in the plays written before he was forced to depart from Uppsala and his student players for the more expansive world of politics in Stockholm. The four plays that he wrote during and immediately after his stay at Uppsala (two others were written later) drew their material largely from Scandinavian mythological and legendary lore so liberally exploited in such early "histories" as those of Saxo Grammaticus in Denmark and Johannes and Olaus Magnus in Sweden. Two of the plays in particular attracted the attention of Messenius's contemporaries and continued for some generations later to be both printed and performed. Their titles suggest sufficiently clearly the combination of entertainment and high historical seriousness which they were intended to purvey — *Disa, Thet är en lustigh Comoedia om then förståndighe och höghberömde Sweriges Drottningh* (Disa, a merry Comedy about the sensible and far-famed Queen of Sweden) and the even more overwhelming *Swanhuita, En lustigh och sandfärdigh Comoedia, om . . . the Stormächtige och Höghborne Herrar, Her Hunding, Sweriges och Göthes, och Her Hading Danmarkz, Konungar* (which may be rendered roughly, Swanhuita, a merry and true Comedy, about the Powerful and Highborn Gentlemen, Sir Hunding, the King of the Swedes and the Geats, and Sir Hading, King of the Danes). In the former of these plays, whose action is represented as occurring in the year 1204 B.C., the audience is treated in the opening scene with the appearance on the stage of Odin, Thor, and Freja, the ancient gods of the Swedes, and later in the play lesser creatures from antiquity appear, including an Amazon who had strayed pretty far afield, finding herself in the Far North after the fall of Troy. Such a lavish display of divinity and near-divinity on the stage convinces one that Messenius's gifts were those of a crude showman rather than a discriminating dramatist, and other features of his plays which we need not go into here certainly confirm this impression.

Though these plays are duly divided into acts and scenes and provided with appropriate prologues and epilogues, they are scarcely more than history presented in the form of dialogue, differing from the biblical drama of the Middle Ages, as a Swedish historian of the drama has observed, merely in the fact that Messenius is dealing with profane rather than religious history. So devoid are Messenius's dramas of any stylistic distinction (the verse in which they are composed is hopelessly clumsy), and so lacking are they in any motivation of character, that it is not easy at first to account for the popularity they enjoyed for many years after their first appearance. One of the reasons for their popularity may well have been the negative one that the Swedish theater had for a long time practically no native repertoire aside from Messenius's plays. Another reason certainly is that the frankly patriotic themes of his dramas flattered the national consciousness of his countrymen during the period of national expansion which came with the advent of the Thirty Years' War. A Swedish public which in the seventeenth century preferred the pseudo-historical fantasies of Johannes Magnus to the historical sobriety of Olaus Petri would hardly fail to respond with enthusiasm to the extravagances of Messenius.

If our interest in Messenius's plays is limited to our recognition of their place as the first fairly considerable body of a native Swedish drama, the same heavily qualified judgment need not be made with regard to the poetry of Lars Wivallius (1605–69). Messenius was certainly not a dramatist by any absolute standards of judgment, but Wivallius was indubitably a poet of considerable talent — in fact, his is the first genuine lyric gift in the annals of Swedish literature.

Though Wivallius was a younger contemporary of Messenius, their paths crossed (or, more correctly, *nearly* crossed) only twice. In his youth Wivallius was a student at Uppsala during Messenius's brief service as a professor at this institution of higher learning, but he seems to have been a disciple here of Johannes Rudbeckius, Messenius's most implacable enemy on the university staff. Years later, by an ironic coincidence, Lars Wivallius, at the time Sweden's most gifted poet, was sent up to Kajaneborg as a prisoner immediately after the aged and broken Messenius, Sweden's then most talented writer of prose, was permitted to depart from his long imprisonment there.

Wivallius's incarceration, unlike that of Messenius, was not primarily for political reasons, though there were suspicions about him also on this point. His imprisonment at Kajaneborg was the final official action of the courts in a judicial affair in which he had become implicated years earlier. This affair, among the more fantastic in Wivallius's bizarre early existence, involved his marriage under false pretenses to the only daugh-

71

ter of an exiled Swedish nobleman of Björkeberga in Skåne, at the time Danish territory.

Born on Wivalla farmstead in the province of Närke, and considered precocious in childhood, Lars Wivallius moved rapidly through his early schooling and soon found himself among the more brilliant university students at Uppsala. But tiring of the sedentary life of the student, he set out, at the age of twenty, on a life of vagabondage on the Continent, penniless and without connections, but combining a Peer Gyntish kind of brazenness with certain subtle social talents which kept him afloat and served for a time to extricate him from such difficulties as his escapades got him into. Ironically enough the irrepressible scamp who had managed to evade military arrest under suspicious circumstances, both at the hands of Wallenstein's forces and Tilly's soldiers, and who had been imprisoned in Nuremberg on charges made by creditors in Strasbourg and Schaffhausen, pursued his pattern of impudence too far when, traveling on the borders of his own country under a false passport and wagging a fast tongue, he came to the estate of Ulf Grijp at Björkeberga in Skåne.

Under the elegant assumed name Count Erik Gyldenstierna he dazzled the simple-minded master of Björkeberga and inveigled himself into the affections of his only daughter to the point where both father and daughter were more than happy to accept him as son-in-law and husband. But the imposture was soon discovered, Wivallius fled from the scene, was hunted, captured, imprisoned, and escaped – this time to Sweden. But the long arm of the law continued to pursue him, and he was again imprisoned, in Stockholm. Here he bombarded the courts with a series of "defenses," which for their logical ingenuity and their rhetorical pathos must be counted among the more curious documents with which judicial bodies have had to deal. His efforts unavailing, the final judgment was banishment to Kajaneborg, where the poet spent five long years. After his release he used his talents — until death came, twenty-eight years later — in safer but scarcely more honorable ways as a shyster lawyer, fleecing his innocent and not-so-innocent clients of such parts of their fortunes as he could get his hands on. It is hardly edifying to note that he even gained a kind of social respectability in his last years. More edifying is the fact that, despite his late ventures into shady legal manipulations of one kind or other, he died apparently without even the remnants of a fortune. His widow had to seek public and private funds to get him decently buried.

The story of Wivallius's life is not calculated to support the assumption that a good character must stand behind the work of a genuine poet, for Wivallius was certainly a genuine poet — at least for a part of his life, the years immediately before and including his Kajaneborg stay. In fact, even earlier he had shown considerable ability at turning out verses in the manner of his day. What poetry existed in his time in Sweden consisted chiefly of either psalms or popular ballads, the latter in a debased, sentimental, half-lyric manner, which in its subjectivity and its preoccupation with love and with nature blended rather easily into the song with religious overtones. To these relatively simple Swedish ingredients Wivallius added, in his early verse, certain more complicated and pretentious baroque elements from abroad, achieving a fresh but highly unstable pictorial and rhetorical quality. And if we mention that, in addition, his early verse was written in any of a number of languages (at times even in a rather unintelligible polyglot jargon), it is easy enough to imagine the difficulties with which Wivallius had to struggle in arriving at a poetic medium which could satisfactorily release his very real poetic talents.

That he finally managed to do so may be said to be an accident, the succession of difficulties he got into in consequence of the Ulf Grijp affair. In Wivallius's case, as with the Milton who penned the noble periods of the *Areopagitica*, immediate personal problems inspired high levels of literary utterance — not in the case of the Swedish poet, admittedly, the insuperably high levels of Milton's famous prose work, but still far above the facile levels of Wivallius's early verse. The result was a group of poems which established a new standard for practitioners of Swedish verse. The most important of these poems are three — "Ack, Libertas, du ädla ting" (Oh, liberty, thou noble thing), written on hearing that he might be released from his Stockholm imprisonment, "Varer nu glad, mina fiender all" (Rejoice now, all my enemies), composed on his being sent up to Kajaneborg, and "Klagovisa över denna torra och kalla vår" (Dirge over this dry and cold spring), composed, it is assumed, on his first setting foot as a free man beyond the sinister confines of his fortress-prison.

Of these three poems the "Dirge" is by far the finest, even though in the other two a remarkably mature skill is reflected both in the handling of verse patterns and in the spontaneous resourcefulness of the imagery. The chief flaw (admittedly an only partial one) of "Oh, liberty" and "Rejoice now" is that the poet does not manage sufficiently to free himself from the petty fetters of his private woes and merge these woes in the

73

larger perspectives of his universal themes. In the "Dirge," on the other hand, the poet's command of technical detail and his sustained development of a noble theme are superb, infinitely above anything in Swedish poetry which had appeared up to this time. In theme the "Dirge" is a prayer for harvest and peace, a prayer which gradually, almost imperceptibly, breaks through the initial note of lamentation over a late springtime of dryness and of cold and issues into an inspired description of nature in its ideal beauty and fullness. In its form the poem brings to a state of perfection that tendency toward the simple art of the lyric ballad of the day, to which Wivallius returns after less happy experiments in his earlier poetry with a sophisticated, hectic baroque manner. In the "Dirge" everything is quiet, unaffected, spontaneous, pure — as natural as the everyday phenomena which the poet describes and as noble as the homely virtues of goodness and industry to which he does obeisance. For once at least in Wivallius's life of duplicity and selfishness and general moral decay, he caught up a vision of truth without guile and of beauty without flaw, and he met the challenge of this vision with a born poet's capacity to depict it with the proper word, the light, ingratiating rhythm, the simple, effulgent image. Generations were to pass before a Swedish poet was again to bring us into such artless regions of poetic beauty as this. Swedish literature during the period of political expansion in the seventeenth century, whose rising cultural tide was contemporaneous with Wivallius's later years, had higher poetic pretensions than the relatively unassuming verse of Wivallius's "Dirge," but the new period produced no poem which realized so perfectly the poetic ideal — in part no doubt because the new period departed so sharply at many points from the simpler, more personal sources of poetic inspiration which moved Wivallius at his best. Scoundrel though he was, living in the shadows of prisons when not actually within their grim portals, he at times somehow caught up a larger vision of existence than the paltry circumstances of his devious way of life seemed to afford; when he caught up this vision his poetic vein *sang* with a freshness and vitality which has not lost its spell even in our day.

CHAPTER 4

Political Expansion and Literary Renaissance

THOUGH Swedish literary historians invariably find in "Stormaktstiden" (the Great Power period following Sweden's successes in the Thirty Years' War) an essentially new secular cultural ferment which supplanted in many ways the almost exclusively religious preoccupations of the Reformation and its aftermath, these literary historians do not always agree as to just when they should date the beginnings of this new age in its specifically literary manifestations. The date usually given is 1648, convenient from a political point of view because it marks the signing of the Peace of Westphalia which established Sweden as a Great Power in Europe, and significant from a literary point of view because it is the year in which Stiernhielm finished his allegorical didactic poem *Hercules*, the most important literary work of the period. The year 1648 may be said, however, to be more convenient than strictly satisfactory in marking the advent of a new literary era in Sweden, for in some ways the beginnings may be moved a generation or so further back in time — to the generous encouragement given to educational institutions and scientific activities by Gustavus Adolphus, whose brilliant career was cut short at Lützen in 1632, and to the literary activities of Messenius and Wivallius, which, though deriving primarily from the limited cultural world of the later Reformation years, manage nevertheless, as we have seen, to point forward in certain ways to a new world of idea and feeling and form. But despite these qualifications it is no doubt best on the whole to accept the usual date, 1648, as marking the advent of a new literary period, for not until something like the total energies of the nation could be devoted to peaceful pursuits, after the extraordinary strain upon its resources during the long war years, does one find the conditions neces-

75

sary to proper cultural expansion, a cultural expansion which could encourage the work of a new type of literary personality and produce new kinds of literary ideals.

Complex as are the conditions which resulted in the new literature and manifold as are the manifestations of the new culture, it may be said without too much simplification that the central fact about Sweden's cultural expansion during the Great Power period is its gradual disengagement from religious domination, its increasing tendency toward secularization. It is true that not until the eighteenth century, under the formidable impact of the Enlightenment, does this process of secularization succeed in definitively extricating itself from the embrace of a long-established clerical cultural domination. But it is equally true that the second half of the seventeenth century took the first bold and adventurous steps in this direction despite the strong religious traditions in Swedish literature from the Middle Ages and the Reformation and the fierce contemporary seventeenth-century rear-guard action of a stubbornly entrenched and still powerful Lutheran orthodoxy.

The ways of history are often devious and paradoxical. The Thirty Years' War, which Gustavus Adolphus entered as a "defender of the faith," produced conditions in Sweden which ultimately led to the triumph of cultural secularization. It did so because it shattered the shackles of cultural isolation under which Sweden had existed since the close of the Middle Ages. During the Reformation and the years after, Sweden's cultural horizon was limited almost entirely to Germany, a country which in itself was hardly one of the more important cultural areas on the Continent. The Thirty Years' War changed all this for Sweden. Though the war was fought largely on German soil, the armies which clashed here were drawn from all parts of Europe, and the cream of Swedish manhood came thus for the first time in direct contact with a large and brilliant outside world drenched in the daring vitality of the Renaissance. Here religious asceticism was forgotten in the bloody clash of arms and the invigorating brutalities of military life. Here wealth beckoned and the glories of this world were to be had by those who sought such glories with single-minded worldly aims. Here military prowess led the able commoner directly to the House of the Nobility. Not that this outpouring of long-pent-up energies and worldly ambitions was done in the *name* of the flesh. Hardly. As in the medieval crusade, the military hero of the Thirty Years' War justified his actions in religious terms, turning to prayer and the divine service during lulls in martial activity with the same alacrity as he rushed into battle. If this was a religious mood, it was scarcely the negative one that denies the flesh and yearns for the intangible spiritual values of another world. It was rather an instinctive, if not unabashed, affirmation of the glories of this world against a lugubrious backdrop of rigid otherworldly religious orthodoxy.

It is little wonder that under the circumstances the triumphant Swedish armies which finally returned home in 1648 brought back with them a mood and a sense of values far different in many respects from those taken with them on leaving Swedish shores some thirty years before. Its leaders had rubbed shoulders with the elite of foreign lands, had seen at first hand much of an elegant way of life abroad, had sharpened their minds in new worlds of idea and accustomed their senses to pleasures scarcely dreamed of by those who penned the severe catechitical and exegetical literature of the Lutheran Reformation. When these military leaders returned to Sweden and took over their estates, their way of life reflected in innumerable ways the new tastes they had developed abroad. The nobility now vied with the royal house itself in the elegance of the castles which it built, the refinements of taste which it displayed, the extravagance of the high social functions in which it indulged. And it was a period in which the sons of the nobility were sent abroad to finish their education — at places, it should be noted, considerably more worldly than the German universities which for more than a century had been the chief training ground for Swedish clerics, who by the middle of the seventeenth century had clamped their severe Lutheran orthodoxy on the Swedish church.

In the years around 1650, when Queen Christina's court became a feverish center of cultural activity with a marked Continental flair, it seemed that a Renaissance mentality would take over completely in Sweden. But the Queen, despite her undeniable intellectual inclinations and her desire to encourage the arts and sciences, found herself, as a Catholic convert, forced to abdicate in 1654 and spent the remainder of her life abroad, chiefly at Rome, where, in her declining years, she wrote in French two volumes of aphorisms in the manner of La Rochefoucauld. These volumes, fascinating as they may be as documents of a personal kind, had no impact on Swedish literary developments, and they need therefore not be examined here.

Though the Swedish aristocracy only in rather rare instances directly and substantially encouraged the intellectual and literary life of the time (Magnus Gabriel De la Gardie is the most important exception), their way of life was broadly conducive to the secularization of culture, and from a literary point of view they provided an outlet for the vast body of occasional poetry (for weddings, baptisms, funerals, etc.) which was so characteristic of the period. Another outlet for this kind of poetry was offered by the middle classes, enriched by war conditions, whose newly established fortunes made them aware of at least the social desirability of some acquaintance with the arts. In general it may be said that the wealth of the upper-middle classes and the nobility provided for the first time in Sweden a relatively large reading public outside the clergy. Before this, higher education had been restricted almost entirely to the clergy, the only exceptions occurring in the royal family and, very rarely, among the highest aristocracy.

Though conditions in the Great Power period were thus favorable for intellectual and literary activities outside the limits of a church culture, the actual advances in this direction were rather slow and the new literature was by no means as vigorous and rich as might have been expected. It had been easier for Swedish military forces in the Thirty Years' War to storm foreign bastions and sack foreign art museums and libraries than it afterward became for a nation at peace to create a new culture of its own. How difficult it was to break down the long-established clerical hold upon the nation's culture is illustrated in the history of the University of Uppsala during the seventeenth century. The firmly entrenched forces of clerical reaction within the university strongly opposed efforts toward curricular and staff changes which would allow for the teaching of more profane subjects than had hitherto been the custom, and even more strenuous was the opposition of this group to the efforts on the part of a few advanced spirits on the faculty — particularly two members of its medical staff, Petrus Hoffwenius and the redoubtable Olaus Rudbeck — to substitute in the teaching of the natural sciences a Cartesian experimental approach for the Aristotelian scholasticism in whose strait jacket of abstractions orthodoxy felt considerably more secure.

It will be remembered that the University of Uppsala was founded in 1477, but that Gustav Vasa had allowed it to disintegrate in the first half of the sixteenth century for lack of financial support. Not much had been done by the later Vasas to make amends — until Gustavus Adolphus, the last male Vasa to occupy the throne, made, in 1624, a magnificent contribution of royal lands to the university. The income from this gift was to provide for all time a sound financial basis for the maintenance of the university's educational and scientific program, and to enable the university to increase immediately the number of its professors in order to secure a more reasonable balance between the profane and religious subjects than had been the case in the past when the university existed largely as an adjunct of the Church. The King's motives, it is clear, were in no sense anticlerical; rather they were guided by the practical demands of his political administration — the necessity of sound advanced training for citizens entering an expanding civil and military service.

But progress in the direction of a more realistic educational program at Uppsala was slow and partial in consequence of the opposition of an entrenched religious-humanistic tradition, and had it not been for the work of such men as Rudbeck and Hoffwenius, who fought all but hopelessly against the solid ranks of professorial mediocrity and reaction, it is doubtful that the seventeenth century would have witnessed any appreciable advances in Swedish higher education. It may be added, however, that outside the ranks of the quarreling academic community at Uppsala, educational matters were somewhat more forward-looking. Certain high ecclesiastical authorities, chief among whom was Bishop Johannes Rudbeckius, father of Olaus Rudbeck, gave much of their time and energy to organizing and directing a broad program of folk education within the diocesan limits of the Church. And in Stockholm, untouched by petty academic squabbles, a considerable amount of scientific and antiquarian research was being conducted, largely under the aegis of a variety of government commissions and institutions.

Though this research had its realistic and practical side, especially the investigations concerned with chemistry and geology and law, most of it was of an antiquarian-philological kind, more often than not concerned with fantastic chauvinistic speculations rather than sober scientific facts. This antiquarian research, at almost every point intent upon demonstrating the pre-eminence of Sweden in terms of its claimed ancient origins and its illustrious history, went under the loose collective label "Göticism" (Gothicism) because of one of its pet theories, the racial identification of the Swedes with the Goths. The beginnings of speculations of this kind are to be found, as we have seen, in the late fifteenth and early sixteenth centuries, especially in such "historical" works as Ericus Olai's *Chronica regni Gothorum* and Johannes Magnus's *Historia de omnibus gothorum sueonumque regibus*. The latter had enjoyed an uninterrupted popularity in Sweden and had exercised considerable influence on Swedish historical writing for nearly a century, but not until the seventeenth century were the "Gothic" historical speculations pursued by a whole host of Swedish scholars representing the collective disciplines of the antiquarian and the historian, the runologist, the philologist, and the literary historian.

The immediate reason for this is sufficiently clear. Sweden, which had almost overnight changed in international status from a relatively primitive and little-known land on the northern periphery of Europe to a Great Power, admired and feared in the political and military councils of the Continent, had somehow to prove that this new-found eminence was not the luck of a political upstart, that it in reality was rather the final and inevitable political attainment of a nation as ancient in its origins and illustrious in its history as any in the world. To document these claims became for Sweden a matter of national honor. Inspired by the sanguine spirit of their age and functioning frequently under the official directives of government-established agencies, some of the best brains of the country were dedicated to the task of reconstructing, stone by stone, the stately edifice of the nation's glorious past. Some of the stones were real enough, others were more or less speculative and hypothetical, still others were sheer figments of an over-patriotic scholarly or literary imagination. Antiquarians and students of esoteric lore like Johannes Bureus and his disciples pored over the evidence of the runes and the Icelandic sagas and pushed their researches even back into archaeological materials. Historians like Messenius spun further on the pseudo-historical fantasies of Johannes Magnus. Literary figures like Gunno Dalstierna and the pseudonymous Skogekiär Bärgbo deplored the influence of foreign tongues on Swedish and in both theory and practice insisted on a vocabulary closer to the primitive language sources of the nation. And the two most remarkable personalities of the day — Georg Stiernhielm and Olaus Rudbeck — became deeply absorbed in the scholarly wilderness of "Gothic" speculations, stamping their strong personalities in the one case on the noble poetry of *Hercules* and in the other on the amazing prose of *Atland, eller Manheim,* works in which both the best and the worst sides of the heady nationalism of the day found their ultimate monumental expression.

Fatuous as much of this nationally inspired speculation is in the light of later scholarship, it may be said in partial defense of those who so assiduously indulged in it, in seventeenth-century Sweden, that they seldom did so for venal reasons and that they were not alone among scholars in doing so. An exaggerated consciousness of a people's national glories was not uncommon in the Europe of the Renaissance, though it must be admitted that this form of national expansiveness manifested itself more extravagantly in Sweden, a somewhat too self-conscious newcomer to the select company of major powers in Europe. But there can be no question that this "Gothic" strain in scholarly speculation nevertheless had a salutary influence in providing the new literature with elevated heroic themes and infusing it with a native realism which had never before been so prominent a characteristic of Swedish poetry. Even more important, the widespread preoccupation of the Gothicists with philological problems led in general to a new appreciation of language as the chief glory of a great poetry and, more particularly, to a new awareness of the necessity of deliberately cultivating the resources of the nation's language if Sweden ever hoped to create a literature worthy of its recently established political eminence. Whatever finer sense of language may on occasion have been present in Swedish literature before this time was seldom conscious or deliberate. The concern of earlier authors was almost exclusively intellectual or didactic, not artistic; on occasion they became artists as if by accident, driven simply by the intensity of their inner visions to use with skill and sensitivity whatever resources of language were available.

In the second half of the seventeenth century, however, language became a central preoccupation of the poet, so central, indeed, that not infrequently the writing of poetry was conceived primarily as an exercise in exploiting the total resources of the poet's language. This seemed especially laudable because of the disgraceful state of decay into which the Swedish of the day had fallen, heavily interpenetrated as it was by other tongues, especially German. So far had this process of interpenetration gone by the middle of the seventeenth century that it appeared to some as if German was rapidly supplanting the national language. Bulstrode Whitelock, the English ambassador to Queen Christina's court, observes with astonishment that German "is commonly known everywhere in Sweden," and a scholar of our century, distinguished for his knowledge of the Swedish seventeenth century, sums up the situation with the words "children said grace in German, psalm books in German were used, and on sign-boards of the time could be read: 'Här säljes Swediskt Bejr' and 'Gut Wein verkaufft man hier.'" Even the poets often wrote funeral odes in German, particularly but not exclusively because the objects of their poetic solicitation were deceased members of German families which during these years dominated the commercial life of Sweden. It is scarcely strange under the circumstances that a patriotically inspired reaction occurred against this neglect of the country's own language. Critics spoke out sharply against the trend and scholars provided dictionaries and other material to guide the language of the land back to its own native resources. How ready the poets of the day were to follow the leads suggested by critics and scholars is apparent even in the titles of some of their chief works: two of the pseudonymous Skogekär Bergbo's most important works are entitled *Thet swenska språketz klagemål, at thet som sigh borde, icke ährat blifwer* (which may be rendered The Lament of the Swedish Language, That That Which Should Be Honored Is Not) and *Fyratijo små wijsor till swänska språketz öfningh för 30 åhr sädan skrivwin* (Forty Short Songs, Written Thirty Years Ago as Exercises in the Swedish Language), and Stiernhielm's collected works appeared in 1668 under the title *Georgi Stiernhielmi Musae Suethizantes, Det är Sång-Gudinnor, Nu först lärande Dikta och Spela på Svenska* (Swedish Muses, Goddesses of Song, Now First Learning to Write and Play in Swedish). The enthusiasm for Swedish had gone so far, indeed, in the hands of that most redoubtable patriot of the day, Olaus Rudbeck, that he did not mind arousing the strenuous resentment of his colleagues at Uppsala by using Swedish instead of Latin, the hallowed academic language, in an official invitation to one of his famous anatomical dissections.

Though the championing of the cause of a pure Swedish by the Gothicists accounts perhaps sufficiently for that strong feeling for language characteristic of Swedish poets during the last half of the seventeenth century, in a larger context this preoccupation with language is simply one aspect of the deliberate concentration on *form* so typical of the later phases of the Renaissance on the Continent. That Swedish poets were aware of this larger Renaissance world and that they learned from it is everywhere apparent, though their immediate access to it was in the main not through Italy, the cradle of the Renaissance, nor from France and England, where the Renaissance attained its greatest literary triumphs in the seventeenth century, but rather through its less impressive intermediaries — Germany and Holland. Because of the unyielding religious orthodoxy in Sweden, the spacious intellectual world of the Renaissance with its adventurous forays into new areas of thinking stirred Sweden deeply only at certain isolated points, especially in a figure like Stiernhielm. Matters of literary form, on the other hand, were not so apt to arouse the suspicions of religious reactionaries, and it is therefore in this respect that the Renaissance came to exert its most effective impact on

Swedish cultural life. Poetry in particular felt this impact in many ways, Swedish prose being satisfied to wait until the early eighteenth century before divesting itself of its awkward, heavy, older forms. So lively was the interest in the technical aspects of poetic form during the seventeenth century that the first Swedish "poetics" appeared in 1651, Andreas Arvidi's *Det svenska poeteri*. Though mainly a pedestrian plagiarization of German and Danish works of a similar kind, it served for many years as the only Swedish work in which the poetic genres were systematically described and discussed.

In the actual practice of Swedish poetry at the time, the primitive doggerel verse (*knittel*) of the earlier chronicles comes to be replaced by the more elegant hexameter and alexandrine with their Classical associations, and the simpler song forms of the past are now largely superseded by a rather bewildering variety of lyrical forms, the ode, reflective poetry, drinking songs and erotic poetry, satiric verse, and — the favorite poetic form of the day in Sweden — a great mass of occasional poetry composed usually to celebrate weddings and burials in aristocratic circles and among the well-to-do *bourgoisie*. Even the difficult forms of the sonnet and the Senecan tragedy find a few exponents, and at the entertainment-conscious court of Queen Christina elaborate masques are written and performed, with the text both in French and Swedish. The intricate allegorical apparatus characteristic of these masques, with its excessive baroque ornamentation, is employed also in certain other of the more ambitious poetic genres of the time, though here the degree of elaboration is usually more restrained.

It is hardly to be expected that the sudden immersion of a little-trained Swedish poetic spirit in the world of subtle artifice and elegant elaboration typical of baroque art would result in any large outpouring of really distinguished poetry. And it didn't. What did result was a much more lively and many-faceted poetic activity than Sweden had experienced before, a great deal of it awkward and imitative, some of it the work of plagiarism (a common practice everywhere during the Renaissance), only a small part of it original poetry of a reasonably high order. It is worthy of note that the best of this poetry — that of Stiernhielm and Lucidor, and certain things by Dahlstierna and Runius — rises above the discouraging level of the current imitative and occasional poetry probably less because of its points of contact with the prevailing late Renaissance traditions of the Continent than because of its immediate native elements, its gutty Stockholm street-life realism and such of its Gothicist-inspired qualities as a strong loyalty to the native tongue and an enthusiastic preoccupation with the Swedish countryside and its solid, unassuming folk culture. But the best of these native elements occur only sporadically and in fragmentary form, struggling under the limitations of a language still half barbaric despite the strenuous efforts of scholars and poets to make it a more adequate instrument of sophisticated poetic expression.

If Swedish literature in the middle and late seventeenth century may be considered important more for what it tried to do rather than for what it actually accomplished, the reason is not that Sweden lacked at this time gifted and strong-willed cultural personalities. On the contrary, in government Gustavus Adolphus's great chancellor Axel Oxenstierna and the nobleman Magnus Gabriel De la Gardie encouraged in many ways serious cultural activities. In ecclesiastical affairs two distinguished churchmen, Jesper Swedberg and Haqvin Spegel, were among the important religious poets of the day. And in belles-lettres and the world of profane learning, two figures, Georg Stiernhielm and Olaus Rudbeck, loom up sharply above all the other cultural personalities of the day in Sweden.

A restless man of the world, many-faceted in his interests and gifted in both the arts and the sciences, Georg Stiernhielm (1598–1672) lived his life to the hilt, busy with innumerable official duties and yet somehow finding time to pursue seriously an astonishing variety of scholarly and scientific interests and to write a body of verse which, though rather small in amount, represents in quality the best Swedish poetry of his age. Born near Falun in the province of Dalarna, in a family of limited means that was once counted among the lesser nobility, he was educated both in Sweden and abroad (in Germany, probably in Holland, possibly in France and Italy also). Upon his return to Sweden in 1626 his talents were first used in teaching, first at Vesterås and later in Stockholm. Four years later he was appointed to a judicial post at Dorpat in the East Baltic possessions of Sweden, where he served as a busy and able government official the remainder of his life except for a number of more or less prolonged stays in Stockholm as a member of special legal commissions or as the chairman of learned institutions such as Antikvitetskollegiet (The Academy of Antiquities). That he took life in stride, despite his share of ugly experiences, and met death with equanimity is evident from contemporary records. The epitaph that he requested be inscribed on his tomb was *Vixit dum vixit laetus* (He was happy as long as he lived). The rather idealized portrait which his Boswellian disciple, the poet Samuel Columbus, has drawn of Stiernhielm's personality and character must be partly modified in the light of modern scholarship. Georg Stiernhielm was no gentle philosophical spirit, nor was he exclusively a man of books and the arts; he was a man with a robust appetite for life in all its manifestations, and at times this appetite took on forms that were neither fastidious nor strictly honorable. But these are minor details in a great man's life, details which serve largely to bring the man alive — the only Swede of distinctly Renaissance spaciousness of mind and complexity of personality.

His learning moved with equal facility in such applied fields as law and engineering as well as in history and antiquities, philological lore, and religious and philosophical speculation of the most esoteric kind. Down to the last days of his life his eager intellectual curiosity was the constant delight of a company of young disciples, though they were at times disturbed that this curiosity did not always show due reverence for the tenets of the prevailing Christian orthodoxy. Stiernhielm's distaste for this orthodoxy derived from his ingrained suspicion of authority in intellectual matters and his insistence upon complete freedom of thought even in religious matters. In 1652, at a public debate at Uppsala University, he went so far in his opposition to the prevailing orthodoxy that he questioned the authority of the Bible on the grounds that the extant text is a product of so many interpolations that it is impossible to know what the original contained. And he was always highly critical of the Neo-Aristotelianism which provided the intellectual frame-work for the Christian orthodoxy of the day. He turned instead to those arch enemies of Neo-Aristotelianism, the Florentine Platonists of the time, and shaped his thought under the influence of Giordano Bruno and others who sought to explain the creation in atomistic terms. Stiernhielm's thought as developed along these lines was incorporated in an unfinished work — entitled variously *Monile Minervae*, *Umbra sapientiae*, etc. — not published during his lifetime and consequently exerting no influence on his contemporaries except insofar as he expounded its theme to his intimate circle.

If Stiernhielm's religious and philosophical views were little known and, when known, hardly acceptable to the great majority of his contemporaries, his poetry came to be known and admired by everyone as the chief glory of the literature of the day. The reading public instantly recognized in it the poetic embodiment of the whole nation's ideals – a high sense of a people's manifest political and cultural destiny expressed in a language both elegant and robust, a language which brought into a fine artistic balance the learned cadences of the Renaissance and the primitive poetic pulse-beat of the Swedish past. Even the crudities of Stiernhielm's verse were accepted with joy, for they could be identified with the proud vigor of a people not completely submissive to the blandishments of foreign cultures. When Stiernhielm's *Musae Suethizantes* appeared in 1668 it was the first collected *volume* of poetry ever published in Sweden. Before this, ballads and songs had appeared on loose sheets and in other ephemeral ways, but practically never with any indication of authorship, for the concept "poet" had been roughly synonymous with "beggar," or something worse, and persons of quality would hardly allow their names to be identified with poetic authorship. But Stiernhielm, a nobleman and servant of the crown, proudly has his name placed, together with one of his more impressive official titles, upon the title page of *Musae Suethizantes*, suggesting a new view of the poet as the practitioner of an art worthy of a high and noble place in the consciousness of man and the affection of his people. The volume itself contained no very large number of poems, and none of such ambitious proportions as not a few Renaissance poets abroad were producing. Nevertheless both the number of poems and their quality impressed Stiernhielm's Swedish contemporaries, and that they were not necessarily overestimating the importance of his accomplishment is clear from the generally accepted position which he has, since his day, been assigned in the history of Swedish literature as "the father of Swedish poetry." The phrase was coined a century ago by the sensitive poet-critic Atterbom, under the fascination of Stiernhielm's verse, and fifty years later another poet-critic, Levertin, equally fascinated, and moved by a strong national feeling, summed up Stiernhielm's personality and work in the following words: "Not many literatures can present a more stately, a more national portal figure. How *Swedish* in the highest sense was this broad-shouldered son of Dalarna, with his healthy view of life, his earth-loving humor, his Viking spirit recklessly setting out on adventures at all points of the compass in the world of idea and art, a man of cheerful versatility whose work bears the impressive though imperfect form of a giant torso."

Stiernhielm's busy career as a civil servant seems to have permitted him in his early years only occasional opportunities to develop his poetic talents. But in the early 1640's he attracted the attention of Christina's court with some verses in the Queen's honor, and in the years which followed he served the court as a talented translator and adapter of the original French texts of a number of the masques and pageants performed at court. Within the framework of the overburdened, often wooden progression of scenes and dances characteristic of court spectacles it was difficult for Stiernhielm to compose poetry of any distinction; but he labored seriously at his task, refused to provide simply a slavish translation (even though the author of one of the pageants was no less a personage than Descartes, then resident at Christina's court), and managed at times to place his own stamp upon the Swedish text, particularly in some of the lyrics so abundantly strewn through the pretentious baroque bric-a-brac of these courtly spectacles.

The mastery of form reflected in these earliest survivals of Stiernhielm's poetry indicates that he was thoroughly familiar with poetic practices from abroad and suggests that he had exercised his pen earlier in the poetic art despite the paucity of documents to prove it. That he had given more than passing attention to current theories of poetry is attested by the publication in 1643 of the first part (no others appeared) of a Swedish lexicon, *Gambla Swea och Götha måles fatebur* (A Depository of the Ancient Swedish and Gothic Tongues), in the Preface to which he expounds at some length the view so dear to the Gothicists that the Swedish language has poetic resources of the first order and that it should be considered a primary duty of Swedish scholars and poets to salvage from an unhappy neglect those words of ancient Swedish origin which could enrich the nation's poetic language and enable her poets to clothe their thoughts in a language free from excessive dependence on foreign tongues. Though only words under the letter A were included in the part of the lexicon which saw publication, the importance for Stiernhielm himself of the ideas he expressed in his Preface is apparent from the consistency with which he applied these ideas in his best and most mature poetry.

Stiernhielm's major poems are two — or, more correctly, *may be* two, for his authorship of *Bröllopsbesvärs Ihugkommelse* (Recollections of Wedding Inconveniences) has been the subject of one of the most spirited debates in Swedish literary history. Without going into the long-drawn-out give-and-take of this debate, we may say that no decisive evidence has been offered which clearly establishes an authorship other than Stiernhielm's, and until such evidence is forthcoming it seems reasonable to assume that Stiernhielm was the author. In any case, if Stiernhielm did not write this poem it was written by a poet whose muse was astonishingly similar to Stiernhielm's.

As the title indicates, *Recollections of Wedding Inconveniences* is an example of that most popular of all poetic genres in seventeenth-century Sweden, the occasional poem, whose purpose was to celebrate weddings or funerals in the castles of the mighty or the homes of the wealthy. But *Recollections of Wedding Inconveniences* is incomparably the best example we have of this overworked and hackneyed genre, whose combinations of comic horseplay and simulated seriousness, lacking grace and originality, are monotonously repeated in innumerable poems of the day. That a genre so limited in poetic possibilities, so banalized by constant reiteration, should include even one example of interest to later readers is an attestation that the man who wrote it was a poet of unusual powers. The moral of the poem, though present, is neither pointed nor overpious. But what impresses us more is the easy mastery of the hexameter, the lusty humor, and the racy realism of the poem.

The handling of verse and the realism of detail are even more impressive in *Hercules* (1658), Stiernhielm's allegorical-didactic poem which is the incomparable poetic attainment of the age. In this poem, using the hexameter with unusual flexibility, the poet ranges with equal ease in a

Copper-plate engraving from the title page of the first edition
of Stiernhielm's *Hercules*

world of sensuous (on occasion orgiastic) descriptive detail and in a world of high moral values, moving from the one to the other with no sense of incongruity and no loss of artistic control. Stiernhielm could do this because to him, unlike the orthodox Christian, the flesh and the spirit were not by necessity enemies. He responded to the world of the senses with the open, healthy sensuousness of the Renaissance, but he had also the high awareness of that ideal world which the best spirits of the Renaissance absorbed from the Classical philosophers and moralists.

Stiernhielm takes the central theme of his poem from the well-known Classical episode of Hercules at the crossroads, and the view of life presented is essentially that of the Stoic idealists; but he uses the Hercules episode merely as a frame in which he arranges his materials and develops his thought, both of which have constant points of contact with an immediate situation, the Swedish scene of Stiernhielm's own day. The central allegorical personages in the poem are three: the young Hercules, restive and uncertain as to the way he shall take in life, and two females, Lusta (Pleasure), who with tempting, provocative words seeks to lead the hero into a way of ease and irresponsibility and the satisfaction of the sensual desires, and Dygd (Virtue), who admonishes him to choose the way of duty and honest labor in the service of his fellowmen. Closely as this outline follows Xenophon, from whom Stiernhielm had taken the Hercules episode, the outline serves in Stiernhielm's poem merely as the basic skeletal structure on which is built a poetic edifice rich in lively turns of phrase, striking visual detail, and virile responses to those variegated phenomena of existence which reflect the way of life in Sweden in a sanguine period of proud political expansion. But this way of life, sound as it may have been in substance, carried with it, the poem suggests, potentialities of dangerous self-assertion and self-indulgence that could, if not restrained, lead to national disintegration and self-destruction. The figure of Hercules is therefore to be considered a thinly disguised young Swedish nobleman of the day, restive in the new-found glories of his nation, attuned to the siren voices of pleasure, not unwilling to be led into paths of self-indulgence and vice. From these ways — described at times in terms of bacchanalian excesses not uncommon in the social life at that time — Hercules is, it is hoped, to be saved by Fru Virtue, a vividly drawn personification of the solid, orderly, and dignified Swedish house mistress of old,

> Cleanly of dress, snow-white, with silver-glistening costume,
> Spotless, fine, and pure, in an honest, old-fashioned manner.

The touch of Gothic patriotism in these lines points up the healthy, positive message of the poem, which by allegorical indirection reminds the young nobleman of his duty to a people who need his gifts of mind and spirit both in the daily life of the citizenry and in the high pursuit of the nation's ultimate destiny. To fail in this duty, the young nobleman is finally reminded, is to dishonor that gift given to man whereby he lifts life to higher ideal potentials. Life is short and ends for the individual in darkness, Stiernhielm concedes, but he also insists that man's glory lies in his striving to triumph over that which is merely mortal — by living the few years of his life aware always of the challenge of the ideal. But Stiernhielm's conception of the ideal was not that of the Christian ascetic. He did not share the ascetic's scorn of the world in which we live, nor did he counsel a severe ideal of self denial. In *Hercules* the young nobleman is not urged to don the hair shirt and castigate the flesh. He is invited rather to partake of the Classical idealist's vision of a better life in the only world which we can know, *a present living world*, with its limitations, its meanness and elements of evil, but also with its good and noble pleasures — above all the pleasure which comes to one who in the paths of duty and of industry seeks to make of this present world as decent a habitation for man as man himself can make it.

If Gothic patriotism meets and nobly merges with Classical idealism in the thought of Georg Stiernhielm, the Gothic strain in its most fantastic form comes to dominate the idea world of that other great seventeenth-century Swedish cultural personality, Olaus Rudbeck (1630–1702). With talents as diverse and in some ways as impressive as those of Stiernhielm, and with even greater energies, Olaus Rudbeck spent his entire mature life as a professor at Uppsala University. But he was no ordinary "professor," content to spend his life among his books and in the laboratory, in a quiet, disinterested pursuit of what scholars call "the truth." To him the profession of teaching and the pursuit of knowledge had an immediate, vital relationship to life. In consequence the sleepy little university community of Uppsala found itself in the last half of the seventeenth century more or less constantly laboring under the spell of Rudbeck's amazing energies, which found their outlet in an astonishing variety of academic intrigues and civic enterprises.

His scholarly career, which began auspiciously in his early twenties with some startlingly significant discoveries in the medical sciences, ended in the bizarre maze of learning which he poured into his *Atland, eller Manheim* (Atlantis, or Manheim), the ultimate extravagance to which the Gothicist speculations of the day were pushed. And between these two extremes of learned activity the restless brilliance of his mind and will expended itself among a score of other things, with intensive botanical investigations, with efforts to improve the mechanics of clocks and organs, with architectural and engineering tasks which included plans for new university buildings and the actual construction of a water system and the paving of streets in Uppsala, and with a multitude of proposals for reforming the university's curriculum, particularly in the applied sciences. The proposals for changing academic practices embroiled him in recurrent internecine warfare with his colleagues, who were prone to react with considerable asperity to the arrogance which he at times displayed in the headlong pursuit of his intentions. His energies sufficed for everything down to the very close of his life. He died, appropriately, in consequence of his herculean efforts to save certain important official buildings from the fire which razed Uppsala in 1702. Large of frame and striking in countenance, with a full beard, long, flowing hair, and a voice and manner which stunted his contemporaries, he for decades dominated the Uppsala scene, the living embodiment of those ancient Scandinavian virtues with which his learned fantasy had been so preoccupied during much of his life.

But before he became all but hopelessly involved in the curious antiquarian speculations of *Atland, eller Manheim* he had attracted the attention and admiration of the learned world far beyond the boundaries of his own country in consequence of his early work in anatomy and had taken some giant strides in the field of botany. Before the age of twenty he had begun intensive medical studies, and within a few years, with practically no assistance from his teachers, he had carried out a program of research (involving an incredible number of dissections of cats, dogs, sheep, calves, goats, wolves, and foxes) which resulted in his discovery of the lymphatic system, one of the most startling medical discoveries of the seventeenth century. A bitter controversy soon arose as to whether the young Swedish scientist's discovery had priority over similar investigations of the Danish anatomist Thomas Bartholin; but the evidence indicates rather clearly that Rudbeck's observations and public demonstrations definitely antedated Bartholin's, though the publication of Rudbeck's findings in the summer of 1653 (under a lengthy Latin title beginning *Nova exercitia anatomica*) seems to have come a few weeks after Bartholin's investigations appeared in print.

In consequence of the sensation produced in Sweden by Rudbeck's anatomical demonstrations he was provided with funds by Queen Christina and Axel Oxenstierna to study in Holland, at the time a country distinguished for its high level of instruction and research both in humanistic subjects and in the physical sciences. Here his interests in anatomy became largely displaced by a consuming passion for botany; and upon his return to Sweden his scientific interests were channeled chiefly in the establishment of a famous botanical garden and in the preparation of an enormously ambitious botanical publication, the *Campus Elysii*. A number of remarkable descriptive catalogs of the plants in his botanical garden which appeared from time to time added to Rudbeck's fame in Europe and encouraged him to plan and carry out the gigantic task of bringing together in one work detailed sketches (whenever possible taken from living specimens) of all known plants. The boldness of the plan was typical of Rudbeck and his era, and his energies were sufficient to the task, though the enormous manuscript of twelve folios including illustrations of nearly seven thousand plants was not completed until he was seventy. Two years later, when the laborious process of printing the *Campus Elysii* had begun, the fire which devastated Uppsala at the time destroyed Rudbeck's home and with it apparently all the notes, manuscript material, and woodcuts upon which the work was based. Only two copies of the printed portion escaped. Later, however, some of the woodcuts were found, ninety of them having turned up in Linné's collections, sold to an English buyer after the famous botanist's death; and nearly two hundred years after the Uppsala fire a handsome hand-painted botanical manuscript was found in a library at Leufsta in Uppland. Though this manuscript may not be identical with the one from which the printing of *Campus Elysii* had been begun, it is one of the manuscript versions of Rudbeck's famous work, and as such it bears witness to a command of botanical materials which made Rudbeck in this field a worthy predecessor of the great Linné, who frequently paid tribute to Rudbeck's botanical labors.

But *Campus Elysii* was not the work by Rudbeck that was of chief interest to his Swedish contemporaries, nor was it the work in which Rudbeck himself became most deeply involved. Though his interest in the physical sciences remained reasonably constant throughout his life, he came gradually — from his early middle-age on — to be more fascinated by those Gothicist antiquarian and philological investigations which sought to bolster Sweden's sense of national eminence by attempting to

Georg Stiernhielm, portrait by David Klöcker Ehrenstrahl,
1663 (photo: SPA)

Title page from Olaus Rudbeck's *Atland, eller Manheim*, 1679,
line engraving by Dionysius Padt Brugge

Emanuel Swedenborg, line engraving by C. A. Bernigeroth

Carl von Linné, portrait by Per Krafft the Elder,
1774 (photo: SPA)

document the claimed glories of the nation's past. These claims, as we have seen, were not peculiar to the Sweden of the seventeenth century. They had already been advanced more or less strenuously in various Swedish works in the Middle Ages, had received their first classical expression in Johannes Magnus's famous *Historia de omnibus gothorum sueonumque regibus* in the middle of the sixteenth century, and had since this time been assiduously nursed for political reasons by the Vasas — not least by Gustavus Adolphus himself, who in his public utterances frequently referred to the ancient "Gothic" lineage of himself and his royal predecessors and who encouraged in many ways the program of antiquarian research whose purpose it was to prove incontestably the truth of these Swedish claims. The success of Gustavus Adolphus's armies in the Thirty Years' War suggested to not a few of the King's contemporaries that his illustrious career was to be looked upon simply as the final definitive evidence of Gothic military valor. It remained for the new Swedish learning of the day to demonstrate clearly that in the peaceful arts as well, in the total context of human culture, Sweden need not feel inferior to any other nation. Among the documents exploited by Swedish scholars of the seventeenth century in tracing Sweden's earlier illustrious history were a large number of Icelandic manuscripts which had recently been acquired for Swedish archives. Though modern scholarship has proved that most of these manuscripts, particularly those containing the late "romantic" sagas, are of no historical value, the scholarship of the seventeenth century blithely assumed that these manuscripts recorded, in the main, historical facts. And especially in Sweden, where historical speculation tended perhaps more than elsewhere to serve immediate patriotic purposes, these documents were eagerly scanned for evidences of the nation's ancient glory.

Rudbeck himself was first attracted to the Gothic speculations which resulted in his famous *Atland, eller Manheim* in consequence of his being asked to prepare a map of Sweden for an edition of the *Hervarar Saga* being prepared by his colleague Olof Verelius in the early 1670's. The moment was a fateful one for Rudbeck, and for the fortunes of Swedish Gothicism in the seventeenth century. The map itself was never delivered, for upon reading the saga Rudbeck became interested in philological rather than cartographical matters — he came upon words in the Icelandic text which seemed to him to have direct equivalents in Greek and Hebrew and other ancient languages. His mind caught fire and his nimble imagination began to raise questions and formulate hypotheses.

93

Why should not these linguistic parallels suggest vast cultural implications redounding to the glory of his own nation? Why might it not be possible to demonstrate that all languages derived ultimately from Swedish? And if this could be established, might one not go further and identify Sweden as the very cradle of European culture, the Atlantis of Plato, the mysterious Hyperborean regions of Greek mythology?

An average mind would have been satisfied with raising such questions, and possibly offering some fragmentary answers. Even Stiernhielm, who had been attracted to these problems, remained content to leave his findings in tentative form. But not Rudbeck. For thirty years he poured his enormous energies and inexhaustible talents into the task of proving his thesis. He went much further than his predecessors in ransacking historical and pseudohistorical records and in pursuing philological evidence and literary parallels; and he added an incredible variety of other evidence, from the physical sciences marshaling the testimony of astronomy, geology, and natural conditions in general, and from archaeology calling to witness the material remains of ancient cultures. The results of his findings were poured into four huge volumes, the first of which appeared in 1679, the last was being printed when the great fire swept Uppsala in 1702. So strong were Rudbeck's convictions about the preeminence of the Swedish language that he was at first determined to publish his work in Swedish rather than Latin, the language of all learned works of the time; but he was finally prevailed upon to compromise by printing parallel texts of his original Swedish and a Latin translation.

Delighted as his Swedish contemporaries were with Rudbeck's *Atland*, the work has since fallen into hopeless disrepute. It is now generally looked upon merely as a historical and literary curiosity, an unhappy testimony to the fatuity of learning when it attempts the impossible and is inspired by other than sober truth-seeking motives. *Atland* is therefore a work which Rudbeck's countrymen no longer like to have mentioned. And yet the work does not deserve to be forgotten or completely ignored, in part because some of its ideas, particularly those concerned with archaeological evidence, are remarkably modern in theory and method of application, and in part because it is the product of an imagination of astonishing fertility and vision. Fatuous as were most of the Swedish Gothicists' speculations, they were at least in the case of Rudbeck conceived with such spaciousness and abandon and executed with such inexhaustible inventiveness and drive that they became in *Atland* something very near great literature. Its prose — concrete, alive, even

94

"folksy" despite its vast accumulation of learning — is at its best distinctly above the level of most of the Swedish prose of the day. *Atland* bears at every point the unmistakable imprint of a great and original personality, taking its place alongside Stiernhielm's *Hercules* as one of the two most remarkable literary products of seventeenth-century Sweden.

Though the far-ranging, opulent spirits of Stiernhielm and Rudbeck tend to dominate the Swedish cultural horizon of their day, they are only the two most important among a rather numerous company of scholars and literary figures who in less striking ways contribute to the Swedish cultural scene. In the field of belles-lettres these lesser figures attempt on occasion ambitious things — the Senecan tragedy, the religious epic, the lengthy sonnet sequence; but usually they are content to nurse their talents in such less pretentious lyric forms as occasional poetry and the religious hymn. During the second half of the seventeenth century, in matters of form nearly all of these genres find practitioners who lift the formal level of Swedish poetry considerably above that attained in more primitive earlier periods. But the same cannot be said of the content of these works, most of which tend with monotonous regularity to repeat in a hundred stale and obvious ways the poetic banalities of their foreign models on such subjects as love, the delights of a pastoral existence, the rewards of virtue, and the practices of piety.

These cautious, pale, imitative literary exercises were hardly the literature envisioned and in part realized by Stiernhielm, who under the influence of Classical models used poetry as a noble means of giving vigorous, pulsing, elevated expression to the vital, surging, larger realities of his day. It is true that even outside Stiernhielm's verse the bland and limited surface banalities of Swedish poetry were occasionally broken by fresher, sharper, and more robust notes, which suggests that those who wrote this poetry were at least dimly aware of the larger idealisms and the more challenging realities of their time. But this awareness on the part of Stiernhielm's successors never results in a poetry of a really high order; they are satisfied to offer merely occasional glimpses into a larger, more immediately active world of idea and of feeling. On the whole we are impressed more by the mere quantity of acceptably skillful verse than by any qualities of freshness and originality and depth of insight which these poets reveal. They are in the main versifiers rather than poets, remaining safely within the limits provided by the poetic conventions of their day. Even in the case of Lucidor, the one really important poetic talent of the time, one comes upon a great deal of posing in the stiff garments of poetic convention; and in a host of lesser figures the pose is maintained with such starched and empty solemnity as to become something of a caricature of what poetry should really be.

That Stiernhielm failed to place his high and noble stamp upon the literature of the day was not because he lacked either admirers or disciples. In fact, an enthusiastic coterie of talented young men gathered quickly around the author of *Hercules*, determined to honor Stiernhielm and serve the cultural ambitions of their country by following the literary program staked out by the master. Unfortunately, neither their energies nor their talents were sufficient for the task, though two members of the original coterie, Urban Hiärne and Samuel Columbus, had some importance in the drama and in lyric poetry respectively, before the medical sciences absorbed the major energies of the former and death came at the early age of thirty-seven to the latter. Outside the Stiernhielm coterie strictly speaking, but under the spell of Stiernhielm's elevated poetic ideals, is the noble religious personality Haqvin Spegel (1645–1714), who found time during a busy church career(he died as the Primate of the Established Church) to compose some of the best hymns of the day and to write *Guds Werk och Hwila* (God's Work and Rest, 1685), the most widely read of a number of ambitious but feeble Swedish efforts to write a religious epic in the manner of the then enormously popular *La Création du Monde ou Première Sepmaine* by Du Bartas. *Guds Werk och Hwila*, with its lofty subject and its occasional flashes of earthy realism, fitted in some ways the ideal of poetry represented by Stiernhielm; but the work is interminably long, helplessly overburdened with learning, and seldom inspired by any spontaneous poetic flight. The fact that it went through four editions within sixty years after its orginal publication suggests how substantial was the appetite of the day for religious literature of the more formidable kind.

Of the two most gifted members of the original Stiernhielm coterie, Urban Hiärne and Samuel Columbus, we shall have occasion later to speak of Hiärne's dramatic and theatrical activities. Samuel Columbus (1642–79), the most devoted of Stiernhielm's disciples, and the one who had the closest personal contacts with the master, was a sensitive, gentle, retiring poetic spirit, in contrast to the vigorous and hearty genius of Stiernhielm. Though Columbus tried the more ambitious poetic genres of the day such as the religious epic (*Den Bibliske Werlden*, The Biblical

World) and — together with Stiernhielm — the ballet (*Spel om Herkulis Wägewal*, A Play about Hercules' Choice), he is at his best in his lyric poetry and in two unfinished prose works, the excellent little study of the Swedish language entitled *En Svensk Orde-Skötsel* (Cultivation of Swedish) and the delightfully chatty *Mål-Roo eller Roo-Mål* with its coyly untranslatable title. *En Svensk Orde-Skötsel* is the most intelligent and realistic of that large number of works from Columbus's day concerned with the uses of the Swedish language for poetic purposes. With Stiernhielm he pleads for a pure Swedish free from foreign contamination, but he doesn't share Stiernhielm's taste for words of distinctly ancient flavor and form, preferring rather the living language of the day as the poetic norm and suggesting even that orthographically the vocabulary of poetry should reflect the phonetic realities of daily speech. From the purely stylistic point of view *Mål-Roo eller Roo-Mål* may be said to illustrate in prose form language ideals of this kind; in subject matter, developed in the anecdotal manner popular in the Renaissance, it consists in part of biographical sketches, by far the most important of which are those on Columbus's two chief literary contemporaries, Stiernhielm and Lucidor. These two sketches — the first literary portraits in Swedish — have such a miraculous aura of "finality" about them that only recent scholarship has had the temerity to question matters of detail in the sketches and to restore to the portraits those more realistic and revealing features which the gentle Columbus had either omitted or softened.

Though he shared the patriotic enthusiasms of his period, Columbus is in many ways the antithesis to the broad-shouldered, full-chested, culturally extroverted Swede of his time. His poetry is in contrast with most of his contemporaries' work extraordinarily refined and elegant, the product of a much more sophisticated poetic talent than was typical of his day. Aside from his religious epic to which we have referred, Columbus published during his life-time a volume of lyrics which, though it bears the title *Odae Sweticae*, has nothing to do with the ode form. In his attitude toward life he is a soft-voiced proponent of moderation and quiet resignation, carefully eschewing the resounding word and the grand gesture; and in his poetic manner he is always the artist, choosing his words with care, refining his lines, ever conscious of the subtle interplay of idea and image and rhythm. His poetry seems at first to lack originality, his form being so unobtrusive and many of his ideas being culled from such respectable Classical sources as Aristotle and Horace and their numerous later imitators; but a closer reading of Columbus's poems makes one aware of a quietly strong poetic personality, a quality which at least partly transforms the borrowed sources and gives to his words a tone and a color which in his best poems is essentially his own. His feeling for nature is unusually sensitive, and his restrained sensuousness in such a poem as "Lustwin" (the title is a personification of a figure who, as the subtitle indicates, "Dances a Gavotte with the Five Senses") reveals that he is neither an abject son of his period's religious orthodoxy nor a participant in the period's more coarse forms of sensuality.

The poet of the day who was most exclusively concerned with matters of form wrote under the pseudonym Skogekär Bergbo, whose identity, which we need not go into here, is one of the most controversial subjects in Swedish literary history. He first appeared in 1658, the year of the publication of Stiernhielm's *Hercules*, with the long argumentative poem *Thet swenska språketz klagemål*, which vigorously and with considerable ingenuity championed the use of Swedish as a poetic language; and more than twenty years later two other works appeared under the same pseudonym, *Fyratijo små wijsor till swänska språketz öfningh för 30 åhr sädan skrifwin* and the sonnet sequence *Wenerid*. The first of these two works contains a group of poems which, as the title indicates, has primarily the purely artistic purpose of exercises in the use of Swedish as a poetic medium, while *Wenerid* is the only sustained sonnet sequence of the day in Swedish, an evidence that its author, whoever he may have been, was prepared to subject the resources of his language to the severe verse disciplines of the Petrarchian poetic tradition. Skogekär Bergbo's verse is not infrequently awkward, falling considerably short of the easy rhythmic fluency of Columbus at his best; but it is skillful enough for its day, and the rather rich sensuousness of certain of Bergbo's sonnets (particularly one describing a surreptitious witnessing of some lovely bathing ladies) reveals that he is capable of rising above the thin-blooded pastoral tradition of the later imitators of Petrarch.

A much greater talent and an infinitely more fascinating poetic personality is Lars Johansson (1638–74), better known under various Classical pseudonyms, the most persistent of which seems to have been Lucidor (The Unhappy One), first used in one of his earliest wedding poems. Lucidor is representative, in a sense, of the tradition of the Swedish poetic vagabond, instituted with considerable success by Wivallius in the first half of the seventeenth century and brought to a magnificent culmination a century after Lucidor's death, as we shall see, by Carl Michael

Bellman. Like Wivallius, Lucidor's personal fortunes (or misfortunes) seem to attract his admirers as much as his poetry, though Lucidor is the more spontaneous and original poetic talent. Around his person has sprung up a host of legends of greater or lesser dubiety, an almost in- evitable result of our lack of precise biographical data and the fascinating waywardness of his poetic career and his sudden violent death. There is a certain appropriateness in the fact that the best book on Lucidor has been written by a great modern poet rather than by a scholar, for in the absence of facts a poet's critical conscience may be less embarrassed than the scholar's. Not that there is no factual record in the case of Lucidor, but the record is sketchy and incomplete — a bare outline of events which must be filled in by a sensitive and honest critical intuition such as Erik Axel Karlfeldt's when, as a member of the Swedish Academy, he pre- pared the monograph *Skalden Lucidor* for inclusion in the "Transac- tions" of the Swedish Academy in 1909.

Born into a middle-class Stockholm family, very early orphaned, cared for by an uncle who died when he was fifteen, educated miscellaneously at Uppsala and abroad (in Germany, France, Italy, and England), Luci- dor returned to Sweden at the age of thirty with a company of strolling players, whereupon he established himself briefly at Uppsala, then at Stockholm, as a language tutor, translator, and popular professional poet, which scarcely exalted occupations permitted him to eke out a precarious day-to-day existence, until one night in a tavern brawl he was stabbed to death. So little did Lucidor esteem his own verses that he did not bother to have them published in collected form. Some years after his death an enterprising printer managed to salvage from the poet's papers and other sources what is probably a reasonably representative group of his poems, publishing them under the artfully touching title *Helicons Blomster plockade och vid åtskillige tillfällen utdelte af Lucidor den olycklige* (Helicon's Flowers, Picked and on Various Occasions Distrib- uted by Lucidor the Unhappy One).

As a personality Lucidor was known especially for his proud and ob- stinate independence, refusing to listen to the worldly-wise importuni- ties of such of his more socially compliant friends as Samuel Columbus who were perturbed by his unwillingness to court the high and mighty in the land in order to gain fame and fortune. Not even Stiernhielm was above this kind of thing. Lucidor's independence of spirit was partly no doubt a form of compensation for his sensitivity to the degrading condi- tions of his daily existence, and his cynicism was only another, more extreme form which his reaction to life's humiliations took. The conditions of life under which Lucidor carried on his existence scarcely permitted him the luxury of Stiernhielm's high conception of the poet, even if his temperament had been other than it was. He turned therefore quite deliberately to "writing for a fee," tossing off occasional poems for weddings and funerals and other formal occasions, at the rate of at least one a month according to the estimate of one authority. Such poems were put together with almost equal facility in a half dozen languages other than Swedish. German he handled with the greatest ease, but when another language like English was for some particular reason called for, he was quite ready to respond, as is illustrated by the copious verses he supplied on the occasion, in July 1669, when Charles XI, the reigning Swedish monarch, received at the hands of the Earl of Carlisle the highest order of British knighthood, the Order of the Garter. Lucidor's talents were particularly sought on the occasion of weddings, which at the time were conducted with unbelievably ostentatious display and accompanied by days-long festivities, the chief feature of which seems to have been gastronomic excesses of incredible proportions. The kind of poetry required for such occasions, and hammered out by Lucidor and a dozen other lesser poets, is easily enough imagined. Convention demanded due reference to the Deity as the true source of marital bliss; but the moralizing element, so prominent in earlier wedding poems, and which persisted in somewhat modified form even in such a relatively realistic poet as the author of *Bröllopsbesvärs Ihugkommelse*, is almost entirely missing in Lucidor. His forte was, instead, a strain of ingenious gaiety and coarse bonhomie. In his wedding poems he catered quite frankly to his public's taste for the equivocal and the suggestive, giving to the biblical injunction "Be fruitful and multiply" applications which have nothing to do with the religious and moral implications of the text as it was used in the earlier wedding poems of the Reformation and the generation or two that followed.

Though Lucidor's occasional poetry at its best is at least as good as such poetry can be, he excels in certain other genres, particularly in the drinking song. The bacchic muse apparently provided him with sufficiently rollicking, if temporary, escape from the bitter realities of his existence; and he found a public adequately attuned to whatever literary graces the drinking song may have added to those alcoholic narcoses which so frequently resulted from the hard drinking of almost all classes in society. How insatiable was the contemporary appetite for the heady

pleasures of strong drink is suggested in the closing verse of one of the
poet's most popular drinking songs:

> If I should die of drink,
> pray I, gin brothers, think
>   to watch my lifeless snout.
> And should me thirst awake
>   beneath the barrel's spout,
> let me such thirst quick slake!

Lucidor is the first genuine master among a rather large Swedish company of inspired devotees of the glass and the mug, taking second honors
in the quality of his bibulous verse only to the incomparable Bellman.
He has only in a slighter degree Bellman's abandoned joy in the alcoholic
state, and he has much of Bellman's rollicking rhythmic crescendoes in
the handling of verse. What he does not have are Bellman's powers of
observation and his ability to gather around the bacchic deity a living
gallery of highly individual topers, catching them up in various gradations of intoxication and intoxicant moods. Lucidor's genius is limited
to a more primitive treatment of the joys of the bottle, though his handling of these joys has its own singular verve and depth.

Modern psychology is not surprised when it finds religious intoxication alongside the intoxication of the bottle, and it is therefore scarcely
astonished when it finds Lucidor writing – apparently for the most part
in his last years – religious poems in which the terrors of dissolution and
the fear of hell are described with a visionary horror that no doubt satisfied the most orthodox of churchmen in a day when the inevitability
of God's judgment was one of the chief subjects of pulpit oratory. Lucidor's eminence in both bacchanalian and religious verse may be explained
in part by the poet's own character, which despite its outward aplomb
had its shoddier sides; but it is also a reflection of the curiously equivocal
habits of mind and spirit of the poet's seventeenth-century Swedish countrymen, who were prone to swing with astonishing agility from the extremes of fleshly bravura to the pangs of the penitent's role, never doubt-
ing the reality of hell even while luxuriating in the pleasures of the flesh.
Because Lucidor combined in his verse the two extremes of this anomaly,
he more than any other poet of his day reflects the immediate conditions
of the daily life of his time. In his religious poetry he is in consequence
no official ecclesiastical hymnologist such as Jesper Svedberg or Haqvin
Spegel. He is merely on occasion a penitent, conscious of his sins and
eloquent in his vision of their consequences. With some changes certain

of his religious poems have been permitted to take their place in the official hymnal of the Established Church.

As a poet Lucidor had one abiding fault, his slovenliness in matters of form. He had little ear for the subtle music of verse, for the finely filed phrase; or if he had, he did not take the trouble to abide by it. He was in consequence a somewhat isolated literary phenomenon in an age when Swedish poets were so conscious of the necessity of rescuing their language from certain of its more barbaric propensities and elevating it to the status of a really cultured tongue. Lucidor's way as a poet was decidedly not that of a careful disciple of Stiernhielm, but rather that of a restless lone-wolf genius, half rollicking, half rueful — true only to himself. That this self had in it, however, more than a little of poetic greatness is clear from the fact that in Lucidor's age only Stiernhielm's poetry is considered greater.

The last quarter of the seventeenth century introduces a new generation of poets, who in some ways continue and further develop the reigning poetic ideals and practices and in other respects bring certain essentially new strains into the Swedish literary world. The death of Stiernhielm in 1672, followed by those of Lucidor in 1674 and Samuel Columbus a few years later, cleared the way for a new generation of poets, who, while doing formal obeisance to Stiernhielm and his poetic program, do not follow him particularly closely. Their sources of inspiration are more frequently than not foreign. Under Italian influences they allow Stiernhielm's relatively restrained baroque form to deteriorate into the artistic excesses of "Marinism," while French burlesque traditions tend to displace Stiernhielm's earthy, realistic Swedish humor. And even when the late seventeenth-century poets follow the earlier Swedish traditions of occasional poetry, in the drinking song, in the hymn, they do so with a difference. The occasional poem becomes more cozy, more bourgeois in the hands of Runius, while it tends to be almost completely displaced in aristocratic circles by Swedish versions of light French society verse in the manner of *les précieuses* of the Hôtel de Rambouillet. The orthodox formalities of the earlier hymn give way in Frese to a warm, highly personal, religious song. The high patriotism of Stiernhielm remains, but it finds expression now in less expansive forms, at its best — as in Dahlstierna — taking on the relatively unpretentious garments of a warm personal feeling for the landscape and a regional culture (*hembygdskänsla*). In short, it may be said that the literature of the closing decades of the seventeenth and the early years of the eighteenth centuries is marked by a kind of uncertainty, moving simultaneously, often awkwardly, in several directions, incapable of focusing its energies, of catching anything like a unified vision of the poet's basic function in the society of the day.

Perhaps this poetry reflects half consciously the coming end of a great age in Swedish history, the age in which Sweden came first to establish and then to consolidate her place as a major European power. In contrast to the sanguine early and middle years of the seventeenth century, the last two decades were marked by a sober political policy which, in the hands of Charles XI, concentrated on practical domestic changes rather than adventurous expansionist dreams. But this tranquil interval proved to be a lull before the storm, the storm generated by the last of the Swedish warrior-kings, Charles XII, who — after a series of brilliant military victories on the Continent — suffered the catastrophic defeat at Poltava which soon led to Sweden's military and political collapse and the loss of the greater part of her proud Baltic empire. Unaccustomed during most of the seventeenth century to tuning their political lyres in a minor key, Swedish poets who lived on into the waning years of the century and later, tended to ignore the gathering storm. Only occasionally — as in the gentle pietist Frese's quiet line, "Here probably shall be, who knows? an evil time" — is the fact of Sweden's gathering political decline faced honestly, in Frese's case in a spirit of otherworldly resignation. In other cases the poets found it more convenient to evade certain of the realities of the day or to express in essentially evasive, noncommittal ways whatever perturbations they may have felt at the disturbing turn of events.

Of the dozen or so poetic talents of some importance at this time, four — Gunno Dahlstierna (1661–1709), Israel Holmström (c. 1660–1708), Johan Runius (1679–1713), and Jacob Frese (c. 1690–1729) — are the chief representatives of the more characteristic poetic practices of their time.

Dahlstierna's claims to literary fame are two: the dubious one of having written the most elaborate baroque poetry in Swedish, and the more worthy one of bringing at times the rather too turgid patriotic poetry of the age down to more everyday folk levels. A relatively successful civil servant (born Eurelius, elevated to the nobility in 1702), Dahlstierna attracted the attention of his contemporaries particularly with two poems, *Kungaskald* (Hymn to the King; *skald*, usually poet, here means hymn, chant, or lay) and *Göta Kämpavisa* (Heroic Ballad of the Goths). The former is an effusive tribute to Charles XI on the monarch's death in 1697, the latter an ingenious allegorical treatment, in popular ballad form, of the great victory of Charles XII at Narva in 1700.

In *Kungaskald* Dahlstierna reveals himself as the most elegant Swedish practitioner of that extreme form of baroque verse known as "Marinism," after its Italian master Giambattista Marini. In fact, the poem is simply a facile adaptation of Marini's *Adone*, whose pompous allegorical ingredients and bombastic language found an eager imitator in the Swedish poet. Though Dahlstierna's poem seems to have been much admired as the ultimate attainment in the then much practiced art of the funeral poem, its baroque excesses proved to be a rather quickly passing vogue in Sweden. Far more important for the future of Swedish poetry was the highly anomalous inclusion in the glitter and artifice of *Kungaskald* of certain passages in which Dahlstierna expresses his profound feeling for his homeland. The local flavor of these lines—they recall the delights of the poet's childhood and youth in the province of Dalsland, or describe the longing for his native province of a Värmland peasant who has lived many years in the far-off Delaware Colony—is a new note in Swedish poetry, but a note that is to be struck again and again in the work of later and greater Swedish poets, culminating in the 1890's in the magnificent regional poetry of Fröding and Heidenstam, and particularly Karlfeldt.

The feeling for folk life and folk traditions, only sparingly used in *Kungaskald*, comes to dominate completely the form and spirit of *Göta Kämpavisa*, a poem which as a propaganda instrument had an enormous popular impact in its day and which continued to be sung for a century or more by the Swedish peasantry. In this poem Dahlstierna pours his merry tale of Charles XII's triumph and Peter the Great's discomfiture at Narva into the late-medieval ballad form, which, as we have seen, had been taken up into the oral tradition of the peasantry after its aristocratic practitioners abandoned it, and which in its new peasant dress had assimilated more homely and coarser virtues. This accounts largely for the extraordinary popularity of Dahlstierna's poem, despite its somewhat involved allegorical machinery and the fact that its hundred and sixteen stanzas make it unconscionably long as ballads go. But its allegory is managed on the whole with such unerring narrative skill and is enlivened with such spirited, coarse-grained humor that it apparently did not disturb the equanimity of the simple, earth-bound mind.

If Charles XII had the good fortune early in his illustrious career to enhance his popularity among the Swedish masses with the lively propagandistic works of Dahlstierna, he had the pleasure in the directly following, more trying years of having in his entourage another poet, Israel Holmström, who provided wryly indelicate literary court fare in the manner of Scarron and *vers fugitives* of the coarser variety. Holmström was not alone among Swedish poets before and after the turn of the century whose literary orientation was French. The poet-statesman Erik Lindschöld (d. 1690) had served up airy society verse for the court of Charles XI, and others, like the diplomat Johan Gabriel Werwing (d. 1715), had continued the tradition. But among these Swedish poets who affected the lighter French manner, Holmström (his official position was that of *generalauditör* of the armies, his unofficial a kind of master of merriment in the royal presence) was the most popular, in part because of his impudent joviality and in part because of his flippancy in dealing with subjects conventionally handled, if at all, with proper circumspection. He scandalized society by the irresponsible airiness with which he treated marital infidelity, and he composed drinking songs in a vein that carried impropriety even farther than usual in this genre. He was most brilliant, however, when he burlesqued the overdelicate love-making in contemporaneous pastoral poetry and the high-blown mannerisms of the baroque poetry of his age. At times, too, he could turn with equal effectiveness to the spoofing poetic epitaph, a delightful example of which is the little eight-line "Gravskrift öfver Konung Karl XII:s hund" (Epitaph on King Charles XII's Dog) — which, despite its harmless gaiety did not escape the protests of those who were disturbed by the startling juxtaposition of the hero king and the faithful-unto-death canine corpse! Humorous poetry is a precarious art, and seems to have been particularly so in early eighteenth-century Sweden.

But the untimely death of another unfortunate dog in the first decade of the eighteenth century, as recorded in Johan Runius's "Deplaisir sur le mort de Plaisir, eller olust öfver Lustens hastiga afgång," doesn't seem to have aroused the same feeling of outrage in certain sections of the reading public as had Holmström's "Epitaph" — this not merely because royal ownership was not involved, but because Runius's humor at the canine bier is warm, almost tender, carefully avoiding the open flippancy of Holmström's gay epitaph. This difference between the humor of Holmström and that of Runius — then the two most popular purveyors of occasional verse — is fundamental, reflecting as it does the difference between Holmström's military world of masculine manners and moods and Runius's bourgeois world of sentiment and simple middle-class reactions. For Runius was the poet par excellence of the middle classes, with their solid virtues and their relatively innocent vices. His duties as tutor, secretary, and a kind of "court poet" in an aristocratic family do not seem to have deprived him of his own unassuming middle-class inclinations and tastes, and his best poems provide us with middle-class interiors of irresistible warmth and fullness. Among his poems of this kind is the inimitable "Friskens och Runii resa til Dalarön, Påskeafton 1712, i et capitel af 17 verser" (The Trip of Frisk and Runius to Dalarö, Easter Eve 1712, in a chapter of 17 verses), which is the most ingratiating picture we have of the manner in which the bourgeois classes in the early eighteenth century paid their respects to plenteous food and drink, not forgetting to sandwich a proper stint of churchgoing between bouts with the fork and the bottle. And the same innocently complacent delight in the pleasures of the flesh is characteristic of Runius's drinking songs, which never sink to the near-bestiality typical of other Swedish drinking songs of the age. Neither the half-desperate conviviality of Lucidor nor the full-bodied joviality of Holmström are to be found in the drinking songs of Runius. His toping took less abandoned forms, though the consumption seems nevertheless to have been considerable. His bourgeois environment may have dictated this relative restraint, though it can be accounted for also no doubt by his bodily limitations. For Runius was never particularly well, and he died quite young, in the arms of his good friend Frisk, who published a posthumous collection of the poet's verse under the title *Dudaim*.

The last of the poets of Sweden's period of political greatness was Jacob Frese, who survived the catastrophic career of Charles XII by eleven years. In his poetry alone in this period, one finds a sense almost of relief at the cumulating difficulties of the fatherland under the bloodletting and the economic strain of the King's long-drawn-out campaigns on the Continent, for Frese, unlike his fellow poets, was a deeply pietistic religious spirit who could find no joy in the boisterous nationalism of many of his countrymen. More important, however, than Frese's relative indifference to the outward fortunes of his nation, was the new intimate and personal strain that he brought into Swedish religious poetry. Aside from the various unhappy attempts to write religious epics in the Renaissance manner of the Continent, Swedish religious poetry since the Reformation had found its form in the Lutheran hymn, a hymn which tended more and more with time to become simply an instrument of sound, orthodox doctrine. The ideal of the hymnologists was to express in simple, measured, austere language the tenets of the Church, eschewing in most cases quite deliberately the expression of any more personal feelings. The hymn became in such hands an instrument of collective worship in which the individual met his God within the organized contexts of the Church and its teachings. Though this concept of the hymn fitted well into the Swedish Church-State orthodoxy, it tended also to formalize religious poetry to the point where it could not serve the more spontaneous forms of late seventeenth-century pietism.

Though Frese himself was not, strictly speaking, "a practicing pietist," his introspective spirit found poetic release in essentially pietistic forms. With the pietists he sought God directly instead of through the offices of the Church, and with the pietists he yearned for the perfection of another, more perfect world beyond the grave, finding little or nothing to rejoice at in the world in which he lived. Among the externals of existence Frese found some pleasure only in nature, a gentle, mystically felt nature, which became in his poetry simply a point of departure for those inner meditations which brought him closer to his God. Most important for the future of Swedish poetry was the fact that Frese's sensitive spirit brought into this poetry new psychological perspectives and depths, something quite foreign to most earlier Swedish verse. Particularly impressive is his quietly restrained subjectivity in a poetic sequence entitled *Verser i sjukdom vid åtskilliga vårtider* (Verses Composed While Ill During Various Springtime Seasons), the successive parts of which were written over a period of more than a decade and a half beginning in 1712, each of the parts reflecting in a gently meditative vein the poet's quiet resignation to the suffering he must undergo during annually recurring attacks of a malarial condition. When he died, in his late thirties, he welcomed death as a release from life's brutal realities, having no fears of those terrors of hell so often described by his more robust predecessors.

It remains to say a word about drama and the theater in this period, and here the record is considerably more modest than in poetry though some advances, particularly in the theater, are made. We have already examined in other contexts Messenius's dramas; and mention has been made of the ballets from the 1640's, largely of foreign origin and adapted for Queen Christina's court. The second half of the seventeenth century provides something quite new in Swedish theatrical enterprise, in that an earlier academic theater with its predominantly pedagogical and moralizing aims comes finally, under the influence of groups of traveling players from abroad, to be replaced by theatrical activities and forms which aimed more or less exclusively to provide entertainment. The first strictly Swedish company of actors was a student group at Uppsala in the 1660's, which arranged its performances in the Hall of State of the old Vasa castle and attracted considerable attention, particularly on the staging of Urban Hiärne's *Rosimunda*, on August 15, 1665, for the delectation of the ten-year-old Charles XI. Though this group broke up after a few years, the interest which it aroused in a new kind of theater was transferred from Uppsala to Stockholm, where the Lejonkulan theater (so-called because its home was an old structure in which a lion had formerly been kept for public observation) was established in 1686 and maintained its somewhat sporadic activities until the early 1690's, when it went under in competition with a newly arrived German troupe, Nordische Comœdianten in hochdeutscher Sprache. In the last year of the century another foreign troupe arrived in Stockholm, this time from France, at the invitation of the Swedish government; and this company maintained itself in the capital until 1706, acquainting the Swedish public with a French repertoire which included Racine and Molière.

This sketch of theatrical activities in Sweden in the last half of the seventeenth century might suggest more than it really should, for the total results of these activities in terms of a native Swedish theater and drama during this period are on the whole rather meager. In a broad sense, however, these ventures, whether Swedish or foreign in origin, did provide certain preliminary conditions for the rise of a more purely Swedish theater in that they brought to the public for the first time professional companies with a reasonably diversified repertoire and established a taste for the theater in at least the higher social classes.

It was natural under these circumstances for Swedish authors to try their hand at writing dramas, though neither in number nor in literary quality are these dramas particularly striking. In number there are in all not more than a dozen Swedish dramas from the pens of five known authors. Among these plays only two or three can be said to be more than mildly interesting to anyone except the specialist. Of these Hiärne's *Rosimunda* is the earliest and in many ways the best. Urban Hiärne (1641–1724) was a typical son of the Swedish Renaissance. Born in the Baltic province of Ingermanland, educated at Uppsala, where his literary and theatrical interests interfered not inconsiderably with progress in his studies, he finally shook off his theater-bitten proclivities and had a long, highly distinguished career in the practice of medicine and research in related fields. His scientific genius brought him international recognition, including a fellowship in the English Royal Society. He is remembered also for his courageous stand against the storm of witchcraft hysteria which burst over Sweden in particularly ugly forms in the late seventeenth century, leaving in its wake scores of sordid tales of wild and witless mass "justice."

Though Hiärne's literary career was scarcely more than a youthful episode in his life, and one quite unrelated to his later scientific career, it was genuine enough while it lasted, finding expression in poetic composition, in an unfinished pastoral-autobiographical novel (*Stratonice*), and — most important — in the drama *Rosimunda*. It has been demonstrated that *Rosimunda* is a Swedish adaptation of a Latin play by the Dutchman Zevecote, but the adaptation is an unusually free one and in most respects greatly superior to its precursor. Hiärne's quite deliberate intent with his drama was to introduce into Sweden for the first time the highly popular "Senecan tragedy" of the time, bloody, revenge-loaded, heavy with portentous moods and dark deeds. The play is based on the oft-told tale of the Longobardian King Alboin, who has murdered Conimund and married his daughter Rosimunda, whom he forces to drink from her dead father's skull. She thereupon murders Alboin before meeting a bloody death herself. As Senecan tragedies go, *Rosimunda* is no mean example of the type. Written for the most part in expressive unrhymed dactyls (a novelty in the Swedish drama), it moves rapidly through its tight series of horror-filled actions, maintains with appropriate consistency its violently brooding mood, and does not burden the theatergoer with uncalled-for moral or religious observations. In this latter respect *Rosimunda* breaks sharply with the post-Reformation drama, which had inherited its didactic elements from a still earlier religious drama. Aside from the excessive violence of the action, punctuated by burlesque interludes calculated to insure comic relief, what the modern reader finds distasteful in *Rosimunda* is its crudely primitive conception of character, dominated by a single overwhelming motive, lacking entirely any subtler, more complex psychological strains. But in this respect Hiärne does not fall below the usual level of tragic writing everywhere in his time, and in any case he created in *Rosimunda* a drama in the Senecan manner which for the Sweden of the day was in a class by itself in dramatic skill and forcefulness.

CHAPTER 5

The Period of the Enlightenment

THE SHOT which brought Charles XII's fabulous military career to an abrupt end in the trenches outside the fortress of Fredrikshald one late November night in 1718 brought to an equally abrupt close the political absolutism established and maintained by the two last kings of Sweden's period as a Great Power. Charles XII's successor was permitted to occupy the throne only on the condition that he agree to a form of government in which parliament was supreme; and not until the successful *coup d'état* of Gustaf III in 1772 did parliamentary government in Sweden yield again – temporarily – to royal absolutism. Though the immediate result of the sharp reduction in royal power after 1718 was to transfer political power to the nobility and the clergy, neither of these two classes could regain the political and cultural eminence which they had exercised in previous centuries. The higher nobility had lost much of its influence already, late in the seventeenth century, in consequence of royal expropriation of the vast domains held by them, and after 1718 a lower nobility, functioning relatively modestly as civil servants, came in the main to represent the interests of the aristocracy. The Church maintained its powers somewhat longer, but gradually during the eighteenth century it had to yield to the inroads of secularization, and by the end of the century it exercised only a modicum of its earlier political power and had even less importance in the intellectual and cultural life of the nation.

This intellectual and cultural life had begun to reflect on the whole either indifference or antagonism to the Church, which came to be looked upon more frequently than not with suspicion in higher cultural circles, at times even with active opposition. No longer did churchmen occupy such central cultural positions in the life of the nation as they so frequently had in preceding centuries. Only two religious personalities, Emanuel Swedenborg and Frans Michael Franzén, made any appreciable literary contributions in eighteenth-century Sweden, and Swedenborg did so completely outside the context of the Church while Franzén was at best a literary figure of only secondary importance. The secularization of literature which had begun in seventeenth-century Sweden comes in the following century to triumph at almost every point.

The reaction against the Church in the eighteenth century derived in part from the central supporting role that this institution had played in the trend toward political absolutism in Sweden during the preceding century or more, but it was at least equally a product of currents of ideas from abroad which swept over the country during the eighteenth century. They were the ideas of the Enlightenment, fanning out over the Continent first from England, taken up, extended, and popularized by the French, operating everywhere in Europe as a liberal leaven, attacking the concept of authority in State and Church and preaching a new gospel of reason and revolt. In Sweden the ground had been well prepared for the new gospel, chiefly because of the smouldering resentment against a political absolutism which, in the person of Charles XII, had dragged the nation to its knees and sacrificed the last remnants of a Baltic empire, whose establishment and maintainance had brought the nation fame but had in the long run also been so costly in both economic and human values. The country was tired of large-minded political adventures; it was exhausted by the efforts necessary to defend a crumbling empire; it wanted peace, and an opportunity to build up again an economy and a way of life more in keeping with the realities of Sweden's position in Europe. Though a strenuous nationalism reminiscent of the Great Power period appeared here and there in eighteenth-century Sweden, this was exceptional, finding little popular support. A new, more sober state of mind displaced the magniloquent will-o'-the-wisp of the Great Power dream.

The ideas from abroad which fed this new state of mind were scientific, philosophical, and literary as well as political. The names outside Sweden's borders that now came to have definitive significance in the new Swedish culture were John Locke, Sir Isaac Newton, Montesquieu, Voltaire, and (late in the century) Jonathan Swift, Addison and Steele, Alexander Pope, and Rousseau. Though neither Locke nor Newton was in principle opposed to traditional religious views, both of them were responsible for ideas which had revolutionary implications for religious thought. Locke's empirical assumption that all knowledge comes to us through the sensations cast doubt in many minds about the reality of the soul, while Newton's rigid law-bound universe seemed to belie the traditional Christian concept of the divine miracle. The devastatingly brilliant Voltaire extended and popularized views of this kind upon his return to France after his English exile, and he together with Montesquieu and the Encyclopedists came to have a marked influence on Swedish intellectual life. The watchwords of the day were "reason," "common sense," "utility," and "progress," words which displaced in many minds the earlier "faith," "tradition," and "authority." Man was now to determine his own destiny by the exercise of reason and common sense, society was to be transformed by man's wisdom and industry, and the "good life" was to be realized within the immediate and practical exigencies of life here on this earth rather than within the framework of some far-off hypothetical "heaven." That such thoughts infiltrated the Swedish scene and eventually exerted a wide and pervasive influence is evident in many ways: in the rise of a parliamentary form of government, in the official encouragement given the applied sciences, in the new emphasis on industry and commerce, in a flood of new cultural ideas and ideals.

All of this comes to be reflected in the Swedish literature of the day, at first only partially and hesitantly, later in the century more sharply and radically. In matters of form this literature remained more conservative than in its ideas. Ranking authors employed by overwhelming preference the relatively traditional poetic and dramatic forms rather than the newer, more typically eighteenth-century genres such as the essay and the novel. No Swedish novel of importance appeared before the end of the century. The poetry of the period reflected in many instances, however, the give-and-take of topical discussion, fulfilling the more practical functions of literature enjoined by the spirit of the Enlightenment. And on the more popular side the lively political debate of the day spawned an extensive, often scurrilous pamphlet literature, while the rise of the newspaper and of a rather flourishing periodical literature supplied some of the demands of a popular taste which found little if any pleasure in poetry or in the serious drama. Though not eliminated by the new parliamentary form of government, censorship was exercised with less rigidity than earlier, and authors could now occupy positions in society less obsequiously dependent than hitherto on the favors of royalty or the higher nobility. Kellgren's case is symptomatic if not typical: tiring of playing the part of a court poet for Gustaf III, he shifted his area of activity to journalism without in any way debasing his critical poetic standards, and he ended his brilliant career as editor-publisher of Sweden's first important newspaper, *Stockholms-Posten.* Such a literary career would have been unthinkable before the end of the eighteenth century. It was possible then only because of the rise of a larger reading public, or, more precisely, the rise of a whole new reading public, a middle-class public which not until the closing decades of the century becomes a factor to conjure with on the literary market.

All in all Swedish literature may be said to have come of age during the eighteenth century, having divested itself almost completely of the archaisms of form and thought of earlier periods and bringing into Swedish literature for the first time a prevailing note of *modernity*, that is to say a literature which can without difficulty be understood and in many cases enjoyed by the reader of today. In its spirit of restless activity, its critical openmindedness, its willingness to experiment, its emphasis on the practical, and its use of a clear and simple modern language (what the philologists call "Yngre Nysvenska," Modern New Swedish), this literature is more closely related to the nineteenth and the twentieth than to the sixteenth and the seventeenth centuries despite its more than occasional points of contact with earlier times. And even in the number of authors of greater or lesser importance, this literature points forward rather than backward. No earlier period in Swedish literature could boast anything like as many literary talents of real distinction. More than a score of authors of more than average attainments appear, two of whom (Bellman and Kellgren) are poets of the first importance, at least two others (Dalin and Anna Maria Lenngren) write brilliantly within the limits of their talents, and still others (among whom may be especially mentioned Creutz and Leopold) produce poetry which in formal grace and elegance is far above any Swedish verse of preceding times. This plenitude of poetic talent permits Sweden finally to realize a mature and diversified literary culture, one that could occupy something more than a modest place in the European cultural community. A new epoch in Swedish letters had come with the eighteenth century.

The work which signalized the arrival of the new epoch was *Then swänska Argus,* an extraordinarily entertaining moralizing periodical in the manner of Addison and Steele's *Tatler* and *Spectator* papers. Its first number appeared in December 1732, its last in December 1734; and upon its demise there was sorrow everywhere among the literate public of

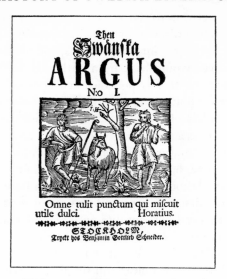

Title page of the first number of
Dalin's *Then swänska Argus*

the land. Nothing remotely approaching its popularity had hitherto appeared in Sweden — a popularity the more intriguing because only after a considerable time was the author's anonymity penetrated. And even then — when it was revealed that a quite unknown young man, Olof Dalin by name, had fathered the delightful literary progeny of *Then swänska Argus* — some contemporaries had their doubts about the alleged fatherhood, preferring to believe that a person of greater consequence was hiding behind the young man's name. That Dalin was directly responsible for practically all of the essays in the periodical has been established by later scholarship, though this same scholarship has also demonstrated that Dalin drew freely on material from the *Tatler* and *Spectator* papers as well as from Continental imitators of these two famous English periodicals.

Olof Dalin (in later years, upon ennoblement, von Dalin), born in 1708, son of a poor West Coast clergyman, had come to Stockholm at the age of nineteen to further his career after having studied for some years at the University of Lund, where one of his teachers was Andreas Rydelius, whose *Nödiga Förnuftsöfningar* (Necessary Exercises in Reason) had introduced the young student to many of the liberal ideas of the Enlightenment. In Stockholm his talents were immediately appreciated by the various aristocratic families whom he came to serve in tutorial and other capacities, and his life settled down into an unbroken series of literary and social successes, culminating in his becoming a central figure in the lively salon of Queen Lovisa Ulrika and his appointment as tutor to the Crown Prince, later Gustaf III. Both as a person and a poet Dalin fitted admirably into the highest aristocratic circles, adding a welcome literary flavor to their social life without presuming social equality with his noble friends and benefactors. The easy facility of his pen, the gay inventiveness of his mind, and his receptivity to the fashionable "liberalism" of the society in which he moved were qualities highly regarded by his contemporaries, one of whom dubbed Dalin "the Voltaire of the North." The label is somewhat misleading. Dalin had Voltaire's facile pen, some of his ability to popularize current ideas, and certain of his satiric gifts; but he lacked Voltaire's intense intellectualism and his white-hot moral indignation. Dalin was in reality a somewhat lukewarm representative of the Enlightenment, inspired by the liberal ideas of the time but only insofar as "good taste" permitted. He took his liberal cues in the main from his immediate aristocratic environment, which was scarcely ready to respond to the more sharply revolutionary implications of eighteenth-century thought as represented by Voltaire and others.

Dalin's temperament was tuned more to the less militant critical genius of Joseph Addison, whose *Tatler* and *Spectator* essays meant so much to him when he tossed together the weekly issues of *Then swänska Argus*. Like Addison, Dalin flayed with controlled good humor the vices and follies of his day, and in the process he at times simply translated material from Addison and Steele without bothering to indicate his source, while at other times Dalin's essays were merely clever adaptations of *Tatler* and *Spectator* material to local circumstances. Sometimes, however, Dalin's essays were entirely original, though they always retained the proper balance of entertainment and teaching which the Swedish essayist's English predecessors had insisted upon. The *Argus* essays were on many subjects, ranging from the vanities of dress and deportment to politics and religion and literary standards.

Dalin's two greatest gifts — fully matured and richly exploited in his essays in *Then swänska Argus* but even more brilliantly employed in his later prose and poetry — were his imitative genius and his narrative skill. As a true son of the Enlightenment he employed the former of these gifts in deftly devastating parodies on the pomposities of the learned pedant and on the soulful rhetoric of the self-important clergyman. His narrative skill was most apparent in allegorical satire, partly in the manner of Jonathan Swift, whose *Tale of a Tub* and *Gulliver's Travels* exerted a direct influence on him.

After his great popular success with *Then swänska Argus*, Dalin turned his attention chiefly to drama and poetry rather than to the prose genres, though he is at his best in some of his later prose. His contemporaries were greatly impressed by his efforts in the higher dramatic and poetic forms, but to later generations he is much more effective in less pretentious forms such as the ballad imitation and the song and in various kinds of light occasional verse. Neither in his two dramatic works from 1738, the comedy *Den avundsjuke* (The Jealous Man) and the tragedy in measured alexandrines *Brynhilda*, nor in his ambitious epic poem from 1742, *Svenska Friheten* (Swedish Liberty), does Dalin produce living literature. Considerably more important is his *Svea rikes historia* (The History of Sweden), the prose style of which is admirably clear and quite free from the awkward turns of phrase characteristic of earlier Swedish historical writing, and which is otherwise noted for its sharp attack on the Gothicist theories about Swedish historical origins which had so long muddied the waters of Swedish historical writing.

Even before Dalin had been commissioned to write a history of Sweden he had, in the sober spirit of the Enlightenment, aimed his satiric barbs at those scholar-fanatics who still persisted, in the third decade of the eighteenth century, in attempting to reconstruct the early history of Sweden in terms of Olaus Rudbeck's *Atland* fantasies. In a merciless satiric essay entitled *Wisdoms-Prof eller Herr Arngrim Berserks förträffelige tankar öfwer et fynd i jorden* (Tests of Wisdom, or Herr Arngrim Berserk's Remarkable Thoughts Concerning a Discovery in the Earth) he had pilloried the pedestrian archaeological learning of the day as represented in the late-born Rudbeckian disciple Eric Julius Biörner. Dalin's prose masterpiece, however, is his *Sagan om hästen* (The Tale about the Horse), in which he relates the history of Sweden in the guise of a horse and its various masters, the horse being the Swedish folk and its masters the succession of Swedish kings from the time of Gustav Vasa. In this allegorical tale he catches the spirit of the folk tale and imitates its form with amazing precision; both the earthy humor and the canny wisdom of folk literature are everywhere present in the magnificently sustained allegorical form of the tale. The folk ballad also interested Dalin as an instrument for conveying ideas, and he employs it frequently to express with a certain indirectness his political views, most successfully in the "Hattvisan" (The Hat Ballad), a contribution to the debate precipitated by a parliamentary crisis in the years around 1740.

Strong judgments have at times been passed on Dalin's last years, the decade and a half before his death in 1763, during which period he served informally as poet and entertainer extraordinary at the royal court. In Dalin's own day clerical indignation was aroused particularly by his impish talents in parodying sermons, while certain later critics have been prone to judge rather harshly the entire literary production of his later years, implying that Dalin during these years prostituted his talents to gain royal favor, that he was untrue to his genius in providing light entertainment for a frivolous aristocracy. A present-day criticism is not apt to concur with either of these judgments, at least not in their totality. Today it seems somewhat gratuitous to demand of Dalin that he be something which he, by temperament and talents, could not be. His was never a heroic temperament and he was not an author of great original talents. Such as they were, his gifts were uniquely adaptable to the gay and elegant tastes of Queen Lovisa Ulrika's circle, the first genuine literary salon in Sweden; and Dalin served his royal benefactors well, lifting the level of court taste far above that which it could have attained without his sharp intelligence and ready wit. Occasional poetry in all its forms had never been so brilliantly exploited by a Swede. It should be remembered also that Dalin had no peer in Swedish literature during the first half of the eighteenth century; not until after mid-century is his ranking position seriously challenged, and even then only with partial success. During the 1730's and 1740's he made certain fundamental contributions to Swedish literature upon which future generations were to build. Aside from his triumphs in such simple poetic genres as folk-song imitations, Dalin wrote the first really *readable* Swedish prose, rescuing that neglected medium from the awkward, heavy-footed habits into which it had fallen. Dalin's prose served also to bring for the first time into the mainstream of Swedish culture many of the most fruitful ideas of the Enlightenment. And finally this prose — because of its clarity and wit and its engaging informality — reached a much larger reading public than any earlier work in Swedish literature. In Dalin's skillful hands literature found its way out of the study into the tavern and the parlor, where delighted readers found that the printed page could compete successfully with gossip, the card table, and sundry other everyday pastimes.

If literature proper had in Dalin its only eminent practitioner in Sweden in the first half of the eighteenth century, the same cannot be said of Swedish intellectual life in general at this time, especially in the physical sciences. In fact, the period is chiefly remarkable for its scientific activity, in which more than a half score minds of great originality were at work. The two most celebrated were Emanuel Swedenborg and Carl von Linné, but others also established international reputations: Anders Celsius and Pehr Wilhelm Wargentin in astronomy, Nils Rosén von Rosenstein in medicine, Johann Gottschalk Wallerius and Axel Fredrik Cronstedt in mineralogy, and Samuel Klingenstierna in mathematics. It is not surprising under the circumstances that the celebrated Swedish Academy of Sciences was founded in June 1739, and that the great tradition in Swedish scientific investigation begun well before the middle of the century should be continued with equal distinction by a following generation which included the entomologist and biologist Charles de Geer, the physicist Johan Carl Wilcke, and the brilliant trio of chemists: Torbern Bergman, Carl Wilhelm Scheele, and Jöns Jacob Berzelius. This remarkable upsurge in scientific investigation was in part a result of the high regard for scientific studies typical of the Enlightenment and in part a consequence of official government encouragement of industrial development, a circumstance which placed high priority particularly on the applied sciences without ignoring fundamental research upon which the applied sciences must build. Scientific know-how was essential to the stepping-up of an industrial production necessary to rebuild the nation's shattered economy after the political collapse of Sweden under Charles XII.

So great was the interest in science and so numerous its eminent practitioners in Sweden at this time that the spirit and methods of scientific investigation came to influence intellectual life at many points, challenging religious orthodoxy, forcing curricular realignments in university studies away from an earlier Latinizing humanistic tyranny, reacting against abstract philosophical formulae, and broadly affecting thought in the direction of more pragmatic and utilitarian ideals. In a sense the scientist became a new kind of high priest of Swedish life and culture, more often than not replacing in the public consciousness the military and political leader as well as the religious official as a spokesman for the spirit of the age. Not until our day was the scientist to occupy again in Sweden as high a place in the life and culture of the nation.

The impact of science specifically on literature occurred in two ways: literary figures like Dalin incorporated in their work points of view, elements of taste, and stylistic ideals that were in harmony with contemporary scientific attitudes and methods; and in two cases especially — those of Swedenborg and Linné — scientists themselves had imaginative gifts which permitted them to contribute directly to the important prose literature of their day. As an essayist Dalin reflects in innumerable ways the sober, practical, scientific spirit of the age, and as a historian he severely attacks the unscientific speculative excesses of earlier Swedish historical writing and its uncritical use of sources. In his treatment of the earlier periods of Swedish history Dalin even goes so far in his scientifically inspired methodology as to employ geological evidence in preference to the tenuous written sources dealing with Swedish historical origins; and he disposes of Rudbeck's *Atland* fantasies about Sweden as the cradle of the nations with the following devastatingly sober observation: "where Plato's Atlantis lay, whether in ancient Svea or in the Promised Land or in the philosopher's brain, or if it was drowned in the flood of Old Testament fame, is and shall always remain an uncertain matter."

Of the two Swedish scientists of the day whose imaginative gifts broke through the barriers of a purely empirical science and in a sense contributed to literature as well as to science Emanuel Swedenborg (1688–1772) fits far less satisfactorily than does Carl von Linné into the pattern of the sober scientific investigator. Though Swedenborg's early career was devoted exclusively to a fanatical pursuit of the natural sciences, midway through his life he experienced a psychological crisis which led to his becoming the most celebrated of eighteenth-century mystics. His genius had in it much of the wide-ranging intellectual restlessness of the Renaissance. Unlike Linné, who was largely content to cultivate with a unique and loving intensity one limited area of science, the world of flowers, Swedenborg's unquiet mind was satisfied with nothing less than plumbing all the secrets of the universe. This led him in his early years into a many-sided program of scientific speculation and research, beginning with mechanics and mathematics, progressing soon to astronomy, geology, and metallurgy, and issuing finally into those physiological and psychological investigations which culminated in the religious crisis that transformed the scientist into a mystic and resulted in that long list of visionary and prophetic works which contain Swedenborg's amazing religious testament.

Swedenborg's religious development was not an isolated phenomenon in eighteenth-century Sweden. Pietistic sectarianism flourished among the lower and middle classes in reaction against an established orthodoxy which had lost all warm, spontaneous, and personal religious qualities. But though Swedenborg's religious drift was perhaps originally inspired in part by a similar feeling of opposition to the Established Church, his final religious position is worlds removed from the current pietistic emotionalism and sentimentalism and is distinguished rather by the emotional sobriety of its spirit and the almost scientific clarity of its verbal formulation. Swedenborg's uniqueness among mystics consists in the combination in him of the scientist and the religious visionary; his final religious position issues as directly *from* his scientific investigations as it develops *in opposition* to them.

Though Swedenborg came from a deeply religious home (his father was the great churchman of mystical anti-orthodox leanings, Jesper Svedberg) and is said to have had strange psychic experiences as a child, he turned to scientific studies upon his matriculation at Uppsala University and continued these studies with fanatical intensity during a five-year stay abroad (chiefly in England), beginning in 1710. Whether he met Newton at this time we do not know, but that he was fascinated by the works of both Newton and John Locke is apparent, and on the eve of his return to Sweden his mind was humming with an astonishing variety of scientific projects, including plans and proposals for the construction of airplanes and submarines. In Sweden he became associated with the great Swedish inventor Christopher Polhem, and was appointed to a responsible position in the Board of Mines. Though this ostensibly involved him in a field of applied science rather than in more fundamental investigations, he found plenty of time to indulge his speculative propensities in astronomy and geology and in cosmological theory. This resulted in a work entitled *Principia rerum naturalium* (published in Germany in 1734), which is remarkable for its thoroughgoing mechanistic view of the universe and for its anticipation of Kant's and Laplace's theory that the planets within the solar system came into existence by being thrown off from the sun. In geology, where he made some of his most significant scientific contributions, he is famous particularly for his investigations of the lowering of the water level on the Scandinavian peninsula. From the purely physical sciences he turned — in a work entitled *Oeconomia regni animalis* (1740–41) — to psychology, intent upon investigating the physiology of the brain and establishing the precise relations between certain areas of the brain and the various muscular reactions of the body. He was the first scholar to localize correctly the motor area in the cerebral cortex.

Latter-day scientists, while ready to acclaim certain of Swedenborg's scientific attainments, are prone to be critical of his general investigative procedures, his tendency to substitute brilliant speculation for the purely experimental disciplines. Both of his more elaborate scientific works, the *Principia rerum naturalium* and *Oeconomia regni animalis*, were as much products of a highly speculative mind as they were the results of scientific investigation and deduction. As such these two works — particularly the latter — point forward to Swedenborg the mystic. In fact, already in 1736 he experienced his first "revelation," and while writing *Oeconomia regni animalis* in the immediately following years Swedenborg became more and more deeply immersed in visionary experiences, which led, in April 1745, in London, to the decisive vision — an experience which resulted in his forswearing all scientific investigation and dedicating his energies entirely to the recording of his ever more strange and increasingly numerous mystical visions. For more than a quarter of a century he busied himself with these materials; only with death did his devoted religious labors cease.

Though devout Swedenborgians (most of whom are to be found in the Anglo-American world) accept without question the view that Swedenborg's visions alone account for the conception of existence in heaven and hell and on the earth which he elaborates and systematizes in his work, others have pointed out that his world of idea and form could have been, and almost certainly has been, derived at least in part from less ecstatic, more mundane sources, from Plato and the Neo-Platonic traditions of the Renaissance and their late theosophist speculations, from the Cambridge Platonist Henry More, from Classical sources and from Milton's *Paradise Lost*. Even Swedenborg's famous "doctrine of correspondences" — the concept that every earthly phenomenon has its exact analogy in the world of the mind and the spirit — has been traced back to similar concepts in Plato and in primitive magic. Swedenborg's restless spirit, it has been said, "sucked nourishment from every convenient source" — chiefly perhaps in his visionary period from direct contacts with what he considered heavenly creatures, but also from a world of idea outside his immediate visionary experience.

Among the works of the visionary years which are of considerable literary interest are *De cultu et amore Dei* (London, 1745), a poetically conceived vision of the Creation which has points of contact both with

Dante's *Paradiso* and the *Paradise Lost* of Milton; *De amore conjugiali* (Amsterdam, 1768), an astonishingly original portrayal of love and sex in both the upper and the nether worlds beyond the grave; and *Diarium spirituale*, a miscellaneous collection of curious memorabilia with appropriate commentaries, published for the first time in seven volumes at Tübingen, 1843–46. The literary quality of these works is not easy to define. So difficult is it, indeed, that a critic as perceptive and sympathetic as Ralph Waldo Emerson, in his essay on Swedenborg in *Representative Men*, at one point describes the Swedish seer's prose as "the highest style of poetry" and at another insists that it is "entirely devoid of the whole apparatus of poetic expression . . . his books have no melody, no emotion, no humor, no relief from the dead prosaic level." The fact of the matter is that both of Emerson's observations are true within certain limits. The Swedish seer's style is singular, if not unique, in its combining imaginative fluidity with ordered logical patterns, poetic fantasy with a concrete down-to-earth realism which was not at all averse to vividly brutal if not brutish effects. His intense early preoccupation with the severe disciplines of the physical sciences did not desert him in his later visionary experiences, and his descriptions of heaven and hell, unlike those of other religious visionaries, frequently have a matter-of-factness which at times makes the reader wonder whether he is describing cities of another world or the London and Stockholm of his own day. If, as Emerson suggests, Swedenborg is the last of the Church Fathers, he is so partly as a son of the Enlightenment, maintaining always a clear and ordered mind in the midst of the strange world of his visionary revelations. This singular quality of Swedenborg's mind perhaps explains the fascination of his work for such diverse spirits as those of Coleridge and Balzac, Goethe and Blake, Emerson and Yeats.

In his own "enlightened" eighteenth century Swedenborg's mystical writings were more often than not looked upon as the products of a severely deranged mind. This was true particularly in Sweden, where his influence, with one exception (that of the poet Thorild), was limited almost exclusively to scattered individuals or isolated groups with pietistic leanings or to amateur theosophists and their ilk. Later, however, his importance in Sweden has been more considerable, particularly in literature, the Romantic poet-critic P. D. A. Atterbom having written a highly sympathetic essay on him, and two later nineteenth-century figures, C. J. L. Almqvist and August Strindberg, regarding him as a major seer and prophet.

To be forgotten or belittled by his countrymen as was Swedenborg, and to meet death in obscurity in a foreign land (Swedenborg died of a stroke during one of his visits to London), was not the fate of that other great personality in eighteenth-century Sweden, Carl von Linné (1707–78). On the occasion of Linné's death all Sweden sorrowed, as at the bier of a beloved monarch. And monarch Linné was, in *his* kingdom — the kingdom of plants and flowers. His international fame had been firmly established before he was thirty, when while temporarily resident in Holland he published in rapid succession a remarkable series of botanical works — in 1735 *Systema Naturae*, in 1736 *Fundamenta Botanica* and *Bibliotheca Botanica*, in 1737 *Critica Botanica*, *Genera Plantarum*, *Hortus Cliffortianus*, and *Flora Lapponica*, and in 1738 *Classes Plantarum*. From this time until his death forty years later, scores of scientific studies flowed from his pen, his reputation grew in the international community of scholars, abroad he was elected to honorary memberships in innumerable scientific societies and at home he occupied the highest of university posts, was the first president of the Academy of Sciences, and became a member of the House of the Nobility. The name under which he is usually known abroad is Linnaeus, the family name which became von Linné on his elevation to the Swedish nobility.

In spite of Linné's many successes he was not, as has often been assumed, a balanced, completely harmonious personality. Genius practically never is, and Linné was not free from moments of moodiness and irritability nor was he unaware of the limitations of his own botanical investigations. In the main, however, he was sufficiently conscious of the basic significance of his work, expressing on many occasions his gratitude to a Creator who had so miraculously chosen him to penetrate certain of the great secrets of creation. Linné's most revolutionary contribution to botanical studies was his classification of plants on the basis of their sexual characteristics. This approach brought light and order almost overnight into a science previously dark and chaotic, and though the approach was in some ways unduly rigid and (as Linné himself recognized) could not account for plant mutations, it was enormously important for all future botanical investigations — probably the greatest single contribution in the field. Botanists since Linné's day have only modified his system; they have not deserted it.

Single-minded as was Linné's devotion to science and enormous as was his scientific productivity, he lived a rich life as an unusually inspiring teacher and academic administrator outside the narrow confines of pure research, was constantly aware of the practical applications of science to everyday life, and found time to speculate interestingly on moral and religious problems. Among his most popular university lectures were those on dietary practices and public health, while his rather frequent botanical excursions during the summer months into the Swedish provinces yielded a series of books in which his observations were of great practical value for his nation's economy. And his posthumously printed notes which go under the title *Nemesis divina* reveal how preoccupied he was in his later years with the laws of morals as well as the laws of nature. Though Linné considered himself a Christian and never deliberately challenged the orthodoxy of his time, his scientific work had implications which were not always orthodox in the religious-traditional sense, and the views expressed in *Nemesis divina* were in substance a reinterpretation in modern scientific terms of Old Testament ideas about "the wages of sin." In this work there is no place for such concepts as "God's grace" or "divine forgiveness" or "Christ's intercession." Moral laws, like physical laws, operate independent of man's hopes or desires; they are immutable.

Though Linné's disciples traveled widely and ransacked thoroughly with the master's encouragement the botanical wonders of many far-flung areas of the globe, Linné's own travels, except for the Holland episode (which included brief visits to England and France), were restricted to extended summer excursions into certain districts of his own country, including Lapland in the Far North, Skåne and Småland in the South, and the mid-Swedish provinces of Västergötland and Öland. Made possible by funds provided from official sources, these summer excursions had in each case the quite practical purpose of investigating natural resources with a view to discovering how they might best be exploited for the national welfare. The published reports of these travels (*Dalaresan*, *Gothländskaresan*, *Skånskaresan*, *Öländskaresan*, etc.) are not, however, merely scientific documents. They are in addition highly personal accounts of Linné's responses to natural phenomena and folk practices and beliefs, and though they are loaded down with factual information they not infrequently include passages which reflect definite literary gifts.

Not that Linné had literary pretensions; he did not. At times his style-conscious academic colleagues cast sharp aspersions on his unpolished Latin, but this has not deterred later generations from recognizing in him one of the two or three masters of Swedish prose in the eighteenth century. Linné's very lack of elegance is what today attracts us to his prose. His directness and concreteness, his reverence for the fact, his scientific economy of phrasing appeal strongly to modern taste and have had their importance for modern Swedish prose, beginning especially with Strindberg and continuing down to our day. Such a prose was possible for Linné because he was essentially a self-made stylist whose ways of thinking and feeling had not undergone the artificial disciplines of the elegant French-inspired prose ideals of the day. Insofar as his prose was influenced by earlier stylistic traditions it is related to peasant speech and proverbial lore and to the relatively primitive language of the so-called Gustav Vasa Bible. Linné's prose reflected perfectly his own personality, with its captivating enthusiasm, its intriguing naïveté, its alternating moods of sly humor and scientific exactitude. This prose keeps its feet firmly on the ground, impressing us by what has been called "the poetry of the fact." When it does take flight it does so only with a sober sense of ultimate responsibility to the fact, never permitting itself to soar freely on the wings of high speculation or pure fantasy. No matter how intense was Linné's experience of the world of nature (and few have experienced nature as intensely) he never permitted himself the emotional luxury of the Romantic poet in the presence of natural phenomena. Even when he is dealing with the mystery of death — as he does in the celebrated passage in the *Journey to Västergötland* which has been called "the Swedish equivalent of Hamlet's graveyard soliloquy" — he manages the appropriate elevation of tone by means more sober and honest than are usually employed in such contexts.

The middle years of the eighteenth century in Sweden, the years in which Dalin was employing his talents largely as a court poet and when Swedish scientific investigations were the chief glory of her culture, witnessed also the rise of a new group of poets who, though their gifts were limited, managed to produce a body of poetry which represents a new phase in the literature of the century. This group of poets — brought together in Tankarbyggarorden, one of the numerous fraternal societies of the day which harbored certain cultural pretensions — consisted of the middle-aged poetess Hedvig Charlotta Nordenflycht and her two young "chamberlains in waiting," Gustaf Fredrik Gyllenborg and the Finnish-born Gustav Philip Creutz. The work of these poets appeared in two literary anthologies, the first, in three small volumes, dated 1753, 1754, and 1756, entitled modestly *Våra försök* (Our Attempts), the second in two volumes from 1759 and 1762 with the more ambitious title *Witterhetsarbeten* (Literary Works). The importance of the group lay less in distinguished poetic skills than in their literary program, though Creutz could at his best write Swedish verse of a finish and elegance never before attained by a Swedish poet. Influenced on the formal side by the canons of French classicism as formulated in Boileau's *Art Poétique* and inspired in matters of idea by the more advanced mid-century thought of Montesquieu, Voltaire, Helvetius, and Rousseau, the literary trio in Tankarbyggarorden were prepared to go much farther than Dalin in accepting the revolutionary philosophical and religious implications of the Enlightenment. Though neither their literary gifts nor their intellectual capacities were sufficient to create in the new, more revolutionary spirit a really significant body of poetry, they pointed a way which later in the century was to be taken up and developed much more successfully by greater poets during the so-called Gustavian era.

Of the Tankarbyggarorden group Hedvig Charlotta Nordenflycht (1718–63) is in some ways the most interesting despite her emotional excesses and her artistic and intellectual pretentiousness. She was the first Swedish literary figure to use poetry purely as a means of giving unrestrained expression to her own inner world — in her case a fluid, oftentimes chaotic world, intellectual and emotional by turn, always intense, passionate, highly personal. Feminist though she was (the first in Sweden), the stages of her inner development seem, ironically enough, to have consisted chiefly of a series of highly charged reflexes aroused by her attachments to a number of men in her life, two of whom in particular inspired directly her most characteristic poetic effusions. The first of these, a Reverend Jacob Fabricius, with whom she experienced a short but very happy marital life, was a sensitive Christian Platonist whose early death resulted in the first profound emotional crisis for the poetess and inspired the tortured sentimental verse in *Den sörjande Turturdufvan* (The Sorrowing Turtle Dove, 1743). Her second — and crucial — experience of love came in her last years, and it resulted in her death — but not before the very hopelessness of this late-born attachment (the object of her love, Johan Fischerström, nearly twenty years her junior, could not reciprocate her love) found expression in the classical simplicity and the tenderly controlled passion of one of her last poems, "Över en Hyacint" (On a Hyacinth). Between the personal crises engendered by her emotional attachments to Fabricius and Fischerström she labored, not very happily, with the intellectual intricacies of the mid-century Enlightenment, searching seriously, at times desperately, to find some philosophical solace in her own emotional dilemma. Genuine though the search was, it had a largely deleterious effect on her poetry, resulting too often in unsatisfactory experiments in the "higher" poetic genres (the ode, epic narrative, etc.) of the French classical tradition. Had she been less ambitious, content to cultivate more modest lyric forms, she would probably have come to occupy a more important place than she does in Swedish poetry. Both her exaggerated emotionalism and her rapt pursuit of "philosophy" tend to amuse rather than impress the modern reader even though these qualities are in their way a genuine enough expression of the poetess's deep-felt personal needs.

The same cannot be said of her two young poetic companions, Creutz and Gyllenborg, both of whom were relatively superficial personalities whose early poetic inspiration was largely a precocious reflection of a youthful mood which largely ceased to exist after they entered into mature manhood. Neither of them wrote significant poetry after Hedvig Charlotta Nordenflycht's death in 1763, Creutz entering upon a brilliant diplomatic career which kept him abroad all except the last two years of his life, and Gyllenborg settling down more modestly to a quiet existence as a happy family man and a minor government official who found some aesthetic consolation in fairly frequent attendance at the elegant court of Gustaf III.

Of the two, Gustav Philip Creutz (1731–85) was the more consistent character and a far more skillful poet. Both in his life and in his poetry Creutz was the born master of the prevailing rococo spirit and an Epicurean philosophy of life, turning out light and graceful verse, living with elegant consistency a graciously irresponsible pleasure-filled life, and dying as an aristocratic son of the Enlightenment should die, "in the bosom of the new philosophy" (*uti den nyare filosofiens sköte*), as one of Cruetz's contemporaries put it. His poetic production was small and fragile but it was executed with a consummate flair for spontaneity and graciousness of form. He is remembered particularly for only three poems, his early "Sommarkväde" (Summer Song), the first broadly descriptive landscape poem in Swedish, and two pieces with predominantly erotic themes, "Daphne," with its slightly disguised sensualism, and his masterpiece, the pastoral narrative sequence in five "Songs" entitled *Atis och Camilla*, in which the splendor of budding young love attains its classical Swedish expression against a natural background of exquisite rococo textures and patterns. Nothing could differ more sharply from the heavy baroque manner of Swedish poetry from the seventeenth century than the light and graceful poetry of *Atis och Camilla*. In this poem the rococo manner of the eighteenth century achieves one of its few really distinguished Swedish triumphs.

The third member of the Tankarbyggarorden, Gustaf Fredrik Gyllenborg (1731–1808), had none of Creutz's light and airy poetic touch nor did he share his friend's elegant, carefree, pleasure-loving leanings. Instead of draping himself in the soft robes of Epicurus he shouldered somewhat self-consciously Cato's severe Stoic mantle. "Virtue's Poet" he has been called in consequence of the high moral tone of his poetry. That his early Stoic moralism was, however, at least something of a pose rather than a fundamental trait of his character he cheerfully admits in his autobiography: "I became a perfect Stoic theoretically if not in matters of practice." And his equally frank account of his later life in general reveals that his earlier Stoicism was scarcely an article of faith in the years of his maturity. For a few short years of his youth, however, Gyllenborg was known and at least outwardly respected as the poet-moralist of the day, castigating contemporary manners and morals in reasonably competent verse of high and noble seriousness of tone, with such Roman satirists as Juvenal and Lucretius as his poetic models. Gyllenborg's moral indignation was directed more or less clearly at conditions in Sweden during the years around 1760, when political morals were at their lowest ebb in Swedish history and when the man in the street cheerfully took his cue from those who were mismanaging the affairs of state. That Gyllenborg's moralizing poems had implications, however, beyond immediate Swedish social and political contexts is sufficiently clear. In such poems as "Världsföraktaren" (Despiser of the World) and "Människans elände" (Man's Misery) they give expression to a kind of philosophical pessimism not usually typical of Stoic thought. But that this is in Gyllenborg's case a momentarily felt mood rather than a consistently held philosophical point of view seems apparent from two of his other most well-known poems, "Ode över själens styrka" (Ode on the Strength of the Soul), in which the poet finds positive values in the liberty-loving traditions of ancient Greece and Rome, and in "Vinterkväde" (Winter Song), a landscape poem, partly in the manner of Thomson's *Seasons*, in which an optimistic Rousseauistic view of nature and the natural state becomes identified with an older Swedish Gothicist patriotism. "Winter Song" calls for a return to "conscience, virtue, courage," traditional virtues of a heroic Gothic age, and reflects sharply at points Montesquieu's

theory of the influence of climate on national character as developed in
De l'esprit des lois (1748).

It is one of the devastating ironies of literary history that Gyllenborg's
preoccupation with Classical Stoic moralists and Gothic heroic ideals
resulted in a poetry of a second order at best, while his contemporary
Bellman's dallying with Swedish tavern sots and ladies of dubious reputation issued into a body of poetry which is the high watermark of eighteenth-century Swedish literature and remains to our day unique and
among the greatest of Swedish poetic achievements. Conditions in Sweden which the serious young moralist Gyllenborg found offensive and
despicable the willful, life-loving poet Bellman found acceptable and
interesting, and out of Bellman's inspired willfulness flowed a poetic
strain of remarkable spontaneity, vitality, and originality. Instead of
being disturbed by the decadent drift of his day, Bellman drifted unabashedly with it, finding a gold mine of poetic materials in the most
unexpected of places — in the tawdry but colorful "low life" of that
desperately pleasure-loving Stockholm which in Bellman's day could
purvey to its seventy thousand inhabitants the alcoholic delectations and
attendant diversions of no less than seven hundred gin-shops and taverns.

Like so many other young men of the time, Carl Michael Bellman
(1740–95) capitulated early to temptations of the street and the tavern
despite the apparent advantages of a sound education and the example
of highly respectable middle-class parents. The world of Stockholm
was the only world he knew except for two short excursions from his
native city early in life, one to Uppsala where he indifferently pursued
university studies for less than a year, the other to Norway to which he
fled for a few unhappy months to escape his creditors, who threatened
to have him incarcerated. Careless with money when he had it, and for
that matter seldom having any, he was throughout his life at the mercy of
his creditors, though he managed somehow to evade their unpleasant
efforts to call him to account — until the year before his death, when old
and broken but famous in his way, he sat out a term of something more
than two and a half months in a debtors' prison before his friends and
benefactors succeeded in gaining his release. His place of incarceration,
the Royal Guards Prison (Slotthögvaktens häkten), had the reputation
of being an especially unhealthy abode.

Bellman's gifts were his fate. Gregarious, a born entertainer with fantastic mimic talents and a remarkable feeling for language and music, he

was more than welcome wherever he appeared, whether in riotous tavern environs or in the outwardly more decorous society of the higher *bourgeoisie* and the younger set of the nobility. His talents even found favor with Gustaf III, who seems to have enjoyed his poetic impudence and saw to it that the poet was appointed to sinecures of one kind or another which would keep him at least partially solvent. But a monarch's recognition, though hardly unwelcome to Bellman, could not in the long run make of him a courtier. His tastes *par préférence* were of a less elevated kind, and though his love for the bottle and boisterous levity never reduced the poet himself to the gutter level of some of the characters his poetry has immortalized, he certainly did not look upon these creatures of the city's underworld with anything but fascination and sympathy. Unfortunately for Bellman's more serious poetic reputation, however, his fascinated preoccupation with the shadier sides of Stockholm life provoked the critical condemnation of those who felt called upon to maintain a proper "tone" in matters literary. Not until 1790, five years before his death, was his incomparably greatest collection of poems, *Fredmans epistlar* (Fredman's Epistles), published; followed a year later by the brilliant but uneven poetic miscellany *Fredmans sånger* (Fredman's Songs). During the preceding decade two fragmentary, quite inferior works had appeared under Bellman's name, the lively, good-natured parodies on the ritualistic excesses of contemporary secret societies in the volume entitled *Bacchi tempel* (The Temple of Bacchus) and a group of largely stillborn religious songs, *Sions högtid* (Zion's Festival). His other poems — until many of them were brought together in *Fredman's Epistles* and *Fredman's Songs* — had been recorded by the hands of admirers in contemporary diaries and "song books" or found their way into ephemeral journalistic sheets.

That the eminent critic and poet Johan Henric Kellgren, who had been among Bellman's early detractors, contributed a highly enthusiastic Preface to *Fredman's Epistles* reveals that nearly all opposition to Bellman's poetry had been stilled by 1790. All except a few of the eighty-two songs included in this volume had come from Bellman's pen during that early magnificently productive period between roughly 1768 and 1774, and it was these songs which Kellgren in 1778 had condemned as coarse and lewd, unworthy of the high inspiration of poetry.

Though Kellgren's later complete capitulation to Bellman's verse in the Preface to *Fredman's Epistles* contains a number of incisive critical observations, it is in some respects misleading, particularly in its assumption that Bellman's poetry consists in the main of freely improvised "creations of the moment" rather than deliberately composed and carefully polished verse. Kellgren's view of Bellman as an inspired "folk poet" was eagerly accepted by a following Romantic generation of critics, and the view persisted down to the end of the nineteenth century in the most brilliant of Bellman critics, Oscar Levertin; but today it is clear that this view must be strongly qualified if not forthrightly rejected. The failure of an earlier criticism to note the careful workman behind Bellman's verse is largely an evidence of Bellman's superb artistic skill, its miraculous blending of the spontaneous and the studied, the unrestrained and the controlled — a verse in which life's pulsing, driving, richly fluid diversity is brought under the control of a rare artistic discipline without the reader being especially aware of the deliberate creative hand.

Unfortunately, Bellman defies translation, and even in Swedish he must be sung, not merely read, for words are wedded inextricably to music in his verse. And so *Swedish* is Bellman that with very few exceptions only Swedes have succeeded in adequately rendering his song. A brilliant exception is the well-known Danish lieder singer, Aksel Schiøtz.

Bellman's verse has demonstrable points of contact both with an earlier Swedish drinking-song tradition (that of Lucidor, Runius, and Dalin) and with a more contemporary French *chanson* development, but it is one of the evidences of Bellman's artistic greatness that he *adds* so much to these forms, transforming them into a mad world of poetic beauty which at all points bears his own inimitable stamp. Bellman's verse is just as jolly and quite as irreverent as the traditional Swedish drinking song or the light French biblical parodies of the day; but in pursuing the moods and themes of his predecessors in the lighter poetic genres he is not satisfied with the limited horizons of a private drinking bout or the immediate joys of a neat satiric thrust. In *Fredman's Epistles* he is satisfied with nothing less than to create a whole motley world of highly individualized characters, each one of whom finds his natural place among his more or less wayward fellows and all of whom play out their precarious, half-desperate roles in a vivid, immediately recognizable environment. These characters were apparently without exception actual individuals of Bellman's acquaintance, and their environment was the Stockholm tavern world which Bellman knew at first hand so well. Bellman's Fredman was in reality Jean Fredman (1712–67), a one-time highly respectable Clock Maker to the Court, whom alcohol and an unfortunate marriage had brought to the sad pass in which we find him in the Epistles

Vignettes by Yngve Berg from an illustrated edition of Bellman's *Fredmans Epistlar*

which bear his name. Ulla Winblad, the gay "queen" of Bellman's oddly assorted, largely male world, was a certain Maria Kristina Kiellström (1744–98), a well-known lower-class demimondaine of the day. Movitz (1721–79), whom Bellman seemed to have a special feeling for, had been in military service but, because of a service-incurred disability, later tried his hand without too much enthusiasm at various occupations, saloon keeper, musician, umbrella fabricator. The redoubtable Mollberg (1734–72), born into a well-to-do family, rapidly degenerating in his youth, having served a turn in the artillery from which derives his military posturing, died completely destitute. And so on down the list of the score and a half of named characters in the Epistles.

What is the secret of Bellman's art which makes of such human derelicts and their scabby, gin-drenched world the fascinating poetry of *Fredman's Epistles*? The question, a very difficult one, can scarcely be answered satisfactorily in the summary fashion demanded in a short history of Swedish literature. But certainly among the central qualities of Bellman's art are its sharp concreteness, its astonishing sense of movement, its richly faceted humor, its amazing variety and range of verse form and poetic mood, and its identity with music at every point.

In Bellman's verse we *see* everything; the poet's visual sense is always present, whether he is describing in sharply naturalistic detail the evidences of physical disintegration of Movitz's moribund body (Epistle 30) or is paying court in a light rococo manner to Ulla Winblad on the occasion of her excursion to Djurgården (25). But the visual detail is never allowed to pile up in a dead mass of concretions in the manner of a latter-day naturalism. Bellman's realism is selective, impressionistic, intensely alive in its dramatic sense of *movement*. Frequently this sense of movement is boisterous, wild, all but out of hand, as in the conflagration in Kolmätargränden (34) or in the episode "concerning Mollberg's Parade to Corporal Boman's Grave" (38) or in the orgiastic bacchanalian concert held at the tavern dubbed The Three Tubs (51). At other times the mobility of scene is more restrained, as in the graceful pastoral on Ulla's return journey from Hessingen of a summer morning (48) or in the melancholy drunken aftermaths to a couple of Movitz's less happy amorous adventures (31 and 44). At still other times, as in the lightly ironic description of Ulla making her morning toilette under the protective care of a tavern keeper (36), the sense of movement is almost minimal — until the fateful arrival of officers of the law, when a madly realistic strain suddenly takes over, dispelling the lovely, half-somnolent pastoral spell of the preceding verses.

Though Bellman's humor frequently indulges in such sudden comic shifts of situation and mood as we come upon at the close of Ulla's toilette piece, his comic resources as otherwise reflected in this poem are capable of much more subtle effects; and in other Epistles Bellman's humor attains a warm, many-faceted spaciousness which reminds one inevitably of Cervantes and Shakespeare.

One of the facets of this humor, perhaps its greatest, is the one which points up by poignant indirection how closely allied are the tragic and comic elements in the daily business of living. The very boisterousness of Bellman's characters suggests something forced, desperate, and broken behind the magnificently maintained comic façade of the Fredman world. Its very bravado, no matter how joyously celebrated in bottle and song, strikes a hollow, empty note. Life is wedded indissolubly to death, and Bellman's alter ego Fredman is no stranger to the thought despite his — or probably *because* of his — strenuous addiction to the pleasures of the bottle and the attractions of female flesh. Not that Bellman-Fredman becomes at the last a moralist — hardly. He becomes rather a humorist-realist, who sees life at times with tired, heavily disillusioned eyes, and at these times he only *barely*, and by desperate last-resort devices, manages to maintain something of his usual devil-may-care equipoise. This complex tragicomic mood, which flashes fitfully so often in Bellman's verse, finds its most impressive and sustained expression in Epistles 23,

30, and 79. The first of these, containing Fredman's famous "gutter soliloquy," is the most gripping, chiefly perhaps because its "comedy" is more
profound, closer to the ultimate sources of tragedy without pretending
to be so. In Epistle 23 we find Fredman in a dark and dirty gutter outside
the gin-shop Kryp-In (literally Creep In!), awakening painfully from a
drunken debauch. Realizing his utter degradation at the moment and
describing its nauseating physical accompaniments in starkly ugly terms,
he breaks out in a savage, broken staccato of indictments against his
mother and father, who in a moment of casual — possibly accidental and
quite blind — passion conceived a son and occasioned Fredman's present
wretched ignominy. Through three harshly gripping stanzas these wild
charges are developed; but as Fredman's befuddled machinery of thought
begins to clear a bit, and the first warm effulgence of dawn penetrates
the dingy alley in which he lies, he pulls himself together as best he can
and staggers back into the gin-shop, now open again for the day. Here
he grasps greedily what joy he can by drinking in loneliness his own
health; and — groping again for life's pleasures no matter how fleeting
or tarnished — he now *blesses* the accident which drove his parents into
passion's blind play. Grotesque as the denouement may seem, it is conceived with an overwhelming visual intensity and power and is born by
a language of aching directness and honesty. It is Hogarth without the
conventional moral.

Such poems as this have from time to time moved Bellman enthusiasts
to attribute to Bellman profound intellectual gifts. This is certainly
nonsense. Bellman is neither an intellectual nor a moralist. He is a pure
artist, little prone to theorizing about life, instinctively responding to
whatever life has to offer, with something of a precocious child's wide-
open greedy eyes. This is why his characters may feel fear but not remorse, why they take poverty, disease, and even death more or less in
stride. Their divinities remain at all times Bacchus and Venus, their pursuits whatever pleasures life may offer. Bellman never seems to have
bothered his brain particularly about a possible "judgment of God," assuming apparently with a disarming naïveté that a good Father God
looks down upon the waywardness of His children with an understanding, generously forgiving heart.

That Bellman was not alone among his literary countrymen in this
childlike lack of concern with higher moral concepts is attested by the
case of Jacob Wallenberg (1746–78), who in the robes of a Lutheran

pastor managed without any profounder compunctions to respond to the pleasures of the flesh quite as completely as Bellman and who wrote a travel book — *Min son på Galejan* (My Son on the Schooner) — which may loosely be called the prose counterpart of *Fredman's Epistles*. Wallenberg's book is a highly original account of certain early phases of a year-and-a-half's sea journey to China and his return as ship's chaplain on the schooner *Finland* under the flag of the Swedish East India Company. Wallenberg's merry book resembles Bellman's masterpiece in its daring realism, its healthy, full-bodied animalism, its boisterous drinking bouts (one of them regularly arranged directly after the Sunday sermon on board!), and its forthright frivolity in matters of the heart. Its humor, however, lacks the warmth and depth of Bellman at his best, and its realism is never cushioned, as Bellman's sometimes is, by the graceful playfulness of a rococo world. Wallenberg's realism was consistently of the bluff, broad-shouldered, deep-chested kind which we associate with the primitive cultural world of the Swedish seventeenth century. *My Son on the Schooner* was touched by none of the over-refinements of the late eighteenth-century Gustavian era. Perhaps because of this it remains among the few Swedish literary works of its century and earlier that are read with pleasure today. Its spontaneous, robust realism has a basic kinship with one side of the modern spirit.

Seldom if ever in literary history has a monarch's name more appropriately been attached to a literary period than those two or three decades in late eighteenth-century Swedish literature which it is customary to call "The Gustavian Era." Gustaf III's character has been both praised and damned, and his politics has been the subject of sharply conflicting judgments; but there have been no fundamental differences of opinion on his importance for Swedish culture. In fact, one of the often repeated charges of his enemies was that the King neglected politics for the arts, and sometimes even confused the two, handling crucial affairs of state with a display of histrionic poses and gestures more fitting to the stage than to the practical arena of politics. However this may be (some truth there is certainly in the charge) there can be no doubt that Gustaf III did love the arts, all of them; and for the arts of the theater he had a consuming passion. In consequence his reign actively encouraged in many ways the pursuit of the arts, as the preceding half century — a more utilitarian period — had encouraged commerce and the sciences.

This royal encouragement of the arts took on many forms and re-sulted in a cultural sophistication in Sweden which the country had never before experienced. Indeed, not until Gustaf III's reign did the program and spirit of the Enlightenment reach its full flowering in the land, largely with France as a model. The aging Voltaire of the radical Ferney period was the Gustavian era's prophet, the graceful rococo of Versailles its formal ideal, a worldly-wise Gallic combination of seriousness and frivol-ity its prevailing mood. So complete, indeed, was the triumph at this time of the ideas and spirit of the Enlightenment over an older Swedish cul-ture that they even penetrated the bastions of the Lutheran Church, where, at least among the upper echelons of the clergy, pulpit oratory took on more polished literary forms than hitherto and a deistically in-spired spirit of tolerance displaced at points the rigid orthodoxy of the past.

The outward and more showy evidences of the new cultural flower-ing — all of them directly initiated by the King or occurring under his protection — are strikingly indicative: the founding of the Royal Opera in 1773, the establishment of the Swedish Academy in 1786, the opening of the Royal Dramatic Theater in 1787. But even more important was the King's imaginative planning and sustained participation in the day-to-day work of these cultural institutions together with his attachment to the Court of artists, sculptors, architects, musicians, and poets whose function it was to create an artistic tradition in Stockholm which might vie with that of Paris and Versailles. Though the program might seem hopelessly pretentious, and certainly was in some respects, it was borne by a contagious enthusiasm and guided by considerable taste and intel-ligence; and thanks to these factors it succeeded in no small measure con-sidering the lack of any mature cultural traditions upon which it could build, particularly in the dramatic arts where Sweden's meager earlier na-tive contribution had to be bolstered by the activities of visiting foreign troupes. It was, in consequence, no mean attainment to establish the be-ginnings of an operatic and theatrical tradition so sound that this tradi-tion has been maintained without serious lapses in artistic standards down to our own day. This attainment was made possible because of Gustaf III's program of recruitment for his theater of the best available artistic talents, native and foreign.

Not the least among these talents were the poets of the day, whom the King used chiefly to turn into competent verse his own operatic and dramatic sketches, but he encouraged them also to translate into Swedish and adapt for the stage both modern and Classical drama and to produce dramatic pieces of their own. Though collaboration with a vain and often capricious royal master became in the long run irksome to the more independent poets of the day, it served to give the poet a considerably higher standing in the community than he had previously been accustomed to, and in some instances — as in the collaboration of the King and Kellgren on the opera *Gustaf Wasa* — the result was a great theatrical triumph.

Of the four poets who became most closely attached to the Court, two of them, Johan Gabriel Oxenstierna (1750–1818) and Gudmund Jöran Adlerbeth (1751–1818), held important political positions and were poets only incidentally, while the other two, Leopold and Kellgren, devoted their entire time and energies to literary pursuits and became, together with Bellman, the chief literary figures of the day. Oxenstierna's rather thin but sensitive and cultivated talent is of interest especially because in his two major works *Skördarna* (The Harvests) and *Dagens stunder* (Times of the Day) he provides the chief link between Gyllenborg's earlier landscape poetry and the later major Romantic poets in whose work we find the most brilliant poetic treatment of the old and persistent notion that the good life is necessarily the unspoiled life of natural primitive man. Adlerbeth is a more impressive and complex figure than Oxenstierna, but his poetic gift is much less supple and spontaneous. Among the most learned Swedes of his day, Adlerbeth was one of the earliest of Gustaf III's literary "work horses." He adapted Racine's *Iphigénie* and Voltaire's *Oedipus* for the Swedish stage, in part by bringing them closer to Euripides and Sophocles, and he composed original librettos (his opera *Cora och Alonzo* was the first piece on the boards of the King's new opera house) and the tragedy *Ingjald Illråda*. As a translator he put into Swedish verse both Latin poetry (Horace, Ovid, Virgil) and Icelandic saga material, and as a scholar-critic he speculated incisively on the relations between Icelandic and "Ossianic" poetry.

Though Carl Gustaf af Leopold (1756–1829) loomed much larger on the Gustavian literary horizon than either Oxenstierna or Adlerbeth, he interests the modern reader little if any more. He is the typical court poet, gifted, obsequious, correct, always at the call of his royal master, who appreciated Leopold's person and talents so enthusiastically that for the six years of their association the King scarcely allowed an evening to pass without availing himself of the conversational talents of his favorite literary man in waiting. Leopold returned the royal compliment by serving his King with exemplary loyalty, a loyalty which remained as absolute in the recesses of his memory after the assassination of the King in 1792 as it had been in life. Unfortunately, this constant preoccupation with the person, the court, and the memory of the King gave to Leopold's verse facility rather than spontaneity, elegance rather than depth, and its facility and elegance, so admired in the poet's own day, are now as dead as a museum collection of courtly garments of the day. The partial shift away from the courtly cadences of Leopold's earlier poetry toward a middle-class sentimentalism in his later work represents no fundamental change in his literary position. He himself apparently placed highest among his works such pretentious moralizing poems as "Det Onda" (Evil), "Försynen" (Providence), and especially "Predikaren" (The Preacher), but later generations have preferred some of his lighter verse, particularly the lively little narrative sketch "Eglé och Annett" (Eglé and Annett) which serves up its moral tidbit with a delectable interplay of sentiment and irony. Leopold is on the whole, however, more important as a critic and theorist, the one who more intelligently and consistently than any of his contemporaries defined and defended Gustavian neoclassical literary concepts, most impressively perhaps in the lengthy critical essay *Om smaken och dess allmänna lagar* (On Taste and Its Universal Laws, 1801). In his late years Leopold, the aging symbol of a disintegrating Gustavian culture, became the obvious target of a youthful and militant early nineteenth-century Romanticism. Despite the overwhelming odds against him and his cause in his declining years, he fought back stubbornly, yielding ground slowly and always insisting that his enemies represented a quite unacceptable literary barbarism. To him the Enlightenment in its Gustavian form represented the noblest of cultural ideals.

The life span allotted to Johan Henric Kellgren (1751–95) was much shorter than that of Leopold, but its duration, just short of forty-four years, was sufficient to encompass a literary attainment of a much higher order than Leopold's. Kellgren, like Leopold, had found his way to Stockholm and Gustaf III's court after experiencing strong feelings of frustration within the limited cultural confines of a provincial university life — in Kellgren's case the Swedish-Finnish university of Åbo. But Kellgren, unlike Leopold, soon tired of employing his talents in providing an elegant poetic form for his King's dramatic sketches, and retired as soon as possible from playing the courtly role of a compliant literary lackey. His genius, incomparably more profound and original than Leopold's, could not indefinitely find itself at home in the cold and oftentimes sterile formalities of the Gustavian world. Kellgren had, it is true, much in common with Gustavian culture: its light-hearted Epicureanism, its dubious morals, its disrespect for religion, its intellectualism, its rococo grace and clarity of form. But these Gustavian attitudes and mores were not for Kellgren mere formalities with which one *plays* at being an enlightened eighteenth-century philosopher or moralist; they were articles of a new and radical faith by which one *lives*. And, more important, if these attitudes and mores proved in practice to be inadequate to the purposes of life they should be modified or rejected in the light of a larger vision of truth. In short, Kellgren never became tyrannized by any fixed set of cultural dogmas; his passionate intellectualism had in it the possibilities of growth. It was capable of pouring into the fragile Gustavian vessels at hand not only the heady Epicurean wines of his youth but also the wholesome, fruitful essence of the poet's maturity.

The headier wines are to be found particularly in his erotic poems, earliest in the blatantly sensual "Sinnenas förening" (The Union of the Senses), later, and more subtly, in the light and playful satiric thrusts of "Till Rosalie" (To Rosalie). An alternately voluptuous and gay dallying with love was not, however, the only note struck in Kellgren's earlier verse. He soon became a master of the mocking poetic vein, in the Voltairean manner, pouring his youthful scorn with irrepressible irreverence on anything and everything which caught his critical eye — on clerical obscurantism and political opportunism, on academic pedantry and fraternal-society humbug, on poetic mediocrity parading as literary genius. He appropriately entitles the best of his early poems in this mocking manner "Mina löjen" (My Laughter). The poem, apparently written in 1777, firmly established Kellgren as the leading poet of his day.

In October of the following year Kellgren became associated with *Stockholms Posten*, an association which he was to maintain in various capacities (critic, editor, and finally owner) down to his death in 1795. Though a competitive journalism was flourishing in Sweden for the first time when Kellgren became active as a journalist, poet, and critic, his brilliant pen rapidly made *Stockholms Posten* the leading newspaper of the day, read avidly by all literate citizens of Stockholm whether or not they approved of the opinions it dished up with a lively, scintillating, controversial flair. Indeed, no livelier Swedish newspaper has ever existed, in part because of Kellgren's journalistic genius, in part because mere "objective" news was no particular concern of a late eighteenth-century Swedish editor. In fact, news as such seldom appeared in Kellgren's newspaper, due largely perhaps to the severe censorship maintained at the time. Instead *Stockholms Posten* was what we now call a "journal of opinion," and as such it became a forum in which Kellgren gave brilliant expression to the cultural ideas and ideals of the Enlightenment in their most advanced and radical forms. While *Stockholms Posten* came to exercise an influence on Swedish life and thought perhaps without parallel in the history of Swedish journalism, Kellgren's work in its columns was also of the utmost importance for his own intellectual and literary development. His activities as an editor brought into his literary work a sense of a living, active cultural awareness, broadening the poet's horizons and deepening his feeling of responsibility to the social and political community of which he was a part. He became more than a poet in the limited sense of the term; he became a citizen who used his literary skills as an effective weapon in the struggle against society's stupidities and injustice.

The severity with which Kellgren expressed his opinions in *Stockholms Posten* involved him inevitably in a great many controversies, the two most sensational of which were the decade-long squabble beginning in 1782 with the poet-critic Thorild about matters of poetic form, and the so-called Pro Sensu Communi furor (1787ff.) in which Kellgren in the name of "common sense" makes a devastating attack on cultural obscurantism as practiced particularly by various sectarian religious fanatics and diverse occultist charlatans of the day. Out of the Thorild controversy came two of Kellgren's most brilliant parodies, "Angående påbudet om snöskottning" (Concerning the Ordinance on Snow Shoveling) and "Nytt försök till orimmad vers" (New Efforts at Unrhymed Verse); and the Pro Sensu Communi campaign resulted in Kellgren's famous "Man äger ej snille för det man är galen" (One Doesn't Have Genius Because One Is Mad), in which the poet discards completely the rather airy mocking vein of his earlier satiric verse and gives vent to feelings of flaming indignation in measured poetic periods of high and noble seriousness. In these works the Enlightenment in Sweden reaches its finest expression. In the heat of journalistic controversy Kellgren had matured into an apostle of reason and of common sense in its most ideal and inspired form.

It is characteristic of Kellgren that his defense of the Enlightenment stopped short of dogmatic assertiveness, never stiffening into sterile, outworn forms. He could in consequence remain open to moods and ideas which essentially challenged some of the more rigid critical concepts of the Enlightenment, particularly those which had to do with literary form and the sources of literary inspiration. The two works which most clearly illustrate Kellgren's openmindedness, his refusal to be tyrannized by the accepted literary conventions of his day, appeared in 1790 — the Preface to Bellman's *Fredman's Epistles* and the greatest of Kellgren's poems "Den Nya Skapelsen, eller inbillningens värld" (The New Creation, or The World of the Imagination). In the Preface to *Fredman's Epistles* he expresses opinions sharply opposed to neoclassical literary dogmas; in "The New Creation" both form and idea break over the boundaries of poetic expression approved by the Enlightenment. The Preface might, indeed, have been conceived if not written by Kellgren's most gifted literary antagonist Thorild, for its central thesis — the right of genius to pursue its own lights independent of all rules and literary conventions — was one of Thorild's favorite critical dictums. In this Preface Kellgren completely reverses his position taken twelve years earlier in "My Laughter," where he condemned in the name of "good taste" what he then considered the coarseness and indecency of Bellman's poetry. In the Preface from 1790 he aligns himself at least tentatively with the Romantic view that genius is a law unto itself, a view which seems to have been funneled into Sweden particularly through Edward Young's *Conjectures on Original Composition* (1759).

Kellgren's readiness in the Preface to *Fredman's Epistles* to challenge literary critical views dear to the Enlightenment made it easier for him to write such a poem as "The New Creation," which in idea and to a lesser extent in form reveals a poet who is establishing vital creative points of contact with late eighteenth-century pre-Romantic trends. That which precipitated the state of mind in which Kellgren wrote "The New Creation" was not primarily, however, his acquaintance with the new literary trends of the day. It was rather an immediate *experience* of Kellgren's, an experience of love — the profoundest of his life — from his last years. Unlike his earlier erotic experiences, which seem never to have progressed beyond the level of the sensuous and the sensual, this new emotional attachment brought to the poet a deeply moving, essentially selfless vision of love. In "The New Creation" the object of the poet's feeling is something far more than a body to be enjoyed in sensuous dalliance: she becomes the very archetype (*urbild*) of creation, a vision of ineffable beauty capable of transforming man's whole view of nature and the physical world. This essentially Platonic view of love is a far cry from the erotic voluptuousness, the radical materialism of Kellgren's earlier verse.

It would be misleading, however, to assume that the poetic vision of "The New Creation" represents a deliberate and complete break with Kellgren's basic loyalty to the ideas of the Enlightenment. It should be understood rather as the inspired reflection of a deeply moving incident in Kellgren's mature life, an incident which allowed him to catch a vision of ideal beauty inconceivable to reason and common sense but which did not result otherwise in a total rejection of these typical eighteenth-century norms of human thought and action. Such satiric masterpieces as "Ljusets fiender" (The Enemies of Light) and "Dumboms lefverne" (The Numskull's Life), written on the verge of Kellgren's final, protracted illness and inspired by his indignation at the political reactionary-ism in Sweden immediately before and after Gustaf III's assassination, reflect as clearly as anything the poet ever wrote his scornful suspicion of emotional obscurantism of all kinds and his firm faith in human reason as man's only adequate guide in a confused social and political world. Kellgren remained down to the end a son of the Enlightenment — the greatest among its Swedish sons, in part if not chiefly because he never permitted its ideas to freeze into forms which denied direct access to life's vital, spontaneous, seminal drives. Tegnér once called Kellgren Sweden's "national good sense" (*nationalvett*). The label is strikingly appropriate.

Within Kellgren's most intimate circle of friends was Anna Maria Lenngren (1754–1817), the coolest head and one of the warmest hearts among Swedish poets. Born at Uppsala, daughter of a Latinist of strong pietistic leanings, she married at twenty-six the solid middle-class Stockholmer Carl Petter Lenngren, a co-editor with Kellgren of *Stockholms Posten*. Though Anna Maria's father had begun to make something of a scholar of his brilliant daughter when she was in her teens, she became in maturity anything but a bluestocking, disdaining the strident attitudes of the feminist and finding her chief pride in fulfilling the duties of a housewife. Her literary talents were exercised sparingly and for the most part privately until 1794, when as a woman of forty she began publishing her verse from time to time in *Stockholms Posten*, apparently in order to assist her husband in consequence of the death-marked Kellgren's inability to contribute regularly to these columns. Her reading public was immediately enchanted, as well it might be, for nothing like these poems had ever appeared in Swedish. And even the august Swedish Academy saw fit to do her special honor. But success did not go to her head. Entirely devoid of literary vanity, she always looked upon her poems (she once call them "trinkets") as something incidental to her life as her husband's wife, and it seems to have been her will that when two years after her death a selection of her poems finally appeared in book form the work was modestly titled *Skaldeförsök* (Poetic Attempts). "She hid her lyre under her sewing table," as one of her contemporaries has put it.

This lyre was tuned to only two poetic genres, the idyl and the satire, but within the limits of these genres her artistic control was complete, manipulating theme and mood with miraculous mastery of verse and phrase and image. Given the subjects which she chose to treat, one cannot imagine a more perfect treatment. As a literary *artist* she has no peer among her countrywomen, and few equals among Swedish male practitioners of the poetic art. Her art has nothing of the abstract and rhetorical, nothing of the artifice and sophistication which we associate with the Gustavian era. In her poetry everything is concrete, clipped, spontaneous, natural. That her realism owes something to Bellman is clear, and that her satiric vein has certain points of contact with Kellgren is equally apparent; but her realism is closer to average human experience than Bellman's and her satire is warmer, more essentially humane than Kellgren's. The special mark of her poetry is its clearheaded sobriety, its sensitive closeness to everyday living, its refusal to take flight either into the speculative intellectualism of the Gustavian tradition or the emotional excesses of a dawning late eighteenth-century Romanticism. She is the canny housewife with wide-open eyes, a brilliant observer of life around her. The latent realism of the Gustavian era had in her its only distinguished representative, except for Bellman whose important work was finished before the Gustavian era got well under way.

Though she is at her best in a satiric or semi-satiric vein, she manages by some kind of poetic magic to pour considerable life into even such an outworn conventional form as the idyl. In fact her idyls take on a certain novelty, all of them departing more or less sharply from the threadbare artifices of the traditional pastoral idyl which she ridicules with high-spirited good nature in "Ett sätt att göra herdekväden" (A Way of Making Pastoral Poems). Usually she combines elements of the simple song with the idyl, as in "Pojkarna" (The Boys) and "Slottet och kojan"

(The Castle and the Cottage). Occasionally her idyls are broadly descriptive, as in the immensely popular idealized picture of life in a country manse "Den glada festen" (The Happy Birthday Party), which is so reminiscent of Goldsmith's *The Vicar of Wakefield* without for a moment losing a specifically Swedish touch.

Fru Lenngren's pictures of the country manse are not, however, always idealized. In one of them, "Grevinnans besök" (The Visit of the Countess), sly touches of good-natured irony add considerable tartness to the sweetness of the scene. The irony is aimed largely at the stupidities of a class-conscious world in which a fatuously obsequious pastor and his good wife entertain a graciously condescending countess and her daughter. But the relatively delicate ironic restraint with which Anna Maria Lenngren's dislike of the nobility is handled in "The Visit of the Countess" takes on much more serious and pointed forms in three of her greatest satiric sketches, two from 1796 "Hans nåds morgonsömn" (His Grace's Morning Nap) and "Portraiterne" (The Portraits), and one from 1798 "Fröken Juliana" (Miss Juliana). In these pieces she becomes the spokesman for the Swedish middle classes against the empty and pretentious claims of a proud and dying aristocracy — in the days, it should be noted, when abroad the French Revolution was writing a poetry of bloody action with the broken remnants of an *ancien régime*. "His Grace's Morning Nap" and "The Portraits" are infinitely clever caricatures, so disarmingly amusing that their political implications are not always immediately apparent, at least not for a later generation. "Miss Juliana," on the other hand, quite brutally points the political moral, when, at the end, the old-maid "Lady" — unlovely, ungainly, and poor — accepts the inevitable by marrying the local sheriff to the unspeakable horror of her proud and penniless family. So pointedly, indeed, is the *déclassé* moral of this poem forced home that "Miss Juliana" was withheld from publication at the time it was written and did not appear in print until years later — when political circumstances in Sweden were less potentially explosive.

That such a well-balanced and naturally restrained person as Anna Maria Lenngren could have written such a poem as "Miss Juliana" is an evidence of how intense was the feeling of antagonism between the classes in the Sweden of the 1790's. Whether she was motivated in her decision not to publish the poem by her good sense or by fear of official reprisal (her husband as a government official was in a delicate position) is difficult to say. In any case her tentative foray into political satire was short-lived, and when in 1798 she wrote her credo in the poem "Några ord till min kära dotter" (A Few Words to My Dear Daughter) she was her usual controlled and sober self, admonishing her imagined daughter to eschew both learned activities and political interests and to cultivate instead, as the sum of all wisdom, the everyday middle-class household virtues of "prudence" and a "sensitive cheerfulness." During the remainder of her life she wrote poetry only sporadically, none of it important and none of it political in implication. She lived her poetry rather than wrote it during these years, reaching out for no mountain tops of human experience, nurturing no dreams of the unattainable, satisfied with the limited adventures of a not very venturesome everyday living.

A few years after Kellgren in 1777 had descended on Stockholm from Åbo across the Baltic to the East and began a career which ultimately made him the most finely critical mind and the greatest poet of the Gustavian era, two other gifted young men, Thomas Thorild and Bengt Lidner, moved into the capital from Sweden's west coast via the University of Lund and other points to the South. Though both Thorild and Lidner early sought favor at the hands of Gustaf III, they proved in the end to be anything but Gustavian in their literary tastes; and before their short literary careers ended, the one in exile, the other in death, they managed to attract sufficient attention to their highly original persons and their almost equally original work to become the symbols of something which struck most of their contemporaries as quite new in Swedish letters. They became the first highly vocal representatives of what for want of a better term we call pre-Romanticism, that congeries of cultural trends in eighteenth-century Europe which was in more or less conscious reaction against French classicism and the Enlightenment, and which toward the end of the century was challenging with considerable success the formalism and intellectualism that had for so long been the chief marks of eighteenth-century literature. Though in Sweden, as elsewhere, pre-Romantic strains had maintained a kind of underground existence during much of the eighteenth century, these strains had existed in such quantity throughout the century that one of the most monumental of Swedish literary-historical studies — Martin Lamm's *Upplysningstidens romantik* (The Romanticism of the Enlightenment) — could quite properly be devoted to a minute study of their various manifestations, religious and philosophical, literary and broadly cultural.

What happened in these contexts in Swedish literature in the 1780's and 1790's is that these half-submerged but persistent pre-Romantic strains came to the surface, not only asserting themselves deliberately as a new literary program in the hands of such authors as Thorild and Lidner but affecting in part the kind of poetry written by typical representatives of Gustavian poetry such as Kellgren, Oxenstierna, and others. Though the new literature owed much to Rousseau's primitivism and Montesquieu's historical relativism, it was even more indebted to a whole host of English authors who in one way or another reflect pre-Romantic tendencies — to the nature poetry of James Thomson, to the "graveyard poetry" of Edward Young and Thomas Gray, to the sentimental novel of Richardson and Sterne, to the bourgeois tragedy of George Lillo and others, to the religious poetry of Milton and his eighteenth-century imitators, to James Macpherson's misty and mystic Ossianic world, and to the new pre-Romantic aesthetics of such critical works as Young's *Conjectures on Original Composition*. And to these English influences were added some related German strains, particularly those provided by Klopstock's *Messias* and by such "Sturm und Drang" works as Goethe's *Werther*. Some of these strains were not entirely new in Swedish letters — both Rousseau's primitivism and the Ossianic moods and themes had obvious points of contact with a long-established Swedish "Gothic" tradition, and religious verse had occupied for centuries its honored place in Swedish poetry. But during most of the eighteenth century these native Swedish strains had either been held suspect or employed with due restraint. The critical spirit of the Enlightenment had frowned upon them and had succeeded in keeping them in check or forcing them beneath the mainstream of literary development. They could not, however, be permanently ignored. In the last two decades of the century they again had their day, encouraged at this time to assert themselves more obtrusively because of the rising tide of English and German reaction against the French classical ideals which had so long prevailed in Sweden. Thomas Thorild (1759–1808) became the strident prophet of the new literature, Bengt Lidner (1757–93) its lacrymose and mellifluous poet.

Thorild may be described as a kind of raging bull in the neat, well-ordered Gustavian china shop. Bursting with new ideas and violently self-assertive, he disliked literary finesses and despised the leering irony, the fashionable negativism of so much of the poetry and criticism of the day. Hating Voltaire and worshiping Rousseau, he found release from an odious Gustavianism in the more spacious imaginative worlds of Milton's *Paradise Lost* and Edward Young's *Night Thoughts*, and in the world of heroic poses and vaguely portentous backgrounds of James Macpherson's *Ossian*.

The poem with which Thorild introduced himself to a startled literary Stockholm in 1781 was *Passionerna* (The Passions), in which a welter of philosophical pronouncements is given expression in turgid, irregular, pretentious hexameters. The work has its chief importance in that it precipitated the Thorild-Kellgren controversy and launched Thorild on his meteoric career as the self-appointed leader of what was generally referred to at the time as "the new sect." Though the celebrated controversy began as a debate on such purely literary matters as the relative values of rhymed and unrhymed verse, it soon burgeoned out into considerations of a much more inclusive kind, chiefly in the hands of Thorild whose undisciplined ego and restless energies envisioned his task in life as nothing less than, as he at one time put it, "to explain all nature and reform the whole world." It is little wonder that a man of such pretensions should find the Sweden of the day too paltry as a base of operations and that he should in 1788 emigrate to England, where he hoped to find a more favorable response to his grandiose reform program. Two years later, perhaps somewhat chastened by British indifference to his person and his work, he returned to Sweden, whereupon he took up again his literary-critical cudgels in the essay *En kritik öfver kritiker* (A Criticism of Critics), in which he chides his old enemy Kellgren for lack of charity in treating literary nonentities and uses this charge as the point of departure for a rather lengthy defense of a historical-relativistic basis for literary judgments. He need not have chided Kellgren at this time, for the latter's Preface to *Fredman's Epistles*, which had appeared a year before, goes in its way just as far as Thorild in rejecting a dogmatic application of neoclassical rules in literary criticism. Both Kellgren and Thorild had learned something from Young's *Conjectures on Original Composition* and a new literature conceived in its liberal non-dogmatic spirit.

Though Thorild became increasingly involved in his last years in political and philosophical writing which need not detain us here, he composed also during these years his best poetry, the so-called "Götamannasånger" (literally, Gothic Men's Songs), which in brilliant aphoristic formulations reminiscent of the ancient Swedish legal style gives concise, concrete expression to certain of his political theories. Thorild's prose style seldom attains the sense of inner discipline characteristic of these poems, but at its best his prose is equally distinguished, chiefly because it has freed itself from the abstract rhetorical patterns of the day, loosening up its syntactical rigidities and bringing prose style closer to the speech of everyday life. Style, Thorild once wrote, is the act of "making something spirited and *alive*, that is: to reveal the beautiful in all its beauty, the ugly in all its ugliness. One does not paint that which is homely beautifully, one does not paint the Devil in golden sunrise tints, any more than the sow in rosy tones." Thorild fashioned his best prose according to this view, that is to say the subject determined his style — a view which points forward to modern realism and finds its great Swedish masters in the nineteenth century, in C. J. L. Almqvist and Strindberg.

Bengt Lidner, who together with Thorild came to represent most unequivocally the pre-Romantic strains of the 1780's, had none of the aggressiveness, the astonishing vitality of Thorild. He has been called "the genius of sensibility" (*känslosamhetens snille*) in Swedish letters. The label is eminently accurate, for Lidner pursued the cult of sensibility with a single-minded devotion that is unique in Swedish poetry, and in certain ways perhaps without parallel in world literature. He is the Laurence Sterne of Swedish letters, without his English contemporary's naughty wit. Both Lidner's life and work are dedicated exclusively to exploiting every most tender resource of human emotion. He quite deliberately proceeds to wring every sad tear of sympathy for the unfortunate ones of this world — including, as not the least unfortunate, himself. A dandy when he could afford to be, an alcoholic most of the time, he was an incorrigible wastrel, living on the limited largesse of those who admired his genius or sympathized with his wretchedness, and dying in desperate poverty at the age of thirty-six. Even Bellman, who had enough of his own troubles, is supposed to have reached out a helping hand to his besotted fellow poet, in part no doubt as a matter of simple humanity, in part probably because he recognized in Lidner a poetic gift of a very high order.

Lidner early experienced the favor of Gustaf III, who hoped to make a dramatist out of him by financing an extended study tour of the Continent. Despite the many irregularities of his life abroad, he managed somehow to complete a tragedy, *Erik XIV*, and to work out substantial portions of an opera, *Medea*, which was finished shortly after his return to Stockholm in 1782. Aside from some magnificent songs in *Medea* — especially the battle song "O, yngling om du hjärta har" (Oh, youth if thou dost have a heart) — neither of these works is intrinsically important. But in form they reflect changing tastes, away from French classical tragedy and toward Shakespeare and bourgeois tragedy; and in mood and theme they provide the poet with ample opportunity to exploit to the hilt sentimental and sensational elements, the twin poles of Lidner's oversensitive genius. Horror is piled on horror, madness and murder heaping up on stage with feverish frequency and abandon. Even the child murders in *Medea* are enacted before our eyes. Though both Erik XIV and Medea are conceived as criminal characters, we are expected to pity rather than condemn them, to weep copious tears over their sad fates in keeping with a late eighteenth-century morality of sentimentalism.

Neither *Erik XIV* nor *Medea* attracted much attention, no doubt because they lacked any really impressive dramatic qualities. Lidner was essentially a lyric poet, and it was not until he poured out his feelings directly in such lyric outbursts as *Grefvinnan Spastaras död* (The Death of Countess Spastara) and *Yttersta domen* (The Last Judgment) that he found a large and appreciative audience and developed a poetic form wholly his own. These two works appeared in 1783 and 1788 respectively, years which mark the period of Lidner's richest poetic creation. His last misery-filled years scarcely permitted sustained poetic production on a high level, as is evidenced by the weak oratorios *Jerusalems förstöring* (The Destruction of Jerusalem) and *Messias i Getsemane* (Messiah in Gethsemane); but the devotion of a woman whom he married a few years before his death brought him some happiness, and an occasional short poem of exquisite quality came from his pen at this time.

In *The Death of Countess Spastara*, from Lidner's middle years, the horror elements and the tear-drenched sentimentalism of Lidner's earlier dramatic works are handled with greater artistic discipline than before, partly under the not always salutary influence of Ossianic poetry, which had taught the Swedish poet to combine heroic pathos with heroic natural backgrounds. These Ossianic elements keep Lidner's sustained effusiveness under some kind of control, albeit the modern reader will still find excessive the poet's desperate lamentations over the death in an earthquake of a Sicilian countess whom Lidner did not know—only knew *of* through a little news item of the pathetic variety which he came upon in a Swedish newspaper. *The Death of Countess Spastara* is chiefly important as an exercise in a free and original poetic form, in which the verse, consisting chiefly of alexandrines, shifts frequently and abruptly into other verse patterns, always in order to meet the stylistic demands of shifts in mood and emotional tensions. Lidner himself calls his poem a "Skaldestycke" (Poetic Piece), no doubt to stress its departure from conventional neoclassical forms and to identify it more or less deliberately with those freer poetic forms of pre-Romantic verse which seem to have been inspired by Ossianic poetry and by Thomas Gray's "bardic" verse. Not by accident did Lidner place a passage from *Ossian* in the original English immediately under the title of his poem.

Lidner's experimentation with freer poetic forms was continued in *The Last Judgment*, but variations in verse patterns are here less frequent and the transitions from one verse form to another are less sharp and abrupt. In *The Last Judgment* Lidner's masters are Edward Young and Milton, in whose *Night Thoughts* and *Paradise Lost* the Swedish poet found an elevation of mood and a religious feeling to which the religious brooding of his later years was perfectly attuned. *The Last Judgment*, like *The Death of Countess Spastara*, is suffused with tears and a sense of horror in the presence of dissolution and death, but in *The Last Judgment* sentiment and terror are not ends in themselves, the ultimate experiences of the dedicated, sensitive spirit. They are rather agencies which lead to religious and moral contemplation, voices which provide guidance and warning in the prospect and presence of a Judgment Day. Lidner's handling of verse and the evocation of an ominous, elevated mood in *The Last Judgment* are superior to Young's and fall not far below the Miltonic level. What gives the poem its peculiar flavor is its note of immediate personal urgency and its intensely conceived "blood mysticism," both centrally characteristic of the widespread Moravian pietism of the day to which Lidner had already been exposed as a child. In the moral bankruptcy of his middle and last years Lidner returns to the religious world of his childhood. In *The Last Judgment*, what Professor Lamm calls "the mystical-sentimental strain in eighteenth-century Swedish literature" attains its most elevated poetic expression.

In the closing years of the eighteenth century another star arose on the Swedish literary horizon, the twenty-one-year-old Frans Michael Franzén (1772–1847), whose early verse seemed to promise another recruit to the pre-Romantic ranks. But before the turn of the century Franzén had already capitulated to Gustavian correctness, and he deteriorated rapidly as a poet in the years which followed. Resigning a professorship in Finland shortly after the ill-fated Finno-Russian War of 1808–9, Franzén moved over to Sweden, where he soon became a member of the Swedish Academy and rose rapidly in a clerical career which led ultimately to a bishopric in Härnösand. His poetic productivity was considerable throughout a long life, but aside from certain of his early poems his claims to literary fame lie largely in some delightful drinking songs of the more innocent variety and a few hymns of no great originality or power. He had from the beginning a remarkable poetic receptivity and an astonishing talent for turning out graceful, crystal-clear verse; but these qualities were scarcely calculated to make him the leader of a new literary school despite the direction which some of his first work took. For a few years he wandered in the pre-Romantic regions in which Thorild and Lidner and the later Kellgren had moved, and his work threatened for a while to go even farther than theirs in this direction. Franzén's early literary orientation, unlike that of his immediate Swedish predecessors, had been almost exclusively English, with some German adjuncts. Milton, Edward Young, and especially Thomas Gray were his early masters. He had a strong distaste for almost everything French.

Kellgren was delighted in 1793 to publish in *Stockholms Posten* Franzén's "Människans anlete" (The Face of Man), which in fresh, graceful, unpretentious dactyls developed a thinly veiled erotic theme in Neo-Platonic formulations closely related to Kellgren's own "The New Creation." But shortly after, when another poem by Franzén, "Det nya Eden" (The New Eden), appeared, Kellgren wondered if the young poet had "gone crazy." Franzén's new piece was a highly Romantic "mood poem," in which a vague, quite undefined yearning is given expression in terms of a subtly mysterious interplay of image and verse-music. The young poet's contemporaries could but guess at what Franzén was trying to do in "The New Eden." But in his "Sång öfver Gustav Philip Creutz" (A Song to Gustav Philip Creutz) — a poem appearing in 1797, shortly after the poet's lengthy tour of Germany, France, and England — his intentions were more apparent. In fact, they were so apparent that the Swedish Academy, to which the poem was submitted in a literary competition, felt obliged to condemn certain of its parts even though it was otherwise prepared to award Franzén its First Prize.

Franzén's "Song to Creutz" is a kind of history of poetry in verse form, in the first version of which bardic "barbarians" are not unfavorably compared with poets of the Classical tradition. It was obviously inspired directly by Thomas Gray's "The Progress of Poesy" and "The Bard," but it has many points of contact also with the whole eighteenth-century bardic tradition in England as well as with the related "Gothic" strain in a centuries-long Swedish tradition. Leopold, who as the leading literary arbiter in the Swedish Academy had been assigned the task of commenting on Franzén's poem, was disturbed chiefly by the earlier parts of the poem, which soar with apparently unabashed enthusiasm into a kind of apotheosis of the poet of bardic cast in his most wild and shaggy form. "This kind of verse," Leopold observes upon his official reading of Franzén's poem — "albeit affecting the imagination of the masses, was nevertheless neither that of Horace or Pope or Voltaire; it was the poetry of some ancient Scots, presumably also of other crude peoples, and has only in later times been summoned back to life by a few German poets." Upon reading Leopold's judgment Franzén drew back from his Romantic heresies, agreed to revise his poem in the direction of more conventional poetic concepts, became "accepted" by those who watched zealously over Gustavian literary ideals — and ceased to live as a fresh, vital poetic force. His genius was scarcely cast in a heroic mould, least of all that of the primitive-romantic. He had merely carried on a youthful flirtation with a new kind of literature which he was scarcely prepared to defend against the attacks of literary convention as represented by the Swedish Academy of the eighteenth century.

Romanticism

THE FIRST YEARS of the nineteenth century were uneventful in Swedish literature. Nothing in particular was happening. Death had come to Kellgren and Lidner, and exile to Thorild, in the 1790's. Fru Lenngren had laid her pen aside except for an occasional minor piece, Leopold was turning out quite uninspired moralizing poems, Franzén was settling down to a comfortable clerical career discreetly punctuated from time to time by the production of inoffensive conventional verse. All was quiet, respectable, and moribund, if not dead, in the world of Swedish letters. But it was a deceptive quiet, the quiet before a storm — a storm which had been brewing quite unnoticed for some time in the little university town of Uppsala and which broke out with considerable violence both in Stockholm and Uppsala at the end of the first decade of the new century.

The most immediate outward evidence of the storm was a flurry of new literary journals, each more or less intent upon promulgating a new literary and cultural program. Of these journals the most militant were *Polyfem* (first issued on December 30, 1809) and *Phosphorus* (1810–13), in both of which a group of young men known as "the New Romantics" (*nyromantikerna*), among whom was the gifted poet P. D. A. Atterbom, carried on a long, caustic, and ultimately successful campaign against the last stubborn remnants of the old Gustavian culture. A third journal, *Iduna* (1811ff.), edited by another poet, Erik Gustaf Geijer, was the organ of opinion for the recently established Gothic Society, which in the name of the ancient "Gothic virtues" had taken upon itself the task to build Swedish national morale after the ignominious loss of Finland in the war with Russia, 1808–9. Effective as was the immediate propaganda program of these journals, they were of even greater importance as publications in which first appeared some of the central poetry of three of the four chief Romantic poets, Atterbom, Geijer, and Esaias Tegnér. Only Erik Johan Stagnelius, whose first work appeared somewhat later than these three, had no direct points of contact with these journals, though Atterbom and other leading figures in the "New Romantic" group were among the first to praise his work when it did appear.

Swedish Romanticism, like Romanticism on the Continent and in England, was a complex, many-faceted cultural phenomenon despite the scarcely more than two decades during which it dominated the Swedish literary scene. These two decades witnessed the creation of a body of poetry whose vitality, range of ideas, and technical virtuosity was up to this time quite without parallel in Swedish literature. The period has been appropriately called "the Golden Age of Swedish poetry." The over-all richness of this poetic production was in part simply an accident — Sweden happened at the moment to be much more than ordinarily endowed with men of extraordinary poetic talents. Equally important, however, were those circumstances of the time which served to release the creative genius of these men from the stultifying backwash of Gustavian literary conventions. The circumstances which effected this release were two: the partial preparing of the ground in Sweden in the late eighteenth century by the introduction of certain pre-Romantic strains of English and German provenance, and — more decisive — the pervasive impact upon Swedish literature of early nineteenth-century German philosophical idealism and German Romantic literature in general. Particularly strong was the German influence on Atterbom and the other "New Romantics," who were wont to follow so slavishly such extremist German Romantics as Tieck, Jean Paul Richter, and the brothers Schlegel that these Swedish poets seemed at times to be simply brilliant northern offshoots of the German Romantic tree. Geijer and Tegnér were more independent, finding their literary ideals less exclusively in German contexts, and when concerned with German cultural trends finding the mature Schiller and Goethe more to their tastes than the gifted though often erratic German Romantics strictly speaking.

Among the most striking general features of Swedish Romanticism is that all of its chief practitioners were born and grew up on the Swedish countryside, and with one exception, that of Stagnelius, their professional careers were largely limited to professorial duties in small university towns — Atterbom and Geijer at Uppsala, Tegnér (until he became a bishop) at Lund. This accounts for their strong speculative bent, their frequent preoccupation with the rural scene, and their political conservatism, which with the single exception of Geijer in his later years led them to ignore, or to react strongly against, the changing social and political realities of the day.

Intellectually they were all more or less profoundly oriented in the direction of the German philosophical idealism which had its point of departure in Kant and whose chief contemporary representatives were Fichte and Schelling. The latter's pantheistic speculations, partly inspired by Plato and the Neo-Platonists, became a veritable gold mine for Swedish Romantic poets, providing as it did a transcendental view of nature and of man in the sharpest possible opposition to the hated eighteenth-century empiricism and materialism. And the strong tendency in Schelling's thought toward mysticism provided a point of departure for a new kind of poetic response to folk culture in all of its ancient, traditional manifestations. A sober and critical eighteenth century had not succeeded in suppressing entirely the poetic uses of such material, as is seen particularly in such famous collections of folk ballads as Bishop Percy's *Reliques of Ancient English Poetry* from 1765 and Herder's *Volkslieder* from 1778–79. But the folk interest reflected in these works was preliminary and limited as compared with the floodtide of such interests in the early nineteenth century. In Sweden, as elsewhere, these interests are now everywhere present both in antiquarian research and in poetic creation. Folk customs and folk superstitions of all kinds are now recorded and studied. Folk ballads and folk tales are collected and analyzed and imitated. To the Romantic, schooled in Platonic thought and Herder's and Schelling's speculations, such materials were especially living and vital, for they seemed to reflect directly how an inspired intuitive folk imagination found its sometimes devious but always sure way to the mysterious heart of nature and the sources of existence. The fact that so many Swedish Romantic poets had their origins on the Swedish countryside made them especially receptive to such folk material. In their childhood and youth in rural Sweden they had heard and read folk ballads and folk tales, enchanted and terrified by turn but always attracted to the strange and the mysterious in this ancient, mystery-filled folk world.

But the preoccupation with the past was by no means restricted to such strange and mysterious sides of primitive man's relation to nature. In two other ways Swedish Romanticism established vital relations with the past: by deriving a modern heroic national ideal out of an ancient Scandinavian saga world, and by applying an organic historical concept to a study of both literary and political history. How fruitful especially in matters of poetic creation the former of these approaches was is evident particularly in the specifically "Gothic" poetry of Geijer and Tegnér, while Atterbom's *Svenska siare och skalder* (Swedish Seers and Poets, 1841ff.) and Geijer's *Svea rikes hävder* (The Annals of the Kingdom of Sweden, 1825) and *Svenska folkets historia* (tr. *The History of the Swedes*, 1832–36) remain to our day as Swedish milestones in applying an essentially historical approach to literary and political matters.

Unfortunately, the preoccupation with the past so characteristic of Swedish Romanticism led quite naturally to political and religious conservatism, a conservatism which ultimately came to identify itself with reactionary trends on the Continent following upon the fall of Napoleon. The military fiasco which in 1809 resulted in the loss to Russia of Finland, Sweden's last major holding in a once great Baltic empire, had violent political repercussions in Sweden, resulting in a new, relatively liberal constitution and the establishment on the Swedish throne of the French marshal Bernadotte after the deposition of the fanatically reactionary Gustaf IV. But Bernadotte – whose Swedish royal name became Karl XIV Johan (Charles John) – found it convenient and personally flattering to ally himself with the prevailing European reaction. There is some evidence that the young Swedish Romantics who in the years around 1810 reacted so violently against traditional literary authority as symbolized by the Swedish Academy at first nursed also certain tendencies toward political and religious liberalism, but this liberalism was tentative and short-lived. In politics the Romantics soon allied themselves with the policies of Karl XIV Johan, and in church matters they at least outwardly were orthodox if not always pious Lutherans. With the years they became members of the once hated Swedish Academy, and even Gustaf af Leopold, whom the "New Romantics" had once looked upon as the very incarnation of moribund academic taste, was forgiven if not entirely accepted. Leopold, a skillful opportunist in things political, was on the side of the Romantics at least in matters of political loyalties. Geijer alone among the Romantic poets managed in his last years to escape from the reactionary political extremes characteristic of Swedish Romanticism in its last stages, in the late 1820's and the 1830's.

But before this happened Swedish poetry had blossomed and flowered as never before in the history of Swedish literature. The four great Ro-

Carl Michael Bellman reading by candle light, sketch by Sergel
from 1790's (copyright National Museum, Stockholm)

Scene from a modern revival of a dramatic sketch by Bellman
at the eighteenth-century Drottningholm Theater

Johan Henric Kellgren, relief by
Sergel (photo: SPA)

Anna Maria Lenngren, engraving
by A. U. Berndes

Erik Gustaf Geijer, unsigned
lithograph from the 1840's

Esaias Tegnér, lithograph from
sketch by Maria Röhl, 1829

Erik Johan Stagnelius, sketch by L. G. Malmberg (The
Royal Library, Stockholm)

mantic poets, not to mention a host of lesser figures, had produced a body of poetry which in substance and variety of ideas, sensitiveness of feeling, and technical virtuosity had no counterpart in earlier Swedish letters. Bellman only among earlier Swedish poets stands indubitably on a level with Atterbom, Geijer, Tegnér, and Stagnelius. Now for the first time a whole *group* of poets of the first rank were simultaneously creating a vitally new literature for Sweden.

This newness manifested itself in many ways, partly in consequence of the differing artistic personalities of the four major poets. Atterbom is the most sensitive, the most delicate of the four, and his poetry has a fragile musical quality so often typical of the earlier Romantics. Geijer and Tegnér are more robust and positive spirits, the former usually abrupt, laconic, and weighty in utterance, the latter spacious and eloquent with a marvelous flair for the flashing, brilliant image and for elevated rhetorical flights. Stagnelius, sick and desperately frustrated throughout his brief career, had a poetic fantasy of extraordinary intensity and visionary power together with a command of verse which some critics place highest among his contemporaries.

Given such an abundance of poetic talent and such diversity of poetic personalities it is little wonder that the Swedish Romantic spirit flowered with a rare sense of inner discipline despite its rich and engaging expansiveness. This discipline enabled it in the main to guard itself against certain of the excesses of German Romanticism even while assimilating those elements from German sources best suited to a Swedish mentality and to Swedish traditions. Swedish Romanticism had few traces of that extreme form of individualism characteristic of one side of German Romanticism, and a native Swedish Lutheran tradition had little difficulty in withstanding the trend toward the religious medievalism with strong Catholic leanings cultivated by certain of the German Romantics. Among the Swedish "New Romantic" group, however, there is something of the German Romantic tendency to elevate the poet to the eminence of a high priest, whose imaginative gifts become the most profound source of truth and who therefore serves as a kind of medium in which philosophical speculation and religious mysticism are supposed to attain an ultimate synthesis.

Though English pre-Romantic literature had considerable importance in determining in the late eighteenth century, as we have seen, the direction which the new Swedish poetic style was to take, German Romanticism was even more decisive in the years after the turn of the century.

These foreign influences operated chiefly in three ways: by introducing a great variety of new verse forms, by encouraging a richly symbolic and image-loaded language, and in pointing the way toward the poetic exploitation of subtle musical qualities in verse. Strongly nationalistic as Swedish Romanticism frequently was, its nationalism did not deter it from developing a wide-ranging cosmopolitan (one might even say eclectic) taste in matters of poetic form. The French classical alexandrine which had dominated Swedish verse in the eighteenth century is now displaced by the much freer English blank verse line, and in addition all manner of stanzaic and rhythmic patterns, ancient and modern, are as never before exploited — alliterative patterns and gnomic laconisms from Old Scandinavian verse, ballad forms from English, German, and Scandinavian sources, the sonnet, the canzone, and the ottava rima stanza from an Italian tradition, and irregular rhythmic experiments of various kinds deriving partly from Ossianic sources and partly from a later Romantic attempt to identify poetry with music. Even the hexameter, popular in Swedish verse for generations before the alexandrine forced it out, is resuscitated with no little success.

Access to such a variety of poetic forms enabled the Romantic poet to avoid the monotony of the alexandrine. The verse form he employed in any given instance came to be determined by the subject matter of his poem or by its mood. At times, it must be admitted, confusion resulted from the poet's failure really to master the poetic form chosen; but in general the poet managed his form wisely and well, not infrequently brilliantly — as, for instance, in Geijer's ballad imitation "Den lilla kolargossen" (The Charcoal-Burner's Son), or in the magic simplicity of line and stanza of Stagnelius's "Necken" (The Nix), or in the magnificent diversity of poetic patterns provided in Tegnér's *Fritiof's Saga*. So masterly, indeed, is the handling of verse by the Swedish Romantics that even on those few occasions when they — Geijer, Tegnér, and Stagnelius specifically — employed the scorned and neglected alexandrine they handled it with such freshness and power that this French classical line came alive again, as if to belie the suspicious attitude toward it maintained so often by the Romantics.

Though lyric and reflective poetry are the genres most frequently used with success by the Swedish Romantics, Tegnér's celebrated *Fritiof's Saga*, by all odds the most popular of Swedish Romantic poems, is a narrative poetic sequence, and both Atterbom and Stagnelius wrote closet dramas of high poetic quality. Of the prose forms fiction receives no serious attention from the Romantics, unless one is to count among them the young C. J. L. Almqvist, who — as we shall see — is more properly to be classified as a late Romantic transitional figure whose work marks most radically the shift in the 1830's toward a realistic liberalism. The two more extensive types of prose which the Romantics cultivate with considerable distinction are history (Geijer particularly) and literary history and criticism (Atterbom, Lorenzo Hammarsköld, and others). The great triumphs of Swedish prose during the Romantic period are, however, essentially incidental products from the hands of genius at moments of particular inspiration — Geijer's *Minnen* (Memoirs), tossed off in four weeks as a means of temporary respite from the severe labors on his *History of the Swedish People*, or Tegnér's scintillating letters and his "Tal vid jubelfesten 1817" (Address on the Jubilee 1817), composed for public delivery on the occasion of the three hundredth anniversary of the Reformation.

The militant, highly vocal group of Swedish critics and poets referred to interchangeably as "the New Romantics" or "the Phosphorists" (*fosforisterna*) were young men full of the self-assurance and arrogance of youth who determined when they first appeared on the literary scene to effect nothing less than a complete revolution in Swedish poetry. Though the group included at one time or another a half dozen or more critics and poets of greater or less distinction, the three most active figures were Atterbom, the only poet of first magnitude in the group, Lorenzo Hammarsköld (1785–1827), indefatigable critic-publicist, and Vilhelm Fredrik Palmblad (1788–1852), whose activities — particularly as an enterprising publisher enthusiastically allied with the New Romantics — provided especially the Uppsala coterie of the group with various publication outlets for the new literary program. The revolution in Swedish poetry envisioned by these young critics and poets involved, first of all, a violent, all-out attack upon "the old school," represented by a moribund Swedish Academy which persisted in attempting to hold inviolate eighteenth-century Gustavian neoclassical ideals and defended these ideals against all attacks by the young New Romantic group. These attacks were as numerous and violent as the defense was stubborn, but the outcome was inevitable. Gustavianism had played out its role and was marked by death, and even if the New Romantics themselves had not been able to muster a force sufficiently powerful to overwhelm the enemy by their method of direct attack other Swedish literary developments in the early nineteenth century were only less deliberately replacing the Gustavian tradition in literature. Geijer and the Gothicists had appeared on the scene. Tegnér had electrified the Swedish public with his early patriotic dithyrambs. And Stagnelius was shortly to pursue poetic paths which in certain ways represented the ultimate development of the New Romantic ideals.

While these developments were taking place as the second decade of the nineteenth century was getting under way, Gustavianism, narcissuslike, was worshiping its own elegant but worn image — and pined away for lack of vital, life-giving sustenance. The defense of its cause was largely given over to an industrious journalistic drone, P. A. Wallmark (1777–1858), editor of the uninspired *Journal för litteraturen och theatern* (Journal for Literature and the Theater, continued 1813ff. as *Allmänna Journalen*), which countered as best it could the blows lustily rained upon it from all directions by the various journals of the New Romantic group. Gustaf af Leopold, who as the grand old man of Gustavian culture was the favorite target of the New Romantic critics, remained for the most part silent and superior, unwilling to cross swords with what he considered on unworthy, upstart, loud-mouthed enemy, though on an occasion or two when he did publicly appear in the lists (most successfully with his devastating satire on an unfortunate translation of Tasso by Atterbom) he did so with a satiric efficiency which reminded the enemy that the Gustavians were no tyros in the game of literary satire.

Such satiric thrusts on the part of the later Gustavians were, however, exceptional. More characteristic was a pose of condescending self-complacency which led them to assume even in the years of their literary impotence that they alone represented good taste and high cultural standards, that before them only barbarism and superstition had existed in the world of letters, and that the New Romantics were but a late-born, particularly objectionable progeny of an earlier barbaric culture. How far the Gustavians had gone in this pose of self-complacency is illustrated by a literary-critical study appearing in the Proceedings of the Swedish Academy for 1809 entitled *Utkast till en historisk och critisk afhandling om svenska vitterheten före v. Dalin* (A Sketch Toward a Historical and Critical Treatise on Swedish Belles Lettres before von Dalin). Its author, Isaac Reinhold Blom, member of the Academy and favorite of Leopold, had no historical critical sense at all despite the promise of such a point of view in the title of his work. Using the most rigid of French classical norms, he dismisses ancient Scandinavian literature as merely rude and barbaric, condemns medieval culture as full of crudities and superstition, and finds hardly anything to admire in the Swedish literature of the six-teenth and seventeenth centuries. Swedish literature does not begin, ac-cording to Blom, until Boileau and the French classicists breathed their spirit into Swedish culture at the beginning of the eighteenth century, and not until the late eighteenth century does Sweden create a relatively mature literary culture. Blom's views, appearing under the official im-print of the Academy, were certainly to be taken as the views of the Academy itself. It is little wonder that the young group of New Ro-mantic mavericks became infuriated by such opinions and gathered themselves for an attack whose first resounding blows appear in the journal *Polyfem* (1809–12), to be followed by a persistent though some-what intermittent attack all along the line in such successors of *Polyfem* as *Phosphorus* (1810–13) and *Svensk Litteratur-Tidning* (1813–25), while lighter, less controversial literary fare was provided by the New Romantics in the short-lived *Elegant-Tidning* (1810) and in the popular *Poetisk Kalender* (1811–22).

It could not be expected that the weapons employed in the attack would always be honorable or that either party in the battle was particu-larly chivalrous. While talented youth is seldom tolerant, old age can indulge in an arrogance that is something less than noble; and when the two struck head on, as they did in the years around 1810 in the contro-versy between the New Romantics and the last defenders of a fading Gustavian culture, it was clear that the conflict could not be maintained on a high level. What is important is that the New Romantics had the sharpest weapons and the largest forces, and before the end of the second decade of the nineteenth century their triumph over Gustavianism was complete.

In one sense, of course, the triumph was an easy one – the New Ro-mantics were attacking a straw man, a literary enemy already dying a slow natural death. Gustavianism was a hopelessly lost cause long before the young Romantics joined battle with it. The triumph of the New Romantics would under the circumstances have been rather empty and meaningless had they not been able to create a significant new poetry to replace the old. At first it seemed that this would be an easy matter, for youthful poetic talent sprang up on every hand in the New Romantic camp. But much of this talent reflected little more than a verbal facility incapable of really vital, original poetic production. In some cases (those of Georg Ingelgren, 1782–1813, and Per Elgström, 1781–1810) death intervened before their talents could mature, in other cases (such as those of Carl Fredrik Dahlgren, 1791–1844, and Erik Julius Sjöberg, pseud. Vitalis, 1794–1828) time proved that the talent was of a second or third order and / or that the talent was not essentially Romantic in kind. Among the New Romantic group proper only Atterbom became a poet of the first order, and he alone bore the burden of creating the new poetry envisioned by his group. Fortunately, however, poetic genius of the highest order existed at this time in Sweden outside the narrower confines of the New Romantic coterie. Even though neither Geijer nor Tegnér nor Stagnelius aligned himself directly with the extremist anti-Gustavian polemics of the New Romantics, the work of each of these poets assisted powerfully in its way to seal the fate of the Gustavian culture. Geijer and particularly Tegnér had their reservations to make about New Romantic excesses, but the work of these two poets served the broader purposes of Romanticism quite as efficiently as did the shrill polemic methods of the New Romantics. It should be remembered, for instance, that Tegnér and only to a lesser extent Geijer were the genuinely *popular* poets of the day. Atterbom's verse, with the exception of the poetic sequence *Blommorna* (The Flowers), attracted no large reading public.

A modest country parsonage in one of the more picturesque parts of Östergötland was the childhood home of Per Daniel Atterbom (1790–1855), who later added with characteristic poetic affectation the romantic Amadeus to his more common baptismal names Per Daniel. His simple, patriarchal, deeply religious countryside origins were of fundamental importance to him. He never forgot these origins, even in the days of his young manhood when he became submerged in the intricate speculative world of the German Romantics; and in the years of his maturity he not infrequently found his way back to his origins, in the spirit of childlike trust seeking its way to the mother's breast. In his letters he often recalls with ecstatic gratitude the days of his boyhood and early youth, and in his *Minnesrunor* (Runes of Memory) he weaves a tender idyllic poetic garland around these early days. The memories of his childhood concern themselves chiefly with loving, understanding parents, with an enchanting natural landscape, and with a world of miscellaneous reading which consisted largely of romantic sagas, folk tales, and legends. All of this fed his sensitive childhood fantasy, but it provided few if any firmer intellectual disciplines. His formal schooling began when he was nine, at the cathedral school in Linköping, and at fifteen the precocious youth matriculated at Uppsala University, where he was to spend the remainder of his life — for some years after his student days in various minor teaching capacities, from 1828 to his death in 1855 as a professor, first in philosophy, beginning with 1835 in aesthetics and poetry. Aside from fairly frequent summer sojourns in his beloved Östergötland and an extended visit to the Continent 1817–19, Atterbom's life for more than a half century was narrowly restricted to the social and academic world of Uppsala. His earlier years at Uppsala were enlivened by participation in literary polemics, but with time this activity tapered off and Atterbom settled down to an academic existence and became with the years increasingly egocentric and petty in his personal relations and increasingly abstract and conservative in matters especially of religion and politics. He became in consequence in his last years an isolated, self-centered, highly querulous figure, not always understood by his friends and incessantly attacked by the rising tide of political liberalism represented in a brutally articulate liberal press.

These late years of intellectual reaction and stagnation were in the sharpest possible contrast to the early days of violent poetic ferment when Atterbom — as the central figure of the Uppsala coterie of the New Romantics — led the charge against the hated Gustavian enemy. The Uppsala coterie did not, however, from the beginning have such belligerent intentions. When Atterbom in the fall of 1805 joined the group of students which called itself Vitterhetens Vänner (Friends of Belles-Lettres), the group was quite innocently concerned with raising literary standards, particularly its own, by coming together for purposes of literary discussion, by arranging poetry contests, and by indulging in various other inoffensive literary pastimes. A couple of years later they were reorganized under Atterbom's leadership, Latinized their name to Musis amici, and otherwise began to develop somewhat greater literary pretensions. But it was not until the following year, when the name Musis amici was changed to the symbolical Auroraförbundet (The Aurora Society), that the group had developed into a militant unit with a whole new program for Swedish literature. They had by this time steeped themselves in German literature, in Goethe and Schiller, and especially in the German Romantics Tieck, Jean Paul Richter, and Novalis. They had come under the speculative philosophical spell of Fichte and Schelling, the latter especially having become their god. And the revolutionary ferment stirring in their own souls had finally to find an outlet, it had to inform a larger public and effect its aim of a literary revolution. The first organ of the Uppsala New Romantics, the journal *Phosphorus*, appeared for the first time, in 1810, with a fiery red cover to announce unmistakably its revolutionary intentions.

Atterbom had written for the first number of *Phosphorus* a poetic "Prolog," a poem which must have startled and bewildered the un-initiated and irritated no end those of conservative Gustavian leanings whose poetic ideals called for tidiness of form and clarity of idea. Loaded with a tortuous, floating, vaguely suggestive imagery, and affecting free, shifting musical verse patterns, the "Prolog" aimed to give its readers not only a sample of a new, experimental Romantic form in poetry but also to introduce them to a new Romantic world of idea. It manages its stylistic experimentation with a certain uneven skill, but its formulation of idea shifts so unashamedly back and forth between symbolical hyperbole and direct statement that the reader is often left confused if not befuddled. In general, however, it is clear enough that the poet is triumphantly announcing a new period of poetry, a period symbolized by the rising effulgence of Phosphorus, the Morning Star. In a sharp jab at a benighted Enlightenment we are assured that henceforth Swedish genius will not "slave in chains hired from a childish time," but the exact nature of the new inspiration which is to free poetry from its eighteenth-century chains has difficulty in emerging with any clarity out of the welter of image and symbol with which Atterbom's poem is weighted. Among some of the vaguely discernible ideas in the poem are the purely Romantic ones that nature is the garment of divinity and that the poet, divinely inspired, commands the secrets of the universe. But if in the "Prolog" Atterbom gives confused expression to certain typical New Romantic ideas, in other poems of a similar speculative kind he more successfully manages Romantic intricacies of form and subtleties of thought, particularly in "Erotikon," "Allegro och adagio," and "Eolsharpan" (The Aeolian Harp), in all of which the sheer *music* of verse maintains such a fine discipline over the disposition of image and idea that ordered poetic impressions are attained and the over-all result is something approaching the Romantic ideal of pure poetry.

It is, however, with another, much simpler type of poem that Atterbom gains a wider reading public — with his *Blommorna* (The Flowers), which began to appear in 1812 in the periodical *Poetisk Kalender* and were added to at various intervals down to 1837–38 when the completed sequence took its definitive form in Atterbom's *Samlade dikter* (Collected Poems) of this date. In these poems Atterbom combines Schelling's pantheistic speculations with a Wordsworthian naïveté of response to nature and simplicity of poetic form. There are forty short "flower poems" in all; each of them, with the exception of a dedicatory piece and the two last poems (one of which tells the tale of Saint Francis's loving care for all helpless natural phenomena), is devoted to a single flower. Atterbom avoids monotony in these poems by an extraordinary descriptive and rhythmic inventiveness which invests each flower with a characteristic personality and mood — the fresh early-spring joyfulness of the anemone, the proud expansiveness of the sunflower, the shy yearning of the forget-me-not, the dignified purity of the lily, the dark melancholy of the poppy, the narcissus, and the hyacinth, the heavy Oriental sensuousness of the rose and the tulip. Behind the poet's warm probing into the secret of each flower lies the mystic assumption that "natural phenomena are a mythic sign-language" capable of being understood by an intuitive childlike mind, but this speculative consideration is never permitted to interfere in the reading of these poems with our spontaneous response to the phenomenon itself in its immediate concrete manifestation. Seldom in Swedish poetry do we experience as in certain of these flower poems such a perfect sense of poetic balance between delicate sensitivity of feeling and an exquisite awareness of fine shadings of language. Romantic naïveté found in them one of its most perfect Swedish expressions.

But exquisite as these poems in some instances are, Atterbom's ambitions could not rest satisfied with perfecting such miniatures. Since youth he had dreamed of creating a major poetic opus, a work into which he could pour the ripe products of his total experience and thought. He had, in fact, already in his mid-twenties contemplated such a work, as is evident from some fragments of a folk-tale play *Fågel blå* (Blue Bird) published in *Poetisk Kalender* in 1813. Though he added later to these fragments, *Blue Bird* was never finished. Instead Atterbom became more preoccupied during these years with another folk-tale motif, worked upon it intermittently for more than a decade, and published the resulting poetic drama *Lycksalighetens ö* (The Isle of the Blessed), in two parts, in the years 1824 and 1827. Impressive as this work is in some ways, it remained comparatively neglected in its day and has never attracted more than a bare minimum of readers. Its contemporary neglect can in part be attributed to the fact that upon the poem's first appearance it had to compete for a public with Stagnelius's fascinating posthumous *Samlade skrifter* (Collected Works, 1824–26) and with Tegnér's enormously popular *Fritiof's Saga* (definitive edition 1825). In part, too, the failure of *The Isle of the Blessed* to win a large contemporary reading public can be accounted for in the same terms as its failure to interest later generations. The poetic drama as a genre has never attracted large numbers of readers, and if such dramas, as is the case with *The Isle of the Blessed*, employ an intricate machinery of symbols to express a rather complicated array of opinions on such wide-ranging subjects as art and politics and religion, they are scarcely calculated to be read by many.

But if one has the patience to read with some attention *The Isle of the Blessed*, one can understand why it is nevertheless looked upon as one of the more distinguished larger Swedish Romantic works. It is rather too long and at times verbose, but its purely poetic quality is uniformly high except for some of the forced caricature in the Fourth Adventure; and among its songs (The Nightingale's Song [beginning "Hopp och Kärlek vila"], The Choir of the Winds ["Upp genom luften, bort över haven"] and others) is to be found some of the most sensitively haunting verse Atterbom has written. Impressive, too, is the sustained skill of some of Atterbom's symbolism and the aptness with which the folk-tale motifs are applied to the drift of the poet's thought in the work. Readers of a speculative bent will be stimulated finally by certain magnificently executed passages (the scene in which Nyx, the mother of Felicia, opposes in macrocosmic contexts her daughter's desire forever to hold Astolf prisoner, and the sublime passage in which Time finally conquers Astolf); but the more mundane reader of today will be inclined to prefer the poem's less grandiose preoccupations, its recurrent concern with the problem of duty as man faces it in the relatively limited conditions of everyday life. Unfortunately, however, Atterbom has too often seen fit in *The Isle of the Blessed* to identify such a concern with contemporary politics, with the result that much of the genuine magnificence of his poetic vision comes to be blurred by animosities unworthy of the elevation of his initial poetic intentions.

The central folk-tale motif in *The Isle of the Blessed* is an old one, and the tale was well known on the Swedish countryside in Atterbom's childhood. It concerns a certain pleasure-loving King Astolf, who, restive in his cold and dreary northern kingdom, flees to southern climes and to the arms of Felicia, but who after three hundred years tires of dalliance and returns to his kingdom — to reality and to duty. If in Atterbom's childhood and youth the tale in itself had fascinated him, in his maturity it is the thematic aspect of the tale — the conflict between beauty and a religiously inspired sense of duty — which he found arresting, particularly because it pointed up a central problem of his own, the poet's relation to conflicting aesthetic and ethical ideals. In the years when *The Isle of the Blessed* was beginning to shape itself in his mind Atterbom was turning away from his earlier Romantic aestheticism and affirming the primacy of a new ethical position — as Astolf in Atterbom's poem departs at last from the arms of Felicia and returns to the world of reality with its claims of conscience and call to duty. In politics and religion Atterbom's "duty" became identified with the Conservative cause of his time, as is evident in Adventure Four of his poem, in which Astolf's return to his Hyperborean Republic (an imagined Liberal Sweden) provides the poet with an occasion for a blistering caricature of liberal social and political trends in the Swedish press of the day. The reactionary stand which Atterbom takes here becomes even more confirmed with the years and accounts for the violent attacks upon him by the Liberal press in the 1830's and the 1840's.

Atterbom did not publicly answer his Liberal critics. He had in his later years wearied of public controversy and withdrew completely into his own poetic world. "With the exception of the decent *Uppsala Korrespondent*," he writes in a letter from 1838, "I no longer read newspapers. I wish to barricade myself behind Poetry and that which concerns itself therewith, and to become blind and deaf to everything else."

That he managed outwardly at least to maintain this position was made possible by his pouring nearly all of his energies in the last two decades of his life into writing the monumental six-volume history of Swedish literature *Swedish Seers and Poets*. This work is often marred by Atterbom's two besetting sins, wordiness and a naïve self-absorption; but it is on the whole surprisingly objective in its judgments and reflects at every point a remarkable sensitivity to literary values. Well schooled in the historical relativism of the Romantics, Atterbom is prepared to find poetic beauty everywhere, in ancient as well as modern times, in worlds of idea and form which were not necessarily his own. Even Leopold, the archenemy of Atterbom's sharply polemic "phosphoristic" youth, is treated with qualified praise in *Swedish Seers and Poets*. And otherwise Atterbom's sympathies and enthusiasm are here all-inclusive, seeking out the primitive beauties of saga, legend, and ballad which the eighteenth century had scorned or neglected, and ranging without prejudice in the literary production of such diverse figures as Saint Birgitta and Dalin,

Stiernhielm and Bellman, Swedenborg and Kellgren. At every point in his work Atterbom maintains the modern historian's sense of context and continuity, delving insofar as documents permitted into the whole complex of a given author's life and times, and seeking always to demonstrate that in the over-all historical process one period grows organically out of a preceding epoch which in turn yields naturally to the next. In these respects Atterbom's *Swedish Seers and Poets* does for Swedish literature what Geijer's *Annals of the Kingdom of Sweden* and *A History of the Swedish People* (both of which had much importance for Atterbom) did for Swedish political history. Atterbom's work has, however, a strong nostalgic backward-looking quality largely lacking in Geijer, whose two historical works have an inner vitality which *joins* a vigorous contemplation of the past with a sense of its profound seminal importance for the present and the future. In contrast Atterbom's *Swedish Seers and Poets* finds in glorious memories (his work has been appropriately called a "literary memorial temple") an object of sensitive, at times ecstatic contemplation — an end in itself as it were.

As colleagues on the Uppsala faculty Erik Gustaf Geijer (1783–1847) and Atterbom had in their earlier years similar intellectual interests and attitudes. They had in common during these years a speculative bent nurtured by German idealistic thought, a distrust of eighteenth-century rationalism and empiricism with its antireligious bias, and a political conservatism rooted in a common historical speculation and investigation. Their temperaments were, however, sharply contrasting, and this came ultimately to account for the divergent paths which they took in the years of their maturity. Close friends though they for many years were, Geijer, a vital, impulsive, masculine personality, could not permanently approve of the effeminate self-absorption, the soft, self-pitying egotism of Atterbom. The final break between the two did not occur until 1838, when Geijer wrote his devastating review of Atterbom's *Samlade dikter* (Collected Poems); but occasions for irritation on the part of Geijer had existed long before, most interestingly perhaps in the episode which occasioned Geijer's famous letter to Atterbom in March of 1820. Here he takes Atterbom to task for the latter's tendency to isolate himself and engage in melancholy, bitter meditation. "To sum up," Geijer concludes with his characteristic yea-saying to life — "my confession of faith: *Sorrow is sin*; because the innermost secret of existence is happiness. I grant gladly, of course, that there is a *purifying* suffering, and perhaps I have all too little felt it. For so inexpressibly glorious has the being that *is* always seemed to me that I have wanted to adore and worship it even in its most impure image, and therefore the earth and the heavens, nature and man have always seemed to me so beautiful that a mortal tongue must falter in expressing the least excellence of their being."

Geijer's healthy, vigorous optimism came to him naturally. The home in which he spent his first sixteen years buzzed with activities, physical and mental. His father was the owner and operator of a reasonably successful iron foundry located deep in the forests of eastern Värmland, where labor and play were pursued with equal intensity and joy. Though the Geijer home lay far from urban centers of culture, literature and the arts were not neglected. Erik Gustaf became particularly attached to music, which with the years became increasingly important to his spiritual well-being and, along with poetic creation, provided him with the necessary outlets for the surging world of idea and feeling which was the mark of his genius. Upon Erik Gustaf's departure from his Värmland home for Uppsala and university studies, he entered upon a gifted youth's difficulties in finding himself. His studies, chiefly in philosophy and history, fascinated him but led very slowly to the coveted degree and in general brought on a rather prolonged inner crisis. But, as Geijer tells us in his *Memoirs*, "directly into the dark, unfruitful irresolution of my being at this time flowed a stream of new points of view." The new points of view resulted from his trip to England in 1809–10. His English experiences enabled him to shake off the narrow world of academic abstraction in which his Uppsala studies had immersed him, and upon his return to Sweden the floodgates of his young genius burst open in the brilliant poetry of his so-called Gothic period, a kind of prose prelude to which was an essay on the importance of the imagination in matters educational, which won a prize in a competition arranged by the Swedish Academy. Into this essay the young Geijer poured the ripe products of his academic studies and his experiences abroad.

Geijer's Gothic poetry was a part of his contribution to the activities of Götiska Förbundet (The Gothic Society), founded in 1811 by a group of young Stockholm patriots in order to bolster a shaken Swedish national self-confidence after the debacle of the Finno-Russian War and the precarious position which Sweden otherwise found itself in because of the ramifications of the struggle between Napoleon and his enemies. The political and military weakness of Sweden at the time was looked upon by the members of the Gothic Society as the outward reflection of an inner moral decay resulting from the nation's failure to maintain its earlier heroic traditions as exemplified in such "Gothic" virtues as simplicity, strength, and honor. Though the purposes of the Gothic Society as defined in its constitution and realized in some of its activities were serious enough, its meetings were not without a lighter touch, particularly after the formal business of the assemblies had been completed and the members (each of whom had an ancient saga name, Geijer's being the mouth-filling cognomen Einar Tambaskälfver!) gathered around the traditional drinking bowl and quaffed many and long toasts from drinking horns of ancient pattern. The impression one gets from rather fragmentary extant accounts is that the meetings of the Gothic Society were conducted in a spirit both serious and gay, the serious vein being more insisted upon by the strenuously doctrinaire Goths (Jacob Adlerbeth, Leonhard Fredrik Rääf, and the formidable "father of Swedish gymnastics" Per Henrik Ling) while a note of lightheartedness was supplied by the large number of merry natives from Värmland, a province long known for its insistence upon combining gaiety with seriousness.

Aside from taking part in the meetings of the Society, each member was expected to conduct investigations in ancient Swedish lore and present his results both to the Society and whenever feasible to a larger Swedish public. Folk customs of all kinds were studied and recorded, sagas were translated and published, and the first serious attempt to provide the nation with the treasures of her ballad literature (*Svenska folkvisor*, I–III, 1814–16) was a product of the collecting enthusiasm of the "Goth" Arvid August Afzelius. Geijer wrote his famous essay on the ballad as an Introduction to this collection. Unfortunately, Afzelius's enthusiasm for ballads was greater than his editorial and critical gifts, and so his pioneering work was soon superseded by the more authoritative *Svenska fornsånger*, I–III (1834–42), edited by A. I. Arwidsson.

Such material, primarily of learned antiquarian concern, interested no very large audience. But when Geijer published his Gothic poems in the first issues of the Gothic Society's periodical *Iduna* (1811ff.) these antiquarian materials suddenly came alive, transformed into a vital modern literature which could be, and was, read with enthusiasm by the learned and the common man alike. Among the most well known of these poems, "Den siste kämpen" (The Last Warrior) and "Den siste skalden" (The Last Skald) are somewhat theatrical pieces in the eighteenth-century bardic manner of Thomas Gray and Ossianic poetry. But others are of a much higher poetic order, particularly "Manhem," the program poem of the Gothic Society, and the twin poems "Vikingen" (The Viking) and "Odalbonden" (The Yeoman Farmer), which brilliantly reflect Geijer's view of pre-Christian Scandinavian character, on the one hand the adventurous, freedom-loving Viking spirit, on the other the solid, earthbound independence of the primitive yeoman farmer.

Geijer creates in "The Viking" the first great Swedish poem dealing with the sea, and no Swedish poet since has given us a more fresh and vivid awareness of the invigorating challenge of seafaring life. All that is young and vital and creative in Geijer's genius is poured into the poem. Even more impressive, however, is "The Yeoman Farmer," with its abrupt, disciplined poetic meter, its measured hammerblow laconisms, and its quiet statement of theme (placed on the lips of the peasant himself) that the constructive processes of history are far better served by the patient, unsung tiller of the soil than by those who in high places presume to shape the destinies of man.

> Though not allured by honor's name,
> My heart well knows its worth.
> I harvest not the field of fame,
> I reap my own good earth.
>
> I love not noise and vain display;
> Great deeds are never loud.
> Few traces mark the tempest's way
> When fades the flaming cloud.
>
> Each sickness wails in its degree
> But health needs no such brawl,
> And therefore no one speaks of me
> Or thinks of me at all.
>
> The mighty lords midst shriek and groan
> Spread ruin all around;
> The silent ploughman and his son
> They till the reddened ground.
>
> *Translated by C. W. Stork*

What is most impressive about Geijer's Gothic poems at their best is the sobriety and restraint with which the Gothic theme is stated, a sobriety and restraint especially apparent if one remembers the mad absurdities of Johannes Magnus's late medieval exploitation of the theme or the chauvinistic excesses of Olaus Rudbeck's seventeenth-century Atlantica fantasies. It is a happy circumstance in Swedish literature that Geijer finally brought these absurdities and fantasies down to earth without destroying that which was healthy and living and sound in the centuries-long Gothic dream.

So self-evident was the triumph of Geijer in his Gothic poems that applause for his accomplishment came from contemporaries of whatever literary persuasion, even from spokesmen for the Swedish Academy, who otherwise instinctively suspected the poetry of the younger generation. Less acceptable to the Academy, and closer to the literary ideals of Atterbom and the New Romantics, were two of Geijer's other poems from these years — "Den lilla Kolargossen" (The Charcoal Burner's Son), the best of the many Romantic ballad imitations, with its subtle evocation of folk superstitions and its haunting refrain "Det är så mörkt långt, långt bort i skogen" (It is so dark far, far away in the forest), and "Bergsmannen" (The Miner), with its vaguely suggestive symbolism and its not especially happy probing, in the manner of German pantheistic speculation, into nature's mysteries. Though Geijer only rarely in his more mature years pursued such poetic strains and never strictly speaking became one of the New Romantics, he did establish rather close contacts with the Atterbom coterie upon his return to Uppsala in the spring of 1811, and in the years which followed he came to be identified more or less closely with members of this group, taking part in their literary *soirées* at the home of Malla Montgomery Silfverstolpe, contributing from time to time to their publications ("The Charcoal Burner's Son" appeared first in Atterbom's *Poetisk Kalender* in 1815), and finding this group a sympathetic audience for the growing political conservatism resulting from his historical investigations. Among Geijer's early work particularly appreciated by the New Romantics was his translation of *Macbeth* (1813), the first play by Shakespeare to appear full length in a Swedish version.

Shortly after his arrival at Uppsala Geijer sought academic advancement in the field of philosophy, but when, in 1815, the incumbent professor in the chair of history wished Geijer to take over his lectures Geijer accepted the proposal, became professor of Scandinavian history two years later, and spent the remainder of his life at this post, his academic activities being interrupted only during those months when he served periodically as a member of the Swedish parliament. Under these circumstances his poetic production languished. Aside from the short songs for which he composed both words and music as a kind of release from his heavy academic duties, he turned to serious verse during these years for the most part only on special occasions, most successfully in the majestic march rhythms of "Viken, tidens flyktiga minnen" (Yield, ye, fleeting memories all), written in memory of Charles XII to be sung by the Uppsala students commemorating the centennial of the warrior king's death, on November 30, 1818.

As a lecturer in Scandinavian history Geijer became at once enormously popular, students and townspeople alike flocking in unheard-of numbers to his lecture hall. The lectures, prepared with considerable care and delivered with a memorable dramatic flair, were the seed out of which soon grew the stately and spacious tree of Geijer's historical composition, the three chief products of which were *Feodalism och republikanism* (Feudalism and Republicanism, 1818–19), *The Annals of the Kingdom of Sweden* (1825), and *The History of the Swedes* (1832–36). Geijer's mastery of prose is everywhere apparent in these works. This prose, like his poetry, is vivid, concrete, factual, concentrated – in a word eloquent without the dubious assistance of the traditional rhetorical flourish. His most famous prose passage is the matchless description of Swedish nature and Swedish folk character which opens the *Annals*.

Though Geijer was not a stranger to the modern historian's insistence upon basic archival investigations and the critical winnowing of sources, his strength as a historian lay more frequently in his intuitive insights and his broad, inclusive view of historical developments. On the whole he sinned less than others of his time and earlier in the handling of sources, and his sense of the continuity of historical developments brought to his historical writing a tight organic quality seldom found in his immediate Swedish predecessors. This sense of continuity was at times, however, somewhat forced and rigid, particularly in the historical essay *Feudalism and Republicanism*, where his early philosophical training led him into the trap of schematic historical speculation so common in much contemporary German Romantic historical thinking. But from such unhappy practices he gradually extricated himself in his later historical work, trusting in his later years only what he came to call "the continuity of *the facts themselves* (Sammanhang! Ja, men *sakernas eget*)."

Geijer's historical studies together with his close contacts with the Uppsala New Romantic group had led him gradually in the 1820's into a political conservatism essentially foreign to the broadly tolerant liberalism of his earlier years. He became in consequence generally considered the leader of "the historical school" in Swedish political theory, the most brilliant spokesman among the Uppsala ultraroyalists who had welcomed the obscurantist Holy Alliance on the Continent and looked upon the rising Stockholm Liberalism as a crass and bloody spawn of the French

Revolution. The shock and dismay among Geijer's friends and admirers was therefore indescribable when, in 1838, their idol published in a new journal, *Litteraturbladet*, his confession of a radically new political faith which in all essentials identified itself with the hated Liberal opposition. Geijer's sensational "avfall" (desertion, apostasy) was scarcely made more palatable to his friends when he insisted with considerable justification that it had long lain dormant in him and that it was a necessary result of his mature historical investigations.

Whatever the justification, Geijer's action was certainly without parallel in Swedish literary history, and the repercussions to it were many and violent. Impulsive and honest to the point of discourtesy, Geijer even went so far in the second issue of *Litteraturbladet* as to indulge in a blistering condemnation of the New Romantics and conduct a merciless dissection of the work and person of his colleague and old friend Atterbom. He conceded that the New Romantics had done a good and necessary work in their earlier years, but accused them of having fallen in later years into the trap of a sterile, egotistic, fantasy-filled subjectivity which deliberately evaded the challenge of reality. Nothing more sensational could have occurred in the cloistered precincts of Romantic Uppsala than Geijer's startling "apostasy."

When Atterbom had recovered sufficiently from the shock of his friend's attack to write a public reply, he did so in a vein of reproachful forgiveness which moved Geijer to reach out a conciliatory hand. But the earlier spontaneous feeling of mutual regard between the two had been shattered beyond hope of repair, as were Geijer's relations with nearly all of his former conservative friends. And among the Liberals Geijer found no real friends. They of course applauded his actions, but with certain reservations, not knowing exactly where they had their man. And well they might, for Geijer was not the man to throw himself without reserve into the arms of his old enemies and accept uncritically every plank in the Liberal program. He remained independent in his thinking, hoping with an optimism which never forsook him that he might without sacrifice of his principles play the role of mediator between the conflicting camps. In this he failed, but he retained the love and respect of those few among these groups who could on occasion rise above the petty concerns of practical politics. The aging King, first of the Bernadottes, even offered Geijer, without success, a place on His Majesty's Council, and the distinguished conservative statesman Hans Järta quotes the King as saying sadly, "J'ai aimé, j'aime Geijer."

The years after his "apostasy" were years of feverish activity for Geijer. In 1838–39 he used the columns of *Litteraturbladet* to state his position on most of the burning issues of the day. In 1840–41, years in which the waves of political controversy ran particularly high, he took a prominent part both in the public deliberations and the more private committee work of Parliament. And in other ways during his last years he made his influence felt in the direction of arousing an informed liberal opinion in the land. His mind was open in all directions, prepared to learn from whatever source. Historian and political theorist that he was, he was particularly sensitive to liberal social, economic, and political developments abroad and to the theoretical considerations which lay behind them. He observed with qualified sympathy such efforts to solve the economic problems of society as the Rochdale cooperative experiment in England and various socialistically inspired theories and experiments both in England and France. Of these latter, Saint Simonism particularly interested him, no doubt partly because of its philosophical-religious pretensions — what its founder called *nouveau christianisme*. Geijer was enough of a realist, however, to avoid being trapped by any simple doctrinaire formula. Specifically for Sweden he advocated direct parliamentary action on a number of crucial reform measures. In matters political he called for an elimination of the Four Estates in favor of a more democratic form of representation, ultimately to be based on universal suffrage. In education he opposed the strong ecclesiastical and Latinizing elements in the schools and identified himself with those reform advocates who wished to reorganize the entire school system and provide educational opportunities for everyone. In social and economic matters he championed measures aimed at eliminating the blight of poverty and encouraging the efforts of the middle classes to raise the level of industrial production. Geijer lived to see only the merest fragments of his program realized, but this program, he knew, was Sweden's inevitable program for the future. He alone among the major literary figures of his generation was not afraid to look Sweden's future in the face and have faith in it.

It was this faith that inspired the new poetic flowering of his last years — a poetic flowering which in originality, depth, and power had no counterpart in his earlier verse. The new poetry did not deal directly with the current social and political scene. It dealt rather with Geijer's mood, his abiding faith in man's future on earth despite the bitterness and rancor aroused by the contemporary social struggle in Sweden. Geijer's faith was a deeply personal one, full of courage and an ultimate trust in life, however dark the shadows were that gathered around his embattled person in the sundown years of his life. He was quite aware upon announcing his "apostasy" of how isolated he would become in consequence of the step he had taken — how the shocked wails of reproach from his Uppsala friends would mount the higher at each new issue of *Litteraturbladet*. To his wife he once said after taking account of the first Uppsala reaction: "It will become worse yet, but it can't be helped. Both cowardice and respect for Järta's political confessions have hitherto stifled my effusions . . . but *now* everything must give way." A lesser spirit than Geijer's would have indulged in self-pity or grown bitter under the pressures of misunderstanding and suspicion to which he was subjected. But his sense of isolation drove him instead down into the fundamental resources of his being, enabled him to discover reality in its richest potencies, to experience in a new and profoundly bracing way what he felt to be God's purposes with him and with man.

> Lone in his frail bark seaward blowing
> The sailor fares on the trackless wave.
> O'er him the starry vault is glowing,
> Grimly below roars his ocean grave.
> 'On!' bids the voice of his destiny,
> 'Here, as in the heavens, God watcheth thee.'
>
> *Translated by C. W. Stork*

This poem, written on New Year's Day, 1838, is Geijer's quiet confession of faith as he plunges into the seething, reef-bound seas of political controversy. It is typical of other poems from the immediately following years, the best of which are "Höstsädet" (Autumn Sowing), "Natthimmelen" (Night Heavens), "Tonerna" (Tones), and "Ord till en gammal hymn" (Words to an Old Hymn).

A tone of chastened optimism infuses these poems, the optimism of Geijer's quiet, manly, at once intense and sternly disciplined maturity. In form they are utterly simple, completely devoid of rhetorical gestures, creating their strong but subdued magic by highly controlled phrasing, by the use of the simplest of possible images and symbols. Geijer's early Gothic poems at their best (as in "The Yeoman Farmer") were moving in these directions; but they had fallen short of the ideal represented in the poetry of the last years — in part certainly because the earlier poems were the too-conscious products of a somewhat forced literary program, that of a Romantic Gothic ideal. In a letter as early as from 1826, to a young Swedish poet, Geijer had condemned both Gothicism and the New Romanticism as guides to a poetry of the future. "As for subject matter," he wrote, "to the devil both with *antiquarianizing* (*antikisera*) and *romanticizing*! Poetry has for so long searched the heavens for subjects that it is about time it turns to *actual life* in the conception, gathering, and perfection of *life's* poetic elements. This is the oldest of poetic wellsprings. It still responds to one whose divining rod nears the hidden vein. The superiority of English poetry of late is simply a result of the fact that it turned its eyes earlier in this direction than other national literatures." Geijer had learned much in his middle and late years from contemporary English literature, from Byron, Scott, and others, but he had learned even more from Goethe and Shakespeare, the two great masters of his later years as Schiller and Rousseau had been in his youth. Goethe's mastery of the highly concentrated "pure lyric" was almost certainly the formal model for the poetry of Geijer's last years, and the idealistic *realism* of these years owes much to that full-bodied response to a living, vital, many-sided existence which Geijer found in such full measure in both Goethe and Shakespeare. Not that Geijer consciously imitated them. He tells us in his *Memoirs* that this is impossible, the two great masters simply "can *not* be imitated." They influence one rather — he says — by "arousing buoyant, spirited self-activity. . . . They stimulate one, providing a sense of spiritual health."

Of the four major Swedish Romantic poets only Geijer and Esaias Tegnér (1782–1846) were personalities of commanding stature. Both played roles in the life of the day far beyond that usually granted a poet: Geijer as professor, historian, publicist, and leading advocate successively of conservative and liberal political points of view; Tegnér as professor, bishop, and as the incomparably most popular poet of the day. But though their outward more or less official roles suggest certain parallels, their temperaments were largely contrasting, their poetry in many ways equally differing, and their lives both private and public moved along quite divergent paths, especially in the years of their maturity. By temperament Geijer was heavy, deliberate, and stable in comparison with the impetuous, mercurial Tegnér. As a poet Geijer was relatively solid, few-worded, earth-bound, while Tegnér was elegant, rhetorical, flashing, soaring. In their private lives Geijer was on the whole balanced and well disciplined, Tegnér hypersensitive, overerotic, alternately expansive and melancholy, and in his last years mentally ill. These differences be-

tween the two men at times occasioned moments of irritation in their relations with each other, but nonetheless they maintained toward one
another a feeling of strong mutual regard and respect. Their paths diverged most sharply in the 1830's and 1840's when each reversed his earlier political position, Geijer turning toward reform and the liberal Left,
Tegnér identifying himself with the reactionary, ultraroyalist Right.
When Geijer in his admiring and yet sharply perceptive memorial address on Tegnér, in December 1846, paid generous tribute to his fellow
poet, he also noted with regret Tegnér's defection from an earlier held
liberal idealism. In Tegnér one thing was "lacking," he observes. "A sense
of history's rejuvenative process was hidden to him. He had no eye for
this, but lived in the antithesis between the *new* and the *old*; and as he
grew older the latter seemed to dominate. And yet it is this rejuvenation
of the old which is the very nature of existence. But an eye for what
really is and exists is in general more rare than one supposes." Geijer's
acute awareness of this "one thing lacking" in Tegnér suggests, without
deliberately pointing up, the central difference between himself and Tegnér.

Like Geijer, Tegnér was born in Värmland, but unlike Geijer his earliest years were spent in the shadows of poverty. His father, a country
pastor, died when the future poet was only nine years of age, and the
widowed mother was in no position to properly support and educate her
children. Fortunately, people of means recognized the boy's talents, provided him with opportunities for a sound early schooling, and continued
to support him while he attended the University of Lund. A brilliant and
hard-working student, he finished work for his degree with despatch and
distinction at the age of twenty-one, was encouraged by the faculty to
pursue an academic career, advanced rapidly on the ladder of preferment, and became at the very young age of twenty-nine professor of
Greek. In the meantime he had taken on the responsibilities of a family
man, marrying in 1806 Anna Myhrman, daughter in the Värmland family
which had befriended him as a boy and assisted him throughout his student years. Tegnér took his professorial duties seriously despite his increasing concern with wider literary and other interests, but in 1824 he
accepted, in part because of the emoluments involved, the chair as Bishop
of Växjö in Småland and spent the remainder of his life as a busy and
conscientious though scarcely orthodox ecclesiastical dignitary.

Tegnér early became aware of his poetic gifts, but his first verse neither
attracted many readers nor impressed the Swedish Academy to which

some of this verse was submitted. Its subjects were as hackneyed as its form was correct. But in 1808 he at last found a grateful audience with his stirring "Krigssång för det skånska lantvärnet" (Battle Song for the Skåne Militia), and the elevated patriotic note which he struck so successfully in this poem was further exploited to the almost universal enthusiasm of his Swedish contemporaries in 1811 in the stirring, aggressively militant "Svea" (Sweden). Both the "Battle Song" and "Svea" sprang from Tegnér's feeling of anger and bitterness over the Finno-Russian War and its humiliating aftermath for Sweden. The poems were in part meant to arouse Swedish resentment against Russia, certain passages in "Svea" going so far in their chauvinistic zeal as to call for a new war of revenge against the enemy to the East.

But Tegnér's "Svea" was not destined to call Sweden to arms. The hard facts of politics intervened and reduced the poet's martial aims to the regions of a poet's dreams, for a reversal of Sweden's foreign policy called for friendship with Russia in a common front against Napoleon. When it became known that the Swedish Academy contemplated awarding to the author of "Svea" one of its First Prizes, certain highly placed persons (including no less a figure than Charles John, the Bernadotte heir apparent to the throne) made their displeasure clear. Whereupon the Academy, ever solicitous to the royal will, asked Tegnér to eliminate the offending passages in his poem or revise them in a way satisfactory to those who were responsible for the new foreign policy line. Tegnér did so with considerable reluctance — and in some cases with an ambiguity which allowed the reader to interpret the revisions in more than one way. When, for instance, Tegnér replaced his "reconquer Finland" demands of the first version with the famous line "och inom Sveriges gräns erövra Finland åter" (to reconquer Finland within the boundaries of Sweden) it might seem that he had completely reversed his earlier aggressive militant position. But the line need not be read in terms of its apparent meaning. Irony may lurk behind the elegant façade of its phrasing. In any case Tegnér remained throughout his life the most implacable of "Russia haters," on all conceivable occasions expressing his antipathy toward the "barbarian" to the East. Always a worshipful admirer of Napoleon, he became particularly critical in the years after the publication of "Svea" of Russia's role in the defeat of the Emperor and heaped scorn on the efforts of Czar Alexander to impress his contemporaries with his Christian piety by clothing a reactionary politics in the deceptive garb of a "Holy" Alliance.

In the years following immediately upon his breakthrough with "Battle Song for the Skåne Militia" and "Svea" Tegnér's poetic production is of a rather diverse kind and somewhat uneven in quality. He seems to be feeling his way with considerable uncertainty toward what to him would be a satisfactory poetic subject matter and form. In the process he maintained points of contact both with the Gothicists and the New Romantics without identifying himself closely with either of these two groups. In fact, he was not too happy about the antiquarian leanings of the Gothic Society even while contributing a number of not especially distinguished Gothic poems to *Iduna*, and he was perhaps even less happy in his relations with the New Romantics though some of his best poems from these years, such as "Flyttfåglarna" (Birds of Passage) and the magnificent "Sång till solen" (Song to the Sun), with their Platonic idealism and flashing, soaring rhythms, are executed in the symbolic-speculative vein of the New Romantic group. But Tegnér was deeply disturbed by the polemic pettiness and the fine-spun metaphysical pretensions of the New Romantics, though he was prepared to concede that there was some justification for their reaction against the unyielding position maintained by the Gustavians.

For some years, however, Tegnér's displeasure with the warring New Romantic and Gustavian factions (he felt that they should vie with one another on the creative rather than the polemic level) found expression only in his letters and other private contexts. It was not until he wrote the celebrated prose piece *Tal vid jubelfesten 1817* (an address on the occasion of the celebration at Lund of the three hundredth anniversary of the Reformation) that Tegnér took a clear public stand on the literary controversies of the day, and though he distributed praise and blame rather equally between the Gustavian tradition and the New Romantic opposition, it is clear enough that the balance of his sympathies tips in the direction of the Gustavians. In his address he disapproves strongly of the materialism and utilitarianism as well as the rationalism and empiricism of the eighteenth century, and yet he feels that the extremist speculative and mystical alternative proposed by early nineteenth-century German thought is equally objectionable. He reserves his strongest words of condemnation, in fact, for the New Romantic literature in Sweden directly inspired by German thought:

In the arts one quite properly demands that which is profound and significant. But as examples of this some wish to force upon us — we sons of the North with the clear heavens above us and a tremendous, sharply distinct nature around us, we heirs of Saga the Deep-eyed, powerful child of Valhalla, with sharp eyes and strong limbs — some wish to force upon us a poetry without form and precision, a sickly figure without marrow or sinews, with the swords of abstraction at its side and a bell-ringed cape over its vaguely outlined shoulders, a wraith which wanders about in the moonlight and paints its confluent images — in the clouds.

In another work, the brilliant versified academic address *Epilog vid magisterpromotionen i Lund 1820* (Epilogue at the Master's Convocation at Lund 1820), Tegnér again takes up his quarrel with the New Romantics — now, however, more elegantly, less sharply, yet with no compromise of his convictions. Vagueness, obscurity, the merely suggestive and allusory — these are not the signature of great poetry, he insists:

> In Phoebus' world, in knowledge or in song
> all is full clear. . . .
> What one can't clearly say, one does not know;
> with thought the word is born on human lips:
> that which is vaguely said is vaguely thought.

Strength, balance, clarity, these are to Tegnér the mark of all great poetry; poetic genius flourishes in a clear, crystal-clear, and light-filled world rather than in the moonlit shades and dim recesses dear to the New Romantic mind.

Tegnér's ideal of poetry became more and more with the years essentially a Classical one, capable, however — and this should be stressed — of assimilating into it certain Romantic ingredients. It might, indeed, best be labeled Classical Romanticism, for the poetic ideal toward which Tegnér was drifting came to identify itself more and more closely in the years immediately before and after 1820 with Romantic Gothicism. In 1820 he submitted for publication in *Iduna* four of the romances which were to be included in the narrative cycle *Fritiof's Saga* (completed 1825), the most popular of Swedish Romantic poems and the incomparable masterpiece of the Swedish Gothic tradition. *Fritiof's Saga* (frequently rendered into English) marks a departure on Tegnér's part from the abstract reflective lyric, often in symbolic form, of his earlier years to a more concrete and objective narrative art — a departure also reflected in two other narrative poems from the *Fritiof's Saga* years, the sensitive religious idyl *Nattvardsbarnen* (tr. *Children of the Lord's Supper*, 1820) and the much less important *Axel* (various English translations, 1822).

Tegnér came upon the idea of casting ancient Scandinavian material into a loose narrative cycle mold with each episode in a different poetic meter when he read his Danish contemporary Oehlenschläger's *Helge*, which had appeared in 1814. In the mastery of varied verse patterns, the handling of descriptive and narrative detail, and the vivid creation of character, Tegnér's narrative cycle equals or surpasses Oehlenschläger's. In his tendency in *Fritiof's Saga* to idealize ancient Scandinavian life Tegnér departs rather markedly from the practices of his Danish contemporary in *Helge*. This strong idealizing tendency in Tegnér derives partly from the nature of the particular Fritiof sources which he uses and partly from his theories as to how ancient Scandinavian materials should be modified to fit modern poetic tastes and needs. The saga concerning Fritiof from Biörner's *Nordiska kämpadater* on which Tegnér based his poem is not a saga of ancient origins. Dating from late medieval times, it is one of the so-called *fornaldarsagor*, and is quite clearly compounded of both Scandinavian and Greek or Oriental sources. The crude, more barbaric elements, the physical violence and the revenge motifs particularly present in the earlier part of the original saga derive obviously from primitive Scandinavian sources, but the spirit of reconciliation and penance in which the saga closes is almost certainly to be accounted for in terms of some non-Scandinavian Near-Eastern source. Feeling that it was the modern poet's duty to further humanize Biörner's saga material, Tegnér eliminated or softened the more brutal barbarities of Biörner's text and developed the theme of penance to the point where it was scarcely distinguishable from the Christian concept of repentance. In Tegnér's version Fritiof, who in his youth had pursued his intentions with little consideration for others and who had violated the sanctity of Balder's Temple in the process, comes at the last to rue his actions, seek reconciliation with his enemies, and rebuild the Temple which his ill-considered actions had once destroyed by fire. Only then does he become worthy of Ingeborg, his childhood sweetheart, who had long been married to King Ring.

If Tegnér's Fritiof had once desecrated and later become the instrument of destruction of Balder's Temple, the poet himself may be said to have equally impiously dealt with the realities of primitive Scandinavian life when he transformed traditional Scandinavian saga material into a sentimental tale of ideal love and Christian reconciliation. That Tegnér himself had compunctions on this score is clear from his letters. He wondered if he might not, by his method of "modernizing" the saga, destroy completely that which was most characteristic of the saga world. A later scholarship can understand Tegnér's compunctions and deplore as quite unhistorical the fuzzy "middle way" between the ancient and the modern which Tegnér took in his poem. But Tegnér's contemporaries — enchanted by his evocation of a world of young romance and heroic adventure and moved by his idealistic moralizing — raised no subtle, learned questions. *Fritiof's Saga* captured the hearts of all Swedes and in a multitude of translations spread the fame of Tegnér's name far beyond the borders of his native country. Among Europeans Goethe praised the poem highly, in America Longfellow translated parts of it and, in 1837, wrote about it in the *North American Review*, and many another foreign hand turned to making the tale about Fritiof and Ingeborg available to those who could not read the original. Unfortunately, the poem often attracted readers for what a modern critic would call the wrong reasons — for its sentimentality, its fondness for artificial, often showy, images, its occasional tendency toward something resembling rhetorical posing. It should be added — partly in Tegnér's defense — that in the hands of awkward, uninspired translators these blemishes, not always immediately apparent in the original, often loom up as grotesque caricatures of the Swedish text.

Tegnér, like Geijer, in his early verse held fast to the view that the sources of poetry are positive and healthy, and that the profession of poetry is therefore an art of affirmation. *Fritiof's Saga* was a monument to this view. But the positive, harmonious note on which *Fritiof's Saga* closes was seldom afterward struck in Tegnér's poetry. In the very year (1825) of publication of the complete Fritiof cycle Tegnér wrote the hopelessly dark-toned, Byron-influenced "Mjältsjukan" (Ode to Melancholy), a poem shot through and through with a despair bordering on cynicism. It is clear that the "Ode to Melancholy" marks a profound crisis in the poet's life — a crisis from which he never fully recovered during the remaining two decades of his life. In July 1840, the crisis broke out into madness, and the poet's remaining years alternated between periods of madness and lucidity. Tegnér himself ascribed the crisis to a strain of hereditary insanity; others have doubted (in some cases denied) this and have sought the reason for Tegnér's mental crisis in a physical condition, or in a series of unrequited love affairs (at various times he was deeply in love with no less than three married women), or in the feelings of frustration which it is sometimes claimed resulted from his taking on the vestments and responsibilities of a bishop while he remained in some respects an unregenerated pagan. Of the efforts to explain Teg-nér's crisis the one which assumes that the bishop's vestments were a kind of Nessus mantle for Tegnér seems least plausible, for high ecclesiastical appointments in Sweden in the first half of the nineteenth century were determined less in terms of the appointee's piety and orthodoxy than on the basis of his intellectual and cultural attainments. Tegnér's conscience need not therefore have been put under any strain when he wrote quite frankly to a friend at the time of his appointment: "A pagan I am and shall remain. Phoebus himself was not baptized." Besides, the record of Tegnér's activities as a churchman reveals that he was in his way a con-scientious bishop, conceiving his duties to consist primarily in improving educational standards within his diocese and raising the cultural level of the relatively unlettered priesthood under his discipline. In pursuing these ends he did not spare himself, devoting a great deal of his time to ecclesi-astical visitations and delivering addresses at school exercises and religious assemblies. These addresses reflect little if any falling off from the very high oratorical level of the celebrated Reformation address of 1817. Some of them are to be counted among Tegnér's best prose pieces, and this is high praise indeed.

But in poetic production Tegnér's last two decades are not rich, whether chiefly because of his inner crisis or because of his many prac-tical ecclesiastical duties it is difficult to say. He did not exactly neglect verse, but only a handful of poems from these years are really notable, the most important of which, aside from the "Ode to Melancholy," being the finely drawn self-portrait and love poem "Den döde" (The Dead One, 1834), and one of the most magnificent of all Swedish occasional poems, the so-called Academy Song from 1836, in celebration of the fifti-eth anniversary of the founding of the Swedish Academy. In "The Dead One" (an imaginary dialogue between the poet and his last serious love Emili Selldén) Tegnér's poetic vein is in part operating under certain self-imposed restraints; but in the Academy Song, a kind of history of Swedish literature in verse, all of the poet's intellectual and imaginative resources are permitted to soar with a majestic fullness reminiscent of the Tegnér before the "dark years" beginning in 1825. The Academy Song contains the last full-throated, proudly triumphant notes from Tegnér's poetic instrument before the shadows again begin to thicken and choke out almost all future inspiration. Only twice during his last ten years, both times during convalescence from outbreaks of madness, did Tegnér write poetry of distinction — an idyllic descriptive piece on a country

wedding entitled *Kronbruden* (The Crown Bride) and the resigned poetic epilogue "Avsked till min lyra" (Farewell to My Lyre).

Though the Academy Song did not limit its concern to the literature
of the Gustavian Age during which the Swedish Academy was founded,
it did quite naturally deal in the main with this period, a period in Swedish
culture whose literary attainments seem with the years to have grown in
Tegnér's esteem despite the efforts of the New Romantics to malign it.
Airily graceful and sonorously majestic by turn, Tegnér's verse in the
Academy Song lends itself effortlessly to the literary portraiture and the
critical formulations demanded by the subject matter. So brilliant, indeed, are Tegnér's critical formulations — often cast in scintillating an-
titheses — that they have in many cases become winged words, determining for generations after they were written our conception of the literary
figures with which they deal. "Wondrous is the power an artist wields,"
one of Tegnér's lines on Gustaf III, might as well be applied to the spell
that Tegnér himself has cast over our picture of the whole Gustavian
epoch. It may be said, in fact, that *one* of the problems of Swedish literary
historians since Tegnér's day has been to disengage the literary figures
dealt with in the Academy Song from the brilliant epigrammatic hyp-
notism of Tegnér's critical formulations. This is true especially of the
two most inspired portraits in the poem, that of Gustaf III, idealized
almost beyond recognition, and that of Bellman, whose realism is barely
hinted at and whose tragic side becomes softly enfolded in the vague
Romantic formula "a Nordic singer's trait, sorrow in rosy red." Such
lovely but half-evasive formulations can be condoned only when it is remembered that the Academy Song was written for a special anniversary
occasion which scarcely called for strict critical honesty. Besides, Tegnér's poetic genius was essentially of the brilliant rhetorical kind, not
always averse to lending itself to an elevated outward show of eloquence
which at least to the modern mind leaves something to be desired.

But if the purely poetic genius of Tegnér at times indulges in what
may be called purely popular effects, and in the process perhaps leaves
us wondering where we have the *man* behind the *poet*, Tegnér's letters
leave us in no doubt at all. These letters, unique in their kind, are of the
highest literary quality. In them Tegnér is completely relaxed, giving
direct, often brutally frank expression to his opinions and his moods. Isolated as he was after 1824 at Växjö from the cultural centers of Sweden
and obliged to occupy himself so largely with routine church matters,
Tegnér found welcome release in an extensive correspondence with a

number of highly cultivated contemporaries, male and female. Among these the one whom Tegnér valued most highly as a friend and correspondent was Carl Gustaf von Brinkman, whose liberal cosmopolitanism in outlook and experience (educated in Germany, he had spent many years as a diplomat in Berlin, Paris, and London) provided Tegnér with a friend who would not be shocked by his most intimate confessions or most violent outbreaks and who had a connoisseur's taste for the high literary quality of Tegnér's letters. And Tegnér was never more brilliant than in his letters. His ideas cascaded down upon his correspondents with a breathtaking inventive abandon in a prose style which was always fresh, flexible, invariably capable of finding the word, the phrase, the image that brought the idea alive. "I can also make a beautiful verse," the aging Gustavian poet-wit Leopold once wrote — "but the devil take me if I can write a single letter like Tegnér."

Despite the highly personal quality of Tegnér's letters, they are never petty. He may make devastating enough commentaries on his contemporaries, but he does so with no ulterior motives, and he nearly always qualifies his judgments with a generous observation or two. On only one subject were Tegnér's judgments on his time adamant to the point of violence — the radical politics of the day in Sweden as represented particularly in the Liberal press. With time Tegnér had become an ultra-royalist, among the most extremist of the kind. Even Atterbom was by comparison reasonable in his political views. The extremes to which Tegnér went in his late years in expressing his political views, in private and in public, can only be understood if we keep in mind his mental condition, the increasing irritability of his later years, and the crudity with which the opposition Liberal press pursued its objectives. It was no accident that the first outbreak of Tegnér's madness occurred upon his return to Växjö from Stockholm after his having taken an active part in the violent political debate of the parliamentary session of 1839–40. Tegnér, as Geijer has said, was a miraculous child of impulse who had no eye for history's process of rejuvenation. By temperament, Geijer concludes, he oscillated constantly between affirmation and negation.

One cannot understand Tegnér without noting in him these oscillations, which came and went without any perceptible cause — because the cause lay within himself. We have said that the great secret of his poetry was its play of *contrasts*. Why? Because *he himself* was a series of contrasts. His art simply reflects his own nature; he blanketed the deeps of his own innermost being by casting over them a whole springtime of flowers. In itself, and fundamentally, his world view was dark, gloomy, yes, tragically dreary. No one has ever born within himself a more profound sense of the power of dissolution than this light-hearted son of impulse.

Truer words have never been uttered about the poetic complex which was Tegnér.

Among Swedish poets of the early nineteenth century Johan Olof Wallin (1779–1839) most closely resembles Tegnér. In his career, in his personality, and in his earlier poetic practices he had much in common with Tegnér without in any sense being his great contemporary's disciple. Wallin's official career was wholly within the Church, leading ultimately, shortly before his death, to the archbishop's chair at Uppsala. By nature he had some of Tegnér's impulsiveness, but he managed with the years to keep this trait well under control. As a young poet he wrote with equal facility gay drinking songs — the best of which is "Lycksalig den, som stödd på eget stop" (Most blessed he, who propped against his stoup) — and reflective poetry in the spirit and manner of Gustavian didactic literature. Throughout his life he retained a fine sense of the *formal* quality in poetry, a quality which had early attracted him to the Gustavians. But in his maturity he reacted strongly against the rationalism and the religious formalism of the Gustavians and in some ways identified himself with the New Romantics and Gothicists, particularly in their feeling for the old, the traditional, the ancient biblical quality of Swedish folk religion. It was largely though not entirely in this anti-Gustavian spirit that Wallin wrote his many hymns and became chiefly responsible for the form which the famous hymnal *Den svenska psalmboken av år 1819* finally took. Lacking the originality of the really great poet, but having a remarkably sensitive ear for traditional religious values, Wallin as a hymnologist paraphrased with due reverence the most well-known of biblical songs, adapted with great skill into Swedish celebrated Christian hymns of various national origins, and "modernized" with a careful, loving hand Swedish hymns of venerable vintage. Moreover, not a few of the items in the new Psalm Book were original with him. All in all he composed some 150 of the roughly 500 hymns in the Psalm Book of 1819. Wallin's greatest purely aesthetic achievement in the hymns is his ability to combine the Oriental magnificence of an ancient biblical tradition with the directness, the simple vigor and gravity of a Swedish folk religion. His most well-known hymn is the majestic "Var hälsad sköna morgonstund" (Be hailed thou lovely morning hour), sung always as the opening hymn at the early morning Christmas service in Swedish churches. With reference especially to Wallin's central eminence as a Swedish hymnologist Tegnér has coined the winged phrase "David's harp of the North" (*Davidsharpan i Norden*).

Wallin was also distinguished as a church administrator, and as a pulpit orator he has had few peers in the history of the Swedish Church. His sermons combined warmth with majesty of utterance and a sense of the fearful disparity between heavenly ideals and our limited conditions of earthly existence. But aside from the finest of his hymns, Wallin's best claim to fame is the magnificently sonorous "Dödens Engel" (The Angel of Death), in which Swedish poetry celebrates its greatest triumph in that religious genre which concerns itself with death and judgment. In this poem Wallin joins hands with that anti-Gustavian Gustavian Bengt Lidner, who had exploited the genre so exhaustively in the 1780's. In Wallin, however, the pre-Romantic excesses of Lidner's fearsome outpourings on death and judgment have come under the discipline of a restrained and dignified art, never resorting for its effects to fulsome tears or wildly catastrophic horror visions. Instead, Wallin's Angel of Death verse moves with the miraculously controlled sonorities of Milton's epic periods and marches with an even-paced majestic solemnity appropriate to its high purposes in a world of disintegration and judgment. The theme of mortality has perhaps never been clothed in more sternly elevated poetic vestments than in those of Wallin's "The Angel of Death."

On September 13, 1822, Geijer wrote from Uppsala to Atterbom who was at the time resident in Östergötland: "In Stockholm I made the acquaintance of Stagnelius, who gave me the first sheet of a new tragedy *Backanterna eller fanatismen*, which is in the press. The subject is Orpheus. I can't say anything about it. Stagnelius is a genius, but a queer, uncouth, unrestrained creature. Warm, but confused, and completely mad when he tries to talk *sense*. His health unfortunately seems to be already ruined and his diet is apparently not the best." Geijer's words concern Erik Johan Stagnelius (1793–1823), the strangest, most isolated, most Romantic of Swedish Romantic poets. Less than a year after Atterbom had received Geijer's letter, Stagnelius's body was lowered one snow-filled April day into a grave. He was only twenty-nine. He has been compared with both Keats and Baudelaire, with the former because of his early death and the rich sensuousness of his poetry, with the latter because of the darkly mysterious splendor of much of his work, its tendency to allow the sensuous strain to drift into a hectic, desperate sensuality even while seeking to retain a sense of ideal, eternal values.

Repulsive in physical appearance and burdened with abnormally active sexual drives, Stagnelius lived out his brief life in alternating visions of forbidden sensuality and ecstatic asceticism. He speaks to us almost exclusively through his verse. What we *know* about his life is very little. Only two letters from his hand are known to exist, he had no close friends and few acquaintances, and though his family did not attempt to suppress the unhappy details of his life story, many of these details have come down to us through devious if not actually dubious channels. We are on sure ground only in sketching the broad outlines of Stagnelius's life. Beyond these outlines conjecture and hypothesis must take over. Even the chronology of his works cannot be determined with any certainty despite the exemplary calligraphic investigations of Stagnelius's manuscripts conducted a hundred years after the poet's death by Professor Albert Nilsson. In life as in death Stagnelius went his close-lipped, solitary way, leaving behind him a fascinating body of poetry — and a multitude of very difficult problems for the scholar and critic.

Practically his entire childhood and youth were spent on the island of Öland in the Baltic, where his father was a prominent clergyman. Private tutors directed intermittently the more formal side of his early education, but much more important for the precocious boy's intellectual development was the opportunity to immerse himself more or less as he pleased in the substantial collection of books, representative of oddly assorted fields, which his rather learned father had acquired. Shortly after the family's move to the mainland upon the father's elevation to Bishop of Kalmar, in 1810, the future poet took up university studies — first at Lund for a brief period and then, from 1812 to 1814, at Uppsala, where he completed work qualifying him for a civil service position in Stockholm, a position he was to fill with no particular distinction and with a number of extended "sick leaves" until his death. At Uppsala he made no overtures to the New Romantic coterie gathered around Atterbom, and during his Stockholm years he maintained such a secluded existence that even the civil servants with whom he worked knew next to nothing about his private life. From the evidence now available it seems apparent that this private life was sufficiently sordid and tragic in its frustrated eroticism, its dark-toned religious crises, and its steadily increasing indulgence in alcohol and (probably) opium to still the poet's conscience and allay the severe bodily pains which ultimately brought on his death.

189

Though most of Stagnelius's important poetry was written toward the end of his life, he had for more than ten years found in the world of his poetic fantasy some compensation for the ugly sides of actual existence which had been his sorry lot. During the last half dozen years of his life he published two dramas, *Martyrerna* (The Martyrs, 1821) and *Backanterna* (The Bacchantes, 1822), and the strange collection of religious lyrics *Liljor i Saron* (Lilies of Sharon, 1821). And shortly after his death the indefatigable New Romantic editor Lorenzo Hammarsköld brought out Stagnelius's *Samlade skrifter* (Collected Works, 1824–26), which in addition to the previously published works included practically all of the rather extensive manuscript material found after the poet's death. Stagnelius's contemporaries almost without exception admired his formal skills, the exquisite musical quality of his verse. But in other respects they differed in their judgments. The tolerant, open-minded Geijer was interested but not prepared to commit himself without reservations. Tegnér — who apparently reflected the general taste of the day — was least impressed, finding in *The Martyrs* a sickly, febrile quality which moved him to hope, not too hopefully, that "God [might] make Stagnelius healthy and sane" again. Only the New Romantics responded with great enthusiasm, recognizing that between themselves and Stagnelius there existed what Atterbom once called a remarkable "harmony in aesthetic studies and ideas."

Little wonder is it that most of Stagnelius's contemporaries were hesitant and disturbed in the presence of his poetry. For here was Romantic *radicalism* in a form possibly dreamt of, but scarcely realized, even by the most militant of New Romantic poets. Here was a poet with no Romantic poses, a poet who *was himself* in good and evil, a poet who followed his own fateful star into the strangest regions of fantasy and idea and whose poetry reflected with startling beauty and precision every last feverish pulse-beat of a torn and wasted soul. Though Stagnelius had points of contact with both the New Romantics and the Gothicists, he never became a captive in their relatively delimited worlds. His genius created a new world — sick and mad, if you will, but a world so intensely conceived and sumptuously adorned that Swedish Romanticism found in this world its most grandiose and haunting incarnation. The erotic and religious themes so central in Stagnelius were not exactly foreign to other Swedish Romantic poets, but these themes are developed in Stagnelius with an intensity and daring scarcely approached by others — unless it be in those erotic poems by Tegnér which have not come down to us.

Because of the uncertainty under which we must labor in dating much of Stagnelius's poetry, it is not always possible to trace precisely the lines of his poetic development. Considerable disagreement exists as to whether some of his works, such as the long narrative poem *Blenda*, come early or late in his poetic production. But the general phases of development are sufficiently clear even though the lines of demarcation between the various periods are scarcely rigid, and at times works essentially representative of one phase fall chronologically within the limits of another. In the first period Gothicist motifs tend to predominate, though these motifs are more frequently than not clad in Classical forms and infused with New Romantic moods and points of view. The second — and crucial — period reflects everywhere the severe religious crisis of the poet. The last phase, like the first, is somewhat heterogeneous, carrying over some of the hectic decadent strains of the immediately preceding period but reflecting on the whole an at least relatively harmonious and objective state of mind. Roughly speaking the early Gothicist-Classical strain is reflected most clearly in the opera *Cydippe*, the narrative poems *Gunlög* (a fragment) and *Wladimir the Great*, and the two tragedies *Sigurd Ring* and *Wisbur*; the religious crisis in *Lilies of Sharon* and *The Martyrs*; and the final relatively objective period in especially *The Bacchantes* and *Thorsten Fiskare* (Thorsten the Fisherman), while other works from the last years — the tragedies *Albert och Julia* (Albert and Julia), *Riddartornet* (The Knight's Tower), and *Glädjeflickan i Rom* (The Roman Prostitute) — reflect willy-nilly poetic strains of quite disparate origins and intentions.

The strong tendency in some of Stagnelius's earlier more ambitious works to superimpose upon ancient Scandinavian materials essentially Classical literary forms and to soften the primitive heroism of these materials by the inclusion of modern Romantic speculative moods accounts largely for the fact that none of these works are really important, except insofar as they suggest certain strains that are later to be handled in more original and profound ways. Stagnelius is already in these early works a master of mellifluous and colorful verse, but his verse has found no focus, it is not anchored in any central personal experience which might give it the integrity and authority which is a mark of all great poetry. But there are signs of what is to come, particularly in what has survived of the opera *Cydippe*, where in the triumph of Venus over Diana the erotic theme is developed with a sensuousness bordering on sensuality, and in *Wladimir the Great*, in which primitive religious ecstasy exists side by side with a colorful Oriental splendor never before seen in Swedish poetry. But the erotic and religious themes are in these poems largely derivative, *Cydippe* being in many ways what may be called a tribute to Ovid, Stagnelius's favorite among the Romans, while *Wladimir the Great* owes a great deal to Chateaubriand's Orientalism as reflected in *Les martyrs* and elsewhere.

That Stagnelius was not merely in these years, however, a virtuoso disciple of others in his poetic treatment of erotic and religious themes is clear from the remarkable poem "Till förruttnelsen" (To Putrefaction), apparently written on the verge of the religious crisis that becomes so exhaustively mirrored in two of his greatest works *Lilies of Sharon* and *The Martyrs*. "To Putrefaction" is one of the most extraordinary Swedish poems, combining as it does in a macabre dream vision the erotic embrace with imminent death spasms. "Rejected by mankind, rejected by God," the poet finds hope only in death, represented as a bride invited to the bridal bed; and in desperate death-marked embraces he and his bride finally find "slumber in golden rest." Death conceived as an ultimate *erotic* experience: this is Romantic eroticism with a difference — dark-hued, decadent, utterly despairing. "To Putrefaction" is verily a poem that would have fascinated Baudelaire, had he come upon it, and received admiring homage from the entire company of *fin de siècle* decadents. It is a matter of some interest that Stagnelius's father revised the line "rejected by mankind, rejected by God" to "rejected by mankind, *accepted* by God" when, after the death of the poet, the manuscript was sent to Hammarsköld for publication. The good Bishop could apparently overlook everything in the poem except the implied blasphemy in the line in question. His religious orthodoxy need not have been shocked by the horror elements in his son's poetic vision — if he did not examine too closely the unconventional erotic form which the horror vision took.

Though Stagnelius was never destined to shake off completely a fatal fascination for the female body, in his later work he did manage to sublimate his abnormal erotic responses — at least theoretically — by constructing a world view which condemned the sin of the flesh and affirmed as man's only means of salvation a radically ascetic religious position. Stagnelius's position was in itself scarcely original, for it is the position of nearly all religions and of much of the philosophical speculation in which so many Romantic poets had become immersed. What was striking about Stagnelius's world view was the intensity and intellectual clarity with which he conceived it and the haunting exoticism of the poetry in which he clothed it — to begin with in the strange lyric sequence *Lilies of Sharon* and in *The Martyrs*, later, and perhaps most impressively, in *The Bacchantes*.

In these works, as in his life, Stagnelius went his own way — and a weird, uncanny, seductively exotic way it was. The world of idea and form which he conjured up was a strange, mysterious, many-colored thing. This world had its immediate philosophical point of departure in Platonic and Neo-Platonic thought, but it fed also on mystical and theosophical speculation (that of Böhme, Swedenborg, and others), and found its ultimate sources of inspiration in Oriental religious speculation, in Greek Orthodox Christianity, in Manichaeism and Gnosticism. Out of this strange conglomerate of philosophical and religious lore Stagnelius built up a religious system which was calculated to satisfy his moral needs and provide a fitting background for his aesthetic tastes. Central in his system was the ancient concept of matter as something which has fallen away from the idea, the divine principle, and not until matter has again identified itself with the idea, or the divine principle, will the world of creation be able to slough off its terrifying burden of evil. To Stagnelius the central symbol of evil is the erotic desire, and not until this desire is crushed can man find his way back to the serenity which is the mark of the divine. Only the way of asceticism, an absolute denial of the flesh, can bring man to God. In *Lilies of Sharon* these ideas become clothed in a sumptuously Oriental symbolism whose central mythical frame is the ancient story of Demiurge (Prince of This World, Anti-Christ) holding as a prisoner in his fabulously appointed, closely guarded castle the maiden Anima (symbol of a lost soul), who sorrows endlessly over her forced physical relations with the Demiurge and yearns constantly for a return to her true love, the idea, the divine, to a union ultimately with Christ. Dominant as is the purely erotic motif in Stagnelius's use of the ancient myth, he employs the myth also in much more inclusive conceptual contexts, drawing a broad parallel in such poems as "Suckarnas mystär" (The Mystery of Sighs) and "Kreaturens suckan" (The Sighing of the Creatures) between the yearning of the maiden for purity and the longing of all natural phenomena, animate and inanimate, for a re-identification with their source, the idea, the divine. Farfetched as the idea might seem, Stagnelius could have referred to a source for his speculations in an immediate Christian tradition, the eighth chapter in Paul's Epistle to the Romans.

What is most interesting, however, about *Lilies of Sharon* is that the ascetic rigorism of its idea world in no way ruled out Stagnelius's poetic sensuousness — in fact it in some ways served to heighten the poet's awareness of the seductive attractiveness of the things of the flesh which in theory he so fanatically attacks. Only some of the *crassness* of an earlier sensuality is missing, with the result that the poet's sensations are now preternaturally alive, at times glowing with a subtle, insinuating, magic incandescence, as in the famous lines from "Rosen i världsfurstens park" (The Rose in the Prince of the World's Park) beginning

> A Moorish glistening Alhambra
> the lordly royal castle stands.

One is tempted to assume that the magnificent stanzas which follow are the product of an opium dream, like Coleridge's "Kubla Khan." Both Stagnelius's and Coleridge's poems describe what the latter calls "a stately pleasure-dome . . . with walls and towers . . . girdled round." Both have a similar floating sensuousness subtly punctuated by a play of musically suggestive Oriental words, especially proper nouns; both have in common falling, crystal-clear cadences; and over both poems hovers a haunting, breathlessly expectant quality, a sense of complete aesthetic absorption in a vision of beauty which seems to be an end in itself. It should be said, however, that Stagnelius never deliberately nurtured a theory of art for art's sake, and least of all in *Lilies of Sharon*, where his thematic engagement is broadly philosophical, more narrowly religious and moral. And despite his undeniable intellectual capacities, his analytic powers, he was a poet born, rather than a thinker, and the poet in him dreamed dreams and caught resplendent visions whose alluring colorations more often than not provide a possessively seductive backdrop for the poet's religious and moral dialectics.

While the poems in *Lilies of Sharon* maintain a precarious, haunting balance between a rigid ascetic dialectic and an excessive erotic-charged imagery, *The Martyrs* (a drama published simultaneously with the second volume of *Lilies of Sharon*) reflects a considerably greater capacity on Stagnelius's part for toning down his poetic preoccupation with thinly veiled erotic motifs drenched in a superabundant exotic imagery. And in his important drama *The Bacchantes*, finished just before his death, the poet manages to maintain a high degree of control over sensuous excesses despite the Dionysian fury of some of its scenes. But that Stagnelius during his last years maintained only a precarious hold upon his late-born asceticism seems apparent from three other plays, *Albert and Julia*, *The*

Knight's Tower, and *The Roman Prostitute*, all of which include an abnormal piling up of horrors around erotic themes which scarcely reflect a healthy and balanced state of mind. Possibly these plays derive in part from an earlier period.

However this may be, *The Martyrs* and *The Bacchantes* are written in quite another key — elevated, relatively serene, Classical in both spirit and form. Both of these tragedies deal with the struggle between the flesh and the spirit, the former in a purely Christian historical context, the latter in a Greek mythic context, that of the Orpheus legend, which in *The Bacchantes* is made to parallel the Christ story. In *The Martyrs* Perpetua meets death gladly at the hands of her Roman persecutors, for to her only in death can the flesh be annihilated and the spirit return to God. In *The Bacchantes* Orpheus is destroyed by the vengeful fury of Dionysian fanatics. Of these two tragic figures Orpheus is the more complex, less the simple martyr of a single cause, and he therefore suggests that the poet was moving away from the rigorous asceticism of *Lilies of Sharon* and toward a more tolerant, humane religious and moral position. Orpheus does not welcome death as the only way back to the divine, as does Perpetua. He is no fanatical ascetic, but a sensitive spirit whose very fineness infuriates the crass-structured Bacchantes and motivates their deed of violence upon him. Orpheus is essentially a Christ-figure, pure in deed and motive, gentle, understanding, and forgiving even when being destroyed by the primitive fury of the Dionysian devotees. In *The Bacchantes* Christian and Classical myth and symbolism fuse, a not uncommon phenomenon in Romantic poetry.

During the long period of convalescence at his parental home in Kalmar from the late fall of 1821 to June 1822, Stagnelius seems to have found some relief from the hectic, feverish world of idea and fantasy of the immediately preceding Stockholm years. The somewhat active part that he took in the "social whirl" of the little provincial town resulted in some unimportant occasional verse in the drinking song tradition of Bellman; but — much more important — he drank deeply during these months from the clear wellsprings of Classical poetry and of Scandinavian folklore. Aside from *The Bacchantes*, the works which most interestingly reflect the convalescence and its aftermath are *Thorsten the Fisherman* and a group of Stagnelius's most exquisite lyric poems, among which "Endymion" and "Necken" (The Nix) may particularly be mentioned. Broadly speaking Stagnelius moved in certain respects during this period closer to the New Romantics than he had previously. In the love poems, of which "Endymion" is typical, there was none of the hot intensity of his earlier erotic lyrics; and in the poetry with folkloristic motifs Stagnelius employed some of the folk sources of thematic inspiration most frequently exploited by the New Romantic poets.

The return to Kalmar — with its proximity to Öland and the folk associations of the poet's childhood and youth — seems to have enabled Stagnelius to divest himself at least in part of the strange Oriental world of idea and image with which he had been burdened, and encouraged him to yield at least for the moment to some of the simpler enchantments of primitive Scandinavian folk materials. The side of folk temperament represented in *Thorsten the Fisherman* is the earthy, the broadly comic, the grotesque. Stagnelius is here indulging in comic fantasy not unlike that of Ibsen upon Peer Gynt's arrival at the Hall of the Mountain King — but without the "moral" that Ibsen tacks on to his bit of grotesque horseplay. In *Thorsten the Fisherman* we are apparently simply expected to *enjoy* the mad gallop of fantastic scenes, completely free from the symbolical circumlocutions so characteristic of much of Stagnelius's earlier work.

In the exquisite lyric "The Nix" Stagnelius employs folk materials in quite another vein than the extroverted fantasy of *Thorsten the Fisherman*. "The Nix" reflects the folk response to the mysterious, the melancholy, the fateful element in life and nature, employing as its theme the tragic inability of the Nix or Watersprite to become "saved" because he is not human. The subject was a commonplace in Swedish Romantic poetry, but in no other Swedish poet has it been handled with the perfect touch of Stagnelius. In his hands the theme becomes pure poetry, simple in form, musical in movement, magical in mood, with whatever "idea" the poem may contain never breaking obtrusively through the sheer beauty of line and image and subtly suggested symbol.

> Evening gilds the sky's expanse,
> The elves upon the meadow dance,
> His harp the laurelled Nix doth play
> In his silver riverway.
>
> A little lad amongst the willows
> Rests on violet-scented pillows,
> Hears the water-rush of springs,
> In the silent evening sings:
>
> "Poor old man, why do you play?
> Can it drive your cares away?

Though you cheer the woodland wild,
You will never be God's child!

The moonlit nights of Paradise,
Eden's flowered plains and skies,
Angels that in heaven be,
These your eye will never see."

Tears the old man's visage lave,
Down he dives beneath the wave.
No more his harp the Nix doth play
In the silver riverway.

Translated by A. Hilen and S. Arestad

Modest as is this little poem, it attains a subtle fusion of Romantic mood and quiet, restrained Classical artistry — a fusion which is the signature of Stagnelius's most mature poetry. "The Nix" takes its place in this respect alongside *The Bacchantes*. Both "The Nix" and *The Bacchantes* give exquisite expression to a twilight mood, calm, serene, essentially undisturbed despite the tragic nature of existence which they portray. Neither the feverish eroticism nor the equally feverish asceticism of much of Stagnelius's earlier poetry intrudes into the world of "The Nix." Stagnelius's poetic fantasy led him during a brief and pain-filled life into many weird and wondrous worlds, none more quietly and sensitively wondrous than that revealed in the magic lines about the Watersprite who sank beneath the wave — never again to pluck the harp as elves danced on nearby meadowlands. For some moments at least in Stagnelius's last years he found a hushed sense of calm, especially in the kind of world he created in "The Nix" and *The Bacchantes*, poetic creations which in their kind have no peers in Swedish Romantic poetry.

CHAPTER 7

Mid-Century Ferment

WHEN Geijer in January 1838 dramatically announced his political defection from the ranks of the Conservatives and aligned himself with the Liberals his announcement created a sensation for a number of reasons, two of which are usually stressed: the circumstance that it was Geijer, the most highly respected of the Conservatives, who took this step, and the fact that his announcement took such sharp form. But equally disturbing to Geijer's conservative contemporaries was the *timing* of his announcement, the year 1838, when a number of recent events had pointed up a growing political crisis in the country and when political controversy had reached a point of acrimony and bitterness seldom if ever before known in Swedish politics. That Geijer at just this time publicly disavowed his former political faith and went over to the liberal opposition seemed to his conservative colleagues and friends a shocking evidence of political irresponsibility on his part. He might have chosen a less charged and potentially dangerous moment to make his announcement. "I am accused of being a revolutionary," Geijer wrote in these days — and his reply to the accusation was: "It has been my chief aim to save my country from revolution."

How close to revolution Sweden may actually have been at this time is a matter of some disagreement, but it is sufficiently clear that a serious political crisis was brewing in the 1830's and that toward the end of the decade the crisis might have precipitated into violent political action had not the government partially yielded during the parliamentary session of 1840–41 to the pressures of the liberal opposition and acquiesced to some reform measures.

The most significant instrument of liberal propaganda at the time was the singularly successful Stockholm newspaper *Aftonbladet*, founded in 1830 and rapidly establishing itself as a highly effective political force. As a newspaper it concerned itself only incidentally with literary matters, but it did not fail on occasion to condemn most Romantic poetry as escapist and reactionary, and it championed with increasing frequency those literary figures who in one way or another came with time to identify themselves with the program of reform which it had taken upon itself to champion. It may be that *Aftonbladet* would have been even less directly concerned with belles-lettres than it was had it not been for the fact that Swedish Romantic poetry had in its late years been so prevailingly conservative in its political position. Romantic poetry was an obvious target for a newspaper with pronounced liberal leanings.

The chief target of the liberal opposition was, however, the King's Council, an obsequious instrument of Charles John's personal politics, a politics which in general attempted to impose upon Sweden the reactionary governmental structure and procedures of the Holy Alliance. The July Revolution in France had in 1830 given the signal for a broad European frontal attack on the Holy Alliance, and the establishment of *Aftonbladet* at the close of the same year had provided in Sweden an effective gathering point for a Swedish liberal opposition. The effectiveness of this opposition is to be accounted for in part by the weakness of the conservative government and in part by the extraordinary skill and dogged persistence of the liberal opposition in pointing up the government's lack of understanding of the crucial issues at stake. Instead of meeting the growing political crisis with measures aimed at satisfying a rising chorus of demands for reform, the King's Council equivocated, evaded the issues, simply marked time. What the liberal opposition called for in general was a greater recognition of the middle classes, whose rising economic status had no sufficient counterpart in political power.

The editor-publisher of *Aftonbladet*, Lars Johan Hierta (1801–72), was both a brilliant journalist and a highly successful business man, and his newspaper became in consequence a natural rallying point for the new middle-class politics. Hierta had journalistic talents of the first order — one is tempted to say he had journalistic genius. His newspaper was eminently readable in every way. Outwardly *Aftonbladet* was modern. Bent on attracting the largest possible reading public, Hierta used every trick of format and general appearance known in his day. *Aftonbladet* articulated the cause of the middle classes in a language which its readers understood — concrete, direct, factual, and, when necessary, sharp, in-

N:o 1.

1830.

AFTONBLADET

i

Måndagen   STOCKHOLM.   den 6 December.

Priset i Stockholm: för helt år 10 R:dr, halft år 5 R:dr, 3 månader 2 R:dr 32 sk. Banko. Prenumeration och utdelning i Linströms bokhandel vid Mynttorget; Bromans bod i hörnet af Drottningatan och Clara Bergsgränd; Linroths bod vid Norrlandsgatan och Esséns bod vid Södermalmstorg. Annoncer mottagas endast i Linströms bod, till ⅓ skilling Banko raden. Utdelningen sker kl. omkring 4 eftermiddagarne.

Post- och Inrikes Tidningen för i dag omtalar följande:

I Götheborg utbrast den 30 November kl. 2 e. m. en häftig eldsvåda i Masthugget. Elden började i Hökaren Ramstens hus och fattade i 2:ne dermed sammanbyggde, allt trähus, hvilka stodo i full låga, innan sprutorna hunno fram. Likväl lyckades man oaktadt en svår lokal, stark blåst och aflägsen vattentillgång, släcka, sedan 6½ hus nedbrunnit.

LEDIG. TJENST.

Skeppsmätare-tjensten i Carlshamn sökes inom 56 dagar efter den 30 October.

LEFVERANS

till Flottan å Skeppsholmen, af: bräder, krita, vadmal, tjära aspik, bultjern. An-

TESTAMENTEN.

H:r Johan Kullbergs och dess Frus, född H. U. Lundgren; communiceradt af Rådh. Rätten i Ystad.

A(l. Bokhållaren P. F. Melldenhauers; communiceradt af Frösåkers H:ds.-Rätt d. 27 Sept.

Afl. Demoiselle Carolina Christina Grubbs; Westerviks Rådh.-Rätt d. 17 Nov.

LAGFART.

3 uppbudet å 3-384:dels Mt:l skattehemman i Öfverklinten; Bygdeå och Nysätra; Tingslag, d. 26 Febr. 1830.

KALLELSE Å

Magnus Samuelsson i Mjölserud till Hvetlanda H:ds-Rätt, efter 1° månad från 16 Nov., ang:de en inteckning i hemmanen Bjädesjöholm och Bjädesjö Karingsgård.

ARF LEDIGT

PRIVILEGIUM EXCLUSIVUM.

För Victor Sjöberg å en handspruta med slang för eldsläckning.

BORTKOMNA DOKUMENTER.

Brandförsäkrings bref: N:o 422¼, å Danviks- Lägenheten Kolbotten i Stockholms Län; N:ris 9359,9748, 10529 å Sölje Bruk'i Veruland; N:ris 13,855. Gladåkers Jernbruk.

Reverser: Å 800 R:dr till Olof Larssen i Munkerud, af Bergs-Rådet J. G. Geyer; å 360 R:dr af afl. fröken Lovisa Fr. Fleming. Bankens pantsedlar N:ris 2519, 3522, 6333, 8088.

SPEKTAKLER.

I dag: *Edlvinski och Floreska eller Polska grifuan;* samt *Mannen och Älskaren.* Nästa Torsdag: (Fru Eriksons rcbett) *Tar-*

Masthead of the first number of Lars Johan Hierta's liberal newspaper *Aftonbladet*

vidious, even brutal. Hierta gathered around him a staff of highly talented and not particularly squeamish editors, who pilloried with devastating mercilessness political personalities close to the King; and not infrequently Hierta himself tossed off some of the more invidious attacks on the government. Hierta's dry humor had a bite that cut even more deeply than did certain of his colleagues' berserk broadsides. His opponents accused him (not always without justification) of inciting the masses by appeals to prejudice and class consciousness, and an incensed King's Council attempted to suppress *Aftonbladet* under a censorship regulation from 1812. But when *Aftonbladet* was confiscated, Hierta took advantage of a legal loophole by having his newspaper appear the following day under the heading *Det Nya Aftonbladet*, and when *Det Nya Aftonbladet* was in turn confiscated the sheet came out as *Det Nyare Aftonbladet*, and the process was repeated until the government, now become a public laughingstock, reluctantly desisted from its unpopular activities as a censor. How effective Hierta and the liberal opposition finally were in political matters is evident from the parliamentary proceedings of 1840–41, which took several steps in the direction of long-delayed reform, including important measures aimed at circumscribing the King's personal power over decisions of his Council.

Though Hierta's newspaper had its most immediate and palpable influence in social and political affairs, it was in many ways equally important in helping to shape literary tastes. Aside from its attacks on the Romantics, it affected literary developments in a number of positive ways, ranging from a general influence on prose style in the direction of greater conciseness, concreteness, liveliness, and realism to a more specific influence on the shorter fictional forms which now for the first time become seriously practiced in Sweden. On its staff Hierta's publication had from time to time authors of greater or lesser distinction, most notably C. J. L. Almqvist in the late 1830's and the immediately following years. Finally, the broad, popular appeal of *Aftonbladet* served to increase appreciably the general reading public in the land and encouraged authors to write on less elevated and exclusive planes than had formerly been the practice. The journalism of the day provided one of the fundamental points of departure for the first great step toward a modern democratic literature.

It would be misleading to assume, however, that what was happening to Swedish literature in the decade or two before the middle of the century was simply, or even largely, a result of the rise of a social-conscious journalism. A general cultural ferment in the land, increasingly wearied by Romantic poses, was becoming evident at many points and moving in the general direction of what may be called a more realistic view of life and the arts. The cloistered cultural hegemony of the universities prevailing during the first decades of the century begins to give way before the miscellaneous practical demands of life in the larger, more forward-looking contexts of urban existence. The tyranny which German speculative philosophy had maintained for a generation over Swedish thinking shifts in part toward an increasing interest in the more utilitarian thought of England and France, and even when a German intellectual orientation is retained, as it often is, it finds its inspiration now more frequently in the objective fact-conscious system of Hegel than in the subjective abstractions of Schelling. In literary taste there are plenty of evidences of change: there is a growing interest in the realistic novel of idea; the political radicalism of French Romanticism acts as a revitalizing agent on Swedish literature; and Scott and Byron, the more "realistic" of the English Romantics, are now for the first time more fully appreciated in Sweden. And periodical literature undergoes a marked change: by the end of the 1830's the last of the many New Romantic journals which had blanketed the Swedish periodical trade for almost three decades had ceased publication, being replaced by a less exclusively "literary" type of periodical publication modeled in part after such British journals as *The Quarterly Review* and *The Edinburgh Review*.

In the light of such evidences of broad social and cultural ferment it is scarcely surprising that literary figures of eminence should feel the impact of the new ideas and accept the implications of these ideas for the future of Swedish literature. It is true that only Geijer among the great Romantics responds favorably to the new ideas, but a year after Geijer's defection from the conservative ranks he is followed into the liberal camp by Almqvist, and several years earlier Johan Ludvig Runeberg, a young Swedish-writing poet from across the Baltic in Finland, had made a slashing attack on much that had been held especially precious in the Swedish Romantic tradition. Almqvist and Runeberg came to occupy central places in the mid-century literature of Sweden, to be joined shortly by Viktor Rydberg, the other major figure of the period. But despite the commanding literary stature of these men none of them succeeded in shaping the literature of the day substantially in his own image, chiefly because the period in which they appeared was essentially a transitional one, in which Romanticism still lingered on, mingling its currents of idea and form in the new literature which was struggling for recognition. Even Almqvist and Runeberg themselves represent essentially, as we shall see, a transitional literary phase, mingling in their work the present and the past, a critical modern awareness with nostalgic moods and traditional forms and themes. The realistic ferment won no clear-cut victory in Swedish literature until the appearance in 1879 of Strindberg's novel *Röda rummet* (The Red Room), almost a half century after *Aftonbladet* had begun its campaign and the cannonading of a beleaguered Romanticism rumbled over the relatively tranquil Swedish cultural scene.

Various circumstances account for the fact that a really modern realistic literature did not come into existence until Strindberg's appearance on the scene, not the least being the stubborn persistence of the Romantic spirit, its ability to retreat from its more exposed positions and to reappear in somewhat disguised forms at points on the cultural scene where the liberal opposition was for one reason or other not prepared to make a frontal attack. Romanticism persisted most obstinately in two forms: its early nineteenth-century Gothic nationalism reappeared in the pan-Scandinavianism and related trends of the two decades after the mid-1840's, and its Platonic idealism served both Runeberg and Rydberg among others to justify their refusal to push their early realism and liberalism to any really radical extremes. Almqvist alone broke radically with the past, but his position was fatally discredited when he disappeared from the literary scene in 1851, a suspected criminal. The liberal opposition itself hastened to disassociate itself from Almqvist after his hasty flight from the country, and it is probably not merely coincidental that beginning in the 1850's a moderate liberalism came gradually to displace the radical liberalism of the preceding decades. The shift is symbolized by the increasing prominence after 1850, in the councils of organized Liberalism, of the moderately liberal newspaper *Göteborgs Handels- och Sjöfartstidning*, for which Rydberg wrote extensively in his early and middle years and with whose publisher, S. A. Hedlund, he maintained cordial relations for many years after the close of his journalistic career. Events on the Continent in 1848 also served to moderate an earlier, more radical Swedish liberalism. Charles Dickens's relatively inoffensive social criticism becomes in the 1850's a norm for the new generation of Swedish liberals.

Rydberg had begun his journalistic career as a writer of serialized fiction in the manner of Eugène Sue and Edward Bulwer-Lytton, who dispensed to the delight of many mid-nineteenth-century readers a due portion of liberal ideas within an exciting framework of melodrama and sensational intrigue. But a quarter of a century before Rydberg wrote his early tales of intrigue set in distant places and times Fredrika Bremer had turned to contemporary daily life in her first *Teckningar utur hvardags-livet* (Sketches from Everyday Life), and it is in the modest realism of these sketches rather than in the flashy melodrama of Rydberg's early novels that Swedish prose fiction was to have its first substantial flowering. Fredrika Bremer herself followed up the success of her early "sketches," as we shall see, with a considerable production of "realistic novels with a purpose," and she was to be joined in exploiting the genre during the two decades after 1830 by two other women, Emilie Flygare-Carlén and Sophie von Knorring, as well as by a number of male practitioners of prose fiction, among whom C. A. Wetterbergh, August Blanche, and especially Almqvist were the most important. Though their "realism" leaves something to be desired from the standpoint of twentieth-century taste, these authors usually managed to avoid the worst excesses of an earlier Romantic tradition and created in many cases convincing pictures of life as actually lived in Sweden, the woman novelists particularly occupying themselves with the middle classes and the lower aristocracy, while Almqvist in his later years was concerned with the lower classes, especially the peasantry.

Though poetry was written with great distinction by Runeberg and Rydberg, and with considerably less distinction by others, the most characteristic — and in some ways the most important — literary accomplishment of the period is the sudden rise of the novel. This rapid rise of prose fiction was something quite new in Swedish literature, where previously the poetic genres had dominated, with only occasional more or less satisfactory ventures into the moral essay and dramatic composition. With very few exceptions — the only notable ones being Fredrik Cederborgh's picaresque novels *Uno von Trasenberg* (1809–10) and *Ottar Tralling* (1810–18) — Swedish readers before well down into the nineteenth century had to satisfy their tastes for prose fiction through translations of foreign novels. Though plentiful these novels were more frequently than not of a dubious kind, and in any case they seldom if ever had any organic point of contact with a living Swedish life and culture. But by the mid-nineteenth-century Sweden could finally boast at least the beginnings of a respectable native prose fiction. What is most interesting about this fiction is that its more important practitioners were with one or two exceptions middle-class in origin, and that some of them were women, who, because of the prevailing social mores, were denied the supposed advantages of a higher education and of necessity approached their material through direct observation rather than through the devious, often abstract considerations of the university-trained mind. The very naïveté of what may be called the "new feminine approach" was refreshing, and not infrequently it resulted in a depiction of life considerably closer to reality than the fastidious profundities of male minds accustomed to the Classical disciplines and to Romantic concepts and turns of phrase. In its mid-century prose fiction Swedish literature dispenses with its traditional academic robes and takes on the simpler garments of everyday realism.

In all of Swedish literature there is no more enigmatic figure than Carl Jonas Love Almqvist (1793–1866), who alone among the novelists of the 1830's and 1840's was a literary genius of the first order. His strange life and the equally strange course of his literary production pose some of the most baffling problems in Swedish literary history. Fantastically productive, and original often to the point of the bizarre, he was in his early years among the most Romantic of Swedish Romantics; but in the late 1830's he suddenly turned against his former Romantic extravagances and wrote among other relatively realistic things his notable peasant tales — and the last pitiful episode in his restless life story was enacted in the German harbor city of Bremen, to which he had come, aged and broken, after a fourteen-year exile in the United States, where he had lived incognito after fleeing from Stockholm, in June 1851, under strong criminal suspicion that he had forged notes and had attempted murder by poisoning his creditor.

This bizarre series of events and the fantastic fluctuations of Almqvist's literary production can be explained in part by the fact that he came upon the scene at a particularly precarious moment and in part by certain profoundly unstable hereditary traits in Almqvist's character. Abnormally sensitive and endowed with an amazing receptivity, he was bound to find himself a victim of that unstable pattern of literary culture typical of the transitional period when Romanticism in Sweden was undergoing its last feverish death-throes and yielding slowly to the new vital and challenging realistic demands of the day. In Almqvist's early work the Romantic ideal is pursued with an all but desperate consistency, and apparently with no qualms as to where it might lead. He is the born radical among Swedish Romantics, prepared to follow with fanatical enthusiasm whatever the inspiration of the moment suggested. Among Swedish authors of the day Almqvist's Romantic exoticism is the most far-ranging, his experiments with form the most extreme, his conception of the purposes of poetry the most emancipated, his ethics the most revolutionary, his religious responses the most original and complex. Out of this congeries of extremes almost anything might erupt, and it is not at all surprising that, in the years around 1840, he finally reacted against Romanticism in equally revolutionary ways. Almqvist was at one and the same time a good deal of a religious mystic and a cold, calculating — sometimes furtively calculating — man of the world, alternating restively between idyllic, contemplative, quietistic states of mind and a nervous, self-consuming, intellectual restlessness.

Almqvist himself has with considerable plausibility accounted for these strange contradictions in his nature as a necessary consequence of the sharply contrasting characters of his highly sensitive mother and his aggressive, practical-minded father. But perhaps equally significant were the circumstances of his childhood and youth. Though he took a degree at Uppsala in 1815, he did not come in contact during his university years with the New Romantic coterie, and his early literary development seems to have been little if at all determined either by this literary group or by his formal university studies. The direction his development was to take was rather determined by his deep attachment to the memory of his mother (she had died when he was only twelve) and to the formative influence of his maternal grandfather, C. C. Gjörwell (1731–1811), who had from Almqvist's earliest years taken a lively interest in his gifted grandson. Gjörwell, who himself had played a modest but worthy role as librarian, publicist, and indefatigable collector of cultural trivia, initiated his grandson into the sentimental religious pietism of the Moravian sect in which he had become a patriarchal figure. Gjörwell's pietism was combined with a gentle nature mysticism of vaguely Rousseauistic origins. To these strains Almqvist himself was presently to add certain darker, fantasy-loaded Swedenborgian ingredients, and the combination of Rousseau and Swedenborg accounts for much that is characteristic in Almqvist's emotional and intellectual world up to his break with Romanticism in the late 1830's. In fact, they persisted, though in somewhat modified forms, in Almqvist's work down to the end.

After his Uppsala years Almqvist combined some rather desultory duties as a civil servant in Stockholm with a number of ambitious but ill-fated cultural activities which included his first literary efforts and his attempts to become the "prophet" of Manhemsförbundet, a religious-patriotic society that proposed to revive the Gothic spirit in Christian-mystical terms under the ritualistic trappings of a secret order. The most characteristic literary piece from these early years was *Amorina*, in which many of Almqvist's revolutionary ideas were poured into a narrative-dramatic work of fantastic richness and inventive confusion. Particularly sharp is his attack in this work on the dead formalism of the Church, on conventional morals and the institution of marriage, on society's traditional views of the freedom of the will and moral responsibility. But when *Amorina* was about to be released in 1822, Almqvist destroyed the edition, apparently under pressure from an uncle who was Bishop of Härnösand. Not until 1839 did *Amorina* again appear in print, and then in a somewhat revised form.

Frustrated in his first major literary venture and forced from the civil service for reasons that are not entirely clear, Almqvist fled in 1824 from Stockholm and established himself as an ordinary farmer in western Värmland, where he proposed to *live* the ideals of a simple life close to nature which he had earlier envisioned in his program for Manhemsförbundet. The experiment was a failure, and after two years of rural solitude Almqvist returned to Stockholm with a considerable accumulation of manuscripts in his baggage as the only visible evidence that his rural sojourn had some practical results. The manuscripts were to be published a few years later. Meantime he turned his hand to various odd tasks to keep the wolf from the door (he had married on the eve of the Värmland adventure). In 1829 he became the principal of a newly founded experimental school in Stockholm, which gave him an outlet for his pent-up energies and provided him for the first time with a respectable standing in the community. In the years which followed he busied himself with writing a number of highly successful school textbooks and with bringing himself to the attention of the Swedish reading public by means of an astonishingly prolific literary activity which he poured, in the form of novels and dramas, poetry and essays, into successive volumes of *Törnrosens bok* (The Book of the Wild Rose), under which collective title nearly all of his literary work was to appear from 1833 until his hasty departure from Sweden in 1851.

Almqvist had waited until he was forty before introducing himself definitively to the Swedish reading public, but then he did so with overwhelming effect, flooding the book market with work after work and rapidly becoming the most talked-of author of the time. Some of the work now published was from earlier manuscripts; much of it, however, was new, and practically all of it delighted Romantics like Atterbom, who found in Almqvist a new and brilliant exponent of a Romanticism that seemed to have had its best days in Sweden by the end of the 1820's. The Swedish Romantic fantasy had never before Almqvist's arrival on the literary scene been so madly inventive, had never before burned with such a mysterious, fitful, strangely incandescent glow. Sweden had finally, in Romanticism's otherwise weary and declining years, produced in Almqvist a Jean Paul Richter, the German prose fantast whom the Swedish New Romantics had so often tried to imitate in earlier years but with only mediocre results.

But Almqvist — like Jean Paul Richter — both fascinated *and* disturbed his readers; and there were those in Sweden, even among the New Romantics, who noted with growing uneasiness the equivocal, the decadent, the tendency toward intellectual and moral anarchy beneath the brilliant surface glitter of Almqvist's art. This tendency manifested itself in many ways, perhaps most subtly and ominously in the extreme subjectivity of this art, a subjectivity quite nakedly expressed on one occasion by Richard Furumo (Almqvist's *alter ego* in *The Book of the Wild Rose*) when he agrees to tell his tales and give vent to his thoughts only on the condition that all his hearers "accommodate themselves to my mood, I, on the other hand, never according to theirs." What this might lead to, and often did, in Almqvist's work from the 1820's and early 1830's, was the pursuit of art as a whim directed solely by the artist's caprice — an art which was in the last analysis an end in itself, passing the time of day, and the long shadow-filled nights, in a more or less insidiously playful pursuit of graceful arabesques and mad, unpredictable fantasies. Almqvist tended during these years to become a prisoner of his own fabulous artistic talents and his own subtle mental agility despite the fact that serious enough purposes lurked within the confines of his art. These purposes only later, however, break clearly out of the web of fantasy in which they were entangled in his early work and assert themselves in boldly didactic forms in the realistic works of social purpose from the late 1830's and the following years.

So rich and diversified is Almqvist's production of tales and other works from the earlier years that each of his readers has his own favorites among them. Some prefer the splendid Italian and Spanish exoticism of the dramas *Signora Luna* and *Ramido Marinesco*. Others favor the historical novels, the concern with the private life of the Folkung monarch Valdemar in *Hermitaget* (The Hermitage), or the brilliant panorama of life at the court of Gustaf III in *Drottningens juvelsmycke* (The Queen's Jewel). Still others prefer the *Songes*, those short, dream-like, subtly charged lyric pieces in which sound and image and idea attain a magical poetic fusion. And some find their favorite works among the allegorical satires such as *Ormus och Ariman* and *Palatset* (The Palace), in which Almqvist castigates the conventional moral structure of society and pleads for a return to individualism and a greater recognition of life's spontaneous natural sources of goodness. If one must single out any one work as most typical from this fascinating literary largesse it would probably be *The Queen's Jewel*, a novel which is on the one hand merely a tale of sensational intrigue but on the other a miraculous recreation of the rococo graces and finely decadent theatrical flavor of life at the court of Gustaf III. Central in this novel is Almqvist's most bewitching creation, Tintomara, *première danseuse* of the day — infinitely graceful, instinctively good though incapable of distinguishing good from evil, a strange hermaphroditic creature who has a fateful attraction for both men and women of the court but who cannot reciprocate affection and ultimately becomes the innocent victim of blind, irrational intrigues.

Many as are Tintomara's literary predecessors (Goethe's Mignon, Fouqué's Undine, Scott's Fenella, and Hugo's Esmeralda), Almqvist's creation is quite worthy of her pedigree — alive, vibrant, subtly and mysteriously enchanting. *The Queen's Jewel* is also reminiscent of Hugo in its central use of the Royal Opera House at Stockholm as the emblem of Gustavianism just as Hugo had employed Notre Dame cathedral as a broadly inclusive symbol of the life and spirit of the Middle Ages.

Upon the publication in 1835 of the sixth and seventh volumes of *The Book of the Wild Rose* Almqvist's amazing literary productivity of the immediately preceding years fell off sharply, not to be resumed until three years later, after Almqvist had undergone a profound personal crisis. Tiring of the daily grind of school work, and seeking without success a university appointment or, failing this, a substantial assignment in the Church, he gradually disengaged himself from the bizarre world of fantasy to which he had been so long committed and worked out for himself a more sober, essentially earth-bound, social-conscious literary program. Though this program came to be pursued both in the analytical essay of social criticism and in prose fiction with a social purpose, the latter is more important in the history of Swedish literature. This prose fiction took on two loosely related forms, the modern folk tale of vaguely "democratic" leanings and the short novel with revolutionary social purposes. Both of these forms, particularly the first, can be said to have more or less honorable Romantic pedigrees; but when Romanticism in Sweden, especially in its later phases, became, as it did in the main, intellectually and aesthetically exclusive and permitted itself to be used by the forces of political and religious reaction, it failed to follow the folk theme beyond its sentimental and picturesque phases and it drew back completely at most points from the revolutionary social and political implications of the Romantic individualism inherent in much folk-inspired literature. But Almqvist, a product of a transitional age and a much more complex, eruptive temperament than most of the Swedish Romantics, could not be permanently lulled into the merely idyllic view cultivated so assiduously by the Romantics. Like Rousseau's "primitivism," Almqvist's becomes intensely revolutionary in its ultimate purposes. He may be said to have disinterred the real Rousseau from the thick overlay of sentimental idyllicism under which two generations of Romantics had managed to bury the author of the *Contrat social*. It was appropriate, considering Almqvist's life-long attachment to the ideas of Rousseau, that when he finally turned in the late 1830's to a reformist-inspired social and political literature he found himself moving in the same direction as two of Rousseau's countrymen, Hugo and Lamennais, who in their reaction in the 1830's against the Legitimists had led a previously conservative French Romanticism into the camp of a liberal political opposition.

Almqvist, however, began his campaign against social and political reaction somewhat hesitantly, twice destroying printings of his most revolutionary political pamphlet, *Europeiska missnöjets grunder* (The Causes of European Discontent), and introducing his new points of view to the public, at first, in the relatively innocuous form of rather moderately realistic folk tales. Then, in a lengthy essay on the national character titled *Svenska fattigdomens betydelse* (The Importance of Swedish Poverty), Almqvist took the aristocracy to task for its foreign affectations and its supercilious attitude toward the peasantry, and praised the common folk as the true representatives of sound national virtues. Though *The Importance of Swedish Poverty* contains a veiled warning that a revolt of the masses could take place if the aristocracy persisted in its antidemocratic attitude toward the serving classes, one remembers the essay rather for its eloquent if somewhat idealized apotheosis of such oftpraised Swedish folk virtues as buoyancy, adaptability, industry, and independence, and for the certainly interesting though rather dubious theory that these virtues derive directly from a fundamental condition of Swedish life down through the centuries — its poverty. "To be poor," Almqvist concludes — "this means to be dependent on one's own resources." The theory builds upon Montesquieu, who, it is clear, had assisted the early nineteenth-century Swedish Gothicists in formulating their Romantic view of folk life. It is scarcely, however, a theory which could serve as a logical point of departure for the realistic modern social prophet Almqvist proposed to be when he formulated his observations on Swedish national character. *The Importance of Swedish Poverty* points curiously enough in two directions simultaneously, despite its predominantly democratic bias. It has become nevertheless a classic among Swedish essays of its kind.

The uncertain blend of traditional-romantic and liberal-realistic elements in *The Importance of Swedish Poverty* is reflected in various ways also in the famous folk tales which Almqvist wrote in the late 1830's, but these tales are nevertheless the first really significant efforts to treat Swedish peasant life realistically, and as such they indicate the direction which prose fiction dealing with the Swedish countryside is to take in the future. They occupy much the same place in Swedish literature as do Björnson's folk tales in the literature of Norway. Of the four most important of these tales, *Grimstahamns nybygge* (Grimstahamn's Settlers), *Kapellet* (tr. *The Chapel*), *Skällnora kvarn* (Skällnora Mill), and *Målaren* (The Painter), the first is a lively piece of pedagogical fiction in which the realistic element is sufficiently sustained; but the other three are each in its way marred at points by the intrusion of Romantic elements of one kind or other — *The Chapel* by occasionally yielding to idyllicism and by an unconvincing "happy ending," *Skällnora Mill* by the inclusion of popular horror features, *The Painter* by using at the beginning hackneyed tricks to create suspense. And all of the tales are burdened with a rather too intrusive moralizing strain. In general, however, these tales move in a recognizably real world, the actual world of the Swedish countryside. And Almqvist's narrative skill never shows to greater advantage than in these tales; his ability to build up a milieu which provides a lively illusion of reality is never more satisfying; and his unassuming, spontaneous, crystal-clear style is the ideal instrument for engaging the reader's interest in the simple folk world of these tales. Almqvist's approximation of something like a genuine "folk style" was far superior to that of any of his Swedish predecessors, thanks to an ear constantly on the alert during his many travels on the Swedish countryside in the years just prior to the writing of his folk tales. Among his successors few are his peers in this respect, and only Strindberg his superior.

The realism of the folk tales — even when, as in *The Chapel*, they contained some rather harsh criticism of traditional Swedish institutions — did not disturb most of Almqvist's readers. The same can hardly be said of another of his works from these years, the novel *Det går an* (It Can Be Done, translated into English under the title *Sara Videbeck*), which created an unprecedented sensation when it appeared in 1839. Not even Geijer's dramatic defection from the ranks of the Conservatives a year earlier had so deeply disturbed the nation. The reason for the uproar around Almqvist's person on the publication of *Sara Videbeck* was his daring to make a radical attack on the institution of marriage as legalized by the State and blessed by the Church. The fact that he held at the time the posts of both schoolmaster and clergyman did not serve to lessen the uproar. Almqvist had previously, and often, expounded some of the ideas central in *Sara Videbeck*, but usually in such fantastic exotic contexts that the ideas seemed hardly to apply to the everyday circumstances of life. With this novel, however, he placed a bomb directly under the foundations of contemporary Swedish society, proposing nothing less than to annihilate one of its most time-honored institutions. He reasoned quite simply that marriage as practiced in modern society was highly immoral because it was more frequently than not entered into as a matter of convenience rather than as a consummation of genuine love and understanding. He proposed in consequence that marriage be strictly a private arrangement between two persons, that neither the State nor the Church had any right to "bind" the arrangement, and that whenever either of the parties wished to break the arrangement he should be free to do so without the necessity of referring the matter to any legal instruments established by State or Church. The bold logic of these proposals shocked all of Sweden and infuriated Almqvist's enemies, who found the proposals no more palatable because they were almost nonchalantly offered to the public in the pages of a highly entertaining novel. In fact, Almqvist had never before written anything more lively, more intriguing, more amusing, more *seemingly* sensible.

Sara Videbeck is the story of a courtship, one of the least sentimental and most ingratiatingly unconventional on record. Its central figure, Sara Videbeck, product of the lower *bourgeoisie*, resident of a thriving provincial town, is the very quintessence of everyday common sense. Intelligent, able, emancipated without being mannish, she develops an affection (the word "love" would certainly be too strong) for Albert, a goodhearted, conservative Sergeant whom she meets on a boat trip; and when Albert reciprocates her feelings she proceeds to clarify for the astonished Sergeant the conditions on which she will consider the kind of relationship called "marriage." After the first shock Albert yields by degrees to the piquancy of the situation, and finally brings himself to accept Sara's conditions — each to have his own work, no constant cohabitation, no daily intrusion upon each other's privacy, and so on. Despite the frequent elaborations of theme, the narrative interest is maintained at a high pitch. Over the whole little novel there lies a freshness, a stylistic verve, a warm, broad play of humor which never ceases to attract the reader, unless moralizing prejudices blind him to such qualities. *Sara Videbeck* is one of the very few Swedish novels before Strindberg's *The Red Room* (1879) which can still today be read with genuine pleasure.

But *Sara Videbeck* was Almqvist's fate.

The uproar which the novel created placed its author definitively outside the precincts of "respectability" and led by devious but inexorable paths to Almqvist's final catastrophe. Deprived of any regular source of income after the publication of *Sara Videbeck* (he was forced to resign his school post and had no success in his efforts to gain university or church preferments), he turned to ill-paid miscellaneous writing. *Aftonbladet* opened its columns to him, but the somewhat limited liberalism of this middle-class newspaper provided only partial support for Almqvist's extremist social and political views. The group of hectic, hastily put together novels from the early 1840's (*Amalia Hillner, Gabrièle Mimanso*, and others) in which he gave expression to some of his most advanced views are chiefly interesting as evidence of his growing desperation. Soon Almqvist found himself inextricably involved with a usurer named von Scheven, an involvement which resulted finally in Almqvist's being suspected of murder by poisoning and his precipitate flight to the United States, where he disappeared from sight under various assumed names, traveled for a couple of years as far west as St. Louis and south to Texas, settled later in Philadelphia where he married an elderly widow, and finally died destitute in Bremen after his return to Europe under the assumed name Professor Carl Westermann "from Westchester in Pennsylvania."

In his utopian youth Almqvist and a group of his friends had dreamed of emigrating to the United States in order to realize the ideal life which they felt a decadent, tradition-bound Europe could not provide. But the early dream of a free and challenging immigrant life in the New World came in fact to be for Almqvist, a generation later, the heavy reality of a fugitive's furtive existence dragged out under tawdry, limited, utterly mortifying circumstances. One can understand why he wrote nothing of importance these last years. The story of Almqvist's life is as fantastic as the fortunes of some of the strangest characters in his early novels and plays — and equally puzzling.

In the very days in the late summer of 1851 when Almqvist as a fugitive from Swedish justice arrived in New York and disappeared quickly into the vast expanses of the New World, another celebrated Swedish author of the day, Fredrika Bremer (1801–65), was preparing to depart from New York for Sweden after having spent a couple of busy years in the United States. It was as a novelist that Fredrika Bremer's fame had preceded her to American shores, but the primary purpose of her visit to the United States was to study American social and political conditions, particularly as they reflected the position of women. To this end she traveled far and wide on the American continent — as far west and north as

St. Paul in the then Minnesota Territory as well as into the deep South, and almost everywhere along the Atlantic coast and in New England. An indefatigable observer of every aspect of American life, she recorded her observations in an extensive correspondence to her sister Agathe, the letters being published in three substantial volumes shortly after her return to Sweden under the title *Hemmen i den Nya världen* (tr. *The Homes of the New World*). What particularly distinguishes Fredrika Bremer among that company of foreign celebrities who in the nineteenth century visited America and recorded their impressions is that she was always intent upon seeing the United States "from within" — she insisted upon establishing direct contact with America's everyday life, meeting all classes of people, feeling the pulse-beat of its immediate ongoing existence. But sympathetic as she was toward America and Americans, she did not allow her enthusiasms to blur her critical sense, even when she was received, as she frequently was, by some of America's most distinguished citizens. Emerson, whom she met on several occasions, she admired greatly and praised highly, but his philosophical remoteness from life's pressing immediate problems distressed her — "I could desire in him warmer sympathies, larger interest in social questions that touch upon the well-being of mankind, and more feeling for the suffering and sorrowful on earth."

In addition to *The Homes of the New World* Fredrika Bremer published two other travel works, one on her two months' stay in England on her return trip to Sweden from the United States appeared in book form first in English under the title *England in 1851 or Sketches of a Tour in England* (1853), the other on her extensive travels of 1856–61 in Switzerland, Italy, and the Near East (*Lifvet i gamla verlden* [tr. *Life in the Old World*] 6 vols., 1860–62). The English observations reflect especially her advanced economic and social interests, the work on Continental and Near Eastern travels her search for a religious solution of the problems of modern man. In many ways the travel books, particularly *The Homes of the New World*, are Fredrika Bremer's most impressive works even from a literary point of view. In them her warm, lively intelligence finds a natural means of direct communication with the reader which has not lost its charm even today. Her novels by comparison are largely of literary-historical importance, serving in their time to provide the first significant impetus to a native Swedish tradition in realistic prose fiction with a strong sense of social conscience.

Born into a family of the higher middle classes, and extremely unhappy in the years of her young womanhood under the formal discipline of a tyrannical father, she came to write her first unassuming tales quite accidentally — in order to get funds to help finance what we today would call "social work" among the cottagers on her family's estate, Årsta, just south of Stockholm. These tales — *Teckninger utur hvardagslivet* (Sketches from Everyday Life, 1828) — attracted so much favorable attention that she soon found herself turning to a more ambitious form of prose fiction, the novel — first in *Familjen H...* (tr. *The H– Family*), which appeared in 1830–31 as the second and third volumes of Sketches from Everyday Life, and in the years which immediately followed four full-length novels, the most important of which were *Grannarne* (tr. *The Neighbors*, 1837) and *Hemmet* (tr. *The Home or Family Cares and Family Joys*, 1839). In later years her growing preoccupation with social problems had a deleterious effect on both the quality and quantity of her literary production, only two novels of some importance appearing after 1839, *Syskonlif* (tr. *Brothers and Sisters*, 1849) and the strenuous social pamphlet in fictional form *Hertha* (1856). That she wrote the first of these on the verge of her trip to America and the second just before she set out for her extended European travels explains why both of these novels are so exclusively concerned with social questions, particularly the place of women in modern society.

Though Fredrika Bremer managed to transfer into her novels from the 1830's some of the lightness of touch, the playful humor, and the realistic impressionism of her early "Sketches," she found on the whole the larger narrative form rather beyond her capacities. Even her best novels, *The Neighbors* and *The Home*, have an uneven quality, a tendency in the midst of an often admirable realism to yield to excessive moralizing and Romantic posing of one kind or another. She cannot, for instance, resist the temptation to introduce into *The Neighbors* a mysterious, demonic Byronic hero, and she is forced finally to resolve the central conflict by resorting to Romantic devices of the most dubious kind. In most other respects, however, *The Neighbors* provides us with a convincing picture of middle-class life on the Swedish countryside, employing with great effectiveness in the early chapters the epistolary manner of presentation, and creating in Ma chère mère her most magnificent character — a character which one suspects haunted Selma Lagerlöf's mind when she more than a half century later conceived the Major's Wife at Ekeby in *Gösta Berling's Saga*. Though Fredrika Bremer's other more important novel, *The Home*, has little of the broad humor, the genuine pathos, and the stylistic verve of *The Neighbors*, it impresses by the quiet force of its realism, by its probing psychological awareness (especially in the case of Petrea, a penetrating portrait of Fredrika Bremer herself as a young girl), and by its ability to restrict itself to the limited everyday world of an ordinary family's history. Its one serious fault is that it trudges on and on and on, being brought to an end finally by thematic exhaustion rather than by any clear-cut narrative necessity.

As a novelist Fredrika Bremer has been called "the Jane Austen of Sweden," a label which is entirely too complimentary, for she has only occasional flashes of Jane Austen's psychological penetration and none of the English novelist's stylistic finesse and coolly ironic view of the human scene. It is as a personality rather than as an author that Fredrika Bremer has contributed most profoundly to Swedish life and culture. But limited in some ways as were her literary talents, she had the creative vitality to lead the way in Sweden into a genre, the novel, which before her time had existed only as a kind of half-suspect stepchild in Swedish letters. What originally impressed readers and critics of her early "Sketches" was the spontaneity and directness of her prose style, a style worlds removed from the involved preciosity of the Romantics. To this literary virtue she added in her later novels an honest, everyday realism, a living attention to detail, and a high sense of the relation between the novel and the central practical problems of society. It is little wonder under the circumstances that she came to appreciate more than all others among Erik Gustaf Geijer's literary contemporaries the great Swedish poet-historian's "conversion" to the cause of social and political liberalism. She was Geijer's feminine counterpart on the Swedish literary scene in the early 1840's, sharing with Geijer what has aptly been called "Christian liberalism" and finding in the family, as Geijer did, the foundation of the modern state. One can but mention finally that Fredrika Bremer in the years after her death came to be the living symbol of the struggle for women's rights – and for recognition of women's responsibilities – in Sweden. The national women's organization in her land is named The Fredrika Bremer Society.

The first Swedish woman to follow Fredrika Bremer in the writing of prose fiction dealing with contemporary life was Sophie von Knorring (1797–1848), who first appeared in print with the novel *Cousinerna* (The Cousins) in 1834. For ten years she was unusually productive, pouring out novels at the rate of almost one a year, after which she wrote only occasionally until her early death in 1848. Her entire life was spent among the Swedish landed aristocracy, from which she had sprung and into which she married. Beautiful and talented, she had dreamed from early childhood of a brilliant marriage and an exalted social existence, but when in young womanhood circumstances forced her to settle down in the country on a social level considerably below her resplendent dreams she found an outlet for her frustrations in the writing of novels about her class.

That she had considerable literary talent was apparent from the outset. She was a keen observer of the life around her, could turn an elegant phrase in the best tradition of her class, and could within the limits of her subject matter spin an interesting tale without resorting to narrative trickery or padding her episodes with extraneous matter. The chief difficulty with her work was that it constantly circled around a single problem, the conflict between desire and duty under the pressures of erotic attraction. And conventional moralist that she was, duty always triumphed, no matter how tragic the fate of the dutiful. In *The Cousins* the lovely heroine, Amalia, wastes away and finally dies for love of the young Axel when her unfortunate *mariage de convenance* gets in the way of her real love; and the theme is repeated with variations in nearly all of Sophie von Knorring's later novels. Sadly as the aristocratic authoress observes these fates, she remains as a moralist always loyal to the conventions of her class, which was elegantly capable of savoring the frivolous conversation and the flirtatious action but withstood firmly any and all attacks on the inviolability of marriage. Both Sophie von Knorring's contemporaries and later critics have observed that there is something equivocal about her apparently pleasurable lingering over the theme of passion when in the end passion has no choice, must dutifully bow to social convention as frozen in the institution of an indissoluble marriage. A prisoner of her class, Sophie von Knorring finds all the answers to the erotic problem within the rigid outward conventions of this class, even while she allows herself in passing the sweet indulgence of many a sad tear over the inexorable fate of innocent young love caught in the web of fatal circumstance.

Inasmuch as Sophie von Knorring's views on love and marriage were directly opposed to those of Almqvist in *Sara Videbeck*, it was inevitable that she should write a novel which engaged Almqvist in debate on the marriage problem. This was done in *Torparen och hans omgivning* (tr. *The Peasant and His Landlord*, 1843), in which for once she departs from

the halls of the landed aristocracy and enters with a partly condescending sympathy into the humble huts of the folk. In this novel the cotter
Gunnar, obliged to marry Lena who had forced her attentions upon him
and borne a child presumably fathered by him, later falls in love with Elin
who reciprocates his feelings. But in keeping with Sophie von Knorring's
desire-duty formula the love of Gunnar and Elin remains "pure," neither
of them being prepared to break the marriage law even though Gunnar
comes to know that the country squire who set him and Lena up with a
household is the actual father of Lena's child. Complications pile up —
Gunnar finally kills the squire and is beheaded for the murder. How confused Sophie von Knorring's thinking could become is apparent from
her feeling that *such* a tale could be the answer to Almqvist's theories of
love and marriage. But aside from the fatuousness of her thinking in this
instance, *The Peasant and His Landlord* is a serious and often impressive
effort at literary treatment of folk life. Many critics, in fact, rank this
work as the best of Sophie von Knorring's novels, but others have with
considerable reason preferred *Illusionerna* (The Illusions, 1836), that
knowing little novel which probes with a deft satiric touch the vanities
and vagaries of life in Stockholm's high society.

Fredrika Bremer and Sophie von Knorring each in her way was a moralist, who neither could nor desired to emancipate story telling from the
serious pursuit of moral ends. In contrast Emilie Flygare-Carlén (1807–
92) as a born story teller was far more concerned in her novels with what
happens than with what should happen. Only occasionally in her best
novels is she concerned with social criticism. Usually she is intent simply
upon *depicting* the living ebb and flow of events within the range of her
immediate creative purposes. Despite her lower middle-class origins and
her natural feeling of solidarity with this class, she did not allow her literary work to become an instrument of social or political criticism except
insofar as her anti-aristocratic bias is reflected in some of her novels dealing with the privileged classes. There is on the whole in her work a kind
of objectivity much more related to a later naturalism than to the realistic
reform literature of her time.

Though the fastidious reader in her day as in ours has noted in her
novels an occasional drifting into Romantic excesses in characterization
and more than occasional lapses of one kind or other, the middle classes
of her day were so delighted with her novels that she rapidly amassed a
fortune in providing them with a literary fare to their tastes. She has been

called "the first professional Swedish author," that is to say a literary practitioner who sensed what her public wanted and produced accordingly.

Unusually productive, Emilie Flygare-Carlén began her literary career with a number of salon novels in the manner of Sophie von Knorring, but she turned soon (at times with the assistance of a brother) to tales dealing with the merchants and fisherfolk of her native Bohuslän, that primitive coastal region stretching south from the Norwegian border and facing the North Sea. Here she had grown up in the town of Strömstad, absorbing with the wide-eyed awareness of a gifted child the colorful miscellany of seafolk life which this district provided. To these experiences were added during her young womanhood a marriage, which ended after a few years with the death of her husband, and a passionate love affair which could not be consummated in marriage because of the sudden death of the man involved. Hers was not the sheltered early life of Fredrika Bremer or of Sophie von Knorring, nor was it a life in which more or less formal literary traditions played any role, and in consequence her novels came to be much closer than did those of the other two women novelists of her day to the immediate concrete realities of human existence.

Though the west-coast novels which are Emilie Flygare-Carlén's chief claim to fame are five in number, two in particular — *Rosen på Tistelön* (tr. *The Rose of Tistelön*, 1842) and *Ett köpmanshus i skärgården* (A Merchant House in the Archipelago, 1860–61) — are most important. In both of these novels an exciting, skillfully ramified plot provides a wholly adequate narrative frame in which the motley Bohuslän coastal world comes to life. Numerous as they are, the characters are vividly, often profoundly drawn, and the rugged sea-coast milieu in which they play out their roles is developed with a naturalistic intimacy and an imaginative sweep which have no counterparts in other Swedish fiction of the time. There is even something of genuine tragic greatness in the over-all conception of these novels, especially in *The Rose of Tistelön*, whose heavy tale of murder and retribution (never stooping to the twin literary vices of the age, sentimentalism and sensationalism) has some of the tragic sweep of ancient drama. These novels also impress the reader of today with their subtle psychological awareness, a sense of the irrational drives in human nature which has a definite ring of modernity. This is particularly true in the treatment of human passion in these novels. There was in Emilie Flygare-Carlén, one senses, literary potentialities of which she

219

herself was probably only dimly aware. It may be that her return to relatively innocuous forms of fiction after the arresting west-coast novels of her middle years involved a half-conscious reluctance on the novelist's part to face squarely the disturbing implications of a view of life often implicit in *The Rose of Tistelön*. Impressive as her work at times is, one has the feeling that she had resources as a novelist which she never fully exploited.

The same can scarcely be said of Emilie Flygare-Carlén's male counterparts in the prose fiction of the day, the most widely read of whom — C. A. Wetterbergh (pseud. Onkel Adam, 1804–89) and August Blanche (1811–68) — worked their literary veins to the limits of their capacities. Their talents were genuine enough within the confines of the short prose narrative genres, but when they attempted the serious novel they floundered hopelessly, frequently resorting in their desperation to obvious moralizing and / or sensationalism to justify their intentions and retain the reader's interest. Wetterbergh's most satisfactory work is the modest collection of satiric sketches *Genre-målningar* (Genre Paintings, 1842), in which a soberly observed reality (Wetterbergh was by profession a doctor) provides perfectly natural occasions for an ironic commentary on the fatuous and ugly aspects of the social and political scene. August Blanche, who has been called the Dumas *fils* of Sweden, had a rather fatal literary facility. In the 1840's he flooded the Swedish literary market with sensational moralizing novels and with popular theatrical pieces, the latter — in the main skillful Swedish adaptations of foreign comedies — being enormously successful with the not so fastidious bourgeois classes of the day. Blanche was the very incarnation of lower middle-class virtues, and in this respect he has his chief importance. Warm, ebullient, "folksy" in the best sense of the term, sentimentally liberal in his social and political views, he was the born spokesman for the mentality of a class which at the mid-century was making its position more and more felt in Sweden. Most of what he wrote is now of interest merely as a reflection of this mentality, and the taste which went along with it. Little of what he wrote has permanent literary importance. Only the picturesque Stockholm tales from Blanche's late years — the four series of "Bilder ur verkligheten" (Pictures from a Real World) published in the magazine *Illustrerad Tidning*, 1863–65 — can still be read with real pleasure. The most famous of the four series is *Hyrkuskens berättelser* (The Livery-Man's Tales), a series of warmly humorous portraits of a motley array of orig-

From *Stockholms Figaro*, 1846, a lithograph showing C. A. Wetterbergh, Fredrika Bremer, Emilie Flygare-Carlén, C. J. L. Almqvist, and G. H. Mellin

Satiric sketch by F. Öberg, 1856,
entitled "The Authoress
and Her Husband"

Sophie von Knorring, sketch by
Maria Röhl, 1842 (The Royal
Library, Stockholm)

Sketch by Fredrika Bremer, 1850, of an Indian village on
the Upper Mississippi (The Royal Library, Stockholm)

Johan Ludvig Runeberg (The
Royal Library, Stockholm)

Viktor Rydberg, portrait by Albert Edelfelt (photo: SPA)

Sketch of Carl Snoilsky as a young man by Severin
Falkman (photo: SPA)

inal Stockholm types as seen through the eyes of a lively livery-man whose occupation has brought him into a particular kind of contact with all levels of Stockholm life.

It may be mentioned in the present context that a generation before Blanche's day another worthy representative of a broad, humorous, middle-class realism, Fredrik Cederborgh (1784–1835), had written a couple of highly popular picaresque novels—*Uno von Trasenberg* (1809–10) and *Ottar Tralling* (1810–18)—in a vein which in some ways anticipates Blanche's sketches of Stockholm life. Though Cederborgh's early venture into a picturesque everyday realism delighted his host of readers, it was denounced by the fastidious New Romantic critics of his day. Appearing more than forty years after Cederborgh's most popular works, Blanche's sketches in a broadly similar vein found more favor with the critics. One of the indexes of a changing critical taste in the nineteenth century is that a middle-class Stockholm realism no longer needed to be particularly concerned with what the fastidious Uppsala New Romantic critics might think of their efforts to serve simple, unsophisticated literary tastes.

Toward the close of the year 1832 there appeared in the Swedo-Finnish newspaper *Helsingfors Morgonblad* an article which sharply castigated certain current literary trends of the day, particularly the tendency in Swedish poetry around 1830 to fall into overflorid rhetorical patterns in the manner of Tegnér. Partly because *Helsingfors Morgonblad* was a local Finnish newspaper with a limited circulation the article had no strong immediate repercussions in Sweden, but its incidental expression of a new, more simple and sober poetic ideal came to serve as a program for its author's own poetic development and to provide a healthy corrective for certain artificial mannerisms which had infected late phases of Romantic poetry in Sweden. The article was written by Johan Ludvig Runeberg (1804–77), who was to become the great national poet of Finland and who soon came to exercise a healthy, sobering influence on Swedish poetry, reflected in the tendency to eliminate those false rhetorical qualities which had so stubbornly persisted with variations down through several centuries, culminating in the many inadequate imitators of Tegnér, the great master of rhetorical verse. After Runeberg Swedish poets have employed rhetorical devices with due caution, even when tuning their lyres to elevated patriotic and religious themes.

It is one of the remarkable coincidences of literary history that just at the time when Finland was beginning to extricate itself from the centuries-long cultural hegemony of Sweden a Swedish-speaking Finnish poet should appear on the scene and presently become Finland's great national poet, a position which he has maintained unchallenged for more than a hundred years. In his formative years as a poet Runeberg was one of the most enthusiastic members of Lördagssällskapet (The Saturday Society), so-called because the group met informally on Saturday evenings to air their opinions on a great variety of subjects, the most actual of which was the necessity of preserving a Finnish national culture under the ominous shadow of the Russian political domination resulting from the War of 1808–9. "Swedes we cannot be," a Finnish patriot Adolf Iwar Arwidsson had said of Finland's position shortly after 1809 — "Russians we do not wish to become, we must in consequence be Finns." Such statements might have been interpreted as treasonable utterances, and Arwidsson found it expedient ultimately to emigrate to Sweden. Those patriots who remained in Finland sought to activate the Finnish national ideal without inciting political action, patiently biding their time while hoping that the day would come when political independence would crown their national efforts. They had to wait more than a hundred years. In the meantime the Finnish people nursed the flickering flame of national consciousness in various broadly cultural ways. Of central importance in these national cultural strivings was The Saturday Society. This group found in Herder's theories about national cultures the point of departure for their national program. They encouraged in every possible way research in matters concerned with Finnish folk culture, the matchless immediate result of which was the publication, in 1835–36, of the first version of the *Kalevala*, a unique national epic based on Elias Lönnrot's tireless collecting activities among the Finnish folk. Runeberg was tremendously interested in Lönnrot's work, and both before and after the publication of the *Kalevala* he employed frequently as the basic subject matter of his poetry the folk life of his country, without however attempting to invest his work with any purely imitative Kalevala qualities. The folk we come upon in Runeberg's poetry are the folk of the poet's own day, earth-bound, patient, quietly heroic — in their modest way worthy human "descendants" of the half-god, half-man Kalevala heroes but in no wise to be identified with them.

Runeberg's birthplace was Jakobstad, halfway up the west coast of Finland on the Gulf of Bothnia. He was of Swedish extraction, both on his father's and mother's sides. His father was a sea captain of some intellectual interests, his mother the daughter in a shipowning family of considerable means. But because of financial reverses and a stroke which incapacitated the father in 1821 at the age of forty-nine, Runeberg had to periodically interrupt his university education in order to earn sufficient funds to continue his work toward a degree. The lengthiest of these interruptions — spent as a private tutor on estates in Finland from late in 1823 to January of 1825 — was of the utmost importance to the future poet. Here for the first time he came in intimate contact with the vast wilderness stretches of inland Finland and the primitive folk life of these regions. How deeply moved he was by the experience is apparent in every line of the magnificent ethnographical essay from 1832, *Några ord om nejderna, folklynnet och levnadssättet i Saarijärvi socken* (Some Words on the Countryside, Folk Character, and Way of Life in the Saarijärvi Parish). He was impressed equally by land and folk, a land which in its quiet, lonely majesty had placed its worthy stamp upon a simple, hard-working, patiently heroic people. In the Saarijärvi years the Finnish national poet was born, though some time was to elapse before the young Runeberg shook off some of his private woes as well as certain extraneous literary modes and definitively found his way back to the Finnish folk.

Outwardly the years following the Saarijärvi sojourn were marked by the completion of work toward a degree, the beginnings of a pedagogical career, a happy marriage, and the publication, in 1830, of Runeberg's first volume of verse, *Dikter* (Poems). Inwardly these were years of considerable soul searching and an uncertain groping toward a poetic form best suited to Runeberg's poetic temperament. The disparate character of the pieces included in *Poems* reflects very clearly the uncertainty with which the poet was feeling his way toward a poetic program, and only in the section entitled "Idyll och epigram" (Idyls and Epigrams), in Runeberg's debut volume, can one discern the direction his poetry is to take in the future. Otherwise the volume is of some biographical interest, especially in the rather hectic poem "Svartsjukans nätter" (Nights of Jealousy), in which an erotic crisis is clad in some rather heavy poetic finery alternately reminiscent of Stagnelius and Edward Young. In "Idyls and Epigrams," however, Runeberg turns quite deliberately away from the luxuriant patterns and melancholy posing of Romantic verse toward a simpler, more spare and realistic poetic medium, largely under the spell of a group of Serbian folk songs which he had taken upon himself to turn into Swedish from the German version in which he had

223

discovered them. Most of the "Idyls and Epigrams" are highly concentrated episodic pieces the locale of whose action is quite indeterminate, but in a few of them, most notably in "Bonden Pavo" (The Peasant Pavo), the characters and scene of action are definitely Finnish. Pavo, sorely tried by a series of catastrophic crop failures, is Runeberg's first inspired portrait of the quiet heroism and natural piety of the Finns.

In various ways Runeberg pursued this Finnish thematic material during the bit more than a decade following upon the publication of his first volume of poetry — in the simple monumental manner of "The Peasant Pavo" in "Grafven i Perrho" (The Grave at Perrho) from 1831, and in larger contexts and with greater attention paid to backgrounds and ethnographical detail in the three extended narrative sequences *Elgskyttarne* (The Elk Hunters, 1832), *Hanna* (1836), and *Julkvällen* (Christmas Eve, 1841). Of the longer poems *The Elk Hunters* and parts of *Christmas Eve* are the most impressive, the former for its lively, at times primitive poetic realism and for its sly undertow of humor, the latter especially for its stirring final tribute to Old Pistol, pensioned veteran of many campaigns, who faces his last years erect and unshaken in spirit despite the news of the death of his only son on a distant battlefield. Offered at the last a comfortable refuge on the estate of the Major under whom he had served in battle, Old Pistol refuses, humble yet proud, prepared to return to his wilderness hut and there face alone the last joust with death in the same spirit as he had served his nation in the years of his manhood's strength. The Major is moved, deeply moved, proud of his old comrade in arms whose will is in no way bent by sorrow and the heavy accumulation of years:

> Finland stood there before him, the bleak, lone, poverty-smitten, idolized land of his birth; and the gray-clad ranks from Lake Saima's shore, the delight of his life, the men he had once been so proud of, marched in review before him, with brothers-in-arms as aforetime — surly, calm, unpretentious, with iron-firm faith in their bosoms.

In these lines the unhurried, earth-bound movement of Runeberg's hexameters (the metrical pattern used in all of his early narrative poems) quickens its pace, lifts itself to an exalted, visionary, hymn-like level, the level of the patriotic anthem. These lines — and for that matter the whole Pistol world in *Christmas Eve* — are a kind of preliminary sketch for the broad, heroic narrative patterns of *Fänrik Ståls sägner* (tr. *The Tales of Ensign Stål*), the incomparable poetic gift to the fatherland which Runeberg was later to pen.

But before he turned to the world of Fänrik Stål he occupied himself with other matters, incidentally with religious controversy, more importantly with literary composition which tended to depart for the time being from his concern with the Finnish folk.

In 1837 Runeberg had settled down not far to the east of Helsingfors in the small city of Borgå, where he taught first Latin and later Greek for twenty years before his retirement in 1857. In December 1863, he had a stroke which kept him bedridden until his death more than thirteen years later. He came with the years to be quite happy in Borgå despite the fact that he had originally moved there because of disappointment in seeking a university post in Helsingfors. His teaching duties were relatively light, allowing him to devote much time to his poetry. Opportunities for social intercourse were sufficient, and he could indulge as he pleased in his favorite sports, hunting and fishing in the areas adjacent to Borgå. So satisfactory, indeed, were the conditions of his life at Borgå that Runeberg never left the town and its environs except for occasional visits to Helsingfors and one or two other Finnish towns and a trip to Sweden, the summer of 1851, where he was so overwhelmingly feted that on his roundabout return journey to Borgå he wrote to a friend: "I am utterly tired of all this world's splendors and yearn for porridge, fish, and quiet at Kroksnäs [his summer place near Borgå]." Pleasant as Runeberg usually found social intercouse, Stockholm hospitality was too much for him. Though the Borgå years were in the main outwardly uneventful, they were not without some inner conflicts, especially of an erotic kind, and they were the years when in such works as *Kung Fjalar* (tr. *King Fjalar*) and *The Tales of Ensign Stål* Runeberg's creative flame burned with its most sustained and brilliant glow.

The first years in Borgå, however, were years which from a literary point of view were relatively fallow, yielding aside from some short pieces only *Christmas Eve*, which is the last of the idyls in hexameters, and *Nadeschda*, a rather slight poetic narrative on a Russian theme. In some ways the most interesting piece from the early Borgå years is the prose piece *Den gamle trädgårdsmästarens brev* (The Old Gardener's Letters), in which Runeberg attacks the pietistic asceticism which at the time was fastening its dark tentacles on Finland, finding converts even among the educated classes. The issues involved were of the utmost importance to the deeply religious Runeberg, who reacted with all the healthy intensity of his being against the pietistic insistence that the flesh and all the things of this world were evil. To Runeberg the flesh was

225

good, our natural instincts the voice of God within us, the whole world of nature a part of God's ultimate revelation. To Runeberg evil existed, but not, as the pietists insisted, as the very condition of existence. The good life to Runeberg was to live in harmony with the world rather than to deny it by flaying the flesh while indulging in dark, fanatical, essentially inhuman incantations. Such are the ideas contained in *The Old Gardener's Letters*. Though it had not been Runeberg's custom to give pointed expression to religious ideas in his poetry, the controversy with the pietists resulted in two poems, "Kyrkan" (The Church) and "Chrysanthos," in which his idealistic religious humanitarianism was given clear expression. And in a broader sense the religious and ethical considerations central in two of Runeberg's major works *King Fjalar* and *Kungarne på Salamis* (The Kings on Salamis) derive more or less directly from the poet's concern with religious problems which first had taken on the controversial prose form of *The Old Gardener's Letters*. *King Fjalar* appeared in 1844, *The Kings on Salamis* not in complete form until 1863 though three acts were written immediately after the completion of *King Fjalar*.

Of these two works *The Kings on Salamis* is a reasonably successful modern attempt to write a Classical tragedy, while *King Fjalar*, a more important work, approximates Classical tragedy in certain ways without slavishly imitating the older dramatic form. In fact, *King Fjalar* is a remarkably impressive experiment in the blending of narrative and dramatic elements. Outwardly the work consists of a series of five narrative episodes which Runeberg calls "Songs," but these episodes are so charged with dramatic life and move so inexorably toward a terrifying tragic denouement that they reflect the spirit of Greek tragedy much more adequately than most modern imitations of Classical drama. Of the Greek tragedies *King Fjalar* resembles most Sophocles' *Oedipus the King*, from which it borrows with some variations such matters as the incest motif and the conception of man's fate as being ultimately determined not by his own will but by decisions of the Gods. A Romantic richness of texture has been added to Runeberg's tragedy of the ancient Nordic King of Gauthiod by introducing the fateful struggle of the King's son Hjalmar with King Morannal's sons on Morven soil of Ossianic fame. Though critics for more than a hundred years have expressed reservations about Runeberg's handling of the Oedipean and Ossianic materials, these reservations are admittedly of secondary importance beside the over-all impression of monumental tragic greatness which *King Fjalar* leaves with even the most discriminating reader. Critics with hardly an exception have adjudged *King Fjalar* as the incomparably most impressive tragic work in the Classical spirit which has come from a Scandinavian pen. Almost equally agreed are the critics in the opinion that *King Fjalar* is Runeberg's greatest work, though some would place *The Tales of Ensign Stål* — a quite different kind of work — on the same general level of poetic attainment as *King Fjalar*. In the light of the differing intentions of the two works it would seem fatuous to choose between the two, except on a purely personal basis. Each is in its way as close to perfection as one has the right to expect.

The incubation period of *The Tales of Ensign Stål* was unusually long. Many years elapsed before Runeberg settled down to the task of bringing to life the hapless but heroic story of his nation's tragic struggle against superior forces in the War of 1808–9. Not until 1848 could his public read in book form the first group of these tales, eighteen in all, and twelve more years were to pass before the seventeen additional pieces were completed and the definitive edition of the work appeared. But Runeberg's interest in the material of his *Tales* went far back in time. As a small boy he had seen on the streets of Jakobstad two of the most colorful figures of the Finno-Russian campaigns, von Döbeln and the jovial Russian Kulneff, and during Runeberg's early manhood at Saarijärvi and Ruovesi he heard tales of the War from Finns who had taken part in it. And in the years which followed he had countless occasions to add to his store of material, for everywhere in Finland tales of military heroism from the closing years of the first decade of the century were treasured by high and low alike among the people of the land. In 1836 and 1837 Runeberg attempted a novel about the War, but the attempt was abortive and the work remained a fragment. Here and there also in Runeberg's poetry from these years we catch passing glimpses of the poet's concern with the memories from 1808–9, most significantly, as we have seen, in the figure of Old Pistol in *Christmas Eve*, but also in scattered shorter poems such as "Molnets broder" (The Cloud's Brother) which are to become included in *The Tales of Ensign Stål* even though in their original conception they were presumably not written for inclusion in the *Tales*. The catalytic agent which finally plunged the poet shortly after the completion of *King Fjalar* into writing the *Tales* seems to have been a Borgå bookseller's suggestion that Runeberg prepare the text for an illustrated work on the heroes of the war of a generation before. Such a work seemed at the time especially desirable because of the general interest in the subject aroused by the appearance in 1842 of G. A. Montgomery's *Historia öfver kriget emellan Sverige och Ryssland åren 1808 och 1809* (History of the War between Sweden and Russia, 1808–9). Though the proposed illustrated work did not materialize, Runeberg was ripe for the task of putting into worthy verse form the most representative tales from the war years, and he began turning out in rapid succession a series of poems which by 1848 numbered eighteen, the series included in the narrative poetic cycle of the first edition of *The Tales of Ensign Stål*. The remaining seventeen were produced more slowly, not being finished until more than a decade later.

Popular as Runeberg's narrative poetic idyls from the 1830's had been, they were completely overshadowed by the acclaim with which *The Tales of Ensign Stål* was received – and not only because of the patriotic theme of the *Tales*. The new work was in every way a superior product. The leisurely, at times monotonous hexameters of the idyls were replaced in the *Tales* by a fascinating variety of metrical and stanzaic forms. The relatively static descriptive quality of the earlier narrative poems gave way to variety and depth in character portrayal and to the rapid dramatic drive and movement of the *Tales*. The somewhat oversweet "realism" of the idyls was abandoned for a bracing world of sweat and blood, of hapless struggle and wild despair, lighted up by moments of supreme valor and heroism. And many of the *Tales* are invested with a warm, engaging humor – broad or sly or elegant or gently ironic by turn, seldom satiric, negative, or critical.

Whether the Ensign Stål who is represented as the teller of the tales has any equivalent in reality we do not know. In all probability he is a fictive figure some of whose characteristics have been taken from certain veterans of the War whom Runeberg had met in his youth. The other characters included in the tales are in part historical personages and in part types representing those qualities of valor and warm humanity which the poet assumed were characteristic of the army and the folk. A constantly recurring theme in the *Tales* is the democratic relation between the common soldier and the officer, a kind of patriarchal relationship which under wartime conditions had been carried over from civilian to military matters. Though the *Tales* deal predominantly with the heroism of both officers and men in the ranks, they reflect at times also a bitter awareness of the weakness of the highest echelon of command, and one of the poems is a furious castigation of treachery in high places – on the surrender of Sveaborg, the proud "Gibraltar of the North."

Modern investigations have demonstrated that Runeberg's depiction of the War was not a little idealized, that the poet's rather exclusive preoccupation with the heroic exploits of the Finnish forces tends to make of the War of 1808–9 something prettier than it actually was — a badly organized and weakly led campaign in which the Swedo-Finnish forces were almost constantly retreating and in which the outcome was nearly from the outset a foregone humiliating defeat. But to Runeberg such realistic concerns were relatively unimportant, or, rather, they served merely to draw into sharper relief a central doctrine of the poet's thinking — that men in certain crucial moments of their experience have the capacity to rise above their normal limitations, become one with the ideal forces of existence. In a citizenry's readiness to sacrifice all for the fatherland Runeberg saw men in active communion with God. Because such a doctrine has been viciously exploited in larger than Finnish contexts by bloody supernationalists of a later day should not blind us to the fact that in the case of little Finland, a century ago, the doctrine served to add strength and dignity to its valiant struggle for national survival. Patriotism need not be a crudely egotistical destructive agent in man's search for the better life.

The popularity which Runeberg had gained among his people long before the appearance of *The Tales of Ensign Stål* became transformed into veneration after the publication of the *Tales*, and this veneration has continued down to our day. Borgå, where the *Tales* were composed, became a place of pilgrimage, the poet a legendary figure around whom a "Runeberg cult" has for generations worshiped — often to the discouragement of those who wish to discover the man behind the national saint, of those who are concerned with disentangling the poet's literary and intellectual orientation from his relations to the congeries of emotional associations typical of the Finnish national temper in Runeberg's time. Modern scholarship has confirmed our suspicions that the poet was more dependent on contemporary philosophical speculation and literary trends of foreign origin than had formerly been assumed and that in his personal relations Runeberg was not quite the serene and harmonious character conjured up by some devotees of the "Runeberg cult." One should add, however, that such scholarly demonstrations do not radically change our picture either of the man or the poet. They serve merely to remove from the Runeberg portrait its purely cultish lines and restore to view the man and poet as he actually was, deeply human in both his eruptive and serene moments, a worthy national poet of a noble and courageous people.

Only one of Runeberg's Swedish contemporaries, Viktor Rydberg (1828–95), can be ranked with the Swedo-Finnish poet in literary importance during the years immediately after the middle of the nineteenth century. In certain general respects the two poets resemble each other — in a crystal-clear poetic style inspired in part by Classical ideals, in firmness and basic solidity of character, in a profoundly felt religious idealism, in the influential role which each played in the total cultural life of his nation. But in two respects particularly Rydberg differs rather sharply from his fellow poet across the Baltic: he was a much more complex and many-sided spirit, given to periods of sharp depression; and he was not destined to dominate so completely as Runeberg his nation's cultural scene, in part because he came upon the scene at a time when certain extremist realistic trends in life and thought tended to make an older idealism seem dated and ineffectual. Though Rydberg struggled intelligently and courageously with the problems of his day, he met the challenge of these problems in terms that only the educated few could really understand and appropriate. His idealism fought a noble but increasingly hopeless rear-guard action against the scientific materialism, the philosophical utilitarianism, and the social and political radicalism of the second half of the nineteenth century.

But Rydberg was by no means a reactionary, and in his early years he was looked upon by many as a radical, particularly in his religious views. The circumstances of his childhood, youth, and early manhood led quite naturally to a liberalism bordering on radicalism. When he was scarcely six he became an object of charity in consequence of the death of his mother and the breakup of the family. Because of the intellectual promise which he early exhibited, he had a schooling of sorts, but poverty permitted him to spend only a year at the University of Lund. Before his short university sojourn he had been involved for some years in journalistic activities in his home town of Jönköping, where for the radical newspaper *Jönköpingsbladet* he turned out sensational serial novels tinged with liberal ideas in the manner of the day. The crucial event in his life occurred in 1855, when he accepted a position on the staff of the west-coast liberal newspaper *Göteborgs Handels- och Sjöfartstidning*. For this newspaper he wrote general political and cultural articles and serialized novels which in historical guise became increasingly concerned with religious and philosophical points of view aimed at modern Swedish conditions. Not until 1862, however, did Rydberg's work attract any great general attention — when he published *Bibelns lära om Kristus* (The

Teaching of the Bible about Christ), an attack on the dogma of the divinity of Christ. The scholarly investigations involved in this work drove Rydberg more and more deeply into wide-ranging humanistic studies and resulted in a number of learned dissertations. In 1876 he had forsaken journalism for the public lecture platform when offered a post as lecturer on cultural history in Göteborg, and in 1884 he became a professor in the same field at the newly established University of Stockholm, which position he held until his death eleven years later. Meantime he had become the ranking poet of his day with two volumes of *Dikter* (Poems, 1882, 1891) and was honored outwardly in many ways, serving as a member of Parliament, being elected to the Swedish Academy, and receiving an honorary doctor's degree from the University of Uppsala. Among Swedish poets only Geijer can be compared with Rydberg in many-sided accomplishments and in the high general regard each maintained among his contemporaries. But while Geijer's path led from conservatism to liberalism, Rydberg's led to a partial rejection of an early radicalism and toward a humanistic idealism not always in step with the more advanced developments of his day.

Though Rydberg was the most intellectual and scholarly of Swedish poets, he was also by nature a man of feeling, moved easily by the fantastic and the mysterious, something, indeed, of a mystic. His insistence that reason is man's primary way to truth in no wise led him to belittle the role of feeling and intuition in human experience. In the history of Swedish literature Rydberg was essentially a late-born Romantic, but the most intellectual of the Romantics, pursuing with a sharper, more critical dialectic than earlier Swedish poets the speculative idealism of nineteenth-century thought without divesting himself of the mystical yearning, the exoticism, and the feeling for the past so typical of an earlier Romanticism. Even Rydberg's liberalism was essentially an off-shoot of the Platonic idealism of early nineteenth-century thought. But these Romantic strains in Rydberg's hands underwent a firm disciplinary process, became as it were sublimated and purified, cleansed of their more excessive and fatuous manifestations, brought into the focus of a subtly critical creative mind. The finest fruits of this disciplinary process are the poems of the 1870's and 1880's. Not until Rydberg was nearly fifty did his poetic vein begin to flow freely and magnificently — and then, paradoxically, at a time when Swedish literature was moving generally in other directions than those indicated by Rydberg's rejuvenation of a Romantic speculative idealism.

231

Meantime Rydberg was feeling his way forward in prose forms — in the historical novel and the extended controversial essay. His serialized novels from the late 1840's and the 1850's (the best of which is *Fribytaren på Östersjön*, tr. *The Freebooter on the Baltic*) combined liberal social criticism with narrative intrigue of a picturesque, often sensational kind, but in *Singoalla* (tr. *Singoalla, A Medieval Legend*, 1857) he managed to rise above the level of cheap sensationalism into a world of sheer Romantic fantasy. This tale of fourteenth-century Sweden centers upon a fateful mutual attraction between Singoalla, a lovely gipsy girl, and a handsome young knight, Erland Månesköld. It is a tale loaded with exotic and mysterious elements, colorful and intense, delicate and brutal by turn, with a profound awareness of those blind, irrational undercurrents of life which may lead man to his tragic destruction even while he is responding to the lovely spell of beauty and the innocent fascination of young love. How deeply attached Rydberg remained throughout his life to the world of youthful dark-stained fantasy which he conjured up in *Singoalla* is illustrated by the care with which he revised the text of the tale in the new editions of 1865, 1876, and 1894, the year before his death. In the years of his maturity he repeatedly referred to the tale as "my favorite child." Of Romantic tales from Swedish pens only Almqvist's *The Queen's Jewel* ranks with *Singoalla* in the subtle reconstruction of the strangely ominous play of natural forces in a beautiful world of the past.

While *Singoalla* is so steeped in sheer poetry that its ideas do not in the last analysis emerge with any clarity and consistency, two of Rydberg's other historical novels, *Den siste athenaren* (tr. *The Last Athenian*, 1859) and *Vapensmeden* (The Armourer, 1891), are works in which Rydberg the *thinker* asserts himself in terms which are relatively free from distracting Romantic moods and backgrounds. Both of these works are deliberately polemic, attacking certain forms of Christianity as represented respectively in the Early Church of fourth-century Greece and in the Lutheran Protestantism of sixteenth-century Sweden. But of the two novels *The Last Athenian*, written in the restive years of Rydberg's young manhood, is the more sharply polemic. "While writing," Rydberg announces in the Preface, "I have felt like a soldier under the banner of ideas for which I breathe and live, and my work is nothing else than a spear which I have thrown against the ranks of the enemy in the warrior's permissible intent to wound and to kill." Fanaticism, intolerance, and dogmatism are the "enemy" against which Rydberg flings his "spear" in his depiction of a barbaric early Christian church riding roughshod over the last noble descendants of Hellenic culture — and he makes it sufficiently clear that a nineteenth-century Christianity shared in certain ways the bloodguilt of the fanaticism and intolerance of an earlier day. In *The Last Athenian* Rydberg is a fighting humanist defending a tolerant Hellenic view of life against a bigoted, power-hungry religious dogmatism. To him the triumph of Christianity over Hellenism, an Eastern-Oriental mysticism over the serene rationalism of a Western-Greek humanism, was a tragedy whose shadows still lingered in the nineteenth century. With time Rydberg came to modify his views somewhat, as can be seen in *The Armourer*, where two kinds of Christianity rather than Hellenism and Christianity confront each other; but it is clear in this novel that a dogma-free humanistic form of Christianity is the religious and philosophical ideal of Rydberg's last years.

The polemic thrusts of *The Last Athenian* aroused no serious outcry among Rydberg's readers, but the same cannot be said of the response to Rydberg's next work, *The Teachings of the Bible about Christ* (1862), in which the doctrines of the Trinity and the divinity of Christ are challenged as having no basis in biblical texts and should therefore have no place in Protestant Lutheran religious teachings. Based on a minute investigation of pertinent biblical texts and related religious literature, Rydberg's work had a profound influence on the educated classes of the day and has had a central place in determining the religious attitudes of these classes in Sweden down to the present time. The Swedish Church had been an object of various attacks in the past, particularly in the eighteenth century, but never before had its doctrinal position been seriously challenged. The controversy with churchmen and theologians which Rydberg's work occasioned necessitated a number of new editions (three in all) of the work, each an expansion and further documentation of the original argument of the first edition. That the time was ripe for a successful challenge of Church dogma in Sweden was evident outside Rydberg's *Teachings of the Bible about Christ* in a number of ways, most strikingly in the appearance two years later of a pamphlet by Christoffer Jacob Boström entitled *Anmärkningar om helvetesläran* (Observations on the Doctrine of Hell). Had Rydberg been open to attack as an upstart journalistic radical, the instance of Boström, Sweden's enormously influential, politically conservative philosopher, made the case against Rydberg's "radicalism" quite untenable. Besides, it was clear to all but the most bigoted that Rydberg's position was that of a deeply religious mind, concerned simply with clearing out an excessive undergrowth of theological thought in order to make Christianity more acceptable to enlightened modern minds.

The studies in cultural and religious history that produced *The Last Athenian* and *The Teachings of the Bible about Christ* led Rydberg, in the years which followed, into extensive investigations in related matters. These investigations resulted in such works as *Medeltidens magi* (tr. *The Magic of the Middle Ages*, 1864), which attempts to demonstrate that the Christian dogma of eternal hell derives from medieval magical formulae of non-Christian origins, and two works on Germanic mythology, *Undersökningar i germanisk mytologi* (tr. in part under the title *Teutonic Mythology*, 1886, 1889) and *Fädernas gudasaga, berättad för ungdomen* (On the Myths of Our Forefathers, Related for the Young, 1887), which in respectively learned and popular forms cover the subjects which their titles suggest. These works reflect a gradual shift of interests on Rydberg's part away from broadly inclusive European religious and cultural subjects to the ancient Gothic-Germanic world, and the new focus of Rydberg's scholarly interests led him to appreciate more and more the significance of primitive Germanic culture for modern life. Not only are these new Germanic interests reflected in the subject matter and to a lesser extent in the form of Rydberg's poetry from these years; they also find expression in a theory of stylistic purism which proposed a radical elimination from the Swedish language of what Rydberg called "the French-German-Danish slag" with which "our golden native speech" had become loaded in the course of centuries. Though there was no general enthusiasm among Rydberg's contemporaries for his language proposals, he himself put his theories into practice, at times with rather awkward results.

Impressive as is Rydberg's contribution in various prose genres, he is considerably more important as a poet. When relatively late in life (in the mid-1870's) his poetic vein began to yield its treasures, it flowed with a clear, strong, often majestic power. His chief distinction as a poet is the all but unique perfection with which he handled the philosophical poem, a genre which for more than a century had been assiduously cultivated by Swedish poets, at times with some success, more frequently with a fatal flair for mere abstraction and rather empty rhetorical bombast. Rydberg rejuvenated the genre by clothing it in verse forms at once varied and highly disciplined and by pouring into these forms a highly sensitive awareness of the mystery and drama of human fate. As the last great Swedish poet-idealist he brought to the genre all of the resources of his massive learning together with an ethical high-mindedness of rare and compelling power.

The world of ideas which gave weight and soaring elevation to his poetry derived originally from Rydberg's extensive familiarity with Classical and Christian religious thought, but that which was primarily responsible for his turning to poetry as a medium of expressing his moods and ideas seems to have been the spell of Goethe's *Faust*, which off and on for more than a decade challenged his critical interpretative capacities and which appeared in his Swedish version in 1875. Among other poets who simultaneously fascinated Rydberg were Shelley and Poe, the latter's technique of repetition and weird powers of poetic suggestion having a special fascination for the Swedish poet. Rydberg's translation of "The Raven" has been judged as brilliant as Poe's original.

In matters of form Rydberg's poetry has little of the rhetorical formalism of traditional philosophical poetry. He sketches an episode, relates a story, creates a fragment of dramatic dialogue — each of which brings into a living, vital focus the idea which a given poem is meant to clarify. Only in poems for special occasions, such as the magnificent "Cantata" for the four hundredth anniversary of the founding of Uppsala University, does Rydberg employ a rigid traditional form. Otherwise he clothes his ideas in a great variety of forms — in the heroic half-Hellenic, half-Gothic garments of "Dexippos," or in the quiet meditative measures of "I klostercellen" (In the Cloister Cell), or in the free, reminiscent strophes of "Träsnittet i psalmboken (The Wood-Engraving in the Psalm Book), or in the clear, warmly humorous stanzas of "Tomten" (The House-Goblin). Often he employs mythological motifs as the structural core of his poems, particularly in poems of larger philosophical and religious implications such as "Den flygande holländaren" (The Flying Dutchman), "Prometeus och Ahasverus," and "Den nya Grottesången" (The New Song of Grotti).

Though at times he employs verse for little other purpose than to give expression to a Romantic mood of yearning or restlessness or vaguely mystical contemplation, he usually uses poetry for more active and profound purposes — to give (as in the Uppsala "Cantata") more or less direct expression to his faith in ideal values, in the indestructible, eternal validity of the beautiful vision, the good deed, the virtuous intent.

> Thy noble thoughts, thy acts of love, thy dreams
> Of beauty — these Time never can devour.

Eternity like some great store-house teems
  With sheaves safe-garnered from destruction's power.
Go forth, Mankind! be glad, thy cares at rest,
Thou bear'st Eternity within thy breast.

Translated by C. W. Stork

With the years Rydberg's early view of the essentially antipathetic relation between Hellenism and Christianity came to be modified, so that in his poetry — in "Prometeus och Ahasverus" particularly — Hellenism and Christianity undergo something of a reconciliation. Simultaneously Rydberg's idealism comes to grips with the philosophical materialism of the late nineteenth century in its various scientific and political ramifications. In "The New Song of Grotti," a poem of violently restive orchestration, he pours out his indignation over the brutal egotism of modern industrialism, castigating both the industrialists who sop their consciences with laissez-faire theories and the rising socialist-labor movement whose program for the future seemed built on merely materialistic foundations. Rydberg's liberalism could not in the last analysis identify itself with the more radical drift of certain late nineteenth-century developments in Sweden. As a member of a jury passing judgment in 1888 on two young labor leaders accused of blasphemy Rydberg voted "Guilty." Hjalmar Branting, who a generation later was to become the first and most distinguished Social-Democratic prime minister, was one of the two young labor leaders. Rydberg's action aroused a storm of protest among the more advanced liberals and became an object of sharp, at times acrimonious, debate among his countrymen. To some he was in his last years admired as "the patriarch of Swedish poetry," to others he was looked upon as a pitiful renegade to the liberal faith of his youth. If today the term "patriarch" as applied to Rydberg's last years seems unfortunate because of its overly conservative connotations, the label "renegade" is certainly unfair in its suggestion that Rydberg had at the last been unfaithful to his early liberalism.

Aside from Runeberg and Rydberg only one Swedish poet, Carl Snoilsky, managed to rise clearly above a modest level of literary attainment during the mid-century and the immediately succeeding decades. The period seemed to prefer prose, and though poets were common enough at the time, neither the level of their talents nor the ideas or events of their day were sufficiently vital to generate any really memorable verse. On two occasions a general poetic flowering seemed imminent, but in both instances the flowering was fleeting and the harvest scant and of little if any permanent importance. In the 1840's a pan-Scandinavian movement emanating from a student group at the University of Lund and feeding on nationalistic trends of the day resulted in a poetic flare-up of some interest, but the phenomenon was short-lived, and its chief poet, C. V. A. Strandberg (pseud. Talis Qualis, 1818–77), soon settled down to a respectable bourgeois existence, permitting himself the luxury of pursuing revolutionary ideas at second hand by translating Byron. Pan-Scandinavianism appealed to both nationalistic and liberal enthusiasms of the day and aroused considerable sympathy in Sweden and Norway for Denmark's struggle against the rising power of Prussia. It was, however, an abortive movement because a sober majority opinion in Sweden was not prepared in the face of political realities to respond actively to the stirring verse of warm-blooded (some said "hot-headed") university youth.

In the 1860's another youthful literary flowering occurred, this time at the University of Uppsala, and though its poetic ramifications were more elaborate than those of the earlier pan-Scandinavian group they were not very much more important. The prophet of the Uppsala group, Lorentz Dietrichson, was an energetic young university lecturer hailing from Norway. The group called itself somewhat self-consciously "Namnlösa Sällskapet" (The Nameless Society), but to the general public its members came to be known as "Signaturerna" (The Signatures) from the title of their first publication *Sånger och berättelser av nio signaturer* (Songs and Tales by Nine Signatures, 1863). Under Dietrichson's leadership they foreswore Tegnérian rhetoric in favor of Runebergian simplicity and realism. Unfortunately, their "simplicity" and "realism" too often amounted merely to an idyllicism bordering on infantilism. Most of the young poets of the "Signature" coterie soon disappeared from the literary scene, reconciling themselves to various ordinary roles in life after the youthful forays into poetic creation of their student days. After their departure from Uppsala only three of the coterie played any part in Swedish literature: Edvard Bäckström (1841–86), whose elegiac lyricism attracted some readers and whose slight historical play *Dagward Frey* was performed in the 1870's when Strindberg's *Master Olof* failed to satisfy the prevailing theatrical taste; Carl David af Wirsén (1842–1912), who as a very active poet-critic became with the years the most persistent and reactionary opponent of the new realistic currents in late nineteenth-century Swedish literature; and – Carl Snoilsky (1841–1903) – the only one of the group whose poetic talents were of a significantly high order and who had the courage in the years of his early maturity to attempt a radical break with the essentially backward-looking Romantic practices of the "Signature" poets.

Snoilsky's origins were socially exclusive. On his father's side he descended from Slovenian Protestant stock, one of whose representatives joined the forces of Gustavus Adolphus during the Thirty Years' War and took up residence in Sweden at the close of the War. On his mother's side Snoilsky was of Banér blood, whose genealogical ramifications were among the most illustrious of the Swedish aristocracy. An only child, whose mother died when he was scarcely fifteen, his father when he was eighteen, Snoilsky bore a Count's title and was destined upon attaining his maturity to pursue a diplomatic career. This career, beginning when he was twenty-five and closing thirteen years later when he had grown desperately weary of the stuffy conventions of high society, was preceded and followed by periods of rich poetic productivity. Even before his student days at Uppsala he had written verse, but not until he became a member of the "Signature" group was he sufficiently encouraged in his literary ambitions to turn seriously to poetry. Within this group he was very active and was looked upon as the group's most promising poetic talent.

But it was not until his departure from Uppsala for an extended Continental tour in 1864 that his poetry almost overnight burst into full bloom. It was a poetry of jubilant youthfulness — sensuous, elegant, borne by contagiously lilting rhythms and impertinently carefree moods. The famous "Inledningssång" (Introductory Song) sets the tone of these poems:

> I stand with roses beside the highway,
>   I pour you beakers of foaming wine;
> On every path and on every by-way
>   I rouse the tambour to rapture fine.
>
> No vapid fictions of dream I bring you,
>   No empty visions for your behoof;
> The world of beauty I fain would sing you
>   My own five senses have put to proof.
>
> Ye learned sages, ye over-cunning,
>   The wares I have to your taste are few.
> You, heart of twenty with blood warm-running,
>   My song will surely accord with you.
>
> Come, heart that thrills in its every fibre,

That loves a tale when 'tis briefly told;
Follow to Brent, yea, and to the Tiber,
Whenever the North may seem too cold.

Translated by C. W. Stork

Such heady poetic wine cast a magic spell over Snoilsky's young Uppsala friends when he sent the first of the "Italian Pictures" to them, and even enchanted an older generation of Swedes when the poems appeared in print, originally in the Signature collection *Sånger och berättelser* (Songs and Tales, 1865), later, and definitively, in *Dikter* (Poems, 1869), the first full volume of Snoilsky's verse to be published. Aside from the breathtaking technical perfection of the verse, what particularly intrigued Snoilsky's contemporaries in the "Italian Pictures" was the poet's refusal to become involved in speculative profundities or to be weighed down by the impressive historical associations of the Italian scene. Not the Italy of ancient traditions and art treasures, but rather the living everyday world of contemporary Italy engages the poet's interest. He seems completely absorbed in what *the moment alone* yields through his "five senses." And on those occasions when the Italian poems do become engaged with historical matters, they celebrate the immediate events of Italian history, Italy's national awakening under Garibaldi, a political phenomenon which arouses Snoilsky's admiration as a link in the chain of the poet's earlier enthusiasm for Poland's and Denmark's struggles for survival against Russia and Prussia.

The "Italian Pictures" bore the mark of sparkling youthful integrity, but these were the last of Snoilsky's poems to bear this mark. Upon Snoilsky's return to Sweden he adjusted himself dutifully to the position in life for which outwardly he seemed destined. He entered the diplomatic service, married advantageously, and attempted to satisfy his sensitive cultural urges by collecting rare books and coins. As a poet he remained silent for nearly a decade after the appearance in 1869 of *Poems* and the publication two years later of *Sonetter* (Sonnets), a volume whose elegantly correct surface only partly concealed persistently recurrent notes of half-expressed frustration and grief, even of bitterness. It is clear to us now though it may not have been to contemporaneous readers of the *Sonnets* that Snoilsky was already during these years growing increasingly restive under the rigid conventionalism of his life; and in 1879 he scandalized Swedish high society by resigning from his diplomatic post, divorcing his wife, remarrying, and settling down on the Continent. Released from the frustrations of the false position in which he had become involved, and inspired in his work by the sensitive and understanding partner of his second marriage, Snoilsky again turned to poetry, three volumes of his verse appearing in the years 1881, 1883, and 1887.

Though the most striking feature of this new poetic production was its effort to identify itself with those literary trends of the 1880's which championed the cause of the underprivileged, Snoilsky's lyric vein was also preoccupied during these years with Swedish historical themes in a series of poetic vignettes, appearing at various times and ultimately collected under the title *Svenska bilder* (Swedish Pictures, 1886; enlarged ed. 1894). He managed to strike something of a democratic note in these poems by employing in them a relatively simple realistic style and by distributing his concern rather equally between the "great" and the "small" in Sweden's history; but despite the brilliance of some of these poems he did not succeed, as he had hoped, in creating a poetic world which appealed particularly to the Swedish masses. The subject in itself was difficult of treatment in a popular realistic vein, and in any case Snoilsky, by birth and training a product of an elegant aristocratic tradition, was hardly the man to interpret Sweden's historical past in terms which would bore their way down into the collective consciousness of the common folk. Snoilsky was no Runeberg, and, besides, the Sweden of the 1880's was politically conscious in quite a different way from Runeberg's Finland of a generation earlier. It was the present and the future rather than the past which engaged the best minds and literary energies of the 1880's, and a radical cosmopolitan spirit had come to replace traditional nationalistic interests no matter how "democratic" such interests might seem to be.

Realizing this, Snoilsky soon turned to poetry in which he seeks to express opinions on social and political conditions, partly under pressure from his friend, the great Danish critic Georg Brandes, who had expressed some dissatisfaction with Snoilsky's preoccupation with historical themes. "As a national poet," writes Brandes at the time, of Snoilsky, "he has appeared in a somewhat different way than I personally have wished. I would rather have seen him write in step with Sweden's present-day life than with her historical memories." In Snoilsky's letters from the early 1880's he is clearly drifting in the direction which Brandes hopes he will. He admires with only minor reservations such sharply radical attacks on modern society as Strindberg's *Röda rummet* (The Red Room, 1879) and Ibsen's *Gengangere* (Ghosts, 1881), and he feels that the literature of the future must move generally in the direction suggested by these works. "Since I finished my last little book," Snoilsky writes to a friend in March 1882, "my aesthetic views have become not a little modified. My belief in the authority of beauty as something independent in and of itself has become shaken, and I lean more and more toward the view of those who hold that literature has no *raison d'être* if it is not capable of reflecting some of the great thoughts and ideas which actually concern our times."

In certain of the poems in *Dikter, tredje samlingen* (Poems, Third Collection, 1883) Snoilsky's new view of literature found its most arresting expression — by historical indirection in pieces on Michelangelo and Olaus Rudbeck, more directly and sharply in such poems as "I porslinsfabriken" (In the Porcelain Factory), "Den tjänande brodern" (The Serving Brother), "Afrodite och Sliparen" (Aphrodite and the Knife Grinder), and "Emigrationen" (The Emigration). In "The Serving Brother" Snoilsky pleads for a greater feeling of understanding on the part of the upper classes for their servants. In "Aphrodite and the Knife Grinder" he warns those who pursue beauty and neglect humane values that a day may come when the slave may rise and destroy the master. In "The Emigration" he mourns the national blood-letting involved in the mass emigration of the times and envisions a day when Sweden through necessary reform measures will become a nation whose citizens will not need to seek the good life in a foreign land far to the West across the Atlantic. And in "The Porcelain Factory" Snoilsky places highest among poets him who can bring to poetry

> The simple form which all men understand,
> The form which offers hearty bread to all,
> To still their hunger, not luxury recall.

But genuine as was Snoilsky's desire to place his gifts in the service of such a poetic ideal, he could not in the long run deny his blood and upbringing and become a popular folk poet. He lacked completely both the simple earthy touch and the sense of profound social indignation necessary to attract the masses in an age of ferment and potential revolt. His verse — even most of his verse which contained a social or political message — was too refined, too much dependent on historical associations, mythological parallels, and over-elaborated symbols to be food for the masses. And Snoilsky himself with sadness came finally to see this: "I know my chief deficiency — that I from my youth have not lived the life of the common folk. Education and upbringing in a narrow Classical direction have made me, as is the case of most of our literary figures, little fitted to speak to the common people in a language which they understand."

The dilemma in which Snoilsky as a poet found himself has points in common with Pastor Rosmer's in *Rosmersholm* (1886), and that Ibsen had Snoilsky in mind when creating the character of Rosmer is quite clear. But in Snoilsky's case, unlike Rosmer's, the dilemma led ultimately to quiet resignation and a kind of compromise with society rather than to desperate frustration and a tragic death. In 1890 Snoilsky returned to Sweden upon being appointed head of the Royal Library in Stockholm, and the somewhat more than a decade before his death in 1903 were years in which he made a kind of peace with his class, occupying himself with the world of rare books and with aspects of the past which were as far removed as possible from the eruptive social and political problems of the day. Only privately did he express himself on political subjects, and then almost invariably in a resigned conservative vein. In an address, in December 1893, before his fellow members of the Swedish Academy he refers sadly to "that wind which blows bleakly on the evening of the century." In these words Snoilsky may have been reacting more against a general *fin de siècle* moral malaise than against contemporary political radicalism in Sweden, but it seems nevertheless clear that the sharply polemic atmosphere of late nineteenth-century Swedish politics was highly distasteful to his fastidious tastes. In some ways he belonged among the Romantics, in other ways among the Gustavians. With the Romantics he shared an interest in history and an essentially conservative bent of mind. With the Gustavians he disliked abstract speculative tendencies of all kinds and cultivated a crystal-clear, elegant poetic style. Among Swedish poets he is one of the most urbane, polishing his verse to the point of perfection without losing an essential sense of spontaneity and warm humanitarianism. Though he is not to be counted among Sweden's great poets, he stands in the front rank of those who have employed their poetic talents short of real greatness.

Strindberg and the Realistic Breakthrough

As THE 1870's came to a close the situation in Swedish literature might have seemed to a contemporary observer as one in which the forces of tradition and conservatism were in complete command. Even the moderate realism and liberalism of the mid-century decades were little in evidence. Politics had to the surprise of some entered into a period of inactivity and reaction after the constitutional changes of 1865 had transferred power to the Agrarian party, and in matters cultural and literary a watered-down philosophical idealism parading under the banner of "healthy realism" (*sund realism*) was being dispensed by the "Signature" poets, apparently to the satisfaction of the general reading public. It is true that Snoilsky found himself in the 1870's drifting away from the limited Signature mentality of his literary apprenticeship and placing his talents in the service of social reform, but his efforts in this direction proved to be abortive, and he soon sank back into the quietistic elegance of his aristocratic background and found in his late years some comfort in the role of elder poet and Royal Librarian. And even Rydberg, who in the 1850's and early 1860's had identified himself with certain of the more advanced ideas of the day, found himself in the following decades increasingly less in step with those general European thought trends which pointed toward a radical revaluation of society and its institutions. Though Rydberg's philosophical idealism was of a much nobler strain than that represented by the slight talents of the Signature poets, he nevertheless found these poets at least relatively satisfactory allies in the cultural program for which in his later years he stood. The evidence is provided in the words with which in 1879 Rydberg welcomed two of them, Carl David af Wirsén and Carl Rupert Nyblom, into the company of "Immortals" in the Swedish Academy. The occasion was not without its unconscious symbolism, suggesting as it did the official triumph of literary mediocrity and reaction in nineteenth-century Swedish letters.

But developments sometimes have a harsh way of defying official occasions no matter how neat and apparently final the patterns of their symbolism might seem to be. A few months before Wirsén and Nyblom were welcomed into the august company of the Swedish Academy, Snoilsky, for some years a member of the Academy, and the only important poet deriving from the Signature group, was preparing to depart from Sweden in protest against his conservative origins and the stuffy spirit of the social and official life in his country of which he had become a part. And — much more important — not many days before the Academy met to receive Wirsén and Nyblom into its membership there appeared in the Stockholm bookshops a novel which marked the definitive breakthrough in Swedish literature of an unmistakably modern realistic spirit. The novel was entitled *The Red Room*, and its author was August Strindberg, every fiber of whose being was violently antipathetic to all formal and official forms of life and literature. Though Strindberg's restless genius was to lead him in his last phase of development far away from the realism and social radicalism of his early work, he never capitulated to reaction, and in the 1880's he became in consequence of his attack on Swedish conditions in *The Red Room* and other early works the inevitable rallying point for a revolutionary realistic literature which has been variously labeled "the Young Sweden" (*det unga Sverige*), "the 1880's" (*åttiotalet*), and "the Modern Breakthrough" (*det moderna genombrottet*). Of these three labels the last, though of Danish origin, is most accurately descriptive of what happened in Sweden at the time. "The Young Sweden" simply refers to a group of authors whom time soon proved to have little real solidarity and less sense of literary continuity, while "the 1880's" is a term which suggests, quite incorrectly, that the decade in question represents an essential unity of literary aspiration and attainment.

Swedish literature in the 1880's was in fact a many-sided phenomenon, in the main revolutionary in origin and spirit but seldom reflecting a unified program or set of ideals and very soon losing whatever sense of inner solidarity it may have had at the beginning. It may therefore best be described simply as a *breakthrough*, a final and complete loosening of contact with tradition and the past, a sharp assertion of values which identify themselves definitively with a living present and a vision of a happy future. Its watchwords were "evolution" and "progress," its faith the assumption that man could create a new and good society if only he could shake off the centuries-long accumulated weight of prejudice and tradition. That the 1880's represents simply a breakthrough rather than a deliberate and systematic establishing of fixed positions is perhaps best illustrated by the fact, frequently reiterated by recent Swedish scholars, that the following decade, which often considered itself to be in fundamental opposition to the 1880's, was in many ways more closely related to the 1880's than to those literary traditions against which the 1880's had so violently reacted. The 1890's, as we shall see later, is in certain senses a child of the 1880's, even though it so frequently denied its paternity. The 1880's prepared the way for the 1890's by clearing away once and for all the heavy underbrush of a long-dead literary tradition and creating an atmosphere in which the poetic upsurge of the 1890's could wing its magnificent way undeterred by overcareful consideration for that which past generations had approved as proper poetic forms and themes and moods.

When in the 1880's a modern realistic literature of strong social protest finally came to Sweden it was long overdue. Such a literature had been flourishing for some time on the Continent and in England and had for a decade and more put out vigorous shoots in the cultural life of Sweden's Scandinavian neighbors Denmark and Norway. When Sweden, too, came tardily to move in this direction its younger generation of authors found inspiration in the example of their immediate Scandinavian and Continental literary predecessors and in the total intellectual life of the time out of which the new European literature had grown. Sweden's own mid-century realism, which had been unprepared to break really radically with the past, seems only tangentially to have influenced developments in the 1880's. The new realism was to find its sources of inspiration very largely from abroad. Aside from the stimulating impact of European ideas on Swedish cultural life at the time, that which chiefly determined the nature of the literature of the 1880's was the changing social and political scene in Sweden, characterized particularly by the rapidly advancing industrialization of the country and its effect on the general social economy of the land. While Sweden had remained essentially an agrarian land, as she did substantially down to the middle of the nineteenth century, conditions could hardly encourage a vital literature of social protest; but when in the late nineteenth century the modern industrialization of Sweden began, conditions became ripe for a literature which recognized its more or less direct responsibility to the masses, to the proletariat or near-proletariat class created by the ongoing industrial developments. It is symptomatic that the year of publication of Strindberg's *The Red Room* was the year of Sweden's first major strike and that the years which immediately followed witnessed the rapid growth of a labor movement which culminated in the founding in 1889 of the Swedish Social Democratic party, followed nine years later by the organization of a central Trades Union Congress (*Landsorganisationen*). Though the younger generation of authors came from middle-class origins, they sympathized deeply with the cause of the rising laboring classes. Literary realism and social radicalism were in the 1880's fighting the same battle on somewhat different fronts. Both called for revolutionary changes in the economic and social structure of the country.

The specifically literary influences of most immediate importance in the 1880's came from Denmark and Norway, where circumstances had been more favorable than in Sweden for literary developments of a modern European kind. Georg Brandes in Denmark and Henrik Ibsen and Björnstjerne Björnson in Norway had in the 1870's and earlier done magnificent pioneering work for a new realistic literature, Brandes as a brilliant critic, Ibsen and Björnson as able and provocative dramatists. For the generation of Swedish authors who appeared in the early 1880's Brandes's *Main Currents in Nineteenth-Century European Literature* (*Hovedströmninger i det 19:de Aarhundredes Litteratur*, 1872ff.) and Ibsen's *Brand* (1866) were sacred canonical works, while the social reform plays of Ibsen (from *The League of Youth*, 1869, to *An Enemy of the People*, 1882) and of Björnson (especially *A Bankrupt* and *The Editor*, both from 1875) became only less sacred to the Swedish literary neophytes of the new realistic gospel. Strindberg had dreamed in the early 1870's of providing the Swedish stage with a realistic contemporary drama, but when Stockholm theater people found his historical play *Master Olof* (composed 1872) too realistic for their tastes he turned for the time being to other matters, and his two Norwegian contemporaries took over the Swedish stage, both of Björnson's social reform plays from the 1870's being performed in Stockholm in 1875 followed by Ibsen's historical play *Lady Inger of Östråt* and *Pillars of Society* in 1877. During the theatrical season of 1877–78 Ibsen was in fact performed in Stockholm, according to the newspaper *Aftonbladet*, more than any other dramatist. And in addition to this Norwegian theatrical vogue Swedish journals and newspapers opened up their columns to lengthy reviews of Danish and Norwegian novels and literary critical works as well as plays immediately upon their publication in the neighboring Scandinavian countries. For a time, indeed, Sweden's younger literary generation, the so-called "Young Sweden" group, existed completely in the shadow of Brandes, Ibsen, Björnson, and other only less celebrated Danish and Norwegian authors such as J. P. Jacobsen, Holger Drachmann, Jonas Lie, and Alexander Kielland. In fact, not until the mid-1880's were there signs in Swedish literary circles of a relatively independent attitude toward these Scandinavian literary giants to the South and West, and by this time Brandes and Ibsen had themselves begun to develop in directions partly opposed to their own earlier work. How central was the importance of Brandes to Swedish literary developments in the 1880's may best be suggested by the words of Gustaf af Geijerstam, in an address in honor of the great Danish critic on the occasion of his lecture tour in Sweden at the close of the decade.

There is certainly no one in this assemblage who does not remember what an impression one experienced from Brandes's works when they first arrived in Sweden and began to be read here. No one among those who at that time dreamed about the creation of a modern Swedish literature has forgotten that the one who showed him the way was Georg Brandes. None of us has ever forgotten the feeling of vitality and desire to create which Brandes's first books aroused in us. And if one reads Strindberg's autobiography one finds also there an expression of homage which the man whom we now honor certainly cannot read without deep emotion. For it is a great thing to feel that one has been the motive power in the intellectual life of a whole movement.

Had Ibsen been the object of homage on this occasion Geijerstam's words would almost certainly have fallen with similar emphasis and enthusiasm.

Because of Brandes's influence on Ibsen it is not always easy to determine which of the two most directly left his mark on the Swedish 1880's. Generally speaking each tended to reinforce the other's influence, both being highly critical of traditional social, political, and religious institutions and both championing at every point the individual's rights over against society. Brandes's massive indictment of Romantic conservatism in *Main Currents in Nineteenth-Century European Literature* was especially instrumental in bolstering the case of "the Young Sweden" against the surviving remnants of Swedish Romanticism, and his insistence that the salvation of the backward-looking Scandinavian literatures was to be effected by disowning their narrow nationalistic patterns and "opening the windows of [their] thought toward the Continent" met an enthusiastic response in Sweden as in Denmark and Norway. But while Brandes represented a kind of modern emancipation which tended to lose contact with any and all ethical norms, Ibsen brought to the literature of his day a sense of moral values of the most rigid and demanding kind. If Ibsen's *Brand* is, as has often been maintained, a dramatization of Kierkegaard's rigoristic ethics, Ibsen's social reform plays which followed are in their way equally insistent that man must live only by the truth, that the spirit of compromise is the ultimate evil, that the "life lie" must be mercilessly branded as such wherever and whenever it raises its ugly or lovely head. The unprecedented popularity of *Brand* among the younger generation of Swedish authors (Brandes found the play quite distasteful) suggests something of the high moral fervor with which the authors of the "Young Sweden" group faced their task of exposing what they considered the many festering sores of the society of which they were a part. They read *Brand*, it is important to note, as a modern social gospel rather than as a religious tract.

Back of Brandes and Ibsen lay the seething contemporary intellectual life of Europe. The Scandinavian literary revolt of which they together with Strindberg are the most challenging exponents found its ideas largely abroad, drawing upon mid-nineteenth-century empirical thought (positivism, utilitarianism) and modern science for the weapons with which it hoped to slay the dragon of prejudice and reaction. Brandes's injunction that Scandinavia must "open the windows of [its] thought toward the Continent" was avidly followed by the more advanced group of Swedish authors and intellectuals. In fact, even before Brandes's ringing words sounded over a rather somnolent Scandinavian literary scene Swedish intellectuals had been reading with ardor the new German biblical criticism and had taken note of such provocative political treatises as de Tocqueville's observations on American democracy. But not until the 1870's did material of this kind become available in considerable quantity to the general reading public, whose ranks were growing rapidly under the impact of the increasing democratization of the country. In the 1870's and 1880's Swedish translations of nearly all of the leading contemporary European thinkers and literary figures appeared. Of scientific, historical, and philosophical works may be mentioned translations from 1871–72 of three of Darwin's most important works and Thomas Buckle's *History of Civilization in England*, from 1877–78 Eduard von Hartmann's *Philosophie des Unbewussten* (in the translation of which Strindberg took part), from 1881 John Stuart Mill's *On Liberty*, and for a decade after 1879 most of the work of Herbert Spencer, who became a kind of Aristotle to the "Young Sweden" group in the early 1880's. Of Continental literary figures who appeared in Swedish translations at this time French and Russian authors seem to have attracted the greatest attention. Flaubert, Zola, and Maupassant, Turgenev, Tolstoi, and Dostoevski became well known in Swedish literary circles. Though the enthusiasm of youth for the ideas from abroad did not remain unchallenged by an older conservative generation, these ideas gained ground from year to year, and before the end of the century they had become for most educated Swedes basic cultural norms.

But for a time the battle between the old and the new was sharp and bitter, for it was clear to all parties concerned that this was no limited foray concerned merely with formalistic literary matters. The contest was joined at many points, most of them involving diametrically opposed positions on philosophical and religious, social and political questions. Neither side was in a mood to compromise, for each felt, quite correctly, that the issue of the battle would have crucial consequences for generations of Swedish life and culture. Inasmuch as the conservative forces were in complete control of what has been called "the official society," that which particularly came to characterize the new literature was its sharply critical attitude toward established institutions of all kinds.

This "official society" had at the time its most unyielding champions in the universities and the Church, and it was therefore inevitable that the younger generation should react strongly against these institutions. As soon as possible after the radical phalanx of young authors had shaken the dust of academic existence from their feet they recorded in literary form their feelings of loathing toward their academic experience. University life at Uppsala was pilloried by Strindberg (in the collection of tales *Från Fjärdingen och Svartbäcken* and in the second volume of *Tjänstekvinnans son*) and Geijerstam (in the novel *Erik Grane*), at Lund by Ola Hansson (in the group of sketches *Studentliv*) and Axel Lundegård (in *Lundastämning*). Even Victoria Benedictsson, who being a woman had not experienced university life at first hand, contributed to the genre the highly amusing tale "Cedergren gör sexa i kväll" (Cedergren Arranges a Party This Evening). University life in general as reflected in these short stories and novels is stuffy and reactionary in spirit, with the average student seeking relief from his ennui in drink and song and dubious escapades preferably of a sexual kind. Not even the serious student is interested in formal university studies, for he can see no relation between his liberal social and cultural interests and the stale varieties of intellectual fare dispensed by a complacent corps of conservative university professors. The only outlet the young liberal intellectuals had for their energies were the radical discussion clubs (Verdandi, founded at Uppsala in 1882, and De Unga Gubbarne, at Lund in 1887), but these clubs were looked upon with strong disfavor by the ruling cliques of the academic community and their members were often considered pariahs.

The two varieties of intellectual fare which especially irritated the young liberals of the 1880's were those which concerned religion and philosophy. In religious matters the young liberals were agnostics or atheists, in contrast to the older mid-century Swedish liberals who sought merely to "reform" the Church by attacking certain of its less acceptable dogmas such as the divinity of Christ and the existence of hell and eternal punishment. The liberalism of the 1880's went much farther, attacking at all points the Established Church as a symbol of prejudice and reaction, and looking upon Christianity as such with distrust if not disdain. Whenever a churchman rears his head in the literature of the 1880's he is either a fool or a knave or both, and the Church is almost invariably looked upon with scorn and indignation. And toward the dominant Swedish philosophical system of the day the attitude of the 1880's was substantially the same. This system, called "Boströmianism" after its founder Professor C. J. Boström (1797–1866), was a late-born offshoot of German philosophical idealism. It had become almost as sacrosanct as the Established Church in the 1860's and 1870's, in consequence of the spell which Professor Boström had succeeded in casting over both his immediate academic community at Uppsala and Swedish cultural life in general. Though Boström had in his later years joined Viktor Rydberg in challenging certain of the dogmas of the Established Church, he was otherwise in his thinking the darling of the conservatives, his social and political philosophy being rigidly reactionary.

Both the political conservatism and the abstract speculative nature of Boström's system were distasteful to the point of nausea to the young liberals of the 1880's. Their thinking was anchored rather in the empirical, social-minded philosophical traditions of the day (Comte, Mill, Spencer) and in the world of modern science, whose theory of evolution suggested a parallel to the envisioned change in social and political conditions. The "idealism" of the younger generation, in sharp opposition to the philosophical idealism of Boström, assumed change as natural and right, looked forward optimistically to a new and better world based on man's own work and his faith in himself. It is true that toward the end of the 1880's the optimism of the young liberals became shaken under the double impact of events and the ideas of Schopenhauer and Hartmann, but the tentative pessimism which resulted did not take on the form of a retreat in the direction of either religious obscurantism or speculative philosophical idealism. Nor did the 1890's, which in certain respects considered itself in conflict with the 1880's, return to the religious and philosophical positions more or less traditional in Sweden since the dawn of the century. By the end of the century Swedish literature had taken the final step in emancipating itself from traditional religious forms and ways of thinking. The secularization of Swedish culture which had taken its first great forward strides in the eighteenth century was at the end of the following century for all practical purposes complete.

The social and political radicalism of the 1880's took on many forms, ranging from demands for fundamental constitutional changes such as universal suffrage to attacks on various particular social evils, poverty, the exploitation of labor, and especially the inferior position of women in society. Of these social problems "the woman problem," thanks to Ibsen's *A Doll's House* (1879) and the rather strong position of female authors in the "Young Sweden" group, came to occupy what may seem to us today a quite disproportionate share of attention. Strindberg's violent reaction against the "woman cult" which flourished at the time need not be accounted for merely in terms of his own unfortunate marital experiences. Practically all of the Swedish literary figures of the 1880's vied gallantly with each other in pitying the presumably defenseless female, and women of the time who wielded the pen (like the talented Anne Charlotte Leffler) exploited the theme of "women's rights" with a thoroughness that must at times have embarrassed the author of *A Doll's House*, whom Strindberg once irreverently labeled "the great Norwegian bluestocking." The proportionately minor attention given to such other social questions as the evils accompanying the rise of modern industry is certainly not to be accounted for by a lack of sympathy for the affected semi-proletariat on the part of the young literary liberals of the day. These young liberals did what they could under difficult circumstances. Coming from educated middle-class origins, they simply didn't *know* enough about the conditions of life among the lower classes to deal adequately with their problems. They felt for these classes, but at a distance, and could not by the nature of things enter more profoundly into their way of feeling and thinking. The approach of the young liberals to these problems lacked concretion and detail, was theoretical rather than actual; and it was therefore doomed to be partial and unresolved despite its enthusiasm and good will. And besides, Swedish socialism and the labor movement were in the 1880's still in their infancy, and even with the best of intentions on the part of the "Young Sweden" group it was difficult to translate these still embryonic movements into vital literary propaganda. The attempts that were made in the 1880's to champion in literature the cause of the working classes were almost without exception fumbling and wooden. The rise of a significant proletarian literature in Sweden had to wait for more than a generation, until the years just before and during the First World War, when a gifted group of authors of what may loosely be called proletarian origins finally made their appearance on the literary scene. By this time the labor movement had reached its maturity and the Social Democratic party was on the verge of taking over the reins of government for the first time in Sweden.

The difficulty the "Young Sweden" authors experienced in attempting to translate into a living literature the struggles of the lower classes was only less apparent in their efforts to write significantly on other social problems of the day. In fact, the authors who in the first years of the 1880's made up what may be called the inner circle of the "Young Sweden" group (Geijerstam, Tor Hedberg, Axel Lundegård, Oscar Levertin, and Anne Charlotte Leffler, in whose salon they frequently met) scarcely got beyond the more or less ephemeral literary sketch in their efforts to make their reading public aware of the evils existing in the social conditions around them. Novels and dramas were written, but outside the work of Strindberg, who maintained only tenuous and increasingly strained relations with the "Young Sweden" group, none of these more ambitious literary forms were managed with any high distinction. In Denmark, and especially in Norway, much more important work was being done in the 1880's in these genres.

A dedicated enthusiasm for "the cause" could not create a great social-minded literature in the absence of effective leadership and literary talents of a really high order. Geijerstam did what he could to provide leadership, but he was scarcely the man for the task of holding together the disparate elements within the "Young Sweden" group, and it was not long before the group disintegrated, its members shaping their individual literary futures in terms which more or less definitely departed from their earlier ideals. Some of them, like Lundegård and Levertin, formally renounced their early literary ideals, while others, Geijerstam and Hedberg, drifted gradually away from their pasts without going through the formality of dramatically announcing a new literary faith. Aside from the fact that the authors of the "Young Sweden" group found themselves unequal to the task of overcoming a strong general public resistance to their advanced ideas, perhaps the chief reason for the rapid disintegration of the group was that the radical literary program which it represented had come so tardily to Sweden. Unlike in Denmark and Norway, the realistic literary program in Sweden which proposed "to put problems into debate" scarcely had time to mature before certain new anti-realistic literary signals from abroad announced the advent of a new symbolism and an attendant mysticism which categorically rejected the ideal of literature as a social and political weapon. These developments abroad served to sow confusion in the ranks of the generation of the 1880's almost before they had deployed for the attack upon social and political injustice. When therefore in 1889 Verner von Heidenstam, "the chieftain of the 1890's," in his essay "Renaissance" called for a literature of fantasy and beauty and national themes in opposition to what he considered the sterile preoccupation in the 1880's with reality and social problems, he found it relatively easy to direct Swedish literary energies into new channels. The 1880's had already in certain ways rejected itself.

But only in certain ways.

What happened in the late 1880's was that the "Young Sweden" as a *group* disintegrated, with its members in most cases modifying their literary ideals rather than completely disowning them. On the whole they found themselves sufficiently at home in the 1890's, which had retained much that was central in the preceding decade — its religious and ethical emancipation, its refusal to accept slavishly traditional ways of thinking, to some extent its poetic realism and its social conscience.

And if the literary generation of the 1880's found itself relatively at home in the 1890's, it would have found itself even more at home in twentieth-century Sweden. For what we know as modern Sweden is to a very considerable extent a product of the ideas which were first boldly proclaimed as a literary program in the early 1880's. If the purely literary skills of the group which championed these ideas were considerably less than distinguished, the ideas themselves had a vitality of their own which carried over into later generations of Swedish cultural life and have played a central role in shaping Swedish society today. The chief significance of the "Young Sweden" group lies in the fact that its members, together with Strindberg, represented a literary and cultural break-through which has had the most far-reaching consequences for many phases of modern Swedish life.

Outside Scandinavia August Strindberg (1849–1912) has been known almost exclusively as the half-mad Swedish genius who wrote a number of highly arresting dramas and autobiographical works and who other-wise distinguished himself by recording some views on women which are anything but gallant. This one-sided capsule view of one of Sweden's greatest authors, and the only Swedish author who occupies an impor-tant place in world literature, has in recent years been somewhat rectified by those critics outside Sweden who have taken the trouble to examine more closely than had previously been the case Strindberg's general sig-nificance for modern drama. But except for Strindberg's work as a dramatist there still exists, and probably always will, an almost complete ignorance outside Scandinavia of Strindberg's total literary production. In Sweden Strindberg's dramatic production is recognized as only his single most impressive contribution to literature, while his sketches and short stories and novels, his autobiographical works and essays, and even his poetry, are looked upon as only less central contributions to modern Swedish literature. Not that everything he wrote (his collected works fill fifty-five volumes) is considered even by his most enthusiastic ad-mirers entirely satisfactory, but it is generally agreed that no Swedish author can be compared with Strindberg in the seething variety and vital-ity of his work and that at his best he ranks, if not first, at least among the select few who occupy the very pinnacle of the Swedish Parnassus.

Few authors are as difficult as Strindberg to fit into a summary literary formula. His genius is too volatile and his interests too many-sided to be accommodated for any length of time to a particular literary group or a fixed literary program. In the course of his career he is continuously in-volved in extricating himself from tentative earlier positions, restlessly searching for a way of life and a literary form which is inherently his own. In every genre which he employs he is the born experimenter, never satisfied with the form as he finds it, always giving to it the stamp of his own restive genius. This is particularly true in the drama, where his mas-tery is most impressive and his experimental proclivities most daring and fruitful. Though not all Swedish critics are equally impressed by some of the more extremely experimental aspects of Strindberg's later work, they are without exception in agreement that his handling of language is one of the chief miracles of Swedish literature. No Swedish author has the stylistic variety and range, the spontaneity, directness, and economy of phrasing that Strindberg commands. He shook Swedish prose completely loose from its earlier ceremonious, rhetorical propensities, bringing to it a pulsing aliveness and driving intensity which have provided the point of departure for all modern developments in Swedish prose style.

Strindberg's stylistic skill is the despair of the translator. It is not mere verbal virtuosity, the plaything of a brilliant mind. It is the perfect reflection of Strindberg's temperament, the inevitable garment of his thought. When a recent Swedish critic observed that "no one has a shorter way from the blood to the ink" (*ingen har kortare väg från blodet till bläcket*) he singled out the great secret of Strindberg's style — its complete lack of formal "literary" qualities, its astonishing ability to all but *identify* itself with the phenomena which it seeks to express. Strindberg can attain this quality because of the incisive intensity of his vision. "I was born," he has his *alter ego* say in one of the Chamber Plays, "without a film over my eyes — and I therefore can see right through things." This hypersensitive directness of vision is so constitutive in Strindberg that it operates constantly on all levels of his experience and thought, determining the nature of his responses to the whole range of human experience which was his. Because of this hypersensitivity he is instinctively on the defense, suspicious of all established practices and institutions, defending his ego fiercely against every variety of those curbs which society in self-defense attempts to force upon its more recalcitrant members.

Strindberg's defiance of accepted patterns of thought and conduct began early and maintained itself with undiminished vigor down to his death. In terms of his literary activity it struck its first telling blow with the novel *The Red Room* in 1879, and its last with another novel *Svarta fanor* (Black Banners) in 1907, followed three years later by a series of newspaper articles around which the so-called "Strindbergsfejden" (The Strindberg Controversy) raged long and bitterly, with almost every cultural personality in Sweden taking sides for or against Strindberg. The controversial storms which had periodically raged about him throughout his career followed him down to the grave.

In his boyhood and youth he resented strenuously both the patriarchal authority exercised by his father and the severe rigidities of early school discipline, and when he came to Uppsala (where he pursued university studies the fall semester of 1867 and from the spring term of 1870 to the spring of 1872) he quarreled with his professors and despised equally the formal intellectual disciplines provided by the university and the easy-going student life of the day. During his second stay at Uppsala he found some pleasure in his associations with a group of fellow students in Runa Förbundet (The Runa Society), whose members affected Old Nordic customs and encouraged one another in literary pursuits center-ing upon ancient Scandinavian themes. Strindberg was looked upon by this group as its one promising young author in consequence of his liter-ary activity during the preceding two or three years, an activity which had resulted in the composition of four little plays, one of which, the slight one-act drama *I Rom* (In Rome), had been performed with some success at the Royal Dramatic Theater in September 1870, and had at-tracted the attention of no less a personage than the reigning monarch, Charles XV, who set aside a small sum from his private purse to encour-age the young Strindberg in his studies and literary plans.

At Uppsala Strindberg wrote during the winter 1870–71 his first rela-tively important play *Den fredlöse* (tr. *The Outlaw*), which manages to include some strongly Strindbergian qualities despite its obvious indebt-edness to the drama of ancient Scandinavian themes as practiced by Ibsen and Björnson. *The Outlaw* is a one-acter. Strindberg's next play, *Master Olof*, is a magnificently conceived and in the main brilliantly executed drama in five acts. In this play, written when Strindberg was only twenty-three, Sweden has its first great drama, but when the young dramatist sent the manuscript of his play to the Royal Dramatic Theater he was advised that it was unacceptable without some radical revisions. Its racy realism and its note of familiarity in dealing with such national saints and heroes as Olaus Petri and Gustav Vasa made the play quite impossible for the cautious theatrical tastes of the day. Besides, it was pointed out, some rather serious historical anachronisms occurred in the play, and it was written in prose, an unthinkable form in high tragedy. To Strindberg these judgments were petty and obtuse, but so sure was he that he had in *Master Olof* the material of a great play, and so anxious was he to have the play produced, that he labored for years over the material, finally completing a new, poetic version in 1878. When the drama was first performed in 1881, however, the original prose version was used, and today it is universally agreed that this version is much superior to the poetic drama. The very qualities of the original version which dis-turbed those who watched over theatrical taste in Sweden in the 1870's are the qualities which appealed to later generations. Particularly impressive is the psychological realism of the play, the treatment of historical characters as something other than heroic semi-legendary figures. In this respect Strindberg goes farther in *Master Olof* than Shakespeare, whom he otherwise follows in using the loose dramatic structure of the chronicle play and including a number of low comedy scenes reminiscent of *Henry IV*.

Before the second period of his university studies, and during the years which immediately followed while he was struggling with the poetic version of *Master Olof*, Strindberg was eking out a precarious existence in various ways — he was a private tutor and taught for short periods in both public and private schools, he pursued spasmodically miscellaneous journalistic activities and translated some of the popular American humorists (Artemus Ward, Mark Twain, Bret Harte, and others), and he worked as an assistant in the Royal Library. Both his journalistic experience and his duties at the Royal Library were of importance in his later literary career, the former acquainting him at first hand with many sides of contemporary Swedish life which he came to satirize so knowingly in *The Red Room* and *Det nya riket* (The New Kingdom), the latter giving him access to a variety of fascinating historical documents which sharpened his interest in the past and became the point of departure for his life-long literary preoccupation with historical figures and events. His personal associations during these years — until his marriage in December of 1877 — were almost exclusively with an irreverent group of young Bohemians, artists and assorted intellectuals of diverse origins and occupations, whose meeting place was the so-called Red Room at Bern's Restaurant and who spent their time in vying with one another in devastating nihilistic commentary on the life around them. From these associations Strindberg was in a sense "rescued" by his marriage, his most fateful step during these years. The marriage to Siri von Essen began with considerable promise once the initial obstacles were overcome — his wife was when he met her married to a Captain of the Royal Guards. But the early promise was short-lived, minor dissonances soon occurring, major discords piling up more and more violently with the years — until the final divorce decree of January 1891 was granted. Which of the two was the more responsible for what happened in this marriage is impossible to determine, though Strindberg has usually been judged the chief offender because of his relentless exposure of Siri in the figures of Maria in *The Confession of a Fool* and Laura and Tekla in the two plays *The Father* and *Creditors*. That Strindberg in spite of all loved Siri von Essen deeply is apparent from the agonizing persistence of his efforts at reconciliation after each of the increasingly serious breaks between the two. The brutality of his charges against Siri when he took up his pen to describe his married life with her is as much an evidence of the depth of his feelings for her as it is an unhappy record of vengeance pursued with satanic literary skill. When Strindberg in the middle and late 1880's wrote these exposures of his first marriage he was so fascinated by them that he was scarcely more conscious of the reality upon which they were based than he was of their extraordinary explosive potential as tragic literary motifs.

The literary career which Strindberg had been attempting to establish for a decade before his marriage had far from fulfilled his dreams. The critics had observed that a couple of his early plays showed some promise, but *Master Olof* had been officially condemned before it reached print or appeared on the stage. The satirical sketches of Uppsala life *Från Fjärdingen och Svartbäcken*, which he wrote in order to defray his wedding expenses, were received with qualified approbation by some critics but scarcely resulted in any general public interest. Strindberg was quietly being forgotten. At this juncture he aroused himself and flung into the faces of the Swedish public late in 1879 *The Red Room* — with startling results. Smarting under the fate of his earlier works, he placed upon the title page of his novel the challenging words of Voltaire: *Rien n'est si désagréable que d'être pendu obscurément.* Strindberg was not this time hanged unknown, in fact he was not hanged at all, for his readers found *The Red Room* so undeniably entertaining that they more often than not chose to ignore or forget the serious satirical intentions of the novel.

Overnight Strindberg became famous. Never before had Swedish prose been written with such engaging verve, with such fresh and youthful satiric aplomb. As a novel *The Red Room* lacked structural tightness, and except for its central figure, Arvid Falk, its characterization was sketchy; but the Stockholm milieu was projected with unexampled variety and concreteness, episodes were handled with unforgettable visual and dramatic flair, and the satiric vein was worked with a combination of high good humor and devastating inventiveness which is the mark of only the greatest satirists. Strindberg's satiric indignation — inspired by his observations of Stockholm life in the 1870's — lashed out in all directions, distributing its blows with equal vigor on political chicanery and religious humbug, bureaucratic irresponsibility and social injustice, philosophical pretentiousness and educational reaction, journalistic opportunism and theatrical intrigues. All of this was something new in Swedish literature. *The Red Room* became inevitably the clarion call to a new generation of authors, all of whom recognized Strindberg as the master.

The success of *The Red Room* having opened up the doors of publishers and theaters for Strindberg and assured him a reading public, he was at last launched on a highly promising literary career. No longer need he fritter away his time on odd jobs of one kind and another while seeking a break in the tight dike which literary reaction sought to maintain around Swedish literary taste. The result during the somewhat less than six years before he departed for the Continent in the fall of 1883 was an almost indecent productivity, book after book coming from his pen, including three plays, a collection of prose satires, a volume of poetry, two rather ambitious historical works (on one of which he was the chief of two collaborators), and a series of fascinating popular tales with Swedish historical subjects. These works reflect in general a curious ambivalence in point of view, balancing precariously between a partial willingness on the part of Strindberg to be reconciled with his contemporaries and a determination to continue the iconoclastic satirical strain of *The Red Room*. Two of the plays, *Gillets hemlighet* (The Secret of the Guild) and *Herr Bengts hustru* (Sir Bengt's Wife), deal with modern themes in historical guise, but they are essentially amicable in spirit and they close on a forgiving, optimistic note, while the fairy tale play *Lycko-Pers resa* (tr. *Lucky Per's Travels*) is similarly disposed to soften whatever satiric intents it may have and to assume that life is in the last analysis endurable if not actually good. Though none of these plays added much to Strindberg's stature as a dramatist, *Lucky Per's Travels* has with the years become a popular children's play, and *The Secret of the Guild* and *Sir Bengt's Wife* served satisfactorily in their day as appropriate vehicles for Siri's appearance as an actress. The latter play is chiefly of interest, however, in its obvious thematic opposition to Ibsen's *A Doll's House* and in the fact that its central character, Margit, provides us in certain ways with an impressive preliminary study of Julia in Strindberg's great naturalistic drama *Miss Julia*.

The generally favorable reception received by these plays was also accorded the collaborative work *Gamla Stockholm* (Old Stockholm) and the first volumes of the historical tales *Svenska öden och äventyr* (Swedish Fates and Adventures). But when in these years Strindberg turned to writing history itself in his *Svenska Folket* (The Swedish People), he found himself involved in a bitter controversy with the professional historians, who irritated Strindberg by pointing out factual errors in his work and by challenging its general historical soundness. The historians reacted strongly against Strindberg's position that a folk-cultural approach to Swedish history was preferable to an account based largely on political and military considerations, and they were especially angered when Strindberg went so far in his polemical extremes as to belittle the great nineteenth-century historian-poet Erik Gustaf Geijer, whose aristocratic thesis that "the history of Sweden is the history of its kings" had become almost axiomatic in some Swedish historical circles. Strindberg refused to budge an inch despite the academic eminence of his critics, and with time he came to feel singled out as an object of persecution. To this was added other irritants, overwork and incipient troubles in his marriage, with the result that he released his growing sense of persecution in one of his most violently outspoken works, *Det nya riket* (The New Kingdom). This work, like *The Red Room*, is a broad satirical exposé of representative Swedish institutions and forms of life of the day. But unlike *The Red Room* its polemic is frequently bitter and personal, satisfied finally with nothing less than singling out certain well-known personalities of the day and mercilessly subjecting them to ridicule and scorn. The enmity which Strindberg had aroused in prominent Stockholm cultural circles in connection with his historical polemics was intensified almost beyond description on the appearance of *The New Kingdom*, and he soon found his situation in Sweden so difficult that he was determined to depart for the Continent to escape from it all and to seek rest and quiet for his overwrought nervous system.

But before he did so he dashed off a volume of verse (*Dikter*, 1883) in which he attacked Swedish conditions anew. This time he was somewhat less bitter but no less devastating. The worst of his gall had been discharged in the withering prose of *The New Kingdom*, and when he discovered that he had poetic talents and that poetry could serve his satiric purposes as well as prose he was so delighted with the new medium that he found himself in a relatively expansive polemic mood. He does not forget those of his enemies who had aroused his ire in *The New Kingdom*, but he castigates them now in swinging, driving, gloriously angry rhythms and in a figurative language so alive and vigorously concrete that we can enjoy his robust mockery without being particularly concerned about its unhappy victims. In "Esplanadsystemet" (The Boulevard System) he employs the tearing down of old buildings to make way for a new boulevard as a symbol of the social and political program of the 1880's:

> Here wreck we to gain air and light —
> Isn't this perhaps sufficient?

In "Lokes smädelser" (Loke's Blasphemies) he compares himself and his work to that arch contriver of mischief and defiance in Scandinavian mythology. In "Olika vapen" (Dissimilar Weapons) he draws on his choicest vein of mockery to ridicule the very personification of Swedish literary, political, and religious reaction of the day, Carl David af Wirsén. But however effective these poems are as instruments of satire, they are in the history of Swedish prosody much more important for their radical break with traditional Swedish poetic forms. In this respect they showed the way toward fresh and realistic poetic ideals which ultimately led to that rejuvenation of Swedish poetry which was to have its first great efflorescence in the 1890's and to continue with only partially diminished vitality down to our own day. Strindberg was a renewer even in the habitations of poetry, where he made only occasional appearances.

The publication of *Poems* took place after the departure of Strindberg and his family for the Continent in September 1883. France was his immediate goal, but after a short visit to an artists' colony in Grèz and a somewhat longer stay in Paris he moved in January 1884 to Switzerland, where he found conditions for work more quiet and satisfying. In the following years, until the late spring of 1889, he shuttled nervously back and forth across western Europe, living for longer periods of time in Switzerland, France, Germany, and Denmark, with a very brief visit to Italy. Finding living costs in pensions and other more or less temporary quarters quite costly for a family of five, he was forced to write as feverishly abroad as he had the immediately preceding years in Stockholm. At first what he wrote is relatively calm and objective in mood by contrast with the hectic Stockholm years. Generally speaking also the first works of his years abroad reflect a marked effort to eschew literary interests in favor of the critical social and cultural essay, and when he uses such traditional literary forms as poetry and prose fiction he does so with a minimum of concern for their traditional formalistic qualities. In a second volume of verse, *Sömngångarnätter* (Sleepwalker Nights), he continues and extends his stylistic experiments in a free modern verse (here based on the loose doggerel verse of the medieval poets) and adopts a utilitarian ethics as the basis for his social and political thinking. In *Likt och olikt* (which may perhaps best be translated This and That) he brings together a group of essays on social and cultural problems originally appearing at various times in journals and newspapers. In the prose tales *Utopier i verkligheten* (Utopias in Reality) he identifies himself with a Rousseauistically tinged socialism. In the first part of the short narrative sketches *Giftas* (Married) he comments — for the most part in a lightly ironic vein — on the difficulties which arise in those marital relations which do not take sufficiently into account economic and biological considerations.

The little volume *Married* seems innocent enough to a present-day reader, and some of its stories — especially the tale of a bachelor's final capitulation to the married state, "Måste" (Must), and the mischievous take-off on Ibsen's Nora entitled pointedly "Ett dockhem" (A Doll's House) — are little gems of the satiric art. But Strindberg's enemies in Sweden were in no mood to be amused by anything he wrote, no matter how remote from incendiarism an innocent tale about a Stockholm bachelor might be or whatever Strindberg's enemies may have thought of Ibsen. They found Strindberg's emphasis on the physical side of marriage offensive, and they became so incensed by the most daring of the tales, "Dygdens lön" (The Rewards of Virtue), that they instigated legal action against its author. The tale deals primarily with the problems of puberty and the consequences of sexual frustration resulting from fears engendered by fanatical religious instruction, but finding no clear legal grounds for proceeding against Strindberg in these matters, his enemies charged him with blasphemy under an ancient paragraph in the Swedish law. The charge was occasioned by a slurring incidental reference in the tale to the Lord's Supper. Strindberg, who at first refused to return to Stockholm to stand trial, was later persuaded to do so when his publisher might otherwise have been held responsible; and though Strindberg was finally acquitted (November 1884) the episode proved to be catastrophic for him. It precipitated anew, and in more violent forms than hitherto, his persecution complex and led directly to a prolonged inner crisis which lingered on in various virulent forms until the middle 1890's, when, culminating in the Inferno experience, it finally at least partially released its ugly hold on its victim.

But the crisis incurred by the legal prosecution of 1884 led directly also to an eruptively rich literary production — to *The Son of a Servant* and *The Confession of a Fool*, *The Father* and *Miss Julia* and *Creditors*, to that whole group of arresting autobiographical works and plays from the late 1880's which loom so large in Strindberg's total literary achievement and which are among those of his works which established his European reputation. And it led ultimately to *To Damascus, The Dream Play*, and *The Spook Sonata*, three of the post-Inferno plays which have especially fascinated the twentieth century and blazed new revolutionary paths in the world of dramatic form and theatrical experimentation. It is misleading, however, to assume, as so often is the case, that Strindberg's mental crisis and what has been called his "genius for suffering" explain his whole work. He had another clear-headed, eminently rational, and robustly healthy side, which not infrequently asserts itself even in his most excruciating moments of self-defense and self-examination. At times, indeed, as in *Hemsöborna* (tr. *The People of Hemsö*, a novel done between two such intensely brooding works as *The Father* and *The Confession of a Fool*), he abandons himself completely to a world of healthy, earthy extroversion. But it is certainly true that Strindberg yielded to such extroverted moods only on occasion, usually to amuse himself or to gain desperately needed funds, and he did so half apologetically. Of *Hemsöborna* he once wrote: "only an *intermezzo scherzando* between the battles."

The Son of a Servant, written in the mid-1880's on the verge of Strindberg's descent into the maelstrom of his so-called naturalistic plays, illustrates how clear-headed and eminently rational he could on occasion be in dealing with himself and his time. It is an autobiographical work which seeks to place its central figure in the total social and intellectual contexts of the day, and it does so with an astonishing objectivity considering the frequency with which Strindberg had earlier come into conflict with the world around him. Though it has sharp things to say about parental tyranny and the backwardness of school and university education, and deals out caustic observations on social conditions, politics, and religion, it does so with little rancor and less bitterness; and in dealing with himself in this work Strindberg maintains a frankness and candor quite unusual in autobiographical literature. It is clear that when Strindberg wrote this work he was as much concerned with honest self-examination as he was with self-defense.

The same cannot be said of those dramas which were gestating uneasily within him at the time he was completing *The Son of a Servant*. The label "naturalistic plays" which has been so frequently used in classifying these dramas is in some senses misleading, for it suggests a rather rigid adherence to the code of French naturalism which Strindberg was not always prepared to accept despite his great admiration for the French naturalists and especially for its master practitioner and law-giver, Zola. Strindberg followed the French in their fondness for the brutal and the pathological, in their biological determinism and their practice of basing their novels and plays on an actual observed reality; but the born dramatic temperament that Strindberg was could not adopt their practice of building up detailed "photographic" backgrounds in order to account for character motivation, nor could he bring himself to maintain that "scientific objectivity" toward the dramatic material which was the first commandment of the orthodox naturalistic author. Strindberg felt that the piling up of detail interfered with the passionate emotional drive which is the essence of drama, and as for "objectivity" he could hardly with the best of intentions maintain an unbiased attitude toward his characters in a group of plays, such as those from the late 1880's, which almost without exception deal with one aspect or other of the tragic marital experience in which he was then involved. Of these plays only in *Miss Julia* and *The Link* is a kind of objectivity precariously maintained. In most of the others (there are fourteen in all) the male protagonists are usually readily identifiable dramatic projections of Strindberg himself in the tortured windings of his first marriage. How close some of these plays are to the realities of Strindberg's marital experience can be seen by a perusal of the autobiographical novel *The Confession of a Fool*, written after *The Father* and before *Creditors* and containing practically every important dramatic motif to be found in these two plays.

Aside from the immediate autobiographical origins of Strindberg's plays from this time, that which particularly distinguishes the best of them from the then prevailing naturalistic drama is their strong psychological emphasis, their almost exclusive concern with the problem of survival as illustrated in the struggle of wills. Strindberg's familiarity with contemporary French and English investigators of hypnosis and mental suggestion (Bernheim, Charcot, Liébault, Maudsley) and his short but violent flirtation with Nietzschean concepts served to deepen and intensify his instinctive tendency to view the human scene as a fierce and deadly struggle for survival, a struggle in which the stronger of two opposed wills inevitably triumphs over the weaker. To these influences were added those of the criminologist Lombroso and of Edgar Allan Poe, the latter fascinating Strindberg as much by his stylistic subtleties as by his preoccupation with the subconscious levels of human experience. So great, indeed, was Strindberg's interest at the time in psychological matters of the most advanced kind that he had gathered what he called in a letter to Heidenstam "a whole literature of madness (*en hel vansinnig-hetslitteratur*)."

In the matter of general form the most striking feature of Strindberg's dramatic development in the plays from this period is the growing trend toward structural concentration. The material in the first of these plays, *Comrades*, is distributed in the then conventional leisurely five acts with appropriate subdivisions into numerous short scenes. The second, *The Father*, is likewise conventional in its act and scene division, but it reduces the number of acts to three and otherwise appreciably increases the dramatic tempo by tightening up the flow of action. Beginning with *Miss Julia* Strindberg's dramatic form becomes much more spare, more skeletal, divesting itself radically of nonessential detail and concentrating with rapt intensity on the core elements of action. The result in its most extreme form is a group of short one-acters, the best of which are the Poe-inspired *Simoon* and *Pariah*, and the fascinating little exercise in dramatic monologue with two characters, *The Stronger*. Of the most important of Strindberg's plays after *The Father* from this period — *Miss Julia*, *Creditors*, and *The Link* — only *The Link* makes some concessions to that slice-of-life doctrine of naturalism which requires the inclusion of detail that has no crucial importance for the central dramatic action. The action of *Miss Julia* is brutally precipitate from beginning to end, its dialogue shorn of all excrescences and its treatment of character nakedly straightforward, while *Creditors* is spare to the point of the schematic both in the development of its theme and in the scalpel-like precision and efficiency of its dialogue. In these two plays Strindberg had gone far beyond Ibsen, who in his plays from the 1880's had been satisfied with modifying and perfecting an older kind of drama rather than creating an essentially new form. Even in *The Father*, where the influence of Ibsen's careful architectonics is often apparent, Strindberg's tempo is nervous and headlong in comparison with the great Norwegian master. How satisfied Strindberg was with his accomplishment in *Miss Julia* and *Creditors* is attested by a couple of letters, one to his publisher Bonnier whom he warns against rejecting the manuscript of *Miss Julia*, "for this play," he prophesies, "will be noted in the Annals," the other to Edvard Brandes in which he cries out exultantly "brand-new naturalistic tragedies, each of one hundred pages, each with three characters, and in a single act without monologues and such things . . . both better than *The Father*. New, you see! brilliant!"

Unfortunately Strindberg's satisfaction with *Miss Julia* and *Creditors* was not shared by the theater directors, and Bonnier did not dare to publish *Miss Julia* because its daring realism would infuriate those Swedish moralists who already had sufficient reason to condemn Strindberg's authorship and make things uncomfortable for those who published his work. Strindberg had to establish his own ill-fated Experimental Theatre in Copenhagen in 1889 in order to have the two plays performed, and even then police censorship forced him to produce *Miss Julia* under the private auspices of the radical, Brandes-inspired Student Society in the Danish capital. Even the presumably sophisticated audience of the Freie Bühne reacted so strongly when *Fräulein Julie* was placed on the boards in Berlin in 1892 that it had to be dropped after a single performance, but in January 1893 *Mademoiselle Julie* was much more favorably received in Paris when, under Antoine's enthusiastic direction, it became "une énorme sensation" at the celebrated Théâtre Libre. Antoine was so impressed on this occasion by the advanced dramaturgy of *Miss Julia* and Strindberg's commentary on it in the famous Preface to the play that he went to the very considerable expense of having the Preface printed in the theater program. In Sweden *Fröken Julie* had to wait for its first performance until September 1906. Meanwhile Strindberg had undergone that prolonged inner crisis which had culminated in the horrors of the Inferno experience, the chief literary result of which was a startling new dramaturgy. Though it had some points of contact with *Miss Julia*, Strindberg's new dramaturgy represented in the main a radical rejection of the spirit and form of the play written almost twenty years before it appeared on a Swedish stage.

The roads which led to the definitive Inferno experience in July 1896 were many and tortuous, and the experience itself very nearly led to hopeless madness before it moderated its harrowing grip on Strindberg and permitted him again to return to significant dramatic composition. The Inferno crisis had its origins, as we have seen, in two tentative earlier crises, particularly the one precipitated by the legal prosecution resulting from the publication of *Married* in 1884. The persecution complex which at that time began seriously to cloud Strindberg's mind became with the years progressively more acute, fed by his sense of growing isolation from the world around him. Various circumstances contributed to this sense of isolation: continuing conservative attacks on his authorship which forced Swedish publishers and theater directors to a near-boycott of his production, deteriorating relations with his friends and former defenders who found his opinions on "the woman problem" and related social questions unacceptable, and finally — and perhaps most important — mounting tensions in his marital relations. When, finally, divorce proceedings were instituted they dragged on for many months under humiliating circumstances for both of the principals, and when in January 1891 the decree was granted on conditions which Strindberg found degrading to himself as a father (all three children were turned over to the care of the mother) his inner world had become a ghastly shambles. During these years he continued at intervals to write, though his literary interests were gradually giving way to scientific investigations of various kinds. How little his heart was in literary creation is apparent in the almost uniformly undistinguished quality of all except two of the plays which he wrote in the agitated years around 1890. The two exceptions are *Leka med elden* (Playing with Fire), a sprightly domestic comedy, and *The Link*, a rather remarkably restrained treatment of the divorce proceedings which in its dramatic form fulfills more satisfactorily than any of Strindberg's other plays the slice-of-life formula of the orthodox naturalistic drama.

But more interesting in a number of ways than these plays is the novel *On the Seaboard*, which Strindberg wrote at intervals during these years. Though this novel has its "dead spots" given over to meaningless flirtations and sundry other mundane inanities, it attains at times an imaginative flight and visionary intensity which presage something quite new in Strindberg, something which points forward to the grotesque and aching fantasy of the post-Inferno dramas. In addition the novel provides the first extensive literary record of Strindberg's new absorption in the physical sciences, an absorption which in the years that follow is to burgeon out into that strange congeries of esoteric speculation of all kinds which is one of the basic intellectual components in the Inferno experience and its aftermath.

Outwardly the years which led up to and included the central Inferno psychosis and its aftermath are characterized by a mad pattern of flights hither and yon across western Europe, beginning with his arrival in Berlin in 1892 and ending in Paris and Lund more than half a decade later, with repeated and sometimes lengthy stays in the two latter cities and on the Austrian estate of the grandparents of Frieda Uhl, whom he had met in Berlin and married on the island of Helgoland in the spring of 1893. Highly favorable opportunities opened up for him in the Berlin theaters when he arrived in Germany's capital in September 1892, but after the great success of *Creditors* at the Residenztheater in January the following year he snubbed theater directors and others interested in exploiting his talents as author and dramatist.

Scientific studies had by this time quite bewitched him, particularly certain fundamental chemical investigations through which he hoped to topple the whole imposing structure of the chemistry of the day by demonstrating that elements can be combined with each other. When he failed to impress chemists he drifted into alchemy and then into an occult borderland between physical and psychic speculation, where he met on common ground several of the most celebrated Parisian occultists of the day and contributed frequently to their journals. But all of this served only to increase his feeling of insecurity, his sense of being pursued, hounded, incessantly persecuted by man as well as by hosts of disquieting little "creatures" from another world. Finally his worn and lacerated spirit turned in upon itself, driven in desperation to seeking answers to such moral and religious questions as *why* he constantly suffered, *why* the terrifying visitations from another world. Some answers to these questions he found in occultist and theosophical teachings, but not until he discovered the writings of Swedenborg did he find what to him was something like clear and definitive answers: he was pursued in fact not by man but by what he came to call "The Powers" because he had done evil, and only in admission of his guilt and in acts of penance could he expect to find release from the ghastly horrors of his inner world. "The Powers" presently came to be identified with a personal God with whom Strindberg, like Job, had to make his peace.

During the years of Strindberg's psychological crisis strange reports from Scandinavian residents in Paris filtered into Sweden — the most strange being that he had become "religious," that he had donned penitential robes. Strindberg a penitent! — the idea was so preposterous that it might have been dismissed as mere gossip had it not been so persistently repeated. That the reports were not gossip became apparent in 1897 on the appearance of *Inferno*, followed a year later by a kind of sequel entitled *Legends*. To those who assumed that Strindberg's long literary silence and his absorption in scientific and occultist studies had permanently removed him from the literary scene *Inferno* seemed to provide a final corroboration. Both the mad miscellany of psychic phenomena recorded in this work and its strongly moralizing religious strain suggested to many that Strindberg was a broken man whose literary career was at an end and who could but live out his remaining years apart from the actual world in some kind of presumably half-mad religious contemplation or discipline. But readers of *Inferno* might also have noted, had they been sufficiently perceptive, that the prose of this strange book had all of the analytical clarity and much of the stylistic skill of an earlier Strindberg, despite the tortured involutions of the experiences described. Strindberg's literary career was in fact far from being finished. The Inferno experience, instead of drawing the curtain on his literary career, became the point of departure for the most extraordinary and in many respects the most impressive literary productivity of Strindberg's life.

The sheer bulk of Strindberg's work in the decade and a half between the publication of *Inferno* and his death in 1912 is sufficiently impressive, including besides twenty-nine plays a volume of poetry and some fifteen volumes of prose (novels, short stories and fairy tales, polemic essays, a sensitive autobiographical sketch, and the amazing miscellany "The Blue Books"). But the variety and originality of this production is much more impressive than its bulk. The Inferno experience seemed somehow to release sources of inventiveness and fantasy in Strindberg which before had welled up only spasmodically in his work. It enabled him to cast off the partial spell which an orthodox naturalism had exercised over his earlier work and allowed his creative energies to create with a minimum of influence from without their own highly original and challenging patterns. Though "reality" has now become to Strindberg an inner world, and life in its external manifestations a fleeting, painful, worthless thing, he does not permit his work to lose contact with the actual world, the scene on which man must play out his earthly fate. Not even in the "dream plays" are we ever very far removed from the actual world, and in the best of Strindberg's other post-Inferno work (*The Saga of the Folkungs, Gustav Vasa, The Dance of Death*) we are at least as much engaged with the actual world as we had been in *The Red Room* and *The Father, Miss Julia* and *Creditors*.

What primarily distinguishes Strindberg's post-Inferno work from that which had gone before is that his intensity of vision has become sharper, more intent upon seeing life "without a film over the eyes," more achingly aware of the total misery of man. This means that his vision has become at once more brutal and more prone to forgive. With Schopenhauer he felt that inasmuch as man's life is a thing of infinite sorrows man's chief virtues must be those of understanding and pity. The sad refrain in *A Dream Play* — Indra's Daughter's "Man is to be pitied" — appears by implication if not by direct statement in most of Strindberg's post-Inferno dramas, even in that most brutal of Strindberg's marital tragedies *The Dance of Death.* Perhaps the most striking evidence from these years of Strindberg's readiness to forgive if not to forget is the relative generosity which he displayed toward his third wife, the young actress Harriet Bosse, during and shortly after the three more or less strained years of their marriage.

Only occasionally in the last years does Strindberg's anger flare up so violently that his sense of pity deserts him completely and he breaks out in a flood of sustained and merciless invective, most savagely in the devastating caricature of Gustaf af Geijerstam in *Svarta fanor* (Black Banners, 1907) and in the attack on other well-known personalities of the day in the so-called Strindberg Controversy (*Strindbergsfejden*) a few years before his death. Despite Strindberg's obvious desire to become reconciled with his enemies after the Inferno "conversion," he never succeeded (nor did he pretend to have succeeded) in rooting out all vestiges of the Old Adam. The penitential robes rested rather precariously on his sensitive, battle-scarred shoulders, and he went to the grave, as he had lived most of his years, an object of discord and strife. It is worthy of note, however, that in the last controversy which swirled around his person he took the same liberal stand on social and political questions that he had forty years earlier in *The Red Room*, his first broad frontal attack on prejudice and reaction. The Inferno experience, with its private woes and its desperate struggle with "The Powers," drew Strindberg into worlds far removed from contemporary social and political problems, but not so far removed that he could not on occasion in his later years identify himself anew with his earlier revolutionary enthusiasms.

Little of social and political criticism is to be found, however, in that part of the post-Inferno production which is most central, the dramas. These dramas are "revolutionary" in quite another sense — in the new experimental *forms* into which Strindberg poured his Inferno experience and the new view of life which this experience brought to him. Aspects of the Inferno crisis itself are directly handled in the group of three plays (*To Damascus*, I–III, *Advent*, and *There Are Crimes and Crimes*) which were written immediately after the autobiographical works *Inferno* and *Legends*, while the dramas which follow in such profusion and variety in the following decade reflect more or less directly the moods and ideas of the crisis years. Strindberg's chief dramatic problem in these plays was to find a form (or forms) which could convey more adequately than did traditional dramatic techniques the ambiguous texture of human experience, what he found to be the strange "dream-like" quality of man's existence. In his new dramaturgy Strindberg everywhere shuns the over-simplified dialectic of the realistic problem play as well as the detailed pursuit of cause-and-effect relationships so fundamental in the naturalistic drama. In place of precise and logical dialogue he substitutes broken phrases, half-articulated thoughts, stylized indirections, dramatic pauses. In place of conventional images he uses the technique of distortion. In place of obvious symbols he prefers those that have vague, indeterminate, often grotesquely ominous connotations. In place of conventional dramatic structure he employs either the schematic structural rigidity of *To Damascus* or the apparently capricious fluidity of *A Dream Play* or skillful variants of these types. The schematic ritualism of *The Crown Bride* and the religious formalism of *Easter* are more closely related to *To Damascus*, the structural fantasy of *The Spook Sonata* to the dramatic fluidity of *A Dream Play*. In the historical plays from the turn of the century (*The Saga of the Folkungs, Gustav Vasa, Erik XIV*) the over-all form is more traditional, not infrequently following Shakespeare; but in *Charles XII*, from a few years later, dream-play techniques are everywhere in evidence, and in two other historical plays, *Kristina* and *Gustav III*, Strindberg has drifted far from the Shakespearean drama without resorting to the formal experimentation particularly reminiscent of characteristic post-Inferno moods.

When Geijerstam in a letter to Strindberg after reading the manuscript of *To Damascus* referred to "the terrifying half-reality" of the play, he put his finger not only on the immediate autobiographical origins of the play, he underlined the strange sense of hovering precariously between actuality and the dream world which *To Damascus* at every point conveys. This quality is not completely absent in Strindberg's earlier work. It is latent at many points in the taut naturalism of *The Father* and *Miss Julia*, and at some points in these plays it breaks out into forms which point unmistakably forward to the terrifying visionary intensity of Strindberg's last period. It is not surprising therefore in *The Dance of Death* to come upon a Strindberg play written in 1900 which might seem to have been composed in the late 1880's. The heightened naturalism of this play, which amounts really to a kind of expressionism, is from one point of view simply a magnificently daring and sustained example of dramatic techniques which had been used more sparingly in Strindberg's so-called naturalistic dramas.

The plays from Strindberg's last period which have attracted the greatest attention are *A Dream Play* and *The Spook Sonata*, largely perhaps

Playbill designed by Carl Kylberg for performances
at Strindberg's Intimate Theater

because they have more successfully than other plays from their period
brought the magic of sharply visual theater back into the drama and have
managed so skillfully to express by means of diverse symbolic indirections a modern view of life. This view of life is profoundly pessimistic,
though in *A Dream Play* the impact of this pessimism is softened by occasional poetic utterance and tempered by the recurrent theme of pity.
In *The Spook Sonata* the pessimism is hopeless and abysmal, hammered
home with a relentless accumulation of ghastly scenes and bizarre symbols. *The Spook Sonata* has been compared with the last book of *Gulliver's Travels* in its all but monomaniacal scorn for the human animal
and the miserable life he must live. But instead of Swift's nimble narrative
inventiveness Strindberg employs all manner of bizarre and theatrical
devices, building them up into cacophonic combinations of grotesquely
monumental explosive force. *The Spook Sonata* is one of the "Chamber
Plays" which Strindberg wrote in order to provide a repertoire for the
Intimate Theatre which he and the young theater director August Falck
established in Stockholm in 1907. Another of the Chamber Plays, *Peli-*

kanen (The Pelican), is less well known but in its way is as arresting a play as *The Spook Sonata*. It impresses chiefly by its unbelievably subtle *blending* of the natural and the grotesque, the spontaneous and the bizarre, the banal and the genuinely tragic. In this play naturalism *eases* into expressionism and back into naturalism, with the enthralled reader or theatergoer being scarcely aware of the transitions or conscious at a given moment of whether he is in a "real" or an "imagined" world. In neither *A Dream Play* nor *The Spook Sonata* is such a subtle fusion of forms attained. *The Spook Sonata* seems somewhat forced by comparison, as if Strindberg had partly lost control of his materials and resorts to wildly fantastic devices in order to bring the mad ingredients of his drama into some kind of focus.

During the three years of its existence Strindberg's Intimate Theater staged with considerable success *The Father* and *The Dance of Death* and scored genuine triumphs with *Miss Julia* and *Easter*, but the Chamber Plays did not fare at all well in the hands of the youthful company of players at Strindberg's disposal. A critic or two had some words of praise for the dramatist's bizarre originality in *The Spook Sonata* and *The Pelican*, but the critics were all agreed that the performances were quite inadequate, and years passed before either of these plays found a director and a cast capable of bringing out their great theatrical possibilities. And it was in Germany rather than Sweden that the first theatrical triumphs with these plays occurred — during the First World War, in the expert hands of that master of theatrical fantasy, Max Reinhardt. When Reinhardt came to Stockholm with German versions of *The Spook Sonata* in 1917 and *The Pelican* in 1920 critics and theatergoers were overwhelmed by the dramatic power of these long-neglected plays, and since then Sweden's most distinguished Strindberg director Olof Molander has scored some of his greatest triumphs with *The Spook Sonata*, *The Pelican*, and *A Dream Play*. In New York in the 1920's, when Eugene O'Neill and the Provincetown Players staged *The Spook Sonata* and *A Dream Play*, O'Neill hailed Strindberg as "the precursor of all modernity in our present theatre just as Ibsen, a lesser man as he himself surmised, was the father of the modernity of twenty years or so ago." If great directors have been most immediately responsible for the ultimate success which Strindberg's daring post-Inferno dramaturgy has experienced in the modern theater, world events — wars and their aftermaths — have had their importance in conditioning theatrical audiences to the grim picture of life which this dramaturgy provides. Neither *The Spook Sonata* nor *The*

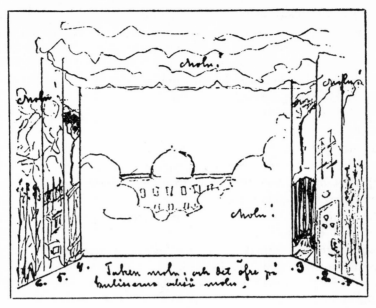

Rough scene sketch by Strindberg for staging of *A Dream Play*, together with explanatory notes by the dramatist

Pelican should seem particularly exaggerated in the lurid Inferno contexts of recent political and military history.

Had Strindberg been less fated than he was to go his own unpredictable ways he might at the beginning of his career have taken over the leadership of that young group of Swedish authors who in the early 1880's were preparing to transform Swedish letters by creating a modern realistic problem literature. As it was, Strindberg's early work served simply as a very heady wine for the "Young Sweden" group, whose leadership, such as it was, fell almost by default into the hands of Gustaf af Geijerstam (1858–1909) and Anne Charlotte Leffler (1849–92). Geijerstam, the most energetic and in some ways the least talented of the group, did what he could to hold the group together and to champion its cause before a largely hostile public by editing in 1885 and 1886 two volumes of a *Revy i literära och sociala frågor* (Review in Literary and Social Questions) and by his assiduous activity as book reviewer and lecturer. As novelist, short story writer, and dramatist he was also among the more productive of his generation, but most of his work in these genres was mediocre, and some of it, particularly the novels and plays from his later years, sank to very low popular levels.

His first works were a couple of collections of relatively callow tales about human misery and social injustice. The title of the first of these collections, *Gråkallt* (literally Gray Cold), sufficiently suggests the prevailing tone of these tales. Considerably more important but scarcely of a high order are Geijerstam's two novels *Erik Grane* (1885) and *Pastor Hallin* (1887), which seek with only limited success to depict the conflict between the older and younger generations in the 1880's. *Erik Grane* is the story (partly autobiographical) of a university student's growing dissatisfaction with and final revolt against his early religious and intellectual environment and the sterile disciplines of higher education as represented at Uppsala. *Pastor Hallin* concentrates more exclusively on the religious conflict of the 1880's without ignoring entirely the larger intellectual and social aspects of the conflict. Strindberg's influence on both of these novels is apparent at many points. Only in the peasant tales of *Fattigt folk* I, II (Poor People, 1884, 1889) and *Kronofogdens berättelser* (The District Attorney's Tales, 1890) does Geijerstam manage to create an impressive living world, in part under the influence of the Russians Tolstoi and Dostoevski whose emphasis on primitive psychology, especially criminal psychology among the peasantry, pointed the way toward a kind of realism which had little to do with the "social problem" purposes of much of Geijerstam's earlier work. In fact, Geijerstam takes the step over into pure naturalism in many of his peasant tales, particularly those like "Fadermord" (Parricide) which are based directly on court records of actual criminal cases and which seek to ferret out the chain of causes that ultimately accounts for the criminal deed. As long as Geijerstam deals with the relatively simple psychology of the peasant he is solid and impressive, but when in the 1890's and later he attempts psychological novels concerned with more complex, sophisticated people — *Boken om lillebror* (tr. *The Book about Little Brother*), *Kvinnomakt* (tr. *Woman Power*), and others — he loses himself in a maze of pretentious profundity and tearful sentimentality. In these novels as well as in his burlesque peasant comedies from the same years Geijerstam gained a wide middle-class reading public but deteriorated so hopelessly as a literary artist that the work of his last decade or two has no importance in literary developments of the day.

Anne Charlotte Leffler, who maintained for some years a kind of literary salon for the "Young Sweden" coterie and kindred spirits, was the only one of the group who attracted a fairly large reading public in the early 1880's. Her collections of short stories *Ur livet* (From Life), the first volumes of which appeared in 1882 and 1883, went through several editions and created around her person controversial eddies exceeded only by the whirlpools of polemics which swirled about the young Strindberg of these years. Though critical of contemporary social conditions, her dramas were on the whole less controversial than some of her prose fiction, partly because the endings of her plays were more often than not so inconclusive that it was difficult to know exactly where she took her stand on the problems involved. Both Ibsen and Strindberg, particularly the former, left strong imprints upon her work, Ibsen's *Brand* and *A Doll's House* and Strindberg's *The Red Room* being decisive in her development in the 1870's and early 1880's. But as the most persistent defender in Swedish literature of Ibsen's Nora-type, the "abused" woman, she came with time to infuriate Strindberg, who aimed some of his choicest satiric darts in her direction. Although many of her tales and plays focus on woman's erotic frustrations in conventional marriages, she handles the theme so coolly, with such apparent detachment, at times so evasively, that her readers might wonder whether she was aware of the nature of human passion. In her work eroticism seemed to be a matter of abstract debate on "women's rights" rather than a primitive, self-forgetful inner drive. Even in one of her better novels, *En sommarsaga* (A Summer Tale, 1886), where she seemed on the way to depicting a great selfless love, she could not finally carry the theme through — perhaps, it has been observed, because her own experience of love and marriage had lacked a decisive quality.

But in 1888 she discovered what "the great passion" really was, when, on a visit to Italy, she met and fell deeply in love with a young mathematician of liberal leanings who was shortly to inherit the title of the Duke of Cajanello. Her own previous loveless and childless marriage with a kind but conventional Swedish government official was dissolved after rather prolonged delays, and in the spring of 1890 she became the Duchess of Cajanello. Her new marital relationship, so breathtakingly happy, had revolutionary consequences for her literary development. Instead of continuing in the rigid patterns of a debate-bound bloodless "problem literature" she now responds jubilantly to those sides of human experience which the moralist looks upon askance if not with a severe condemnatory mien. Italy taught her how to exorcise the spell which a rigoristic Scandinavian ethics had long maintained over her work. But the first literary product of her new-found joy, the novel *Kvinnlighet och erotik, II* (Womanliness and Love, II, 1890), was also her last, for in 1892 death suddenly cut off her life at a moment when the new wellsprings of inspiration began to flow. *Womanliness and Love, II*, is a kind of tale retold, or, more precisely, the reconstruction of a character sketch contained in *Womanliness and Love, I*, composed many years earlier. Alie, the heroine in both stories, has in her second fictional incarnation become transformed from an independent, half-mannish feminist, acutely aware of her "rights," into a warm, spontaneous, full-blooded woman so absorbed by her experience of love that theories about women's marital rights have no meaning for her. Her exulting conviction that love alone is all, that the individual loses his identity in the experience of love, is a far cry from one of the cardinal tenets of the problem literature of the 1880's, that love and marriage should in no way encroach upon "a woman's right to develop her own personality." With all its freshness and vivacity, its engaging warmth and spontaneity, *Womanliness and Love, II*, is structurally amorphous and stylistically very uneven. It is but a promise of what might have come had its author been permitted to gain the perspective of additional years in the handling of her new material. From a purely literary point of view her best work is to be found neither in her serious problem prose nor in her last literary joy in a new-found life, but rather in some of her least ambitious stories such as "Gusten får pastoratet" (Gusten Gets the Parish) and "Moster Malvina" (Aunt Malvina), lively little tales about simple people whose modest claims on life preclude all concern with "problems" in the 1880's sense or with the resplendent glories of "the great passion."

The most sober and objective of the "Young Sweden" coterie, the one who least identified himself with its challenging social call to arms, was Tor Hedberg (1862–1931). Though his loyalty to the group was genuine enough, he was by temperament little disposed to engage in literary debate on social questions, and after dutifully turning out a story or two in the manner of his "Young Sweden" colleagues (most notaby in *Högre uppgifter*, Higher Tasks, 1884) he went his own quiet way, writing a variety of short stories and novels and plays in which the focus of our interest is invariably maintained on purely psychological conflicts and broad ethical problems. In keeping with a realistic literary ideal, however, this focus does not exclude a reasonably careful building-up of milieu, particularly in such of Hedberg's more impressive novels as *Johannes Karr* (1885) and *På Torpa gård* (On Torpa Farm, 1888). But intelligent and sensitive as such novels are, they fall short of the tragic greatness they seek to attain. In these novels as in nearly all of Hedberg's later creative work there is a sense of artistic integrity that tends to bind rather than release, a sober honesty of approach that too often invests his prose (and for that matter his verse) with a certain stiffness, even heaviness. Only in a few of his many dramas does he come close to greatness, closest in *Johan Ulfstjerna* (tr. *Johan Ulfstjerna*, 1907), an inspired dramatic glorification of the political murder in 1904 of the Russian tyrant Bobrikov at the hand of the aging Finnish poet-patriot Eugen Schauman. It is perhaps not unfair to say that Tor Hedberg's single most important contribution to Swedish culture lay in his work as a critic rather than as a creative literary artist, despite his long and honorable career as a writer of prose fiction, verse, and drama which reflect at every point a sensitive and intelligent awareness of the problems of his day. In 1897 he began to share with Oscar Levertin responsibility for literary and art criticism in the columns of *Svenska Dagbladet*, established at this time, and in the decade which followed he devoted himself to the task with a conscientiousness, solidity, catholicity of taste and breadth of view rare in Swedish criticism. His colleague Levertin was more brilliant and popular but not always as sound or reliable in his critical judgments. The range and quality of Hedberg's contribution are reflected in the representative selection from his criticism republished in 1912–13 in the three-volume *Ett decennium: uppsatser och kritiker i litteratur, konst, teater m.m.* (A Decade: Essays and Criticisms in Literature, Art, Theater, etc.). Hedberg's reputation as a person of high integrity and broadly inclusive cultural attainments came with the years to be recognized by his appointment in 1910 as director of the Royal Dramatic Theater, in his election in 1922 to the Swedish Academy, and in his appointment in 1924 as director of the famous Thiel Art Gallery in Stockholm. His work as director of the Royal Dramatic Theater resulted in a refreshing though not too successful effort to rejuvenate that hitherto staid institution, among other ways by opening its doors more than had previously been the case to Strindberg's plays.

The original "Young Sweden" group, not overly provided with literary talent within the limits of its base of operations at Stockholm, had occasion from time to time to welcome in its midst those young authors from other parts of the kingdom who in the early 1880's had intellectual and literary affinities with the Stockholm group. Among the most promising of these young authors were those who from time to time came up to the capital from the southern province of Skåne. None of them remained long in Stockholm, for they did not find conditions entirely to their liking; but their direct contacts with the "Young Sweden" group at least helped them to recognize their own partial variation from the distinctively Stockholm form of literary realism, and enabled each of them on his return to Skåne to develop his talents free from the immediate demands of a coterie-inspired literature. All of the Skåne authors were originally in essential agreement with the realistic social-problem program of the "Young Sweden" group, but they had arrived at their literary position independent of their colleagues to the north, and each was ultimately to pursue lines of development in more or less conscious opposition to the Stockholm group. Aside from a natural sense of rivalry with their Stockholm contemporaries two circumstances determined from the start their deviation from the Stockholm realists: their attachment to the native province of Skåne and their closer proximity to Denmark and the Continent. Particularly in their early work did the Skåne authors find inspiration and subject matter in the landscape and the folk culture of their province, while their later work reflects a considerably greater sensitivity than was characteristic of the Stockholm group to the rapidly shifting intellectual and literary currents of the Continent in the late

1880's and the 1890's. They were able in consequence to detach themselves with relative ease from the more orthodox forms of an earlier literary realism.

Of the four Skåne authors of chief importance only one, the poet A. U. Bååth (1853–1912), had no direct personal contacts with the "Young Sweden" writers. He had appeared on the literary scene before the Stockholm group had come into existence and had written practically all of his significant verse before the group had become sufficiently articulate to make its voice generally heard. Though his poetic productivity stretches over some three decades, only the first five years are of importance. The first volume of *Dikter* (Poems) appeared in 1879, the second, *Nya dikter* (New Poems) in 1881, the third, *Vid allfarväg* (On the Highroad) in 1884, after which five other volumes of verse came from his pen, all five distinctly inferior to the earlier three volumes. Bååth's significance lies in the fact that he brought Swedish poetry *sharply* down to earth after its long, many-winged flight into regions more or less distantly removed from the everyday cares and conditions of man's actual existence. Other poets — Bellman, Geijer, Almqvist, and especially Runeberg — had pointed the way; but none of them had so completely dispensed with traditional poetic accouterments as Bååth was to do in his early poetry. In part this can be explained by the spirit of the times, but certainly more important was Bååth's own solid, heavy, earth-bound temperament. In his early verse he had learned to "put problems into debate" from such Danish contemporaries as Holger Drachmann, whose flaming "socialistic" poems from the early 1870's had stirred up the placid waters of Danish verse and had attracted some young admirers in the neighboring Swedish province of Skåne. Following this lead, Bååth wrote in a rather less inflammatory mood about poverty, inequality, and the rumbling dissatisfaction of the masses in such poems as "En Pingstdagsmorgon" (A Whitsunday Morning), "Vid Café du lac" (At the Café du Lac), and "Ett socialistmöte" (A Socialist Meeting). Such poems were, however, relatively peripheral in Bååth's work, a reflection simply of a warm humanitarian strain in his character rather than a deliberate poetic dedication to a program of social protest. Bååth's poems dealing with the landscape and folk life of Skåne are more important, more central. The very limitations of these poems are their virtues. Lacking entirely the musical qualities and the large imaginative perspectives of traditional Swedish verse, they can concentrate the more intently upon what the poet *sees* and what he *hears*. The result is a simple, direct poetic realism, which at its best — as in "Vinterstämning" (Winter Mood), "Sydskånsk sommarkväll" (Summer Evening in South-Skåne), and "Nyårsafton på skånska slätten" (New Year's Eve on Skåne's Prairies) — has an artistic integrity of rare impressiveness. And even when this poetic realism is not at its best it has a solid honesty and a concrete, factual quality which the modern mind must admire. Though Bååth is certainly not to be counted among Sweden's great poets, he fills his own minor niche with a good deal of the robust dignity of the Skåne peasantry whose character and way of life so frequently inspired his modest muse.

The case of another poet, Ola Hansson (1860–1925), who counted many generations of Skåne peasants among his ancestors, is far more complex. He shared Bååth's admiration for the folk of his province, but endowed with a much more subtle poetic sensibility he came to go quite other literary ways. At first it might have seemed that he was treading in Bååth's firmly planted footsteps — thematically in his first volume of poems he indicted social injustices even more sharply than Bååth and wrote with warm feeling about the countryside of Skåne. But Ola Hansson's touch in the Skåne poems had none of the heaviness, none of the sturdy earthiness or rugged poetic phrasing of Bååth's. It was by contrast soft, subtly probing, full of delicate nuances, in its more advanced forms highly sophisticated, in its tone and implications essentially decadent. In Ola Hansson the peasant blood of Skåne had begun to thin out, a hypersensitive intellectualism had largely taken over. This resulted in a poetry of extraordinary refinement, hovering always on the brink of decadence and not infrequently yielding completely to its darkly fastidious fascinations. As one peasant-born he felt in his blood the slow, rhythmic pulse of nature, the steady succession of the seasons, the continuous ebb and flow of decay and renewal in all organic life. But as a highly cultured modern spirit he also had in his blood the restive, nervous, irregular tempi of modern man. His poetic sensitivity was combined with an unusual intellectual and literary receptivity, and in the unhappy union of these two qualities is probably to be found the explanation of his life's tragedy. But back of this almost certainly lay an inherited pathological condition, heightened through the years by a growing feeling of literary isolation. In the period of his intellectual and literary maturing, the late 1880's, the only Swede of stature with whom he came in reasonably close personal contact was Strindberg, whose own highly developed feeling of insecurity at this time could hardly give comfort to Ola Hansson. For a few hectic years beginning in the late fall of 1888 Strindberg and Ola Hansson fed each other's sickly discontents — with unhappy consequences for both of them. The coolness not unmixed with irritation (at times, indeed, with horror) that Swedish critics almost without exception maintained toward Ola Hansson's early works precipitated a crisis in his development and led directly to his decision, in 1889, to emigrate to the Continent, where until his death more than thirty years later he (together with his German-born wife, Laura Marholm) carried on a busy miscellaneous literary activity. During the first decade and a half of his exile he published largely in German, after which he found some outlets for his essays and poems, short stories and autobiographical sketches also in Sweden. His autobiographical works *Före giftermålet* (Before the Marriage), *En uppfostrare* (An Educator), and *Resan hem* (The Trip Home), all from the mid-1890's, and *Rustgården* from 1910, are of considerable importance to those interested in Hansson's early points of conflict with Swedish conditions, but his critical essays are of much more permanent importance. Though some of these essays deal with Scandinavian authors, most of them are concerned with larger intellectual and literary contexts, by preference with contemporary French and German figures (Paul Bourget, J. K. Huysmans, Jean Richepin, Barbey d'Aurevilly, Garschin, Stirner, Nietzsche, and the painter Böcklin) and with Edgar Allan Poe. In most of these essays Ola Hansson has a polemic purpose, a discrediting of the literary program of the Swedish 1880's insofar as this program persisted in its naturalism and its social reform aims, its utilitarianism and its political awareness. Ola Hansson's voice was, however, hardly discernible in the Swedish literary debate of the day despite the unusual perceptiveness and the daring modernity of his critical contribution. Berlin, where he had first settled, was rather distant from the Swedish cultural scene, and other voices with largely other ideas determined the directions to be taken by Swedish poets when in the early 1890's Swedish literature "changed its signals" and broke all but completely out of the bonds of an everyday realism and the demands of a social conscience.

It was as a poet that Ola Hansson made his basic contribution to Swedish literature — in the two thin volumes *Dikter* (Poems, 1884) and *Notturno* (1885). That he did not continue as a poet is perhaps largely to be attributed to the hostility of the critics and the indifference of the public for his *kind* of poetry. Especially in *Notturno* the verse is subtle and refined far beyond anything hitherto attempted in Swedish nature poetry. Though the subject matter of this verse is in one sense the Skåne countryside, this immediate physical world is not employed as an object for "description" or abstract "commentary." It is simply a point of reference for finely felt perceptions, distillations of sensory experience, mysterious intimations of parallels and relations between man's subconscious and unconscious urges and nature's eternal processes of growth and decay, its alternating patterns of life and death. Nature in this poetry has become spirit without losing its direct sensory appeal, as if physical and psychic phenomena were actually one. In Ola Hansson's hands we witness the transformation of naturalism into a kind of psycho-physiological mysticism. It is little wonder that neither critics nor the Swedish reading public of the time found this to their liking. Conditioned as they were either by a conservative idealism or by a realistic radicalism they found such studied subtleties either suspect or unintelligible or both. And the form of these poems was as disconcerting to contemporary Swedish critics as their moods and ideas. Ola Hansson's free metrical patterns with their unusual use of dactyls and their sinuous enveloping quality seemed somehow to take indecent liberties with the traditions of Swedish prosody.

When therefore in 1887 *Sensitiva amorosa* appeared with its daring series of case studies in erotic abnormalities, clothed in a garment of delicate poetic prose, the outcry against Ola Hansson in Sweden was almost universal. His treatment of the erotic experience in purely aesthetic terms seemed excessively overrefined, and his conception of love between the sexes as a fathomless succession of frustrations was worlds removed both from the sentimental bourgeois idealism and the radical feminist realism of the day. Today we are not so disturbed by Ola Hansson's decadence and stylistic refinements. In fact, we find the prose of *Sensitiva amorosa* an extraordinarily stimulating stylistic experiment in a day when Swedish prose in general was anything but subtle, and we can now see that the poetry of *Notturno* was a very important step forward in the freeing of Swedish verse from overrigid metrical patterns. Had Ola Hansson's early poetry met with more understanding and sympathy he might have become one of the really great Swedish poets. As it is his poetry remains but an absorbing torso. He had poetic sensibility of the highest order, an intelligence unusual among poets, and a finely disciplined command of language. How finely disciplined his command of language was is nowhere in his work more apparent than in *Notturno* and *Sensitiva amorosa*, two of the most arresting works which appeared in Sweden in the 1880's.

In addition to the poets from Skåne, A. U. Bååth and Ola Hansson, two writers of prose fiction from this southern Swedish province are worthy of attention. The one, Axel Lundegård (1861–1930), was at the beginning of his career the most radical of the Skåne authors, but with the publication of the novel *Röde prinsen* (The Red Prince) in 1889 he disavowed his earlier loyalty to a democratic realistic ideal of literature and devoted most of his energies during the remainder of his life to the writing of a series of not particularly important historical novels. A more important work, and one which Lundegård carried out with admirable taste and considerable candor, was the task he performed as literary executor for his friend Victoria Benedictsson (1850–88), one of the most remarkable Scandinavian personalities of her day and a literary talent appreciably above most of her Swedish contemporaries. At the time of her death by her own hand she had published (under the pseudonym Ernst Ahlgren) a couple of interesting novels, some of the best short stories we have from the 1880's, and (together with Lundegård) the drama *Final*. After her death Lundegård completed a novel and a drama which she had left unfinished and published a considerable portion of her other literary remains, including large parts of her journals and letters, in the somewhat unreliable essentially autobiographical work *Victoria Benedictsson, en sjelvbiografi ur brev och anteckningar* (1890; 3rd rev. ed., 1928).

No Swedish author has fought more fiercely against greater odds for literary recognition than Victoria Benedictsson. Brought up as a child under difficult circumstances on the Skåne countryside, and living out her young womanhood in a stuffy provincial community with a husband more than twice her age and five stepchildren, she had always met with misunderstanding and opposition in her desire to develop her artistic and literary interests. Her first contact with a larger world came when she met a free-wheeling Swedish-American radical named Quillfeldt, but much more important was her meeting with Lundegård, who introduced her to the literary worlds of both Stockholm and Copenhagen and who became her literary confidant and co-worker. With the "Young Sweden" coterie she did not find herself particularly at home when late in 1885 she visited Stockholm, but in the Danish capital a year later she found things somewhat more to her liking. Among the Danes to whom Lundegård introduced her was Georg Brandes, with whom she fell desperately in love and who reciprocated her love for him by finding in her but one of the more "interesting" of his many "conquests." This shattered her

Strindberg at Lund in the 1890's

Stockholm production of *Fröken Julie* during the Strindberg
Centennial, January 1949

University of Minnesota Theater production of *The
Dream Play*, November 1948

Sketch by Carl Larsson of the Hasselbacken restaurant, Stockholm, 1885,
depicting animated conversation among well-known
artists and authors

Gustaf af Geijerstam, portrait by
Carl Larsson, 1901 (photo: SPA)

Victoria Benedictsson in 1888 (The
University Library, Lund)

Tor Hedberg, portrait by Eugène
Jansson, 1910 (photo: SPA)

spirit and occasioned her suicide at the age of thirty-eight, four years after her first modest literary success.

Victoria Benedictsson like Ola Hansson bore within her two strongly conflicting strains, one sound, earth-bound, and healthy, the other over-sensitive, intensely passionate, potentially sickly. But unlike the case of Ola Hansson, the sound and healthy strain dominates in what she wrote — until the Brandes episode crushed her proud will and placed the mark of tragic desperation on her work. Then driven by the furies within her she poured out in her last months a number of terrifying, dark-hued, erup-tively primitive works, some in only fragmentary form. Under various easily penetrated disguises they lay bare her feelings in the shadow of what to her was inevitable, death by her own hand. The most impressive of these are the short stories "Förbrytarblod" (Criminal Blood) and "Livsleda" (Satiety), with the unfinished drama *Den bergtagna* (The Be-witched One) falling little short of the same high creative level.

The works for which Victoria Benedictsson is better known, how-ever, are her short stories and novels from days when she was less des-perately preoccupied with personal problems and more concerned with the living, pulsing, external world around her. The two volumes of sketches and short stories and the two novels written in these days fall naturally into two categories: the shorter fictional forms are almost ex-clusively objective treatments of everyday life on the Skåne countryside, while the novels provide Victoria Benedictsson's contribution to the "problem literature" of the time. In the two problem novels, *Pengar* (Money, 1885) and *Fru Marianne* (1887), she is concerned with that most persistently recurrent of problems in the literature of the 1880's, love and the institution of marriage. But it is characteristic of Victoria Benedictsson's independence of judgment that she only in part falls in line with the views typical of the 1880's on the subject. In *Money* she may be said to be in essential agreement with these views, when she elo-quently defends divorce as the only decent means of escape from the marital hell in which her heroine finds herself. The appearance of this novel delighted the "Young Sweden" writers and that highly vocal femi-nist phalanx in Stockholm which propagandized busily at the time for "women's rights."

But when *Fru Marianne* appeared it was evident that Victoria Bene-dictsson was not the uncritical feminist Sir Galahad that she had seemed to be, for in this novel she examines — and condemns — the more extreme developments in what may loosely be called the feminist literature of the

day. Particularly did she condemn that radical offshoot of feminist literature called "free love," which had recently been so brutishly championed
by the Norwegian Hans Jaeger in the novel *Fra Kristiania-Bohêmen* and
which flourished in more sophisticated forms in Copenhagen literary circles. Even Victoria Benedictsson's closest friend, Axel Lundegård, had
publicly identified himself with the "free love" advocates. Against such
views the whole healthy side of Victoria Benedictsson arose in revolt. To
her, love was not an episode, or series of episodes, to be enjoyed for the
moment whether in merely sensual or more fastidious forms. It was man's
and woman's definitive experience, compounded in its only justifiable
form of utter devotion and loyalty while resting on a solid basis of biological attraction. As such the supreme insult to love is the mere flirtation,
the handling of love as a plaything, as something to pick up or drop as
one's whims dictate. In *Fru Marianne* the heroine is at the beginning a
spoiled creature married to the simple, strong peasant Börje, whom she is
quite incapable of appreciating, let alone really love. In her indolent, self-
indulgent existence she is attracted for a time to her husband's friend Pål
Sandell, an incarnation of the decadent aesthete; but she finally tires of
Pål's flirtatious subtleties and finds a rich and satisfying love in Börje's
arms and in his solid workaday world. Marianne's story is that of
Emma Bovary, with a different ending. Victoria Benedictsson might have
weathered the storm of protest among liberals and radicals on the publication of *Fru Marianne* had not the Copenhagen newspaper *Politiken*
published a scornful review which she assumed had been written by
Georg Brandes. She considered this review to be her literary death sentence.

    In Victoria Benedictsson's collections of tales and sketches, *Från Skåne*
(From Skåne, 1884) and *Folklif och småberättelser* (Folk Life and Short
Tales, 1887), her admiration for the sound and healthy life of the Skåne
countryside is evident without her making a particular issue of her admiration as she does in *Fru Marianne*. And it is in consequence more
impressive. Her folk tales have points of contact both with the programmatic realism of her immediate Danish predecessors (Sophus Schandorph
and Henrik Pontoppidan) in the genre and with a native contemporary
folkloristic realism as represented in August Bondeson and Henrik Wra-
nér, but she manages in most of her tales to create her own folk world,
chiefly because she knew this world at first hand and refused to make of
it anything either better or worse than it was. In the little sketch "En
studie" she sharply satirizes the kind of folk literature which used lovely

words to hide a fundamental ignorance of its subject, and she found equally false that kind of folk literature which emphasized only the brutish sides of peasant life. She can on occasion lean a bit toward idyllicism and the sentimental, as in the highly popular tale "Mor Malenas höna" (Mother Malena's Hen), but almost always her folk tales are straightforward, simply phrased, eminently honest pictures of folk life as she knew it. Her realism is quite unstudied, never going out of its way to shock the reader and yet never hesitating to use the strong word or the gross detail when the situation called for it. And even though she never tired of depicting the qualities of honesty, industry, and loyalty in the folk character of her native Skåne — see "Vid sotsängen" (At the Deathbed), "Historien om en näsduk" (The Story of a Handkerchief) — she recognized without being unduly disturbed the cruder traits which in their way were equally characteristic of the folk. "Giftermål på besparing" (Thrifty Marriage), for instance, is a priceless yarn about the crass self-interest of a peasant in matters matrimonial. Nearly always Victoria Benedictsson's realism is tempered by a brusquely controlled humor, the kind of slyly meaningful humor practiced by the folk whom she depicts. How close she felt to these simple folk and how much they meant to her she expressed one time in these words: "I have grown up among the folk, among coarse farm workers and their children. I know their faults, but in spite of this there are bonds between their class and me which shall never break. They have given me much; yes, I dare say that the most healthy strains in me have their roots among the common folk."

The Poetic Renaissance of the 1890's

THE SWEDISH 1890's liked to think of itself as in opposition to the 1880's, and literary historians have until fairly recently been disposed to perpetuate the view that the relation between the 1890's and the 1880's was very largely a negative one. But it has become apparent that this long-held view has to be modified. It is of course clear that in certain respects the 1890's moved quite deliberately in directions other than those typical of the preceding decade. In place of the earlier predilection for social problems and photographic realism, the 1890's tended to cultivate a cult of beauty and stressed a freely creative imaginative art. In place of an emphasis on the present and the predominant use of prose, it found a new interest in the past and displayed a strong preference for poetic forms. In place of the cultural cosmopolitanism of the 1880's, it returned to national themes and regional materials of all kinds. But despite such differences the 1890's did not represent the complete break with the 1880's which has frequently been assumed.

We have seen that the 1880's was not *merely* a period of prose and realism and social propaganda, that it bore within itself literary potentials which not infrequently came with time to break over into worlds of idea and form that in certain ways denied its own original literary program and pointed forward to things to come. None of the Swedish authors who in the early 1880's had enthusiastically embraced the doctrine that literature should serve primarily the purposes of social reform remained completely loyal to this doctrine very long. Well before the end of the decade they had one after another begun to release themselves from the more rigid implications of the dictum that "literature should put problems into debate," and by 1890 most of them were identifying themselves with literary ideals which diverged more or less definitely from their earlier almost exclusive preoccupation with social problems. Geijerstam had abandoned "the novel with a purpose" in favor of a more objective kind of prose fiction and was finally to write psychological novels with "mystical" overtones. Anne Charlotte Leffler had found in her second marriage a world of values which had little to do with her former strenuously feminist literary bias. Ola Hansson, with the assistance of the French decadents, had categorically condemned naturalistic materialism and found a kind of spiritual refuge in a rather curious combination of pseudo-mystical and Nietzschean ideas. And Strindberg was at the close of the 1880's descending into that private hell of his which led to the Inferno crisis and a new religious-tinged "dream world" art. The 1880's, which at the beginning had so optimistically accepted the challenge of rebuilding society in terms of a radical social gospel, found itself before the decade had run its course steeped in a variety of points of view and involved in a diversity of problems which were often far removed from the social pathos of its early years. It was not therefore so strange as it might seem, that when Verner von Heidenstam published in 1888 the volume of poems *Vallfart och vandringsår* (Pilgrimage and Wander-Years), with its colorful exoticism and its impudent avowal of other gods than those of realism and utility and social pathos, he was enthusiastically hailed in almost all quarters — including those of the so-called *80-talister* who had begun their literary careers under the sign of quite other literary constellations than did the young aristocrat Heidenstam.

When Heidenstam a year after the appearance of his first volume of poems published the polemic essay "Renässans" (Renaissance) he deeply offended some of the *80-talister* by disparaging much of the literature of the 1880's, but the essay included also words of appreciation on the role that the naturalism of the 1880's had played in permanently removing from the Swedish literary scene the sentimental idealism and empty imitative verse of the immediately preceding period. With the years, it is true, Heidenstam and others among the chief figures of the 1890's became increasingly critical of certain aspects of the literature of the 1880's and more and more conservative in their political thinking, but their general view of life retained essential points of contact with the 1880's and their poetic form incorporated elements of realism which would have been unthinkable before that decade. It is important to keep in mind that all of the major authors of the 1890's had their formative years in the 1880's, and they could not (and for that matter did not wish to) cast off completely the intellectual and literary radicalism of the Sweden of their youth. They shared, for instance, the religious emancipation of the 1880's and brought to completion the secularization of literature which had taken such giant strides just before 1890. They accepted in the main the scientific world view of their immediate predecessors. They despised, as had the authors of the 1880's, the legitimist reactionarianism of the permanent secretary of the Swedish Academy, Carl David af Wirsén, who in the name of Lutheran orthodoxy and ancient aristocratic social and political prerogatives attempted vainly to stem the tide of modern thought which was revitalizing Swedish literature in the closing decades of the nineteenth century. And even in their social and political thinking the authors of the 1890's leaned for a time toward the liberalism of the 1880's, though under the pressure of events and in keeping with their essentially conservative instincts they came ultimately to identify themselves more or less clearly with those forces which sought to preserve traditional Swedish forms and values.

Though the 1880's was in its closing years feeling its way toward literary horizons not envisioned in the program of its early years, the event which finally triggered the magnificent flood of creative activity which is now generally called "the 1890's" (*nittiotalet*) was the appearance of Heidenstam's first volume of poems and his polemic essays and sketches which immediately followed. The way toward a new poetic renaissance which Heidenstam envisioned in these works was eagerly followed by an extraordinary galaxy of new literary talent. Heidenstam's example as a poet and his skill as a polemicist shattered the partial spell which the rigoristic realism of the early 1880's had managed to exercise over cultural developments, and a new group of authors took possession of the Swedish literary scene. Never before in Sweden had so many literary figures of the first order appeared in such a short period of time. By the middle of the 1890's three major poets, Heidenstam, Fröding, and Karlfeldt, together with Sweden's greatest story teller Selma Lagerlöf, had made their appearance, and two figures of lesser stature, Oscar Levertin and Per Hallström, had joined "the great four" on the slopes of a rejuvenated Swedish Parnassus. A new Golden Age had burst into a brilliant bloom almost overnight to take its place with the Gustavian and the Romantic eras as one of the three high points of Swedish poetic creation.

Among the charges which Heidenstam had made against the 1880's was that its effort to cultivate a photographic realism had stultified the creative individuality of the poet, and he called instead for a literary freedom

which would allow the poet to follow the bent of his own genius undeterred by doctrinaire demands which sought rigidly to define the nature
and purposes of literature. The authors of the 1890's, whether immediately under the influence of Heidenstam or not, came to exemplify his
view — Selma Lagerlöf's naïvely canny narrative fantasy recapturing the
magic of the folk-tale tradition, Fröding's complex, alternately gay and
tragic genius pouring out verse with a melodic virtuosity unique in
Swedish poetry, Karlfeldt's sturdy masculinity identifying itself with the
deeply rooted folk culture of his native province Dalarna, Heidenstam's
aristocratic tastes finding in the great national traditions a chief source of
poetic inspiration, and Levertin's sensitive talents adding a note of studied, elegant decadence to the many-voiced chorus around him. All in all
the variety and splendor of the literature which in the 1890's flooded the
Swedish book market was overwhelming in its effect. But the reading
public found this rich literary fare more than welcome after the rather
Spartan diet to which they had been subjected in the 1880's; and the new
authors managed to enhance further their standing with their reading
public when they came to have at their disposal two highly influential
organs of opinion, the distinguished cultural journal *Ord och Bild*
(1892ff.) and the newspaper *Svenska Dagbladet*, the latter taken over
and reorganized in 1897 under the aegis of a group whose central figure
was Heidenstam. Though those who determined the editorial policies of
Ord och Bild and *Svenska Dagbladet* insisted that their publications were
not intended to represent any particular cultural point of view or favor
any literary coterie, it was inevitable that both publications had a rather
strong bias in the direction of works typical of the 1890's. It is true that
Levertin, who together with Tor Hedberg was responsible for the book
reviews and critical essays in *Svenska Dagbladet*, was highly critical of
Fröding's at times folksy poetic vein, but otherwise Levertin's judgments
were almost invariably favorable toward the work of the major authors
of the decade. As to Strindberg's post-Inferno drama, which in its way
departed as sharply from the literary ideals of the 1880's as anything
written by the poets of the 1890's, Levertin was either cool or sharply
condemnatory. On *The Dance of Death*, for instance, he passed the astonishing judgment: "a more monstrous, and what is worse, a more dull
drama has never come from Strindberg's pen."

While the authors of the 1890's accepted the scientific world view of
the 1880's and sympathized generally with its social program, they were
not inclined to pursue with the persistence of their predecessors all of

the revolutionary implications of these new ways of thinking. In their religious and ethical views they were in fundamental agreement with the preceding decade, but unlike the young radicals of the 1880's they seldom made a sharp issue of their opposition to the Established Church and traditional moral concepts. Their early social and political radicalism was sporadic and rather halfhearted, and it soon yielded either to indifference or to an actively conservative attitude toward actual developments of the day. It is one of the paradoxes of Swedish cultural history that at the moment when the social conflict in Sweden becomes for the first time really acute, literary developments turn rather sharply away from the immediate realities of the conflict. The years around 1890 were tense with demands for reform. An extension of the suffrage was being urged by many groups at this time, and the rise during these years of an aggressive, highly organized labor movement, together with the founding of the Social Democratic party, emphasized the need for change. But the literature of these years only occasionally reminds us of these matters. Only on the issue of universal manhood suffrage do the authors of the 1890's take a generally positive stand. Otherwise — with the partial exception of Fröding — they tended either to ignore or react coolly to the mounting popular protests against social and economic injustice. Rich and significant as the literature of the 1890's in many ways was, its sources of inspiration and its prevailing interests and lines of development were on the whole rather far removed from actual contact with the more burning issues of the day.

Instead of concerning itself with these actual issues, most of the literature of these years and immediately after tended to gravitate toward the past or to stress the values of poetic individualism or to champion forms of aestheticism which oscillated uncertainly between the extremes of "joy of living" (livsglädje) and decadence. Of the ways in which the 1890's conceived its literary function and program, neither its call for "joy of living" nor its "aestheticism" proved in the long run to have any great artistic vitality. They served more as literary catchwords in the campaign of reaction against the realism of the 1880's than as significant permanent elements in the new literary program. Long before the close of the 1890's the carefree amorality implicit in the phrase "joy of living" had been replaced by concepts more in keeping with heroic ethical ideals. And as to the "aestheticism" of the 1890's it is now clear that it was never as prevalent as had earlier been assumed. Certainly the Swedish 1890's had few serious points of contact with that radical form of decadent and semi-decadent aestheticism typical of *fin de siècle* developments on the Continent and in England. Only Ola Hansson and Levertin were strongly attracted to this kind of aestheticism, and Ola Hansson at least partially extricated himself from its subtle blandishments at the close of the 1880's under the influence of Nietzsche, while Levertin ultimately drew back from its more paradoxical manifestations as represented particularly in Oscar Wilde's last tragic years. Heidenstam, Levertin's closest friend, reacted vigorously against all forms of the decadent aestheticism of the day, and neither Fröding nor Karlfeldt nor Selma Lagerlöf seems to have been much more than generally aware of its existence. Sweden's *fin de siècle* literature was both too robust and too humane, too positive and too creatively vital to identify itself in any significant way with the ultimate in aesthetic refinements and decadent subtleties from abroad even though cultured Swedes of the day were sufficiently cognizant of the literary implications of the work of Baudelaire, Paul Verlaine, and J. K. Huysmans, Dante Gabriel Rossetti, Swinburne, and Oscar Wilde.

In fact, Sweden's intellectual and literary dependence on foreign importations, so marked a feature of the 1880's, largely disappears in the 1890's, to be replaced at least for the time being by a vigorous sense of creative independence. This was made possible by a general reawakening of a national spirit in the land and by the high quality of original genius among those authors who came to represent centrally the literature of the new decade. The foreign prophets of the Swedish 1880's, particularly Ibsen with the ascetic moral rigorism of *Brand*, are rejected in favor of less otherworldly, more earth-bound voices — voices which find indigenous inspiration in the glories of the national past and in the pulse beat of folk life and the diverse patterns of folk culture. Insofar as foreign influences operate in the Swedish 1890's they are relatively incidental. They are only in exceptional cases reflected in particular phases of development in individual authors, never determining the basic patterns of general literary development. Swedish literature becomes again in the 1890's a *Swedish* literature, after a period in which it had rather too slavishly followed foreign prophets and had sworn allegiance to foreign gods. No period in Swedish literary history is so essentially Swedish in its orientation as is the 1890's.

That this orientation was not an accident, that it reflected a deeply felt cultural need of the time, is apparent from the fact that the late 1880's and the 1890's were years in which a rising tide of interest in all aspects of the Swedish past is everywhere apparent. At this time, for instance,

Artur Hazelius (1833–1901) was busily engaged in establishing Skansen, the great Swedish outdoor ethnographical museum, and a brilliant group of Swedish painters (Anders Zorn, Carl Larsson, and others) were rediscovering folk life and the glories of the Swedish countryside after a period of early training in Paris. Poets and painters and enthusiastic students of the roots of an ancient Swedish folk culture join in the 1890's in the common task of reminding a not inattentive public that it should cherish the patterns of its early culture in a world on the verge of rapid change under the impact of modern industrialization. These poets and painters and ethnographical enthusiasts felt that a changing Sweden would be infinitely poorer if it did not somehow carry over into its modern way of life those values from its past capable of exercising a vital, continuing influence on the shape and substance of its present and future.

The danger was of course actual that this preoccupation with traditional national values might deteriorate into mere antiquarianism or sentimentalism or sterile conventionalism, or — worse — become a rallying point for chauvinistic excesses or an instrument of political reaction. And the literary level of the 1890's was not always above such ways of using the materials of a folk tradition. But on the whole this literature maintained even on its folk-inspired side a high level of creative activity, thanks chiefly to the extraordinary originality and vitality of its poetic talents. Each of the four major figures of the 1890's, not to mention less important figures, was a genius of marked originality and power. In general their originality is perhaps most impressively demonstrated in their ability to pour new wine into the old bottles of an early nineteenth-century Romantic tradition. But the label "Neo-Romantic," which has been applied to the 1890's, is justified only in certain limited senses. The authors of the 1890's, like the Romantics, cultivated by preference the poetic genres, they found in nature and folk life one of their chief sources of inspiration, and they exploited at times for purposes of political propaganda the shades of a great Swedish national past. But the authors of the 1890's manipulated these forms and materials in fresh, often strikingly original ways and managed to avoid some of the unhappy pitfalls of the Romantics. They substituted for the speculative propensities of the Romantics a robust, sharply sensed, earthy concreteness which amounted to a kind of poetic realism. They avoided the stale "Gothicism" which the Romantics had inherited from a centuries-long heroic tradition and replaced it with an essentially new, more complex and profound interpretation of the historical process which had created and sustained the Swedish nation. They enriched the concept of the nation's folk culture by recognizing much more than had the Romantics the regional diversity of this folk culture. And they managed in the main to avoid the relative solemnity of the Romantic poets by infusing into the poetic fabric of the 1890's a rich strain of humor, gay or whimsical or warmly human by turn.

But in particularly one respect the literature of the 1890's struck a false note, at least in the judgment of a later, more sober generation. It was at times too self-conscious, too affected, too merely decorative. It was not always averse to evading reality and seeking poetic effects, acting an artificial literary "role." It sometimes confused poetry with high-flown and empty rhetorical periods. All of this is naturally distasteful to present-day critical standards, so distasteful, indeed, that some critics are prepared to dismiss the 1890's as largely a brilliant episode in Swedish literary history. Surely, however, such a judgment is unduly harsh: it does not sufficiently take into account the real substance behind the glittering façade. Selma Lagerlöf may seem hopelessly naïve to some modern readers, but her naïveté was certainly not completely lacking in those complex ingredients of which a modern world view is made. Fröding and Karlfeldt are each in his way profoundly seeking souls, the former torn by inner conflicts of the most tragic kind, the latter potentially eruptive beneath the deceptively calm surface of his robust personality. And Levertin's aestheticism builds its delicately precarious superstructure of sensuous beauty on foundations compounded of modern pessimism and a clear-headed materialistic determinism.

When some critics of our day charge the 1890's with self-consciousness, posing, and a weakness for decorative effects, they usually (and with considerable justification) have particularly in mind the case of Verner von Heidenstam (1859–1940), whose work tends always to be cloaked in an aristocratic panoply whether it is indulging in the sumptuous imagery of his early verse or is cast in the severe Classical forms of his mature poetry. Heidenstam could not — nor did he wish to — deny his aristocratic heritage. He was proud of his origins in a privileged class, so proud that his fatuous attempt in the years around the turn of the century to play the role of a national leader was bound to founder on the shoals of the changing social and political realities of the day. Heidenstam's tragedy, if it can be called a tragedy, lies in the fact that he never attracted the great popular attention of which he had dreamed, despite the position of leadership that he early attained in the poetic renaissance of the 1890's. As the twentieth century dawned he had become the *grand seigneur* of Swedish letters rather than the hero of the masses, and he continued in this role until his death forty years later even though the last twenty-five of these years he remained silent as a poet. Events had gone past him. With the years he became increasingly critical of developments around him, withdrawing into himself and unable (or unwilling) to turn his hand to significant literary creation. He refused to make the necessary adjustments to the changing world of the new century.

Except for some posthumously published fragments Heidenstam's literary work falls between the years 1888, when the volume of verse *Vallfart och vandringsår* (Pilgrimage and Wander-Years) appeared, and 1915, when he published *Nya dikter* (New Poems). His production also includes a volume of semi-journalistic travel prose (*Från Col di Tenda till Blocksberg*), an autobiographical novel (*Hans Alienus*), a brilliant book of verse (*Dikter*), several volumes of historical fiction — the most important of which are *Karolinerna* (tr. *The Charles Men*) and *Folkungaträdet* (tr. *The Tree of the Folkungs*) — a sheaf of short stories, a few dramatic fragments, and a considerable number of essays, some of a polemical kind. As a poet he ranks among the greatest in Swedish letters, and he is otherwise chiefly important in his historical fiction, *The Tree of the Folkungs* being perhaps the most distinguished of Swedish historical novels, and in his polemical prose, which in its hard-hitting attack upon the 1880's provided a point of departure for the new literary program of the 1890's.

Heidenstam's youth and early manhood were spent almost entirely abroad; an illness necessitated his living in more moderate climates than Sweden could provide. The earliest of these years took him to the central and eastern Mediterranean countries (Italy, Greece, Syria, Egypt), the later years largely to France and the Swiss Alps. Of his early years he once wrote: "I was fortunate enough to inhale the cosmopolitanism of the more southerly lands when my being still possessed all of youth's receptivity. Instead of studying the world of antiquity in Uppsala's confined small-town lecture halls, I, already scarcely grown up, stood upon the Acropolis at Athens. Instead of growing up in a modern Christian culture, I was permitted to visit the Orient." At first the young Heidenstam intended to become an artist, and studied under Gérôme at Paris; but soon he abandoned these plans and turned to poetry. He matured slowly, nearing thirty before he finally had a volume ready for the printer, but when this volume — *Pilgrimage and Wander-Years* — appeared, it was received with jubilation by both critics and the Swedish public. Not since Snoilsky's Italian poems had burst upon the Swedish reading public in 1869 had Swedish readers of verse been so enthralled, and partly for the same reasons. Both Snoilsky's and Heidenstam's early poems were borne on the wings of youth — spontaneous, vital, sensuous, gaily irresponsible, confronting Swedish readers with fabled lands to the South which took their morals relatively lightly and accepted the days as they came. Heidenstam, however, did not possess the elegant technical facility of Snoilsky, but his verse was more varied, more sensuous, more rich and substantial in its motifs and ideas. He had traveled more widely, observed more acutely, and thought more profoundly than Snoilsky — and his genius was of a higher order. All the brilliant color and the sleepy Oriental profusion of the Near East flashed and soughed through Heidenstam's early verse, in the sharpest possible contrast to the drabness and strenuous utilitarianism so prevalent in Swedish literature in the 1880's.

The dominant anti-utilitarian tone of *Pilgrimage and Wander-Years* was quite deliberate. To the young Heidenstam the ancient "backward" East, with all its limitations, had found a way of life quite superior to an ugly, practical, money-mad, industrialized Western civilization — a point of view developed further but on the whole less satisfactorily in the slight book *Från Col di Tenda till Blocksberg* and the more important *Hans Alienus*, the two prose works which appeared in 1888 and 1892 respectively. As an autobiographical novel *Hans Alienus* is somewhat pretentious and rather confused in its thinking. Its significance lies in the visionary splendor of certain of the passages in which Heidenstam's inspired prose breaks inevitably over into verse, most impressively in "Pilgrimens julsång" (The Pilgrim's Christmas Hymn), which attains heights of poetic utterance that hitherto had only been hinted at in Heidenstam's production. The theme of this poem, the Pilgrim's return to his homeland after many years abroad, has its obvious parallels in the poet's life: Heidenstam had taken up permanent residence in Sweden in 1887, and he seeks to express in the poem one side of his feelings on that occasion. These feelings were melancholy, heavy, hopeless, for the Pilgrim had lived out his life in a foreign "shadow land" whose Kingdom of Beauty had enthralled his soul to the point where he feels unable to identify himself with a vital new life toward which he nevertheless yearns.

> Chained fast to life my staff I bear,
> Restless, move on from place to place.

Ever a stranger, everywhere,
Yearning hopelessly on I pace.

But this was a passing mood for Heidenstam, if for that matter it ever existed for him in the extreme form it takes in this poem. In any case, when "The Pilgrim's Christmas Hymn" appeared in the last section of *Hans Alienus* in 1892, Heidenstam had long since cast off the spell of his Oriental "shadow land" and returned to the challenge of a very real "life" — to the strenuous, partly polemic activities which were to place him in the forefront of those forces which sought to establish in the 1890's a new era in Swedish literature.

Before Heidenstam settled down to the creative task of contributing in poetry and fiction to the dream of a new Swedish literature, he dashed off a group of critical pamphlets in which he announces "an approaching new crisis in literature" and suggests in broad outline the lines of development which Swedish literature in his view should follow. Of these critical pamphlets the most important, and the first to appear (in the late summer of 1889), was the essay "Renaissance." While admitting at the outset of this essay that naturalism had been a "healthy and necessary" protest against certain debilitating trends in mid-nineteenth-century literature, Heidenstam goes on to point out that naturalism had in the 1880's run its course, deteriorating especially in Swedish literature into a drab and inconsequential prose which he disdainfully labels "shoemaker realism." Only Strindberg among Swedish realists and naturalists had risen above the dead level of literary mediocrity, "but no one," Heidenstam reminds us with reference to Strindberg, "had so subjectively transformed [naturalism] according to his own temperament." The chief reason for the deterioration of naturalism in Sweden, it is argued, is that its rigid doctrinaire spirit is essentially foreign to the Swedish national temperament. The literary ideals of the Renaissance rather than those of nineteenth-century naturalism are best suited to Swedish tastes and Swedish genius. Sweden's literature of the past in contrast with that of the 1880's, Heidenstam maintains, is characterized by a bold imaginative freedom, by an earthy, colorful realism, by an expansive, frequently festive and opulent affirmation of life. Such a literature is Heidenstam's dream for the Sweden also of his own day. "If my dream were to become more than a dream," he writes at the close of his essay — "if a current actually breaks out in the direction I have suggested, what name could we give it? Might it not best be characterized by the term *renaissance*? It should justify such a name in part because of the peculiarities of our national temperament that should then become honored, in part because of its readoption of the methods of the older schools, in part also because of its own inner nature, its favoring of the subjective, of personal independence, its uniting of the imagination, the sense of the beautiful, and bold, racy realism."

Heidenstam is concerned almost exclusively in the essay "Renaissance" with literary form rather than with subject matter, theme, and point of view. He does not suggest that the new literature should deal predominantly or by preference with Swedish motifs and themes, but in his subsequent development he gradually comes to occupy himself more and more with matters Swedish, and in the period of his greatest productivity, the decade beginning with 1897, his preoccupation with Sweden present and past consumes almost all his energies. The first fairly considerable evidence of Heidenstam's interest in specifically Swedish subjects is to be found, in fact, a couple of years earlier, in *Dikter* (Poems, 1895), though it cannot be said that Swedish themes really predominate in this volume. Actually the greatness of *Poems* — perhaps Heidenstam's supreme literary achievement — is to be found in the richness and amazing variety of its themes and the striking originality of their treatment. The poet conceives of himself in many situations and responds with equal intensity and sensitivity to all of them — in "Malatestas morgonsång" (Malatesta's Morning Song) he ventures into a defiant Nietzschean mood, in "Morgonen" (The Morning) he composes an elegiac hymn to the quiet joys of the summer season, in "Barrikadsång" (Barricade Song) he erupts in a flaming revolutionary strain, in "Den nioåriga freden" (The Nine-Year Peace) he finds war preferable to a complacent condition of peace, in "Djävulens frestelse" (The Devil's Temptation) and "Jairi dotter" (The Daughter of Jairus) he employs New Testament motifs with turns of thought that are quite other than those of the biblical text. And so on, and so on. . . . .

Overwhelmed as one is by the opulent diversity of motif and theme in *Poems*, one does not at first note that through this diversity emerges a stubbornly recurrent subject, the poet's persistent preoccupation with his forebears and his homeland, with all those ties which bind him to his people and to a national heritage. The volume opens with two poems of this kind and closes with two others, and scattered within the volume are half a dozen or more pieces which turn to the Swedish countryside and Swedish history for their material. As yet, however, Heidenstam only samples this subject matter, almost by the way as it were; but the brilliant results he attains in a number of these poems suggest how deeply the subject has moved him. Though some of the pieces in *Poems* deal with nature and the countryside (most notably the magnificent opening poem, inspired by the primitive majesty of Tividen forest), the mood or drift of thought that most persistently recurs is a deeply sensed aware-ness of man's relation to his past, to his family's heritage and his nation's traditions. In poems dealing with the family heritage such as "Hemmet" (Home) and "Vid kistan med familjereliker" (At the Chest of Family Relics) Heidenstam conceives of man's relation to his past as an essen-tially passive one — the dead live on with us, shaping our lives and deter-mining our destinies. But in those poems concerned with larger national contexts such as "Pingstnatten" (Pentecostal Night) and "Den sovande systern" (The Sleeping Sister) — the two pieces which close the vol-ume — man's relation to past ages is conceived more actively: the past becomes to us a vital challenge, a symbol of youth, the primary source of national regeneration in years of national eclipse and decay.

This note, struck tentatively in *Poems*, becomes the all-pervading theme in Heidenstam's work in the following years, now however in prose forms, though the short poetic cycle *Ett Folk* (One People, 1902) has its honored place in the production of these years as an evidence of Heidenstam's desire to contribute directly to certain aspects of contem-porary political discussion. The circumstances of Heidenstam's child-hood had early tended to funnel his thoughts into historical channels. Östergötland, his native province, was the cradle of medieval Folkung power; and Olshammar, the Heidenstam family estate on the northern shores of Lake Vätter, had its name (originally Ulvshammar) from Ulv, husband of Saint Birgitta, the greatest personality of the Swedish Middle Ages. Legends about the Swedish saint still circulated by word of mouth during Heidenstam's childhood in the regions around Olshammar. Dur-ing his long residence abroad Heidenstam had shared at least outwardly the critical attitude toward the Swedish past fashionable among young intellectuals of the 1880's, but when he returned to Sweden his country's past again began to exercise its early fascination over him. In 1897 and 1898 he wrote the two volumes of *The Charles Men*, celebrating the tragic heroism of Charles XII and his people, and during the same years he participated in the cultural debate of the day with a number of critical essays — "Om svenskarnas lynne" (On Swedish National Temperament), "Dikt och historia" (Literature and History), "Klassicitet och german-ism" (Classicism and Germanism) — in which he develops his theories of history and offers views on the relation between literature and history.

After the turn of the century he turned to the Middle Ages in the novels *Heliga Birgittas pilgrimsfärd* (Saint Birgitta's Pilgrimage) and *The Tree of the Folkungs*, and at the request of educational officials wrote a Swedish history for school use entitled *Svenskarna och deras hövdingar* (tr. *The Swedes and Their Chieftains*).

The interpretation of Swedish history we come upon in the work of Heidenstam's maturity differs sharply from that which Heidenstam had earlier held. In his essay "Renaissance" from 1889 he had justified the title of the essay in part by maintaining that the Swede was, more than other Scandinavians, earthy and carefree, sensuous and pleasure loving, expansive and adventurous, with a taste for the resplendent (*det lysande*) and the elegantly chivalrous. But in the essay "On Swedish National Temperament" as well as in *The Charles Men* from less than ten years later, he emphasizes other qualities of Swedish character — its less showy, everyday virtues, its quiet heroism in times of crisis, its capacity for suffering and sacrifice, its willingness to meet death without flinching when the fate of the nation is at stake. In *The Charles Men* the tragic heroism of Charles XII becomes the royal symbol of the hard-pressed Swedish armies and a long-suffering Swedish folk. It has been said that the Swedish people rather than their King is the hero of the diverse assortment of tales which makes up *The Charles Men*. In one sense this is true, for we learn to know them and admire their reticent heroism almost more than the heroic figure of the King. But the King nevertheless remains the dominant figure, iron-willed, uncommunicative, mysterious, pursuing his tragic destiny without complaint, without wavering, and by some strange power molding his not always willing people into his own selfless heroic cast. Though Charles XII was the last of the great Swedish warrior kings, and Heidenstam had in his earlier years been guilty of entertaining chauvinistic moods, he had no intention of exploiting such moods in *The Charles Men*. It was not an accident that Heidenstam in this work turned to the last tragic chapter in Sweden's Great Power period, nor was it an accident that the phase of Charles XII's career with which he chiefly deals covered the long, difficult, increasingly desperate years following upon the definitive defeat of the Swedish armies at Poltava. Heidenstam's essentially tragic view of history would scarcely have permitted him to concentrate — as had Tegnér and others — on the young, triumphant Charles XII of the Battle of Narva. To the Heidenstam who wrote *The Charles Men* those moments in Swedish history when the nation attained its supreme greatness were the moments when — daring and sacrificing all — it went down to defeat. Nations as well as individuals attain their greatest stature in the tragic experience. Moments of victory and success are by contrast banal, indifferent, meaningless.

How thoroughly Heidenstam had come to free his nationalism from pretentious chauvinistic excesses is evident also in *One People* (1902), the poetic cycle in which he speaks directly to the Swedish people on matters of immediate national concern, and in the two historical novels *Saint Birgitta's Pilgrimage* (1901) and *The Tree of the Folkungs* (1905, 1907), in whose searching analysis of religious experience and of Swedish political origins Heidenstam's mature humanism is everywhere apparent. In "Invocation and Promise," the brilliant closing poem of *One People*, the poet is resigned to Sweden's playing a minor political role in the future, but he envisions another "great Sweden" in coming years, a Sweden that will distinguish itself among the nations of the world "in science, in the arts, in literature." In his treatment of Saint Birgitta he ignores almost completely her political role (which at one time was not inconsiderable), concentrating rather on her inner struggle, her confrontation with her God. Harsh and demanding in her relations with her fellows, imperious, even bitter in the early years of her spiritual "pilgrimage," Heidenstam's Birgitta grows gentler and more understanding with time, and in this spirit she makes her peace with man and God. To Heidenstam Birgitta's sainthood is attained not in an ecclesiastical act of "elevation," it lies rather in her purely *human* transformation, in her final selfless devotion and dedication to the good life.

In *The Tree of the Folkungs* we witness a similar humanizing process, though in much more complex contexts — in the broad, surging, vigorously conflicting ramifications of a primitive society which in the course of some centuries was to undergo the disciplines necessary to the founding of a social and political unit, the Swedish nation. Heidenstam does not sentimentalize his picture of national origins. He depicts the legendary figure of Folke Filbyter, founder of the Folkung family which was to unite Sweden, as a crude, barbaric, insensitive creature, whose consuming passion is an insatiable greed for land. Only his love for a lost grandson raises him in his declining years a step above the level of a brute. Heidenstam's conception of this legendary, only half-human figure is repeated a generation after the appearance of the novel in the ruthlessly expressive bronze of the famous Linköping fountain by the Swedish sculptor Carl Milles. In Heidenstam's final view, however, the ill-gained possessions of this base creature ultimately provide the economic foundation upon which the Folkungs build their power and finally come to occupy the throne – first the soft, pleasure-loving Valdemar, who prefers dalliance in love to the responsibilities of political power, and then his brother Magnus, who displaces Valdemar by acts of deceit and treachery but who brings order to a land torn for centuries by bloody, internecine strife. Magnus himself, as we come to know him in *The Tree of the Folkungs*, is not a happy man, but he follows the star of his destiny without wavering, to see in his closing years the promising beginnings of an orderly and humane state. Devious if not dastardly was the road of the Folkungs to the throne, but it was a road which in the end led beyond the chaos of barbarism to a conception of society based on law and justice.

The art of Heidenstam's prose fiction is that of a great poet rather than a born story teller. It is colorful, concrete, concentrated, depending more often than not for its effects on brilliantly conceived scenes and a sharply focused stylistic flair. What it lacks in the leisurely narrative progression typical of so much historical fiction is compensated for by the incisive use of striking episodes and symbols. In over-all form *The Tree of the Folkungs* follows closely the line of its thematic development – primitive, potentially violent, crudely mysterious in the early parts where the brutal individualism of Folke Filbyter dominates the center of the stage, but more artistically restrained in later parts, particularly those toward the end of the novel which concentrate on the struggle of Magnus to realize his dream of a society which seeks to curb an irresponsible individualism and protect the rights of all. The extremes of these forms are most apparent in the novel's opening and closing scenes, the one harshly monumental, ominous, overcast with darksome prophecies and pagan superstitions, the other essentially calm and harmonious, infused with a warm and elevated humanism. The one describes Folke Filbyter's return from a bloody Viking foray, gloating heavily over his booty. The other sketches in warmly human colors the chivalrous ideal as represented by the newly established knightly forces of Magnus gathered in a courtyard in the presence of the King:

There seemed no end to the growing host below. It was the whole knighthood of the country, his sworn body-guard, which he had conjured up from wild bands and filled with noble purpose. There waved the gauntlet, on a hand that would never be raised to harm a woman. There gleamed the ring and the belt, symbols of loyalty. There the black sole under the mailed hose constantly reminded the overweening of the grave's mould. And the arms displayed on every shield had made an end of every treacherous ambush. All the knights were bareheaded and looked before them, full of confidence. They had dropped their reins and held their swords upright in both hands like tapers, and the steel points flashed like flames for the suppression of war and violence. And as the numbers grew, the song of victory from Hofva rose ever louder to the clear autumn sky:

> Jesu, grant Thy servants' boon.
> Children of this world are we,
> Crying to Thee every one:
> Give us rest and peace with Thee.

It was not granted the later Folkungs to pursue the ideal in the pure self-lessness of this vision; but bloody as was their course in the somewhat more than a century of their rule, they had been the first of Swedish chieftains to establish a relatively civilized community, to create some kind of unity in the midst of disorder, to invest the Swedish people with a sense of its national destiny.

If Heidenstam's picture of the rise of the Folkungs was because of its subject partly brutish and partly humane, his last major work, *Nya dikter* (New Poems, 1915), breathed at every point a pure, elevated humanism. Though some of the poems in this volume are rather slight in subject and others have formal flaws, the majority of them are among Heidenstam's greatest. Their mood is one of serene maturity, their spirit one of resignation and magnanimity, their form one of classical simplicity and clarity. They remind one inevitably of the Goethe of the "pure lyrics," and at their best do not fall much if at all below the level of Goethe's poetry of this kind. In Swedish poetry Runeberg is Heidenstam's greatest predecessor in the genre, but there is no slavish following of the Swedo-Finnish poet. In these poems glimpses of otherworldly splendor flash out sharply only to be quickly extinguished, and yet they leave no sense of emptiness or frustration despite the transitoriness of their appearance:

> A trembling in remotest space: in vision
> a garden gleaming bright among tall trees.
> What was my name? who was I? wherefore wept I? —
> All is forgotten — like the tempest's song
> soon with the rolling worlds to blend, and vanish.

Translated by C. D. Locock

Of frequent occurrence is the motif of death, of journey's end, that final stage in man's search for happiness when his perspectives have become widened and when he seeks reconciliation rather than strife, when humil-

ity and resignation become basic virtues and the ideal condition is one
of quiet contemplation of the earthly scene.

> Already I'm on the bridge that leads
> from Earth unto a land beyond my ken,
> and far to me is now what once was near.
> Beneath, as formerly, the race of men
> praise, blame, and forge their darts for warlike deeds;
> but here I see that true and noble creeds
> even on foemen's shields are blazoned clear.
> No more does life bewilder with its riot.
> I am as lonely as a man may be;
> still is the air, austere, and winter-quiet;
> self is forgot, and I go forward free.
> I loose my shoes and cast aside my stave.
> Softly I go, for I would not defile
> with dust a world so pure, all white as snow.
> Beneath, men soon may carry to a grave
> a wretched shape of human clay, the while
> mumbling a name — 't was mine once long ago.
>
> *Translated by C. W. Stork*

Heidenstam's genius had traveled a long road since the defiant Epicureanism of his youthful *Pilgrimage and Wander-Years*, a road which led to
the maturing artistic and ethical disciplines of *Poems* and the national
preoccupations of the prose fiction and which culminated in the quiet,
elevated serenity of *New Poems*. Whether *Poems* or *New Poems* is the
greater poetic achievement is a matter of taste. Those who value more
highly variety of theme and surging richness of execution will prefer
Poems. Those who demand of poetry simplicity, clarity, and elevated
restraint will find in *New Poems* Heidenstam's most distinguished work.
Each of the volumes is in its way the perfect reflection of the poet's level
of maturity at the time of its conception and execution.

In 1891, two years after Heidenstam's Renaissance-call for a new, more
colorful and imaginative Swedish literature, the call was answered by
the appearance of no less than five works from the pens of four Swedish
authors, two of whom, Selma Lagerlöf and Gustaf Fröding, were not
only soon to become major representative figures of the 1890's but also
with time to be counted among the greatest of Swedish authors. Selma
Lagerlöf even attained world-wide fame long before her death, a distinction which placed her together with Saint Birgitta and Fredrika
Bremer among Swedish women. Both Selma Lagerlöf and Fröding have

their roots deep in the soil and traditions of Värmland, the west-central Swedish province earlier made famous in literature in the work of Geijer and Tegnér. Neither Selma Lagerlöf nor Fröding are "regional," however, in the narrowly limited sense of the term, though Selma Lagerlöf's best work is more frequently localized on the Värmland countryside than is that of Fröding, who in consequence of an inherited mental taint could only in part and for a relatively short time escape from the dark shadows of his tragic private destiny.

Though the genius of Selma Lagerlöf (1858–1940) is hardly as complex as Fröding's, it had depths of feeling and areas of questioning and conflict which have not always been recognized. The popular assumption that she was simply an inspired story teller who evaded the realities of life by yielding to the legendary enchantment of her native province is quite misleading. The glittering surface features of her work are frequently deceptive. They tend to hide her strenuous struggle with matters of literary form and delude the unwary into assuming that she had no inner conflicts, that her world was a genial child's world capable of ignoring more or less completely the problems with which modern man is beset. She came early to struggle with the religious and ethical implications of "socialism." Her fabled "optimism" was not unalloyed. Especially in her later years she had her moments of doubt, of skepticism, of spiritual weariness just short of despair. She found some of the traditional elements of Christian belief unacceptable. With the years she became something of a "spiritualist" but guarded herself cannily against its excesses. Such evidences of what may loosely be called "modernity" in her way of thinking are admittedly never allowed to dominate, to bring about a revolutionary change in her manner of responding to life or to art; but they recurred with such stubborn persistence that they cannot be ignored in any final judgment of herself and her work.

Selma Lagerlöf's early years were spent at Mårbacka, the modest family estate, in the parish of Östra Ämtervik in the heart of Värmland. These years were to her delightful beyond compare, filled with play and study and lively contacts with the gay life of the surrounding countryside. But this carefree existence could not go on forever. In her early twenties she attended at Stockholm a teachers' seminary, after which, in 1885, she took a position as a teacher in a girls' school at Landskrona on the shores of Öresund in southwestern Sweden. It was during the Landskrona years that she broke through as an author with *Gösta Berling's Saga* (1891), an ultimate consequence of which was that she could devote herself exclusively to her literary work. Aside from her rapidly growing fame both at home and abroad, particularly after the turn of the century, she became in the first two decades of the new century the recipient of many honors, the most impressive of which were the Nobel Prize in Literature in 1909 and her election in 1914 as the first woman member of the Swedish Academy. Some years after her departure from Mårbacka in the early 1880's the family estate had to be sold, to her great sorrow, but her later success as an author and the Nobel Prize award enabled her to fulfill a long-cherished dream of repurchasing Mårbacka (the dwelling house and other buildings in 1907, the entire property in 1910) and settling down in her beloved Värmland for the remainder of her life. Here she took an active part in improving the land and increasing its economic yield, built an imposing manor house on the spot where the original modest family dwelling stood, busied herself with the affairs of the parish, and — as a world-famous figure — received as graciously as her time and energies permitted an endless stream of visitors from every corner of the globe.

Outwardly she bore her fame with a quiet, patient dignity through years of recurrent illness, decreasing creative energies, fantastic demands upon her time and economic resources, and deepening inner struggles of various kinds, not the least of which centered upon religious questions. Behind the gleaming white façade of the world-famous Mårbacka manor house a tired world-famous woman fought out her last spiritual battles, certain in but a few things, secure only in one article of faith: that man is by nature good and that her own primary duty was to live and write to the end that the light of goodness in man should not permanently be dimmed by the growing darkness settling down upon a brutal war-torn twentieth-century world. As a child of Värmland she had early found joy and beauty in life, but a joy and beauty joined indissolubly to goodness. Beauty to her could not exist outside a moral context, and she became in consequence the great moralist among the Swedish literary figures who appeared in the 1890's.

But her didactic purposes seldom interfered seriously with her art, an art which at its best is superb. It has nothing of the vaunted "objectivity," the factual sobriety, the stylistic impersonality, and little of the minute analysis of cause-and-effect relations which the 1880's sought to attain in prose fiction. Instead Selma Lagerlöf's prose tended to be unashamedly subjective, its characters are moved by impulse and by inner visions, its style often favors rhetorical effects and is loaded with per sonifications, hyperbole, exclamatory interjections, free rhythmic patterns. Selma Lagerlöf wrote no verse after reaching maturity, but her prose was in its way as poetic as most of the great poetry of her contemporaries. Aside from its avoidance of formal verse patterns it took an honored place in the poetic renaissance of the 1890's. This was particularly true of her early tales and novels.

Highly original as Selma Lagerlöf's work may strike the modern reader, it has its prototypes in traditional literary forms, chiefly in the folk tale, the saga, and the legend. With these forms it has in common a sense of concreteness, an interest in the supernatural, a naïve delight in the purely narrative side of the story. As one of the two incomparably great Scandinavian *story tellers* Selma Lagerlöf takes her place alongside Hans Christian Andersen, and like her famous Danish predecessor she has retained much of the wide-eyed naïveté which goes with an oral literary tradition. The folk tale and the saga played central roles in her imaginative childhood days at Mårbacka, while the flourishing legendary Mediterranean world came to fascinate her in the later years of travel abroad. The Icelandic saga world provided some of the materials for *Drottningar i Kungahälla* (tr. *The Queens of Kungahälla and Other Sketches*, 1899), and southern European lore played a more or less important part in such works as *Antikrists mirakler* (tr. *The Miracles of Antichrist*, 1897), and *Kristus legender* (tr. *Christ Legends*) and *Legender* (Legends), both from 1904.

In the main, however, Selma Lagerlöf turned to the folk tale as it flourished in her native Värmland for the material of her novels and tales. Much of this material had a relatively late local provenience, dating back to episodes which occurred on the Värmland countryside only two or three generations before they became immortalized under the magic of Selma Lagerlöf's pen. In the case of the material which ultimately became the brilliant group of tales included in her first novel, *Gösta Berling's Saga*, she insists that she served simply as a kind of medium through which the tales came almost by themselves to find their definitive form in her work.

Once upon a time there was a saga which wished to be told and led out into the world. This was quite natural, for it knew within itself that it was as good as finished. Many had been instrumental in creating it through remarkable actions; others had added their bits to it by time and again recounting its episodes. What was necessary was that it be carefully composed so that it could travel comfortably about in the whole land. It was still only a strange medley of tales, a formless cloud of adventures, which drifted back and forth like a swarm of stray bees on a summer's day, and did not know where they might find someone who could gather them into a hive.

The "hive" into which Selma Lagerlöf gathered the "stray bees" was a long time in the making, ten years in all; for the form which it finally came to take in *Gösta Berling's Saga* ran so counter to the prevailing notions of how novels should be written that only after numerous abortive efforts to cast her materials into sober "acceptable" forms did she throw all prudent considerations aside and allow the materials to find a form in keeping with their own mad, fantastic spirit.

Carlyle gave Selma Lagerlöf the courage to be herself rather than to write as she "should" in depicting the activities of the pleasure-loving, irresponsible Cavaliers and the redoubtable Major's Wife at Ekeby. On reading in the mid-1880's Carlyle's *Heroes, Hero-Worship, and the Heroic in History* and *The French Revolution*, with their expansive rhetoric, their flaming imagery, and their passionate apostrophes, she found her form; and when Mårbacka had to be sold in 1888 she felt that she owed it to the memory of her childhood home, where she had heard the Gösta Berling tales so often told, to bring the tales together in a novel which in form would be true to their wild, abandoned, unruly spirit. Though a section of the novel won a first prize in a fiction contest arranged by the women's magazine *Idun* in 1890, and the novel as a whole was published the following year, the reading public responded to it slowly and most of the critics were cool, in some cases scornful, in dealing with it. Among Swedish critics only Oscar Levertin gave it high though somewhat qualified praise. In a letter to Heidenstam he calls it, quite properly, "the first work in accordance with the Heidenstam-Levertin aesthetics," that is to say the new aesthetics of the 1890's. Only after Georg Brandes, in a review of the Danish edition of the novel in 1893, had been highly impressed by "the startling strangeness of [its] material and the originality of [its] form" did Sweden capitulate to *Gösta Berling's Saga*, and since then it has become the most popular of novels with the Swedish reading public.

In general structure *Gösta Berling's Saga* is a group of loosely related tales which are brought into a kind of focus by a recurrent primary concern with the central characters Gösta Berling and the Major's Wife, by the time limit of a year and a day rigidly delimiting the action, by the scene being restricted to the valley region of Lake Löven, and by the theme, that a light-hearted individualism — no matter how brilliant its affirmation or how brightly insouciant its manifestations — bears within itself certain ultimately dark and destructive elements. The odd assortment of variously gifted Cavaliers who live at Ekeby on the largesse of its owner, the Major's Wife, enter into an agreement with "the dark One" to take over the estate and its foundries, with the understanding that if they do "anything sensible or useful or effeminate" the devil may take all twelve of them "when the year is out." They proceed to keep their promise, with devastating results for the estate and the whole countryside; and at the end their leader Gösta admits that "the garden where butterfly-winged joy abounded" had become "filled with destructive caterpillars, and . . . its fruit was shrivelled." The penance which Gösta finally proposes for himself is a life of work rather than play, of service to his fellows rather than the way of carefree self-indulgence. The difficulty with Selma Lagerlöf's application of such a moral to her tale is that she had made lightheartedness and self-indulgence so delightful and engaging in the novel. We have at the end of *Gösta Berling's Saga* something of the same feeling that we harbor at the close of Ibsen's *Peer Gynt*: the feeling that a sprightly, impudent, inventive rascality has its charms in spite of everything, and that a strong flavor of didacticism is rather unpalatable in such essentially comic psychological contexts. *Gösta Berling's Saga* maintains throughout a precariously ambivalent attitude toward such normally contrasting "values" as play and work, the beautiful and the useful, and the reader has under the circumstances some difficulty in making his choice between evil and good. Perhaps the attachment which Selma Lagerlöf had nurtured since childhood for the tales centering upon Ekeby made it particularly difficult for her in this case to pass judgment without a lingering fondness toward those to be judged.

Selma Lagerlöf's work from the years immediately following *Gösta Berling's Saga* reflects considerable uncertainty as to where it should turn next. Värmland material is used only very sparingly in the two collections of tales *Invisible Links* (1894) and *The Queens of Kungahälla* (1899) and is abandoned completely in *The Miracles of Antichrist* (1897), a half-sympathetic, half-condemnatory treatment of modern socialism in a south Italian milieu. In *Jerusalem* (1901, 1902), the first major work after *Gösta Berling's Saga*, she returns to the Swedish countryside, but to the province of Dalarna bordering on Värmland to the north and east.

The world we enter into in *Jerusalem* is quite different from that of

Gösta Berling's Saga. It is a sober, solid, deeply religious, and relatively primitive world. Its characters are of hard-working ancient peasant stock whose chief "pleasure" lies in working the soil and fulfilling their destiny as dictated by a deeply rooted sense of loyalty to ancestral traditions. But early in the novel there enters into the quiet, tradition-bound world of this ancient peasant stock a foreign, disruptive element, which comes to turn their world topsy-turvy and drives many of the people to sell their ancestral farms and follow a returned Swedish-American sectarian preacher to Jerusalem to await the imminent coming of the Lord. The story is based on actual events originating in the parish of Nås not many years before Selma Lagerlöf heard of the events and studied them with great interest in preparation for the writing of her novel.

Material of this kind enabled Selma Lagerlöf to fashion a novel largely devoid of the looseness of structure and the stylistic excesses of much of her earlier work. This is particularly true of the first volume of the novel, entitled *In Dalarna*, a monumental study of the clash between an ancient conservative peasant traditionalism and modern religious sectarianism. The second volume, in which the scene of action shifts from Dalarna to Palestine, is considerably less impressive, though not a few of its episodes are handled with that sovereign narrative skill and intuitive understanding of the human psyche which seldom desert the genius of Selma Lagerlöf. Though *In Dalarna* gradually burgeons out into the story of a whole parish, it maintains a fine narrative and thematic focus by its central use of the Ingmarssons, the family most ancient and honored of all in the parish and the least affected by the insidious sectarianism of the Palestine vision. The Ingmarssons are in their way deeply religious, but their religion is conservative and earth-bound rather than fanatical and visionary, and their loyalties are to the soil and to an ancestral sense of reverence for the good deed. The language of these tales of the Ingmarssons and their neighbors is appropriately simple and restrained, considerably closer to the Icelandic saga than is Selma Lagerlöf's earlier work. She had in her new novel learned to catch in modern prose the stylistic spirit of the saga world by following in the paths of Runeberg and Björnson. And like her immediate Scandinavian predecessors she did not shun lyrical effects and symbolical usages, though unlike in *Gösta Berling's Saga* these effects and usages are now employed with a finely disciplined sensitivity and restraint. How sensitive and restrained she can be in these respects may be illustrated by the last scene in *Jerusalem*, in which Barbro, young Ingmar's wife, comes to find a deep-rooted sense of joy and strength, after a period of uncertainty and trial, in the simple immediate *objects* which surround her in the great hall of the substantial old peasant home of the Ingmarssons:

But then she looked about her, embraced with her eyes the entire room, the long, low window, the benches along the walls, and the open fireplace, where generation after generation had sat at their tasks in the light of the open fire. All of this enveloped her in a tranquil feeling of security. She felt that it would shelter and protect her.

No mention is made here of God, but the room is filled with the quiet, unassuming, solid divinity of the daily task well done through generation after generation, far back in remembered and unremembered time. In this sense God most profoundly existed for the Ingmarssons.

Jerusalem firmly established Selma Lagerlöf as the incomparably greatest novelist who had written in Swedish. The years which followed its publication were filled with diverse literary labors, official honors of all kinds, and a gradual gravitating back to Värmland both in her literary concerns and in the outward circumstances of her life. The two most important works in the years immediately before her return to Mårbacka were *Herr Arnes penningar* (tr. *Herr Arne's Hoard*, 1904), a dark tale of murder and retribution from sixteenth-century west-coast Sweden, and *Nils Holgerssons underbara resa* (tr. *The Wonderful Adventures of Nils*, 1906, 1907), a fabulously inventive and enormously successful "geography book" which — though written for school use at the suggestion of the National Association of Teachers — has become not only a precious jewel to Swedish children but also a children's classic throughout the world. Kipling's *Jungle Book*, with its fascinating assortment of acting and talking animals, has something of the importance for *The Wonderful Adventures of Nils* that Carlyle's *Heroes and Hero-Worship* and *The French Revolution* had for *Gösta Berling's Saga*.

The year 1908 marks both Selma Lagerlöf's actual and her literary return to Värmland. It was in this year that she re-established her residence at Mårbacka — at first only during the summer season, in 1919 as her permanent all-year-round home. She had in many instances wandered far afield in her search for literary materials in the seventeen years since the publication of her great Värmland novel *Gösta Berling's Saga*; but she had never forgotten her first love, Värmland, as is evidenced by its cropping up at the most unexpected places in her writings during these years — and now at last she finds the fascination of Värmland stirring strongly in her again as she comes to make her home in the midst of the places

Drawing by Bertil Lybeck for an illustrated edition of Selma
Lagerlöf's *The Wonderful Adventures of Nils*

filled with the countless voices of old, still vigorously living memories.
The result is a mellow late harvest of new Värmland novels and tales.
None of these stories achieves the sparkling literary triumph of *Gösta
Berling's Saga*, but each of them has an undeniable charm of its own.
They are for the most part less spontaneous than the tales included in the
Saga, and yet in their quietly pulsing, finely mellowed tone and in their
subtly modulated humor they reflect the mature Selma Lagerlöf's in-
gratiatingly delicate art and her rich and warm humanity.

Already in *En saga om en saga och andra sagor* (tr. *A Saga About a
Saga and Other Tales*), the volume which came out in the year of the
purchase of Mårbacka, we come upon evidences of the author's desire
to return to Värmland materials. Three of the eight tales included in this
volume have Värmland settings and characters, two of them dealing
with the locally famous itinerant "fiddler" Jan Öster. The title-piece, "A
Saga About a Saga," is a reprint (originally published in 1902) of the
author's delightful account of how *Gösta Berling's Saga* came to be written. In *Liljecronas hem* (tr. *Liljecrona's Home*, 1911) Selma Lagerlöf
deals directly with a past generation of her own family. The "Lövdala"
of the novel is Mårbacka; the central character, Liljecrona, is the author's
grandfather; and the details of narrative conflict, particularly those between Maia Lisa and her stepmother, are a free handling of actual situations in an earlier generation of the Lagerlöf family. In *Kejsarn av Portu-
gallien* (tr. *The Emperor of Portugallia*, 1914) we find another example
of the free handling of an actual Värmland character, a pathetic, harmless old madman whom Selma Lagerlöf had seen occasionally during her

313

childhood at Mårbacka. Difficult as is the subject of this novel, with its harmlessly insane father and prostituted daughter, the materials are handled with genuine tragic pathos; and in the early chapters the author is at her best in humorous characterization, much of the humor being conveyed (only to the Swedish reader, alas!) by the skillful use of dialect.

A tale which occupies a unique place in Selma Lagerlöf's work from these years is *Körkarlen* (tr. *Thy Soul Shall Bear Witness*, 1912), in which an imaginative intensity unusual in her work is permitted to cast its eerie phosphorescent glow over a modern version of the ancient moralizing folk-tale motif about the coachman who goes about gathering in the souls of those who die. The action takes place in the slum district of a modern city, and the moral is pressed home with devastating force. The art of this tale resembles expressionism in its strange blending of realism and fantasy, its stark, terrifying visionary quality.

The First World War dealt a crushing blow to Selma Lagerlöf's creative energies. The first volume of *Troll och människor* (Trolls and Men) was published in the second year of the War. It is a curious miscellany of tales, legends, addresses, and essays, very uneven in quality, several of the stories revealing that strange fascination which grim peasant superstitions and the horror theme have on occasion held for Selma Lagerlöf. Only one of her stories from the War years — *Bannlyst* (tr. *The Outcast*, 1918) — uses the War as a background; and this tale is not one of the author's best, though some Swedish critics have disposed of it somewhat too summarily. The tale proves how profoundly the War had shaken her — so profoundly apparently that she was unequal to the task of using it as the basis for really memorable literature. The second volume of *Trolls and Men*, which appeared in 1921, was something of an improvement on the earlier miscellany with the same title.

In 1925 the most ambitious work after the publication of *Jerusalem* came from Selma Lagerlöf's hand — the first two volumes of a trilogy generally known as the Löwensköld Cycle. The first two volumes are entitled *Löwensköldska ringen* and *Charlotte Löwensköld*, the third, which appeared in 1928, *Anna Svärd*. The trilogy has appeared in English under the collective title *The Ring of the Löwenskölds*. A planned and partly executed fourth volume was among Selma Lagerlöf's literary remains. Though the Löwensköld Cycle has its setting in Värmland, the province which had most consistently stirred its author's best creative efforts, the novel is on the whole disappointing despite its recurrently rich vein of humor and its creation in Charlotte Löwensköld and Anna

Svärd of two of Selma Lagerlöf's most alive and ingratiating female characters. The central male character, the thin-blooded idealist-fanatic Karl-
Artur Ekenstedt, with whom both Charlotte and Anna fall in love to
the dismay of the reader, serves merely as a rather wooden point of departure for the author's accounting with an otherworldly religious fanaticism. Long before the end of the trilogy we grow weary of the fatuous asceticism of this would-be Brand of the Swedish countryside, who
very tardily, after innumerable stupidities, comes to recognize the error
of his way and embraces a more humane way of life. Karl-Artur Ekenstedt, Charlotte assures us, had finally "learned to love people. This was
so important, for it was this that he lacked. He had loved Christ, and had
shown that he could sacrifice everything in the world in order to follow
Him. But he had never experienced a true love for his fellow men. And he
who wishes to be a follower of Christ without loving his fellow men will
lead both himself and others into misery." The observation endears us
less to Karl-Artur Ekenstedt than it does to Selma Lagerlöf, whose own
warm religious humanism it so beautifully sums up. The two women,
Charlotte and Anna, who each in her way loved Karl-Artur, deserved
better of fate than to find the object of their love in a priggish clergyman-
moralist with the unstable emotional drives of the religious fanatic.

If the Löwensköld Cycle is something less than satisfactory, the years
just before and after its appearance brought among other things three
volumes of considerable autobiographical importance — *Mårbacka* (tr.
Mårbacka), *Ett barns memoarer: Mårbacka 2* (tr. *Memories of My
Childhood*), and *Dagbok: Mårbacka 3* (tr. *The Diary of Selma Lagerlöf*).
The chief charm of these autobiographical fragments lies in their utter
self-forgetfulness. It is doubtful that autobiography has ever been written with a more complete exclusion of self. The three volumes deal with
life at Mårbacka, with Selma Lagerlöf's parents, her brothers and sisters,
and the family servants, with the originals of some of the characters in
Gösta Berling's Saga, and with legends and tales current among the coun-
try-folk in the neighborhood of Mårbacka; but none of the three volumes, curiously enough, can be said to deal immediately with *Selma
Lagerlöf herself* — except insofar as her childhood is revealed indirectly
through these memories of the past.

This artistic reticence is one of the most ingratiating elements in Selma
Lagerlöf. It is natural with her. It would never have occurred to her to
take a reader into her confidence in the self-conscious manner so frequently practiced since the vogue of Romantic egotism first swept the

literary world with its confessional vein – a manner which in so many of its practitioners came to harden into a confessional pose or degenerate into confessional hysteria. Selma Lagerlöf's artistic reticence grew naturally out of her essential modesty of person. She has always been ready to give to others the credit for her own success as a teller of tales. Perhaps the most charming example of her literary modesty is to be found in the little address of acceptance delivered before the distinguished audience gathered to do her honor in December of 1909 on the awarding to her of the Nobel Prize in Literature. The entire address is a simple, unassuming confession of her deep feeling of indebtedness to a host of *others* who in one way or another had made her work possible: first, to her parents, especially her father, who had read to her when she was a child from Bellman and Tegnér, Runeberg and Hans Christian Andersen, in whose pages she had first learned "to love the old tales and the deeds of heroism and the life of man in all its greatness and all its weakness" . . . then to Värmland, to its many good and simple people who had opened to her the rich store of her province's peasant tales . . . also to Dalarna, the region which had brought to her the profoundly gripping story of the Swedish "peasants who took their way unto the Holy City" . . . then to that varied host of literary figures "who have cultivated the language, who have forged and hammered out the good instruments and taught me to make use of them" . . . and finally to her readers and to her critics, "both to those who have praised and to those who have found fault." Selma Lagerlöf's own genius and industry are not mentioned here, but her genius was in its kind very rare, and her industry never failed her. Almost always a superb craftsman as a story teller, she on not a few occasions was so gripped by her subject that the craftsman became an artist on the highest level of artistic performance. Her prose at its best ranks with the finest poetry of that distinguished generation of Swedish poets who appeared in the 1890's.

Among these poets was Gustaf Fröding (1860–1911), who like Selma Lagerlöf was born in Värmland, wrote in part about the Värmland countryside, but whose literary career, unlike Selma Lagerlöf's, spanned only a few years, a half dozen in all, before an inherited strain of madness snuffed out his brilliant poetic talents and necessitated his being cared for during the last twelve years of his life as a hopeless mental patient. But limited as were the number of years during which Fröding's poetic flame burned they were years filled with an almost incomparable poetic

Verner von Heidenstam as his hero in *Hans Alienus*, portrait
by Hanna Pauli, 1896 (photo: SPA)

Olshammar, the Heidenstam family estate, with the Birgitta
Church and its multitude of historical associations

Selma Lagerlöf (photo by B. Goodwin, ca. 1920)

Erik Axel Karlfeldt, portrait with national romantic
background detail by Carl Larsson

Gustaf Fröding, detail from a portrait by
Richard Bergh (photo: SPA)

magic. In Swedish poetry only Bellman can be compared with him in the mastery of verse forms, and only Bellman and Runeberg in brilliant character portraiture in verse. And among all Swedish poets he stands alone in his warm and direct humanity, his instinctive compassion for all whom life has dealt with harshly. As in the case of Stagnelius, circumstances made a tragic shambles of Fröding's life, denying him normal outlets for his drives and dreams and impelling him to seek tawdry recompense in sexual and alcoholic excesses. But his personal degradation never touched the *core* of Fröding's being. Humiliated by his own irregular way of life, and often burdened by a heavy feeling of guilt, he was always ready to understand if not condone those acts of others who erred without deliberately cultivating evil. Except for a short, half-mad, Nietzschean interlude in the late 1890's his poetry reflects everywhere a gentleness and humility of spirit frequently deepened and enlivened by a warm, all-forgiving humor.

Fröding was born with a profound feeling of insecurity in the presence of reality, and this feeling of insecurity led him ultimately to look upon himself as a social outcast, a pitiable pariah. He somehow never "fitted" into an everyday, normal world. Only in his poetry could he exist without a feeling of inferiority. In his childhood and youth he lived in his own dream-world peopled by such phenomena as he found in the Arabian Nights and Sir Walter Scott's novels. His university years at Uppsala in the early 1880's, and the following years of provincial journalistic activities at Karlstad, temporarily led him into the camp of the literary realists and radicals of the day. But he had difficulty in adjusting himself to literary realism and lacked entirely those qualities which the social reformer must have. At Uppsala he took no degree because of his inability to adjust himself to the "prescribed courses," and at Karlstad the first serious signs of mental degeneration became noticeable, necessitating his seeking treatment for nervous disorders in various hospitals abroad. Meantime he wrote verse and dreamed of becoming a poet as the only way out of the dilemma in which he found himself. But, as he writes to his sister Cecelia, in April 1889,

it is almost impossible to be a poet in these times, when one must, whether one wishes to or not, place the dissecting knife upon one's feelings and is not permitted to abandon oneself to them as in the past . . . Literature has lost contact with music and has tended instead to identify itself with science. I myself am an unhappy conglomeration of romantic moods and naturalistic convictions, and I don't know whether such a half-man is fit to be either a romantic poet or a naturalistic author [literally "describer," *skildrare*].

Though he read widely during these years in the great poets (Goethe and Heine, Byron, Shelley, and Burns, Tegnér and Stagnelius), it was not until Heidenstam had shown the way for modern Swedish poetry with *Pilgrimage and Wander-Years* that Fröding had the courage to pull himself together and compose the poems published in 1891 under the title *Guitarr och dragharmonika* (Guitar and Concertina). The great success of this volume encouraged him to follow through with *Nya dikter* (New Poems) in 1894 and *Stänk och flikar* (Splashes and Rags) in 1896, after which only a few gripping poetic fragments — appearing chiefly in the two thin volumes *Nytt och gammalt* (New and Old Pieces, 1897) and *Gralstänk* (Grail Splashes, 1898) — provide evidence that his creative gifts, though not totally beclouded by his mental crisis, had lost forever their magnificent earlier mastery of form and substance. After Fröding's death in 1911, some inferior verse written in his last years was published under the title *Reconvalescentia*.

The prose which Fröding from time to time wrote is of little importance aside from the light which it throws on certain crucial areas of his thinking, particularly those areas which include his break with literary naturalism in the years around 1890 and his later titanic struggle with his conscience and with religious and philosophical thought. Of chief literary interest are the two essays "Naturalism and Romanticism" and "On Humor," which appeared in the periodical *Ur Dagens Krönika* in 1890, and the life of Burns (*Folkskalden Robert Burns*) published in the series Verdandi småskrifter in 1892.

In "Naturalism and Romanticism" Fröding joins Heidenstam ("Rennaissance," 1889) in rejecting naturalistic theory as a basis for creative literature. Using *La bête humaine* as his point of departure, Fröding demonstrates with telling effect that Zola's work in general is more closely related to Victor Hugo and E. T. A. Hoffmann, Bulwer-Lytton and Hans Christian Andersen than it is to the scientific ideals which it purportedly follows. That which is best in Zola, his imaginative flair, his subjectivism, is, Fröding insists, Romantic rather than Naturalistic. Zola is in reality a highly imaginative author despite his insistence that literature should be based on sober scientific observation. In "On Humor" Fröding takes issue with the moral rigorism of the Scandinavian 1870's and 1880's, pleading for a more flexible and humane view of the human scene than that which draws absolute distinctions between good and evil and insists on "the famous ideal demand" of Kierkegaard and Ibsen and their pale brood of followers. Such distinctions and demands result in self-righteous fanaticism rather than genuine ethical pathos. Under the circumstances, Fröding argues, man is in desperate need of the sense of reconciliation with life provided by a warm, understanding, all-embracing and all-forgiving humor, the kind of humor so magnificently represented in Shakespeare's Falstaff and Bellman's Fredman. Such humor will release the literary imagination while it brings a spontaneous solace to the broken human spirit. It will serve both aesthetic and moral ends without indulging in either overprecious poetic effects or overzealous preachments.

In all except some of Fröding's last, most madly visionary verse he retained his faith in the releasing and reconciling powers of humor. In his early verse this humor tended to be broad and playful, essentially a humor of scintillating surfaces; but with time — as darkness settled down over the poet's spirit — his humor took on increasingly dark-hued tones not infrequently bordering on profoundly tragic poetic utterance. At times there is in his later verse a note of harshness, of bitterness, but this note enters his poetic world usually as a tentative, furtive visitant rather than a welcome, long-time guest. Fröding had a desperate faith in life's healing, restorative powers despite the grim realities of his own fate. His poetry, as one Swedish critic has put it, is "essentially an expression of his *healthy* self's (*friska* jags) struggle against madness. Suffering has taught him to worship that which is good and healthy in life and to propound its ideal values."

Fröding's great popularity was from the beginning based on his broad vein of humor and the flawless felicity and facility of his verse, but readers today are apt to be more impressed by the thematic range and variety and the profound humanity of his poetry and by the stark visionary quality of some of his later verse. Despite Fröding's sympathy with certain sides of the social program of the 1880's — most apparent in such poems as "Salomos insegel" (Solomon's Seal), "Takt" (Tact), "Bollspelet vid Trianon" (Ball Play at the Trianon), "Tronskifte" (The New Regime), "Atlantis," and "Den gamla goda tiden" (The Good Old Times) — he indulges comparatively rarely in social satire, and when he does so he tends to couch his satire in the guise of good-natured banter. How tolerant in comparison with the 1880's was his view of the worldly clergyman is apparent in "Våran prost" (Our Dean), and how different from the 1880's was his approach to "the woman question" is equally apparent in

"Indianer" (Indians), "Äktenskapsfrågan" (The Matrimonial Problem), and "Mannen och Kvinnan" (Man and Woman).

The so-called Värmland poems were those that early attracted popular attention. Each of Fröding's three major volumes of verse included a group of poems with provincial motifs, depicting for the most part droll local types and situations in a language frequently flecked with lively local dialect. These types and situations are approached from infinitely varied points of view and clad in verse forms which fit perfectly the subject and mood of each. Among the most unforgettable of the provincial poems in a lighter vein are "Jonte och Brunte," the lazy tale of a weary hired man and a broken-down horse; "Our Dean," a slyly understanding portrait of a worthy though earthy prelate and his appreciative parishioners; "Det var dans bort i vägen på lördagsnatten" (There Was a Dance on the Roadside on Saturday Night), a rollicking description of a wild country dance, and "Ett gammalt bergtroll" (An Old Mountain Troll), a poem which manages to invest even a supernatural denizen of the wilds with comic human attributes by having it indulge in rueful ruminations over its massive ugliness and beastly stupidity. A special dimension is added to the Old Mountain Troll's ruminations when we realize that it is Fröding's *alter ego*. Among the more quiet and meditative Värmland poems are such sensitive mood pieces as "Strövtåg i hembygden" (Homecoming) and "Ett gammalt förmak" (An Old Drawing Room), which contain recollections from the poet's childhood and youth and from the family life and manor house existence of Fröding's better days.

In sharp contrast both with the broadly comic poems and the gently reminiscent autobiographical pieces are a number of Fröding's more deeply personal poems — poems in which he pleads for sympathy and understanding among men and gives more or less direct expression to his own immediate tragedy. Among the most moving of the poems which plead for sympathy and understanding on the human scene are two dealing with the relation between man and woman, one entitled "Jägar Malms hustrur" (The Wives of Hunter Malm), the other called simply "Mannen och kvinnan" (Man and Woman). Harsh as is the outlawed Hunter Malm's defense of himself in the first of these poems, and hard as his words fall, a momentary note of tenderness finally breaks through, suggesting how difficult it is for him to maintain an attitude of indifference toward his last love, Eli-lita, during her final illness and death. Bitter as he has become toward life, which had driven him to acts of violence and the ways of a pariah, he has preserved at least for Eli-lita a gruff but genuine sense of solidarity in love. "Man and Woman," one of Fröding's many "biblical fantasies," employs the Adam and Eve motif in dealing with the relation between the sexes as an eternal, often bitter and vengeful conflict; but as the poem closes the two are driven together in a common feeling of pity for one another — life being what it is.

> Then the woman softened, and flinging
> Her arms out wide, she grasped him,
> With all her soul to him clinging
> As she hung to his neck and clasped him,
> Crying, "Nay, when thou weepest there lives not
> Desire for this cursing and pother:
> Since the Lord in Heaven forgives not,
> We must e'en forgive one another!
> We are doomed from our lives' beginning
> To wrangle and never content us,
> We are even as dogs in our sinning,—
> Let us sin then still, and repent us!
> Let our woes be a bond uniting
> Our lives in misery blended,
> And brawling and hating and fighting,
> And love, — till the world is ended!" —
>
> *Translated by C. D. Locock*

Though "The Wives of Hunter Malm" and "Man and Woman" are "objective" in the sense that Fröding is not in these poems dealing directly with his own case, one feels nevertheless how personally the poet's feelings become engaged here with the tragic materials he uses.

In other poems Fröding presents his own tragic case under certain rather easily penetrated disguises: by means of animal and mystical symbolism in "En ghasel" (A Gazelle) and "Fylgia," through fictive parallels of various kinds in "En fattig munk från Skara" (A Poor Monk of Skara), "Prins Aladdin av lampan" (Aladdin of the Lamp), and "Fredlös" (The Pariah), under the guise of a buffoon in "Clown Clopopisky." In most cases these poems express the poet's despair and remorse over a way of life which was to stunt and finally destroy his creative powers, but occasionally, as in the gripping confessional strain of "A Poor Monk of Skara," he admits no personal guilt and seeks comfort in the dream of a day

> When none is evil, none is good,
> but all as brothers breast the flood,
> each lending each a hand
> while struggling to the strand.

More relentlessly and without any special pleading, Fröding deals with his own case in "Skalden Wennerbom" (The Poet Wennerbom) and "Flickan i ögat" (The Girl in the Eyes), the former a sketch of alcoholic degradation, the latter a broken, darkly fragmented portrait of sexual frustration made the more tawdry by constant use of the bottle. In "The Poet Wennerbom" the title figure seeks sottish solace in a drunken stupor, and finally forgetfulness in sleep:

> Drowsy is he now: soon sleep is calling:
> Kindly tree-tops filter the light falling
> On the head of Poet Wennerbom,
> Tenderly the chestnut rains its bloom.
> Empty, neath the gloom,
> Lies the flask, mid caterpillars crawling.
>
> Rich and deep the glow that o'er him creeping
> Floods his soul, — into far limbos sweeping
> Stings of conscience, thoughts of crime and ruth;
> Gone into the dreamland of his youth,
> Sleeps he well in sooth: —
> Good it is when Poets can lie sleeping.
>
> *Translated by C. D. Locock*

Beautiful as are the sun-drenched, midsummer-filled final lines of "The Poet Wennerbom," they only in part reconcile us to the sordid realities with which the poem otherwise deals. They serve chiefly to point up the utter state of degradation into which Wennerbom had drifted. More deeply moving, on the other hand, are the simple, selfless words of comfort offered the besotted, miserable poet by the shop-girl in "The Girl in the Eyes."

"The Wives of Hunter Malm" and "The Girl in the Eyes" were published in *Splashes and Rags*, the volume in which Fröding's poetic greatness and personal tragedy are most powerfully reflected. In 1894, when he was reading proof on *New Poems*, the first serious schizophrenic symptoms occurred, symptoms which multiplied dangerously in the following months and led directly within a few years to Fröding's final mental deterioration. But while this deterioration was taking place he composed those terrifying other-worldly visions and naked confessional poems which most impress the modern reader of *Splashes and Rags*. Somehow his formal skills, his mastery of language and his metrical magic, remained for the time being unimpaired even though his world of idea was gradually lapsing into a seething, chaotic, at times quite mad and unintelligible aggregate of dream sequences and thought fragments. The pure dream sequences are perhaps most satisfactorily represented in the subtly modulated visions of "Dreams in Hades," while the drift of Fröding's thinking at the time is most clearly articulated in such pieces as "Sagan om Gral" (The Story of the Grail), "En morgondröm" (A Morning Dream), and "I Daphne" (In Daphne). During Fröding's years of incipient mental disintegration his thought world — often grotesquely fragmented but only apparently directionless — gyrated unsteadily but persistently around the problem of good and evil. Torn between a strong feeling of guilt and remorse and a desire to defy a traditional ascetic ethics, he ransacks ancient and modern religious and philosophical thought on the subject of moral responsibility. He immerses himself in esoteric speculation of all kinds, theosophy, spiritualism, Swedenborgianism, and among modern thinkers he is alternately fascinated by Tolstoi and Nietzsche, with the ascetic dualism of Tolstoi ultimately yielding in Fröding's thought to the amoral affirmation of life characteristic of Nietzsche.

In his poetry from these years a free, unfettered Nietzschean ethics, with its dream of a perfect future for man when he has cast off all rigoristic moral claims, finds expression in two ways: in the sin-seared symbolistic ambiguities of "The Story of the Grail," which gropes uncertainly toward a day when man has attained a synthesis between good and evil, and in the daring visions of "A Morning Dream" and "In Daphne," which triumphantly glorify the sexual act as the ultimate expression of man's emancipation and his entering into the good world. The very extremes to which Fröding goes in such poems as "A Morning Dream" and "In Daphne" suggest that his brain had reached its breaking point, that he felt his hold upon reality — and with it some of his poetic skills — slipping. Even as he dreamed so aggressively of a vital, healthy, new world for man he recognized that he himself had become "a cinder-pit of burned out desires."

The event which hastened his final mental collapse and left him a harmless madman for the remainder of his years was the legal prosecution on charges of immorality lodged against "A Morning Dream." Even though the jury's decision was "Not guilty," Fröding suffered fearfully under the accusations of "moral rottenness," "erotomania," and "moral and physical insanity" which were hurled against him by his critics, and he never recovered from the public stigma of these accusations. Two years after the court prosecution he became a patient at the mental hospital at Uppsala and spent the remainder of his life under psychiatric supervision there and elsewhere. During these years he continued to struggle with the gods, to brood over the problem of good and evil, to experience strange and terrifying visions, and to try his hand — with less and less skill as the years wore on — at poetic composition. As a poet he had only fugitive flashes of inspiration during the first gloomy years after the crisis which reached its climax with the publication in 1896 of *Splashes and Rags* and its aftermath. After the turn of the century the darkness which had settled down over his spirit cut off almost completely any literary communication with an outer world.

When Fröding died in 1911 Sweden mourned as she has never mourned the passing of a poet. On the occasion of his passing Heidenstam penned one of his most inspired poems, a majestic dirge whose closing lines intone a nation's sense of wonder and of terror in the presence of the poetry and the life story of one of her greatest sons:

> How wondrous great is man's destiny:
> Dreams and old tales and the flowing sea,
> Floods and flames and the choir of the storm! —
> But weak as a reed is his own frail form.
>
> . . . .
>
> Pass, O bard, erect as a king,
> To the host of the shades through the darksome portal!
> Still we cherish
> Your limpid-silvery notes immortal
> Singing to us as they used to sing.
>
> *Translated by C. W. Stork*

No Swedish poet has sung as spontaneously, with such apparently effortless ease and depth of both comic and tragic feeling as Fröding. It has been said that to his predecessors poetry was "conscious song, to Fröding it is simply breathing." The observation is as true with regard to the warm humanity of Fröding's verse as it is with reference to its phenomenal felicity of form.

Upon turning from Fröding to Erik Axel Karlfeldt (1864–1931), the last of the great poets of the 1890's to appear on the literary scene, we come into a poetic world which has some points of contact with Fröding's but which in the main has a flavor all its own. Its chief point of contact is the relatively superficial one that Karlfeldt writes of the Dalarna countryside as Fröding does of the province of Värmland. But Karlfeldt's identification with Dalarna is at once more complete and profound than is Fröding's with Värmland, and in most other respects Karlfeldt differs sharply, both as man and poet, from Fröding. As a man he was robust, reticent, stable, firmly rooted in the ancient traditions of his peasant forbears. As a poet he was a solid master-craftsman, rarely given to direct confessional expression of his private inner world, nearly always looking upon himself as the voice of others, his forefathers, with their sturdy self-confidence and independence, their quiet acceptance of the conditions of life, their love of the soil upon which so many generations of their ancestors had toiled. The drift toward literary regionalism (*hembygds-diktning*), one of the most characteristic features of the literature of the 1890's, has in Karlfeldt its most satisfactory interpreter. Compared with Karlfeldt's Dalarna-regionalism Heidenstam's relation to Östergötland is largely a matter of surfaces, and though Fröding and Selma Lagerlöf penetrate rather deeply into certain sides of the spirit and folk life of Värmland, Karlfeldt's poetic treatment of Dalarna is at almost every point more intimate, more profound, more essentially organic. Indeed, Karlfeldt *is* Dalarna in as absolute a sense as it is possible for a poet to be the collective expression of a region's folk and its way of life.

A number of conditions in Sweden at the close of the nineteenth century account for the fascination which her ancient folk life exercised over the cultural life of the day. Perhaps chief among these conditions were the revolutionary changes in Swedish social organization resulting from the growing industrialization of the country. As population shifts toward urban centers accelerated in the closing years of the century, there arose among many Swedes who had moved from rural areas to the cities an inevitable tendency to idealize the forms of life they had abandoned. Under the impact of the new industrial developments an ancient peasant culture was dying before men's eyes, and artists, composers, and poets, scholars and amateur antiquarians joined with folklorists and museum directors, among whom Artur Hazelius was the born leader, to save what they could of the record and the spirit of this ancient culture. Dalarna in particular became the focal point for cultural activity of this kind. Its countryside, rich in matters reminiscent of the past, was ransacked for primitive furniture and wall paintings, peasant costumes, woven articles, tools and implements; and these examples of the arts and crafts of the folk of Dalarna together with those of other Swedish provinces were catalogued, arranged, and displayed, first in the newly established ethnographical museums in Stockholm (Nordiska museet and Skansen), later in more modest local collections everywhere around the country. Leading artists of the day filled canvas after canvas with Swed-

Old country fiddler (vignette
by Bertil Bull-Hedlund)

ish landscapes and Swedish folk types, and in the case of some of them,
Anders Zorn, Carl Larsson, and Gustaf Ankarcrona, enthusiasm for the
older ways of life as represented in Dalarna led them to maintain resi-
dences in this province and surround themselves with authentic examples of its folk art and crafts. In fact, Zorn and Ankarcrona collected
such enormous quantities of ancient objects representative of the Dalarna
folk culture that their collections became with time impressive permanent ethnographical museums. Zorn in addition encouraged a revival of
folk music in Dalarna by arranging a series of old fiddlers' contests.

Swedish cultural history has had its share of happy coincidences, none
happier than that concatenation of circumstances which, as if by accident, provided the Dalarna folk culture in the days of its decline with a
poet, in the person of Erik Axel Karlfeldt, capable of articulating with
vigor, dignity, and rare imaginative sensitivity and intensity the rich
ebb and flow of life on the Dalarna countryside. Among all Swedish
provinces celebrated in history and literature Dalarna has come to have
in Sweden a special place. It has been called "the Swedish ideal," in part
because of the role its sturdy peasant stock played in the long and bloody
struggle for national independence in the fifteenth and early sixteenth
centuries, and in part because it has preserved longer than any other
Swedish province a way of daily living deeply rooted in local ancestral
traditions. Geographically also it is perhaps most typically Swedish. Its

326

broad river valleys hemmed in by a vast wilderness area and low mountain ranges to the west and north have for centuries rewarded man's ingenuity and labors with such typical Swedish products as copper and iron, timber and the yield of field and meadow. The native of Dalarna has been for centuries a blend of miner and peasant, something of an aristocrat of the soil, quietly conscious of his worth, normally conservative in his ways but capable in moments of stress to meet new situations in new — if need be in revolutionary — ways.

Karlfeldt was a true son of Dalarna, born in Folkärna parish near the southern boundary of the province, with an ancestry both on his father's and mother's side of pure Dalarna stock. His childhood and early youth were unusually harmonious, but just before he was to take up university studies the most fateful event of his life took place — the loss of the family property, Tolvmansgården, in consequence of financial defalcations on the part of his father. Heavy as this blow was to the future poet's pride, and difficult as it made his pursuit of a higher education, he managed to take two degrees at Uppsala during a dozen years' stay at the university broken by a number of spells as a teacher in private and public schools. Instead of turning permanently to teaching in 1898 upon the completion of his university studies, he accepted in 1900 a minor appointment at the Royal Library in Stockholm and a few years later became the librarian at the Institute of Agriculture. He remained a citizen of Stockholm the remainder of his life, returning frequently to Dalarna, however, during the summers, and late in life establishing a permanent summer residence at Sjugareby in the northern area of his native province. After the difficult university years his life was outwardly uneventful, dedicated quietly to the task of shaping a solid, honest body of poetry, as solid and honest as had been the work of his forefathers in their centuries-long task of breaking the soil and fashioning the conditions out of which could grow a sturdy peasant culture. The dates of publication of Karlfeldt's six volumes of verse mark therefore the chief "events" of his life — in 1895 *Vildmarks- och kärleksvisor* (Songs of the Wilderness and of Love), in 1898 and 1901 *Fridolins visor* (Fridolin's Songs) and *Fridolins lustgård* (Fridolin's Pleasure Garden), in 1906 and 1918 *Flora och Pomona* and *Flora och Bellona*, and finally, in 1927, four years before the poet's death, *Hösthorn* (The Horn of Autumn). Though he turned his hand only rarely to prose, his address on the occasion of Fröding's burial is a masterpiece of its kind, and his monograph on the seventeenth-century Swedish poet Lucidor combines scholarship and a poet's insights in a way seldom attained in literary criticism. Karlfeldt's poetic reputation, firmly established with the two Fridolin volumes, grew steadily with the years, and many high literary honors came to him, including his election as early as 1904 to the Swedish Academy, whose Permanent Secretary he became in 1912, and his being the recipient of the Nobel Prize in Literature in 1931.

So great was Karlfeldt's popularity throughout his career that some critics of liberal leanings have been disturbed that a poet of his stature employed his gifts so exclusively in the service of a dying local culture. In the 1890's such essentially regional, tradition-bound poetry might have been appropriate, but in the rapidly changing world of the twentieth century it came to be looked upon in some quarters as an unhappy anachronism. The phrase "Karlfeldtfaran" (the Karlfeldt danger) was coined by one Leftist critic, and spokesmen for a new, more modern, forward-looking literature disclaimed any loyalty to the kind of poetry of which Karlfeldt was the most distinguished representative. That such an attitude toward Karlfeldt's poetry had a certain validity is apparent, but when it was propounded, in the early 1930's, Swedish poetry — if not popular poetic taste in Sweden — had for some time been moving in directions other than those suggested by the work of the chief regional poet of the 1890's. The reason for this shift in poetic ideals was not merely that the new intellectual climate was antipathetic to a regional romanticism such as Karlfeldt represented. It was also the fact that Karlfeldt himself had carried certain thematic and technical trends in Swedish poetry to such a point of perfection that no poet could go farther on the road he had traveled. Karlfeldt's primary distinction as a poet lies in the amazing originality and skill with which he extracted hitherto unimagined poetic values from what in the main was a rather limited regional material. Regional loyalties in no wise restricted his imaginative potentialities. They provided the firm foundations on which his genius could build a brilliant superstructure of poetic form and motif.

Though Karlfeldt's poetic production maintains a high level of creative vitality for nearly a half century, it undergoes during this time no fundamental change, reflects no basic shifts in point of view or in stylistic manner. His ideational presuppositions and aesthetic standards were essentially the same at the close of his career as at the beginning. In his poetry Karlfeldt seldom got outside his Dalarna world, and when he did so, he tended to react to the larger outside world in terms of the norms determined by his feeling of kinship with an ancient Dalarna culture.

This made him instinctively suspicious of many developments in the modern world, not least the tendency to assume that all social problems can be solved by means of political action. It is only in his later work, however, that he directly offers his opinions on such subjects, and the few poems in which these opinions are expressed are scarcely among Karlfeldt's best. Not even in the flaming indictment of the modern war spirit in "Till Bellona" (To Bellona) and "En pest hymn" (A Pest Hymn) does Karlfeldt *quite* achieve real poetic greatness in his poems dealing directly with the evils of a modern world.

If Karlfeldt's poetry reflects no basic shifts in point of view or in stylistic manner, it underwent with the years an increasingly impressive *maturing* process. Its recurrent motifs and themes took on with time new dimensions, plumbed new depths of feeling and of thought; and its form became more subtle, more complex, more richly and finely orchestrated. This constantly growing poetic maturity can be illustrated in a number of ways, most strikingly in matters of theme and motif by examining his handling over the years of three of his most persistently recurring subjects — love, nature, and the way of life of his peasant forebears. Though he attained a level of poetic utterance on each of these subjects second to none in Swedish poetry, he did not from the outset bring to these themes the touch of the master. The love theme as handled in such early poems as "Vild kärlek" (Wild Love) or "Intet är som väntanstider" (Nothing is like times of waiting) is engaging rather than impressive, its level being that merely of young love, by turn sensually possessive and full of an indefinite dreamy yearning. With the years, however, Karlfeldt's love poetry matures, becomes more complex, more moving and profound, as reflected in a preliminary way in "Dina ögon äro eldar" (Your Eyes Are Flames of Fire) and in its full maturity in the fateful, darkly demoniac, mystery-weighted periods of "Nattyxne" (Dame's-Violet) and "Häxorna" (The Witches).

In the primordial symbolism and the sexual mysticism of the last two of these poems is also reflected Karlfeldt's mature awareness of nature's mysterious, primitive, frequently destructive drives, a view of nature nursed by the poet's increasing preoccupation as the years go by with all manner of strange and portentous folk supersitions. Much of the indefinable, almost unbearable sense of horror that we feel on reading "Nattyxne" and "The Witches" derives from the thoroughness with which the poet exploits primitive man's imaginative life as peopled by grotesque creatures of forest and stream and conceptualized in terms of a crude and bloody dualism. Though the view of nature reflected in such poems did not exclude from Karlfeldt's mature nature poetry elements of the idyllic or the merely healthy and robust, it added an impressively disturbing note to many of his later nature poems and served as a necessary corrective to the optimistic animalism of much of his early verse.

The poems concerned primarily with the folk culture of Dalarna are not so dark-hued, so eruptively earthy as some of the love lyrics and nature poems, but primitive qualities are certainly not lacking in these poems, for the peasantry of Dalarna had retained far down into modern times a deep sense of partial identity with their nature-bound heathen origins. They were in their way good Lutherans of the old school, but beneath the heavy overlay of Lutheran orthodoxy existed a disquieting residuum of pagan beliefs and superstitions which played a not inconsiderable role in their daily lives. They at times resorted in consequence to the tricky subterfuge of exorcism when pressed by the primitive powers of darkness, but normally they made ineffectual the machinations of those powers by more positive means — by simply putting their hands to the plow, the sledge, and the axe, fashioning from the wilderness a solid peasant culture which by its quiet strength of *character* kept destructive forces at a respectable distance. The folk culture of Dalarna pursued its ideal ends down through the centuries without shaking off completely its contact with the soil and with an immemorial past. The result, as we come to know it in Karlfeldt's poetry, was a native culture of extraordinary balance and stability, a culture in which the flesh was not denied in the service of the ideal, a culture in which a finely disciplined traditionalism grew naturally out of partly disparate origins and conditions of existence.

Of the poems dealing with the Dalarna peasant and his culture, the most memorable are some of what are known as the Fridolin pieces, the "Dalarna Wall Paintings in Rhyme," and a group chiefly of a reminiscent kind which in a more or less direct programmatic vein extol the virtues of the Dalarna way of life. The Fridolin figure, Karlfeldt's slightly disguised *alter ego*, was dictated by the poet's desire to speak in the third rather than the first person. He appears extensively in the two early volumes whose titles include his name, and reappears occasionally in later volumes. A learned man of peasant extraction, he is represented as having returned to the countryside of his forefathers and established himself as a kind of poet-peasant who "talks with the peasantry in the peasant's manner but with men of learning in Latin." As a part-outsider he responds to the peasant way of life with extraordinary discernment and enthusiasm. The poem in which he reveals most richly his feeling of identity with the life and culture of his ancestors is the magnificent "Sång efter skördeanden" (Song after Harvest), whose sensuous play of imagery and full-bodied rhythms are perfectly attuned to Fridolin's warm responses to love and harvest-time fertility and his proud awareness of those ancestral values which lend meaning and elevation to the scene and the occasion. To Karlfeldt, Fridolin is the ideal type in his harmonious adjustment to the quiet, stable, dignified form of life of his ancestors. That Fridolin does not, however, sum up all sides of Karlfeldt's own character is apparent from the fact that the poet feels obliged in the two Fridolin volumes to create, as a kind of fleeting foil to Fridolin, the restless, darkly defiant figure of The Vagrant (*Löskerkarlen*), a creature who in his all but anarchistic individualism despises society's efforts to tame him, listens alone to the proud, wild voice within himself. And in the superb measures of "Jag är en sjungandes röst" (Voice of a Singer Am I) the motif is developed with a poetic immediacy which discards completely the metaphorical indirections behind which Karlfeldt partially disguises himself in the Vagrant type:

Voice of a Singer am I, through empty spaces calling,
Where ear is none to hear, scarce echo seems to be.
Will-o'-the-wisp am I, when night on the mere is falling,
A fitful fire soon quenched in dark — the dark which
    fostered me.

I am a whirling leaf mid Autumn's wide-flung shadows,
My life-day but a toy for the winds' revelry.
Shall I come to rest on a hill-top? or down in a ditch
    in the meadows?
I cannot tell — I hardly care — no help for that have I.

Translated by C. D. Locock

The mood in which these lines are conceived takes over only fitfully in Karlfeldt's verse. What may be called the bucolic humanism of Fridolin yields only rarely to this mood. Of Karlfeldt's Dalarna poems the most original are those included in *Fridolin's Pleasure Garden* under the group title "Dalarna Wall Paintings in Rhyme" (*Dalmålningar, utlagda på rim*), in which the poet succeeds miraculously in turning into verse the religious moods and naïve aesthetic effects of those peasant artists who had recorded on the walls of Dalarna farmhouses many a dramatic scene from biblical history and ancient legendary lore. The idea in itself

331

of transferring to words and poetic meters the vivid brush strokes of the primitive artists of his province was sufficiently original. But even more original was the *manner* in which Karlfeldt rendered in poetic form the traditional motifs and themes of the wall paintings. Whether or not in a given poem he has a particular painting in mind (in most cases he does), he employs the motifs from this quaint world of art with complete imaginative freedom. "As a Dalarna artist," he writes with regard to these poems, "I insist on the modest right of my fellow-craftsmen of old: to paint as I wish, with a whimsical brush, mixing jests with gravity – in the spirit of my predecessors even though with partly differing techniques." The result in Karlfeldt's case is a remarkably fresh recapturing of the religious tone and the aesthetic naïveté of the originals. Though "Yttersta domen" (The Day of Judgment) provides evidence that Karlfeldt could on occasion respond deeply to some of the more somber motifs of the Dalarna paintings, most of his poems in the manner of these primitive paintings suggest that he was more fascinated by their homely everyday realism and their apparently unconscious humor. "Elie himmelsfärd" (The Assumption of Elijah) reflects his delight in the naïve anachronisms of the peasant painters who clothed Old Testament worthies in Dalarna dress and placed them in recognizable Dalarna environments, and "Jone havsfärd" (The Voyage of Jonah) reveals how far Karlfeldt was prepared to go in transforming the relatively restrained humor of his predecessors into a deliberate exploiting of broad comic effects. In "Jungfru Maria" (The Virgin Mary), on the other hand, he creates a delicate poetic vision far removed from the rude archaisms of the typical wall painting though its motif is biblical and its milieu is an identifiable localized Dalarna landscape.

If the "Wall Paintings in Rhyme" reflect Karlfeldt's specific delight in an art form particularly characteristic of Dalarna culture, other poems such as "Fäderna" (My Forefathers), "Uppbrott" (Departure), "Träslottet" (The Wooden Castle), and "Klagosång över en landtman" (Threnody for a Peasant) concern themselves more broadly and inclusively with the life and culture of the poet's Dalarna forebears. Each of these is a deeply personal poem, essentially confessional and credo-like in spirit and form. In "Departure" the poet immerses himself greedily in the beauty of nature and landscape. In "The Wooden Castle" (the original of which was Hyttbacken, the childhood home of the poet's mother) he lingers particularly in the festive hall, where the gay and colorful wall paintings and the heavy oak chests with their treasures of dress and ornament come gradually to symbolize those qualities of spirit and character from the past which instill in the poet a deep feeling of veneration. "My Forefathers" and "Threnody for a Peasant" may be called collective portraits of the Dalarna peasantry, portraits full of admiration and affirming the poet's grateful sense of loyalty to the way of life which this peasantry represents.

> On history's page their names do not shine,
> For humble and peaceful were they,
> And yet I can see their long, long line
> Stretching back through the ages gray.
> Yes, here in the ancient iron-rich land
> They tilled in their fields by the river-strand
> And smelted the ore in their day.
> Neither thralldom nor pomp could they understand,
> But, dwelling each like a king in his house,
> They quaffed at their festal carouse.
> They kissed their sweethearts in springtime's pride,
> As husbands their faith they revered,
> The king they honored and God they feared,
> And calmly they died, satisfied.
>
> . . . .
>
> I see you in dreams, ye sires of my race,
> And my soul becomes faint and afraid;
> Like a plant I've been torn from my sprouting-place
> And I feel that your cause I've betrayed.
>
> *Translated by C. W. Stork*

But the "cause" which the poet felt he had "betrayed" in his youth when he left his countryside and his people to settle in the city among strangers was a cause which he championed in verse throughout a long poetic career. His poetry was in part his penance for once having outwardly broken with the past — the past he had never betrayed in spirit. In the declining years of an ancient Dalarna folk culture Karlfeldt appropriately penned a last, living poetic testament both to its colorful, picturesque externals and to its solid, abiding human values.

In the handling of verse and other formal poetic concerns Karlfeldt is one of the great Swedish masters. He has neither the elegance of Tegnér and Heidenstam nor the facility of Bellman and Fröding, but he has a stylistic quality peculiarly *his own*, one more rare and in some ways more impressive than the poetic manners of those who had before him been counted among the select few of the great Swedish poets. That which particularly distinguishes Karlfeldt's verse is its deliberate, conscious artistry, its solid, honest, and yet richly imaginative craftsmanship — qualities which the poet admired above all else in the arts and crafts of his Dalarna forefathers. Karlfeldt wished to build with words as his ancestors had built with timber and stone. Though he was capable of writing quiet, meditative verse as well as majestic, intricately orchestrated ode-like poems — his "Vinterorgel" (Winter Organ) is superb in this latter manner — he is usually at his best in more earth-bound contexts and forms. His verse has a sturdy masculine drive and thrust, marked by strong rhymes and lusty rhythms, and his imagery and symbols are of the earth earthy, drawn from wood and field and the concrete everyday realities of the folk life of his native province. His Pegasus, he reminds us in the Prelude to *Fridolin's Pleasure Garden*, "dwelleth not on Parnassus" but moves rather like

> A colt of our own mountain breed.
> With iron spurs gleaming and jangling
>   We stumble through thicket and brake,
> Like the grouse cock my lyre is a-twangling,
>   And oh, what a clatter we make!
>   *Translated by C. W. Stork*

He is fond of the strong word from daily speech and of gutty archaisms drawn from the Peasant's Calendar (Bondepraktikan) or from the Charles XII edition of the Swedish Bible. Traditional as Karlfeldt's poetic style in many ways is, it is traditional with a difference. Its traditionalism is not imitative: it is alive, virile, profoundly primitive in its inner drives, employing old words in new and fresh ways, refashioning conventional metrical patterns with an inventive flexibility and vitality always appropriate to mood, motif, and theme. Perhaps the chief secret of Karlfeldt's poetic style is the sense of tension between the old and the new which it builds up in the reader — a quality, it is worthy of note, which the most advanced modern verse frequently seeks to attain. His traditionalism points both backward and forward, using in the service of modern poetry that which is most alive and vital in the old. It is characteristic of Karlfeldt that in his search for a modern poetic ideal he finds himself most at home among the *earliest* important Swedish poets. Neither the Romantics nor Bellman appeal to him as profoundly as do the two at once learned and passionate Renaissance figures Stiernhielm and Lucidor, worthy literary representatives of an expanding, adventurous, power-conscious seventeenth-century Sweden. In the poetry of Stiernhielm and Lucidor, Karlfeldt admires particularly the audacious use of language, the willingness to experiment with verse forms, and what he calls "the genuine *furor poeticus*," qualities which he finds too little present in the more finished poetry of later generations of Swedish poets.

Though the 1890's is popularly thought of as the decade of Heidenstam, Selma Lagerlöf, Fröding, and Karlfeldt, it should not be forgotten that other talents were active during this period and made more or less significant contributions to the cultural complex of the years around the turn of the century. Among these talents were a strenuous feminist and a quietly forceful philosopher as well as a couple of artists-turned-short-story-writers, and two purely literary figures whose talents and productivity were so considerable that they must be ranked only somewhat below "the great four" of the day. The feminist, Ellen Key (1849–1926), and the philosopher, Hans Larsson (1862–1944), influenced literary developments in various ways, Ellen Key through her vigorous, often even vociferous championing of a rather naïve cult of beauty and individualism, Hans Larsson by his nice balancing of realistic and idealistic values and his sensitive studies (*Intuition*, *Poesiens logik*) on the nature of poetic inspiration. The one-time art student Pelle Molin (1864–96) and the great caricaturist Albert Engström (1869–1940) added Norrland and Småland to the areas exploited by the literary regionalism of the day. Their concern was chiefly with the purely primitive sides of folk life in these regions in contrast to Karlfeldt's emphasis on the folk cultural aspects of the Dalarna countryside. Engström later also became fascinated by the picturesque peasant-fisherfolk of Roslagen on the shores of the Baltic to the north of Stockholm. The short stories and sketches of Engström and Molin have been variously labeled "realism" and "wilderness romanticism" (*vildmarksromantik*). Both terms are applicable to their work, which has strong affinities with the comedy of realistic exaggeration practiced by Mark Twain and Strindberg and the fondness for the primitive and picturesque of Jack London and his followers. But neither Engström's hundreds of tales nor the single posthumously published volume, *Ådalens poesi*, by Molin has made much more than a minor impact on Swedish letters. Albert Engström made his major contribution to the arts as an incomparably witty caricaturist, and Pelle Molin died before his early literary promise could ripen into a mature literary art.

It remained for Oscar Levertin (1862–1906) and Per Hallström (1866–1960) to bring to the 1890's the only considerable literary production of high quality outside the work of Heidenstam, Selma Lagerlöf, Fröding, and Karlfeldt. In some ways Levertin and Hallström pursued lines of development similar to those of "the great four," but in other ways each of them asserted his own literary individuality by either rejecting or modifying certain typical literary trends of the day. Both Levertin and Hallström were Stockholm-bred and represent essentially cosmopolitan attitudes and states of mind which were difficult to adapt to the nationalism and regionalism of the 1890's. By temperament and conviction they were both also profoundly pessimistic in contrast with the optimistic affirmation of life which was generally characteristic of the work of their contemporaries. And though they at times were prepared to surrender to the claims of fantasy, they did so with such reservations as were decreed by a philosophical determinism inherited from the 1880's. In fact, neither Levertin nor Hallström succeeded completely in shaking off the 1880's despite strenuous efforts to identify themselves in certain ways with the literary program of the new decade. If in their maturity they did not share the social pathos of the 1880's, they retained for the most part its cosmopolitanism, its healthy skepticism, its refusal to lend itself to comfortable illusory attitudes. Not far beneath the surfaces of that part of their work which may seem excessively Romantic in its leanings lie moods and points of view which derive ultimately at least as much from the 1880's as from the 1890's.

Levertin was the first Jew to occupy an important place in Swedish literature. His ancestors had come to Sweden at the close of the eighteenth century via Holland, where they had found refuge some two centuries earlier in their flight from anti-Semitic persecution on the Iberian peninsula. His father became a Stockholm art dealer, liberal in his views and only modestly successful in his business because of a tendency to neglect his customers in favor of his own interest in some of the art objects around his shop. The father's liberalism and art interests reappeared in the son, who before young manhood had become an enthusiastic devotee of the realistic social-minded Scandinavian literature of the 1870's and 1880's. In his last school years, when awarded a prize which permitted him to add to his library a work of his own choice, he quite logically chose Georg Brandes's *Main Currents in Nineteenth-Century European Literature*. Equally logically his first serious literary efforts, the two collections of the short stories *Småmynt* (Small Coins, 1883) and *Konflikter* (Conflicts, 1885), were concerned with contemporary social problems entirely in the manner and spirit of the 1880's. Upon taking up university studies at Uppsala in 1882 he joined the radical Verdandi Society, became identified with the "Young Sweden" literary coterie, and was apparently launched on a literary career dedicated to a realistic critical treatment of the problems of contemporary life.

But it gradually became clear to Levertin that his talents were ill-adapted to the methods and purposes of a radical realistic literature, and by the close of the 1880's he had come under the direct influence of Heidenstam and adopted a literary program in sharp opposition to that he had previously espoused. The death of his young wife in 1887, and his own serious tubercular condition during the years which followed, forced Levertin in upon himself and made it relatively easy for Heidenstam to convince him that his talents could best serve a poetic program whose watchwords were beauty rather than utility, fantasy rather than fact, the glories of the past rather than the limited horizons of the present. Besides, Levertin's university studies and art interests had driven him more and more into an exclusive, bookish world, where the magic of words and the subtle fascination of the brush strokes of the old masters had come increasingly to displace his concern with the everyday world around him. His academic studies, which resulted first in a dissertation on French comedy from the Renaissance to Molière, led him ultimately into the gracefully artificial rococo world of the Gustavian era in Swedish art and letters, a world in which he found himself completely at home and which became the subject of some of his most inspired scholarly and critical work. From the year of his appointment as an assistant professor at Uppsala in 1889 until his premature death in 1906 he was a very popular academic lecturer (after 1893 at the University of Stockholm), a scholar, and a highly productive critic and poet. As a scholar he was not always held in the highest esteem by his colleagues, but as a critic he was phenomenally successful, and as a poet he had his share of readers in a decade when greater lyric talents than his were lifting poetic utterance to levels rarely attained in Swedish poetry.

That which sets much of Levertin's poetry apart from that of his fellow poets in the Swedish 1890's is its relatively extreme aestheticism, its highly sophisticated preoccupation with moods and motifs whose counterparts are to be found among the English Pre-Raphaelites and the French symbolists and decadents rather than in the Swedish poetry of the day. This *fin de siècle* aestheticism is particularly dominant in Levertin's first volume of verse, *Legender och visor* (Legends and Songs, 1891), but it is by no means absent in the three volumes of poetry which follow — *Nya dikter* (New Poems, 1894), *Dikter* (Poems, 1901), and

Kung Salomo och Morolf (King Solomon and Morolf, 1905) — even though these volumes cultivate a somewhat less exclusive tone than *Legends and Songs* and in some of their central poems seek to establish points of contact with such typical thematic material of the 1890's as a Nietzsche-inspired Dionysian affirmation of life and a Heidenstam-influenced Swedish nationalism.

The two pieces (both in the volume *New Poems*) which most boldly give expression to Levertin's triumphant affirmation of life in all its sensuous glory and rich variety are "De visa och de fåvitska jungfrurna" (The Wise and Foolish Virgins) and "Sång före natten" (Song before the Night). The first of these poems reverses the scriptural moral of the tale about the Wise and the Foolish Virgins by bowing in reverence before the "Foolish" ones, who are good, Levertin suggests, because they are prepared to *give* of that which is theirs — their lovely, pulsing beauty, their soft, responsive bodies.

> Ye sit in the rushes in waters below
> And loosen ribbon and buckle,
> And mirror your shoulders white as snow
> In sky-blue pond's soft ruffle.

In contrast to the softly sensuous contours of these lines (they have been said to be reminiscent of a Burne-Jones painting) is the frankly defiant mood of "Song before the Night," a kind of love song in which man in the presence of his beloved develops the theme that heroic struggle, not happiness, is man's destiny, and that man should welcome all which life provides — not least its heavy blows and ugly frustrations, for these conditions of life temper the soul and enable us "to measure the world" and ourselves "with our own claims and by our own standards." But the Nietzschean heroism of "Song before the Night" was a passing mood in the poetry of Levertin, who by temperament was passive and receptive, a sensitive artist-dreamer rather than an aggressive, extroverted activist. Therefore Levertin soon came to substitute for the heroic individualism of "Song before the Night" a cultural nationalism which finds its most memorable expression in certain parts of the historical novel *Magistrarne i Österås* (1900) and such pieces in *Poems* (1901) as "Moderspråket" (Mother Tongue), "Folket i Nifelhem" (The People of Nifelhem), and "Gammal svensk julkantat" (Old Swedish Christmas Cantata).

Levertin's most characteristic poetry is to be found, however, in his debut work, *Legends and Songs*. "My verse," he reminds us in the Epilogue to this volume, "is black with purple-reddish seams." It is verse of a man who had early experienced the nearness of death, a verse fashioned by a hypersensitive artistic spirit steeped in the painting and poetry of the past, by preference seeking its motifs and themes in the medieval world of Christian legend and symbol. But it is not the poetry of a Christian *believer*. It is the poetry of a highly sophisticated modern spirit who responds with extraordinary sensitivity and sympathy to the aesthetic charm, the simple piety, and the quiet ecstasy of medieval art. In many of these poems Levertin, like the Pre-Raphaelites, simply attempted to transfer to words and meters medieval paintings which had moved him by the direct naïveté of their composition, the haunting mystery of their moods. But like the English and French decadents of his own generation Levertin's poetry reflects also a fondness for the artificial and the hectic, for subtly stylized imitative effects, alternately indulging in the studied simplicity of the Pre-Raphaelites and the lurid, sensuous complexities of a Baudelaire. At times, however, Levertin extricates himself from the merely derivative and imitative sides of these artistic mannerisms and creates a poetic world of sheer, spontaneous, original beauty — most satisfactorily in such a poem as "En gammal nyårsvisa" (An Old New-Year's Song), with its strangely moving series of symbolical personifications, or in "Monika," with its bittersweet interplay of disillusionment and yearning, or in "Flores och Blanzeflor," with its exquisitely delicate retelling of the ancient tale of innocent young love, or in "Ithaca," with its insistent dreaming, despite life's harsh frustrations, of "a spring-white isle on the sea" which possibly *may* exist for man in another, happier incarnation. None of these poems is borne by a triumphant, overwhelming eagle-flight of inspiration, but each of them soars in its own finely restrained, marvelously phrased way, bearing its lovely thematic freight on graceful, softly floating, gentle-winged poetic pinions.

Levertin's poetic wings had neither the spacious spread of Heidenstam's nor the magic sweep of Fröding's nor the sturdy drive and thrust of Karlfeldt's, but at his best Levertin as a poet occupies a not unworthy though admittedly subordinate place in the company of his great contemporaries.

As a critic Levertin had in his day no peer.

In his criticism is combined the sensitivity of the poet, the learning of the scholar, and the immediate cultural awareness of a responsible working journalistic-critic. Among Swedish critics before Levertin only Atterbom can be compared with him in perceptiveness and learning, but Levertin, thanks to his French intellectual and literary orientation, has a lighter touch and a broader general appeal than Atterbom. Chief among Levertin's French masters were the Goncourt brothers — whose studies in the arts and morals of the French eighteenth century became the inevitable prototypes for Levertin's investigations in kindred phenomena of the Swedish Gustavian era — and Renan, whose subtle urbanity, gentle skepticism, and catholicity of taste never failed to fascinate the Swedish critic. Renan's definition of wisdom as a refusal to hate or love *absolutely* appealed especially to Levertin's naturally tolerant temperament, sometimes, it may be admitted, to the point where he praised with only slight qualification literary work of a distinctly inferior quality. Besides this readiness to find some good in dubious literary performances, Levertin's chief vices as a critic are his tendency toward the rhetorical and flowery in formulating his appreciative judgments and his occasional blindness in failing to recognize the greatness of work which disturbed his highly cultured tastes. He found Fröding, for instance, too "folksy," and rejected the best of Strindberg's post-Inferno work as crude and barbaric, the more or less distasteful spawn of a genius gone astray in the mazes of superstition and ill-digested religious mysticism.

But otherwise Levertin's far-ranging critical intelligence is sensitive and discriminating, capable of finely perceptive judgments on figures as diverse as Lucretius and Dante, Nietzsche and Renan, George Sand and Edmond de Goncourt, J. K. Huysmans and Selma Lagerlöf. He is at his best, however, in those essays and studies devoted to his chief love, eighteenth-century Swedish culture. The collection of critical essays entitled *Svenska gestalter* (Swedish Figures, 1903) deals chiefly with authors of the eighteenth century, and three other works — *Teater och drama under Gustaf III* (Theater and Drama under Gustaf III, 1889), *Gustaf III som dramatisk författare* (Gustaf III as a Dramatic Author, 1894), and *Från Gustaf III's dagar* (From the Days of Gustaf III, 1896) — concentrate exclusively, as their titles suggest, on the rococo world of Gustaf III's court. Though his famous Bellman essay and his treatment in general of the Gustavian era have been accused of over-idealization, it is undeniable that these studies capture with astonishing grace and sureness of touch *one* important side of the courtly culture of the Stockholm of Gustaf III. So hypnotized was Levertin by this Gustavian world that, in addition to the numerous essays and studies which he devoted to it, he wrote also a group of tales (*Rococonoveller*, 1899) which attempt *stylistically* to recreate this world.

Levertin had on occasion in his early career contributed book reviews

to various publications, but it was not until 1897, when he became associated with the reorganized *Svenska Dagbladet*, that he employed his
critical talents extensively in book reviewing. As a reviewer of current
literature he attained in the following years a popularity never before or
since enjoyed by a Swedish critic. Without prostituting his talents he
managed to meet daily deadlines and delight a wide reading public. Nothing quite like Levertin's glowing language and largely appreciative judgments had ever regularly appeared in the review columns of a Swedish
newspaper, and readers responded with appropriate enthusiasm. It is true
that some of the reviews (there are hundreds) deal with books of no importance, and others reflect rather too sharply the haste with which they
had to be composed, but in most of them Levertin writes with his usual
mastery of word and phrase and image and maintains more than a modicum of his critical insights and standards. In their day his reviews served
admirably to lift the cultural level of their readers, and even today not a
few of them may be read with profit by those who indulge seriously in
the study of Swedish literature. A large number of them have been reprinted in two volumes under the title *Svensk litteratur* in Levertin's
collected works.

Of the authors of the 1890's Levertin was the first to die, prematurely
in 1906. Per Hallström, on the other hand, outlived them all, not passing
away until the present volume was on the press. During the years of
his richest productivity, the somewhat more than two decades before the
First World War, Hallström attracted an appreciative though not over-
large circle of readers and became generally recognized as the first great
Swedish master of the short story. Considerably less important is his
work in other genres, poetry, the drama, the longer tale and novel, and
criticism, though he produced rather extensively and not without occasional distinction in these forms. Hallström's failure to attain really
marked distinction outside the short story can perhaps best to be attributed to his inability finally to resolve the conflict within himself between
an innate intellectualism and a rich imaginative resourcefulness. He was
a creature of sharp critical instincts in the manner of the 1880's and of
many-faceted, varicolored fantasy in the fashion of the 1890's, and in his
work he more often than not failed to attain a happy synthesis of these
disparate elements in his character and personality.

The conflict of gifts in Hallström showed up early. In his youth he
pursued scientific rather than humanistic studies despite strong leanings

toward poetry and the arts, and upon graduation from the Institute of Technology at Stockholm he spent two thoroughly disillusioning years as a chemical engineer in a large factory in Philadelphia. When in 1890 he returned to Sweden and turned gradually from science to literature (he finally deserted the profession of engineering in 1897), he was prepared to accept — with some reservations — the new literary program being promulgated by Heidenstam and Levertin and which soon was to count among its most brilliant representatives Fröding and Selma Lagerlöf. Hallström's first volume of poems, *Lyrik och fantasier* (Lyrics and Fantasies), was published, unfortunately, in 1891, the year which witnessed the appearance of three of the most important books of the 1890's, Selma Lagerlöf's *Gösta Berling's Saga*, Fröding's *Guitar and Concertina*, and Levertin's *Legends and Songs*. Gifted as Hallström was, he could scarcely compete successfully for public favor with work of such striking originality. His early poems were by contrast largely imitative exercises, most markedly reflecting an unusual familiarity with English poets, Shelley, Keats, and Swinburne. The most impressive poem in his debut volume deals with the tragic early death of Chatterton. With the years his interest in English literature deepened perceptibly and exercised a more salutary influence on his later work than it had on *Lyrics and Fantasies*. His critical essays included in the volumes *Skepnader och tankar* (Forms and Thoughts, 1910), *Levande dikt* (Living Literature, 1914), and *Konst och liv* (Art and Life, 1919) are frequently concerned with English authors (Robert Herrick, Shelley, Keats, Byron, Carlyle, Thackeray), and in 1922 he began the monumental task of translating into Swedish all of Shakespeare's plays, a work completed with high literary distinction some ten years later.

Having attracted only slight attention in 1891 with his first volume of verse, Hallström waited three years before again courting the favor of the Swedish reading public — this time with the collection of sketches and short stories *Vilsna fåglar* (Strayed Birds), which immediately found favor with both critics and public and still today can be read with considerable pleasure. In their kind these stories are little gems of narrative concentration, and in their subtle blending of realism, moral pathos, and psychological finesse bear their creator's own stamp at every point. They quietly but clearly signalize Hallström's "arrival" as a mature literary talent, a writer of prose fiction second only to Selma Lagerlöf in the mid-1890's. In the two decades following the publication of *Strayed Birds* Hallström was among the most productive of Swedish authors, turning out a half dozen plays, a second volume of verse (*Skogslandet*, 1904), five novels, and seven volumes of short stories. With two exceptions his dramas are philosophical "idea plays," draped in legendary or historical disguises and containing little of really "living theater." The exceptions are the two modern problem plays *Erotikon* (1908) and *Nessusdräkten* (The Mantle of Nessus, 1919), in which Hallström with telling irony vents his anger on a current Swedish cult of eroticism and on certain forms of political hypocrisy of his day. None of Hallström's novels rise to the level of really significant literature. They are serious, honest, usually realistic accounts of Swedish life, but they seldom come alive in terms of character and narrative movement, chiefly because the action is so often cluttered up with unnecessary commentary on the part of the author. We admire his penetrating analysis of human foibles and are compassionate with him in the presence of human tragedy, but we are not in the last analysis gripped by his bloodless, essentially abstract vision of life.

Something of this fondness for an abstract, overintellectualized vision of life carries over also into Hallström's short stories, particularly in the rigidly schematic symbolistic patterns of *De fyra elementerna* (The Four Elements, 1906). But in four of his first five collections of short stories — *Strayed Birds*, *Purpur* (Purple, 1895), *Briljantsmycket* (The Jeweled Brooch, 1896), and *Thanatos* (1900) — Hallström's art strikes such a fine over-all balance between the natural and the studied that we accept without serious objection whatever manipulatory devices he employs. Though some of his short stories, especially those included in *Strayed Birds*, are realistic and satiric in the manner of the 1880's, his tales differ markedly from those of his immediate realistic predecessors in their analytical psychological emphasis. The 1880's had dealt essentially with surfaces, pointing up scene and milieu in great detail. But Hallström concentrates on what goes on inside the human animal, particularly in moments of stress, of near-tragedy or genuine tragedy. His profoundly pessimistic view of life had fed deeply on Schopenhauer, with whom he shares the ethical doctrine that compassion is the chief, perhaps the only, virtue. He does not, however, share Schopenhauer's bitterness, his essentially cynical view of man's potentialities. Man, Hallström feels, is capable of a great selfless love, and not a few of his tales focus their attention on those moments of decision when man realizes this kind of love — not infrequently, it should be remembered, in the presence of death. In fact, Hallström's mature thought world is constantly hovering between the two poles of love and death, fascinated by the mysterious potentialities of their interaction.

In Hallström's short stories one can trace a broad thematic and formal development. In *Strayed Birds* he muses with gentle irony over certain half-pathetic examples he had observed in America of the way in which a materialistic society callously tramples underfoot those sensitive spirits who for one reason or other cannot "adjust" themselves to life's brutal conditions. In *Purple* he deliberately departs from the "realism" of the contemporary American scene, and in the romantic fantasy-filled manner of the 1890's turns to the hectic, sensuous, image-burdened decadence of the Italian Renaissance, with its dark undertow of heavy, brooding, mysterious forces. In *The Jeweled Brooch* he moves in an essentially quiet, meditative, balanced and idealistic world, where moral values manage to assert themselves against what at times might seem insuperable odds. And in Hallström's most profoundly impressive work — the tales brought together under the name of Thanatos, the Greek god of death — we are ushered repeatedly into the presence of death. *Thanatos* may be described as a theme with variations. The theme — the ennobling effect of the presence of death — is examined in these tales from various angles of vision as exemplified in the experiences of diverse characters in various conditions of existence. Hallström's artistic control of the material in *Thanatos* is so complete that the reader's interest never flags despite the brooding repetitive pattern of the tales. He wrings rich poetry out of the theme of death at a time when it was not uncommon among his Swedish contemporaries to acclaim a proud, pulsating cult of life. To Hallström life's final meaning can be understood, if at all, only in the presence of death.

In the years during and after the First World War, Hallström's literary productivity fell off sharply. He had early become politically the most conservative of Swedish authors of the 1890's, and when the War broke out he was an outspoken defender of the German cause against the Allies. He became in consequence an isolated figure in the liberal and progressive Swedish community of the twentieth century, and the sources of his literary inspiration gradually dried up. This accounts for his turning to the task of translating Shakespeare into Swedish, the only important work of his later period. Today he is a forgotten author, read only by those who wish for one reason or another to tarry occasionally in regions somewhat off the main highway of Swedish literature just before and after the opening of our century.

CHAPTER 10

Realism Renewed and Challenged

THE LABEL "the Oscarian idyl" which has been applied to the Swedish social, political, and cultural scene during the thirty-five years (1872–1907 of the reign of Oscar II is rather difficult to understand — except perhaps against the background of later developments, the fluid, shifting, often even agitated circumstances of Swedish life in the half century after the King's death. Actually the last two decades of the nineteenth century were, as we have seen, anything but placid and idyllic even though the literature of the 1890's did serve in some ways to act as a corrective against both the literary radicalism of the 1880's and the rising tide of socialistic economic and political agitation of the decade which followed. But in other ways the 1890's had its own kind of "radicalism," what may loosely be called an "aesthetic radicalism," which was in many respects quite as objectionable to such inveterate champions of religious and political orthodoxy as Carl David af Wirsén and his kind as had been the social reform literature of the 1880's. And outside the literary scene strictly speaking, forces were at work which presently — in the twentieth century — were to transform the face of Sweden, to break down the last vestiges of a conservative patriarchal Swedish society and make of the country a modern democratic state.

On the surface it might seem that the transformation of Swedish society in our century was a rapid, revolutionary phenomenon dictated by extremist social and economic theories and brought about by a series of ruthless political maneuvers. But this is scarcely the case. The transformation was in fact gradual, essentially evolutionary. Though a Social Democratic labor party has been most directly responsible for the social and political changes in twentieth-century Sweden, it should be remembered that a liberal political tradition had been active in the land for the greater part of the nineteenth century. But because this tradition had been nurtured by a politically conscious middle class pursuing its own limited political ends, it became with time relatively conservative; and it was therefore inevitable that nineteenth-century liberalism should be superseded by a more radical social and economic program when industrial developments toward the close of the century had created a new politically conscious group, the laboring classes. The new social and economic program formulated by the newly organized Social Democratic party early adopted a sharply Marxist materialistic ideology, which emphasized its opposition not only to the religious and political conservatism of its own day but also to the idealistic political liberalism of an earlier generation. In the years of their later political success, however, the Social Democrats have receded rather sharply from the doctrinaire materialism of their Marxist origins and have become less exclusively a class-conscious, internationally oriented "labor party." In cultural matters also their earlier suspicion of traditional values has given way, at least in part, to an appreciation of those attainments in Swedish arts and letters which derive ultimately out of deeply rooted national traditions. In brief, a finally triumphant Social Democratic party matured with age, steering a middle course between political and cultural extremes.

The new political alignments and changes of the last half century were accompanied by equally fundamental changes in practically every side of Swedish life. The twentieth century ushers in an enormously expanding economy, revolutionary changes in communications, sharp shifts of population from the countryside to the cities, better working conditions for the masses and "welfare state" privileges for all, diversified educational opportunities tailored to every need of the new society, and a gradual elimination of the older rigid class distinctions which had in the past determined the patterns and the directions of Swedish culture. Everything is fluid, impelled by new forces, struggling to find new forms and to realize new communal ideals in the shifting ebb and flow of modern life. Not least important is the impact of world developments on Swedish life, an inevitable consequence of vastly improved communications and the crucial import-export aspects of Sweden's rapid industrial growth, a growth which has been called Sweden's new "Period of Greatness," comparable in economic matters to the Great Power period of Sweden's political expansion in the seventeenth century.

Everywhere in the Swedish literature of the new century these changes

346

are reflected. The very tempo of this literature, its inner pulse and rhythm, differs markedly from the literature of the past despite the operation of certain cultural lags which emphasize traditional values and counsel conservative ideals and practices. Though this new literature at times takes on the nervous, uncertain pace of a self-conscious modernity, it moves on the whole aggressively and confidently once it really finds itself during and after the First World War. It is not averse, particularly in its later manifestations, to defying literary convention, reaching out for new forms to express new moods and points of view. The most important immediate conditioning factor in the new literature is the enormously expanded reading public resulting from the spread of educational opportunities among the masses and the growing importance of the daily press and of popular magazines and journals. The vastly increased appetite for books on the part of a culturally conscious reading public is reflected both in the size of editions and the number of authors dispensing their wares to this reading public. Before 1900 a Swedish book was considered "successful" if an edition of two or three thousand was exhausted. In our day an edition of ten thousand or more is quite common. The "best seller" phenomenon was not at all uncommon in the Swedish 1930's and 1940's, a number of novels having sold in several tens of thousands of copies. Even some poets during these years enjoyed great popularity, the works of both Hjalmar Gullberg and of Nils Ferlin, for instance, were published in numbers nearing a hundred thousand. Only Fröding among earlier poets had enjoyed anything approaching such popularity, and the sixty-five thousand copies of his work published before 1905 included a large inexpensive edition, a publishing practice later abandoned in Sweden.

These inexpensive editions (single volumes became available at the remarkably low price of one crown) whetted an alert reading public's appetite for great literature in the early years of the century. And this appetite for good reading was further stimulated in the years which followed by the highly favorable attitude toward books and reading on the part of a burgeoning folk-movements development. For the first time in Swedish cultural history literature became a significant preoccupation of the masses. From their beginnings such popular folk movements as the temperance lodges, the cooperative movement, the folk high schools, and the labor movement actively encouraged their members to follow literary developments, and by the time the new century was well on its way a variety of study opportunities, including such a specifically Swedish phenomenon as the "study circle," became available to the masses. Among the features which provided a quality of maturity to popular education was the readiness on the part of the liberal intellectuals of the day to join forces with the masses in their study pursuits. The role played by the Verdandi Society of Uppsala is illustrative, particularly in the series of popular booklets which this Society made available as late as the early 1930's at the very low price of twenty-five *öre*, about five cents. These booklets, written by distinguished specialists in all fields of scientific and humanistic studies, include today well over five hundred titles.

One of the fruits of these growing educational opportunities for the masses was bound in time to be the rise of a new kind of literature, a literature deriving directly from the conditions of life of the masses and written by those self-educated poets and novelists and dramatists whose early years had been filled with deprivation, misery, and frustration. To begin with, these "proletarian authors" (the term is used to connote their common origins among the working classes) struggled awkwardly up the slopes of the Swedish Parnassus, exhibiting to begin with more energy and originality, it must be admitted, than finesse and profundity. But during the 1920's they had established for themselves a position not far below the ranking authors of the day, and in the 1930's they threatened to take over command of Swedish literary developments. The majority of the more important novelists and several of the leading poets of the 1930's were of lower-class origins, and they have also contributed significantly to the drama. The rise of a literature of what may loosely be called proletarian origins is, indeed, the most important fact about Swedish literature in the twentieth century. It has poured into the bloodstream of a literary culture which had long been the special if not exclusive holding of the academically trained middle classes certain new, vital, distinctly forward-looking elements. The conditions of existence out of which the proletarian authors came, their early struggles and their literary purposes, can be examined at first hand in the fascinating series of autobiographical sketches from their pens included in the two volumes *Ansikten* (Faces, 1932) and *Avsikter* (Intentions, 1945).

The recent rise of this new class of authors has made of the literature of today a more completely *representative* literature than Sweden had enjoyed before. All classes of Swedish society are now represented in Swedish letters, a circumstance both appropriate and inevitable in a society which has undergone in the last half century fundamental changes in the direction of total democratization. But before the culminating phases of this process of democratization came to be realized Swedish literature continued to maintain a great many of its more exclusive middle- and upper-class qualities. These qualities yielded their cultural priorities only by degrees under the pressure of the new social forces of the twentieth century. It may in fact be said that they never yielded completely, that what actually happened as the century progressed was a gradual *merging* of apparently antipathetic cultural elements, until today it is in many cases no simple matter to distinguish on the basis of class origins the work of one author from another. Both Eyvind Johnson and Harry Martinson, for instance, are among the more sophisticated literary practitioners of our day in Sweden, and yet their social origins were hardly high, and they grew up familiar with poverty and private miseries of various kinds.

This is one of the many reasons why it is such a precarious task to write literary "history" about the literature of the last fifty years. So subtle are the interrelations among authors and groups of authors, so frequently does a given author come ultimately to identify himself with trends that in some ways belie his origins, and so close to us are those complex forces which determine the general trends of literary development that one must always be aware of the provisional nature of any generalizations about these developments. In dealing with earlier periods the literary historian has little difficulty in singling out significant patterns and trends, in identifying those authors whose work is of basic importance, in recognizing the particular works of each author which are most significant and representative. In fact, the mere passage of time has done much of this work for us. But the literature of our century is an immediate part of ourselves, clamoring from all sides for our attention, offering its diverse wares with an urgent insistence that tends to dull our critical discrimination and defy our efforts to bring some kind of order into the shifting patterns and conflicting claims of contemporary literary developments. And our dilemma is the greater because of the enormous increase in the *number* of competent authors who in our century have the right to claim our critical attention. In a recent book on Swedish literature from 1900 to 1940 more than a hundred authors have been deemed worthy of some attention, about half of them being given more than summary notice. Although the inclusion of so many authors may seem somewhat generous, it is not always easy to say which of these authors can be ignored without the risk of misrepresenting at one point or other the course of Swedish literary developments in our century.

And yet the risk must be taken in the limited space at our disposal. We shall by necessity have to ignore some authors completely, others we can only mention in passing or give highly summary treatment. And to extract some kind of order out of the fermenting multiplicity of contemporary literary trends we shall have to be somewhat schematic — even at times arbitrary — in the grouping of authors, knowing full well the dangers of proceeding in this manner. There is, unfortunately, no alternative.

Aside from what we have previously said about the general transformation of Swedish society in the last half century, with a resulting shift in the nature of the reading public and conditions of authorship, we should sketch very briefly the general over-all lines of specifically literary development in our century before going on to a more detailed treatment of this development.

As the new century was ushered in prospects for a significant literary renewal seemed dim, chiefly because the literary splendor of the 1890's still maintained its magic hold on the Swedish reading public. With the exception of Fröding, all of the central figures of the 1890's were still at the height of their creative powers. The regionalism and nationalism of the 1890's celebrated, in fact, some of its greatest literary triumphs in the early years of the new century in Selma Lagerlöf's *Jerusalem* and *The Wonderful Adventures of Nils*, in Heidenstam's *The Tree of the Folkungs*, and in Karlfeldt's *Fridolin's Pleasure Garden* and *Flora and Pomona*; and in various other ways, most brilliantly in the work of such artists as Anders Zorn, Carl Larsson, and Bruno Liljefors, the traditionalism of the 1890's maintained its hold on Swedish cultural life. Even relatively radical labor groups in the early years of the century sensed no essential antagonism between their program of reform and the literary developments of the 1890's. Heidenstam's early "revolutionary songs" ("Barricade Song," "Citizen's Song," and others) were often quoted with enthusiasm by labor agitators at the turn of the century, and Fröding was considered "one of *our* poets" (*en av de våra*) by the laboring classes.

Under the circumstances it was scarcely surprising that the generation of authors who immediately succeeded "the great four" of the 1890's did not strike out in new and fresh directions. What they did was to temporize, rendering established melodies with skillful tonal variations, pursuing the cultural fashions of their predecessors with slightly disguised emphases. Some, such as Hjalmar Söderberg and Bo Bergman, maintained a little of the aesthetic pose of the 1890's, though with elegantly skeptical and melancholy deviations. Others, such as Vilhelm Ekelund and Anders Österling, retained the regionalism of the 1890's but bereft of much of its historical orientation and most of its gay, gusty, boldly assertive elements. Only in one case, that of K. G. Ossiannilsson, did they identify themselves boldly with revolutionary social and political programs; but Ossiannilsson proved to be more loud-spoken and superficially radical than finally loyal to the laboring classes who in the early years of the century were stirred by his militant Kiplingesque verse. A few years after his appearance as a poet-agitator he broke ostentatiously with his socialist comrades, and since then he has drifted into a kind of rightist activism of dubious origins and dangerous ultimate implications. His break with socialism is described in the polemic novel *Barbarskogen* (The Barbarian Forest, 1908).

It was not the young Ossiannilsson but an aging Strindberg who gave the decisive signal for literary change. And Strindberg did so at a fateful moment in Swedish social and political history. In 1909 the first General Strike took place in Sweden. In 1910 Strindberg, who for nearly a quarter of a century had been absent from the social battle, took up the polemic cudgels again in a series of highly provocative newspaper articles in which he vigorously attacked political conservatism in Sweden and heaped scorn on the literature of the 1890's in general and its "chieftain" Heidenstam in particular. That neither Strindberg nor his adversaries were particularly squeamish in their choice of weapons should not obscure the fact that a fundamental issue was joined in the contest. Both the General Strike and the controversy stirred up by Strindberg brought into sharp relief elements of social and cultural conflict which had previously been ignored or neglected by those who dominated the political and literary scene in the early years of the century. Though the working classes suffered a crushing defeat in the General Strike, their first great organized effort against a powerfully entrenched employer class, they showed in 1909 a sense of group discipline and a loyalty to their cause which, after they had reorganized their broken forces, became an increasingly important instrument of popular reform. The General Strike served to suggest to all thinking Swedes the necessity of re-examining an economic and social structure which had been so sharply challenged by the masses; and the strike, together with Strindberg's attack on the literary traditionalism of the day, combined with other contemporary realistic critical trends to create at least the beginnings of a new literary climate in the second decade of the century.

This new literary climate was reflected chiefly in the novel, a genre which now for the first time in Swedish literature becomes a really effective instrument of social criticism on a high literary level. All of the Swedish literary figures whom we are accustomed to place in the decade beginning with the year 1910 (the collective term is *tiotalister*) write by overwhelming preference in prose fictional forms, and all the really representative figures are of middle-class origins. As yet the "proletarian" authors do not seriously challenge the literary hegemony of the middle classes despite the appearance during these years of such arresting literary figures as Martin Koch and Dan Andersson. Without being directly inspired by the dogmatic radicalism of the 1880's, the literature of the second decade of the twentieth century is in its way as conscious as was the 1880's of economic and social conditions and as aware of the social function of literature. The historical and rural orientation of the 1890's, and of some of the literature of the succeeding decade, comes in consequence to be replaced after 1910 by a critical examination of a modern urban society — by preference the world of the Swedish provincial city. Among the authors of the new decade, Sigfrid Siwertz concerns himself with Stockholm and the Stockholm area, but Hjalmar Bergman introduces us to the merchant-banking world of Örebro in central Sweden, Gustaf Hellström to the urban culture of the southern provinces, and Ludvig Nordström to the rapidly expanding industrial activities of the Norrland coastal regions. The best work of each of these novelists reflects a sensitive awareness of an urban culture undergoing the stresses and strains of modern life, an urban culture which for better or worse is changing its older patterns of existence under the persistent pressures of modern economic and social developments. Realistic and oftentimes sharply critical as is the point of view of these novelists, they are not (with the exception of Hjalmar Bergman) disillusioned pessimists. They have retained a faith in the ultimate possibilities of human progress as determined by man's intelligence and his sense of justice and human decency.

This is not always true of later generations of Swedish authors, whose fate it was to sit out two world wars and to become engulfed in the economic and political chaos of a desperately groping between-the-wars world.

Though Sweden was not a participant in either the First or the Second World Wars, her literature could hardly escape being affected by the wars and their general European aftermaths. The hectic, highly accelerated pace of life and the desperate, catastrophic mood of Europe during and after the war years are reflected in both the ideas and form of Swedish literature, whether this literature attempts to identify itself with the catastrophic mood or seeks solace in escapism or attaches itself to some kind of social or humanistic gospel which might seem to give promise of a better society and a better life. In the years immediately following the First World War the dominant note was one of anguish and despair, represented particularly in the early work of Pär Lagerkvist, the central portal figure in Swedish literature of the last three or four decades. Two other figures, Hjalmar Bergman and Birger Sjöberg, represent during the war years and immediately after only less directly and extremely a dark and disintegrating modern mood. In all three of these authors one finds also a more or less deliberate experimenting with literary forms (expressionism, cubism, daring symbolistic variations, etc.) in an effort to fit form to the fluid, irrational, often revolutionary patterns of human response and human action. In the work of Lagerkvist and Sjöberg particularly do we come upon the first indubitable evidences of a revolutionary literary "modernism" in Swedish literature. Aside from the claims of this literary modernism in the 1920's, the decade witnesses the final breakthrough of a realistic and partly radical literature of proletarian origins and the appearance of a rather exclusive cult of poetic idyllicism inspired in part by the English Georgians and practiced by a group of middle- and upper-class traditionalists.

If the 1920's took the first significant steps toward literary modernism and witnessed the final breakthrough of a proletarian literature, the 1930's and 1940's continued to move along the lines suggested by these developments. To some extent, in fact, these two developments came to coincide in the years around 1930, particularly in the arresting experimental prose fiction of Eyvind Johnson and in the primitivistic poetic program of a group called "five young men," from the title of an anthology in which they jointly appeared in 1929. A more intellectual and sophisticated poetic modernism than that represented in the early work of the "five young men" is to be found among such products of an early university environment as the poets Karin Boye and Hjalmar Gullberg, Johannes Edfelt and Gunnar Ekelöf. All in all the literature of the last three decades in Sweden has a rich, kaleidoscopic quality, oscillating violently between literary extremes while managing somehow to maintain at least a semblance of that solidity and cultural balance which is the mark of much Swedish literature of earlier periods.

The change in literary patterns was inevitable, given the disillusioned mentality of a postwar Europe desperately stumbling from one economic and political crisis to another. Several of the leading literary figures of the day lived for longer or shorter periods in the war-torn countries of the Continent, and those who did not could scarcely ignore the ominous developments to the South which led to Mussolini and Hitler and finally to another world holocaust in 1939. To the credit of Swedish authors in the 1930's it should be noted that no major and few minor figures among them were blinded by the developments of the time to the point of hailing either Fascism or Nazism as a way out of the contemporary European dilemma. In fact, both novelists and dramatists were early aware of the dangers implicit in the rise to power of the two dictators, and when Hitler finally struck, in 1939, a number of Swedish literary figures were in the vanguard of those who strenuously counseled a less neutralist position than the official one of the Swedish government. Typical of the antitotalitarian and antineutralist literature of the day were Pär Lagerkvist's *Bödeln* (The Hangman, 1933) and *Mannen utan själ* (tr. *The Man without a Soul*, 1936), Eyvind Johnson's *Nattövning* (Night Training, 1938), *Soldatens återkomst* (The Soldier's Return, 1940), and the three so-called Krilon novels (1941–43), and Vilhelm Moberg's *Rid i natt* (tr. *Ride This Night!*, 1941). The central point of departure for these and other antitotalitarian works was Sweden's sharpened wartime awareness of her political and cultural affinity to Western humanistic traditions with their respect for the individual's rights, their insistence upon freedom of thought and expression. In the Swedish literature of the day there could be no doubt on which side Sweden stood, despite her government's official position of neutrality.

Culturally Sweden had for decades been veering rather sharply toward an Anglo-American orientation, despite the highly vocal pro-German activities on the part of such formidable personalities as the world-famous explorer Sven Hedin and the influential literary critic Fredrik Böök. This Anglo-American orientation had its roots far back in nineteenth-century social and political liberalism, but not until the twentieth century did it bear fruit in really significant literary ways — first among the novelists in the second decade of the century (Ludvig Nordström, Gustaf Hellström, Elin Wägner), and later among both the poetic idyllicists of the 1920's (Gunnar Mascoll Silfverstolpe, Karl Asplund, Sten Selander) and the primitivists of the early 1930's (Artur Lundkvist, Harry Martinson, and others). During the between-the-wars years and later some German and more French authors (Kafka, Proust, Gide, the surrealists) were of importance for certain Swedish novelists and poets, but considerably more important were such English and American figures as D. H. Lawrence and T. S. Eliot, Walt Whitman and Sherwood Anderson, Carl Sandburg and Ernest Hemingway. The vogue for William Faulkner did not come about until well into the 1940's, the first of his novels to appear in a Swedish version being *Light in August* in 1944. Many Swedes read the Anglo-American authors in the original, and for those who hesitated to tackle in English such difficult stylists as Eliot or Faulkner competent Swedish translations were available. Not a few of these translations were the work of distinguished Swedish literary figures. Besides, Swedish critics provided the interested reading public with informed and discerning analyses of the work of particular Anglo-American authors and with critical works on these authors of a more inclusive kind, including admirable surveys of modern English and American literature. Among the more competent of the general critical works are August Brunius's *Modern engelsk litteratur* (Modern English Literature, 1923) and *Engelska kåserier* (English Causeries, 1927), Artur Lundkvist's *Atlantvind* (Atlantic Winds, 1932) and *Diktare och avslöjare i Amerikas moderna litteratur* (Authors and Exposers in Modern American Literature, 1942), and Thorsten Jonsson's brilliant little book *Sex amerikaner* (Six Americans, 1942). Of these critics Brunius lingers by preference among the gentlemanly Georgians without neglecting earlier English authors, while Lundkvist and Jonsson find themselves particularly at home among the less confined and conventional literary practices of the American moderns.

So great has been the interest among Swedes since the First World War in foreign literatures that the Swedish book market has in recent years become flooded with foreign works. "Translations are no longer a mere contribution to our book market," observes a recent Swedish critic, "they are beginning more and more to overshadow it." To what extent the reading public's interest in translations has affected the patterns of literary development is difficult to say. But that it has not resulted in changing fundamentally the course of Swedish letters in our century seems sufficiently clear despite a rather confused floundering in the maze of international literary modernism on the part of some of the younger Swedish authors of today.

In the main Swedish literature in the last half century has had a sufficient inner vitality to assimilate a heady international diet without denying its own native cultural traditions. Even such bold poetic experimenters as Pär Lagerkvist and Birger Sjöberg, Harry Martinson and Gunnar Ekelöf, have never lost contact with their Swedish origins. It may, indeed, be said that Swedish literature in our century has in a sense taken the same "middle way" that Sweden's social and political developments during the last half century have taken, maintaining always an open attitude toward advanced ideas and new cultural currents from abroad while quietly conserving those elements of national strength which have their roots deeply imbedded in the best of the nation's traditional values. It is a literature which looks backward and forward simultaneously, knowing instinctively that only in such a double perspective can it survive, create vitally, and make its solid contribution to a national literature whose foundations are one with the nation's political and cultural beginnings. It is this double perspective — with its sensitive awareness of loyalties to the past as well as to the present and the future — which chiefly distinguishes the Swedish literature of our century from the brilliant but essentially backward-looking literature of the period which preceded it, the 1890's. The literature of the last half century consequently tends to become in contrast with the 1890's more sober, more restrained, more self-critical, less given to the grand gesture, the Romantic pose, the self-conscious preoccupation with a great and glorious past.

How much more sober and restrained and self-critical the literature of the new century was to become is strikingly illustrated in the work of Hjalmar Söderberg (1869–1941) and Bo Bergman (b. 1869). Though both of these authors have points of contact with the 1890's, these contacts were with the pessimistic lyricism of Levertin rather than with the expansive historicism of Heidenstam or the vigorous regionalism of Karlfeldt. And even Levertin's pessimism becomes in the hands of Söderberg and Bergman shorn of most of its showy Romantic accouterments and all of its poetic flirtation with the past, its fond lingering in the world of legendary lore and brooding religious symbolism. The disillusionment of Söderberg and Bergman has a brittle, spare, essentially restrained quality not present in Levertin. But it is a disillusionment with its own kind of lyricism, quiet, subdued, skeptical, subtly ironic, deceptively impersonal. Its literary paternity is to be found primarily in Heinrich Heine and Anatole France and in the Danish decadents Jens Peter Jacobsen and Herman Bang, rather than in the Swedish 1890's. It reflects a view of

life not too far removed from the Swedish 1880's, in certain ways reminiscent of the disillusioned, humbug-hating, acid-tongued young Strindberg of *The Red Room*, *The New Kingdom*, and *The Son of a Servant*.

In Söderberg's novel *Martin Bircks ungdom* (tr. *Martin Birck's Youth*,
1901) we have the classical Swedish literary incarnation of the melancholy *fin de siècle* mood. It contains the oft-told tale of man's frustrations and ultimate resignation amidst the petty limitations of existence.
Its hero, whose life story we follow from early childhood to middle age,
is sensitive, something of a poet, but will-less and helpless, a dreamer who
must give up his early dreams of a successful career and a great passion.
He settles finally for the limited everyday existence of a clerical drudge
in a government office and a pale erotic liaison with another creature
whom life's ways have brought to a pass roughly identical with his own.
Aside from the fascinating opening section on Martin Birck's childhood,
this depressing tale holds our interest for two reasons: the exquisite sensitivity and economy of its prose style and the absolute authenticity with
which it captures the local color of Stockholm in all its subtle gradations
and moods. No Stockholm novel can approach Söderberg's in its miraculous evocation of the "poetry" of the city, its streets and squares, its
waterways and building complexes, especially as these urban externals
are caught up in dim lights and drifting mists and the unobtrusive fluctuations of the seasons. In Söderberg's work a sophisticated urban regionalism comes to replace the primitive provincial regionalism of the 1890's.

Neither Söderberg's total literary production nor his range of subject
matter and mood was very large, chiefly because he was a stylistic per-
fectionist of the first order and because he refused to look upon life as
anything more than a fatuous, highly delimited tragi-comedy. Wisdom
to him consisted in demanding as little of life as possible. In addition to
Martin Birck's Youth he wrote three short novels, three plays, four volumes of short stories, and, in his declining years, a number of controversial religious works. One of his novels, *Doktor Glas* (1905), created
a sensation with its apparent justification of a deliberate ethical murder.
In some ways his most mature works are the drama *Gertrud* (1906) and
the novel *Den allvarsamma leken* (The Serious Game, 1912), both
of which are profoundly tragic in their implications despite the arch
urbanity of their dialogue and the sophisticated treatment of erotic
themes. In *Martin Birck's Youth* love somehow asserted itself, and survived after a fashion, in a world otherwise strewn with the paltry flotsam
of disillusionment. In *Gertrud* and *The Serious Game* love itself becomes

357

an illusion, the last and most devastating in the experience of man and woman. "I believe," reads the title-page motto of *Gertrud* — "in the lust of the flesh and the incurable loneliness of the soul." The brilliant surface wit of Söderberg's work has often misled his readers into assuming that he is merely a scintillating cynic, a frivolous purveyor of elegantly salacious tidbits. *Gertrud* and *The Serious Game* should prove how wrong such assumptions are. Not far beneath the surface banter of Söderberg's accomplished prose style there lies a relentless effort to get at the truth about life. He is a satirist-moralist whose weapons are alternately the stinging rapier thrust and the deadly stiletto.

It is in his short stories that Söderberg's probing, fastidious, fabulously witty genius operates at its best. As "the Anatole France of Sweden" he had a flair for penning naughty tales in a gay and elegant manner and mocking man's self-complacency and self-deceit with withering ironic turns of phrase. Among his favorite targets was the clergy, whose stupidity and hypocrisy he belabored with the savage joy of a Voltaire. In many of Söderberg's tales ("Pälsen" [The Fur Coat], "En herrelös hund" [A Dog Without a Master], "En kopp te" [A Cup of Tea], "Vox Populi") the realism is unrelenting, merciless, sharply disillusioning. In other tales ("Blom," "Oskicket" [Misbehavior]) a kind of half-forgiving lyricism envelops the action, an element of warm human sympathy breaks through the harsh realities of scene and situation. In still others ("Sotarfrun" [The Chimney Sweep's Wife], "Historieläraren" [The History Teacher]) there is a note of genuine tragedy. In form the tales are usually very short, consisting in most cases merely of a highly charged episode, with implied meanings which open up large perspectives and provide by quiet indirection the author's usually caustic commentary on the human scene. They are essentially narrative *sketches*, depending for their effect more on economy of line and skillfully selected detail than on the element of narrative progression. In their kind they represent a perfect but limited form of the narrative art. Söderberg himself was aware of his strengths and limitations as a literary artist. "My ray of light (*stråle*)," he once said of his art, "is narrow but clear." He could not manage with complete mastery larger literary forms such as the novel and the drama, and he had little capacity for literary growth; but within the limits of his genius he produced work which in its kind has never been surpassed and seldom approximated by Swedish authors. In mentality and manner he has come closer to the Gallic spirit than any other Swede.

Among Söderberg's countrymen who most closely resemble him is his friend Bo Bergman, whose first volume of poetry, *Marionetterna* (The Marionettes), which appeared in 1903, may be said to be a verse counterpart to Söderberg's novel *Martin Birck's Youth* of two years earlier. Bergman's early poetry is inspired largely by the same hopeless deterministic view of life as is Söderberg's novel, the same disillusioned moodiness, the same subtle use of Stockholm local color, the same stylistic clarity and precision. The first of Bo Bergman's volumes of short stories, *Drömmen* (The Dream, 1904), is also strongly Söderbergian in mood and method. But as Bergman matures as man and artist he reveals a capacity for growth which Söderberg lacked or at least refused to exploit for purely literary purposes. Söderberg's sharper mind and finer artistic sensitivity together with his highly provocative satiric predilections became his own fate. They permitted no compromises and issued finally into a proud but creatively sterile withdrawal from potential sources of vital renewal for his art. Söderberg found the developing spiritual climate of the twentieth century so foreign to the fastidious sources of his literary inspiration that his creative vein became exhausted thirty years before his death. Bo Bergman scorned, too, much that the twentieth century came to admire and widely accept, particularly its radical democratization and certain vulgarizing aspects of its mass culture. But he expressed his scorn in less aggressive ways than Söderberg and did not withdraw petulantly into an intellectual and literary ivory tower. Bo Bergman's poetry shed fairly early, in fact, some of its exclusive, over-fastidious quality, and with time it became an effective instrument of attack against brutalizing political developments, especially the political totalitarianism of the 1930's. Without disowning the pessimistic determinism of his early years, Bergman came to recognize the necessity of extricating himself from the attitude of passivity which in the early years of the century had resulted from his deterministic view of life. He recognized the deadly danger to man's hard-won civilization in the political and cultural barbarism of certain post-World War I developments, and spoke out sharply against these developments.

In the placid early years of the century when a poet's alternatives seemed to be either a disillusioned aesthetic passivity or a vulgar bourgeois activism it was natural enough for Bo Bergman to pen his famous "marionette philosophy":

> We eat and we drink, we love and we fight,
> We die, — for the earth to swallow;

We carry the lantern of reason bright,
Great words, scant deeds to follow.
We live in honour or live in shame,
Come death, come life, it is all the same,
For all that our good or our ill luck brings
Is just a pull of the strings —

or lose himself in the exquisite imagery and the soothing, sad-toned rhythms of the "Adagio":

Waters stirring, soft winds playing —
Wind and water meet and kiss.
Yonder past the wood's thin shadows
Sway the golden meadows —
All were bliss,
Save for thee, dear, still delaying.
Through my slackened pulses creep
Strains of music softly playing,
Singing me to sleep.

White swans sail across the heaven,
Floating thro' the azure sky,
Silent on their travels lonely —
Swans, they say, sing only
When they die.
Years in slavery have I striven,
Hard the road of beggary.
I would sail too through the heaven
With the swans to thee.

Translated by C. D. Locock

But the melancholy preciosity of such verse was soon to be abandoned by Bo Bergman for a less exclusive poetic world, first, and tentatively as it were, in his second volume of poetry, *En människa* (A Human Being, 1908), where the poet establishes contact with a larger world than that bounded by a self-conscious aesthetic egotism, and later, more whole-heartedly, when he commits himself unreservedly to man's active struggle for freedom and justice and other positive civilizing values in the firmly vigorous verse of *Elden* (The Fire, 1917), *Livets ögon* (Life's Eyes, 1922), *Trots allt* (In Spite of Everything, 1931), *Gamla gudar* (Old Gods, 1939), and *Riket* (The Kingdom, 1944). In particularly the last three of these volumes of verse Bo Bergman is battling strenuously in the ranks of "the fighting humanists" of his day in Sweden.

In the history of Swedish prosody that which is most important in Bo Bergman's verse is its showing the way, to later generations of poets, toward ideals of poetic simplicity and clarity. The tendency of twentieth-century Swedish poetry to shun rhetorical effects owes a great deal to the example of Bo Bergman's simple, unadorned, straightforward verse. Heine, whom he has translated with great distinction, meant much to him. Likewise Ibsen, and the French Parnassiens, whose concentrated, epigrammatic, medallion-like poetic art is not infrequently approximated in Bergman's verse. Though he admired his countrymen Heidenstam and Fröding, he did not go their ways, Heidenstam's expansive, often grandiose manner having no appeal for him, and Fröding's tragic visions being beyond his ken. Instead he found his Swedish poetic ideal in Count Snoilsky, "the master," he once wrote, "who was forgotten too soon." The combination in Snoilsky of aristocratic taste with warm human sympathies, of the elegant and yet simple and clear poetic style, never ceased to attract Bo Bergman. He has on the other hand reacted sharply against the Strindberg of the Chamber Plays and the young Swedish primitivists of the early 1930's, whom he finds too aggressive and violent, betrayers of Apollo, of a balanced humanistic ideal of art. Bo Bergman identifies himself in his own unassuming way with the great classical tradition in Swedish poetry, the tradition of Kellgren and Tegnér, Runeberg and Rydberg.

Though Bo Bergman's poetry weighs more heavily than his prose, the prose has a distinction of its own. It is the prose of a cultivated man, conservative but not reactionary in his tastes. Aside from his substantial contribution to what may be called cultural journalism as represented in a more than thirty-year-long stint as theater critic for a leading Stockholm newspaper, Bo Bergman's prose production includes four volumes of short stories, three novels, a volume of autobiographical fragments entitled *Skyar* (Clouds), and, as part of his duties as a member of the Swedish Academy, three monographs, one of which is on his old friend Hjalmar Söderberg. Bergman's short stories, written in a delicate, finely probing prose reminiscent of Chekhov, deal largely with ordinary people whom life has crushed or at least sadly abused. The novels and autobiographical fragments represent a mellow late prose harvest from the pen of a clear-headed, tolerant, warmly understanding man of advanced years. The first of the novels, *Ett bokslut* (A Balancing of Books), appeared when Bergman was well over seventy, the last, *Den förrymda själen* (The Escaped Soul), when he had attained his eighty-sixth birthday. Concerned with elderly people and their fates, these novels breathe a quiet dignity of spirit entirely free of sentimentality or querulousness, and they are couched in the crystal-clear prose which is Bo Bergman's distinctive literary mark.

Reflected with a finely stubborn persistence throughout Bo Bergman's work has been what may be called his "local patriotism," his quietly phrased, nicely perceptive loyalty to his native Stockholm. "I Am a Stockholmer" is the title of a short sketch which he contributed to *The American-Scandinavian Review* some twenty years ago. In this sketch he is concerned at least as much with his city's spirit and moods, and its way of life as conditioned by the centuries, as he is with its pulsing modern outward drives. And though the poet in him finds some of the modern drives vulgar and distasteful, he prefers on the whole not to judge them harshly, but rather to look upon them with resignation if not enthusiasm as vital and necessary components of the ongoing historical process in which his city has been involved since its origins.

In addition to Bo Bergman, four other more or less distinctive voices joined in the Swedish lyric chorus of the early years of the century. Two of the voices, those of K. G. Ossiannilsson and Sven Lidman, were aggressive, blatant, full of youthful defiance, but fated in the long run to play only minor roles in Swedish letters. The other two, Vilhelm Ekelund and Anders Österling, came with time to occupy positions of considerable if not exactly central importance in Swedish literature of the last half century — Ekelund as a brilliant exponent of free verse and as a persistent practitioner of elevated aphoristic prose, Österling as the most gifted of those figures who cultivated a poetry of realistic idyllicism.

Never in Swedish literary history have two poets drawn sharper attention on the occasion of the appearance of their first volumes of verse than did K. G. Ossiannilsson (b. 1875) and Sven Lidman (1882–1960), the former by the sheer energy of his poetic performance, the latter by the strained and florid symbolistic erotomania of his early verse. Ossiannilsson was the absolute antipodes of the typical *fin de siècle* poet. He was an unbridled activist, whose stirring, militant, hammered-out verse was the perfect poetic form for his worship of force and the strong personality. His early volumes bore such telling titles as *Masker* (Masks, 1900), *Hedningar* (Heathen, 1901), *Örnar* (Eagles, 1902), and *Amerikaner och byzantiner* (Americans and Byzantines, 1905). Willy-nilly he justifies in his early verse all manifestations of force regardless of its motivation, its degree of bloodiness, or the political persuasion of the personality who exercises the force. Cromwell and Marat, Napoleon and Bismarck, Kitchener, Cecil Rhodes, and American millionaires — all are glorified with equal enthusiasm. For a moment in his early years Ossian-nilsson was even persuaded to enlist his talents as an agitator in the service of the incipient Swedish labor movement, but he soon found himself at odds with his new-found "socialist comrades," and after his characteristically ostentatious break with them (recorded in the novel *The Barbarian Forest*, 1908) he has had no importance in Swedish literature despite a rather considerable literary productivity largely in the service of various rightist political causes. Typical of the mentality represented in this literary productivity is the enthusiasm for Mussolini and Fascist doctrine reflected in Ossiannilsson's novel *Fädernas arv* (Our Forefathers' Heritage, 1925).

Sven Lidman, who was also swept into conservative activist propaganda activities after the unrestrained poetic sensualism of his early years, underwent in the years around 1920 a profound spiritual crisis which led to a religious conversion and his identification with the Pentecostal movement. His poetry from the first years of the century was hysterically decadent, and the long series of nationalistic novels which followed were only less hysterically patriotic and activist in tone. The group with which he associated as a student at Uppsala called themselves "Les quatres diables," and as its most extreme representative Lidman dreamed of emulating in life and poetry the provocative decadence of Rimbaud and Oscar Wilde. To the work of the Pentecostal sectarians he dedicated his life throughout four full decades, serving as a kind of lay preacher and writing collections of sermons, devotional books, etc. Since his conversion he has permitted himself to stray from deliberate sermonizing and allowed his literary talents relatively free play only in some brilliant, utterly candid volumes of memoirs, the first two of which appeared in 1952 under the titles *Gossen i grottan* (The Boy in the Grotto) and *Lågan och lindansaren* (The Flame and the Rope Dancer). As a novelist of some importance during the decade preceding his conversion Lidman had been concerned with the fortunes of the Silfverståhl family, whose gentleman-officer representatives are employed to glorify the ideals of loyalty to family traditions and a heroic awareness of responsibility to activist political principles. It is not, however, in the aggressive heroic traditionalism of the Silfverståhl series that Lidman is at his best as a novelist, but rather in the quiet everyday heroism of the aristocratic but poverty-marked ladies in *Huset med de gamla fröknarna* (The House with the Elderly Ladies, 1918). In this sensitive, humorous novel, which owes a great deal to Dickens, heroism is equated with the unobtrusive ethics of the Sermon on the Mount rather than with baronial pretensions and military exhibitionism. The novel was completed during the years of Lidman's religious crisis and breathes the atmosphere of the better moments in this crisis.

Swedish literature has in Vilhelm Ekelund (1880–1949) its most exclusive and severe spirit, a figure who deliberately cultivated isolation from the multitude and lived in the most rarified aesthetic and intellectual atmosphere. His circle of readers is small, but among those who turn to his work with enthusiasm are to be counted not a few of contemporary Sweden's leading poets and novelists. Ekelund is difficult of access, especially in his later aphoristic volumes, but those who persist in the task of deciphering his often cryptic prose assure the less hardy reader that the effort is richly rewarding. For forty years before his death he wrote only prose though he had been highly admired in his early years as a poet. He forsook poetry for prose in 1906 after publishing *Dithyramber i aftonglans* (Dithyrambs in Evening's Splendor), his seventh volume of verse, because he had found poetry an inadequate instrument for expressing the elevated purity of feeling and of thought which he looked upon as the artist's unique creative function.

During the period before which Ekelund turned from poetry to prose he had undergone a rapid and, for Swedish conditions, a radical development. As a native of Skåne he had been influenced to some extent in his earliest verse by the regionalism of A. U. Bååth and Ola Hansson, but this regionalism never struck deep roots in him, and very soon it disappeared entirely from his poetry. More important from the very beginning was the young poet's thematic concern with himself, with his own frustrations and dreams and the nameless yearnings of youth. In the volumes *Vårbris* (Spring Breeze, 1900), *Syner* (Visions, 1901), and *Melodier i skymning* (Melodies in Twilight, 1902) such thematic material is exploited in a verse of extraordinarily sensitive musical quality, after which in *Elegier* (Elegies, 1903), *In Candidum* (1905), *Havets stjärna* (The Star of the Sea, 1906), and his last "Dithyrambs" Ekelund moved sharply in the direction of a less personal, more severe and objective poetry, a poetry elevated, visionary, and hymn-like in quality. In these last volumes he had come under the spell of the Greek-inspired German Romantics Hölderlin and August von Platen and the solemn symbolistic world of Stefan George.

At the moment when Ekelund discarded poetry for prose he had become the incomparable Swedish master of a free, flexible musical verse. His mature poetry was a final step in freeing Swedish poetry from the rigidities of conventional verse patterns and the use of rhyme. The great poets of the 1890's had moved a few steps in this direction, but it remained for Ekelund to become the first clear-cut and consistent Swedish representative of what may loosely be called "free verse," a verse completely divested of rigid rhyme schemes, its rhythmic patterns determined exclusively by the inner drift of thought or emotion. From this kind of poetry to Ekelund's concentrated, often rhythmic and image-loaded prose is but a step — the next, almost inevitable step in a completely free expressive use of language.

The step was taken in *Antikt ideal* (The Classical Ideal, 1909), the first in a long series of aphoristic volumes of essays in which Ekelund offers to his devotees the fruits of his bookish meditations with the great spirits of the past. In his long and persistent search for truth and beauty (the former was but a part of the latter to Ekelund) he became a kind of secular monk, who — often literally in poverty — devoted all his energies to *willing* and *living* a sternly disciplined inner life. He lived alone with the select spirits of the past, immersing himself in their works and distilling his own aphoristic pronouncements out of the severe spiritual exercises which contact with these works inspired. In his early collections of essays Ekelund is inspired chiefly by the harsh heroism of Nietzsche and the kind of austere pursuit of Absolute Beauty to be found in Stefan George, but not many years elapsed (as is evident in *Vera similia*, I–II, 1915, 1916, and *Metron*, 1918) before a Classical conception of moderation tempered the early severity of Ekelund's thought, and Emerson and Goethe taught him the ways of a calmer, more humane, and actually realizable idealism. "Goethe," Ekelund has written, "attained much with a mild heart. . . . He who has seen beauty can perhaps dispense with indignation." Emerson, he observes, has "succeeded in uniting the heroic and the idyllic." And in the elevated presence of Emerson's rich and gentle personality his Swedish admirer raises the wondering question: "If now the best and strongest human being really looks like this? So flowing with milk and honey? Who can know." Among other great spirits who fascinated Ekelund without having a decisive importance for him were Swedenborg, Carlyle, and Dostoevski.

If Vilhelm Ekelund had early divested himself of earth-bound regional poetic motifs in his search for beauty and truth in the absolute sense, his fellow poet Anders Österling (b. 1884) has taken a less heroic literary way. It is apparent from the hectic profusion and the sacral solemnity of the youthful Österling's *Preludier* (Preludes, 1904) and *Offerkransar* (Sacrificial Garlands, 1905) that he, like Ekelund, had early been strongly attracted to both French and German symbolists. But unlike Ekelund he came to feel that the abstract aesthetic heroism of such poets as Stefan George led in time to poetic sterility, and he turned instead for his poetic materials to life itself in its immediate, palpable, everyday aspects, particularly as they were to be found on the countryside of his native Skåne. This regional material was exploited extensively for the first time in Österling's verse in the graceful bucolic arabesques of *Årets visor* (The Year's Songs, 1907) and in the more varied and substantial measures of *Blommande träd* (The Blossoming Trees, 1910). But not until his later years did he attain the rich regional effects which are his abiding poetic signature — first in the graceful charm and impressive variety of *Idyllernas bok* (The Book of the Idylls, 1917), then in the deepened sense of contact with the soil and ancestral values as reflected in *Jordens heder* (The Honor of the Soil, 1927), and finally in the large perspectives and the simply phrased faith of *Tonen från havet* (Tones from the Sea, 1933) and *Livets värde* (The Worth of Life, 1940). In only two of his volumes of verse after 1907 — in *Facklor i stormen* (Torches in the Storm, 1913) and *Sånger i krig* (Songs in War-time, 1917) — does Österling break sharply but tentatively out of the quiet calm of his regional poetry, in the first of these volumes because of an unhappy passion, in the second because of the catastrophic developments of the First World War.

Strictly speaking Österling did not grow up on the Swedish countryside as had so many other regional poets. His ancestors had for centuries tilled the soil of Skåne, but his father had left the ancestral acres and established himself as a printer and publisher, and the young Österling was brought up in Malmö, the chief city of his native province. In his early manhood he took up residence in the city of Lund, where he served as a university librarian for a decade before he finally established permanent residence in Stockholm while maintaining a summer home in the tiny village of Falsterbo not far from Malmö. In Stockholm he served for many years as literary critic for a couple of Sweden's more important newspapers, and since 1941 he has carried on the duties of permanent secretary of the Swedish Academy, a member of which he had become at the early age of thirty-five. His sensitive, cultivated, conscientious

366

literary criticism has appeared in book form at various times, most extensively in the three volumes of *Dagens gärning* (The Day's Work, 1921, 1926, 1931).

Though Österling's regional poetry was first inspired by his Skåne predecessors and contemporaries A. U. Bååth, Ola Hansson, and Vilhelm Ekelund, it came to take on its definitive spirit and form under a number of non-Swedish influences, those of the Basque poet Francis Jammes and a group of Danish lyricists (among whom the most important was Sophus Claussen), and especially Wordsworth. It is to the poetic ideals and practices of these poets that Österling refers with particular warmth in an essay from December 1909, entitled "Dagens lyrik" (Poetry of Our Day), in which he condemns contemporary Swedish poetry for its hyper-elevated solemnity, its fondness for the artificial and the elegant, its excessive sophistication. In Sophus Claussen he confesses admiration for "the sly, enchanting smile," in Francis Jammes the affectionate lingering over "things, the banal everyday things," and in Wordsworth he responded deeply to "the quiet attitude of things" and found delight in "a fantasy which from the simplest rural realities has created a miraculous world of poetic beauty." The work of these poets released Österling's own quietly earthy poetic gifts, enabling him to depict the life of the Skåne countryside in measured iambic pentameters (his favorite verse form) of remarkable flexibility and charm. The open, intensively cultivated countryside of Skåne, spreading its fertile acres far as the eye can see and peopled by a substantial peasant stock, lent itself ideally to the calm, leisurely, for the most part meditative pace of Österling's mature verse. In his poetry he catches up the life of this countryside in both its realistic and its dreamy moods, in its robust complacency and its moments of ethereal beauty, in its daily tasks and its festive diversions, in its alive immediacy and its sensitive awareness of close ties with an ancient past, in its arching heavens and its sweeping shore-lands lapped by Baltic waters. Toward all of this — and particularly toward life's simple human realities on this countryside — Österling feels a sense of profound poetic dedication:

> Time was when speech of men to me was vain
> As the trees' sighing when the June wind blew;
> O Life, I thank thee for the gentle pain
> That made its age-long meaning seem as new!
> Yon fisherman, rocked on the waters wild
> Of the sea's desert, 'tending to his gear:

Or the young mother nourishing her child
With breast laid bare — find we no meaning here?
O Conservation, path decreed of fate
For quiet happening and peaceful task —
To thee, Life's will, my song I dedicate,
My soul, my life-blood, whatsoe'er thou ask!
Take thou me in thy service: be my star:
Thy solemn radiance more and more let fall,
E'en though the beams that light me from afar
Be but a part, and very far from all.

Translated by C. D. Locock

Had Wordsworth lived in our day he would certainly have recognized in the quiet elevation of this "Credo" an entirely worthy Swedish disciple.

Österling has lived long enough to be accused of Romantic escapism by a younger generation of Swedish critics, whose ideas, hammered out on the anvil of modern social strife in the shadows of catastrophic world conflicts, demand of literature something more than the Skåne poet's nature worship and admiration for a life close to the soil. Österling has answered his critics with dignity and restraint, refusing to repudiate his conviction that man's salvation, if it is to be attained, will come through a state of mind in which a humanistic culture recognizes its ultimate source of strength in what Wordsworth called "the quiet attitude of things." That Österling's "realism" was of a limited — or special — kind is apparent even to those who are not prepared to denounce it as merely escapist. Its literary origins are clearly Romantic and it identifies itself almost exclusively with non-contemporary phenomena, with moods and ideas that at least on the surface are foreign to the drives of modern life. He had quite early disengaged himself from the symbolistic preciosities of *fin de siècle* poetry, but he did not substitute for this a realism of sharply modern social awareness, a realism which seeks to come directly at grips with the actual conditions of a rapidly changing contemporary world. This task became the special concern of a number of Swedish authors of prose fiction who in the somewhat more than a decade after 1910 produced the most considerable body of important novels which Swedish literature up to this time had seen.

Though only Hjalmar Bergman among the generation of novelists appearing in the first decade of our century is a genius of the first order, four others — Sigfrid Siwertz, Gustaf Hellström, Ludvig Nordström, and Elin Wägner — have made contributions to Swedish prose fiction of only less distinction. Of these both Siwertz and Hellström began writing under the decadent star of Hjalmar Söderberg, but they soon shook off the disillusioned passivity of their early master and came actively to grips with the problems of contemporary life. Nordström and Elin Wägner had never indulged in the Söderbergian manner of over-refined negativism. Aside from the highly original work of Hjalmar Bergman, who shall be dealt with in later contexts, the characteristic work of the new generation of novelists is essentially positive in spirit, inspired by the assumption that a sober, critical examination of the conditions of life can serve to effect a genuine improvement of man's lot. Unlike their immediate predecessors the new practitioners of prose fiction are neither deterministic fatalists nor self-absorbed egotists. Though they are in their social and intellectual thinking primarily late-born middle-class liberals of a nineteenth-century stamp, two of them, Siwertz and Hellström, particularly the former, find in the Bergsonian concepts of *élan vital* and "creative evolution" additional reason to have faith in man's potential to shape a better world than the one in which he finds himself. Without being unduly optimistic, they believe more or less consciously in the possibilities of progress, in the transforming power of the intelligent creative *will*.

In their novels they range widely and boldly over the whole contemporary Swedish scene, probing, questioning, judging, laying bare social evils and suggesting ways by which man might realize better forms of communal existence than those dictated by convention and tradition. And their awareness of social problems does not exclude a fundamental concern with psychological matters, with those deep-lying frustrations and complexes which often determine the tragic drift of individual human fates. The label "social reporters" which has been applied to them is particularly appropriate, both because three of them were practicing journalists for longer or shorter periods of time and because in their literary work they have "covered" the contemporary Swedish scene with the wide-open critical eyes of the best journalistic tradition. Aside from the specifically Bergsonian influence on some of these novelists, their social and intellectual orientation is predominantly English, with occasional American elements. Nordström's mother was English, and he greatly admired English industrial genius and commercial talents. Elin Wägner was attracted to various Anglo-American phenomena, in her maturity especially to the sober, undemonstrative religious ideals and practices of the Quakers. Hellström spent long periods of time in England and the United States as foreign correspondent for a leading Swedish newspaper, and though his best literary work is Swedish to the core it reflects not infrequently English literary influences in matters of mood and form. What is generally important in the case of these novelists is that their relatively cosmopolitan orientation provides them with a fresh, more balanced perspective on the Swedish life which they depict, enables them to view Swedish society from the outside as it were — with the relative objectivity which such a view permits.

In terms of more strictly Swedish literary contexts these novelists continue the work of social criticism of the 1880's, which had for a time been interrupted by the poetic renaissance of the 1890's with its individualism, its interest in the past, and its preoccupation with exclusive aesthetic values. The new generation of novelists succeeded where in a sense the 1880's had failed, that is to say they brought intellectual maturity and high literary competence to the writing of the novel and managed in consequence to create a large body of prose fiction of considerable distinction. Except for Strindberg and Victoria Benedictsson, the 1880's had no literary talent of a really high order, and Strindberg did not consciously cultivate the novel as a serious literary form while Victoria Benedictsson did not live long enough to fulfill her literary promise. Besides, those who wrote novels in the 1880's were on the whole so obsessed with the concept of scientific determinism and the notion that literature must be the handmaiden of social reform that their prose fiction had little independent existence outside the dogmatic rigidities of current scientific and social doctrine. The novelists who three decades later came to dominate the Swedish literary scene were far less hedged about by extra-literary dogma. Their social pathos, in contrast to that of the 1880's, sprang more directly and spontaneously out of their immediate experience of life and lent itself more readily to the purposes of imaginative literary treatment. Their novels could in consequence be something more than mere scientific demonstrations or slightly disguised social pamphlets. They could at their best — as in Siwertz's *Selambs* (tr. *Downstream*), in Hellström's *Snörmakare Lekholm får en idé* (tr. *Lacemaker Lekholm Has an Idea*), in Elin Wägner's *Åsa-Hanna*, and in any of a half dozen or more of Hjalmar Bergman's novels — rise to a very high creative level.

The most elegant and facile of the new generation of novelists is Sigfrid Siwertz (b. 1882), who in addition to an extraordinarily prolific production of prose fiction has provided the Swedish public with several volumes of competent verse and prose sketches and essays and written a number of highly successful plays. Stockholm born, he occupies a not unworthy place in that brilliant galaxy of literary depicters of Stockholm and its environs (in Siwertz's case especially the Stockholm waterways) which counts among its earlier practitioners such famous names as Bellman, Strindberg, and Hjalmar Söderberg. After a brief period of Söderberg discipleship in his early work, Siwertz found his own form and mood, partly under the influence of Bergson, whose lectures he had attended, together with Österling and a young Swedish philosopher-critic, John Landquist, at the Collège de France in 1907. Landquist was to become an enthusiastic exponent of Bergson's philosophical theories and a leading critical champion of the new realism in Swedish literature before and during the First World War. Though Siwertz's final formal accounting with *fin de siècle* aestheticism is to be found in a novel from 1914 entitled *En flanör* (An Idler), he had only less fully analyzed and found wanting the passive aesthete type in earlier tales, particularly in "Räddningsbåten" (The Life Boat), included in the collection *De gamla* (The Old Men) in 1909. The title *The Old Men* is in a way misleading, for the volume is concerned primarily with glorifying such active virtues of youth as daring, adventurousness, courage, and the will to act freely without conventional compunctions. These virtues celebrate their ultimate literary triumph in Siwertz's work, however, in the brilliantly fresh and invigorating chapters of *Mälarpirater* (The Pirates of Mälaren, 1911), a kind of Swedish *Huckleberry Finn*, in which the author's ability to enter enthusiastically into the juvenile world of boyish seafaring adventurers is to be accounted for at least as much by his own love for the sea and his experience as an accomplished yachtsman as by his Bergsonian intellectual predilections.

But Siwertz soon became confronted with more brutal, adult realities, with the repercussions in Sweden of the First World War. These realities forced him to modify his earlier Bergsonian optimism, which seemed to assume that the active will is always *good*. Despite the ambiguities of Siwertz's "war novel" *Eldens återsken* (Reflection of the Fire, 1916), it is sufficiently clear from its pages that he has come to recognize that the will need not *necessarily* be good — that it may in fact be a devastating instrument of evil. And in Siwertz's one indubitable masterpiece, the novel *Selambs* (tr. *Downstream*, 1920), he provides us with a terrifying study in the ways of the evil will, of rapacious egotism run amuck. *Downstream* is the unsavory tale of a family, the Selambs, all of whose members are dominated by the acquisitive instinct in its most selfish, inhuman, parasitic manifestations. The novel is a relentless exposé of capitalistic mentality as reflected in the lurid lights of modern wartime profiteering. It is written in an appropriately corrosive prose enriched by symbolistic detail of rare pregnancy and power and intensified by a recurrent vein of harsh, searing, at times grimly grotesque irony which reminds one of the aging Strindberg. Psychological depth is achieved by an incisively discreet use of Freudian conceptual patterns. "This is a tale," we are told at the outset, "of people whose childhood was passed in the shadow of the wolf – and who never could escape from their childhood." Complexes built up in the brutish, fear-filled early years of the Selambs brood account largely for the egotism, the rapacity, the spiritual sterility of their mature years. In their single-minded pursuit of wealth they become animals who "preferred to hunt alone," to use the novelist's grim formulation of modern capitalism's cult of the rugged individualist. The moral of the sordid Selambs tale would seem to be that capitalistic individualism must be replaced by a democratic social-conscious way of life, but Siwertz does not clearly draw this conclusion – at least not in a simple either/or form. He admits merely, in the closing sentence of the novel, that "the best days of the Selambs are over," and then adds – "the egoism of the masses is perhaps now the greater danger."

The observation is an interesting one (even prophetic, judging by political developments since the words were written), but it is hardly the kind of conclusion one expects at the close of a novel so charged with moral indignation against capitalistic excesses as is *Downstream*. Siwertz's position at the end of *Downstream* is not inconsistent, however, with the rather convenient relativism which, it has been observed, not infrequently crops up in his work. His sharp intelligence raises questions and exposes issues, but it does not take unequivocal stands on the issues it poses. In at least one instance, indeed, in "Fellow Travelers," the title story in a collection of short stories from 1929, he seems to be saying that one "truth" is quite as good as another.

Though nothing in Siwertz's work since the publication of *Downstream* approaches this novel in brilliance of conception and intensity of execution, he has continued to produce a steady stream of short stories and novels, poetry and plays, essays and sketches, which by any ordinary literary standard are almost uniformly competent, alive, and provocative.

These works frequently are as "actual" as the columns of the latest newspaper, but like these columns they often merely *report* daily phenomena for the delectation of the reader rather than provide a clear-cut judgment on the issues which may be involved. In such novels as *Det stora varuhuset* (tr. under the title *Goldmans*, 1926), *Jonas och draken* (Jonas and the Dragon, 1928), and *Sex fribiljetter* (Six Complimentary Tickets, 1943), and in the plays *Jag har varit en tjuv* (I Have Been a Thief, 1931), *Ett brott* (A Crime, 1933), *En hederlig man* (An Honorable Man, 1933), and *Spel på havet* (Gambling at Sea, 1938), Siwertz is an elegant reporter, a penetrating but scarcely profound thinker, who skillfully adapts to his literary purposes current newsworthy personalities and events to the delight of that segment of the reading public which wishes such material served up by a fastidious master of literary effects. In these and other works of Siwertz there is often an equivocal, half evasive quality, a kind of tacit skepticism, a form of resignation which is only more mature and sophisticated than was the melancholy aestheticism of his earliest work. But in two of his most recent books, *Den goda trätan* (The Good Quarrel, 1956), an essay collection, and *Trådar i en väv* (Threads in a Fabric, 1957), which skillfully combines the forms of the novel and the short story, Siwertz strikes at times a more sober, less evasive note without departing from the essentially resigned and relativistic position which is characteristic of most of his prose fiction and his plays. In these two works, and a third, the collection of memoirs and sketches entitled *Få-fäng gå . . .* (1959), Siwertz retains a stylistic verve and liveliness of mind which reflect an inner vitality little touched by his advancing age or by such disillusionments as inevitably come to those who have lived through the violent dislocations of the twentieth century.

The massive heavy-jowled bulk and expansive prophetic propensities of Ludvig Nordström (1882–1942) have little in common with the cat-like agility of Siwertz, except broadly similar middle-class origins and a lively interest in the contemporary Swedish scene. Nordström's father was a banker at Härnösand in Norrland, his mother English. Both of these circumstances proved to be of the utmost importance in his development. Norrland became the region around which his fantasy constantly circled, England the country which to him embodied those virtues most necessary to survival and world progress. Nordström's humor has much in common with Laurence Sterne and Dickens, his gospel of work resembles Carlyle's, his religious speculation parallels at many points H. G. Wells and G. K. Chesterton. Add to this liberal doses of Rabelais and Strindberg, especially in Nordström's early work, and one has suggested those authors who have meant the most to him outside the immediate literary traditions of his native Norrland. He reacted sharply against the tendency to "romanticize" the Norrland region as exemplified in Geijerstam's essay of 1897 on Pelle Molin, and identified himself rather with the more realistic and social-conscious trends in the work of his fellow Norrlander Olof Högberg, whose monumental but oftentimes grotesque and shapeless novel *Den stora vreden* (The Great Wrath, 1906), became the point of departure for Nordström's life-long effort to impress upon his countrymen the central importance for modern Sweden's economy and way of life of Norrland's expanding industrial potential.

Nordström more consciously than any of his contemporaries enlisted his literary talents in the cause of the new industrial society. Unfortunately, his enthusiasm for the cause was so great that his work as *literature* inevitably suffered. In fact, nearly all of his best work came early, before his very considerable literary talents were sacrificed to the grandiose socioeconomic speculation which he came ultimately to call "totalism" and which he pursued with stubborn persistence throughout his career despite the failure of his countrymen to respond to his vision of a triumphant technological society. In its strenuous anti-individualism, its stress on group and communal values, and its mystical predilections Nordström's totalism has a great deal in common with Jules Romains' unanism, but Nordström arrived at his views quite independent of his French contemporary.

Nordström is at his best in the short story and in the journalistic genre which provides broad studies in current social and cultural matters. Though he at times dreamed of emulating Balzac in writing a kind of Swedish *Comédie humaine*, he lacked Balzac's capacity for sustained creative effort, and as a novelist he is on the whole unsatisfactory. Only two of his novels, *Landsorts-bohème* (Small-Town Bohemia, 1911) and *Planeten Markattan* (The Monkey Planet, 1937), are important, the former as a lively Rabelaisian study in provincial degeneration, the latter as a sensitive account of the Nordström family tragedy. His most ambitious venture in prose fiction, the several-volume strenuously "totalist" work entitled *Petter Svensks historia* (The Story of Petter Svensk, 1923–27), can only in the loosest sense of the word be called a novel. In his short stories, on the other hand, Nordström is a master in the direct line of

374

descent from Strindberg, particularly in *Fiskare* (Fishermen, 1907), a worthy successor to Strindberg's gusty tales of folk life in the Baltic archipelago, but also in many of the stories in *Borgare* (Burghers, 1909), *Herrar* (Gentlemen, 1910), and *Lumpsamlaren* (The Junk Collector, 1910) as well as in other collections of tales with which Nordström at intervals continued to delight his readers down through his entire career. For his material Nordström draws on an apparently inexhaustible fund of lively, picturesque memories from his childhood, youth, and early manhood. The tales are characterized by a remarkable freshness of observation, a knowing use of everyday speech patterns (dialect, slang, colorful oaths), a rapid, sometimes headlong narrative tempo, an ever active fantasy, and an unabashed joy in every evidence of life's vital concreteness in Norrland's sprawling provincial world.

Nordström's Muse is neither beautiful nor gracious. She is Gumman Ångerman (Old Lady Ångerman), a woman of Norrland fisherfolk stock, ugly and gnarled and sharp of tongue, but cheerful, hard-working, courageous, and human — the creature, Nordström tells us, "who first and foremost gave me insight into the Swedish people. When I looked at her almost black, liver-spotted hands, with their broken nails and their knuckles swollen by hard labor, when I saw how she was the first one up in the morning (between 3 and 4), the last to bed at night (between 9 and 10), when I saw her staggering under the yoke of water buckets for the cattle — then I felt within me what one perhaps otherwise only can feel for one's mother; and one's throat quickened so that one had to run forward and take the buckets and jest with the old lady and reproach her for her tirelessness." Great as was Nordström's admiration for the quiet heroism of the common folk, he was not at all prone to praise the limited conditions of their existence, as can especially be seen in *Bondenöden* (The Distress of the Peasantry, 1933) and *Lort-Sverige* (Dirt — with the connotation "dung" — Sweden, 1938), the latter a devastating exposé of hygienic conditions on a supposedly "clean" Swedish countryside. *The Distress of the Peasantry* and *Dirt Sweden* were highly effective journalistic "social studies" based on extensive first-hand observations of rural conditions in Sweden in the 1930's. They aroused nearly as much discussion as Gunnar and Alva Myrdal's ominous study in Swedish population trends (*Kris i befolkningsfrågan*, 1935) and had something of the same importance as the Myrdal book in triggering reform measures through direct political action. Nordström's hard-hitting social reportage attracted more serious attention than his fantastic "totalist" speculations.

The only Swedish woman of considerable literary importance in the first two decades of our century was Elin Wägner (1882–1949), who found herself in the early years of the century doing yeoman duty as an enthusiastic literary feminist during what was perhaps the most strenuous period in the history of Swedish feminism. The measure of her literary talent is to be seen, however, in the fact that her early novels managed to be something more than feminist pamphlets, and the best novels of her maturity are concerned with universal moral problems far beyond the doctrinaire confines of an early twentieth-century Swedish feminist movement with its persistent and well-organized agitation for "women's rights," particularly women's suffrage. Born in Lund and having struggled through a rather unhappy childhood and early young womanhood in Hälsingborg on Sweden's west coast, Elin Wägner came to Stockholm in her early twenties and embarked on what was to be a successful career as a journalist, chiefly in feminist publications like *Idun*, from time to time as a contributor to the prominent newspaper *Dagens Nyheter*. Her first novels, *Norrtullsligan* (The Norrtull Gang, 1908) and *Pennskaftet* (The Penholder, 1910), created an immediate stir, partly because of their subject matter and partly because of their pert, playfully malicious satiric vein. The Norrtull "gang" is a plucky little band of working girls who live and dream together as best they can in a dull, gray, work-a-day world, a world made the more melancholy by the more or less dishonorable efforts of men to penetrate their innocence or break down their sense of independence and feminine solidarity. The world that we are introduced to in *The Norrtull Gang* is the same as that of Sigrid Undset's early novel *Jenny* (1911). But Elin Wägner, unlike her Norwegian contemporary, does not in her novel permit a tragic denouement — chiefly no doubt because she has an abiding faith in the feminist cause. This cause, nurtured in the brave though "frostbitten" camaraderie of the little Norrtull coterie, purrs with a warm undercurrent of the working girls' group-awareness and makes its claims against man's encroachments in a delightfully aggressive youthful jargon. But these are in a sense external matters. In the last analysis the women who make up the Norrtull group have warm motherly instincts which seek — and often find — outlets in other directions than the drudgery of their daily work. Elin Wägner joins the world-famous Swedish feminist Ellen Key (1849–1926) in vigorously opposing the doctrine that there is no constitutive difference between man and woman. It is however in *The Penholder* that Elin Wägner writes the classic novel on the Swedish feminist movement. In this novel she provides us with a thoroughly documented and very lively account of the Swedish feminism of her day, its theoretical foundations, its organizational form, its political program, its missionary fervor and widespread field of operations. Particularly does she stress the ideal of solidarity among women, an ideal which, she insists, must make the voices of women heard in the future counsels of humanity.

But in her feminist zeal in defending "the cause" Elin Wägner does not in *The Penholder* ignore completely the element of passion, and this element, together with the problem of evil in its more inclusive aspects, crops up with increasing persistence and emphasis in the later novels, where her view of life has in part freed itself from its more limited immediate feminist preoccupations. One of the sides of the feminist movement which had particularly interested her was its peace program, but when the First World War demonstrated how ineffectual this program was in reality, Elin Wägner was driven to a more realistic and critical examination of humanity's ethical potential than had been permitted by her early rose-tinted feminist idealism. During the War years she wrote two novels, *Släkten Jerneploogs framgång* (The Jerneploog Family's Success, 1916), a bitterly ironic arraignment of war, and *Åsa-Hanna* (1917), the greatest Swedish peasant novel since Selma Lagerlöf's *Jerusalem*. While *Åsa-Hanna* has the monumental simplicity and the moral impressiveness of *Jerusalem*, its depiction of human fate on the Swedish countryside dispenses almost entirely with the romantic lyricism and colorful antiquarianism of Selma Lagerlöf's novel. Elin Wägner in her novel deals head-on with the problem of evil in some of its most sordid forms, when her healthy, morally sound heroine Åsa-Hanna becomes enmeshed by marriage in a family of sly, petty, blood-sucking criminal types. We are reminded early of their kind when we are told that the copperware in their kitchen was polished only on the front side – the side which can be *seen*. Åsa-Hanna inevitably degenerates in this environment, becomes a deceiver and covers the ugly tracks of her kinfolk by marriage – until her burden of guilt becomes too great to bear and she does bitter penance for her sins under circumstances that are as morally impressive as any scene in Swedish fiction.

Åsa-Hanna is the first of Elin Wägner's novels whose action takes place in rural Småland, the province to which she as a child had become attached during many happy summer holidays and to which she ultimately returned to live and came to interpret in her maturity. Though she admired in general the way of life in rural Småland, she did not become enamored of it in the uncritical way characteristic of so many of her predecessors who had dealt with the Swedish countryside. Her concern with rural Sweden was in the last analysis ethical and religious rather than aesthetic and antiquarian, and it is therefore that she is able so convincingly to pour into her best Småland novels the larger human problems of her own day — the ethical and religious problems of a sick, wartorn, often despairing world. With these problems she was acquainted at first hand in consequence of her extensive postwar relief activities on the Continent in the early 1920's. Her impressions from these years were recorded in a book *Från Seine, Rhen och Ruhr, Små historier från Europa* (1923). In connection with her relief work she had come in contact with the Quakers, whose religious forms and practices profoundly impressed her and served to bolster both her pacifistic convictions and her leanings toward a simple non-confessional type of Christianity as distinguished from certain traditional religious formulations and usages.

At times Elin Wägner's Continental experiences are directly exploited in her prose fiction, particularly in the strongly pacifistic novel *De fem pärlorna* (The Five Pearls, 1927); but in her best postwar novels — *Den namnlösa* (The Nameless One, 1922), *Silverforsen* (The Silver Rapids, 1924), *Genomskådad* (Unmasked, 1937), and *Hemlighetsfull* (Mysterious, 1938) — these experiences become so organically a part of the ethical and religious conflicts of her characters that only those readers who are in some detail aware of her humanitarian labors can discern the part that these experiences have played in her interpretation of life in Småland and on the larger Swedish scene of her day. *The Nameless One* and *The Silver Rapids* are in matters of form highly charged, sharply focused, half-realistic, half-symbolical treatments of unbridled passion and its consequences in the light of moral and religious considerations, while *Unmasked* and *Mysterious* (both partly autobiographical) pursue the theme of unhappy marriage beyond its dissolution and on into the identification of the heroine with humanitarian causes as envisioned by an ideal, selfless women's movement. Written in the years just before the Second World War, *Unmasked* and *Mysterious* are inspired by a burning sense of urgency not present in her early fiction.

Aside from these novels, Elin Wägner wrote during her Småland years a number of works specifically about the folk life of her adopted province, among which may be mentioned the general historical and ethnographical work *Tusen år i Småland* (A Thousand Years in Småland, 1939) and two novels — *Svalorna flyga högt* (The Swallows Fly High, 1929) and *Gammalrödja* (Old Clearing, 1931) — both of which are concerned with the impact of modern forms of existence on an older communal culture. Her last work, the sensitive though not always satisfactory biography of Selma Lagerlöf (1942, 1943), was commissioned by the Swedish Academy, the second woman member of which she had become in 1944. She was at work on a biography of Fredrika Bremer when death came in 1949.

Though Elin Wägner's talent is not of the first rank, she is certainly to be counted among the half dozen women who have made the greatest contribution to Swedish letters. She had much of the impulsive femininity and warm-hearted humanitarianism of Fredrika Bremer, Selma Lagerlöf, and Ellen Key. But she also had the critical sharpness and much of the witty common sense of Anna Maria Lenngren together with something of the religious mysticism and capacity for moral indignation of Saint Birgitta. Of all women who have occupied prominent places in Swedish cultural developments she is in some ways one of the most interesting.

The novelist of the generation with which we are concerned who had the most extensive experience abroad is Gustaf Hellström (1882–1953), who served for more than a quarter of a century as foreign correspondent for *Dagens Nyheter* — in London 1908–10, 1927–33, in Paris 1911–17, and in New York 1918–23. His production includes — in addition to a corpus of brilliant journalistic commentary — the long series of only slightly disguised autobiographical novels concerned with the life and inner struggles of one Stellan Petreus and more than a dozen volumes of short stories and novels some of which were in essence only less autobiographical than the Stellan Petreus series. Despite the fact that Hellström's first work *Ungkarlar* (Bachelors) appeared as early as 1904 and his literary activity for more than two decades following his debut was quite considerable, he did not break through as an author of serious literary consequence until 1927 with the fascinating family novel *Snörmakare Lekholm får en idé* (tr. *Lacemaker Lekholm Has an Idea*). The reasons for his late literary maturing seem to have been two: the necessity of his having to expend so much of his energy in journalistic activities, and his sensitive, highly self-critical literary temperament. In his years abroad he had written nearly a thousand lengthy and often penetrating articles on conditions in Europe and America during a period which included the ominous preliminary maneuvering of nations before two world wars and the actual conduct of the first of these wars. How seriously he took his duties as a foreign correspondent and how sensitively he performed them may be seen in his half dozen reportage volumes from the years between 1914 and 1933, dealing with France at war, with a postwar England and America, and with conditions which led to Hitler's rise to power. Though Hellström's sympathies were always with the Western Powers (he was a strong Anglophile throughout his career), he had both admiration and scorn for the America he came to know after the First World War. In the first of two works he wrote shortly after his arrival in America entitled *Förenta staterna och världsfreden* (The United States and World Peace) he provided his countrymen with an intelligent and sympathetic account of Woodrow Wilson's peace plans and their political backgrounds together with a generally favorable orientation in American life and mentality. But in the second of these works — the corrosively entertaining novel *Ett rekommendationsbrev* (A Letter of Recommendation) — Hellström appears concurrently with the Sinclair Lewis of *Main Street* and *Babbitt* as a sharply perceptive prober of middle-class mentality in the United States. In Hellström's novel, however, the focus is more dispersed, and its central action together with its conditioning milieu is upper middle-class on the eastern seaboard. Its more serious portions deal with such crucial matters as the Negro problem, while its light but sufficiently deadly wit plays often by preference in a sly Freudian manner around such phenomena as idle American social matrons who devise apparently ideal "humanitarian programs" in order to escape from sexual frustration and general boredom. As a grimly ironic reminder of his point of view in *A Letter of Recommendation*, Hellström places as a motto on his title page Emerson's words on America, "Our whole history appears like a last effort of the Divine Providence in behalf of the human race."

If Hellström could make sophisticated sport of female frustrations on the post-World War I American scene, he could not with equal aplomb dispose of his own persistent emotional and intellectual frustrations. In fact, much of his work reflects an only half-successful effort to resolve his own inner problems. His return to Sweden in 1923 seems to have been directly dictated by a strong desire, after a quarter of a century of preoccupation with world events and world cultures, to come to grips with himself and with the Sweden of his childhood and youth. And even

Anders Österling

Sigfrid Siwertz

Hjalmar Söderberg, portrait by Gerda
Wallander (Thielska galleriet)

Hjalmar Bergman (courtesy of fru Stina Bergman)

Pär Lagerkvist (copyright Lennart Nilsson)

Birger Sjöberg

Gustav Hedenvind-Eriksson

Dan Andersson

before his return he had begun the long autobiographical Stellan Petreus series, the first three volumes of which fall under the collective title *En man utan humor* (A Man without Humor, 1921–25). These were followed at rather long intervals by five more volumes, the last of which, *I morgon är en skälm* (Tomorrow Is a Rascal), appearing in 1952. From a narrowly literary point of view the Stellan Petreus series has its faults, but as a psychological and moral document and a thoroughgoing inventory of Swedish life and culture in a given period it has few counterparts in Swedish literature. In these volumes Hellström examines dispassionately his own inner problem within the intellectual and ethical contexts of the Sweden of his own generation. Primarily he is concerned with the related problems (so basic to his generation) of the freedom of the will and of moral responsibility, and he takes a stand which may be described as a kind of qualified Bergsonism, that is to say he maintains a healthy critical attitude toward "activist" doctrine, accepting its central thesis with certain reservations but remaining much more on guard against its potential excesses than did some of his literary contemporaries.

How balanced, sensitive, and essentially humane Hellström's judgment could be in matters of ethical import rooted deeply in the social and psychological conditioning factors of his day is most impressively demonstrated, however, in the best of his prose fiction — in the three social-conscious early tales about London street life included in *Kuskar* (Coachmen, 1910) and in the three important novels of his maturity, *Lacemaker Lekholm Has an Idea* (1927), *Carl Heribert Malmros* (1931), and *Storm över Tjurö* (Storm over Tjur Island, 1935). In these three novels Hellström was finally able to create living segments of actual life out of the mass of material with which he struggled in vain to give satisfactory artistic form in the Stellan Petreus series. Of the three novels the story of Police Commissioner Malmros's struggle with his conscience is closely related to the ethical problems so often broached in the lengthy narrative sequence concerned with Stellan Petreus. In the Police Commissioner's moral dilemma Hellström also points up sharply an immediately actual social problem in Sweden, the rights of labor to take strike action as illustrated in the famous Ådal strike of 1931, the year of the appearance of Hellström's novel. In *Storm over Tjur Island* the petty quarrels, backbiting, and general cantankerousness of the human animal within the limited confines of a primitive fisherfolk Baltic island community are employed to suggest telling parallels with a larger world of social, economic, and political bickering — the whole between-the-wars world with which Hellström through his international journalistic experience was so intimately acquainted. "To what extent," an observer in the novel asks, "can these folk who are trying to destroy one another, and in the process annihilate themselves, be considered representative of mankind in general? Are they an exception, an atavism, determined by special geographical conditions and a special social mentality? Or are they a manifestation of mankind as a whole, of something terrifying and profoundly human, which under certain circumstances broke out and spread itself like an epidemic in spite of all developments, 'all progress'?" Harsh as are the implications of such questions as these, they serve only recurrently to disturb our otherwise essentially pleasurable response to such qualities in Hellström's novel as its lively narrative drive, its unafraid everyday realism, and its rollicking though at times half-bitter humor.

In contrast with some of the humor of *Storm over Tjur Island* the comic element in *Lacemaker Lekholm Has an Idea* is consistently open and expansive, warm and understanding — in the manner of a Fielding and a Dickens. From Fielding and English eighteenth-century traditions Hellström has learned how to employ brilliantly mock heroic satire, from Dickens he has discovered how to lay bare a character's central inner quality by means of emphasizing a physical trait or two. And Dickens's warm, often sentimental humanity almost certainly has had something to do with the forgiving strain of humor characteristic of *Lacemaker Lekholm Has an Idea*. But Hellström's novel also goes the way of a more modern literary tradition, that of Thomas Mann's *Buddenbrooks* and Galsworthy's *Forsyte Saga*, in terms of its broad social purposes as reflected in a minutely documented concern with the fates of an entire family through successive generations of development and decay. The central action of Hellström's novel takes place in a typical Swedish provincial town, with appropriate periphery material from other localities being employed to provide the broader outlines of a highly ramified family picture. The Lacemaker's "idea" (around which the action of the novel swirls in both comic and half-tragic profusion) is that the lower middle-class family of which the Lacemaker is the fatuous progenitor must raise the social level of its members by seeking university training, by pursuing the learned professions. So rigid were Swedish social mores regarding class distinctions that the Lacemaker's "idea" failed of realization in his immediate offspring, but the social barriers were eventually broken down by members of the Lekholm family in the third generation. Some of them had managed in one way or another to gain a higher education and others had raised their social level by other means. "It is not likely," we are reminded late in the novel by a Lekholm of the third generation — "that grandfather had even the faintest notion of how *genuinely Swedish* he was when he got it into his head that his sons should be learned men. One can surely safely maintain that this idea, which apparently was the only idea the Old Man had in his head, has been responsible for eight-tenths of Sweden's cultural values and Sweden's cultural history. The fact is that the old Lacemaker counts among his descendants practically all of the types which Swedish society can exhibit." This commentary both pays its fond offhand respects to the old Lacemaker and brings into a sharp focus one of the central concerns of a novel which, in the breadth and depth of its treatment of Swedish small town provincial life on the threshold of our time, has few counterparts in Swedish fiction. With *Lacemaker Lekholm Has an Idea*, and the two later novels *Carl Heribert Malmros* and *Storm over Tjur Island*, Gustaf Hellström comes to take his honored place alongside such competent and representative practitioners of prose fiction in the years after 1910 as Sigfrid Siwertz, Ludvig Nordström, and Elin Wägner.

But Hellström does not rank, nor do Siwertz nor Nordström nor Elin Wägner, with another literary contemporary, the novelist and dramatist Hjalmar Bergman (1883–1931), an original genius of the first order, a genius who breaks new ground and becomes together with Pär Lagerkvist and Birger Sjöberg one of the three portal figures in contemporary Swedish literature. Of these three Pär Lagerkvist is the key figure, the central portal figure in the literature of our day; but Hjalmar Bergman is only less important in pointing the way toward a new kind of novel and drama, while Birger Sjöberg's precipitate shift in the mid-1920's from poetic idyllicism to expressionistic verse provides one of the immediate points of departure for a new kind of Swedish poetry. It is not customary to apply the term "literary modernists" to Pär Lagerkvist, Hjalmar Bergman, and Birger Sjöberg, but it is clear that the generation appearing in the years around 1930 to which the term "modernists" has been applied learned a great deal from the three Swedish predecessors in whose work can most clearly be discerned a desire to break sharply with older literary forms. Aside from the work of these three figures, Swedish poetry and prose in the first quarter of the twentieth century moves almost entirely in conventional literary forms. The representative novelists of the second decade of the twentieth century took their cues from the past, chiefly from the Swedish 1880's; and what they did in their novels was largely to perfect a genre formerly handled in a fashion relatively crude and unsatisfactory. Instead of being concerned with experimenting in new points of view and new forms, Siwertz and Nordström, Elin Wägner and Hellström wrote solid, well-documented, nearly always intelligent and at times brilliant realistic novels about contemporary society and contemporary problems.

Among these sober, systematic, highly rational novelists of his generation Hjalmar Bergman was a strange, often disturbing phenomenon — strange because of his fabulous fantasy, his unpredictable narrative verve, disturbing because of his persistent concern with abnormal human types and his brooding awareness of the dark and fearsome undertow of life. The Swedish reading public, conditioned by the more normal, predictable world of Siwertz and Nordström, Elin Wägner and Hellström, didn't know quite how to respond to Hjalmar Bergman's work; and though the critics bowed respectfully in Bergman's direction, they did not for a long time really come to grips with his deep-dredging, complex, highly disturbing modern art. It was not, indeed, until Bergman, well along in his literary career, deliberately capitulated to popular taste in 1919 with the brilliantly comic novel *Markurells i Wadköping* (tr. *God's Orchid*) that he finally found — a decade and a half after his literary debut — a large and demonstratively appreciative audience. The dozen years which followed before his death in 1931 were years of feverish productivity in prose fiction and the drama, a productivity accompanied by pyramiding success with readers and theatergoers alike. But this "success" was bought at least partly at a price which strained Bergman's creative energies to the breaking point and brought him to the desperate state of final disillusionment which erupted in the broken fragments of confession and judgment of his last work *Clownen Jac*. In the central symbol of this work, the Clown — a creature who stumbles into exploiting commercially his own terror when he by accident discovers man's perverse comic pleasure on witnessing the grotesque outward evidences of the Clown's terror — Bergman provides a ghastly ironic commentary on one side of his own final literary development. In much of the work of his late years Bergman, too, had become in a sense a clown, had gone through with his grimly pathetic act — because this was what his public wanted in its insistent, blind demand for entertainment, for pleasure. But the comic act became to Bergman a leering tragedy, a desperately weary admission of his own dark dilemma as an artist — and a bitter commentary on his public, which with diabolic unconcern had forced him to play the part of a mere entertainer when he would rather have followed the honest inner dictates of his genius. "I was born a human being," the Clown confesses — "I lived as a clown — I sold my heart — I shall die poor . . ."

That Hjalmar Bergman had extraordinary talents as a literary entertainer is apparent in nearly everything he has written. His teeming gallery of queer and yet credible characters operates in contexts of comic inventiveness and narrative fertility that are unique in Swedish literature. And his dialogue — direct, alive, varied, loaded with unexpected turns of phrase — is the perfect stylistic instrument for the world which Bergman has conjured up in his work. But underneath the glittering surfaces of Bergman's art lurked drives and moods of another kind, drives which identified themselves more often than not with the darkly destructive forces of life, moods which maintained a constant flirtation with an all but hopeless fatalism. That which is perhaps most characteristic of Bergman's best work is the uneasy balance maintained between the comic and tragic, the expansive and sinister elements — *both* Dickens and Dostoevski were among the novelists whom he most admired.

Though such early works from Bergman's pen as the Maeterlinckian drama *Det underbara leendet* (The Wonderful Smile, 1907) and the Renaissance novel *Savonarola* (1909) might indicate that his disillusioned attitudes derive largely from typical *fin de siècle* literary moods, the persistence with which such moods continued to pursue Bergman and the fixed forms which his pessimism ultimately took suggest that they have more deep-lying, essentially constitutive sources. These sources can be traced back to Bergman's preternaturally sensitive childhood. While he enjoyed all of the outward privileges which could be provided by loving parents in a wealthy home, he felt in his childhood and youth constantly on the defensive against his environment — a defensive attitude which with the years often took on abnormal forms. He had great difficulty in associating in normal ways with people outside a narrowly limited circle, was constantly "on the move," living during the thirty years of his mature life largely abroad (by preference in Italy though not infrequently in France, Switzerland, and Germany) in hotels, pensions, and other temporary quarters. To Sweden he would usually return only during the summers, settling down to his work on a small island, Segelholm, in the Stockholm archipelago. He lived in his work, driven by his creative furies, pouring out an apparently inexhaustible succession of novels and short stories and plays. Late in 1923, at the height of Bergman's popularity in Sweden, he was inveigled over to Hollywood by his Swedish friend Victor Sjöström, then active as a director in the American film capital. Bergman was under contract to turn out film scripts, but he disliked everything about Hollywood and escaped shortly to European shores again. *Clownen Jac* is in part Bergman's devastating commentary on the Hollywood mentality and the publicity aspects of high pressure American business procedures.

After having experimented in his early years with various literary genres and themes, Bergman published in 1910 a novel, *Hans nåds testamente* (His Grace's Last Testament), which becomes in a number of crucial ways the point of departure for almost all of his later work. In *His Grace's Last Testament* Bergman appears for the first time as a comic genius of the first order and moves the locale of his prose fiction to the Bergslagen foundry and mining areas of central Sweden, a district whose life he had observed so closely in his youth and whose local history had been aired so frequently in his presence by members of his immediate family and other informed people of prominence in the area. Bergslagen now becomes to Bergman what "Wessex" was to Thomas Hardy, a reasonably limited geographical area within which the action of most of his novels is to take place, a roughly homogeneous local life and culture which provides the necessary material for the author's commentary on the human scene. In more than a dozen novels Bergman now comes to concern himself with the affairs of middle and upper class Bergslagen families whose fortunes ebb and flow in often violent patterns of conflict through more than two hundred years of time on the local countryside and in that urban center of population which does not get its name, Wadköping (in reality Örebro), until the publication of *Markurells i Wadköping*, the ninth in order of appearance of the Bergslagen novels.

Unlike the Balzac of the *Comédie humaine* or the Zola of the Rougon-Macquart series, Bergman does not attempt to provide his readers in the Bergslagen novels with an inclusive and systematic account of the world with which he is dealing. Nor does he emulate the Selma Lagerlöf of the Värmland novels and tales in providing us with precisely localized regional detail. In any given novel Bergman simply descends upon his material at any point and proceeds intuitively rather than by deliberate design to lay bare some segment of Bergslagen life which through some accident of local tradition had fastened itself upon his memory. Situations and characters and dialogue fall into place as if by magic as he spins out his narrative patterns. The situations are often mad, the characters eccentric, the dialogue apparently a mere crazy-quilt of alternately gay and macabre indirections. So utterly brilliant, indeed, are the surface features of Bergman's art that they tend in some of the early Bergslagen novels to obscure somewhat the author's more serious purposes — his central concern with the tragic drift of character in a world of petty, directionless, meaningless conflict. One's impression on first reading some of the earlier Bergslagen novels is mixed and somewhat bewildering. Bergman seems so delighted with the rich fictional potential of the Bergslagen material, and his brilliant narrative gifts operate with such scintillating abandon, that his more serious intentions are not immediately apparent in such less important though in part arresting works as *Loewenhistorier* (Loewen Tales, 1913) and *En döds memoarer* (Memoirs of a Dead Man, 1918). But in some of these early Bergslagen novels, particularly in *Knutsmässo marknad* (Knutsmässo Fair, 1916) and in *Mor i Sutre* (Mother at Sutre, 1917), Bergman attains a well-nigh perfect fusion of narrative brilliance and ethical intention though early readers of these works had difficulty in discerning the novelist's serious intentions beneath the scintillating surface artistry of these works.

In the later novels, especially in *God's Orchid* and in the two masterpieces *Farmor och Vår Herre* (tr. under the title *Thy Rod and Thy Staff*, 1921) and *Chefen fru Ingeborg* (tr. *The Head of the Firm*, 1924), Bergman's ethical intentions are underlined more distinctly without sacrificing either brilliant narrative inventiveness or psychological penetration. These and other later novels are less consistently macabre in manner and less hopelessly fatalistic in mood than Bergman's earlier work. They operate in a somewhat more sharp and bracing atmosphere, and they employ more clearly defined patterns, the central characters apparently pursuing more positive and constructive ends than do the half-mad eccentrics and the will-less drifters of so many of Bergman's earlier novels. I say "*apparently* pursuing more positive and constructive ends" because on closer examination we discover that Bergman in the novels beginning with *God's Orchid* is no less a fatalist than he was before, no less grimly aware of how fatuous is man's assumption that he by an act of will can alter the irrational drift of life. "Any person whosoever," Bergman reminds us in a famous paradox, "may commit any action whatsoever at any moment whatsoever." *Any* person — the strong as well as the weak of will. Each of the strong-willed central figures in Bergman's more important later novels, Markurell in *God's Orchid*,

Grandmother Borck in *Thy Rod and Thy Staff*, and Ingeborg Balzar in *The Head of the Firm*, lives long enough to discover that goodness is not readily identifiable with common sense, business acumen, and a determination to establish order and decency in family relations, particularly as they have to do with parental relations to children. In *God's Orchid* this theme is handled relatively crudely in the midst of much comic horseplay capped by some late-born "tragic" scenes of a not very subtle kind. In *Thy Rod and Thy Staff* and *The Head of the Firm* the theme is developed with a psychological incisiveness and moral sensitivity which mark in some ways Bergman's highest fictional attainment. But it is typical of Bergman that he arrives at his "moral" in these two novels not by superimposing upon life certain predetermined moral standards but by sensitively probing the complexities of the human psyche. He digs deeply down into the unconscious and subconscious layers of the human spirit in order to create credible characters who *will* to do good but because of life's ironic irrationalities end up in profoundly disturbing moral dilemmas.

The redoubtable (in many ways delightful) Grandmother Borck in *Thy Rod and Thy Staff* does evil because her busy efficiency is so inconsiderate, runs so roughshod over less thick-skinned people about her. She brings order into the affairs of the ineffectual Borck family into which she marries, but she does so by destroying whatever rudiments of self-sufficiency and self-respect the Borcks had managed to preserve. Grandmother Borck is an angel with a sharp tongue and over-officious wings. Like all egotists she assumes in her years of vitality and success that even God must admire her readiness to order everybody and arrange everything within her field of operations. But God, unfortunately, remains silent, unresponsive, when she finally in her hour of despair all but demands His official seal of approval upon her actions. In her way she has to do penance . . . in *her* way, it should be noted — and this way is not on bended knee. Grandmother's concept of penance as Bergman develops it in one of the most original bedroom scenes in literature is as richly comic as it is psychologically revealing and morally true to life.

In *Thy Rod and Thy Staff* Bergman's humor retains much of its gaiety and warmth despite its more than occasional yielding to grotesque effects and its way of serving the author's ethical intentions. In *The Head of the Firm* the humor is by contrast sophisticated, sharp, essentially brittle, serving by its tonal vacuities to accentuate the relentless development of the novel's tragic theme, the disintegration of Ingeborg Balzar's character under the impact of an irresistible passion for her daughter's fiancé. None of Bergman's novels, with the possible exception of *Memoirs of a Dead Man*, owes more to Freud than *The Head of the Firm*. Sensational as his subject is, Bergman handles it with exemplary delicacy and profound understanding and sympathy, employing all his analytical resources in tracing the tenuous unconscious origins of Ingeborg's sexual compulsion and accounting for its final tragic consequence — her suicide as the only decent way out of an intolerable situation. She, like the Phaedra of Euripides' *Hippolytos*, finds herself "struggling to pluck honor out of shame," and finds the struggle equally hopeless. The overall form into which Bergman pours these tragic materials is stark, rigid, schematic. It has the inexorable drive and the artistic economy of Greek tragedy, departing sharply from those freer, fantasy-filled, often unpredictable narrative patterns which Bergman elsewhere employs with such sovereign skill.

Though Bergman as a dramatist does not perhaps weigh as heavily on the literary scales as Bergman the novelist, he is the only Swedish dramatist of importance between Strindberg and the mature Pär Lagerkvist, and the first after Strindberg to be played extensively in Stockholm theaters. Unfortunately, theatrical recognition came to him even later than acceptance by a large novel-reading public. It was not until he met an entertainment-minded theatergoing public more than half-way, in 1925 with the "smash hit" comedy *Swedenhielms*, that he finally broke through in the theater. In this play, as in the novel *God's Orchid*, Bergman laid aside temporarily his macabre moods and brooding fatalism and created a delightfully warm and waggish comedy. The overwhelming success of *Swedenhielms* on the Swedish stage may be accounted for in two ways: first, the play stands alone in the whole range of Swedish dramatic tradition as the single indubitable creative triumph of the pure comic spirit in this tradition; and, second, in the two central characters of the play — the elder Swedenhielm and his housekeeper Boman — the dramatist has created with a sure touch for theatrical effect two warm human caricatures of those sides of Swedish national temperament which all Swedes like to think are essential.

It is not difficult for those familiar with the comic tradition in the theater to recognize that in *Swedenhielms* the dramatist is quite deliberately exploiting (often to the hilt) all of the common technical ingredients of this tradition: its love of complications in plot, its tendency to-

389

ward farce in the conception of scene, its brilliance of dialogue, and its sudden transitions in mood from that of the veriest high jinks to that of heartwarming pathos and an at least implied moralizing. *Swedenhielms* would not be the scintillating tour de force it is, however, if it did not handle each of these ingredients with superb skill and if it did not combine them into an organic whole which gives to the total comic conception that peculiar potency which at one and the same time both entertains and moves. In *Swedenhielms* Bergman's inexhaustible inventiveness and his unpredictable fantasy, the twin marks of his narrative genius, escape for the moment from the strait jacket in which he had been encased in his earlier tragic dramas, and the result is a comedy as spontaneous and unforced as the processes of nature or the play of imaginative children.

But, like all great comedy, Bergman's playful imaginative arabesques in *Swedenhielms* have their profounder purposes, though these purposes may not be apparent at first sight and are never permitted to intrude so sharply as to break the spell of pure comic entertainment which the dramatist has created for us. These profounder purposes are intimately tied up with the characterization of the expansive elder Swedenhielm and his dour housekeeper Boman, who represent, each in his way, two sides of Swedish national character: Swedenhielm the irresponsible fantast of brilliant mental attainments and traditional concepts of honor; Boman the solid, practical, self-effacing Swedish servant of stable unimaginativeness and everyday virtues. It may be a question at the end of the play whether we are more entertained by the fascinating vagaries of Swedenhielm or the canniness and common sense of his housekeeper. But it is hardly a question as to which of these characters finally impresses us the more. We may love the magnificently irresponsible, and irrepressible, Swedenhielm in spite of his momentary discomfiture in the presence of a "moral law," but we come to see nevertheless that it is Boman who represents, in her grimly triumphant manner, those virtues necessary to maintain at least a semblance of balance in the queer and oddly assorted world of the Swedenhielm family. It is in Bergman's impish lightness of touch in handling the moral issue of the play — his refusal to judge either man or the world in which man must exist, even while he gently satirizes man's rather fatuous pretensions — that we find the comic spirit operating in its subtlest ways in *Swedenhielms*. When, at the end of the play, the redoubtable Boman sits down to her coffee and rusks, with a formidable cane in her hand, grimly awaiting the arrival of the usurer Eriksson, the spectator can hardly avoid a chuckle of delighted comic recognition as he recalls the immediately preceding action in which this same redoubtable Boman uses with only partly tender relish another kind of cane on the whole Swedenhielm clan, whom she has loved and served so well down through the years, and whom she still loves so deeply that she does not hesitate to apply the cane when it seems appropriate and necessary.

But the stage success of *Swedenhielms* in 1925, together with that of another important comedy, *Patrasket* (The Rabble), which followed in 1928, was a somewhat hollow triumph for Bergman, who for twenty years had attempted, and failed, to break into the theater with plays of much more serious intent, plays which clothed his tragic view of life in subtly suggestive modern experimental forms partly reminiscent of Maeterlinck and the Strindberg of *The Dream Play* and *The Spook Sonata*. The most arresting of Bergman's serious experimental dramas are the three "Marionette Plays" from 1917 entitled *Dödens Arlekin* (Death's Harlequin), *En skugga* (A Shadow), and *Herr Sleeman kommer* (tr. *Mr. Sleeman Is Coming*, 1944), and a group of plays published in 1923 in a single volume which included *Spelhuset* (The Gambling House), *Vävaren i Bagdad* (The Weaver of Bagdad), and *Porten* (The Portal). With *Swedenhielms* these plays have in common only the element of the fantastic, the operation of the irrational on the human scene. But in these plays the irrational element is charged with terrifying tragedy in the sharpest possible contrast to *Swedenhielms* where the irrational is employed *playfully*, entering into the action merely as a temporary irritant, as a momentary obstruction in the otherwise at least relatively happy tangle of human fate.

Of Bergman's early plays *Mr. Sleeman Is Coming* most subtly evokes the mood of fatalistic brooding over the tragic theme of human destiny as being determined by irrational, darkly evil forces which man is incapable of either controlling or understanding. This play, a brief three-act tragedy, is a little gem in a subdued Maeterlinckian terror mood, sharply stylized in its technique, but lacking almost entirely the exaggerated, grotesque *bizarrerie* of tone and general procedure so typical of much of Bergman's prose fiction. The story upon which the action of the play is based is a simple one: a beautiful and innocent young girl, Anne-Marie, who stands in a somewhat vaguely defined relation to two elderly spinsters in whose home she lives, is forced to entertain, and finally to accept, a proposed marriage tendered indirectly through the spinsters by a lecherous old man, Mr. Sleeman, though she is in love with a handsome, dashing young forester and its quite naturally revolted at the idea of marriage with Mr. Sleeman. Out of this naïve fairy-tale motif, apparently little suited to the dramatic expression of a modern mood, Bergman evokes gradually, by means of a number of skillfully manipulated symbolistic techniques, a dramatically intensified spirit of pure horror which gives utterance with terrifying indirectness to a thoroughly modern conception of the tragic irrationality of human fate. Every detail of dramatic technique is purposely stylized, thrown out of normal focus, in order to suggest the essentially marionette-like nature of human fate: something or someone seems to be drawing wires behind the scene of human activity in this world of ours, and that something or someone is blindly irrational, if not deliberately evil, in its sardonic, apparently meaningless play with human life. As in the case of Maeterlinck there rests, however, over the action of Bergman's little play a soft, almost evanescent shimmer of poetry. The action of the play is steeped in symbolistic indirections, and the unselfish, ideal love of Anne-Marie for her forester remains unblemished and, spiritually at least, triumphant over the clammy approaches of lustful senility. Mr. Sleeman finally "comes" at the end of the play to claim his bride, but he does not triumph over Anne-Marie's spirit. She accepts him — mechanically, only as the inevitable, as fate itself.

Hjalmar Bergman's sense of terror in the presence of life's apparently meaningless brutalities, as well as his warm sympathy for its helpless victims, is shared by his younger contemporary Pär Lagerkvist (b. 1891), in whose person and work Swedish literature in the last half century has its greatest and on the whole most representative figure. That which chiefly distinguishes Lagerkvist's work from Bergman's is, first, what may be called its metaphysical and religious preoccupations to the almost total exclusion of narrowly psychological considerations, and secondly, its persistent search for new, more effective literary forms, a search which in Lagerkvist's case finds expression both in deliberate theorizing about matters of form and in constant creative experimentation designed to discover and perfect only those forms which are most *expressive*. Lagerkvist is the first great Swedish literary "expressionist" after Strindberg, and he remains down to our day its most brilliant and consistent representative in Sweden. Lagerkvist had from the start of his career nothing but scorn for the prevailing realism of the day with its careful documentation and its emphasis on environmental conditioning factors, and though in later years his attitude toward conventional literary forms became less belligerent he has never in any essential ways departed from the literary program which he envisioned from the beginning. In fact, so consistent has been the pattern of Lagerkvist's literary development that the pattern retains at all times its basic core while only its more peripheral elements remain relatively flexible, undergoing such partial transformations as are determined by the tense interplay between his high artistic standards and the uneasy, at times grotesquely fearsome ebb and flow of contemporary life. So intent has he always been on finding the ideal form for his vision of life that he has written extensively in all the recognized literary genres — lyric poetry, drama, prose fiction of various kinds, autobiographical sketches, aphoristic prose, etc. But he never leaves these genres where he finds them, he subjects each of them to the demands of his *expressive* ideal — always with interesting, not infrequently with impressive, results. Lagerkvist went his own way in Swedish letters from the start, lighted only to begin with by French cubistic art and by fitful flashes from the formidable workshop of Strindberg's dramatic expressionism. Only with time did Lagerkvist's countrymen recognize in his work a spirit and a technical daring strangely appropriate to the crisis-filled realities of the contemporary world, but when his work became thus recognized it served as a basic — if not actually *the* basic — point of departure for a revolutionary renewal of Swedish literature.

In his personal life Lagerkvist has always chosen to remain isolated, never identifying himself with any literary coterie, shunning public appearances as a matter of principle, limiting his personal contacts to a few friends. What is necessary for us to know about his early life he has provided in the sketch of his childhood and youth in *Gäst hos verkligheten* (tr. *Guest of Reality*, 1925). In this work he draws a sharp contrast between the spirit of quiet religious assurance which suffused his childhood home and the growing feeling of terror in the presence of life's realities and death's potential horrors which came to dominate his childhood fantasies. His parents, both of poor but solid Småland peasant stock, had moved to the cathedral town of Växjö, where his father was employed on the railroad, with the family inhabiting a small apartment on the second floor of the railway station. Attracted though the young Lagerkvist was to the protective comfort of loving parents and a pious home, he could not accept their God, and before the end of his schooldays he had under the impact of modern scientific ideas broken with the religion of his forefathers and tentatively identified himself with the advanced socialistic radicalism of the day. His earliest literary efforts were conducted partly under the banner of the new workingmen's cause, but his active identification with its program of economic and social radicalism came soon to be displaced by a campaign of literary radicalism which attracted in some quarters considerable attention. This campaign may be said to have lasted the better part of a decade beginning in 1912, and included the publication of two highly provocative critical essays — *Ordkonst och bildkonst* (Word Art and Pictorial Art, 1913) and *Modern teater: synpunkter och angrepp* (Modern Theater: Points of View and Attacks, 1918) — together with a number of volumes of poetry, prose, and drama which were intended more or less deliberately to provide examples of the new kind of literature which Lagerkvist champions in the critical essays.

Though to begin with Lagerkvist's work aroused enthusiasm only here and there in the Swedish reading public and among critics, it served to introduce an author of disturbing modernity and to announce with unequivocal importunity the claims of an expressionistic literary ideal — an ideal which thundered, like the cannonading of the World War to the South, over those literary ranks in Sweden which preferred complacently to continue employing in their work a relatively conventional literary realism. But ultimately — in the years after the War — the expressionistic seed which Lagerkvist sowed during the war years bore fruit at many crucial points on the Swedish literary scene. He was a voice crying in the wilderness for only a limited period of time. He had finished his *Sturm und Drang* years and attained literary maturity at just the time when his public, conditioned by catastrophic world developments, was prepared to listen seriously to his strangely phrased but sharply arresting modern parables on man and God and the grim mysteries of existence.

In *Word Art and Pictorial Art* Lagerkvist pleads for a return of literature to the abstract mathematical ideals of contemporary cubistic painting and certain related forms in primitive art and literature. He recommends as models for the modern poet those literary works which are simple and straightforward in manner and which are concerned with man's direct, unsophisticated "feelings in the presence of life's eternal powers." Among the works he recommends are: from the East, the Old Testament, the Rig-Veda hymns, the Avesta canon, and the Koran; from the Nordic tradition, the Eddic poets and the Icelandic sagas, the ancient

Vignette by Isaac Grünewald for Pär Lagerkvist's
Word Art and Pictorial Art

Swedish provincial laws, and the folk ballads. When Lagerkvist in *Motiv, dikter på vers och prosa* (Motifs, Poems in Verse and Prose, 1914) first seeks to apply his theories, he is not particularly successful. But in the war-conscious volumes *Järn och människor* (Iron and Men, 1915) and *Ångest* (Anguish, 1916) he is considerably more impressive, partly because he has sacrificed some of the more rigidly formal literary ideals which he championed in *Word Art and Pictorial Art*. Especially in *Anguish*, the collection of poetry which is Lagerkvist's first major work, he is moving away from the abstract formalistic ideals of cubism toward the fragmented, violently explosive patterns of expressionism, the literary ideal which becomes central in his long critical essay *Modern Theater* and the group of dramatic sketches and plays written toward the close of and immediately after the First World War. In *Modern Theater* Lagerkvist attacks the realistic-naturalistic tradition in the theater as represented particularly by Ibsen's one-wall-away drama with its limited perspectives and its "silent treading on carpets through five long acts with words, words, words." Ibsen, he feels, can be ignored by the dramatist of today — but not Strindberg. The Strindberg of the religious-expressionistic plays, Lagerkvist insists, "stands in the middle of the way, and one cannot slip past him except by understanding him." Besides Strindberg's post-Inferno plays, Lagerkvist feels that the vivid, primitive, highly pictorial qualities of the medieval drama can be studied with profit by the modern dramatist.

Lagerkvist's eagerness in his early dramas to follow Strindberg, together with his early lack of familiarity with dramatic composition, led him in these plays into certain theatrical excesses and into unfortunate obscurities of one kind and another. But on the whole these plays reveal a dramatist of an imaginative intensity and power seldom found in the Scandinavian theater. The best of his early plays is *Himlens hemlighet* (The Secret of Heaven, 1919), in which the dramatist conjures up a ghastly vision of life upon the earth. Upon the stage emerges, with ominous deliberation, a vast convex surface representing the earth, on which one discerns through the shadows a motley and pitiable array of human beings, emaciated in body and warped in spirit, sitting listlessly or crawling aimlessly about in brutal disregard of one another, incapable of a noble thought or an ideal emotion — whilst God, a helpless old man, observes the scene passively, if not indifferently, from a great distance in the heavens. Into this scene of creeping horrors enters for a fleeting moment a single clear note of love, only to be drowned in the fearful cacophony of moans and shrieks and lamentations that emanates from the assemblage of the damned. Such is life, the dramatist would suggest — mean and low, hopelessly indifferent, utterly brutal in its darksome, meaningless, fateful drift. Goodness and love are but transitory guests in the pitiful household of man: they serve perhaps but to mock mankind in its otherwise complete and ultimate misery. It was the philosophical implications of a deterministic science, forced into terrifying relief by the holocaust of the First World War, that had driven the brooding speculative genius of Lagerkvist to such a view of life.

But in Lagerkvist's work in the 1920's his desperate pessimism comes by degrees to be displaced by a relatively positive view of life, in which he gives expression to his faith in the human spirit's ability to rise above evil and to cast off at least in part the shackles of the material world. Lagerkvist gradually becomes reconciled, not to life, which he still finds evil, but to man, whom he comes both to sympathize with and to revere. In 1927 appeared the great prose monologue *Det besegrade livet* (The Triumph over Life), which gives magnificent aphoristic expression to Lagerkvist's faith in man and becomes the positive point of departure for much of his later work. At the same time that his view of life changes, Lagerkvist's plays undergo a gradual technical change away from the purely visionary, somewhat obscure manner of the early plays and toward a more simple, tangible form, which may perhaps best be described as a kind of expressionistic naïvism. Symbols and diverse expressionistic devices are employed more sparingly, and the episodic element is simplified by permitting the action to take place in a world of immediate recognizable actuality. But the dramatist's primary preoccupation remains man's *soul*, in the metaphysical and religious senses of the term; he is still concerned centrally with the problem of good and evil. The first play that reveals the shift in Lagerkvist's dramatic form is *Han som fick leva om sitt liv* (He Who Was Permitted to Live His Life Over Again, 1928), the action of which takes place in a shoemaker's shop, with the dramatist employing only two bits of visionary technique, both of which could be eliminated with no fundamental loss in dramatic effect. It is with a subtle, quietly unassuming art that Lagerkvist in this play manages to give universal human significance to the struggle between good and evil that goes on in the shoemaker's soul. By careful self-discipline the shoemaker controls the evil within himself, but when in an unguarded moment he criticizes his son, he brings about the young man's self-destruction. The point seems to be that goodness and evil are infinitely pervasive forces, maintained in the most delicate and precarious balance in the human soul and in all human relationships; one man may destroy another even as he is concerned with saving his own soul.

In the 1930's Lagerkvist's art and thought undergo in general a process of further maturing in the directions suggested by the play *He Who Was Permitted to Live His Life Over Again*. His concern with the problem of good and evil finds expression now, however, with reference particularly to contemporary political developments as reflected in the rise of political totalitarianism. The two plays which most directly express Lagerkvist's indignation with Fascism and Nazism are the dramatized version of the short novel *Bödeln* (tr. *The Hangman*, 1933) and *Mannen utan själ* (tr. *The Man Without a Soul*, 1936). Of these two works *The Hangman* represents a temporary return to Lagerkvist's earlier horror moods and visionary techniques while *The Man Without a Soul* is finely representative of his later more subtle and delicate art. In many ways, indeed, *The Hangman* is the most sensational of Lagerkvist's works, both in its highly experimental form and in the savage force with which it drives its message home. The central figure of the play is The Hangman himself — grisly symbol of the idea, born of medieval superstition, that good may come of evil, that violence, brutality, and bloodshed are in some mysterious way the instruments of progress. The play consists of two striking scenes, with no pause between them: the first scene, a dimly lighted medieval tavern, the second, a brilliantly lighted, garishly furnished modern jazz restaurant-dance hall. In the first scene ignorant beer-guzzling workmen react half in fascination, half in horror to the sinister figure of The Hangman, sitting alone in one corner of the tavern; in the second, men and women dressed in evening apparel, with a scattering of gray field military uniforms, work themselves up into a frenzy of admiration for The Hangman, who symbolizes for them the essence of the modern political spirit. The application to Hitler-dominated Nazi Germany is unmistakable. The play gains much of its terrifying power of utterance by the skillful use of modern cinematic devices and startling lighting effects as well as by the focal use of The Hangman, a huge hulk of a man, silent, brooding, massively portentous with his blood-red cloak and sepulchral features.

In sharp contrast with the effective use of sensational theatrical tricks in *The Hangman*, the art of *The Man Without a Soul* is quiet, controlled, starkly bare in outline and movement. Its dialogue is laconic, abrupt, charged with between-the-lines meanings, in which that which is not said is frequently as important as that which is said. Its characters are conceived only in their essential selves: we know next to nothing about the mere outward accidents of their existence. The central emphasis of the play is an inner ethical one, concerned solely with the moral consequences of a recently committed political murder. The chief character, "The Man," who has committed the murder, comes by accident to fall in love with "The Woman" who bore the child of the murderer's victim. Though the murderer's love is not, cannot be, reciprocated, it effects by degrees a fundamental change in his character — from a callous instrument of a mechanical political doctrine (a man "without a soul") to one who comes to see that only in the mystic humanism of brotherly love and sacrifice can life ultimately fulfill its mysterious and elevated mission. The story of the drama contains Lagerkvist's uncompromising protest against the brutalizing tendencies of modern political trends, particularly that tendency to manipulate forms of hysterical sophistry in order to deny the moral worth of our common sense of humanity. That which is meant by "soul" in *The Man Without a Soul* is the belief in a sense of common humanity in times which are frequently inhumane, in times when the loudmouthed catchwords of propaganda are so apt to obliterate those fundamental humane values which man's soul cries out for in its best and purest moments. "The Man" in Lagerkvist's play never finds peace in his life, in part because his offense has been so great, in part because life, as Lagerkvist sees it, is scarcely capable, at least in our stage of development, of bringing peace to mankind. But the restless longing which fills The Man's breast at the close of the play symbolizes man's *search* for truth down through the ages, and the promise is held out that this restless longing in the heart of man may be the instrument which the world of creation in some mysterious way may use to effect its ultimate salvation.

In the 1940's three plays came from Lagerkvist's pen, the philosophical drama in medieval dress with modern ethical overtones *De vises sten* (The Philosopher's Stone, 1947), and two plays — *Midsommardröm i fattighuset* (tr. *Midsummer Dream in a Workhouse*, 1941) and *Låt männ-iskan leva* (tr. *Let Man Live*, 1949) — which reflect in addition to the dramatist's concern with universal moral questions his continuing interest in modern dramatic experimentation. On the theme of *The Philos-opher's Stone*, Lagerkvist remarked in a letter to the present writer immediately after he had completed the play: "It deals with a medieval alchemist and a rabbi, the West and the East, and many other things — especially about other things. It is the work of my old age [*mitt 'ålder-domsverk'*], and many years of thinking lie behind it." Among the "other things" to which he refers is the problem of human responsibility as it often *isn't* observed by the scientist and theologian — so intent on their narrow search for "truth" that they lose contact with human values and more or less unwittingly become instruments of evil and destruction. Not least is Lagerkvist concerned here with the moral implications of the atom bomb. The play has a number of thematic points of contact with Maxwell Anderson's *Joan of Lorraine*. In form it is the most conventional of Lagerkvist's plays. In *Midsummer Dream in a Workhouse*, on the other hand, Lagerkvist experiments with a strange blend of delicate dream elements and a coarse realism of situation and dialogue to produce a dramatic fantasy of haunting beauty, while in *Let Man Live* he departs completely from conventional dramatic forms, creating an intense series of dramatic tableaux in which is developed (with variations, as in musical composition) the theme that man should not be so eager to judge man, that he frequently in the process commits evil rather than serves the purposes of truth and justice.

As *Let Man Live* opens, fourteen characters, ranging from Christ and Socrates down through Giordano Bruno and Jeanne d'Arc to a Second World War underground fighter and an American Negro, stand in a semicircle before a backdrop of darkness on an absolutely bare stage. Diverse as are their origins, their stations in life, and their identifications with historical periods, they are all related to one another in their common fate as martyrs, victims of man's readiness down through history to judge his fellows and condemn them even to death. Each martyr in his turn steps forward, giving his name and the bare facts on the occasion of his martyrdom, and returns to his place in the background. Then each returns (in some cases on two different occasions) to the front of the stage, relating in some detail the story of his martyrdom and commenting — in some cases bitterly, in others with varying degrees of resignation — on the inhumanity of man to man as it affects his case. Neither dialogue nor action nor scene in the usual dramatic sense is employed in *Let Man Live*, yet the play has undeniable dramatic qualities. What Lagerkvist is seeking to do is to cut away all dramatic excrescences and to present each character in his innermost self, spiritually *naked* as it were. He does not perhaps always succeed in this intention, but in several cases at least — such as those of the peasant, put to death for stealing a shoulder of mutton, and Comtesse de la Roche-Montfaucon, full of aristocratic scorn for the rabble and its crude instrument, the guillotine — the dramatist manages by use of a concentrated, highly explosive language and by the employment of suggestive gesture and powerful mimicry to create a sense of starkly focused dramatic intensity. Continuity and a sense of rising dramatic movement are attained by employing a kind of musical technique in the development of theme. The label "stage oratorio" which has been applied to the play is superficially descriptive in the formal outward sense that each actor (as the soloist in an oratorio) delivers his words directly to the audience; but the label "theme with variations" is more profoundly descriptive in its implication that the idea central in *Let Man Live* is first introduced, like the theme of a musical composition, in a simple, relatively naked form, and then taken up under other circumstances in more complex contexts, with finally the whole "development" being pulled together in a logically acceptable form. The fact that Lagerkvist's "thought" in *Let Man Live* is not always "clear" may suggest another sense in which this little drama provides a literary counterpart to the technique of musical composition.

The quality of unadorned directness of utterance which becomes with the years increasingly characteristic of Lagerkvist's dramatic composition may be said to be even more the distinguishing mark of his poetry and prose fiction. His nine books of poetry and ten volumes of prose fiction to date reflect at almost every point a striving toward utter simplicity of diction and syntax and imagery, of rhythmic qualities and over-all patterns of form. It is in this respect that his poetry departs most sharply from that of his great Swedish predecessors of the 1890's, who moved so readily in a rhetorical, colorful, image-loaded poetic world. Though Lagerkvist at times modeled his earliest poetry (that of the volumes *Motifs*, 1914, and *Anguish*, 1916) too consciously after the rigidly controlled cubism, the primitive naïvism, and the violently explosive expressionism of the day, he soon perfected an expressionistic naïvism of his own which became an ideal instrument for expressing the conflicting interplay between affirmation and skepticism, light and darkness, the ideal and the earthbound, which is the mark of so much of Lagerkvist's mature poetry. It is a far cry from the demonstrative near-hysteria of the lines from *Motifs*,

> My prayer speaks no caressing words. No
> supplinat hands it lifts.
> My prayer is a roar which slobbers from the
> mouth —

or the opening stanza of the title-poem from *Anguish*,

> Anguish, anguish is my heritage,
> my throat's wound,
> my heart's shriek in the world.
> Now stiffens lathery skies
> in night's coarse hand,
> now rise the forests
> and rigid summits
> barren against the heaven's
> stunted vault.
> How stark is all,
> how stiffened, black, and silent —

to the cryptic, utterly unadorned solemnity of the closing stanzas in "I stället för tro" (In Place of Faith) from *Kaos* (1920),

> I am no one. I am yearning
> now to darkness, then to light.
> I was no one, but a yearning
> stifled, stunted by a blight.
>
> I must die so you may live,
> all shall die that is not you.
> On that grave you smiling live,
> all forgot which was not you.

So skeletal is the art of these two four-line strophes that neither the concretion of a clear image nor the embellishment of a haunting rhythm is permitted to interfere with the direct humanity of their utterance.

In matters of verse form Lagerkvist employs with equal skill free, un-rhymed verse and conventional poetic patterns, but he never uses meter and rhyme as obtrusively as had been the practice of his Swedish pred-ecessors. Poetry to him is primarily an exercise in extracting from ex-perience its essence, and as such it must not parade obvious metrical pat-terns which tend to call attention to themselves. Whatever "music" his verse may have serves simply to provide a quiet undercurrent of accom-paniment for the profounder purposes of his art. These purposes being in the last analysis metaphysical and religious, the imagery and symbolism in Lagerkvist's poetry tends to be drawn from larger cosmic phenomena without losing contact with terrestrial realities, the simple things of everyday life. At times his poetic naïvism drifts almost imperceptibly over into pure idyllicism, as in such exquisite reminiscential distillations of his mother's simple faith and scenes from the Småland countryside as are evoked in "Det kom ett brev" (A Letter Came), "Nu vänder mor sitt bibelblad" (Now Mother Turns the Bible Page), and "En mor som hämtar in en kväll" (A Mother Who Fetches in One Eve) from *Den lyckliges väg* (The Way of the Happy One, 1921) and *Genius* (1937). But much more often Lagerkvist's poetry is more complex, a poetry in which his inner tensions are caught up in alternately agitated and quies-cent symbols — that of a desperately frustrated humanity in "Torso" (*Hjärtats sånger*, Songs of the Heart, 1926), or that of a brooding, truth-seeking wanderer on the earth in "Ej bjudes till fest" (Uninvited to Festivities) and "Staven faller ur vår hand" (The Staff Falls from Our Hand) from *Vid lägereld* (Beside the Watch-Fire, 1932), or that which views existence as a vast enigmatic desert area as in many of the poems of Lagerkvist's last volume of verse *Aftonland* (Evening Land, 1953). Among the *Evening Land* poems which depart from the recurrent desert symbolism of the volume is one of the most powerful, the one which em-ploys an arresting theatrical symbol to suggest the essential pettiness of man's life and the apparently final devastation of his fate:

> All shall be forgotten. All human destinies
> shall shuffle down oblivion's murky stairs
> and be extinguished in the final darkness.
> All shall be extinguished. The tragedy has ended,
> footlights darkened, all the stars of heaven
> which witnessed have the cruel action,
> meaningless and meager in its evil.
> Empty stage, with shabby wings,
> and the poisoned dagger men have used

'gainst one another tossed aside on rubbish
heap.

Oblivion, silence. Nought to live in memory.
None who can remember.
Emptiness.

Was this all?
That we know not.

The quietly questioning final lines of this poem are as typical of Lagerkvist's mature prose as of his poetry, as characteristic of the finely chiseled novels *Barabbas* (tr. *Barabbas*, 1950) and *Sibyllan* (tr. *The Sibyl*,
1956) as of the verse of *Evening Land*.

But Lagerkvist's way to the prose perfection of *Barabbas* and *The
Sibyl* was long and somewhat devious, a way which in his earlier prose
moved by preference in various shorter fictional forms. Because of his
aversion to detailed sociological documentation and the piling up of
psychological minutiae, he had from the start no use for the conventional realistic novel of the day. Of the five volumes of prose in which
his shorter narrative pieces have appeared, the first two, *Människor*
(People, 1912) and *Järn och människor* (Iron and People, 1915), pour
their anguished narrative material into rigid cubistic and writhing expressionistic molds, while the remaining three, *Onda sagor* (tr. *Evil
Tales*, 1924), *Kämpande ande* (Struggling Spirit, 1930), and *I den tiden*
(In That Time, 1935), clothe their shifting moods and points of view in
an astonishing diversity of narrative patterns: in the symbolical episode
and the fable, in moralizing fairy tales and grimly satiric sketches, in
simple realistic tales and lurid episodic sequences reminiscent of Lagerkvist's violently visionary early works. In many of the shorter pieces he
has learned from such masters of the concise narrative genres as Swift
and Voltaire and the Baudelaire of *Petits Poëmes en prose*, but he has
learned so well that only occasionally is the influence of his masters as
apparent as in the Swiftian piece "The Children's Campaign," which
owes so much to both *Gulliver's Travels* and *A Modest Proposal for Pre-
venting the Children of Poor People from Being a Burden to Their Parents*. Among the best of the pieces from *Evil Tales*, *Struggling Spirit*,
and *In That Time* are "Father and I," with its skillful use of a deeply
disturbing childhood experience to symbolize man's sense of terror in
the presence of darkly inexplicable phenomena, "The Elevator Which
Went Down to Hell," with its brutally scabrous pointing up of the cheap
expedients of sexual promiscuity, "The Basement Apartment" and "The

Marriage Feast," with their simple realism and their warm understanding of the "little people" of the earth, and "The Venerated Bones" and "The Children's Campaign," with their devastating commentary on misplaced patriotism and the heroic pose in the conduct of war.

Except for the two recent novels *Barabbas* and *The Sibyl*, Lagerkvist's prose fiction in the larger forms has appeared at rather lengthy intervals — *Det eviga leendet* (tr. *The Eternal Smile*) in 1921, *Bödeln* (tr. *The Hangman*) in 1933, and *Dvärgen* (tr. *The Dwarf*) in 1944. The shifting attitudes toward life and the diversity of forms among these works were determined largely by the differing sets of circumstances in which each was conceived and executed. *The Eternal Smile*, written in a relatively calm mood after the violent negativism of Lagerkvist's early work had spent its force, reflects a desire to become reconciled to life despite its many stupid, frustrating limitations. *The Hangman* and *The Dwarf*, conceived under the bloody skies of European political developments in the 1930's and the Second World War which followed, are profoundly pessimistic works, studies in the darkly destructive instincts of man. *Barabbas* and *The Sibyl*, written during the quiet early-evening years of Lagerkvist's development, are simply phrased but many-faceted works in which life's mysterious ebb and flow between sterility and relative fruitfulness, frustration and partial attainment, is reflected in a prose at once delicately sensitive and sharply — at times harshly — intense.

In general these works reflect a constant search for the most expressive over-all structural form, *The Eternal Smile* employing a free cosmic-fantasy manner with the addition of naïvistic and realistic ingredients, *The Hangman* reducing the elements of scene and action to a couple of visionary, highly explosive central symbols, *The Dwarf* providing a corrosive focus for its disillusioned view of life by limiting our area of vision to that determined by the extended monologue of the central character, *Barabbas* and *The Sibyl* building up their thematic sequences by means in each case of a short series of carefully selected tableau-like symbolical episodes. Such highly original narrative patterns did not always find favor with Lagerkvist's reading public and his critics, some of the latter, for instance, being disturbed by what they considered an unfortunate (that is to say un-Dante-like) blending of the sublime and the trivial in the vast cosmic contexts of *The Eternal Smile*, others being moved to protest against what they felt to be the excessive brutalities of *The Hangman*. But such judgments were by no means universal. And in any event whatever critical dissent had existed with regard to *The Eternal Smile*,

The Hangman, and other prose works was silenced on the appearance of *The Dwarf* and *Barabbas*. All Swedish critics bowed in the presence of these two masterpieces, and so great was the success of *The Dwarf* with the reading public that Lagerkvist, after thirty years of going his own way without concerning himself with public taste, finally achieved with this thoroughly Lagerkvistian work a "best seller." With *Barabbas* in 1950 and the Nobel Prize a year later he achieved world recognition.

Of all the problems with which Lagerkvist has wrestled through a long literary career, the problem of evil occupies a central place. In his early work he tended to identify evil with a condition of life outside man, and he in consequence condemned life and revered man, life's desperately helpless victim. But later, particularly under the impact of European political developments in the 1930's, he came to see that in man himself existed a destructive instinct, a basic drift toward that which is evil. During the years which preceded the outbreak of the Second World War, Lagerkvist's primary concern was with this brutalizing drift and with those human potentials for good which might counterbalance man's destructive instinct. In *The Hangman* and *In That Time* he depicts some of the most terrifying manifestations of man's suicidal drift toward darkness and evil. In *Den knutna näven* (The Clenched Fist, 1934), a group of essays inspired by a visit to Greece and other Eastern Mediterranean lands, he pleads humanity's ancient cause against the rising totalitarianism of a latter day. In the shadow of the Parthenon he defies modern barbarism in the name of a "fighting humanism," with its ideals of sanity and reason, freedom and justice for all. But his cries of defiance were scarcely heard in the rapidly gathering darkness over Europe which led to the Second World War. *The Dwarf*, which appeared toward the end of the War, is Lagerkvist's crushing commentary on human evil as manifest in the war spirit whenever and wherever it has flourished and gathered its sinister harvest of death and ghastly mutilation.

Never before had Lagerkvist been as completely in control of his artistic instrument as he was in the measured probing of the ways of evil in *The Dwarf*, which has been described quite correctly as "the coldest, most disciplined of Swedish prose masterpieces." Even in its most lurid scenes (and these are not a few) Lagerkvist's artistic control of his material is absolute, calculated to lay bare with the utmost precision the ways of evil on the human scene. The central figure of the novel, a Court Dwarf, is in many ways the very incarnation of evil. Hunchbacked and revengeful, he spies on all manner of human folly around him, feels superior to it, and yet in his own spiritual sterility he becomes the most destructive of all the forces loosed in the fearsome, festering, bloody tale of life in Renaissance Italy of which he is a part. The story would not be from Lagerkvist's pen, however, if the Dwarf were in the last analysis a simple character, merely the incarnation of evil. He is something more — or less. He hates everything that is good, elevated, pure, particularly the purity of young love — *because* he himself cannot attain to virtue. His destructive desperation results from a sense of isolation, from his having been "left outside" by the accident of being born dwarfish and hunchbacked. He has no means of communication with the community of man.

The same is true in a somewhat less absolute sense of the central figure in *Barabbas*. The brutish outlaw-outsider in whose stead Christ had died lives in Lagerkvist's novel in a world of shadows and dies in an hour of impenetrable darkness, but he senses less dimly than the Dwarf the presence of good and he gropes blindly toward a faith which he cannot achieve. The Christ whose death he had witnessed exercises a strangely persistent spell over him, a spell which forces him to break with his criminal past and wander restlessly over the face of the earth in a fumbling, ever-shadowed, finally hopeless search for a truth which might set his spirit free. He lives his life outside the community of man and the communion of God despite his ill-defined yearning toward both, and in the end — when by an ironic turn of fate he dies what appears to be a martyr's death — he meets death as the Great Unknown if not actually the Great Nothingness.

When he felt death approaching, that which he had always been so afraid of, he said out into the darkness, as though he were speaking to it:
— To thee I deliver up my soul.
And then he gave up the ghost.

Harsh were the conditions of life for Barabbas, bitter and lonely his way, but his tragedy had its moments of half-belief bordering precariously on serenity of spirit. His soul could not soar because he was too earth-bound, too human, blinded by the very resplendence of a triumphant faith. The novel which sketches his fate is born by a monumental simplicity of phrase and symbol and episodic progression, always rooted to the earth (at times brutally so) and yet suffused with a sense of larger perspectives, those of a tortured soul seeking largely in vain its God.

In *The Sibyl* the problems propounded and the questions raised in *Barabbas* are pursued further, now in primitive Apollonian rather than early Christian contexts. But the problems remain equally complex, the questions elicit equally indecisive answers. Lagerkvist is in his latest work no more a prophet with a final message for man than he was at the beginning of his career. He remains the constant questioner, the eternal seeker — eruptive and serene, earthy and elevated by turn, never cynical, ever profoundly human. He is a visionary deeply rooted in the things of the earth, for to him man's search for truth is not in the last analysis an abstract leap beyond the circumscribed conditions of existence but rather an immediate grappling with the confused profusion of life. Though the sharp limitations of existence seem to Lagerkvist often brutal and terrifying almost beyond human endurance, he feels that man's spirit, no matter how sorely tried, manages somehow, at least in its best moments, to rise above these limitations and create, albeit gropingly and only step by step, positive moral values which transcend the confines of a merely outward existence. This is the miracle of life, unpretentious and only partly triumphant though it may prove to be.

Contemporary Swedish literature's third portal figure, Birger Sjöberg (1885–1929), appeared on the literary horizon with rocket-like suddenness in his thirty-eighth year, maintained a brilliant glow for a brief period, and passed on almost as suddenly as he had appeared. The work published during his lifetime spanned but five years and included two volumes of poetry, *Fridas bok* (Frida's Book, 1922) and *Kriser och kransar* (Crises and Laurel Wreaths, 1926), and one novel, *Kvartetten som sprängdes* (The Quartette Which Was Broken Up, 1924). After his death two other volumes appeared, a second series of Frida songs (1929) and a selection from some three thousand poems and poetic fragments which he left behind, and which came to be published under the title *Minnen från jorden* (Memories from the Earth, 1940).

Born in West Central Sweden at Vänersborg on the southern tip of Lake Väner, Sjöberg left school at an early age and tried his hand at a number of occupations, settling down finally to a journalistic career, first, for a year at Stockholm, then permanently in Hälsingborg, on the west coast. Though he took his journalistic duties seriously enough, he became known chiefly in west coast circles as a person of unusual social talents, one who could always be depended upon to add a lively waggish note to private and semi-public parties with his remarkable mimic and musical gifts. For many years he entertained friends and a large circle of acquaintants with songs of his own composition which he sang to the accompaniment of a guitar, but it was apparently not until he was well up in his thirties that he considered seriously appearing before a larger public with a published volume of these songs. The step was finally taken with *Frida's Book*, which turned out to be fabulously successful among practically all segments of the Swedish reading public. Sjöberg was hailed as a twentieth-century Bellman and found himself launched on a triumphal "Frida songs" concert tour which took him to many parts of Sweden. But neither the comparison with Bellman nor the public adulation pleased him, and in violent reaction against being thus labeled and lionized he withdrew into himself, determined to demonstrate that his poetic resources were equal to something far more significant than the amiable felicities of *Frida's Book*. The result — after he had unburdened himself of the relatively unimportant but highly popular Dickensian novel *The Quartette Which Was Broken Up* — was *Crises and Laurel Wreaths*, a volume of verse so volcanic in its naked confrontation with life and so startlingly original in form that it has become a focal work in modern Swedish poetry.

The Vänersborg of Sjöberg's childhood and young manhood provides the material of *Frida's Book*, with its lively but eminently respectable middle-class miscellany of lodge meetings and choral rehearsals, picnics and circus performances, "learned" homilies on nature and the universe, and romantic promenades in the city's environs. It is a peaceful, limited, complacent lower-middle-class world as seen through the fond spectacles of a poet's memory, which manages to avoid excessive sentimentality of recall by a gently judicious use of parody and playful irony. The "Frida" of this book was in reality a Karin Lustine whom Sjöberg had in his early years courted in vain, and the shy but ambitious and aspiring young clerk who in the book remains unnamed is the young Sjöberg himself. Aside from the happy combination of words and music in *Frida's Book*, that which in particular distinguishes the work is its remarkable concretion and precision in depicting the banal activities of a small provincial community and its subtle blend of genuine tenderness and sly parody in its affectionate probing of the harmlessly naïve, self-complacent mentality of this community. Though a half-superior note breaks through at many points, it is clear that Sjöberg loves even the faults of his Vänersborg folk.

But this was the sleepy, self-contained, patriarchal Vänersborg of Sjöberg's childhood and youth, not the aggressively alive, viciously competitive, sanguinary reality of the world today. And in *Crises and Laurel*

Wreaths the idyllic harmonies of *Frida's Book* exploded into the ghastly cacophonies of a tormented modern verse. Abrupt as the shift from the idyl to a brutal modernity of mood and utterance may seem, it is quite understandable in terms of Sjöberg's temperament and the pressures to which he was subjected in his last years. Sjöberg was an extraordinarily sensitive genius, with schizophrenic tendencies and subject to recurrent periods of profound depression. *Frida's Book* reflects only one side of his temperament — the more superficial side, which sought desperately for a world of light in a world of gathering darkness. But even in *Frida's Book* the world of darkness is not completely excluded, for this work includes the gripping poem "Bleka Dödens minut" (Pale Death's Moment), in which the shabby reality of death is depicted with unforgettable starkness and force. And in *The Quartette Which Was Broken Up* elements of the macabre now and then break through the fantastic surface grotesquerie of dialogue and action — to remind us, as it were, that man's mad play with life is conducted over areas where Death is master and a madcap escapism no longer permits the illusion of joy and happiness.

In *Crises and Laurel Wreaths* two circumstances combined to bring into almost unbearable focus the gloomy view of life of which we are only peripherally aware in *Frida's Book* and *The Quartette Which Was Broken Up*. The fearful carnage of the First World War and its hectic aftermath, together with the strain occasioned by the fabulous success of Sjöberg's first two works, precipitated in the poet a nervous condition bordering on madness. Out of this erupted a new art form, a poetry of broken cadences, of fierce concentration of phrase, of darkly fragmented imaginative splendor. So violent was the upheaval within Sjöberg when he poured out the agony of his soul in *Crises and Laurel Wreaths* that the work is uneven in quality, sometimes all but hopelessly obscure, at other times confused and fumbling to the point where a sense of sustained artistic creation is difficult to discern. But the best of the poems in the volume (and they are not a few) are startlingly impressive both as human documents and as highly original modern art. Absent — or transformed to a point where they are difficult of identification — are nearly all of the distinguishing features of Sjöberg's earlier poetry: its sinuous or merely "lively" rhythms, its precise concretion of image and situation, its clear episodic sequences. These are replaced in *Crises and Laurel Wreaths* by irregular, nervously pounding rhythms, by unfinished, angular blocks of imagery, by narrative sequences so loosely tied together that only the alert reader is apt to discern the over-all narrative pattern. And all of this operates against a background of shifting, frequently shadow-like substance, a dream world limbo of predominantly ominous mood and coloration.

In a few of the more calm pieces such as "Min fordran är ej ringa —" (My Claim Is Not Small), "Drömmar famnas" (Dreams Embrace), and the lovely return to Frida's world entitled "Cantilena comunale," crystal-clear rhythmic and imagistic patterns drive home the poet's thought with unerring economy of phrase and serene elevation of spirit. But much more often the subject matter of a given poem in *Crises and Laurel Wreaths* so overwhelms the poet that he is forced to resort to technical innovations of the most modern kind in order to give adequate expression to the tortured agitation of his spirit. In the poems in which this emotional turmoil does not get completely out of hand Sjöberg has given us modern poetry of the very first order. Among the most impressive of these poems are "Statyernas samkväm" (Meeting of the Statues), "Av raka linjen" (Straight of Line), and "Konferensman" (Conference Man), in each of which the poet is concerned in one context or other with the often grotesque disparity between outward form and inner spirit, between the world of evasive convention and the world of brutal reality. In pregnancy of utterance and sustained development of theme "Conference Man" stands alone in Sjöberg's production. In narrative outline this poem sketches the professional career of a conscientious clergyman who is driven to desperation and finally to madness by the outward pretentiousness and the inner sterility of the ecclesiastical organization of which he is a part. His awareness of ecclesiastical pretension and its evasive mentality reaches madly climactic proportions at a world religious conference (obviously the Stockholm Ecumenical Congress of 1925), where the petty protocol and politely abstract doctrinal discussion are dutifully pursued while the crying immediate needs of a ravaged post-war humanity are neglected.

The inner agitation and growing madness of the clergyman in the presence of life's grotesque anachronisms as reflected in his Conference experiences provide the psychological and moral conditions out of which the poem's modernistic techniques inevitably erupt. So highly charged is the clergyman's state of mind, so desperate his feeling of anger and frustration in "Conference Man" that only the ultimate refinements of a modern poetic art can serve Sjöberg's purposes. When the clergyman's madness finally breaks out in full fury, a kaleidoscopic confusion of associations, broken images, and fragmented ideas overwhelm him:

> Dredges with dripping scoops
> heaved constant visions from the mud.
> Look, a blue-meat coarseness there!
> Look, a white and hard-crushed hand!
>
> There on blackened swell is lifted
> shattered limbs of fallen Gods,
> riven proclamation placards.
> Time's secreted terror news-bits
> naked stand up now again,
> threatening with spectral hands,
> staring, empty, eyeless sockets.
> Fled was all — and yet not fled.
>
> Futuristic school —
> evening salons, wild, sear pieces
> here exhibit of the heart:
> Lips that cowardice closed in silence,
> hands that killed for filthy lucre,
> eye that stings with cruelty . . .

In addition to such deliberately futuristic patterns as are used in this passage, Sjöberg employs throughout "Conference Man," as elsewhere in *Crises and Laurel Wreaths*, an astonishing variety of modern poetic devices — stylistic anachronisms, macabre distortions, abrupt transitions, antithetic juxtaposition of ideas and images, sharp concretions of abstract concepts, passages with double-level meanings, language stretched to its expressive breaking point. In his search for intensely expressive modern effects the poet has not, however, ignored some of the uses of traditional poetry. In fact, fleeting reminiscences from many poetic sources abound in Sjöberg's later verse. Shakespeare particularly has left his mark on Sjöberg, showing the way toward a completely free and flexible use of blank verse and demonstrating the rich possibilities of the daring image, of unusual poetic concretions of all kinds. Some critics feel also that more than the mere *shadow* of Hamlet's mentality falls over "Conference Man" — and for that matter over the whole of Sjöberg's final tragic poetic world.

Like so many of the central poems from Sjöberg's last years "Conference Man" is both satire and confession, both a withering attack on convention and dogma and a desperate search for some meaning in an existence which seemed but to mock man in his ghastly misery. As the clergyman of the poem tosses feverishly on his bed of convalescence and searches the secret places of his own heart, he finds vanity and pretension also there — not least in his insistence that God give him final, clear-cut answers to his questions about life and death, good and evil, the prospects of heaven and hell. But at the moment when his spirit is most darkly clouded a child's voice from out the refulgence of a dawning day pours light into his lacerated soul —

> Your yearning strong suffices, seems to me,
> to lighten bonds of clay and of existence.
> Intention good lifts earth's mold toward the light.

This yearning, this intention, is man's justification before God. Man's purity of heart rather than his groping toward deceptive dogma is his only hope in life's "tumultuous swarming toward the grave." The closing mood and formulation of theme in "Conference Man" offers a striking parallel to the final scene in Pär Lagerkvist's *The Man without a Soul*. But Sjöberg's development of the theme is more tense and more fraught with a sense of decay and dissolution — probably because he felt more immediately the actual nearness of death, which came to him but a few short years after he had written his most moving and powerful poem.

During the years when Birger Sjöberg's tormented spirit was shaking itself loose from the complacent middle-class idyllicism of *Frida's Book* and pouring its heavy brooding into the explosive modernism of *Crises and Laurel Wreaths* another Swedish literary development was taking place — the rise of what is sometimes called "a proletarian literature" — which in its way was to have an equally great importance for contemporary Swedish letters. In matters of form, however, its way was not on the whole the way of literary modernism, revolutionary as its social and political point of view proved to be. It is, indeed, scarcely surprising that the authors of working-class origins did not begin by experimenting with new literary forms. The remarkable thing about these authors was that they wrote at all, considering the poverty-stricken conditions out of which they derived and the sharply limited educational opportunities of their childhood and youth. Only by dint of the most heroic efforts in the direction of self-education, and by taking advantage of such limited intellectual opportunities as were provided by the folk high schools, study circles, and other cultural outlets available to the less favored classes, were they able to cultivate their talents and assert their rights to a place in the literary sun.

It has been pointed out that the aggressive class-conscious term "proletarian literature" (*proletärdiktning*) is somewhat misleading as applied to the literature of working-class origins in Sweden, for this literature reflects only in part strenuously class-conscious attitudes. It is true that in the early years of the Swedish labor movement authors from the working classes published fiction and collections of verse with such disturbing, in some cases bitter and inflammatory titles as *Ur djupet* (From the Depths), *Bubblor från botten* (Bubbles from the Bottom), *Hunger* (Hunger), *Vid svältgränsen* (At Starvation's Boundary-Line), *Arbetare, En historia om hat* (Workers, A Story About Hatred), and *Hatets sånger* (Songs of Hatred). But as time went on the extremist attitudes suggested by such titles became less common among working-class authors. The class-conscious literary agitator tended gradually to disappear because the rapidly accelerating pace of social democratization characteristic of twentieth-century Sweden served with the passage of time to eliminate most of the social evils which had at one time provided the literary agitator with convenient targets for his activities. By the 1930's, when the process of social democratization was all but complete, most authors of working-class origins needed no longer to feel like "outsiders" either in matters of social acceptance or in matters of literary recognition. They had finally become an integral part of Swedish culture, living out their years and writing their books as the equals or superiors of those among their literary colleagues whose social origins had been more distinguished.

But the road which led to social acceptance and literary recognition was for years strewn with all manner of obstructions for those who came "from below." Particularly difficult was the road for the first generation of working-class authors, who appeared on the literary scene around 1910 and whose chief representatives were to become Martin Koch, Gustav Hedenvind-Eriksson, and Dan Andersson. Authentic and at times impressive as was their depiction of a world of poverty and struggle and heavy labors in field, forest, and factory, they had to force their way toward literary recognition more often than not against unsympathetic critics and an only mildly responsive reading public. Only after a decade of persistent knocking at the door of literary recognition did they succeed — with the assistance of another, younger, group of working-class authors — in partly dissipating the centuries-old assumption that the making of literature was the exclusive business of the educated classes. Even the working-class movement out of which these authors in almost every case sprang did not always understand and encourage their work, and this not only when their work happened to stray somewhat outside the rigidities of party discipline and Marxist orthodoxy as it so often did.

To Martin Koch (1882–1940) must go the honor of having first among the "proletarian authors" made a relatively deep impression on Swedish readers, though his first important work, *Arbetare, en historia om hat* (Workers, A Story about Hatred, 1912), was preceded a few years by the publication of Maria Sandel's collection of proletarian tales *Vid svältgränsen* (At Starvation's Boundary-line) and Gustav Hedenvind-Eriksson's examination of ruthless industrial exploitation *Ur en fallen skog* (From a Felled Forest). Strictly speaking Martin Koch was not of working-class origins. Resident in Stockholm, his family's social status was lower middle-class, but the father's bohemian tastes led to his deserting the family when the children were very young, after which the mother had to support her family as best she could. Though the young Martin turned out to be brilliant in school, he soon tired of its rigid disciplines, took summer work as a laborer's helper, studied art with considerable success, became active in the Good Templars Lodge, and identified himself more and more as time went on with the temperance and labor movements, in part by contributing articles and sketches to their journals and newspapers. His first and richest period of literary production begins with the novelette *Ellen* in 1911 and continues for a full decade with a steady stream of books, the most important of which are the three central novels *Workers* (1912), *Timmerdalen* (The Timber Valley, 1913), and *Guds vackra värld* (God's Beautiful World, 1916), and the sensitive study in the folk psychology of religious sectarians entitled *Fromma människor* (Pious People, 1918). Upon his return to Sweden in 1928 after a lengthy stay in Paris, he tried his hand again at literary composition, now in a quiet, meditative, partly reminiscent manner. The only important work from this last period is the charming collection of autobiographical tales *Mauritz*, published the year before his death. This little work is the finest product of that idyllic strain in Martin Koch's character which asserts itself in less pure forms almost everywhere in his work, even in such harshly realistic contexts as we come upon in his three arresting proletarian novels.

The first of these novels, *Workers*, depicts the dull monotony of daily existence in a Stockholm working-class quarter in the years after the

General Strike of 1909 when the struggle between workmen and employers was particularly bitter. The novel has no central figure, no individual "hero" — its hero is the masses, the collective will and sense of solidarity which a group of workers is striving to realize against all but insuperable odds. Its subtitle, "A Story about Hatred," suggests the author's own sense of solidarity with the masses, his belief in their cause and sympathy with their attitude toward an employer group which uses every subterfuge to crush their efforts to organize and gain a decent wage. But this does not mean that Martin Koch approves of all the extremes to which some of the workmen are prepared to go. He has a sharp eye out for signs of irresponsible extremism, of incipient anarchism, of certain criminal or near-criminal tendencies which were the ugly by-products of an otherwise idealistic labor movement. Despite the heavy stress on theme in *Workers*, everything in the novel is concrete, active, alive, especially the handling of milieu and dialogue. Even the gray monotony of the workingman's neighborhood environs and the distressing drabness of his domestic existence are indelibly imprinted on the reader's memory, and other, more lively scenes are in their way quite unforgettable, especially those depicting the seamy, often alcohol-drenched sides of human misery. It has been suggested that the brutal manner in which proletarian living conditions are handled in *Workers* owes something to Upton Sinclair's *The Jungle* and Jack London's *The People of the Abyss* which had been rendered into Swedish in 1906 and 1910 respectively. Though stylistically Koch stoops at times to banal and merely rhetorical expressions, he employs in the main in *Workers* a language which is direct, racy, colloquial, the gutty language of the street and of the places where men labor and sweat and on occasion bicker and carouse and plan acts of violence in order to forget their misery. Koch's dialogue at its most powerful has a harsh ring of everyday reality unique for its time in the Swedish proletarian novel and seldom approached in a latter-day Swedish prose fiction.

When Koch in *The Timber Valley* left the Stockholm scene which he knew so intimately and moved up into a modern industrial Norrland for his fictional material he did not succeed so well, even though he spared no effort to acquaint himself with the area both by firsthand observation of contemporary conditions in this northern region and by extensive studies in the region's social and industrial history. But if, as a novel, *The Timber Valley* is uneven in quality and fails to maintain a sustained narrative interest, it is a social document of the first order.

Koch's novel attempts nothing less than a social history of an entire region during forty years of revolutionary changes in its way of life, a period during which a primitive agrarian society of essentially medieval forms becomes suddenly transformed into a modern industrial empire. That side of the transformation which especially interests Koch and arouses his indignation is the rapacious exploitation of the local peasant freeholders by the giant sawmill corporations, an exploitation which ultimately reduced great numbers of solid peasant families to the status of a landless proletarian class. Though some of the more memorable action of the novel is concerned with such violent industrial conflicts as the notorious Sundsvall strike of 1879 and the nasty developments in the Sandö conflict of 1907, the novel's profounder concern is with the tragedy of a whole regional culture being sacrificed almost overnight to the greed of modern industry. In the main Koch's depiction of conditions in Norrland at the time was not overdrawn. His novel served to dramatize a national scandal which was being discussed everywhere in Swedish newspapers during the first decade of our century and which had become a central concern in parliamentary debate and legislative action at the time. Nowhere in Sweden had industrial growth been as rapid as in Norrland, nowhere were the social and economic dislocations more disturbing. Around the so-called Norrland problem scores of short stories and novels and reportage books of one kind and another came to be written by authors of greater or lesser distinction. Among these works none has the combined thoroughness and sweep of *The Timber Valley*, and few measure up to its over-all literary quality.

A superior work on the whole, however, is *God's Beautiful World*, Koch's one undeniable masterpiece. Though *God's Beautiful World* brings us again into a world of capitalistic exploitation of both peasant and the urban proletariat, its primary concern is with the problem of right and wrong independent of immediate economic, social, or cultural considerations. In form Koch's new work is a genealogical novel, a deeply disturbing study in three generations of a family's history which begins relatively hopefully on the Swedish countryside and ends all but hopelessly in a jungle of degeneration and proletarian misery in Stockholm. Misfortune first comes to the family in consequence of an unjust act on the part of the male founder of the family, an honest, hard-working Vestmanland peasant. Forced finally from the land, the second generation drifts to the city and becomes grist for the proletariat-fed mill. On one side the family degeneration pursues its destructive purposes in its most repulsive forms, primarily in the criminal, sexually perverted person of Frasse Karlsson-Gyllenhjelm. On the other side a struggling spirit of idealism tries to assert itself, seeks as best it can to retain a sense of decency in the midst of a reality which seems on almost every hand to belie the dream of "God's Beautiful World." In this novel Koch comes closer to Zola's naturalism than anywhere else in his work, but the dark desperation of the novel derives at least equally from Koch's horror at the First World War, whose outbreak had shattered for the time being his faith in man and brought into grim focus the problem of evil in the modern world. Koch's social optimism had been severely shaken, so severely that he toyed in the latter portions of *God's Beautiful World* with the possibility of a religious way out of man's ugly dilemma. But this possibility is left in a vague, unconvincing form — whether because Koch was not himself convinced of its validity or because he was unable to give it a satisfactory literary form is difficult to say.

If Martin Koch in *The Timber Valley* made an impressive but temporary excursion from Stockholm and its environs into the surging Norrland world of industrial expansion and social change, his contemporary Gustav Hedenvind-Eriksson (b. 1880) has lived a large part of his life in this area and devoted large segments of his literary work to its folk and the role they have played in its dramatic transformation from a relatively unimportant half-arctic region to a central theater of operations in the development of modern Swedish industry. Though peasant born, Hedenvind-Eriksson left his home at the age of fifteen and wandered widely over the face of the earth (Europe, Africa, even America) as a construction worker (*rallare*) and at other jobs for a quarter of a century, during which time he systematically gathered an enormous dossier of material for his books, the first half dozen of which were written whenever time permitted while he was engaged at heavy labor on one construction job or other. Though his first published work, *Ur en fallen skog* (From a Felled Forest), appeared in 1910, it was not until the early 1920's that he could devote himself more exclusively to literature, residing for a decade largely in Stockholm and its environs, after which he bought a small farm and became a peasant again, an experiment which was abruptly terminated in 1938 when an accident forced him to give up heavy physical labor. He has continued throughout his career to write prose fiction, but in his later years he has also turned to the extended prose essay and the autobiographical sketch, most successfully in *En bondes dagbok* (A Peasant's Diary, 1937) and *Med rallarkärra mot dikten* (With a Rallar-Cart toward Literature, 1944). Though he has always maintained a sense of solidarity with the working classes, and at times has identified himself directly with organizational activities among the workers, he is by temperament and by virtue of his long experience as a *rallare* (that most individualistic of worker types) an author who in the main does not allow himself to become simply an instrument of a class-conscious workers' point of view. And in his literary form, too, he is essentially himself, the most original of Swedish proletarian authors.

In subject matter it may be said that Hedenvind-Eriksson completes a full circle in the more than a score of volumes which he has published during the near half-century of his literary career. Beginning with a study in the disruptive impact of industrialization on the Norrland peasantry in *From a Felled Forest* in 1910, he moves on to the purely industrial *rallare* world with *Vid Eli vågor* (Beside the Waves of Eli) in 1914 and many following works, and returns finally to the Norrland forests and their folk in a number of works, the most important of which are three volumes of Jämtland folk tales, 1941, 1946, 1949, and the finely executed trilogy begun with *Silverskogen sydväst om månen* (The Silver Forest Southwest of the Moon) in 1950 and brought to a close with *Snöskottning i paradiset* (Snow-Shoveling in Paradise) two years later.

Among all of Hedenvind-Eriksson's novels only *From a Felled Forest* is highly class-conscious, a bitter denunciation of capitalist exploitation of the peasantry and the working classes. The other novels contain here and there passages inspired more or less directly by a class-struggle mentality, but such passages are subordinated to the larger artistic and thematic purposes of the novels in question. Hedenvind-Eriksson is a born story teller and something of a philosopher. In the latter capacity he is usually prepared to accept life on its own terms without pretending to understand it in all its multifarious manifestations. In terms of scene and action his world is extraordinarily alive, vivid, colorful, exciting, peopled with a vitally mobile type of workman who faces his daily task and its lurking dangers with taut muscles and a come-what-may camaraderie of spirit. It is a vigorous, fluid, fresh-air world, contrasting sharply with the drab monotony of the workingman's world which we come upon in most proletarian fiction. Though Hedenvind-Eriksson's art is usually straightforward, delighting in lively externals and the surging vitality of the life he has known, it moves also in areas of mood and expression seldom characteristic of literature dealing with the realities of the workaday world and its immediate problems. The novels have much of the sweep and spaciousness and the expansive quality of the world they depict, and at times they are impressively symbolic or visionary in form, operating in borderland areas between reality and dream and myth. The symbols are not always clear, but they are almost invariably arresting, loaded with impressive visionary concretions and allusive in ways that alert our attention and retain our interest despite their refusal to yield all their secrets.

The *rallare* novels which occupy Hedenvind-Eriksson's almost exclusive attention down to 1930 combine a picaresque joy in lively externals and fantastic adventures with a symbolic probing into life's deeper meanings. In some of these novels, particularly in *Beside the Waves of Eli* (1914), the interplay between action and symbol is maintained in fine balance. In others — *Tiden — och en natt* (Time — and One Night, 1918), *En dröm i seklets natt* (A Dream in the Century's Night, 1919), and *Orions bälte* (Orion's Belt, 1924) — patterns of outward action tend to give way to impressive but only partly intelligible symbolic and visionary detail. And in still others of the *rallare* novels — *De förskingrades arv* (The Heritage of the Dispersed, 1926) and *Det bevingade hjulet* (The Winged Wheel, 1928) — an almost endless succession of fascinating narrative sequences take over nearly to the exclusion of symbolical elements. *Beside the Waves of Eli*, the first of the important *rallare* novels, provides a vivid and imaginatively conceived account of the building of the great power station at Älvkarleö near the mouth of Dalälven in northern Uppland, while *The Winged Wheel* follows a *rallare* gang from construction job to construction job at such widely scattered points on the Continent as Copenhagen and Riga, the Ural mountains and the mines of Sulitelma. Wherever these *rallare* go and however heavy and hazardous their work, they retain the irrepressible appetite for life in all its forms as summed up by the defrocked priest-philosopher Hejlamb in *Beside the Waves of Eli*: "Look ye, my friends, everything is distorted, absurd, lovely and alluring all at once. And it is perhaps in the last analysis just these multi-changing nuances which in spite of everything make life so attractive, strange — I was about to say — interesting even in harsh moments of sorrow and hardship."

This all but devil-may-care elasticity of spirit doesn't carry over in equal measure into *Time — and One Night*, *A Dream in the Century's Night*, and *Orion's Belt*, the *rallare* novels which record First World War repercussions in the semi-arctic regions of the northern perimeter of Europe. Depicting strange events, often in a lurid half-dream-world atmosphere, these novels reflect Hedenvind-Eriksson's brooding over a world at war as he came in contact with it as laborer and seaman in and near such far northern border towns as Haparanda and in fantastic adventures at sea on board a highly unseaworthy fishing schooner manned by a motley array of landlubbers and commanded by a half-mad skipper. *Time — and One Night*, the most arresting of the war-inspired Swedish novels, details the misery of refugees fleeing the horrors of a world aflame across the wintry wastes of Lapland-Sweden. Even here, in a neutral land, these victims of modern warfare must struggle desperately to survive against man's meanness and greed. But in the end humane acts and feelings flash fitfully in the Arctic darkness, suggesting that man *may* have learned something from the catastrophic whirlpool of evil into which he had drawn himself:

Perhaps they finally began to surmise the depth and breadth of the condition man found himself in — a restless, blind wandering through a starless night — a bitter struggle of all against all toward a terrible, self-inflicted suffering which made their selfish faith in man's all-powerful intelligence and noble striving a faith without deeds — and thereby merely an empty bubble. Then the evil they had seen, the bitterness they had felt — in a word all the harsh and desperate things they had experienced — had verily not been in vain.

The impressive but only partly intelligible symbolism of Hedenvind-Eriksson's other war novels, *A Dream in the Century's Night* and *Orion's Belt*, have points of contact both with modern expressionism and with an ancient folkloristic world of myth and legend which in the 1940's the author brings to life in the three volumes *Jämtländska sagor* (Jämtland Sagas), *Sagofolket som kom bort* (Saga Folk Who Disappeared), and *Jorms saga*. It was scarcely an accident that Eyvind Johnson, who was to become in the years around 1930 and later one of the most brilliantly experimental of Swedish novelists, had taken with him on his Continental wanderings in 1921 Hedenvind-Eriksson's *Time — and One Night* and *A Dream in the Century's Night*.

The only poet among the three chief pioneer figures in Swedish working-class literature was Dan Andersson (1888–1920), a restless, vagabond spirit, who if he had not died so young might well have played a more important role in Swedish literature. Besides a considerable body of poetry and prose published after his death, six volumes of his verse and prose appeared while he lived. He became quite early one of the few

Swedish poets really beloved by the folk (joining Bellman and Fröding and perhaps one or two others in this respect), and since his death a kind of cultish admiration for Dan Andersson has until recently made it difficult to distinguish that which is true and false about him and his work. Born in extreme poverty in the so-called Finnmarken district of southern Dalarna, he had to labor early as a woodsman and charcoal burner, broke out of this primitive way of life for a spell in early manhood by serving as a temperance lecturer, returned to his home district to write a first collection of charcoal burners' tales, attended the famous Brunnsvik Folk High School for a part of the year 1914–15, after which he devoted himself more or less exclusively to literature, maintaining in his last years a precarious existence, in part through the generosity of friends and well-wishers. Though his native Finnskogen was the fixed point in his existence during the last years, he quite frequently sought intellectual and literary stimulation on visits to friends at Brunnsvik and Stockholm. Death came to him in a cheap Stockholm hotel room which had not been sufficiently ventilated after fumigation for vermin.

A new class of workman, the charcoal burner, is introduced into Swedish literature with Dan Andersson's first two published volumes, *Kolarhistorier* (Charcoal Burners' Tales, 1914) and *Kolvaktarens visor* (The Charcoal Watcher's Songs, 1915), the second despite its title containing both poetry and prose. The stories included in *Charcoal Burners' Tales*, we are told in a prefatory note, were "in part written in a sod hut (*jordkoja*), often under the dim light of a sooty lantern hanging from a smoke-blackened roof." Both the circumstances under which these tales were written and the care taken by the author to verify every detail in the tales, guarantee their integrity. They are heavy tales of lonesome men deep in snowbound forests, men who labor month after month in freezing darkness and semidarkness at the onerous task of seeing to it that the smoldering fires of the charcoal kilns do not get out of hand. Only once during the winter-long kiln-watch of these men does anything really dramatic happen, when one of the kilns erupts and threatens to destroy itself before the heroic labors of the men bring it again under control. Otherwise the dead monotony of existence for these men is made endurable only by a crude camaraderie of spirit and by the stories of trolls and Finnish sorcery and strange apparitions bandied about during long winter evenings in their wretched huts lighted only by the flares of wood fires. Though some of the tales about the charcoal burners reveal that Dan Andersson is sufficiently aware of the fact that these men

are being deliberately exploited by the large timber and foundry interests in Dalarna, the tales in general are hardly inspired by a modern
class-conscious point of view.

It is clear especially from Dan Andersson's three last volumes of prose,
the narrative sketch *Det kallas vidskepelse* (It Is Called Superstition,
1916) and two autobiographical novels, *De tre hemlösa* (The Three
Homeless Ones, 1918) and *David Ramms arv* (David Ramm's Heritage,
1919), that he was never impressed by those popular cultural and social
prophets of the day who proposed to solve all man's problems by
means of intellectual enlightenment and/or political manipulation. He retained a healthy skepticism toward some of the forms of folk education
represented in the Brunnsvik Folk High School, and he never identified
himself with an organized labor movement or with the Social Democratic party. In *It Is Called Superstition* (the word "called" is to be emphasized) he subjects to rather sharp ridicule that kind of enlightenment
represented on the Brunnsvik faculty by those who in the name of science belittled life's mysteries or assumed that science would in the course
of time lay all mysteries bare. To Dan Andersson life's essential problems were personal rather than social, and they involved primarily man's
confrontation with "the beyond," with God and the problem of good
and evil. What is sometimes *called* superstition, Dan Andersson suggests,
may very well be life's ultimate reality, whether it take on the form of
primitive folk superstitions as they existed on the Dalarna countryside
or a pietistic faith as represented by Dan Andersson's deeply religious
father or some other form of consciousness into which man has poured
or shall pour his religious yearning.

While the slight narrative piece *It Is Called Superstition* provides but
a sketchy point of departure for such speculations, the two autobiographical novels *The Three Homeless Ones* and *David Ramm's Heritage*
pursue these ideas with considerable thoroughness in the total context
of the author's experience from early childhood to mature manhood.
Though neither of the two autobiographical works is a literary masterpiece, both are profoundly moving human documents, inspired as they
are by a desperate desire to find some kind of peace in a world full of
frustration and suffering. So desperate, indeed, is this desire that in
David Ramm's Heritage hysteria sometimes takes over and the drift of
thought becomes often highly confusing. *The Three Homeless Ones*,
on the other hand, is at almost every point a genuinely gripping and relatively clear study in the inner development of its hero as determined

particularly by the early conditions of his existence on the Swedish countryside. That Strindberg's *The Son of a Servant* was one of the models for Dan Andersson's autobiographical novels seems apparent. Other models were almost certainly such works of purely proletarian origins as Gorki's *My Youth* and Jack London's *Martin Eden*, both of which had appeared in Swedish a few years before the first of Dan Andersson's autobiographical novels. But the most important of the literary influences seems to be Dostoevski, whose wandering unfortunates and noble prostitutes and whose terror-inspired moments of religious ecstasy recur in Dan Andersson's novels. Nowhere among contemporary "faiths" as mirrored in the Swedish society of the day does the hero of these novels find the peace for which he is searching — neither among the Pietists nor among the priests of the Established Church nor among the Socialists nor among the Temperance enthusiasts. "I had been everywhere," David Ramm concludes, "and I was homeless." Of these "faiths," however, that of the Pietists attracts David Ramm most strongly, for "these people are the only ones who are interested in what we call the soul." But what disturbed him about the Pietists was their overwhelming sense of sin and guilt and their concept of God as a stern and vengeful judge. It is therefore that David Ramm becomes interested in certain sides of Indian religious speculation — in, for instance, the Bhakti concept, which in its view of the universe as a revelation of Love refuses to recognize any difference between good and evil and cannot accept the concept of a divine power which metes out punishment for a transgression of its laws. To what extent such speculations brought peace to David Ramm is not, however, clear. His spiritual heritage was in the last analysis the stern pietism of his father, a pietism which seems finally to triumph in the closing symbolical scene of the novel.

If in his prose fiction Dan Andersson only in part brings his world into a satisfactory literary focus, he succeeds much more with his poetry, particularly with some of the central poems in *Svarta ballader* (Black Ballads, 1917), a work of darkly haunting poetic splendor. But also in *The Charcoal Watcher's Songs* and in some of the posthumously published poems one comes upon verse of rare and abiding beauty. As the titles of Dan Andersson's two volumes of poems suggest, he uses by preference the simple song and ballad forms, but he employs these with considerable imaginative flexibility, his "ballads," for instance, being invested with a strong *lyric* quality, some of the best of them drifting over into the form of the dramatic monologue. He had learned something from Fröding, but Kipling, whose *The Seven Seas* he had translated, seems to have been a more important technical influence. Kipling's free-swinging rhythmic line frequently appears in his verse, though with a less sharp, less obtrusive beat, with a more softly musical, essentially Swedish tone. A certain Swedish quality in Dan Andersson's verse is also reflected in its more than occasional fondness for the elegantly colorful, the lushly exotic. Flower imagery, particularly that of the rose, is apt to crop up even in the most harshly realistic contexts. Happier is Dan Andersson's poetic use of such Finnish proper nouns as Pajso, Hattomarja, Sami, Raiski, Savona, and Luossa, with their mysterious euphonious associations, and his blending of landscape and wilderness detail with the weird primitive world of Finnmarken violence, superstition, and dark-hued sorcery.

Even though abject poverty and human misery are often sketched in detail in these poems, poverty as a social problem is seldom allowed to emerge — and then permitted to assert itself in only the most oblique and fragmentary terms. Human misery in the most impressive of Dan Andersson's poems always has a religious dimension. Its immediate source may lie in poverty and social injustice, but its ultimate ramifications raise questions of guilt and universal human responsibility in the presence of heaven and the gods. This is why the hour of death or visions of the afterworld are so often central in the greatest of Dan Andersson's poems — "Sista natten i Paindalen" (The Last Night in Paindalen), "Omkring tiggarn från Luossa" (On the Beggar from Luossa), "En spelmans jorda-färd" (A Fiddler's Last Journey), "Gillet på vinden" (The Feast in the Garret), and "Angelika." Of these "The Last Night in Paindalen" is the most realistic and earth-bound, in some ways the most profoundly moving. The others have each in its way more poetic flight, more free imaginative sweep, whether it takes on visions of heavenly splendor as in "On the Beggar from Luossa" or provides a subtle blending of comedy and moments of ineffable beauty as in "The Feast in the Garret" or suggests the compassion which nature offers to man as in "The Fiddler's Last Journey."

The most frequently recurring theme in these poems is a plea for divine understanding of man's moral limitations, together with the hope that the "other world" will deal less harshly with man than the one in which he is pursued by misery and plagued by a sense of guilt. In "The Feast in the Garret" the poet, engaged in an imaginary conversation with a departed friend,

> . . . ventured on a question — rather shyly forth it
>   came —
> "I wonder — now — is it truth they tell — that tale of our
>   Lord and Shame?
> Do only the saintliest saints of all in the Blessed Islands
>   dwell?
> Or is there a Heaven for those who are *not* . . . quite up to
>   the mark, as well?"

And the ghost of the poet's friend answers:

>   "I am Joiner Johnson, not learned at all, as you
>   see;
> Much trouble I gave in my life on earth by my self-taught
>   carpentry.
> And the learned wanted to hang me, for I knew no Latin
>   or Greek,
> And when I was dead an Angel said, 'You might give all
>   *you* know to Old Nick!'
>
> "But I heard a lay on a Star one day — I remember a bit of
>   it still —
> Of the pains for sin that the world must win by the Lord of
>   Heaven's will.
> But one of the singers told me this was merely an earthly
>   lay
> Which an Angel learnt for practice' sake when he fetched
>   up a soul one day.
>
> "Then the noblest song of all their songs — a theme as of
>   infinite peace.
> Not a word could I catch, but the tears ran down as if they
>   would never cease.
> 'Twas beyond all hearts, on a planet-path where none had
>   ever been:
> 'Twas a thing no ear had ever heard, nor eye had ever seen."
>   *Translated by C. D. Locock*

In other of Dan Andersson's poems, "Fången" (The Prisoner) in particular, the problem of sin and guilt is handled with greater severity and concentration, but not without hope of better things in another, less imperfect world:

> Three stairsteps lead to Sunlit Gate,
> Three stairsteps of musty stone —
> I'll mount them one day, all penance done,
> Through the iron-wrought door, will I step forth wan
> And weep in the sunlight's sheen.

In my dark cellar hole I have spoken with God —
He stood sublime and stern.
So wrathful, severe, the commands He gave —
But dazzling the glory of His garment hem
In a prison of deep despair!
Three stairsteps of sin I have long since gone,
Three stairsteps of penance remain,
Slow will I pace them, year after year,
And one day will bask my greying old head
In a sun that never goes down.

Translated by Caroline Schleef

Short as was Dan Andersson's life-span, it was in its way rich enough both in the pleasures of the flesh and the desperate searching of the soul. His poetry at its best gives sensitive expression to the taut tensions within his restless spirit, tensions between that which drew him to the earth and that which sought peace "on a planet-path where none had ever been."

The years in which Dan Andersson was breaking through as a poet rather far removed from the world of direct social conflict were years in which a number of other labor-marked young authors were fashioning verses and more or less actively identifying themselves, as Dan Andersson did not, with the rising organized social and political radicalism of the day. These years, just before and after 1920, were among the most stormy in the history of the Swedish labor movement and the Social Democratic party, marked by a sharp struggle between the older "reform" element and the more radical "Left Socialist" revolutionary wing of the party — a struggle which resulted finally, in 1917, in the Left Socialist group breaking with the mother party and establishing a splinter Social Democratic party of the Left. Whipped into a fury of resentment by a wave of unemployment resulting from the economic recession which swept over Sweden at the time, the Left Socialist falange hailed the Bolshevist Revolution in Russia, championed the cause of the Reds in the Finnish Civil War, and in general dreamed of radically refashioning Swedish society along communistic lines. An even more radical group, the Young Socialists (Svenska socialistiska ungdomsförbundet), which had as early as 1897 broken with the Social Democratic party, nurtured strong anarchistic ideas. Neither of these splinter groups had much political power, but they were highly articulate, in part because their journalistic organs *Brand* and *Stormklockan* succeeded in attracting the literary talents of young working-class authors who had difficulty in finding

426

other outlets for their poetry and prose. Though a number of these worker-authors spent some time at Brunnsvik Folk High School, where a middle-of-the-road social liberalism obtained, they were readily swept up in the whirlpool of European revolutionary currents which had been temporarily checked by the First World War but released again as the War drew to a close. So provocative were some of the young Swedish proletarian authors, particularly in their pronouncements on religion and national defense measures, that no less than three of them served prison terms for "blasphemous and treasonable utterances." With time, however, these young Hotspurs abandoned almost without exception their extremist positions and made their peace with society. In fact, some even underwent religious "conversions" of one kind or other, and in semi-confessional works did a kind of public penance for "the sins of their youth" committed in the name of a revolutionary social idealism. From the pens of the young radicals of the years before 1920 who had deliberately employed such incendiary class-conscious titles as *Till kärleken och hatet* (To Love and Hatred) and *I revolutionstid* (In Revolutionary Times) there afterward issued such inoffensive, quietistic titles, preferably with religious overtones, as *Den trånga porten* (The Narrow Way), *Det stilla året* (The Peaceful Year), *I ny jord* (In New Earth), *Vi måste börja om* (We Must Begin Over Again), and *Med stort G* (With a Capital G), the last of which titles calls for the re-establishment of the use of the capital "G" in referring to the deity, a practice which for some years had been discontinued by a number of the more radical of the proletarian authors.

Of the rather numerous works by repentant or half-repentant proletarian authors devoted to an accounting with their radical past one of the most representative is the finely ironic novel *Gröna riddare* (Green Knights, 1926) by Ivan Oljelund (b. 1892), who was also responsible for the religious-confessional piece *With a Capital G*, and who in a series of autobiographical novels beginning with *Det hände på Kungsholmen* (It Happened on Kungsholmen, 1951) and ending with *Dans med stormen* (Dance with the Storm, 1954) depicts again and in a more sober, factual, and detailed manner Oljelund's relation to Swedish radicalism during the years immediately following the First World War. His work otherwise since the break with his early radicalism consists largely of lively causeries on broad cultural subjects contributed to certain moderately liberal or conservative newspapers.

A poet of some importance who had begun his literary career among

the Young Socialists was Erik Lindorm (1889–1941). Quick-witted, re-
sourceful, and fabulously successful at almost anything to which he
turned his hand, Lindorm became a public favorite, particularly in the
1930's, through his contributions to the popular weekly *Veckojournalen*
and with his "film books," ingeniously edited "histories of our times"
consisting of brilliantly arranged series of newspaper clippings and
photographs. Even in his earlier years he had demonstrated a flair for
popular journalism in the comic satire of *Naggen*, a paper which he
founded in 1913 and edited for ten years.

But Erik Lindorm's literary importance lies almost completely in his
poetry, six thin volumes of which appeared between the years 1908 and
1934. Only the last of these, *På marsch* (On the March), departs somewhat from the simple everyday realities of the working-class world
which Lindorm has depicted more convincingly than any other Swedish
poet. With no "literary" effects, with the simplest of rhythms, with no
excessive imagery and with an appropriately limited vocabulary, he
manages to invest the everyday world of the worker with a subtle magic
of idea and feeling. He creates a kind of proletarian idyl in the Stockholm slums. He deals with poverty and the limited conditions of existence of those who labor long and sometimes bitter hours for a mere subsistence, but except for some of his earliest poetry he does not directly
employ his verse in the service of social agitation. He allows his theme to
take care of itself — or, rather, he allows the reader to draw his own conclusions from the quietly compassionate undercurrent of his verse. And
he is always sensitively aware of those moments of fumbling, inarticulate
warmth which can well up from hidden human sources in the midst of
the dead monotony experienced daily among the poor and less favored.
This lends to Lindorm's poetry a measure of idyllicism without stooping
to sentimentality or false pathos. Lindorm's subjects are limited, his
themes few, but in the handling of these themes his touch is perfect. He
wrings just the right amount of realism and romance from such everyday subjects as concern about the monthly rent or the mixed banalities
and joys of an ordinary weekday evening or the awkward state of mind
of adolescent confirmands. In his ability to maintain a fine balance between stark realities and an unobtrusive warmth of feeling he is definitely
among the most original of the Swedish poets of his day. Seldom does
he permit us to catch a glimpse of his own inner life, but when he does
so — as in the poem "Invaliden" in his last volume of verse — we suddenly
realize that Erik Lindorm's finely balanced realistic idyllicism gives ex-

pression to only one side of his experience of life. With its tattered imagery, its nervous rhythms, and its dark, desperate intensities, "Invaliden" *might* have been written by the Birger Sjöberg of *Crises and Laurel Wreaths*. Success — or what a young leftist critic once labeled the "massive middle-class mentality" of Erik Lindorm's later years — had apparently not brought the mature poet complete peace of mind.

Less gifted and original than Lindorm but in some ways more representative of the first generation of proletarian authors were Ragnar Jändel (1895–1939) and Harry Blomberg (1893–1950). Jändel and Blomberg were among the working-class poets who published verse with revolutionary implications in the politically precarious years just before 1920, and both of them rather precipitately lowered their Red banners in the following years, retired from the political barricades, and transferred their idealistic loyalties to certain religious or religiously inspired attitudes which permitted them to retain certain points of contact with their earlier social indignation. Jändel was born in the southeastern Swedish province of Blekinge, turned early to painting as a trade, and became very active as a young man in the working-class movement and in extreme leftist political activities. His published work is rather extensive, including, besides thirteen volumes of poetry, three autobiographical works (*Det stilla året*, The Peaceful Year, 1923; *Den trånga porten*, The Narrow Way, 1924; and *Barndomstid*, Childhood, 1936), two volumes of essays on literary and general cultural subjects (*Vägledare*, Guides, 1921, and *Jag och vi*, I and We, 1928), and a volume of sensitive nature studies (*Blommor*, Flowers, 1937). Neither his prose nor his poetry is particularly distinguished, but at their best they give sensitive expression to a fine spirit's search for ultimate values, and even in their less inspired moments they may serve as valuable documents to those interested in the literary-proletarian contribution to contemporary Swedish culture.

Jändel's first two volumes of poetry, *Till kärleken och hatet* (To Love and Hatred, 1917) and *De tappra* (The Courageous Ones, 1918), give unrestrained expression to his enthusiasm for a Leftist revolutionary action in Sweden, inspired in part by the successful Bolshevist revolt in Russia and the struggle of the Reds against the Whites in Finland. In *The Courageous Ones* Jändel unreservedly defends the Finnish Reds. But in these early volumes there is to be found also poetry conceived in a quiet, personal, confessional strain, concerned with other matters than urgent social themes — with the home, the Swedish countryside, and with nature in some of its unassuming idyllic manifestations. It is this strain that rapidly gains dominance in Jändel's later work, though on occasion he gives indignant direct expression to his sense of solidarity with the working classes, most strikingly in "Två dikter till minnet av Sacco och Vanzetti" (Two Poems in Memory of Sacco and Vanzetti) in *Kämpande tro* (Fighting Faith, 1928). The serene confessional strain which is the mark of most of Jändel's later poetry borders at times dangerously on the sentimental, on the traditionally idyllic; but for the most part he maintains a reasonably healthy sense of realism, a warm, intimate, unassuming closeness to the folk and to the earth. His religious speculation has in it none of the primitive mysticism of Dan Andersson, nor does it yield to heroic or ascetic religious moods. On the negative side it reacts strongly against institutionalized religious forms, especially as represented in the Swedish Established Church, and it is equally suspicious of most forms of modern sectarianism. On its positive side it finds its most characteristic expression in a quiet undogmatic acceptance of a religious-ethical interpretation of life, not without points of contact with Quakerism on the one hand and an Emersonian religious idealism on the other.

Harry Blomberg, as well as Hedenvind-Eriksson and Dan Andersson, was one of the restless vagabond spirits in Swedish working-class literature. But his vagabondage was of a relatively superficial variety, a product more or less at second hand of what has been called "wilderness romanticism" and related semi-exotic phenomena. He never really knew the life of the wilderness and the ambulatory worker as did some of his literary contemporaries. The extent of his vagabondage amounted to the fact that he did "take to the road" for a short time in his early manhood, and has lived most of his life a rather itinerant existence, partly as a popular folk lecturer. Stockholm born, brought up by a sternly pietistic aunt, trained in his youth as a printer, he came early to write radical poetry (*I revolutionstid* [In Revolutionary Times, 1919]), but soon deserted the ranks of the young revolutionaries without becoming a renegade to the working-class cause.

The facility with which Harry Blomberg wrote resulted in a productivity so extensive that it could only on occasion rise above a relatively low literary level. In this respect his poetry especially suffered, though it continued for a long time to attract a large body of readers. Among his prose works which are most likely to be remembered are four novels — *Tiden och en människa* (Time and a Man, 1921), *Landets lågor* (The Country's Flames, 1930), *Babels älvar* (Babel's Rivers, 1928), and *Det brinner i snön* (It Burns in the Snow, 1935), the first two of which deal with contemporary problems, the last two with Swedish historical subjects — and the extended autobiographical religious essay *Vi måste börja om* (We Must Begin Over Again, 1937), which gives an account of Blomberg's conversion in the 1930's to the Oxford Group (Buchmanite) movement. *Time and a Man*, like Oljelund's *Green Knights* and Jändel's *The Narrow Way*, is an autobiographical novel dealing with the hero's final break with the radical Young Socialists, while *The Country's Flames* is an inspired delineation of the far-flung educational activities carried on among the Swedish masses. *It Burns in the Snow*, concerned with the work of the missionary to the Lapps Lars Levi Laestadius, has in its religious emphasis certain points of contact with *We Must Begin Over Again*. Of his four more interesting novels, however, only *Babel's Rivers* attains much of the epic breadth and moral sweep of really distinguished prose fiction. In this novel Blomberg takes up the heroic tale of a group of Esthonian Swedes who in the late 1920's had returned to Sweden after a century and a half's existence as immigrants in southern Russia. Though the popularity of this novel on its appearance was in part determined by the actuality of its subject, it is apt to survive on its own literary merits long after most of its author's poetry and prose has been forgotten. Blomberg is genuine enough in his way, but he had neither the sensitive contemplative bent of Ragnar Jändel nor the poetic intensity of Dan Andersson, without either of which great literature is seldom written.

Space scarcely permits more than a passing mention of such other authors of proletarian origins as Maria Sandel (1876–1927) and Maj Hirdman (b. 1888), two novelists who have given us intimate and gripping accounts of the struggles of working-class women, Albert Viksten (b. 1889) and Ragnar Holmström (b. 1894), both of whom have included in their wide-ranging and rather miscellaneous production some interesting studies on the impact of industrialism on Norrland, Ture Nerman (b. 1886), who as provocative poet and lively literary critic has never deviated from his early political radicalism, and Fabian Månsson (1872–1938), a major figure in Social Democratic journalism and politics who also found time to write some arresting prose fiction, most happily in the novel *Rättfärdiggörelsen genom tron* (Justification by Faith, 1916), an earthy, knowing, half-satirical, half-sympathetic study of the pietistic contribution to contemporary Swedish religious life and social developments.

431

The idyllic element which interpenetrates some of the proletarian poetry of the 1920's takes over almost completely in the verse of another group of poets whose origins and cultural backgrounds contrast sharply with those of their working-class counterparts in the literature of the day. This group — which includes the two highly cultivated art connoisseurs Karl Asplund (b. 1890) and Gunnar Mascoll Silfverstolpe (1893–1942) and the equally cultivated poet-critic-journalist Sten Selander (1891–1957) — had a remarkable homogeneity of interests and tastes and was bound together by strong ties of friendship. So close, indeed, have been the relations of the members of this group that they have with some justification been referred to as a cultural coterie, warmly admiring one another and not infrequently influencing each other's poetic production. They are relatively pure idylists, the last in Swedish poetry — with Runeberg, Bo Bergman, and Österling as their Swedish literary ideals and the English Georgian poets as their primary foreign source of inspiration. The example of Runeberg provided them with a quiet heroic ideal, Bo Bergman with a touch of sophistication and an impeccable poetic style, while Österling pointed the way toward Wordsworth, which when combined with a later Georgian idyllicism and a proper Etonian sense of grace and elegance resulted in the cultural ideal of the "gentleman" admired so much by Swedish idylists of the 1920's. The poetry of Asplund, Selander, and Silfverstolpe is admittedly a "miniature art," limited, fastidious, often fragile, but within the limits of idea and utterance which it proposes to reflect it is genuine enough. The verse particularly of their maturity is always competent, intelligent, sensitive, at times sufficiently inspired to add a dimension or two to the modest poetic world of mood and feeling which they cultivate.

Asplund is the most facile but in some ways the most engaging of the group, Selander the most intelligent and wide-ranging in interests, Silfverstolpe (the only blooded aristocrat among them) the most genuine and irreproachable in taste. Though Asplund entered the University of Uppsala at the age of nineteen "to study to be a poet," he came partly by accident to study art history, spent some time in London gathering material for his doctoral dissertation on the expatriate nineteenth-century Swedish painter Egron Lundgren, wrote art criticism for *Dagens Nyheter* and *Svenska Dagbladet*, and became the manager of one of Stockholm's most distinguished art shops. As a poet he matured slowly. Not until the publication of his fourth volume of verse *Hjältarna* (The Heroes) in 1919, six years after his debut volume, did he throw off the wordy poetic sentimentalism of his youth and find a subject and a form which suggested that he had a genuine if limited poetic potential. Later volumes, particularly *Klockbojen* (The Bell Buoy, 1925) and *Skuggorna* (The Shadows, 1929), confirm the impression of a certain poetic maturing without in any essential way breaking out of the mood of the idyl. Though the theme of First World War "heroism" in *The Heroes* is not unmixed with bits of cynicism and disillusionment, it is conceived largely in the quietly tragic tradition of Rupert Brooke but not infrequently clad in something of the vigorous rhythmic patterns and expansive realism of Rudyard Kipling and Robert W. Service. Many of the poems in *The Bell Buoy* and *The Shadows* are deeply personal, concerned with the poet's private sorrow over the early death of his wife. They are for the most part gently elegiac rather than tragic in tone, and in form they are usually delicate and fragile, like *objets d'art* of the finest line and mold. But in some cases, as in "Ångest" (Anguish), "Nattsegling" (Night Sailing), "Vågorna" (The Waves), and in the title poem in *The Bell Buoy*, the poet's sorrow breaks out in sharper, more stirring forms, by preference seeking an outlet for its brooding in the sweeping symbolism of the sea. Karl Asplund is a connoisseur of art and a passionate devotee of sailing, and it is more often than not his experience with rudder and sail at sea which lends to his poetry those buoyant rhythms and daring symbols that at times depart from the fastidious gentility of most of his verse.

Sten Selander likewise loved the sea, but — as is evident from his poetry — he is more at home on land. Born in Stockholm and trained as a botanist before he settled down to a career in publishing and journalism, he devotes most of his poetry and prose to his home city and to the flora of the Swedish countryside. Aside from his activities as a literary and drama critic for a number of leading Stockholm dailies, he has distinguished himself in prose chiefly as a warmly sensitive author of perspicacious nature essays, a genre not much cultivated by Swedish authors despite the brilliant example of Linnaeus and the widespread enthusiasm among Swedes for the forests and fields and the innumerable waterways of their land. Selander served for years before his recent death as national chairman of the Swedish Society for the Preservation of Nature.

After years of persistent but only modestly successful poetic productivity, Selander established himself among the more popular poets of the day with *Staden* (The City, 1926), followed five years later by *En dag* (A Day), perhaps his most satisfactory volume of verse. These two vol-

umes reflect both the strengths and the weaknesses of the "idyl of everyday life" (*vardagsidyll*) as represented in the tight little group of poetic
idylists of which Selander was a member. Selander's strength lies in his
literary inventiveness, which in *The City* manifests itself in variations
on the theme of Stockholm's quietly pulsing daily glories, and in *One
Day* manipulates with unerring skill a motley progression of everyday
scenes within the rather rigid poetic "frame" of a poet's day in the city.
The weaknesses in these volumes derive largely out of the ambivalent
social attitude of the author, an attitude which at times reflects strong
compassion for the unfortunate and the socially ill-favored classes but
which resolves the moral problem involved by apparently assuming that
compassion alone erases the element of guilt. I say "apparently" because
one cannot be sure, so delicate is the balance in these volumes between
the poet's social conscience and his artistic self-preoccupation. In any
case Selander is capable of moments of high poetic creation in these volumes, particularly in the finely democratic humanism of "En bonde-
student" (A Peasant Student), a noble reminder of the struggles of gifted
but poor students who down through the centuries have often in the
years of their maturity made central contributions to Swedish life and
culture. That Selander has not himself been entirely satisfied with the
predominantly idyllic strain maintained in *The City* and *One Day* seems
apparent in some of the poems in *Sommarnatten* (The Summer Night),
a volume from 1941 in which he tries his hand at verse of a relatively
dark-hued kind, a verse which suggests some awareness of the fateful
undertow of forces which play their part in man's destiny. This verse
drifts far from the world of quietly optimistic humanism that had been
typical of Selander's earlier work, but it may be doubted that it represents anything more than a momentary mood, a sensitive and intelligent
poet's experimenting with moods and ideas that were everywhere in the
air when Europe for the second time in our century was aflame with
war.

Even Gunnar Mascoll Silfverstolpe, the most correct and socially impeccable representative of poetic idyllicism, was shocked into an awareness of realities outside his own "beautifully rounded world" when war
clouds began to gather over Europe in the middle 1930's, and in 1940, in
the volume of verse *Hemland* (Home Land), he protested strongly
against totalitarian violence and injustice, and expressed his faith in the
Western humanistic tradition which had been so blatantly challenged
by a belligerent Fascism and Nazism. In keeping with his aristocratic

fastidiousness his protest was not couched in violent terms, but it left its mark for all of that.

Silfverstolpe was a nobleman to his fingertips, born into a class highly conscious of its position and having a strong sense of responsibility toward traditions and country. He became in consequence a poet of the rarest refinement and dignity, publishing only five volumes of exquisitely finished verse over a period of twenty years. His life and work otherwise was mainly that of a modern courtier-connoisseur. In his official capacity as Keeper of the Royal Wardrobe he busied himself with art history, and outside court environs he served for sixteen years as a respected literary and art critic for *Stockholms-Tidningen*. A year before his death he was elected to the Swedish Academy. Of literary influences on him A. E. Housman and Thomas Hardy seem to have been most important, Housman's verse because of its identification of the youthful idealism of modern England with ancient Greece, Hardy's apparently because in his poetry a tragic modern spirit triumphs over a self-absorbing romantic melancholy.

A meticulous sense of duty dominated everything Silfverstolpe did, whether it was accounting for the royal household's possessions or preparing art monographs or dashing off newspaper copy or writing elegantly restrained verse. This sense of duty, combined with a profound feeling of loyalty to his family and a narrow circle of friends, determined largely both the themes and the literary quality of Silfverstolpe's poetry. His world of experience and idea was a more limited one than that of either of his friends Asplund or Selander, but it was of its kind an absolutely genuine world, and the poetry which emanated from it was in its way equally genuine. This world being a world sharply delimited by tradition, it was quite appropriate that Silfverstolpe's first poems appeared under the collective title *Arvet* (The Heritage, 1919). Gunnar Mascoll Silfverstolpe was always conscious of "the heritage," a heritage in his case intimately identified with Stora Åsby, his family's modest landed property in Sörmland, one of the relatively pastoral rural areas in central Sweden. He clung throughout his life with a never failing loyalty to the memories of his childhood and youth on the countryside of his ancestors. In the best of his poetry — that included in the volumes *Dagsljus* (Light of Day, 1923), *Vardag* (Weekdays, 1926), and *Efteråt* (Afterward, 1932) — he sings with quiet simplicity and restrained ecstasy of the charms of this countryside and the cultural values which its fine old landed traditions had preserved from generation to generation. This poetry is elegantly disciplined and prefers to lose itself in a quiet contemplation of things past, but tensions exist in it, tensions determined largely by events over which the poet had no control, events in a war-torn, war-conscious modern world. In *Light of Day* and *Weekdays* these tensions appear sporadically and in certain poetic disguises which blunt their force, but in *Afterward* they more frequently disturb the calm surface of Silfverstolpe's verse, and in *Homeland* (1940), published a year after the outbreak of the Second World War, the poet's sense of a bloody storm over the world and the homeland tends to take over almost completely. In the years of his first poetic bloom Silfverstolpe was vaguely aware of the precarious hold which the past maintained on the average twentieth-century mind and the apparently hapless position of tradition in the presence of modern industrialization and man's mania to conduct war. This is why he clung fast to traditional values with such unswerving loyalty. To him Stora Åsby with its way of life was not merely his childhood home, a pinpoint on the world map — it was a symbol of humane values and as such a way of salvation for a disintegrating modern society.

But in the form which the Stora Åsby tradition nearly always took in Silfverstolpe's verse it was also a fragile idyl, a poetic recollection of things past — and as such it lacked the vitality to stem the formidable tide of modern developments. His poetry was a lovely requiem over a dying local culture rather than a vital support and guide for man in a brutal modern world. Silfverstolpe's "everyday realism," like that of his fellow idylists in the 1920's, represents a last graceful and charming chapter in the history of poetic traditionalism rather than a significant source of inspiration for a literature of the future. The times may have needed Silfverstolpe's poetry but found little use for it because it had not kept pace with the brutally accelerated social and cultural drives of modern life. For better or for worse, cruder but stronger and more virile spirits than Silfverstolpe and his kind were destined to take over the burden of guiding Swedish literary developments through the deeply disturbing maze of feeling and idea which is the spiritual dilemma of man today.

The fact that Swedish literature of the last three or four decades has, instead of yielding to the blandishments of an idyllic traditionalism, matured with the challenge of modern times and modern problems is an evidence of its continuing vitality, its willingness to meet the spiritual contingencies of our day on their own terms and to ferret out those literary forms best suited to the modern spirit. In the process many stylistic sins have been committed, many stillborn poems and novels and dramas have been written; but on the whole it can be said that recent Swedish literature — particularly that which came to fruition in the late 1920's and the 1930's — reflects a creative sensitivity and vigor worthy of the extraordinarily complex world with which it was confronted.

CHAPTER 11

The Modernistic Ground Swell and Attendant Social Criticism

THOUGH Sweden lay on the periphery of postwar developments on the Continent in the 1920's, she could not wholly escape the impact of these developments. At the close of the War economic conditions and an inflamed political situation forced the Conservatives to yield to the long-standing demand for universal suffrage, the almost immediate consequence of which was the rise to dominant political power of the Social Democratic party, a power which this party has maintained with only occasional breaks down to the present day. Universal suffrage spelled out the definitive democratization of the country. Economic conditions improved rapidly after 1922, but ten years later Sweden's fabulous financial manipulator, Ivar Kreuger, took his own life under circumstances which had international reverberations, and with Kreuger's demise Sweden found itself drawn deeply into the whirlpool of world depression of the 1930's. But by skillful political maneuvering and a series of social reforms calculated to satisfy the masses the Social Democratic party in cooperation with the Agrarians managed to ride out the storm of depression with a minimum of complications. Sweden made in consequence a remarkably rapid economic recovery. New dislocations inevitably took place during the Second World War, which Sweden sat out as a neutral; but with the passing of the War the country again went forward economically by re-establishing its substantial position in world trade.

Aside from these crucial political and economic phases of development Sweden has in the last four decades undergone many changes, changes which have tended to transform the face of the land and sharply affect its cultural temper. A rapidly stepped-up industrialization of the country has not only substantially increased the size of cities, it has modernized them in many ways, and it has in part revolutionized conditions on the countryside. Farms have been electrified. Railroads and busses, the automobile and radio, the growth of rural cooperatives and improved educational facilities have to a very considerable extent eliminated the sense of isolation which farm folk had experienced in the past. A flood of newspapers and magazines and books calculated to satisfy all levels of intelligence and taste has become easily available. With leisure for the masses provided by a shortened work week and compulsory vacation allowances, sports have flourished and adult education has attracted increasing thousands of those who previously had neither the time nor the energy for intellectual pursuits. The "welfare state," a concept strongly supported by the parties in power in the 1930's and later, accounts only partly for the transformation of contemporary Swedish society. Private initiative has been equally important, providing products and services hitherto unavailable to many, employing effective modern advertising techniques, and introducing generally streamlined procedures in the conduct of business and industry. Private capital has even ventured with at times considerable success into such a sharply competitive field as modern film production. At almost every point the tempo of Swedish life has been accelerated, the pulse-beat of the nation has perceptibly quickened, a thoroughly modern spirit has come to pour its heady components into the life-stream of the nation. This has meant that Sweden has in a sense become less Swedish, that it has become more and more in recent years a part of the world community, has taken on more than a little of what may be called an international way of life, an international mentality.

Fortunately in literature and the other arts the less desirable features of this internationalization of man's way of life have been largely avoided, chiefly it would seem because a centuries-long cultural discipline has provided the nation with an ability to absorb fairly large doses of foreign matter without fatal results, that is to say without losing its national identity. In the last three decades the doses have simply been more severe than before, and generally more pervasive in their effects, influencing not only such relatively exclusive manifestations of the nation's culture as literature and the arts but tending to transform the daily life-patterns of the whole nation. In literature and the other arts a strong ground swell of what may be called cultural modernism has asserted itself. No longer

439

are such modern literary spirits as Hjalmar Bergman, Pär Lagerkvist, and Birger Sjöberg relatively isolated figures, impressive and massively disturbing but attracting only a limited, half-willing audience. Now a whole host of young Swedish authors feed eagerly on modernistic fare and have come with the years to dominate more or less triumphantly the literary scene.

Though it is scarcely possible to indicate with precision exactly when this cultural modernism made its first strong bid for public favor in Sweden, one can with some feeling of assurance say that this occurred in the years leading up to and including 1930. Two events in particular dramatize the bid for public favor on the part of the modernists at this time: the appearance in 1929 of the deliberately provocative volume of experimental poetry entitled *5 unga*, and the opening in 1930 of the equally provocative Stockholm Exposition of the applied arts. Of these two events the Stockholm Exposition inevitably attracted the larger public attention and aroused a more violent and widespread controversy. Its daring defense of a partly Corbusier-inspired functionalism as applied particularly to the home and its furnishings had at first as little popular appeal as the "new poetry" of the young poetic mavericks who had banded together in the *5 unga* group. But the early efforts of both the functional modernists and the young experimental poets threw open doors from which new creative perspectives could be descried, and these doors have remained open, permitting a steady flow into the world of the Swedish arts of fresh, forward-looking ideas from far and near. The results have not infrequently been happy. What the world now calls "Swedish modern" as applied to furniture design and related matters has its immediate origins in the Stockholm Exposition of 1930, and Swedish architecture of the last quarter century is equally indebted to the ideas first dramatically promulgated in the same exposition.

Though Swedish literature in the last few decades reflects certain parallels to these developments in the applied arts, it is both in its origins and its creative ramifications a considerably more complex phenomenon. The constantly shifting surface features of the new literature suggest something of the complex inner play of forces out of which it grows. At times these forces are instinctively conservative, essentially tradition-directed; but much more frequently they are radical, intent upon questioning and defying, prepared to experiment with such advanced literary forms as the chaotic times seemed to demand. The representative authors of the period find encouragement for their departures from conventional thinking and literary practices by immersing themselves in the world of idea and form of the most advanced spirits of the day. In immediate Swedish literary contexts they learn from Hjalmar Bergman, Pär Lager-kvist, and Birger Sjöberg, who each in his way, as we have seen, had broken with convention and sought new paths for literary expression. Just across the Baltic also, in the highly modernistic Swedo-Finnish verse of Edith Södergran (1892–1923) and Elmer Diktonius (b. 1896), Swed-ish poets find much to admire and emulate. And in larger, international contexts the new generation of authors feeds on Freudianism and Marx-ism, on primitivism and surrealism, on experimental trends in poetry and prose ranging from "free verse" and diverse symbolistic techniques to hard-boiled laconisms and sophisticated stream-of-consciousness prac-tices. While the immediately preceding generation of Swedish authors had found inspiration in such relatively simple modern spirits as Jack London and Upton Sinclair, Kipling, Housman, and Rupert Brooke, the new generation feeds on the more subtle and heady, the more sharply challenging literary fare of Proust and Gide, D. H. Lawrence and James Joyce, Edgar Lee Masters and Sherwood Anderson, Kafka, T. S. Eliot, Hemingway, and Faulkner. The result is a literary mentality in Sweden which is more often than not prepared to strike out boldly in new direc-tions along a broad front. In the years around 1930 these developments came to a head, and though some of the more extreme tendencies had to be modified under the pressures of world events, it is clear that Swedish literature in the decades which followed has in the main moved in the directions suggested by those poets and novelists and critics who first came into prominence around 1930.

The developments at this time can be studied most directly in the rash of critical essays published in a number of short-lived periodical publica-tions which became what may be called "house organs" for the various groups then seeking to impose upon their reading publics the particular way of literary salvation which each of them promulgated. Three jour-nals in particular dispensed modernistic doctrine of one kind or other — *Spektrum*, an organ of radical social and political opinion whose con-tributions were largely from the Clarté falange, *Fönstret*, which de-fended among other things the primitivism and poetic experimentation of the *5 unga* group, and *Fronten*, which provided a prominent pulpit especially for Sven Stolpe (b. 1905), the most prolific and vociferous of the modernist evangelists of the day. Stolpe's later change of heart, which led him first to the Oxford Buchmanite group and then to conversion to the Roman Catholic faith, has resulted in an only partly modulated cocksureness of manner, with little diminution in the precipitate flow of essays, novels, and dramas from his pen. While *Spektrum, Fönstret*, and *Fronten* met the usual fate of small coterie publications with special missions and small financial resources, another periodical which came into existence at the time, *Bonniers Litterära Magasin*, has had a continuous flourishing existence down to our day. The flexible, open-minded editorial policy of *Bonniers Litterära Magasin*, together with the economic backing of Sweden's most successful publishing house, has guaranteed its long life and permitted it to take its worthy place alongside the distinguished, more than half-century-old cultural journal *Ord och Bild*. Though the "cultural debate" which swirled for a few years around *Spektrum, Fönstret*, and *Fronten* was often strident and at times confusing, it reflected a critical vitality and an awareness of modern literary trends which were of the utmost importance for Swedish literature in the 1930's. Among the contributors to these journals were some of those who were to become (or already had become) the leading poets and novelists of the day, and the columns of these journals not infrequently provided the Swedish reader with his first decisive introduction to certain central figures on the international literary scene. D. H. Lawrence was one of the "discoveries" of *Fönstret*, and T. S. Eliot's *The Waste Land* appeared for the first time in a Swedish version in *Spektrum*.

It should be mentioned in connection with the role that the journals of the time played in acquainting the public with literary trends and helping to form literary tastes that newspapers also in the last quarter century have performed a similar service. Swedish newspapers had, indeed, for at least two or three generations previously opened their columns to serious literary criticism — for the first time dramatically in the case of Oscar Levertin and *Svenska Dagbladet* in the years around the turn of the century. After Levertin's death this practice became more general, until today it would be unthinkable for a prominent Swedish newspaper not to have on its staff two or three distinguished cultural personalities whose task it is to provide the newspaper's readers with a sensitive and mature account of what is going on in the world of literature and the related arts. Today the larger Stockholm newspapers vie with one another for the services of the best available literary talents, and these talents are in many cases among the more distinguished poets, critics, and literary historians of the day.

We have noted above how from the earliest years of our century the very *number* of competent Swedish authors is on the increase. This phenomenon accelerates sharply with the passage of time and becomes in our day one of the most characteristic features of the Swedish literary scene. It may be that no one of the authors who rose to literary prominence in the 1930's ranks with the major literary figures of the past, but no earlier period in Swedish literature can boast so many at least near-distinguished poets and novelists, and beneath this near-distinguished group a score or more of quite competent authors jostle one another for a place in the literary sun. So numerous, indeed, are the literary talents of our day and so extensive and varied their total productivity that the contemporary literary scene in Sweden at times reminds one of the teeming fertility of the jungle. Some of this rich literary flora will seem familiar enough to readers acquainted with the literature of preceding decades — poems that have contact with the past or certain readily identifiable relations with the present outward scene, novels that deal realistically with social problems, plays that do not depart sharply from an older tradition in the drama. Then again one comes upon what seem to be new and often strange phenomena — distorted, "unnatural" forms, symbols that open up curious, oftentimes ominous vistas, words and phrases and rhythmic arrangements that seem to be ends in themselves, worlds of mood and idea which become entangled in bewitching Freudian conceptual patterns. But the knowing reader will recognize that not all of these phenomena are new, that they derive in part both from Classical and Romantic sources, that they at least in some cases represent a deliberate effort on the part of the author to bring the past and the present together in fresh poetic syntheses.

If the drift toward modernism is more pronounced in lyric poetry than in other genres, it comes also to have especially in the late 1930's and the 1940's an increasing importance in the novel and the short story. The Swedish drama, however, largely tends to resist more stubbornly the pressures which clamor for radical change, despite the impressive contributions made by Hjalmar Bergman and Pär Lagerkvist to a symbolistic-expressionistic drama which had the post-Inferno Strindberg as its chief source of inspiration and point of departure. The failure of the contemporary Swedish drama in general to pursue a radical program of renewal along the lines suggested by the Strindberg of *The Dream Play* and the "Chamber Plays" did not mean, however, that it was prepared to capitulate meekly to theatrical convention and be satisfied with the modest minor role which a native Swedish drama had before Strindberg played in Swedish literary developments. On the contrary, dramatic composition on a reasonably high level of achievement has flourished far more in contemporary Sweden than at any other time in the nation's history. Not a few of the last generation or two of ranking Swedish poets and novelists have been encouraged by favorable developments in the theater as well as in the film and radio to seek fame (*and* fortune) in one or the other or all of these theatrical media. In both the legitimate theater and the film Sweden experienced during the 1920's and later a genuine theatrical renaissance, marked not only by the appearance of several great directors (Per Lindberg, Sandro Malmquist, Olof Molander, Alf Sjöberg) and a number of brilliant actors and actresses (Lars Hanson, Gösta Ekman, Inga Tidblad, Tora Teje, and others) but also by an active participation in matters of scenic design on the part of a number of highly talented artists (Isaac Grünewald, Otte Sköld, Jon-And, Sven Erixon, Stellan Mörner) and by certain developments in the film. The Swedish film in the 1920's, in fact, attracted such favorable international attention that Hollywood felt obliged to send hurry-up calls to a number of Swedish film figures of the day, two directors, Mauritz Stiller and Victor Sjöström, and three Swedish "film stars," Lars Hanson, Karin Molander, and — Greta Garbo.

It has been observed that these theatrical developments in Sweden insofar as they involve a serious approach to the dramatic arts were from the beginning characterized by a conflict between the spectacular, colorful, Reinhardt-inspired theater of the young directors and stage designers on the one hand, and a more intimate, realistic Stanislavsky-motivated art favored by actors and the theater-interested public on the other. However this may be, the Swedish theater was shaken to its foundations by the daring vision of the young moderns led brilliantly by "the foremost disturber of the theatrical peace," the young Per Lindberg (1890–1944), and out of the storm which swept over the Swedish theater in these years came fresh ideas which in part transformed acting and staging practices, aroused generally a new interest in theater, and encouraged as never before those who had dramatic talents to write for the theater. The new interest in drama was reflected in the establishment of several (today eight in all) municipal theaters in provincial cities and in the founding of the highly successful National Touring Theater called *Riksteatern*. This latter organization, which recently celebrated its twenty-fifth anniversary of highly successful activities, brings theater

444

of the highest class to many communities which cannot afford permanent theaters of their own. Among the rather considerable number of Swedish authors of the last two or three decades who have been encouraged by these developments to contribute to the new theatrical repertoire are the two novelists Vilhelm Moberg and Björn-Erik Höijer, the novelist-dramatist Rudolf Värnlund, the journalist-critic Herbert Grevenius, the poet Karl Ragnar Gierow, the art historian Ragnar Josephson, and three more or less precocious young men from the 1940's, Stig Dagerman, Ingmar Bergman, and Lars Levi Laestadius, the latter two as theater directors approaching playwriting primarily from within the theater. Of these dramatists I shall deal in other contexts with Moberg, Höijer, and Dagerman, for the basic work of the first two lies chiefly in prose fiction while Dagerman's contribution to Swedish literature can best be considered in terms of his literary developments generally in relation to the 1940's.

Of the remainder, Rudolf Värnlund (1900–45) and Herbert Grevenius (b. 1901) have turned more often to social questions than their fellow dramatists. Värnlund, the more original of the two, is the only Swedish author of proletarian origins who has managed to write something approaching great drama on proletarian phases of life. In both his novels and his plays he is a restless experimenter in matters of form, but in the novels he is usually rather diffuse and ineffectual though he often gives us vivid glimpses into the mentality of talented young workmen in times of extreme social stress. In the 1920's the mood of his novels is one of sharp desperation, but in the following decade this desperation yields to less somber moods and permits him to write his one completely satisfactory novel, *Hedningarna som icke hava lagen* (The Heathen Who Have Not the Law, 1936), a significant contribution to the broadly documented autobiographical novel so typical of the Swedish mid-1930's. As a dramatist Värnlund had a surer touch, and when death suddenly cut short his career he was counted among the most effective of the more advanced dramatic experimenters in Sweden. Though *Sångare* (Singers, 1933) reveals that he was capable of writing folk comedy in a warm, essentially idyllic vein, he is really impressive only in such tragic working-class drama as *Den heliga familjen* (The Holy Family, 1932) and *U 39* (1939), the former a sensitively sketched history of the Swedish labor movement culminating in a bitter strike, the latter a gripping psychological study centering on a U-boat catastrophe, its social ramifications and ethical implications. Värnlund's dramatic form reflects his direct con-

445

tact with German expressionism and constructivism, both of which he had observed at first hand in the crisis-torn Berlin of the early 1920's.

Herbert Grevenius is by contrast with Värnlund a more skillful but a less stirring dramatist. His working-class origins were far less degrading than Värnlund's and do not seem to have left any sense of class consciousness in him. After studies at the University of Stockholm he drifted into journalism, becoming with time one of the more diligent of Swedish theater critics as attested by the three volumes of his collected articles on theater and reviews of performances *I afton kl. 8* (This Evening at 8, 1940), *Offentliga nöjen* (Public Entertainment, 1947), and *Dagen efter* (The Day After, 1951). His dramatic production, beginning in 1927 and continuing with no discernible loss of creative energy down to our day, reflects a flair for lively, telling dialogue and genuine local color together with a born journalist's interest in subjects of current interest. In *Sonja* (1927) and *Första maj* (The First of May, 1935) he concerns himself with working-class home life and its problems, in *Tåg 56* (Train 56, 1936) with the Swedish birthrate crisis as actualized by the sociological investigations of the Myrdals, in the comedy *Krigsmans erinran* (Warrior's Reminder, 1947) with some of the human situations which arise in periods of military mobilization. In plays such as *Som folk är mest* (As People for the Most Part Are, 1941) and *Lunchrasten* (The Lunch Pause, 1952) Grevenius is satisfied on the whole to provide us with group sketches of ordinary people in their essentially drab but somehow engaging everyday milieus. *As People for the Most Part Are* has been to date his most popular play despite (or possibly because of) its failure to maintain a sharp dramatic focus. This play and *The Lunch Pause* contain a full measure of Grevenius's special flavor as a dramatist, a dialogue of extraordinary naturalness and a finely human way of projecting the exact quality of given Stockholm milieus. Grevenius knew his city well and catches up its face and spirit with uncanny precision and aplomb.

The relative hurly-burly of the contemporary scene out of which the plays of Värnlund and Grevenius directly and unashamedly grow is hardly characteristic of the drama of Karl Ragnar Gierow (b. 1904) and Ragnar Josephson (b. 1891), whose origins and backgrounds have dictated a literary approach to the contemporary scene and the problems of modern man which does not permit crude patterns of conflict or a coarse-grained modern vocabulary. In fact, in Gierow's most important plays the heavy historical and legendary disguises in which he envelops

446

his treatment of modern problems is so overwhelming that few readers or theatergoers are especially aware of the fact that he is deliberately manipulating these disguises as a means of throwing light on certain timeless dilemmas of man — but dilemmas, it should be noted, which manifest themselves particularly in the stresses and strains of contemporary life. Josephson does not employ the machinery of historical disguises in his examination of man's fate, but he has a fondness for the poetic phrase, the indirection of the symbol, and an occasional brittle or sentimental comic effect which reflects a constitutive unwillingness to come at grips *directly* with the conditions of existence. The somewhat circuitous ways in which Gierow and Josephson approach their problems are to be accounted for by the fact that both are highly intelligent academic talents, Gierow approaching dramatic composition only after a rather long literary apprenticeship as a poet with strong cerebral predilections (four volumes of verse coming from his hand before his appearance as a dramatist in 1941), and Josephson turning to the drama as a kind of avocation in the midst of a brilliant career as a professor of art history at the University of Lund. That both Gierow's and Josephson's dramatic composition ultimately led to appointments as chief of the Royal Dramatic Theater is natural enough, Gierow having in 1951 succeeded Josephson who had occupied the post for the preceding three years.

Two circumstances conspired to make Gierow the kind of dramatist that he became — his facility at writing verse and his profoundly pessimistic disillusionment in the presence of European between-the-wars developments. Gierow represents in the Swedish theater today the only serious attempt to renew the drama in terms of poetic drama on the grand scale. As such he takes his place in the contemporary world drama alongside such exponents of a poetic drama as T. S. Eliot and Maxwell Anderson, combining in his work some of the intellectual qualities of the former with the colorful rhetoric of the latter. Though Gierow has experimented with half-gloomy folk fantasy in *Färjstället* (The Ferry Place) and tried his hand at light comic satire on a contemporary theme in *Av hjärtans lust* (With All My Heart), he is considerably more impressive in his two serious verse dramas *Rovdjuret* (The Beast of Prey, 1941) and *Helgonsaga* (Saint Legend, 1943), in which his sonorous, image-laden blank verse lends an appropriately elevated tone to the tragic view of human destiny that these dramas reflect. But impressive as these two plays in general are, they suffer at times from an excessive preoccupa-

447

tion with grisly manifestations of human cruelty and the author's somewhat pretentious insistence upon using his dramatic materials more or
less directly in the service of abstract reasoning on such thorny subjects
as the problem of evil. The philosopher-moralist tends to take over from
the poet-dramatist, sometimes with unhappy consequences.

Josephson's plays are less pretentious, closer to life's immediate realities than Gierow's, but in their relative sobriety of conception and form
they have their own kind of theatricality. Josephson is at once more
sophisticated and popular than Gierow. As an art historian he has an
eye for telling external effects, subtle or "stagey" by turn; but underneath such surface matters in Josephson's plays there runs an undercurrent of serious enough intention — an incisive probing of certain sides of
the human psyche, a probing which raises ethical questions without insisting upon sharp judgments. Before taking up his duties as chief of the
Royal Dramatic Theater, Josephson had attracted theatergoers' attention particularly with two plays, *Leopold, luftkonstnär* (Leopold, Acro-
bat) and *Kanske en diktare* (performed 1932; tr. *Perhaps a Poet*), of
which the latter is the more important. Written as a starring role for
the fabulous Swedish actor Gösta Ekman, *Perhaps a Poet* was one of the
distinct theatrical successes of the 1930's. It lays bare with gently incisive
dramatic skill the soul of a man whom life has passed by, as it were, and
who therefore has to create in his own imagination a life which he is not
permitted otherwise to live. He is a poet with no public except himself.
The man, Filip by name, is an ordinary *portier* by occupation, but a sensitive man, a man of exalted worth in his own highly developed imaginary world. Nothing happens to him, however, in the drab round of
his daily existence — until one day he takes upon himself, in an excess of
misdirected feeling, the guilt of a murder committed by another, a young
woman who had merely spoken kindly to him on occasion in the past.
The real motive of Filip's apparently heroic act of gratitude, we come
to know, is to give to his pathetically empty make-believe life some kind
of moral content; but in the end he realizes that even this act was based
on a lie, that his whole imaginary world has been but a tissue of evasion
and illusion. Coming face to face with this fact in all its stark mockery
at the last, he shoots himself, unable any longer to maintain even with a
tatter of dignity the pathetic life illusion which he had built up with such
fatuous dissimulation down through the years. The role of Filip is a
challenging one for a great actor, one who can play with undiminished
virtuosity the whole gamut of human emotions from the depths of

pathos to the extremes of willful self-exaltation; but otherwise the play provides only minor, rigidly subordinated character parts. The play in general falls into the category of tragicomedy, composed in a sensitive poetic vein not without some elements of the sentimental and the sensational.

Swedish theatergoers have not often been so startled as they were in the 1930's and 1940's when the two talented and brash young men Lars Levi Laestadius (b. 1909) and Ingmar Bergman (b. 1918) burst in upon the Swedish theater with ambitions to reshape it more or less radically. In a sense they came to continue the demand for change championed since the early 1920's by Per Lindberg, whose death came early, at the height of his brilliant career, shortly after Laestadius's debut as a young director. Both Laestadius and Ingmar Bergman first attracted attention as directors of student-performed plays, Laestadius in Uppsala in the early 1930's, Bergman in Stockholm a decade later. After these beginnings they moved quickly into the professional theaters outside Stockholm — to Göteborg, to Hälsingborg, to Malmö, and finally to Stockholm, Bergman as a director of the Royal Dramatic Theater in 1959 and Laestadius as chief of the new Stockholm City Theater in 1960.

Laestadius first attracted general attention in 1943 with a comedy entitled *Herr Blinck går över alla gränser* (Mr. Blinck Breaks Over the Traces), whose hero, an ordinary office drudge, defies the banal tyrannies of his everyday existence and launches out for the time being into a mad pattern of existence of which he had always dreamed. The play is replete with unexpected turns of episode, lively dialogue, and warm poetic fantasy. It might have gained even more favor with the Swedish public than it did had not the Danish dramatist Kjeld Abell employed several years earlier the identical theme of Laestadius's play in the highly popular lyric comedy *The Melody That Got Lost*. Two of Laestadius's later plays, *Herrgården* (The Manor House, 1945) and *Melodi på lergök* (Melody on a Toy Ocarina, 1948), are comedies with a rather sharp and definitely effective satiric thrust, the former playfully castigating aristocratic pretensions, the latter exposing fraudulent manipulations on the art market.

Ingmar Bergman was from the beginning a more brash and many-sided figure in the theater than Lars Levi Laestadius, and has remained relatively brash down to our day — so brash that he has continued, at least until recently, to be a thorn in the flesh of theater critics, who have admitted his brilliance but have often deplored the manner in which he

449

uses his talents. For years, Swedish critics accused him of having never really grown up, of having persisted in retaining an essentially adolescent mentality long after he should have moved on to more mature levels of response to life in his art. However this may be, Ingmar Bergman has been enormously productive as a playwright both for the theater and the film, and as a director he has been equally active in both of these media. The result of such an intensive theatrical activity has by no means always been happy, but in his best moments as a playwright and scenario writer he approaches Strindberg and Hjalmar Bergman in dramatic intensity, and as a director he is invariably arresting if not always distinguished. In the film Ingmar Bergman ranges widely and often brilliantly in mood and theme, his first film script *Hets* (entitled *Torment* in the form released for English showings) being a grim study of a schoolboy's writhings in the hands of a sadistic schoolmaster, while in later years he has scored international successes (including the Grand Prix at Cannes in 1956 and a similar award at Berlin in 1958) with two fascinating comedies and the medieval morality with modern cinematic techniques known among English-speaking film viewers as *The Seventh Seal*. Of the two comedies, *Sommarnattens leende* (Smiles of a Summer's Night) and *Smultronstället* (English title, Wild Strawberries), the former handles madcap farce ingredients with something of the touch of Classical comedy and the latter exploits a vein of warm human feeling just short of the sentimental.

As a serious dramatist for the legitimate theater Ingmar Bergman has cultivated much more exclusively than in his films a view of life of a grimly macabre kind. Among his more arresting plays are *Mig till skräck* (Dread Unto Me), *Dagen slutar tidigt* (The Day Closes Early), and *Mordet i Barjärna* (The Murder at Barjärna), all of which are bizarre modern morality plays reminiscent of but scarcely attaining the fierce dramatic economy of Strindberg's *Spook Sonata*. As a man of the theater Ingmar Bergman cannot resist the temptation of employing all the modern stage tricks at his command, and as a kind of adolescent Strindberg he all but outdoes the master in stripping man of his pitiful masks and conjuring up macabre visions of human evil. Frenetic and utterly bizarre as these visions often are, they are nevertheless not infrequently visions of genius or near-genius. One objects less to the visions in themselves than to the monomaniac persistence with which they are repeated. As a dramatist Ingmar Bergman, like not a few of his fellows today, immerses himself more and more deeply in one mood, tends to play endless variations on a single gruesome theme. He is in his serious drama so hyp-notized by his grisly view of life that he at times seems incapable of breaking the dark spell which it maintains over him. He has for years managed to hold his public in the legitimate theater by the sheer virtu-osity of his creative performance, but unless in the future he can renew his dramatic vision as he has his film instinct, widening his thematic mood and range, it is doubtful that as a dramatist he will succeed in realizing his early promise. To date certainly his chief contribution lies in the theater and the film rather than in dramatic composition.

If one is compelled finally to conclude that developments in the Swed-ish drama during the last three or four decades are impressive but scarcely distinguished, one need not be so reserved in generalizing about Swedish lyric poetry during the same period. In fact, not since the 1890's has lyric poetry flourished in Sweden as it has since the 1920's, and not even the 1890's can boast the number of poets of reasonably high dis-tinction who are writing today. Though it is difficult to determine the relative importance among Swedish poets who have appeared in the last three or four decades, one can say with some confidence that at least five of them — Karin Boye, Hjalmar Gullberg, Harry Martinson, Gunnar Ekelöf, and Erik Lindegren — are poets of high distinction, and a half dozen or more others — Erik Blomberg, Bertil Malmberg, Johannes Ed-felt, Artur Lundkvist, Nils Ferlin, and Karl Vennberg — rank just below the first five.

To this listing of contemporary Swedish poets might be added a dozen or more others, all of whom are talents of some distinction but none of whom has to date come to occupy an important place in Swed-ish poetry. Aside from the extraordinarily large number of poets of greater or lesser stature, that which particularly impresses one in the poetic renewal of the last decades is its awareness — its often painful, tragic awareness — of the dark complexities of modern life and its often eager readiness to experiment with such new poetic forms as might best give expression to a questioning, skeptical, sometimes desperately pessi-mistic modern spirit. Faith and hope exist in this poetry, but usually as a kind of residual element or as an in-spite-of-all note of defiance in the presence of the cumulative banalities and brutalities of the contemporary scene. Though one may at times grow weary of the predominantly nega-tive tone in this verse, one cannot fail to be impressed by its honesty and by its finely expressive quality, the variety and originality of its form. This verse has some points of contact with Swedish poetry of the past, but in the main it reflects a radical departure – especially in matters of verse form – from Sweden's great lyric traditions.

Some signs of the departure appear already in the 1920's, and more in the 1930's; but not until the early 1940's do we witness a veritable flood-tide of poetic renewal – a flood-tide which has continued with little if any abatement down to our own day. During the years after the First World War, when the Swedish poetic idylists had lulled many a reader into a synthetic mood of quiet and security, certain other Swedish poets, more modern and critical in spirit, were far less prepared than the idylists to assume that humanity had learned its lesson from the War and that society would somehow solve its problems by only slightly modifying the social and political status quo. It should be noted, however, that these other Swedish poets – among whom may especially be mentioned Bertil Malmberg and Erik Blomberg, Hjalmar Gullberg and Johannes Edfelt – did not in the 1920's break radically with the traditional poetic forms even though their poetry breathed a spirit and at times took on forms which were scarcely traditional. Their verse may be labeled "conventional poetry with a difference," that is to say they poured more or less modern ideas and moods into only partially transformed verse forms. Unlike the poets of the 1930's and 1940's they were not prepared to create a radically new kind of Swedish poetry.

In fact, one of them, Bertil Malmberg (1889–1958), is the last Swedish poet who has deliberately written in the "grand manner" typical of one of the main lines of development in earlier Swedish verse. In later years Malmberg on occasion experimented with simply phrased, highly concentrated verse, but such occasions were relatively few and scarcely characteristic of his usual practices. After having made some impression on the Swedish reading public before and during the First World War years with verse in an exaggerated *fin de siècle* manner which soon drifted paradoxically into activist heroic moods, Malmberg left Sweden in 1917 for Germany, not to return to his native land until ten years later. During his stay abroad he was drawn more and more deeply into the stream of Platonic idealism represented particularly by Schiller and Stefan George. In the elevated Classical concept of Absolute Beauty implicit in this poetic idealism Malmberg seems to have found a degree of control over the discordant elements within him which had been sharply intensified during his years in a chaotic postwar Germany. The volume of poems *Orfika*, from 1923, reflects a strenuous effort on the part of the poet to swing himself up to the serenity of the Platonic ideal world. But in the two following volumes, *Slöjan* (The Veil, 1927) and *Vinden* (The Wind, 1929), it is apparent that the ideal of abstract beauty could provide for Malmberg no final protection against the destructive forces within himself and the immediate world of reality around him, and in *Illusionernas träd* (The Tree of Illusions, 1932) and *Dikter vid gränsen* (Poems on the Boundary, 1935), the volumes which first attracted widespread admiration for Malmberg's poetry, the impression was confirmed that the poet could find no final comfort in a dream of pure beauty. In *The Tree of Illusions* a number of arresting love poems provide a temporary escape from the world of brutalizing reality, but in *Poems on the Boundary*, whose magnificent doomsday visions are inspired in part by Spengler's *Untergang des Abenlandes* and certain of Thomas Mann's works, the poet's gloom is absolute. An abortive effort to escape this gloom via fellowship in the Buchmanite Oxford group is recorded in the confessional moralizing poems of *Sångerna om samvetet och ödet* (Songs About Conscience and Destiny, 1938), after which Malmberg returns to his poetic isolation and his private struggle with fate in the brooding visions of *Flöjter ur ödsligheten* (Flutes in Desolation, 1941) and *Under månens fallande båge* (Under the Moon's Descending Arc, 1947). For those interested in the personal backgrounds out of which Malmberg's poetry has grown the poet has provided two revealing volumes of memoirs, *Ett stycke väg* (A Bit of the Way, 1950) and *Ett författarliv* (An Author's Life, 1952).

None of Malmberg's Platonic abstractions, apocalyptic visions, and resounding verbal sonorities is to be found in the verse of Erik Blomberg (b. 1894), who insists always that man's life is for better or for worse a thing of this world and who refuses to allow his poetic Muse to soar into imaginative worlds "that never were on land or sea." While Malmberg was essentially an isolated figure, an egocentric poet struggling with his own private destiny, Erik Blomberg has always been driven by a sense of social mission deeply rooted in a Marxist philosophy. University trained, an art historian and cultural critic of high distinction, Erik Blomberg has never in his prose or poetry veered from the social idealism of his youth. In his work a mind of rare range and critical penetration is always finely sensitive to aesthetic values and constantly attentive to the demands of a warm human conscience. Though small in amount his poetry weighed heavily with the younger generation in the 1920's, and it impresses readers today more than most of the poetry of its day. So severe has been Erik Blomberg's poetic standard that when in 1944 his collected verse was to be published he permitted only a hundred poems to be included from a production which had spanned a quarter of a century. Six modest volumes in all had contained the poems from which the collected edition was drawn — five volumes from the years 1918 to 1927; the sixth, after a long pause, in 1943. Of these volumes *Den fångne guden* (The Imprisoned God, 1927) is the most important though *Jorden* (The Earth, 1920) and *Visor* (Songs, 1924) attracted in their day a great many enthusiastic readers.

Simplicity and clarity of utterance are stylistic ideals which Erik Blomberg always realizes in his poetry, whether in his short songs and concentrated proverb-like pieces or in the more ambitious, almost ode-like poems in which he gives deeply felt expression to the deliberately earth-bound social gospel which he has most exhaustively developed in the brilliant essay "En ny livskänsla" (A New Feeling for Life, 1925). Dreamer though he in some ways is, Erik Blomberg insists that our dreams must face up to reality, that they must derive their strength from the earth rather than from the stars.

> Night upon Earth has fallen —
> Quivering, starry gleams.
> Distant the bright worlds wander:
> Boundless the darkness seems.
>
> Meadow and mould and darkness,
> Why do I love them so? —
> So far the bright stars wander:
> Earth is for men below.
>
> *Translated by C. D. Locock*

Out of such moods as this simple confession of faith expresses, there is ultimately derived both Blomberg's sense of solidarity with man and his belief that God exists only in Man, that Man's struggle to attain goodness and virtue is the key which opens the prison vault in which God himself is imprisoned:

> How vainly we cry to the heavens, "Deliver mankind,
>   O Lord!"
> For our God himself is captive — not he may loosen
>   the cord;
> And his form lies bound in darkness mid the star-fields,
>   viewless, vast, —
> But his living heart is Earth itself, where the scene
>   of our strife is cast. . . .

In our hearts is his spirit hidden as a priceless stone
   in the mine;
'Tis ours from the depths to release it — that pure,
   white light divine.
Yea, his thought ourselves would chisel, tho' the
   ruinous acid sears,
So the conquering light mount upward like fire thro'
   the shadow-spheres.

Translated by C. D. Locock

In these lines the poet joins with H. G. Wells (*God the Invisible King*) and others of the day who rejected a dualistic universe and a personal God in favor of a divine immanence resident only in man's heart and mind. The concept fitted well into Blomberg's youthful belief in human progress, in the possibilities of man transforming his conditions of life by means of an enlightened Marxist social and economic program. Though Blomberg has never substantially lost his faith in these possibilities, his last volume of verse *Nattens ögon* (The Eyes of Night, 1943), with its more than occasional notes of frustrated yearning, and even bitterness, indicates sufficiently clearly that the catastrophic world events of the 1930's were responsible at least in part for the sixteen-year-long interval between his two last volumes of poetry, and for the less hopeful tone in the latter of these volumes. But that Erik Blomberg has not lowered his Marxist colors and denied his early faith is apparent from the active part which he has taken as an eloquent Leftist voice in cultural and political debate down through the years. The record of his contribution to this debate can be examined in such collections of his essays and book reviews as *Tidens romantik* (The Romanticism of Our Times, 1931), *Stadens fångar* (Prisoners of the City, 1933), *Efter stormen — före stormen* (After the Storm — Before the Storm, 1938), *Mosaik* (1940), and *Från öst och väst* (From the East and the West, 1951). So balanced and sane has Erik Blomberg's loyalty been to his early faith that even those unable to share his faith respect the courageous consistency and good taste with which he has championed it. As a knight in modern Marxist armor he has been, and is, without fear and without reproach.

If Erik Blomberg represents in its noblest form the social pathos and faith in progress of the 1920's, Harriet Löwenhjelm (1887–1918) appealed to those airily skeptical spirits of the day who preferred to deal with serious matters in an only half-serious manner. Her playfully ironic verse struck a new chord in the Swedish poetic tradition, a chord which other Swedish poets were not slow to adopt and further develop. During

Vignette by Harriet Löwenhjelm for
the cover of her *Poems*

Harriet Löwenhjelm's lifetime her poetry was known only to her family
and immediate circle of acquaintances, but when the year after her
death a first fairly liberal portion of her verse was published she immediately found enthusiastic readers, and when in 1927 a new and enlarged
edition of her poems appeared both the number and the enthusiasm of
her readers sharply increased. The thirty-one years of her life were all
spent within the protective precincts of the higher landed aristocracy,
one of whose harmless social pastimes was to indulge in the writing of
elegant satiric verse. Had she been destined undisturbed to live out her
years within the conventional patterns of existence dictated by her class
she might have been known only during her lifespan by an intimate family circle as the most talented and gaily caustic of those who manipulated
poetic metres for the amusement of this little group. But when, in her
late twenties, a tubercular condition marked her for an early death her
poetic vein matured and deepened without losing much of its innocent
spontaneity and freshness. Her irony retained its tripping lilt in the very
shadows of death. The result was a deeply personal religious poetry of
the rarest vintage, devoid of all pretension and severity, a meeting of the
soul with its God on a level of almost playful intimacy. Only occasionally in this poetry does the near presence of death cast a sharp shadow
over the verse pattern, tighten the free rhythmic movement of the line,
or take ominous possession of the imagery. Usually the serious and the
playful blend in beguiling combinations of phrase and image and mood.
By some miracle of her inner creative resources Harriet Löwenhjelm

closed out her poetic account with life without indulging in either sentimentality or bitterness or heroics, creating almost as freely in the sani-
tarium as in the drawing-room and meeting death soberly if not quite
willingly. It has been observed that when she wrote her own epitaph
(in English by the way) —

> May we be happy and rejoice
> on this green earth, my son!
> But tired and smiling we leave our toys
> when it's over and life is done —

she had in mind Robert Louis Stevenson's "Requiem."

Harriet Löwenhjelm was in her subtle ironies a modern spirit. Her
slight but genuine poetic talent reminds one of Emily Dickinson in many
ways, especially in its delightful whimsy, its irreverent reverences, its
unexpected turns of phrase, and its striking originality of total poetic
conception. It has been said that Emily Dickinson "wrote as though no
one had written poetry before." The observation might as aptly be applied to Harriet Löwenhjelm.

The unconventional manner in which Harriet Löwenhjelm deals with
religious matters recurs in Hjalmar Gullberg (b. 1898), though in the
case of Gullberg the naïvistic clarities of Harriet Löwenhjelm give way
to complex patterns of feeling and of thought deriving more or less directly from his sophisticated awareness of man's grim dilemma in a
brutally disillusioned between-the-wars world. Among the more ur-
banely sensitive and facile of Swedish poets of his day, Gullberg attracted
some attention in the late 1920's with two volumes of verse, *I en främ-
mande stad* (In a Foreign City) and *Sonat* (Sonata). But it was not until
1932, on the publication of his *Andliga övningar* (Spiritual Exercises),
that he firmly established himself as one of the ranking poets of the day.
Since then he has added seven volumes to his poetic production, in
addition to being responsible for a substantial number of distinguished
translations, from Racine, Lorca, Gabriela Mistral, and others, but most
notably from Aristophanes, Euripides, and Sophocles. His appointment
as chief of the theater division of the Swedish National Radio in 1936
and to the seat in the Swedish Academy left vacant by the death of
Selma Lagerlöf in 1940 are outward evidences of the distinction which
he rather early attained and has since maintained in general Swedish cultural contexts.

Gullberg's two chief volumes of poetry from the 1930's, *Spiritual*

457

Exercises (1932) and *Att övervinna världen* (To Overcome the World, 1937), are predominantly religious in theme and tone, combining a spirit of restless yearning for the state of mystical ecstasy with a sense of heavy world-weariness and contempt for man. Sandwiched between these two volumes are the ironically sophisticated observations on modern love included in *Kärlek i tjugonde seklet* (Love in the Twentieth Century, 1933) and the rather slight but undeniably engaging tragicomic verse of *Ensamstående bildad herre* (Cultured Gentleman Bachelor, 1935). During the dark war years of the early 1940's Gullberg issued *Fem kornbröd och två fiskar* (Five Loaves and Two Fishes) as his contribution to what has been called "mobilization poetry" (*beredskaps-diktning*), which sought to build Swedish morale at the time. In *Döds-mask och lustgård* (Death Mask and Pleasure Garden), appearing in 1952, ten years after *Five Loaves and Two Fishes*, he has to date written his most profound and moving volume of verse, providing his readers with a series of impressively rigorous modern reinterpretations of Greek and Hebraic myths in which an achingly naked severity of tone banishes definitively from his poetic horizon that elegant irony of spirit which had so often earlier been his poetic signature.

That Gullberg's irony had been at least partly a mask behind which his essential seriousness uneasily lurked is fairly apparent even in his earliest volumes of verse, and becomes more apparent with each succeeding volume. During the years of his early manhood he had been nurtured alternately on the postwar chaos of the Continent (where he traveled extensively) and the airy skepticism and disillusionment of university life at Lund in the 1920's, a combination of circumstances which produced in him a brittle Heinesque ironic pose that persisted for many years despite a strong religious undercurrent in his genius. On the surface Gullberg seems to be an artist of few complexities. Except for certain anachronistic experiments in diction and the rather original use of symbols, the form of his verse is conventional, distinguished by its clarity and economy of phrase and by an intellectual balance which is a reflection of his Classical studies. But beneath the prevailing conventionalism of his poetic form there stirs a subtle modernity of spirit, ready to respond to the claims of contemporary developments while refusing to be inundated by a flood of catchwords or impressed by hectic latter-day ways of salvation. His skepticism provided an antidote to excessive modernity, his intuitive taste and intelligence led him to seek a poetic middle way, in which traditional and modern components unite to create a poetry of often magic freshness and pregnancy of feeling and utterance. The attraction which he exercises over his reading public derives not from time-tested popular effects but rather from the elegantly intriguing manner in which he merges seriousness and irony, the Classical and the modern, elevated poetic diction with an everyday vernacular. Gullberg's "modernism" is a modernism with a light, at times impertinent, but always disciplined touch, ever conscious of the dangers that lie in burning one's bridges with the poetic past. His art is quietly eruptive, finely restrained, never yielding to those blatant and vulgar drives which sometimes take possession of modern poetry.

Though his disillusionment can at times be bitter and take on harshly brutal forms, as in some of the "Kindergarten" poems in *Spiritual Exercises* and the utterly cynical sewage symbolism of "Cloaca maxima" in *To Overcome the World*, it is never inspired by a desire simply to wallow in a mire of poetic horrors. The only fault one is apt to find in Gullberg's disillusionment is its rather detached inhumanity, its refusal to pity man in his desperate struggle with the petty web of fate. Even when he draws on Classical myth and biblical legend for thematic material (and this he does often) Gullberg tends to be coolly collected, matter-of-fact, essentially skeptical if not subtly ironic in spirit and point of view. God to him apparently exists, and man has responsibilities to the Divinity, but man can merely in his best moments *approach* God, not know him nor experience his grace and rest triumphantly in his glory. And man in his spiritual poverty has no recourse of his own, no deeper insights and flashes of goodness — such as one comes upon in Pär Lagerkvist's world. So ingrained is Gullberg's skepticism that only when he approaches Christ and the mystery of Golgotha, as he does frequently, is he completely reverent and does he seem to harbor hope. But he only seems to: the mystery of the Cross escapes him despite his reverence and his yearning. Gullberg's religious dilemma is that of modern man, honestly in search of a way of salvation amidst the heavy drumbeats of a catastrophic age but unable (or unwilling?) in his honesty to believe finally in the possibility of finding God. In all of Gullberg's poetry except his most recent he is more or less concerned with the possibilities of a Christian tradition, and the door is left open for a possible Christian faith. But in *Death Mask and Pleasure Garden* he moves in a world of skepticism which has dispensed with the aesthetic compensations of irony and refuses to seek the possible comfort of a Christian tradition. In two series of poems, one entitled "Gudasaga," the other "Paradismyt," he returns again to the most primitive Greek and Hebraic myth, but in a vein of utter though quietly resigned disillusionment. "Gudasaga" opens with the magnificently defiant lines on Orpheus's bloody death:

Singing head driven to sea with its hair's
black sail hoisted, with extinguished eyes —

but it closes on a less grandiose note. And "Paradismyt" is a modern re-telling of the Garden of Eden tale shorn of its Genesis grandeur. But most disconcerting of all the poems in *Death Mask and Pleasure Garden*, because the poem is so direct, so nakedly personal, is "Dialog i en gry-ning" (Dialogue at Dawn), in which the poet's total work is judged vain and futile in turns of phrase as raw and crushing as those that Birger Sjöberg hammered out in the gloomy verse of *Crises and Laurel Wreaths*. In such pieces as "Dialogue at Dawn" neither stylistic tricks nor an ele-gant poetic irony has a place. The searching soul of the poet is at the end of a road — and he knows it. What impresses one in such a piece is the honesty of the confession, the willingness to face reality without subterfuge. Gullberg's poetry in general is an adventure of the soul in a complex, disordered modern world, an adventure which had early sought tentative solace in an ironic pose behind which Christian sym-bols and a Christian world vision hovered, but an adventure which in *Death Mask and Pleasure Garden* seemed at least for the time being to have foundered helplessly on the shoals of something resembling total disillusionment. Whether Gullberg could clear the shoals and move out into open waters remained to be seen. In any case he would almost cer-tainly, like Orpheus, sing to the end — whether serenely or darkly Gull-berg's readers waited to see. He was only a few years past fifty on the appearance of *Death Mask and Pleasure Garden*, and the disturbing ex-igencies of modern existence had not in the past succeeded in silencing his voice.

Nor have they, indeed, in the present, for during the writing of the present history, Gullberg again appeared in print — twice in fact, first with a volume entitled *Terziner i okonstens tid* (Terza Rima Verse in Inartistic Times, 1958), and most recently with *Ögon, läppar* (Eyes, Lips, 1959). Of these two works, *Terza Rima Verse in Inartistic Times* is the more impressive, haunting our poetic sensitivities with eerie Dan-tesque associations both in its skillful modern variations on the terza rima form and in its Inferno-like vision of modern man's fate. As total as in *Death Mask and Pleasure Garden* is the poet's sense of disillusion-ment in *Terza Rima Verse in Inartistic Times* — in fact more so, for the verse in the latter volume, grimly compressed, relentless in its pursuit of truth unadorned, is never permitted to lift itself to the elevated tragic vision which in spite of all is sometimes attained in *Death Mask and Pleasure Garden*. The mood of *Terza Rima Verse in Inartistic Times* is such that it refuses to entertain even the kind of fragmented solace of the Orpheus myth or other moving motifs from ancient lore.

Though Johannes Edfelt (b. 1904) shared for years with Gullberg certain thematic moods and stylistic practices, he ultimately, a decade after his poetic debut, extricated himself from the embarrassments of constant comparison with a distinguished contemporary poet and created a poetic world which was clearly his own. Edfelt's first two volumes of verse, *Gryningsröster* (Voices of Dawn, 1923) and *Unga dagar* (Young Days, 1925), were juvenile in spirit and imitative in manner and not without sentimental and rhetorical qualities, while the following two, *Ansikten* (Faces, 1929) and *Aftonunderhållning* (Evening Entertainment, 1933), suggested real poetic promise without being genuinely impressive. But with *Högmässa* (High Mass) in 1934 he broke through as a poet of marked distinction, and during the more than two decades which have followed he has added solid stone upon solid stone to a poetic edifice which is one of the more original and impressive in contemporary Swedish poetry. As for the claims of Edfelt's early dependence on Gullberg one wonders if the critics have not overemphasized it, and in any case the dependence such as it may have been has left few if any marks on the poetry of Edfelt's maturity. Actually, from fairly early in his career Edfelt's disillusionment had a more desperate and profoundly anguished tone than Gullberg's, and when his poetic form divested itself of its early imitative garments it became, in opposition to Gullberg's elegantly ironic verse, increasingly more naked, more brutal, more angular and severe in both phrase and structure. Edfelt, like Gullberg, early cultivated a disciplined, fastidious verse which contrasted sharply with the untidy wordiness and swelling rhythms of the poetic primitivists of the day, but Edfelt's phrasing is almost from the beginning more severe, more rigorously and harshly concentrated than Gullberg's.

Even though one can understand Harry Martinson's observation that Edfelt's extreme stylistic severity amounts to "a kind of aesthetic Calvinism," one may not be prepared to agree with Martinson in his feeling that this poetry is at times really oppressive in its severity. Edfelt has

461

had greater difficulty than Martinson in resigning himself to life's stupidities and coarseness and its apparent meaninglessness. His poetry is in consequence considerably less prone to lend itself to the kind of meditative idyllicism which characterizes so much of Martinson's verse. When Edfelt does yield to an idyllic meditative mood, and this he does on occasion, especially in his later verse, he does so warily, with reservations. One of his most lovely poems in the idyllic genre is entitled significantly "Förbjuden musik" (Forbidden Music). What has been called Edfelt's "formal fanaticism," that is his extreme concentration of phrase and deliberate rigidity of structure, is to be explained, it has more than once been pointed out, as a more or less conscious means of forcing some kind of order and discipline upon the disorder and chaos of modern life. His stylistic severity serves to stay the processes of dissolution within his own soul. Edfelt looks upon the naïvistic and most of the idyllic strains in modern Swedish poetry as essentially escapist, but he does not assume, as have some of his contemporaries, that the alternative is an aggressive primitivism or a form-denying surrealism. "Personally," he once wrote, "I am no adherent of the doctrine which maintains the necessity of rendering a fragmented world of feeling in an immediately and directly equivalent form. That the extent of the world's destruction should exactly correspond to the degree of a given art form's destruction is a romantic doctrine, worshiped chiefly by the surrealists. Granted that it is perhaps unavoidable in our time that a poet's consciousness becomes more or less tragically dark and fragmented, yet a poet is medium *and resistance*, not *merely* a seismograph recording the condition of the world."

Among the more arresting ways in which Edfelt attains a sense of tightly disciplined line and over-all poetic structure is his fresh and original use of such traditional forms as the chorale and other strictly ritualistic patterns. In *High Mass*, for instance, not only is the title itself broadly ritualistic in connotation, the subdivisions within the book are labeled respectively "Preludium" (Prelude), "Kalla koraler" (Cold Chorales), "Dagens evangelium" (The Day's Text), "Betraktelser" (Meditations), "Gravpsalm" (Funeral Psalm), "Sakrament" (Sacrament), and "Heiliger Dankgesang" (Thanksgiving Hymn). And even individual poems in the volume bear such titles as "Missa solemnis," "Förklaringsberg" (Mount of Transfiguration), "Husandakt" (Family Devotions), "Fromma önskningar" (Pious Wishes), and "Altartjänst" (Altar Service). Usually, however, these labels are harshly ironic in their implica-

462

tions, for the poems thus labeled are more often loaded with mockery and scorn than inspired by reverence and prepared to offer spiritual comfort. But in one of the subdivisions of *High Mass* — the one entitled "Sacrament" — the tone is positive, elevated, proudly triumphant, though the sacrament here being observed treats of man's love for woman rather than man's obeisance to God. In their magnificent tenderness of feeling, their profound sense of gratitude, and their surging elevation of spirit the "Sacrament" poems attain a level of utterance all but unique in the Swedish erotic poetry of the day, and very little Swedish love poetry down through the centuries approaches the passionate intensity and purity of perception of these poems. By comparison Gullberg's alternately ecstatic and ironic handling of the love theme in *Love in the Twentieth Century* is only at points really impressive while the erotic verse of the Swedish primitivists of the 1930's is crudely overassertive and seldom capable of lifting itself appreciably above its immediate sexual origins. Of the Swedish poet who wrote the "Sacrament" lyrics, on the other hand, D. H. Lawrence himself might well have been envious, for in them, as in Lawrence's vision of man's relation to woman, the union of the sexes becomes an essentially religious experience, a triumphal entering into a mystic union with the very sources of life.

In the "Sacrament" group of poems, and in one or two other pieces from *High Mass*, Edfelt had taken a step away from his earlier isolation and frustration, had found in the experience of love a point of contact with certain positive values which served to mitigate for the time being some of the heavy gloom that had taken possession of his earlier verse. But that the step Edfelt had taken was not conclusive is apparent in *I denna natt* (In This Night, 1936) and *Vintern är lång* (The Winter Is Long, 1939), whose verse is prevailingly severe and heavy despite an occasional willingness on the part of the poet to seek sources of positive poetic renewal in nature and in a sense of sympathy with a quietly heroic humanity. It was not until the two wartime volumes *Sång för reskamrater* (Song for Traveling Companions, 1941) and *Elden och klyftan* (The Fire and the Chasm, 1943) that these sources of poetic renewal enabled Edfelt to lift himself significantly out of his sense of isolation and attain something of a feeling of comradeship and solidarity with man.

He did so diffidently, it should be noted, but firmly and genuinely — partly in connection with his opposition to Fascist and Nazi forms of totalitarianism. He did not, however, have much more faith in any of the other current social and political nostrums, be they liberalism or socialism or communism. In his search for values in the chaos of the times Edfelt sought quite outside narrowly political contexts to immerse himself in man's common experiences — man's joys and pains, his quiet visions, his will to maintain a sense of decency despite the blatant stupidities of those who presumed to order society and rule the world. In the verse of *In This Night* and *The Winter Is Long* Edfelt had on occasion employed the fresh-welling waters of a spring as a symbol of life's healing and renewing force. In *Song for Traveling Companions* this symbol, together with that of deep rootedness, becomes central, the two symbols complementing each other in suggesting a means of solace, if not a way of salvation, in nature's quiet ways and vital processes of growth and renewal. Even in pain and suffering Edfelt now finds the possibility of positive values, and life's very gathering darkness invites to a search for its hidden sources of vitality and rejuvenation. The search is not, however, an easy one, yielding easily accessible treasures to the sanguine spirit. It must struggle over stony paths through heavy underbrush, and even then it yields only fleeting flashes of insight, never a Mount of Transfiguration vision. Such is the drift of thought in Edfelt's wartime verse, a drift of thought which also carries over in a softer, more idyllic vein into a volume from 1947, *Bråddjupt eko* (Sharply Deep Echo).

But how hedged about with misgivings on the poet's part is even such a limited confidence in man's and nature's potential toward good becomes apparent in Edfelt's two volumes of poetry from the 1950's, *Hemliga slagfält* (Secret Battle Fields, 1952) and *Under Saturnus* (Under Saturn, 1956). In these volumes Edfelt returns to something of the sense of isolation and futility of his early years, admitting with little reservation that man's fate must remain a dark mystery, visited by anguished hours which man must face alone as best he can, lighted only now and then by fleeting moments of elevated otherworldly beauty. Such moments are caught up into words in the prose poem "Missa papae Marcelli" in *Under Saturn*:

From the church the song reaches me standing on the street outside. I do not enter, for the fragrance of the incense from the censers swung by the choir boys and the sight of the priest's sacramental magic nauseate me. But I listen to Palestrina's music: the song lifts itself, strives constantly upward like a broad, dazzling marble stairs. It does not torment me with the fanaticism and vulgarity of dogma: it is a rising toward needlessness and freedom. For a moment I stand there on the street enveloped in a breath of timelessness and peace. Only a moment, but that is enough. Alas, no footing, sufficiently firm, no place of abode, sufficiently enduring, is there for the soul — this I know well. But moments of liberating devotion — such as this one — there are in any case. And this is happiness enough on the journey toward the leafless forests of autumn and the snow crystals of winter.

Edfelt's poetry is in its development down through the years profoundly organic. His motifs are few, and often repeated, but in the repetition there is always growth and deepening, a stubborn search for values and perfection of form which with the years becomes ever more impressive in idea and subtle in phrase. Simple, severe, finely chiseled, his best verse reminds one of pure, utterly unadorned sculpture.

> Pain is a sculptor,
>   greater than Phidias:
> shapes from shadows and blood
>   monuments of regret.
>
> Darkness which steeps our hearts
>   is its living stuff.
> The hand, sensitive, skilled,
>   shapes the statue's line.
>
> Inward its art,
>   strange its material:
> all who have met their doom
>   shape its enduring form.

Such lines bear Edfelt's stamp at every point, breathe his spirit and realize his finely disciplined sense of form at its very best.

Aside from his eminence as a poet Edfelt has rendered into Swedish a considerable quantity of foreign verse, and as a critic and editor he has become one of the best informed Swedish students of German and Russian literature and has edited Hjalmar Bergman's complete works as well as the work of the brilliantly controversial novelist Agnes von Krusenstjerna. That he has edited two such Swedish pioneers in modern psychological fiction and written a book about Dostoevski is not an accident. His own subtle poetic probing into life's tragic areas of experience and vision has found an apparently not unwelcome nourishment in the novels of three such profoundly representative modern observers of the darkly irrational aspects of human consciousness and conduct.

Though both Gullberg and Edfelt have departed to some extent from the ways of poetic traditionalism, neither of them, as we have seen, has been prepared radically to reshape poetic form in the direction of a definitive poetic "modernism." They are essentially transitional figures, ready to experiment in matters of detail of form but unwilling to deny the essential validity of an earlier poetic tradition. The same cannot be said of a number of other Swedish poets who appeared in the years around 1930 and in whose work earlier tendencies toward change break out into open revolt and mark the advent of a militant poetic modernism. Many are the sources out of which this poetic modernism grew. Purely Swedish points of departure were to be had in the work of such major figures as Hjalmar Bergman, Pär Lagerkvist, and Birger Sjöberg, while from abroad — from the arresting Swedo-Finnish poetic modernists of the early 1920's as well as from such far-flung frontiers of literary modernism as France and England and the United States — an avalanche of modernistic -isms poured in upon the Swedish literary scene. Freudianism and primitivism and surrealism, together with a variety of radical social and political nostrums, jostled one another for the attention of the eager young Swedish modernists, whose capacity for assimilating such advanced fare was matched by a creative vitality of equal variety and range. So radically experimental were the resulting literary products that the Swedish reading public was at first either puzzled or hostile or both, but with time it adjusted itself to the new poetry and prose — and came, indeed, to take it for granted, particularly when it became evident that the new literary modernism in one form or other was here to stay. What may have seemed to broad segments of the Swedish reading public in the early 1930's to be merely a temporary literary vogue has persisted with only minor modifications down into the 1940's and continues in the main to dominate Swedish poetry today. Though changes have occurred during the last quarter of a century, these changes are scarcely fundamental. Everywhere in contemporary Swedish poetry the spirit of daring experimentation reigns, the spirit out of which modernistic verse from the beginnings had erupted.

In the late 1920's the new trends tended to crystallize in Sweden at two points, in a circle of young intellectuals banded loosely together in the radical socialist Clarté falange and in the group of five young authors of nonacademic origins who pooled their preliminary poetic resources in the little volume of poetry and poetic prose issued under the title *5 unga*. The Clarté group was a very active Swedish branch of the international organization launched in the postwar years by the French author Henri Barbusse and dedicated to a pacifistic program in the name of a radical political socialism. The Swedish Clartéists originated among a group of students and young faculty members at the University of Lund, spread rapidly among academic groups in Göteborg and Uppsala, and maintained during the peak years of activity a central base of operations in Stockholm, where efforts were made to work with the politically conscious labor groups, toward the end particularly of establishing a kind of United Front among the various socialist-minded groups including the Communists. Though social and political radicalism of a strenuously Marxist kind seems to have been the original driving force among the members of the Clarté group, not a few of them — among whom were the profounder literary talents of the group — became equally if not more interested in the ethical and aesthetic implications of Freudianism. Of the more purely Marxist-inspired poets from the Clarté ranks such as Stellan Arvidson (b. 1902) and Arnold Ljungdal (b. 1901), none has made much more than a passing literary impression on the Swedish reading public, while Clartéists and kindred young literary radicals like Karin Boye, Artur Lundkvist, and Harry Martinson, who from the start tempered their Marxism with Freudianism and ultimately discarded more or less entirely their Marxist predilections, came with time to occupy increasingly important places in the development of modern Swedish literature.

Among the more active and central figures in the Clarté group in Stockholm during the 1920's only Karin Boye (1900–41) is a major poet. Born in Göteborg and educated at Uppsala, she had before coming in contact with the Clartéists been recognized as one of the few Swedish women poets of high distinction. One must go back to Anna Maria Lenngren in the late eighteenth century to find a Swedish poetess of equal distinction, and to Anna Maria Lenngren's immediate predecessor, Hedvig Charlotta Nordenflycht, to find a woman poet of comparable emotional intensities. But Karin Boye has none of the cool satiric vein of Anna Maria Lenngren nor does she affect the outwardly impassioned manner of fru Nordenflycht. Her art is profoundly personal but is for the most part couched in severely disciplined verse patterns which half hide the intensities of the inner crises to which Karin Boye was from the beginning subjected. How profoundly personal her poetry is can be seen in the fact that it so rarely reflects the social and political interests of her Clarté period.

Her first volume of poetry, *Moln* (Clouds, 1922), attracted considerable attention with its bell-like clarity and its seriousness and elevation of mood, and the two volumes which shortly followed, *Gömda land* (Hidden Lands, 1924) and *Härdarna* (The Hearths, 1927), reflected a poetic growth which not only increased the circle of her admirers in Sweden but led the formidable Hagar Olsson, critical firebrand of Finnish modernism, to hail Karin Boye's verse as the first indubitable evidence among the generation of the 1920's of a spirit of genuine renewal in Swedish poetry. Without being aggressively modern in form Karin Boye's early poetry inwardly reflects a tense modern spirit, aroused to strenuous affirmations of absolute ethical loyalties but prone also to drift passively back into regions of the subconscious and the unconscious where mysterious natural forces take possession of the human spirit. The conflict within Karin Boye between an active-heroic idealism and a passive-natural drift is caught up in her poetry in a variety of telling symbols, none more telling in formulation and magic in poetic execution than that of the Aesir and the Elves, who in one of the central poems of *Hidden Lands* agree to a division of powers in the world, the Aesir to organize and control all outward phenomena, the Elves to govern those things

> Which never a name have had,
> and all that they have and all that they give
> spells power of fertility.

The Freudian implications of this nature symbolism are unmistakable, and these implications carry over even more clearly into Karin Boye's most mature volume of verse *För trädets skull* (For Love of the Tree, 1935), in which the formal simplicity of her earlier verse partly gives way under surrealistic influences to irregular rhythms and verse patterns, and the poet's identification with nature's dark but knowing and fertile instincts is complete.

But quietly serene as is the poet's faith in nature's purposes as symbolized by the vast root system of a flourishing, wide-spreading tree, this volume also contains a number of tensely ecstatic poems which suggest that Karin Boye's serenity of spirit in *For Love of the Tree* is not unmixed with ominously dark and strained elements. These elements derive primarily out of a number of hopelessly tangled erotic relationships, the first of which forced Karin Boye to seek psychiatric advice, and the last of which seems to have led directly to her suicide. The state of mind in which she found herself in her last desperately searching years finds arresting expression in the posthumously published *De sju dödssynderna* (The Seven Deadly Sins), in the long title poem of which the sacral earth-bound elevation of *For Love of a Tree* gives way to a more intense and abstract chorale mood and form that may in part have been influenced by T. S. Eliot's *Murder in the Cathedral*. Though "The Seven Deadly Sins" is an unfinished fragment, enough of it was completed before Karin Boye's death to make clear that the poet's central intention was to deal with the problem of good and evil in terms of modern psychiatric investigations — to raise the question, in the light of such investigations, whether man can be held morally responsible for his "sins."

During her short life span Karin Boye experienced a number of shattering inner defeats, and finally self-immolation, but her singularly honest poetry rose above these defeats both in clarity of vision and nobility of utterance. Much of her mature verse has a strenuously angular quality which reflects with naked candor the harsh realities of her tragic inner struggle. In one of her finest poems she employs the striking phrase "struck down by purity," a phrase appropriately employed as the title of a biography of the poet written with deep understanding after her death by a long-time friend.

In addition to her poetry Karin Boye wrote a considerable number of short stories and four short novels, none of which, with the possible exception of *Kallocain*, ranks with her poetry. Her prose fiction is of interest chiefly in terms of its experimental form or because it quite frequently throws light on her personal crises. *Kallocain*, the novel that appeared the year before her death, has both an autobiographical and a political significance, dealing simultaneously as it does with Karin Boye's desperate search for a satisfactory basis of communion with her fellows and with her flaming indignation in the presence of current totalitarian efforts to degrade the individual by making him simply a cog in the wheel of a monstrous Absolute State. In the novel a pale green drug called "Kallocain" is used by the State to force its citizens to reveal their innermost feelings and thoughts — inevitably to their destruction. Though *Kallocain* has certain obvious surface features in common with Aldous Huxley's *Brave New World*, its terrifying vision of man's tragic fate in a totalitarian modern world is much closer to Arthur Koestler.

In the years around 1930 when the Clartéist intellectuals were enlisting literary talent in the service of a radical social and political program, a predominantly proletarian fringe element of the Clarté group became involved in pursuing the Freudian psychoanalytic predilections of one wing of Clartéists in the direction of social and political indifference.

While Karin Boye approached the "open" Freudian "way of life" with some hesitation, the Five Young Men (as Artur Lundkvist, Harry Martinson, Erik Asklund, Josef Kjellgren, and Gustav Sandgren came to be called in consequence of the volume *5 unga* in which they collaborated) rushed headlong into the embrace of a vitalistic "primitivism" — jubilant, unashamed, with no conventional specters dogging their steps or complicating their joyous, quite uninhibited acceptance of life in all its manifestations. With one exception the origins and experience of life of the Five Young Men were those of the least favored classes, their formal education largely nonexistent, their literary Gods the hearty yea-sayer Walt Whitman and the "sexual mystics" Sherwood Anderson and D. H. Lawrence. Their violent opposition to literary traditionalism in any form and their gusty affirmation both of the "dynamic" inner drift of nature and the rich potential of modern industry were the absolute antipodes of the poetic idyllicism of the 1920's. That Österling and his fellow idyllicists found the early poetry and prose of the Five Young Men woefully lacking in essential poetic qualities is understandable; but their work soon came to be more or less accepted — in part because its primitivism became with the years less aggressive and vociferous without losing its essential freshness and vitality. The immediate outward circumstance which served to check the excessive nature cultism of their early years was the use by Nazi propagandists of a related cultism of *Blut und Erde* to justify the expansionist politics of Germany before the Second World War.

The leader of the Five Young Men group, one of its chief poets and its most effective critical champion, was the astonishingly vital and productive Artur Lundkvist (b. 1906), who descended on Stockholm from a farm in the south of Sweden in the late 1920's and forthwith began a literary career which in poetic vigor and intellectual receptivity and liveliness has few parallels in Swedish letters. His voracious appetite for life, his astonishing energy, and his restless, wide-ranging, often incisive mind have made him one of the most arresting if not one of the major figures in contemporary Swedish literature. In addition to a dozen volumes of poetry Lundkvist has written some fascinating travel sketches and has been very active as a critic both in the literary "little magazines" and in book form. He has always been especially responsive to literary developments abroad, most notably those in the United States and France. That he knows more about contemporary American literature than any other Swede is evident in his three works *Atlantvind* (Atlantic Wind, 1932), *Amerikas nya författare* (America's New Authors, 1940), and *Diktare och avslöjare i Amerikas moderna litteratur* (Authors and [literally] Exposers in Modern American Literature, 1942), and in the essays on Faulkner and Henry Miller in *Ikarus' flykt* (The Flight of Icarus, 1939), a book which also contains notable essays on Rimbaud, T. S. Eliot, James Joyce, and the surrealist movement in France. Of Lundkvist's two most recent books, one, *Ur en befolkad ensamhet* (From an Inhabited Loneliness, 1958), part travel book, part veiled confession, with its Baudelaire-borrowed title, might suggest that he finds himself in some kind of inner crisis after thirty years of what certainly has been the most amazing expenditure of creative energy in contemporary Swedish letters, but the expansive novel *Komedi i Hägerskog* (Comedy in Hägerskog, 1959) is so charged with a lively narrative inventiveness and descriptive gusto that it belies the assumption that his creative aplomb if not his creative vitality has appreciably diminished in freshness or force.

Lundkvist's early poetry — appearing in volumes with such assertive titles as *Glöd* (Glowing Embers), *Naket liv* (Naked Life), and *Svart stad* (Black City) — all but inundated his readers under surging free-verse crescendos and massive accumulations of lusty, often sex-inspired images. There is more than a grain of truth in the comment of a recent Swedish critic that the young Artur Lundkvist's confession of faith might be formulated in the statement "there is no God except *Libido* and D. H. Lawrence is its prophet," but it may be added that Walt Whitman is another of Lundkvist's prophets and that he has learned also from Carl Sandburg and others. He glories in his early verse in being what he calls a "poetic desperado . . . mocking all broad-legged cautiousness and stifling respectability." He flaunts his young poetic limbs with deliberate abandon to the embarrassment of the squeamish, those who wish their verse served up in fastidious conventional forms. As a spokesman for an emancipated younger generation he asserts that

> Something new has come into the world —
> we sense it, we glimpse it in the crowded throng.
> We must seek it, seek it ceaselessly.

> We shall play life's new melody for man,
> the intoxicating, rising life-rhythm,
> swift,
> daring,
> steel-glistening.

In Lundkvist's early career "life's new melody for man" was often that of the dynamic modern city, of industrialism and the worker; but in *Nattens broar* (The Bridges of Night, 1936), and in succeeding volumes, he has under the influence of French surrealism sought out by preference his own inner melodies — and these melodies, seeking fluid concretions in a subconscious drift of sensory associations, have become in later years increasingly rootless, disillusioned, and desperate in tone. How far this development has gone can be seen in Lundkvist's complete rejection in 1947 of even a partly disciplined logical art in favor of what he calls "panic poetry: an abrupt and convulsive verse, flinging itself forward in surprising leaps, fragmentary but intensive, not least in its omissions." That this is not, however, Lundkvist's final word on his ideal of poetry would seem apparent from his last volume of verse *Vindrosor, moteld* (Wind-Roses, Backfire, 1955), in which the aggressively vitalistic quality of much of his earlier verse gives way in part to a more measured manner, and the "panic" note is at least on the surface toned down. In this volume a somewhat diffuse aphoristic form seems to be bent upon bringing some order into the excessive play of sensory associations which had been the most marked quality of his verse from the beginning. In Lundkvist's work in general the clearheaded critic and the creative poet are often at cross purposes, a circumstance which accounts for its brilliant but not always happy effects. In his precipitate desire to find a satisfactory modern form for his vision of life he has tended at times to lose himself in the myriad mazes of extremist poetic experimentation.

This is not the case with Harry Martinson (b. 1904), the finest literary talent among the Five Young Men and the most sensitive and freshly original of the entire company of poets who were storming the Swedish Parnassus in the 1930's. Not that Harry Martinson lacked the sophisticated skills of the more advanced modernistic poets. In fact, he had these skills to a pre-eminent degree and has exercised them on occasion with a daring and subtlety equal to that of any of his contemporaries. But he has done so with a fine inner discipline unusual among the poets of his day. In the chaotic contexts of a literary world aflame with new ideas and revolutionary experimental trends he has maintained an exemplary poetic balance, recognizing the pressing claims of artistic modernity but never allowing these claims to take complete possession of his spirit or his art. There is in consequence in most of Harry Martinson's poetry an emotional maturity as rare as it is impressive. A quietly resigned serenity infuses much of his poetic world despite an early experience of life which might easily have led to bitterness and despair. "Life betrayed you but you did not betray life" were the words with which Martinson was welcomed as the first author of proletarian origins to occupy a chair in the Swedish Academy. "Life betrayed you" are words which refer to Martinson's childhood, youth, and early manhood.

No Swedish author has had to endure more harsh and unpromising conditions of existence during childhood, youth, and young manhood than Harry Martinson. Born in the southeastern province of Blekinge, he was left homeless at the age of six upon the death of his father and the desertion of a mother who disappeared in an America-bound emigration stream. For ten years of his boyhood he was a public charge, shifted from farm to farm and tolerated only because meager parish funds provided for his keep. He escaped from these humiliations to sea at the age of sixteen, "seeing the world" from the "vantage point" of a common sailor — for the most part below deck as a coal stoker on ships of diverse national origins and often dubious seaworthiness. Miraculously he managed to retain an elasticity of spirit through all this, as is evidenced by the rich literary vitality of a half dozen books from his early authorship which draw upon his experiences on land and at sea. Two of these books, *Nässlorna blomma* (tr. *Flowering Nettle*, 1935) and *Vägen ut* (The Way Out, 1936), provide a sensitive account of his difficult childhood years, while the others — the two prose volumes *Resor utan mål* (Aimless Travels, 1932) and *Kap Farväl* (tr. *Cape Farewell*, 1933) and the two verse collections *Spökskepp* (Spook Ship, 1929) and *Nomad* (1931) — deal largely with the seven years at sea and experiences in strange exotic climes.

The first of Martinson's verse volumes attracted no great attention, nor did his contributions to *5 unga* in 1929. But his second volume of poetry, *Nomad*, was hailed by the critics as a work of very considerable promise — a promise which was confirmed by the resounding success of the two travel sketchbooks, particularly *Cape Farewell*, and by the two autobiographical works *Flowering Nettle* and *The Way Out* which followed. Since the mid-1930's Harry Martinson has perhaps more than any other Swedish poet of his generation fascinated large segments of the Swedish reading public. His three highly original volumes of nature observation and commentary, *Svärmare och harkrank* (Dreamers and Daddy-Long-Legs, 1937), *Midsommardalen* (Midsummer Valley, 1938), and *Det enkla och det svåra* (The Simple and the Difficult, 1939), have attracted many readers; his warmly human "tramp novel" *Vägen till Klockrike* (tr. *The Road*, 1948) was one of the memorable events in the recent Swedish book trade; and even those "difficult," only half-intelligible poems which occur so persistently in such volumes as *Passad* (Trade Winds, 1945), *Cikada* (1953), and the ominous space-ship fantasy *Aniara* (1956) have found favor with a constantly increasing majority of those Swedes who read poetry. When in 1949 Martinson became the first of the "proletarian authors" to be named one of "the Eighteen Immortals" in the Swedish Academy, his election was hailed on all sides as eminently appropriate.

The charge which has in some quarters been made against Martinson's poetic style as tending toward the "coy" and the "affected" has some basis in fact, especially in his early verse; but this quality results quite naturally from that insistence on verbal *precision* which makes him one of the great renewers of language in Swedish poetry. Harry Martinson's amazing sensitivity simply *forces* him to seek the unusual word, the fresh, frequently startling image, the flashing interplay of verbal associations which mirror the poet's wayward, lightning-like rapidity of response to sensation and idea. As a "self-made poet" with an imagination untrammeled by conventional ways of seeing and responding, he can achieve such magic effects as the following in a stanza from the poem "Skönhet" (Beauty):

> I see at a distance women.
> They bathe in a summer-flecked sea.
> Hear their glass-clear cries
> dance over the water's blue membranes. See
>   like a
> flower torch and a saint cry
> the praise of their white nakedness
> raised in the Japanese ghost of a blossoming
>   wild apple.
> Sunsmoke. Sunsmoke.

Or the haunting tender-sharp accents of "En väns död" (Death of a Friend):

> Your trip is over —
> they are airing out your clothes —
> the window is open;
> stretched on the line is a coat
> with flapping arms.
> It waves toward the stubble of the field,
> smells of stable,

is like a hung-up past —
It flaps out, fast,
like the crane taking wing to Africa.
                    Translations by Richard B. Vowles

Most of Martinson's verse has the fresh impressionistic brevity of these
two pieces, but as he matures, and in the process develops something of
a speculative, "philosophical" vein, he feels compelled to write poems
of greater length and complexity, poems "with a message for modern
man." These longer poems lack on the whole the freshness and spontaneity, the playful grace and movement of his shorter pieces, but they
give arresting and at times deeply moving expression to the poet's profound distaste for certain aspects of modern life, its hectic tempo, its
sterile artificiality, its tendency to lose all sense of contact with nature's
indwelling sources of growth and renewal.

In Martinson's early work, in *Cape Farewell* and *Nomad* particularly,
he develops a somewhat shadowy "nomadic" theory, suggesting that
man can save himself from the deadly tyranny of a bureaucratic technological civilization only by "keeping on the move," by deliberately
refusing to identify himself with those fixed forms of existence often
characteristic of modern society. But in later years Martinson has abandoned as rather too Utopian his early "nomadism" without forsaking his
strongly antipathetic attitude toward most modern forms of existence.
Mild and gentle by temperament, and blessed with a finely quizzical
humor, he prefers in the years of his maturity to reason calmly about
man's and nature's ways, as is evident in the wisely whimsical commentary of *The Road* and in the sober meditative vein of such central pieces
in *Trade Winds* as the title poem, with its use of the trade winds as a
symbol of life's ultimate source of strength, and the quiet commentary
of "Li Kan talar under trädet" (Li Kan Talks Under the Tree), with its
serene, mild-mannered Oriental wisdom. But at times Martinson is less
calm, stirred by a sense of sharp moral indignation in the presence
of man's blundering stupidity and callous insensitivity, especially as
these are reflected in the tragic misuse of technological "advances." In
Verklighet till döds (Reality to Death, 1940) he castigates Russia's in-
dustrial-military crushing of little Finland in the Russo-Finnish War of
1940, in the grim *Trade Winds* (1945) piece entitled "Hades and Euclid"
he depicts with loathing the heartless triviality of modern life, and in
the ghastly cosmic vision of the verse-epic allegory *Aniara* (1956) he ex-

amines with rising horror the destructive violence actual and potential in an Atomic Age.

That Martinson could distill cosmic contents out of the most minuscule natural phenomena had for long been apparent to those who were familiar with his early work. That he can also manage poetically the vast reaches of the universe with its overwhelming magnitude and its celestial variety becomes clear in some of his later work, most clear in the eerie, awe-inspiring tale of the huge space-ship Aniara which, after evacuating some eight thousand humans from a world ripe for atomic annihilation, gets off its course within the solar system and plunges endlessly on into the empty darkness of interstellar space, while its occupants, reacting variously to their strange fate, receive periodic reports on the step-by-step destruction of the earth from which they came. In *Aniara* the ultimate paradox of technology, its atomic "triumph," effects the annihilation of all forms of life upon the earth. In imaginative sweep and tragic implication only Pär Lagerkvist's *The Eternal Smile* ranks with *Aniara* in contemporary Swedish literature. Both of these works are written with gentleness and compassion within the heavy shadows of their visions of man's fate, and both of them hold out a *slight* hope that man may somehow, and before it is too late, grope his way out of the dread conditions of existence which have trapped him. Martinson's space-ship Aniara moves through spatial eternities in the direction of Lyra — a constellation which gives off light, but light which emanates from an infinitely distant point in space.

Martinson's *Aniara* (which has recently been turned into an appropriately modernistic opera and staged at Stockholm) is the central book in what has been called the "black period" in his work, the other two volumes of verse in this period being *Cikada*, which preceded *Aniara* by three years, and *Gränsen i Thule* (The Boundary in Thule, 1958), his latest collection of verse. *The Boundary in Thule*, with its title reference to the northernmost part of the habitable world, grows in a sense out of the mood of desperation characteristic of *Aniara*, but it offers its readers — with a kind of diffident persistence — something more of hope than did Martinson's grim space-ship fantasy. In *The Boundary in Thule* man is still in an infinitely hostile world, that of an atomic age, but Martinson nevertheless, in spite of all, seeks to provide such solace as still may exist for man, and he finds such solace in the contemplation of nature in its more intimate aspects and in the pursuit of certain traditional poetic values as reflected in earlier Swedish poets, Wivallius and Bellman,

Agnes von Krusenstjerna, sketch by Olga Raphael
Linden (photo: SPA)

Hjalmar Gullberg (copyright
Lennart Nilsson)

Johannes Edfelt (copyright
Harald Borgström)

Eyvind Johnson (copyright
Harald Borgström)

Karin Boye

Gunnar Ekelöf

Vilhelm Moberg

Lars Ahlin

Erik Lindegren (photo: Bo Dahlin)   Harry Martinson

Stage design by Sven Erixson for the space-opera based on Harry Martinson's *Aniara*, with music by Karl-Birger Blomdahl and libretto by Erik Lindegren

Heidenstam, Karlfeldt, and Fröding. Without courting the world of illusion, in *The Boundary in Thule* Martinson succeeds in part in exorcising the sense of almost total horror caught up in the apocalyptic modernism of the Aniara vision. Harry Martinson's genius, it is clear from his latest book to date, has not become a captive of the cold terror of an Atomic Age even though it is so fraught with disquieting implications for man and the future of his culture.

Of the remaining three of the Five Young Men who burst upon the Swedish literary scene in 1929, neither Erik Asklund (b. 1908) nor Gustav Sandgren (b. 1904) nor Josef Kjellgren (1907–48) has succeeded in competing successfully for the reading public's favor with their comrades Martinson and Lundkvist. Asklund has experimented with only limited success in prose fictional forms which seek to reflect the trivial, fragmented quality of contemporary life, while the very productive Sandgren has in such often allegorical short stories as are included in *Skymningssagor* (Tales of Eventide, 1936) developed a somewhat striking but rather exclusive prose style which has its undeniable fascination but has not proved to be especially capable of growth and development. Sandgren is the most persistently primitivistic of the group, having pursued in the most extremely Romantic forms the moods and motifs of his early work long after his fellows among the Five Young Men had qualified if not rejected their early primitivistic attitudes and programs. Josef Kjellgren is in some ways the most appealing personality among the three minor figures of the Five Young Men and the only one who retains throughout his career a strong sense of loyalty to the working classes. His most important works are the "collective novels" *Människor kring en bro* (People and a Bridge, 1935) and the series beginning with *Smaragden* (The Emerald, 1939). In each of these the "hero" is the masses, the group rather than the individual, and in each case Kjellgren manages to give something of heroic stature to the struggles of a group of individuals tied together in a common enterprise and a common fate. Though *People and a Bridge* deals with the construction of the famous Västerbron, pride of all Stockholmers, Kjellgren seems originally to have come upon the idea for his novel upon hearing a tragic tale connected with the building of Brooklyn Bridge. Like Harry Martinson, Kjellgren had traveled far and wide as seaman and laborer, and these travels provided him with some of the raw materials as well as the symbols and points of view of his literary work.

Though much of the more advanced literary modernism of the 1930's found its early practitioners within the ranks of those authors whose origins were marked by poverty and limited cultural conditions, one of the major modernist poets — Gunnar Ekelöf (b. 1907) — comes from the well-to-do middle classes and has, like Gullberg and Edfelt, enjoyed access to academic training and a culture of the most sophisticated kind. But while neither Gullberg nor Edfelt, as we have seen, has pursued the precarious ways of poetic modernism to the near-exclusion of conventional forms, Ekelöf came early to identify himself with those who had little if any use for such traditional usages as rhyme and rhythmic regularity, and throughout his career he has remained in the vanguard of those Swedish poets who during the last three or four decades have been prepared to experiment with all manner of poetic moods and forms.

Despite his privileged middle-class origins Ekelöf early sought contact with those Stockholm literary circles in the early 1930's out of which the poetry of the Five Young Men issued. From the beginning, however, Ekelöf was interested exclusively in what may be called the "psychological wing" of the literary radicalism of the day, the wing whose prophet was Freud rather than Marx and whose avant-garde journal was *Spektrum*. It was in this group that Ekelöf first came into contact with Artur Lundkvist, together with whom he was to cooperate in founding the short-lived surrealistic journal *Karavan* in 1933. Though Ekelöf's early verse and a number of early critical essays on French surrealism resulted in his being labeled a surrealist, he was never an orthodox follower of André Breton and the Parisian surrealists, and in 1940 he formally announced his definite break with the surrealists, a movement, he concludes, which "we must now look upon as a completed chapter" in the history of literature.

Ekelöf is among the most restless and elusive of Swedish poets. As a matter of principle he does not allow himself to settle down for long into any one poetic manner. His points of departure are extraordinarily diverse and fluid, deriving as they do from his interests in music and painting as well as from literature and from esoteric lore often of Oriental provenance. Because he is an eclectic in principle, he shifts both thematically and stylistically from work to work with no easily discernible lines of development. In general, however, one can discern in his poetry a gradual shift away from the amorphous surrealistic drift of image and symbol characteristic of his early verse toward the more

478

disciplined form and spare intellectualism (partly influenced by T. S. Eliot) of his poetic maturity. He rendered into Swedish as early as 1941 Eliot's "East Coker" from the *Four Quartets*.

Behind Ekelöf's restless experimenting with poetic form lies a desperate search for a meaning in existence — a meaning which, however, he never attains, at least not in clearly definable terms. Born in a Stockholm family of considerable wealth and some mental instability (his father, a stockbroker, lived for years as a mental patient), Ekelöf early became centrally concerned with the problem of reality, and his world of poetry may be said to be one long struggle with this problem. His first two volumes of verse, *Sent på jorden* (Late Upon the Earth, 1932) and *Dedikation* (Dedication, 1934), with their chaotic surrealistic dream sequences, seem to reflect a deliberate flight into a non-real world, a flight which in *Sorgen och stjärnan* (Sorrow and the Star, 1936) is moderated in part by the presence of a strong strain of otherworldly Romantic mysticism. In *Köp den blindes sång* (Buy the Blind Man's Song, 1938), however, Ekelöf seeks tentatively to identify himself with man and society and is apparently ready to accept the admittedly harsh conditions of existence in an outward objective world. In one of the quietly disillusioned "Elegies" of this volume he is for the moment prepared to throw in his lot with man and "cling fast to life" despite its limited, tightly closed-in perspectives, its dim, little-lighted horizons:

> One after another
> I see them extinguished, the lights,
> one after another, throughout life
> toward death, the last.
>
> And yet 'tis here I choose to live,
> here have my dwelling,
> here on the earth, among men.
> Little wonder I remain,
> cling fast to life.

But that Ekelöf could not finally hold fast to his resolve to reconcile himself with life, to accept existence on its own terms, in its immediate common humanity, becomes apparent in the severe analytical intellectualism of the poems in *Färjesång* (Ferry Song, 1941) and in the subsequent almost total retreat into the poet's purely subjective world as unfolded in the four volumes of verse, *Non serviam* (1945), *Om hösten* (In Autumn, 1951), *Strountes*, (1955), and *Opus incertum* (1959), which have come from his pen in the last decade and a half.

Though Ekelöf in the main goes his own way in these volumes of his maturity, creating a world of darkly haunting image and symbol and of subtle musical effects not without moments of ecstasy and magic enchantment, his poetic craft has perhaps learned from T. S. Eliot and others more than he is willing to admit (cf. the essay "Självsyn" in *Poeter om poesi*, 1947). But like other Swedish poets who in recent years have been attracted to Eliot, Ekelöf is attracted to the *poet* Eliot rather than the cultural critic and religious traditionalist. And even the poet Eliot by no means determines the final quality of Ekelöf's verse, in which the moments of unutterable ecstasy quite beyond the limits of sensation and thought are reminiscent not of Eliot but of Shakespeare and Hölderlin and such Swedish Romantic mystics as Stagnelius and the C. J. L. Almqvist of *Songes*. What Eliot seems chiefly to have done for Ekelöf was to suggest the possibilities of an allusive literary and learned language and to point the way toward a relatively rigid poetic discipline as a counterpoise to the deliberate formlessness of his early surrealistic verse. The opening lines of *Ferry Song* echo Shakespeare's "Those are pearls that were his eyes" from the lovely poem on death, "Full fathom five thy father lies," in *The Tempest*, a source alluded to twice in *Waste Land*. Ekelöf does not, however, work out elaborate allusive mosaics in the manner of Eliot. Like the Romantics he finds his world of image and symbol more frequently in nature, in the sweep of landscape and the skies, and particularly in the sea and its strange marine phenomena. Though some of Ekelöf's more recent poetry is bitter, astringently satiric, its primary note is one of quiet, restrained passivity in the presence of life's frustrating mysteries. "All consciousness is fleeting," he observes in the opening poem of *In Autumn* — but, he adds, "that which is fleeting is not vain and empty." Perhaps the final measure of Ekelöf's place in contemporary Swedish poetry is the fact that among the poets of the 1930's he has been the most important for the following decade's generation of Swedish poets, the so-called *40-talister*.

If Ekelöf is one of the most esoteric and exclusive of modern Swedish poets, his contemporary Nils Ferlin (b. 1898) is the most popular and profoundly "folksy." In fact, no Swedish poet appeals more directly to popular taste than Ferlin, who after a belligerent, brawling youth and a restless young manhood became for some years an actor of sorts and began what may loosely be called a "literary career" as a facile purveyor of satirical "hit songs" (*schlager*) for revues and the gramophone industry. Not until his early thirties did he appear formally as a poet, in the volume *En döddansares visor* (Ballads of a Death-Dancer), whose impertinent self-assurance and grotesque strain of melancholy cast in free-swinging rhythms enlivened by a catchy, slangy diction made Ferlin at once accepted by far larger numbers of the Swedish reading public than any of his poetic contemporaries. And even some of the more fastidious critics like Sten Selander were at first impressed by the originality of his talents, though most of the critics had difficulty in swallowing some of his excessive folksiness. But despite the reservations of some critics *Ballads of a Death-Dancer* was followed by two more resounding successes, *Barfotabarn* (Barefoot Children, 1933) and *Goggles* (1938), after which a somewhat "tamed" Ferlin has turned out six more volumes of verse, only two of which, *Tio stycken splitter nya visor, tryckta i år* (Ten Brand-New Ballads, Printed this Year, 1941) and *Med många kulörta lyktor* (With Many Chinese Lanterns, 1944), maintain something of the poetic level of his earlier work. His latest volume is entitled *Från mitt ekorrhjul* (From My Squirrel Wheel, 1957). Ferlin does not seem capable of poetic growth. What he did from the beginning he did well enough, but when in later years his early poetic aplomb begins to falter and he fumbles vaguely in less vigorous poetic directions he loses his touch and produces more frequently than not pale commonplaces in flat doggerel patterns of no particular distinction.

At his best through most of his career, however, he is arresting and not infrequently impressive. Though he is in many ways the least "literary" of Swedish poets, he has definite points of contact with a long Swedish literary tradition, the tradition which began with the seventeenth-century ne'er-do-well poetic vagabond Lasse Lucidor, became most brilliantly represented a century later in the inspired drinking-song verse of Carl Michael Bellman, found fascinating expression at the close of the nineteenth century in some of the verse of Fröding and Karlfeldt, and had its last worthy representative before Ferlin in Dan Andersson's restless poetic personality. This tradition was that of the poet as an "outsider," an essentially asocial, ill-adjusted creature of bohemian tastes and wayward vagabond predilections who, while looked upon askance by his "betters," takes his revenge on society in the role of a free-speaking, wisely bantering individualist, by preference clownish in pose. How thoroughly Ferlin has assimilated this tradition is suggested by the fact that its mentality as well as its characteristic literary mannerisms are more or less constant in Ferlin's poetry. In *Ballads of a Death-*

Dancer it takes on directly imitative forms, echoes of Fröding, Karlfeldt, and Dan Andersson occurring with disturbing frequency, while in Ferlin's later verse it is less obviously derivative, more fresh and original in its spirit and poetic formulation without departing sharply from the literary sources of its original inspiration. What Ferlin adds to the tradition is what may loosely be called a note of "modernism," a brutal, bitter, wryly cynical quality which is one of Ferlin's few points of contact with the disillusionment of the Swedish 1930's. In this respect, as well as in his use of stylistic anachronisms within the frame of traditional verse patterns, Ferlin reminds one at times of Hjalmar Gullberg, but Ferlin's cynicism has none of the elegant ambiguity of Gullberg's nor do his vigorous rhythms and pounding rhymes have much in common with the sense of Classical neatness which watches over Gullberg's choice of poetic accents.

Ferlin is a kind of proletarian troubadour, i.e., a poet with undeniably proletarian instincts and sympathies without a ready-made proletarian social and political creed. He is just as critical of one kind of political spellbinder as another and is prepared to satirize with equal pleasure (if not savagery) all breeds of social theorists and social workers. Neither the Leftist Clarté group nor the Salvation Army is safe from his barbs, as we know from one of his more celebrated poems; and other social-minded groups are even less apt to find mercy at his hands. His refusal to take seriously even well-meant organized efforts to mitigate man's misery derives in part from his ingrained individualism and in part from his views on the hopelessly indifferent conditions of man's existence. In formulating such views Ferlin is by preference deliberately offhand, as in the "poetically sublimated ditty" of the following lines:

> It's hard to keep track of them all,
> each proverb and each saying . . .
> It's said that the fall of a star
> means that a man is dying.

> The frozen refrain of the wind
> sounds over the chilly torps,
> the dogs are out and baying,
> as dogs generally bay for a corpse.

> I hear the widows shrieking
> children sobbing for bread —
> The stars get along all the same,
> whether one's alive or dead.

Translated by Richard B. Vowles

Coldly matter-of-fact as these lines at first glance seem to be, they are not without a faint implication of compassion; and in other of Ferlin's poems this implied compassion becomes warmly explicit, particularly as it applies to those whom life has dealt with harshly — children in despair, the forgotten aged, social outcasts of various kinds, and those to whom he refers as "these, the very poor" in one of his most famous poems. For most others — especially for the *streber* type and the man of success and influence, for those who are looked upon as pillars of society — Ferlin reserves his choicest scorn in poem after poem, and in one of the most devastating, "En boaorm" (A Boa Constrictor), a live-rabbit-devouring boa provides a gruesome parallel to man's rapacious habits and serves as Exhibit A among the Wonders of Creation:

> Oh, Lord, you who create without surcease,
> your boa, he's still your masterpiece!
>
> He is in all the great menagerie
> that which stirs most the human fantasy.
>
> Lies like a highly polished ring now
> and scarcely thinks of anything at all now.
>
> A boa, a boa who has such charming habits
> digesting sleepily his small white rabbits.

The grim and macabre in a poet's vision of the law of the survival of the "fittest" can scarcely be pushed farther. Tennyson's "nature red in tooth and claw" and "nature so careful of the type, so careless of the individual life" are restrained, properly Victorian generalizations on the subject of survival in comparison with Ferlin's brutal drawing of the parallel between an efficient live-rabbit-eating boa constrictor and an efficient live-man-eating human monster. So fond is Ferlin, especially in his early poetry, of drawing such grim likenesses between the animal and the human worlds that Hjalmar Gullberg once observed that Ferlin's world tended actually to *be* a menagerie. It is, however, a menagerie with a difference, a menagerie which more than merely entertains a gaping crowd. In its fierce satiric purposes it breathes a warm compassion for those who are daily victimized by the insensitive and indifferent masters of creation.

The grim note which is so often struck in Ferlin's satiric verse suggests that behind the grotesque clown mask which he so frequently dons there lies something of a sensitive, uncertain, tragically serious modern spirit. Not without reason he has been called the Chaplin of modern

Swedish poetry. Not infrequently a note of anguish lurks just beneath the surface of his verse, and at times, as in such poems as "Månen är hygglig och lyser" (The Moon Is Gentle and Shines), "Jag fryser" (I Am Freezing), "Av ständig oro" (Because of Constant Restlessness), and "Analys" (Analysis), the note of anguish breaks out in a nakedly confessional, frankly self-critical strain. In "Because of Constant Restlessness" Ferlin explains his caustic satirical practices as a means of bolstering his own hypersensitive, vacillating spirit. He likens himself in this poem to "a queer porcupine" whose quills have pierced his own exposed self even as they are employed against others as a means of self-defense. And in "Analysis" the poet, referring to himself in the second person, observes laconically:

> He, God, who lives above on high
> gave you a wretched heart,
> also an owl-sharp, captious eye —
> restlessness is your part.
>
> Better might be your heart,
> free from your anguished plight,
> if from the very start
> you'd had a more normal sight.

In some of Ferlin's later poetry this defensive restlessness in part recedes, and in its place comes a not very convincing note of passivity, of quietism, an almost idyllic preoccupation with certain near-sentimental childhood memories and a rather spineless flight into a vague kind of meditative, mood-inspired landscape poetry. And simultaneously Ferlin's rhythms and rhymes become bereft of much of their earlier boldness, dash, and vigor. The change is not for the better. The earlier Ferlin may not in the last analysis have been a great poet, but he had at the time a remarkable poetic vitality and an extraordinary ability to reduce some of the complex facets of modern experience to levels of poetic expression which were understandable to the multitude. It was such qualities as these which led to his winning in 1942 the coveted Fröding Prize, the highest tribute that Swedish university youth can pay a Swedish poet. But Ferlin has since 1942 done little to maintain the level of poetic production and promise which led to the distinction of the Fröding Prize. He was perhaps too facile as a verse-maker? too much a *merely* bohemian vagabond spirit? too easily aggressive and contrary in dealing with his environment? too little really sensitive and profound either as artist or man? — whatever the reason, or reasons, he has shown of late years little capacity for genuine poetic renewal. Among the half dozen more important poets of the 1930's he has seemed the least capable of really fruitful poetic growth.

Two other poets should be mentioned at least in passing before we have done with the poetry of the 1930's — Olof Lagercrantz and Karl-Gustaf Hildebrand, both born in 1911 and both having distinguished themselves as much as critics and scholars as they have as poets. Neither of them has the creative originality or vigor of the important poets of the day, but each in his modest way has contributed to the rich lyric flowering of the 1930's, in their cases particularly in the direction of poetic refinement. Lagercrantz is definitely the more "modern" and catholic in taste of the two, finely sensitive as a poet and warmly perceptive as a critic-scholar. Besides his poetry (*Den döda fågeln*, The Dead Bird, 1935; *Den enda sommaren*, The Only Summer, 1937; *Dikter från mossen*, Poems from the Swampland, 1943), he has written a delicately penetrating *Dagbok* (Diary, 1954) and has been among the more active and intelligent of literary critics in a number of leading Swedish newspapers and journals, on some of whose staffs he has served also in editorial capacities. In 1951 he attained the doctorate in literary history at the University of Stockholm on the basis of a brilliant dissertation on Agnes von Krusenstjerna, and most recently he has written a sensitive monograph on his late friend Stig Dagerman. Lagercrantz's verse is crystal clear in form, employing, as does Gullberg and Edfelt, conventional poetic patterns but handling them in a less sharply disciplined manner than his contemporaries. His first volumes of verse were rather pale exercises on such subjects as illness and convalescence and recollections of things past, but in *Poems from the Swampland* he shakes off most of his reminiscent-tinged, subdued romantic manner, pouring out folk-legendary material and landscape impressions in darkly brooding periods constantly remindful of death and disintegration, of the ominously mysterious play of fate as symbolized in a bog-land world.

Aside from his poetic production, which is confined to three volumes, *Nödvärn* (Self-Defense, 1933), *Vårdagjämning* (Vernal Equinox, 1937), and *Djupt under ishöljet* (Deep under the Ice Cover, 1950), Karl-Gustaf Hildebrand has devoted himself exclusively to cultural criticism and historical scholarship. His criticism, given early expression in a book of essays entitled *Kristna perspektiv* (Christian Perspectives, 1935), is conceived in a spirit of intelligent Christian humanism. His study

Bibeln i nutida svensk lyrik (The Bible in Contemporary Swedish Poetry, 1939) is a little classic in its kind. His poetry has little spontaneity
or flight but it has an honesty and precision of utterance which is in its
way refreshing. Despite his Christian traditionalism he is neither prudish
nor dogmatic, and he is capable of meeting the literary secularists of his
day (be they socialists, nihilists, primitivists, or surrealists) on their own
terms without submitting to their modernistic blandishments. Among
the relatively small group of younger Swedish authors with serious religious interests Hildebrand is the most balanced. He is in almost every
way the antipodes of that other religious-motivated author-critic Sven
Stolpe, who, as we have seen, was plucked from the embrace of literary
modernism in the mid-1930's by the Buchmanites (the Oxford Group),
and later became a convert to Catholicism, to whose service he now
devotes the considerable literary energies and polemic gifts which have
always been his somewhat dubious hallmark. Stolpe's recent biography
of Jeanne d'Arc has appeared in an English translation.

Though future historians of recent Swedish literature will probably
agree that the chief glory of the 1930's is its poetry, its prose fiction is
on the whole only less impressive. The novelists of this period, with two
or three exceptions, are not as boldly experimental in matters of form
as the poets, but they are equally prepared to come to grips with the
central problems of the day, and they do so with a directness and thoroughness and a sense of social values that the poets can scarcely match.
The novelists of the 1930's have not drifted so strongly as the poets
toward a kind of literary internationalism. They have maintained strong
points of contact with the Swedish scene, continuing the traditions of
the realistic social-minded novel of the two preceding decades by providing a kind of literary inventory of modes of existence on various
social levels in various geographical areas of Sweden. But unlike their
predecessors, the novelists of the 1930's are less prone to be regional in
their emphasis or class-conscious in their points of view and bases of
judgment.

Even though authors of proletarian origins are decidedly in the majority among the ranking novelists of the 1930's, they are less concerned
than were their working-class literary colleagues of an earlier generation
with writing novels which directly reflect the class struggle. By the
1930's the working man with literary talents no longer stood outside the
crucial areas of Swedish cultural developments. He had by virtue of his

talents and in consequence of rapidly changing social patterns come to take a central place in Swedish literature. Before 1930 the working classes had gained two of their chief objectives, universal suffrage and near-majority political power, and during the depression-wracked 1930's social change followed rapidly upon social change as a matter of course — a development which amounted to the writing of the last, decisive chapter in the total democratization of Sweden. Under the circumstances the working-class author of the day no longer felt forced to employ his gifts primarily as an instrument of propaganda and social criticism, though conditions even in the 1930's were admittedly not so ideal that novels of radical social purpose were not by necessity written. In fact, at least three of the novelists of the day, Ivar Lo-Johansson, Moa Martinson, and Jan Fridegård, made some comfortably situated Swedes wince under the whiplash of their revelations on conditions among the least favored of agricultural and industrial workers. But in general the earlier direct attack on existing conditions came in the 1930's to be superseded by novels in which the thematic material was remotely if at all identifiable with a class-conscious attack on the contemporary social scene. Novels with titles like *Workers*, *A Story About Hatred* needed no longer to be penned by Swedish authors.

It is on the other hand symptomatic of the changing social mentality of authors of working-class origins that in the 1930's one of the favorite fictional forms was the lengthy autobiographical novel in which social criticism, insofar as it was included, tended either to be oblique rather than direct or had to do with the past and could therefore be sifted through the softening perspectives of time instead of exposed to the blazing light of immediate social conflict. Among the more or less deliberately autobiographical novels of the 1930's are Ivar Lo-Johansson's *Godnatt, jord!* (Good Night, Earth! 1933), Eyvind Johnson's so-called "Olof-romanen" in four volumes (1934–37), Harry Martinson's *Nässlorna blomma* (tr. *Flowering Nettle*, 1935) and *Vägen ut* (The Way Out, 1936), Jan Fridegård's "Lars Hård" series (1935–37), and Vilhelm Moberg's *Knut Toring* (tr. *The Earth Is Ours*, 1935–39). So rich, indeed, in possibilities did the autobiographical novel prove to be, that some of the novelists who cultivated it in the 1930's continued to exploit the genre later, Moberg, for instance, in *Soldat med brutet gevär* (sharply condensed English version *When I Was a Child*, 1944) and Lo-Johansson in a still-unfinished series which up to 1958 includes *Analfabeten* (The Illiterate, 1951), *Gårdfarihandlaren* (The Peddler, 1953), *Stockholmaren*

(The Stockholmer, 1954), *Journalisten* (The Journalist, 1956), *Författaren* (The Author, 1957), and *Socialisten* (The Socialist, 1958).

Despite the undeniable impression of critical honesty of recall which these novels leave with the reader, they suggest also that even working-class authors can enjoy creatively the *luxury* of reminiscence, are quite capable of indulging without sentimentality or falsification in some of the comfortable creative *clair-obscur* which tends to take possession of those who write about their past. In the case of most of these novelists their "hard years" were over when they wrote their autobiographical works, and they were in consequence less liable than they might earlier have been to swing the polemic sword. They had become "accepted" in the literary counsels of their nation and no longer felt compelled to assert themselves against an entrenched literary and social traditionalism. They were themselves creating a new literary tradition, unfettered by the past and unhampered by a consciousness of inferiority in the presence of those of their contemporaries whose road to literary distinction had not been strewn with the early hardships and frustrations of the proletarian authors. What the working-class novelist had to offer from the very beginning was a whole new world of experience and a fresh way of looking at this world of experience. Though he came to do this during the 1930's in various fictional forms, the autobiographical novel was the form in which he attained some of his greatest triumphs, chiefly perhaps because in this form he was least hampered by the demands of more narrowly disciplined fictional forms. He was free to follow the dictates of his memory as determined by the nature of his experience of life, and this experience was in many cases so rich and diverse, so replete with unexpected turns of fortune, comic or tragic or both, and so often instinct with the mad miscellany of existence that it was all but bound to yield a fascinating literary harvest once the workingman author had learned to use his literary instrument with sufficient finesse and precision and imaginative sweep.

Curiously enough the Swedish novelist who at the time most bitterly attacked certain social conventions and institutions was a person of the most exclusive aristocratic origins, Agnes von Krusenstjerna (1894–1940) — and the conventions and institutions she attacked were those of her own class. In her last work — the unfinished but formidable novel sequence which includes *Fattigadel* (Poor Nobility, 1935), *Dunklet mellan träden* (Shadows Among the Trees, 1936), *Dessa lyckliga år*

(These Happy Years, 1937), and *I livets vår* (In the Springtime of Life, 1938) — she wreaks merciless revenge not only on her class as such but also on members of her own family with whom she had been at odds for many years, partly because of a marriage outside her class with a gifted literary critic of dubious reputation, and partly because of the subject matter which her novels occupied themselves with from the very beginning. Her novels were concerned more daringly with sexual problems than any Swedish prose fiction to date — with sexual frustrations and sexual perversions which were to be found particularly in a degenerate aristocracy such as her family represented. In fact, her first novel (the so-called Tony books) is, we now know, a thinly disguised account of her own girlhood and young womanhood, an intimate study in a precarious early awareness of sex, which in Agnes von Krusenstjerna's own case, as in the novel, led to nervous hysteria and finally to a private mental institution in Stockholm.

Agnes von Krusenstjerna's entire mature life (she died of a brain tumor in her mid-forties) consisted of alternating periods of extraordinary creative vitality and of severe psychic crises, the latter often requiring extended professional treatment. At times creative activity and psychic crisis overlapped, as in the case of *Poor Nobility*, portions of which were written in a mental institution in Spain. Much of her work was written abroad, though nearly all of it deals with the Swedish conditions which she had known in her childhood and young womanhood. Hers is almost exclusively a reminiscential work, one of the most fearsome and tormented which has come from a Swedish pen, and yet one in which a crystal-clear, delicate precision of style often belies the sick, hysterical eruptivity of the world which she describes. It is clear from manuscript revisions that her husband, a scholar-critic of Gallic interests and tastes, is responsible for most of the sharp satiric turns of phrase and many of the pointed stylistic concretions which punctuate her otherwise relatively quiet and measured prose. To what extent he otherwise contributed to her work is impossible to say, so closely have wife and husband hidden the secrets of their literary collaboration.

Though Agnes von Krusenstjerna deals constantly with sexual problems of the most delicate and disquieting kind, she was not a devotee of Freudian lore nor did she cultivate contacts with those of her literary compatriots, the primitivists and surrealists, who had found fundamental points of departure for their work in Freudian investigations into the subconscious and unconscious levels of human experience. She did, however, in certain ways share — without apparently having been influenced by — the "sexual mysticism" of such figures as D. H. Lawrence and some of his Swedish admirers. The literary enthusiasms of her early years (enthusiasms which in some cases carried over into her years of maturity) were astonishingly enough Louisa May Alcott, Fredrika Bremer, Hans Christian Andersen, Selma Lagerlöf, and above all Dickens, authors who would seem scarcely calculated to lead her very far in the directions which her own work was ultimately to take. In any case the world of Agnes von Krusenstjerna's literary creation, though it has points of contact especially with Dickens among her predecessors, derives primarily out of her instinctive — and violent — reaction against the world of rigid social convention in which she had grown up. Her novels are her means of escape from that world of convention — often, in addition, an act of bloody revenge against it.

Aside from some unimportant early tales about young girls, and a scattering in later years of some reasonably competent short stories, Agnes von Krusenstjerna's work includes three several-volume novels — the three "Tony books" which appeared at two-year intervals between 1922 and 1926, the more ambitious seven-volume work (1930–35) about the von Pahlen family and its various social ramifications, and finally the series beginning with *Poor Nobility* in 1935 and left unfinished at the author's death. Of these novels the one which centers upon the girlhood and early womanhood of Tony Hastfehr is in the main a sensitive and relatively inoffensive treatment of sexual awakening and sexual frustrations, but its last section, which introduces us to the harrowing agonies of a mental hospital, is a disquieting warning of more sensational things to come from Agnes von Krusenstjerna's authorship.

These things came with unmistakable emphasis in the early 1930's when *Fröknarna von Pahlen* (The Misses von Pahlen) began to appear, and before the von Pahlen series was completed Agnes von Krusenstjerna became the storm center of a violent controversy focusing upon the problem of an author's rights and responsibilities in the literary treatment of sex in its various manifestations. Halfway through the von Pahlen series Agnes von Krusenstjerna had become so daring in detailing the ways of eroticism — particularly perverse forms of eroticism — that her publisher, Bonniers, refused to continue publication unless certain changes were made in the manuscript. The last four volumes of the work were in consequence brought out by Spektrum, a publishing house which prided itself in encouraging the literary activities of the young radicals of various stripes. Though Bonniers' action may have been motivated partly by the political situation in Europe (as a Jewish publishing house, the firm was in an exposed position in the Hitler-triumphant early 1930's), there was otherwise some reason for the publisher's decision. *The Misses von Pahlen* is definitely not pornographic, but it comes at times precariously near the line of demarcation between art and mere pornography. Seldom if ever has an artist of Agnes von Krusenstjerna's distinction and high intentions brought together in a novel as motley and nauseating an assembly of hopelessly perverted males and females as we come upon in the later volumes of *The Misses von Pahlen*, and what takes place among them amounts at its culmination point to a lurid bacchanal whose resources of degeneracy seem bottomless.

Aside from Agnes von Krusenstjerna's never failing stylistic virtuosity, that which enables us to endure the vision of aimless sex-inspired evil in *The Misses von Pahlen* is the fact that it is conjured up by the novelist in a spirit of white-hot scorn and indignation. To Agnes von Krusenstjerna sex as mere play, as flirtation, as egotistically motivated pleasure leads inevitably to sterility, the ultimate insult to sexual passion, whose healthy drives are always drives toward fertility, toward the reproduction of a healthy race. Only in two of the women in *The Misses von Pahlen*, Angela and her aunt Petra, are healthy drives central; but the manner in which these women ultimately seek to realize these drives — in a matriarchy which uses men merely as an instrument of insemination — suggests that Agnes von Krusenstjerna's constructive intentions in this novel are hardly equal to the task of formulating an acceptable alternative to the sickly drift of misdirected passion which she so devastatingly castigates.

But the author's indignation, which in *The Misses von Pahlen* tended to lose its focus and issue into monomaniac visions of sexual promiscuity, recovers some of its critical precision and balance in the family novel usually referred to as *Poor Nobility*, from the title of its initial volume. Though stuffy family traditions and rigid social conventions frequently crop up in both the "Tony books" and the von Pahlen series, they do not move into the focus of the author's attention until *Poor Nobility*, in which is examined with deadly precision the ways in which the dead weight of convention on the highest social levels snuffs out all spontaneous forms of life and growth. Degenerate heredity together with morbid sexual fears and frustrations also play a part in *Poor Nobility*, but they no longer occupy the center of the stage. All in all *Poor Nobil-*

ity is a fascinating work, not least because its subtly modulated prose, only on occasion breaking out into phrases dripping with relentless hatred, suggests to the perceptive reader how the social class with which Agnes von Krusenstjerna had broken dramatically in her young womanhood still maintains over her as she approaches middle age a subtle half-attraction. She could not completely emancipate herself from her past.

The curious contradiction which one notes between the unconventional ideas and the essentially conventional art of Agnes von Krusenstjerna does not exist in Eyvind Johnson (b. 1900), who together with Agnes von Krusenstjerna shares the distinction of cultivating intensively, already in the 1920's, certain of the moods and themes and points of view that came to be widely accepted in the literature of the following decade in Sweden. But Eyvind Johnson also cultivates new experimental *forms* — a new prose style and new fictional techniques of the most advanced kind. He is, in fact, the first Swedish novelist who almost from the start of his career deliberately sought those modern prose forms which in the hands of Proust and Gide and James Joyce had resulted in a new kind of novel. Eyvind Johnson had no difficulty in finding his way to such modern masters, for his early formal schooling was so slight that it could scarcely channel his literary tastes in the direction of traditional forms, and when he had grown up he had no direct points of contact with established Swedish cultural institutions, not even with the folk high schools, which had often led an earlier generation of working-class authors into a world of idea and form that in some ways was highly traditional. The generation of working-class authors to which Eyvind Johnson belonged had for the most part educated itself in the school of hard knocks, and this school was hardly inclined to encourage a sense of loyalty to literary convention. Besides, Eyvind Johnson had an artistic temperament which instinctively went its own way, ever alert to modern literary developments, ever prepared to try his hand at whatever stylistic and structural experiments were being advanced abroad, and yet always capable of rising above mere imitation of his foreign contemporaries and of creating a form which was unmistakably his own. Among the gifts which enabled him to create his own kind of "modernity" in the novel are a lightning-like quickness of mind, a fabulously inventive fantasy, a magic way with words, and a satiric point of view which ranges effortlessly from waggish irony through grotesquely mad caricature to searing sarcasm.

492

But before these gifts were to burst into full creative flower Eyvind Johnson had to fight his way through a bleak boyhood and a grim, unpromising, restless young manhood. Born in upper Norrland near the Polar Circle, he already knew what hard and dangerous labor was when as a boy of fourteen he was taken on as a helper at a timber boom. At the age of fifteen he was sweating through long months of toil in a brickyard, followed by brutal labors in a sawmill, after which he was employed in various capacities in a village movie house, from which relatively light work he presently found his way back to what he considered "more honest proletarian labor," that of a ditch digger for a sewage contractor. All this time he was reading, reading, reading anything he could put his hands on — as a means of escape from the desolate limitations of his existence. Meantime he dreamed vaguely of becoming an author. Finally, at the age of nineteen, he fled south to Stockholm, and a few years later to the Continent, first to Berlin and then to Paris. At Stockholm he took what work he could find on a labor market made uncertain by the prevailing economic crisis around 1920. By this time his interests had become definitely literary, and he found some outlet for these interests in writing short stories and collaborating with a couple of proletarian comrades in a short-lived *avant-garde* journal, *Vår nutid* (Our Times). His first stay abroad, two years in duration, were years lived on the borderline of starvation, but during these years he read widely and discovered Freud. Most important, however, as he himself has told us, was the fact that during these years on a war-devastated Continent he "met a great many strange people, cast up like flotsam by a swirling world. And this gave me, more than all else, living documents in the history of the times." Upon his return to Sweden in 1923 he felt ill at ease at what he considered his country's comfortable self-complacency, its readiness to ignore misery on its borders and to find in the idyl the literary genre most to its taste. He soon fled again to Paris, this time remaining abroad for five years.

Before departing from Sweden the second time he had his first novel accepted for publication, and during his stay in Paris he established himself firmly in the literary consciousness of his countrymen by turning out four arresting novels — *Stad i mörker* (City in Darkness, 1927), *Stad i ljus* (City in Light, 1928), *Minnas* (Remembered, 1928), and *Kommentar till ett stjärnfall* (Commentary on a Falling Star, 1929). Though these novels, with the exception of *City in Light* (which first appeared in French under the title *Lettre recommandée*), deal with Swedish conditions, they are conceived and executed in a manner which at almost every point reflects Eyvind Johnson's fascinated familiarity with the most advanced of Continental practitioners of fictional art, particularly with Proust, Gide, and Joyce. We are reminded of Proust in the very title of *Remembered*, a novel which in other respects also betrays definite Proustian leanings. Gide's ironic intellectualism and skeptical challenging of all accepted "values" are reflected in all of Eyvind Johnson's early novels, and Gide's practice of writing stories within stories as well as Joyce's use of inner monologue are skillfully adapted by Johnson for his own immediate purposes. Among Swedish novelists only Nordström and Hjalmar Bergman, especially the latter, seem to have had any early importance for Eyvind Johnson. He has often gratefully admitted his indebtedness to the more advanced practitioners of the modern novel, most fully in an essay from 1945 entitled "Romanfunderingar" (Meditations on the Novel), in which he observes that they are important not merely because they have introduced "new spheres of action (*motivkretsar*) . . . but new ways of examining man and his conditions of existence. Each of them has in his way opened the eyes of others to new or only partially realized possibilities in the art of the novel."

Of the novels which appeared during the Paris years *City in Light* is the most derivative, reminding one in both theme and mood of Hamsun's *Hunger* and in its dialectic subtleties of Gide. *City in Darkness*, a tale about life in the far northern city of Boden, is far more Eyvind Johnson himself, employing all manner of new techniques but subordinating them skillfully to his over-all purpose, a half-satiric, half-sympathetic and understanding picture of human destinies in a little city perched precariously on the edge of the Arctic wastes. Insofar as literary influences played a part in the conception of this novel, Hjalmar Bergman's treatment of the small Swedish provincial town must have been of importance. *City in Darkness* is on the whole one of Eyvind Johnson's less pretentious but most perfectly wrought novels. By contrast *Commentary on a Falling Star* is ambitious and highly complex in design, and it leaves us with a less unified and organic impression — perhaps deliberately, for in this work the novelist is concerned with the most intricate psychological and ethical ramifications of modern man's experience in a disintegrating capitalistic community. The tone of the novel is in consequence grim; its satire often harsh, in the last analysis corrosive; its probing into the hidden areas of human motivation at once trenchant and darkly disillusioning. *Commentary on a Falling Star* is all in all the most disquieting of Eyvind Johnson's first group of novels, all of which are concerned centrally with man's frustrations and somber inner conflicts — with what the novelist was to call man's Hamlet-character.

When, in 1930, he gives the title *Avsked till Hamlet* (Farewell to Hamlet) to a new novel he takes a first step toward a less negative position, even though this novel and its immediate successors *Bobinack* (1932) and *Regn i gryningen* (Rain at Daybreak, 1933) are in their way sufficiently critical of man and the world he has fashioned. But in these novels Eyvind Johnson is not so immersed in a world of psychological determinism that he is incapable of envisioning a possible solution of man's dilemma. Upon his return to Sweden in 1930 he had established some tentatively fruitful contacts, on the one hand with the reform politics of the Social Democrats and on the other with the literary primitivism of the day. These contacts helped him to shed the melancholy introspective Hamlet mask of his early novels and led him to take part in the social and cultural debate of the day on the side of those who optimistically assumed that radical changes in economic and social institutions and/or a frank recognition of man's natural, sex-inspired motivations would bring about a better world. The result in *Bobinack* was a fantastically demoniacal exposé of the machinations of modern capitalism, and in *Rain at Daybreak* an attack on the stultifying effects of modern office drudgery and a glorification of life in the bosom of nature. Polemic in purpose as were these novels, the polemics did not deter the author from indulging in his usual sophisticated exercises in literary form, *Bobinack* being a novel of extraordinarily tricky construction and *Rain at Daybreak* employing for purposes of depth-analysis a rather complex multiple point of view reminiscent of André Gide.

In Eyvind Johnson's next work, however — the series of autobiographical novels usually referred to as "Romanen om Olof" — sophisticated modernistic structural devices are almost entirely absent. The narrative patterns are allowed to take care of themselves, to spring directly out of the exigencies of episode and the nature of the human material, to move rapidly or slowly, intensely or calmly, depending upon the mood or immediate interpretative purposes of the author. Spontaneous and richly diverse in style, original in point of view, profoundly personal in tone, this series is certainly one of Eyvind Johnson's finest works. Its first volume, *Nu var det 1914* (Now It Was 1914), appeared in 1934, followed at yearly intervals by three others, *Här har du ditt liv!* (Here You Have Your Life!), *Se dig inte om!* (Don't Look Back!), and *Slutspel i ungdomen* (Youth's Finale). The first volume gave promise of the series' becoming, when completed, a broad social epic of Norrland during the second decade of the twentieth century as reflected in the life and folkways of the working classes, and though the later volumes did not fail to give us many vivid, often brutal, sometimes tragic glimpses into the life of the masses struggling grimly against the cold and darkness of an inhospitable semi-Arctic region, these later volumes are chiefly fascinating for their sensitive study in the psychology of timid boyhood moving precariously through the complications of puberty to a restless, questioning, essentially uncertain young manhood. Free as is the narrative form of the Olof novels in almost all matters of detail, the detail is held together by a kind of thematic development in the musical sense, each volume treating a given, rather sharply distinguishable stage in the hero's growth toward intellectual and emotional maturity and each volume containing at some point within its realistic frame of action a kind of fairy tale, a poetic-symbolic "saga" which provides a profoundly imaginative distillation of a central aspect of folk life in Norrland. Of these "sagas" the one in the first volume, entitled "Sagan om dimman och lungsoten" (The Saga About the Fog and Tuberculosis) is the most moving — a tale about the swampland woman who after losing her children by the dread killer tuberculosis comes to believe that the swamp fog *is* her children, whereupon she breathes in its chilling dankness and dies. Such a "saga" would have fascinated the modern Swedish master of the genre, Selma Lagerlöf, though she would not have been capable of telling it with the unrelenting realism of Eyvind Johnson.

The last volume of the Olof series is the least satisfactory, which may be accounted for at least in part by the fact that at the time Eyvind Johnson was writing it he was becoming increasingly disturbed by the triumphant progress of political totalitarianism on the Continent in the late 1930's and the threat which this held for humane values as represented in Western culture. He felt compelled to counteract the totalitarian evil with all the talent and energy at his command. During the War as well as in the immediately preceding years Eyvind Johnson's novels took on the form of flaming protests against totalitarian terror, and outside the field of literature proper he identified himself more or less actively with such propagandistic journalistic ventures as *Trots Allt*, *Nordens Frihet*, and *Håndslag*, all of which openly and sharply opposed certain of the neutralist policies of the Swedish government and served as rallying points for those who sought to buttress the morale of Danes and Norwegians whose countries fell before the Nazi invaders. *Håndslag* (the Norwegian word for "handclasp") was an illegal sheet issued by Eyvind Johnson and designed specifically for illicit distribution in Norway.

Though all Swedish authors of any distinction sooner or later recorded their opposition to Nazism and Fascism as well as Soviet totalitarianism, and defended a humanitarian idealism which they identified with Western culture, none was more outspoken or persistent in both attack and defense than Eyvind Johnson. Of the three novels which he dedicated to the cause of democratic freedom in its struggle against tyranny (*Nattövning* [Night Maneuvers, 1938], *Soldatens återkomst* [The Soldier's Return, 1940], and the Krilon series, 1941–43), *Night Maneuvers* provides us with a terrifying picture of Nazi exploitation of all that is low and mean, the beast in man, and as such the novel is also Eyvind Johnson's accounting with the primitivism of his earlier *Rain at Daybreak*. Some attention is also given in *Night Maneuvers* to incipient Swedish forms of Nazism, the subject which occupies the center of the stage in *The Soldier's Return*, a story about what has been called "Scandinavia's Unknown Soldier," who after having served in freedom's forces in three wars, in Spain, Finland, and Norway, meets death one lovely summer night on an idyllic Swedish countryside at the hands of a petty malcontent, a human type ripe for the crude blandishments of totalitarian propaganda. The grim irony of the murder scene in *The Soldier's Return* rises to grotesque crescendos of harsh and relentless satire in the scene which follows the murder — a scene in which typical representatives of the nation's citizenry, gathered around the soldier's maimed body, are concerned much more with their own private everyday desires and woes than with the larger ideal issues incarnated in the passing of the hero-stranger. But over the dead ditchwaters of their pettiness rises finally the dream-vision of the dying man, a dream of *decency* among men — "one can also call it," we are reminded, "cultural freedom. Here in the North and the West the possibility of decency exists; to the East and the South are its enemies."

This "possibility of decency" among men is what a group of friends in the Krilon series (*Grupp Krilon*, 1941, *Krilons resa*, 1942, and *Krilon själv*, 1943) fight for, at times against great odds, in neutralist Sweden during the war years. The Krilon series adds up to a magnificently devious allegorical mosaic, a brilliant, fascinating, but rather uneven work springing directly out of immediate conditions in Sweden during the early war years. Its allegory is infinitely inventive, infinitely varied, infinitely *charged* — satire at its mad and holy best. But the allegorical patterns are often so intricate that the reader has great difficulty in following its mazes and deciphering its details. Brilliant in many of its parts, the Krilon series becomes at times almost a caricature of Eyvind Johnson's always sharply alert style, his restlessly inventive narrative practices, his often roundabout manner in the handling of theme. Possibly the extremes to which he goes in these directions in the Krilon series were deliberate — a way of confusing the enemy. In any case it is a matter of record that Nazi censors did not confiscate the Krilon books at Danish ports of entry during the wartime occupation of Denmark.

The allegory which supplies such a precarious structural base for the action and development of theme in the Krilon series is, as a technical device, related not too distantly to the "narrative frame" employed in *Strändernas svall* (tr. *Return to Ithaca*, 1946), the novel which together with the four Olof volumes represents Eyvind Johnson at his best. In *Return to Ithaca* the "narrative frame" device is handled with superb skill, directing us step by step (despite the intrusion of subtly sketched interludes and fabulous digressions of various kinds) into the core of "meaning" which the novel pursues. The novel is ostensibly a retelling of the Odyssey tale in modern terms, and can be read as such with the delighted pleasure one feels upon examining something old and revered through the eyes of a skillful modern narrator and observer. But more seriously *Return to Ithaca* is a modern "quest" novel, in which its hero is in search of "values," of whatever "meanings" life may have to offer. The Ulysses tale in the hands of Eyvind Johnson constantly suggests to the perceptive modern reader ancient parallels to problems faced by contemporary man — the problems of war, of guilt, of the conflict between desire and duty, even of the concept of duty itself and the ambiguously skeptical attitudes toward it which man is frequently tempted to adopt in our complex modern times. In Eyvind Johnson's novel, however, these "problems" are never forced into rigid dialectic molds. They are approached subtly, obliquely, quizzically, oftentimes in a humorous or in a grotesque vein — as if to suggest that "truth" is infinitely coy and must be approached with something less than an overpossessive, pretentiously serious mien. In the creation of *Return to Ithaca* Eyvind Johnson has learned much from Joyce and from the Thomas Mann of the Joseph books, but he is himself everywhere in his version of the Ulysses tale, employing Joyce's inner monologue with an impish offhand skill of his own, adding to Thomas Mann's laborious reconstruction of the past a note of lightness, of sly, infectious humor, and yielding without hesitation when occasion permits to the pleasures of spinning a tall tale or irreverently reducing to proper proportions our traditional way of looking at such matters as mythical heroes and ancient religious rites. These — and many, many other things — make up the variegated, fluid, thoroughly modern fabric of *Return to Ithaca*, a novel whose quality even in its most bizarre moments is so subtle and many-faceted that only a finely perceptive reading of it can provide an adequate awareness of its superb artistry and its alertly searching analysis of man and his fumbling but stubbornly persistent pursuit of truths which so often have a mocking way of eluding him.

During the last ten years Eyvind Johnson has shown no falling off in narrative resourcefulness, though the note of disillusionment which has seldom been far from the center of his world seems in the last years to have become more marked. And with this his style and narrative verve have lost some of their freshness and vitality. Of his more recent novels *Drömmar om rosor och eld* (Dreams About Roses and Fire, 1949) antedates Aldous Huxley's novel on the 1643 witch trial against the French Catholic priest at Loudon, and *Lägg undan solen* (Put Away the Sun, 1951) deals with contemporary conditions on the Continent as they are affected by two catastrophic world wars, while *Molnen över Metapontion* (Clouds over Metapontion, 1957) operates simultaneously on two planes, the world today and the Greece of around 400 B.C. The best of these novels, *Clouds over Metapontion*, skillfully combines elements from *Return to Ithaca* and *Put Away the Sun*. The note of disillusionment in the recent novels is often harsh and bitter, and the form of these novels tends to be so loose as to border at times on the chaotic; but they retain, in spite of all, their creator's profound sense of solidarity with the West and with Western culture. Eyvind Johnson has been in the 1950's one of the sharpest critics of those particularly among the youngest generation of Swedish authors who have been attracted to the so-called third alternative in the Cold War — an alternative which identifies itself with an absolute neutrality between the forces of the East and the West. When, in April 1957, Eyvind Johnson was elected to the Swedish Academy, the election was merely an official outward recognition of the high place which he has held for many years in Swedish letters.

Of Eyvind Johnson's deliberately Continental orientation, his literary internationalism, there is very little in the most read of contemporary

Swedish novelists Vilhelm Moberg (b. 1898), whose roots are always firmly implanted in Swedish soil even when he is most critical of Swedish institutions — as he has been particularly of late in his vigorous attacks on what he feels to be the tendency of Swedish bureaucracy to swallow up the individual in the State, and in certain cases, even, to obstruct justice by the manipulation of legal technicalities in protecting people in high (in fact in the highest) places. Moberg's recent concern with such immediate social and political matters might seem to be carrying him rather far from the peasant world of most of his novels, but actually this concern grows naturally enough out of what was from the beginning the central preoccupation of his literary work, the soil and those who labor on it. That which he most admires in the Swedish peasant of ancient stock, whose way of life he has depicted more satisfactorily than any other novelist, is the sturdy individualism combined with respect for law which this peasant to him represents. That this sturdy individualism has its drawbacks, its darker reactionary sides, is sufficiently clear to Moberg from the very beginning, but with time it becomes equally clear to him that such an individualism in its ideal form is the only answer to the excessive bureaucratism of modern society. The specific evils which Moberg attacks in his purely polemic works of the last decade (in his public addresses and essays and in the satirical novel *Det gamla riket* which owes much to both Strindberg and Swift) are simply the worst fruits of a system which he feels has gradually sapped man of his dignity as an individual, has reduced man to a creature who passively accepts and quietly dozes rather than asserts himself and creates for himself and for society vital, forward-looking, positive values.

Few Swedish authors have such a profound sense of identity with the class out of which they grow as does Moberg, whose ancestry on both sides for many generations had eked out a meager living on small and stony holdings on the southern slope of the great Småland plateau. In his young manhood Moberg had reacted against some of the stultifying features of life on this countryside, had moved to urban centers and become first a journalist and then an author; but he never forgot his origins, and his best work grows as directly out of the Småland countryside as had his ancestors down through the centuries. How deeply Moberg feels his identity with this countryside and its folk he has expressed in the autobiographical essay "Brodd" (Germination):

One may be transplanted any number of times, but in a deeper sense one cannot obliterate the stamp of one's origins. One has indestructible roots left in the earth where one first began to grow — at least when the whole of one's childhood was spent in a single place. An affinity of the blood, a solidarity of feeling with this folk remains with me, even though I clearly recognize that there is not always reason to prefer these people above all others. Among them there were no doubt persons whom I should have difficulty in liking if I now could see them as they really were. But I own them as one owns those closest to one, whom one under all circumstances observes with a wary eye. They belong permanently to a phase of life. They are *my* people. And I react against the city-dweller's tourist view of them — as one reacts in case those closest to one are put on public display in some menagerie. On the other hand they are ill served by that female sentimentality which makes of them God's angels and figures in conventional wall hangings, edifying pictures for those who love "nice people."

"They are *my* people" — the words apply specifically to what is called in Sweden the *småbonde* (the peasant with small holdings), in whose ranks Moberg was born and grew up and about whom he was the first of important Swedish authors to write. "This folk has lain asleep — resigned, patient, forgotten, mute, not conscious of its strength and its possibilities," Moberg observes in the pages of *Soldat med brutet gevär* (Eng. adaptation *When I Was a Child*, 1944), the autobiographical novel in which he describes his discovery of them as material for literary treatment. And he adds: "I now want to provide a picture of that illiterate race, which I still have not been able to recognize in any printed book. I myself am so closely related to it that I have illiterates in the generation nearest me. I wish to describe its deeds, explain its reticence, give to it a voice and take part in its striving to discover itself. In my mind's eye I feel that this could be my true calling — *that this henceforth could be my class struggle.*" The italics are Moberg's.

Those of his novels which first attracted serious attention — *Raskens* (1927; the title defies translation) and the two volumes about Adolf Bengtsson in Ulvaskog, *Långt från landsvägen* (Far from the Highway, 1929) and *De knutna händerna* (The Clenched Hands, 1930) — concern themselves exclusively with peasant life in Moberg's Småland. In *Raskens* this life has retained a quality of healthy vigor despite its undeniably limited, at times brutish aspects, but in the two volumes which concern themselves with Adolf in Ulvaskog the picture of life on the Småland countryside takes on heavy, somber, deeply tragic qualities. It is the Småland that we have come to know as one of Sweden's least favored, most poor and hard-bitten provinces. Down through the centuries nature had yielded her treasures here very sparingly, and as a rule only at the price of arduous, cruelly persevering human labor. It is a province of forbidding expanses of deep forests, broken at intervals by natural valleys and man-made clearings of stubborn rocky soil. Its peasant population was, in consequence, for centuries stolid, hard-working, essentially primitive in its innermost character. The Småland peasants whom we meet in Moberg's novels therefore differ from their counterparts in the literature on Värmland or Dalarna as Moberg's heavy prose differs from the lyric intoxication of Selma Lagerlöf's Värmland prose or the warm vitality of Karlfeldt's Dalarna verse. There are, it is true, some lighter sides to the picture that Moberg gives us of Småland in his early novels, especially in *Raskens*. The sober matter-of-factness of Moberg's narrative progression has its occasional flashes of lyricism, its momentary surges of those high animal spirits that even a stolid, careworn peasantry cannot indefinitely deny itself. But on the whole the picture of life that we get in these novels is severe, constrained, often darkly brooding, with tragedy lurking grimly near at hand ready to sink its claws into a struggling humanity.

One wonders at times, as one follows the relentless piling up of minute physical detail in the broad epic movement of Moberg's early novels *Far from the Highway* and its sequel *The Clenched Hands*, if he has not felt the impact of Sigrid Undset's narrative genius. And one is almost convinced when one notes the laborious care with which Moberg penetrates into the desperate brooding consciousness of its central character. This is the manner of *Kristin Lavransdatter* and *Olav Audunssøn*, though one need certainly not assume a conscious effort on Moberg's part to imitate Sigrid Undset's narrative manner in his novel dealing with the tragic destiny of Adolf Bengtsson in Ulvaskog. In several basic respects the Swedish novelist goes quite a different way from that of his Norwegian contemporary. The religious element — to mention but one of the important differences — is incidental rather than central in Moberg's novel; and when it is introduced it tends to operate toward destruction rather than toward salvation. Adolf Bengtsson's wife, for instance, ultimately commits suicide, against a background of dark religious brooding. She did not, as did Sigrid Undset's Kristin, find ultimate solace in religious penance, in a dignified though hard-won acceptance of a "divine justice" impossible to fathom but capable of being experienced even in moments of deepest trial.

Human destiny in Moberg's novel, magnificently conceived as ruthless and primitive, is terrifying to behold. We become convinced as we read the uncompromisingly honest pages of *Far from the Highway* and its sequel that man has lived and died in this manner, though we may shudder to admit it and wish that it were not so. Thomas Hardy's title *Far from the Madding Crowd* echoes unmistakably in Moberg's *Far from the Highway*, and not a little of Hardy's spirit breathes in the pages of Moberg's early novels. Hardy and Shakespeare. The fate of the Småland peasant Adolf Bengtsson in Ulvaskog has something of the hopeless, tragic pathos of Lear, though in Moberg's novel there is no Cordelia to bring a last sad measure of comfort to a broken man. Moberg's narrative moves toward high tragedy without perhaps finally achieving it, chiefly because as a modern realist he insists upon keeping his feet on the earth, envisioning his hero in a limited, everyday, commonplace existence. There is honesty in Moberg's picture, and at times flashes of hauntingly somber beauty, of genuine poetic insight, which make us realize that a genuine artist is handling the brush. But detail piles up into almost unmanageable masses, and the shadows lie so deep, so seldom relieved by light, that we tend to grow restive under the gloomy monotony of it all. The characters have courage, and they struggle with praiseworthy persistence for those things which seem to be of importance to them. But their courage is too frequently that of a mere beast of burden, and they struggle against such hopelessly dreary odds that their efforts tend to strike the reader, at the last, as essentially meaningless, the aimless, unseeing struggle of matter with matter. As a result we leave this early novel not wholly satisfied, despite the undeniable honesty of its vision of life on an isolated Swedish farmstead in the years after the turn of the century, when youth was moving in droves to the cities in protest against rural isolation and the stern patriarchal traditionalism of their elders. The title *The Clenched Hands* symbolizes the refusal of Adolf Bengtsson of Ulvaskog to change his ancient ways, to open his hands to youth and to the future, and in the end, in desperation, he kills his youngest daughter who proposes to flee to the city as had his other children.

When we get into the pages of Moberg's next novel dealing broadly with the Småland countryside — the *Knut Toring* trilogy (tr. *The Earth Is Ours*, 1935–39) — we feel more satisfied even though this novel is not heroic in the traditional sense and the problems of form are not handled with the sureness and fine consistency of the earlier novels. Its rather loose structure is suited, however, to its material and its thematic purposes, the treatment of a rural community in a state of flux, adjusting itself slowly and laboriously to the altered conditions of modern society.

It is a soberly rich picture of Småland and its folk that we come upon in this new novel, more rich and full and diversified than we had before become accustomed to in Moberg's work. But its richness and fullness and diversity are unobtrusive. And a warm, vigorously alive prose lyricism is more often encountered here than in the earlier Moberg, especially in the lyricism of natural scene and of human passion as they are to be found on the Swedish countryside. But Moberg also introduces not infrequently into these pages what may be called the lyricism of the machine, the poetry of modern invention — modern developments of one kind and another which bring a lightening of the burden of daily toil to the countryside. One does not easily forget, for instance, the passage in which the arrival of the first piped running water is celebrated in the village of Lidalycke:

Standing beside Betty and watching the water pouring from the tap, Knut lost himself in the vision that irresistibly took possession of his mind. Past ages were revived in a sequence of images.

It was the true legend of the peasant women and the water. He saw them coming from the well carrying the huge buckets of water. Laboriously they made their way through piles of drifted snow. The cold was bitter. Icicles formed glistening fringes along the hems of their skirts. He saw them coming from the well or spring, slipping on the icy path, fighting with bent bodies against the wind, soaked to the skin by the autumn rains, puffing and sweating in the heat of summer, groping through the wintry darkness. Then the crowd of village women merged into a single figure. He saw his mother as he remembered her from the earliest childhood years, burdened with heavy buckets of water, walking through snow and rain and weather of every kind. He saw her when she had been young and upright, and had moved swiftly on firm legs. He saw her back bending under the weight of years and buckets. He saw her still carrying the same burdens, but stooped over, and now increasingly slow of step, her swollen legs tottering under the weight. He saw her having to stop again and again for a rest on her way from the well to the house. And finally he saw her as he had seen her one evening in the moonlight, prostrate on the ground: "I simply fell down."

Here a great gain had been made in saving human beings from a misery of such long duration that it had come to be taken for granted. Here a step had been made toward that mastery of the earth which was Knut's dream in behalf of mankind, the dream that would not perish. This was the way to follow. Sacrifices should be made only to save man from evil. Life should be the object of all sacrifices.

This is what Wordsworth would have called "the poetry of common life": a poetry breathing human sympathy, a poetry in which depth and

504

spontaneity of feeling inspire a warm, living vision of universal human values.

Man's age-long struggle for freedom becomes the central theme of *The Earth Is Ours* though we are not at first aware of this as the novel's primary concern. The opening pages of the novel seem to be concerned exclusively with an immediate personal problem of primarily psychological interest. We meet Knut Toring, a man in his late thirties, in Stockholm, as the successful editor of the widely popular magazine *Hearth and Home*. He is, it seems, happily married, with two children. But despite his professional success he broods excessively and sleeps very restlessly. Upon consulting an eminent physician he is told that he has no organic difficulties, that his general physical condition is excellent. And he is provided by the specialist with the usual formula for combating a serious case of insomnia. But his restlessness continues, and he finally has to admit to himself that his unsettled state of mind derives from the fact that he finds no satisfaction in his work, that in adjusting himself to his journalistic career he is untrue to his deepest instincts. His profession has brought him what is called "success," but at the cost of a gnawing inner restlessness. He realizes finally that he is prostituting his talents to earn a living; he cannot really *live* in his work. For months he tries to rationalize his case, to avoid the issue, to plead to himself the necessity of supporting his wife and children on the level to which they have become accustomed. But his restlessness continues, grows more and more disturbing, until finally he resigns his position in the city and returns to Lidalycke, his native village in Småland, there to seek rest and happiness in identifying himself once again with the soil and with the ancient traditions of his Småland ancestors. His roots were in the soil of Småland, and the soil has drawn him back to itself.

When Knut Toring returns to Lidalycke village, and adjusts himself as best he can to the simple life and labor there, the psychological emphasis, so marked in the early portions of Moberg's trilogy, gives way largely to a broader concern with the varied problems of communal life in a modern Swedish rural economy. Knut Toring comes now to divide his time between farm labor and writing for newspapers and journals about farm conditions and farm prospects. He joins gladly, though with some mental reservations, in the program of the back-to-the-soil youth movement. He champions agricultural cooperatives. He concerns himself with the difficult economic and social problems of the rural population among whom he now lives. And in all of this he seems to be finding a kind of final happiness: in serving his fellows directly on his native soil and in working on a modern program of rural development he seems satisfied. He even begins to work out a kind of Testament of Faith, which he entitles "The Earth Is Ours" and in which he hopes to define the ideal of life which seems to him to be The Good Life. But unfortunately, far beyond the confines of Knut Toring's rural Sweden, forces are at work that are to upset with little ceremony the relatively simple calculations about The Good Life which had filled Knut Toring's dreams in the early years of his return to Lidalycke. It is 1938, and dark, sinister clouds are gathering rapidly on the European horizon to the south, clouds that have their fateful meaning even to an apparently isolated peasantry on a quiet, industrious Swedish countryside. These clouds, Knut Toring realizes all too well, can scarcely be ignored in his dream of man's future; for how can man say without ghastly mockery: "The earth is ours," when his freedom is being threatened and totalitarian might is beginning to thunder ominously along the not very distant horizon? Knut Toring has to seek an answer to this question — if he believes at all in the possibility of human happiness based on human freedom. He does seek an answer. And so a new chapter in his Testament of Faith has to be written, a chapter not included in the original plan. "When it was done," we are told, "he thought that perhaps it might prove the most essential chapter in the whole book." The chapter is entitled "A Dream Worth Dying For" and gives eloquent expression on the verge of the Second World War to the necessity of free men everywhere opposing the oppressor even unto death.

If *The Earth Is Ours* issues in its final chapters into an eloquent attack on tyranny and oppression, Moberg's next novel — *Rid i natt!* (tr. *Ride This Night!*, 1941) — dramatizes the issues involved by depicting men *acting* in the cause of freedom. Moberg's style in his new novel is more spare, more lean, more angular than it had been before. No longer do we have the leisurely epic sweep, the careful, unhurried lingering over detail of action and of scene that we had become accustomed to in Moberg's pages. *Ride This Night!* is a compact, hurried, intensely concentrated narrative; it achieves throughout a dramatic concentration of form, and little beyond the central skeleton of action is provided. Moberg's purpose in writing this novel had to him a vital urgency, and the tone and tempo of the narrative are determined directly by the urgency of his purpose. Though *Ride This Night!* is a historical novel, with its action placed in the middle of the seventeenth century, its central theme

— man's age-long struggle for freedom against powerful forces of oppression — had when the novel appeared so many obvious parallels in contemporary world conditions that no reader could fail to recognize the author's immediate polemic purposes. Moberg is sufficiently conscientious in his effort to depict life in central Sweden as it was three hundred years ago. The language in the novel has strong archaizing qualities, old-time superstitions are woven skillfully into the fabric of the action, and the whole economic and social structure of the society of the day is carefully worked out. But still it is clear that these things hardly interest Moberg for their own sake: they merely provide an appropriate world of idea and fact out of which emerges a vitally actual and pressing message for all free men in the war-torn world of the early 1940's.

The story is that of a tiny rural village (Brändebols by) of a dozen peasant families who find their ancient freemen's legal rights at first challenged, and then openly violated, by one Bartold von Klewen (a foreign-born landed gentleman) who has established himself on a property near Brändebols village at the close of the Thirty Years' War, and who claims certain services from the native peasantry in consequence of privileges granted him by Queen Christina. At first the peasants of the village resist, appealing to their ancient freemen's rights. But von Klewen's bailiff is wily, skilled in the tricks of handling "a stubborn peasantry"; and, exacting the bitterly hated forced labor on the master's estate, he ultimately imposes von Klewen's will upon the freemen of Brändebols village. But even as these freeborn peasants bow physically to the oppressor, their spirit is not broken — chiefly because one of their number, young Ragnar Svedje of the old and honored Svedje farmstead, resists to the end, though driven to seek the dark protection of the surrounding forests by the overwhelmingly superior numbers of Bartold von Klewen's men. Living a dangerous, hounded life in the forest, young Svedje becomes the living symbol of opposition to von Klewen and all that the oppressor stands for in the minds of the villagers; and though he loses his life at last, buried alive by von Klewen's deputies, his spirit of resistance lives on as a stern and somber inspiration to those who knew him and the justice of his cause. With *Ride This Night!* Moberg joined the Pär Lagerkvist of *The Hangman* and the Eyvind Johnson of *Night Maneuvers, The Soldier's Return*, and the Krilon series in employing the novel as an eloquent polemic weapon against the rise and spread of totalitarian tyranny in the Europe of the 1930's and early 1940's. Shortly after the appearance of *Ride This Night!* Moberg's novels were placed on the proscribed list in Nazi Germany.

Aside from his very active participation in anti-Nazi journalism in the years following the publication of *Ride This Night!* Moberg finished, in 1944, the autobiographical novel *Soldat med brutet gevär*, the composition of which had been interrupted by his work on the novel about the seventeenth-century peasant freedom fighters, and in 1946 appeared one of his most arresting and original works, *Brudarnas källa* (The Brides' Spring), a prose-poetic fantasy concerned with ancient Scandinavian rites centering upon the symbolism of sex and fertility. Moberg had never in his novels been averse to handling without circumlocution the facts of life as they involve sex, but in none of his works before *The Brides' Spring* had he immersed himself so completely in the world of sex symbolism. *The Brides' Spring* has been appropriately labeled "a hymn to fertility," and as such it may be looked upon as a late-born but not unworthy child of the sexual primitivism of the Swedish 1930's. To Moberg, however, sex never becomes a point of departure for an all-embracing literary program, as it had once been to such Swedish primitivists as Artur Lundkvist and his group. The treatment of sex in Moberg's novels has been considered by some readers and critics as excessive and tasteless, but it is rather a quite natural ingredient in novels which concern themselves honestly and realistically with folk life and the spontaneous animalism of the countryside.

Curiously enough *The Brides' Spring* did not upon its appearance arouse the ire of self-appointed moral censors, perhaps because its symbolic fantasy was sufficiently indirect to cloak the sexual implications of the novel. But when in 1949 the first volume of Moberg's great epic sequence on Swedish immigration to America appeared, a storm of protest descended on the author for what a small but highly articulate group of religious and political conservatives felt to be the indecency of certain portions of the work. Moberg's realism, which is undeniably open and frank in all matters, including the treatment of sex, infuriated those on both sides of the Atlantic who insisted upon sentimentally idealizing the folk migration from Sweden to America. Fortunately, the uproar around the initial volume of Moberg's work soon subsided; and he was left in peace, so far as his moral censors were concerned, to continue his work about the group of Småland peasants who in 1850 departed their Swedish shores and embarked on the great American adventure. The work, when completed a full decade after the publication of its first volume, *Utvandrarna* (tr. *The Emigrants*), included three more volumes, *Invandrarna* (tr. *Unto a Good Land*, 1952), *Nybyggarna* (The Settlers, 1956), and *Sista brevet till Sverige* (The Last Letter to Sweden, 1959). *The Emigrants* provides, in its first half, a detailed account of the conditions in the homeland which drove the group of sixteen emigrants, children included, from Ljuder parish in Småland, and, in the second half, brings these emigrants safely across the Atlantic after a long and arduous passage. *Unto a Good Land* follows the little group from New York halfway across the American continent to the sparsely settled Minnesota Territory, where as the first Swedish settlers in the area they establish land claims and begin to break the soil. The third volume, *The Settlers*, carries the story forward some seven years, to 1860, by which time Karl Oskar Nilsson, the born leader of the original party of immigrants, has become an American citizen, has proudly exercised his first voting rights by casting his ballot for Abraham Lincoln, and would have used in his daily relations with his fellows the name Charles O. Nelson had his wife not warned him against the sin of pride! In *The Last Letter to Sweden* he does change his name to Charles O. Nelson, an incidental symbol of his definitive Americanization, though in his last days, broken by his wife's death and his labors with the soil, but still stubbornly heroic in stature, his thoughts return to the homeland, to Ljuder parish in Småland, whence forty years earlier he and his neighbors had emigrated. The circle was completed — "the last letter to Sweden" was written by an immigrant neighbor (in a Swedish partly contaminated by the language of the new land) to announce his passing to relatives and neighbors of the past in the homeland, who had not followed him and his family across the Atlantic to a new land.

His lot as an immigrant had not from the beginning been an easy one. He had toiled long and hard in order to establish himself in the new land. But this new land to him was the land of opportunity where free men could carve out their own destinies, and as such it appealed to Karl Oskar's deepest peasant instincts. He, like Knut Toring in *The Earth Is Ours* and Ragnar Svedje in *Ride This Night!*, was a freedom fighter, though Karl Oskar's enemy was the chaos of the wilderness rather than the tyranny of social convention and political oppression. But unfortunately Moberg labors too heavily the theme of American freedom versus European oppression, with the result that his novel suffers from an overidealized view of American conditions a hundred years ago and an overeager desire to glorify this America in contrast to the Europe of the day. One wonders if Moberg's current crusade against present-day Swedish bureaucracy and its not always tasty fruits has not carried over into the polemic America-versus-Europe attitudes of his immigrant novel — at least to the extent of forcing these attitudes in the novel into much sharper relief than would seem necessary or desirable. The reader in any case tires of the repetitious appearance of this polemic element in a novel which in almost every respect otherwise is magnificently impressive, certainly the work by Moberg that will live longest in the consciousness of his countrymen.

What is most impressive about the novel is the way in which Moberg gets under the skin of his characters, the way in which he looks at everything in the new world through the immigrant's eyes. He is able to do so in part because of his long apprenticeship in a prose fiction which had concerned itself so intimately with his own people, the Småland peasantry, and in part because of a life-long contact with immigrant mentality as reflected in the "America letters" which poured into his home from dozens of relatives who had emigrated. Among his earliest childhood memories were these America letters. They haunted his youth and young manhood (on one occasion almost convinced him that he himself should emigrate), and they never drifted far from the center of his consciousness. He seemed in consequence fated to write the great novel about the first Swedish immigrants to the Middle West — the novel that waited a full century for its author. The research which Moberg conducted in the late 1940's "on the spot," on the American scene and in Swedish-American archives, was all that he needed to complete his preparation. When he finally put pen to paper the story of the Swedish immigrants from his own native Småland all but told itself.

Moberg had such distinguished predecessors in the immigrant novel as Willa Cather and the Norwegian-American O. E. Rølvaag, but he seems not to have learned from them. In all essential respects he goes his own way, deriving his narrative methods largely from his own earlier Småland novels, simply transferring his peasant characters and their ancient way of life to a new and in some respects more primitive scene, the mid-nineteenth-century American frontier. But he adds something to his earlier narrative methods, he adds the epic sweep which the story of one of history's greatest folk migrations demanded. In doing this he did not, however, allow his story to take on purely legendary qualities or to lend itself to stylistic effects of conventional epic design. Biblical language is not uncommon in Moberg's immigrant epos, but it is an ancient, down-to-earth mode of speech with biblical overtones, one that rested naturally on the rough tongues of a Swedish peasantry.

Moberg's story is rooted at every point in the earth, in the everyday commonplace tasks of the immigrant. Its narrative pace is deliberate, plodding, toil-bound — the pace of the actual pulse of life which it depicts. And its language is simple, bare, earth-bound — the language of the folk who people this immigrant world. At times, of course, the narrative pace quickens, is lighted by glints of racy humor, or takes on momentarily heroic proportions, or gathers itself into a strikingly expressive symbol. But the racy scenes are relatively exceptional, as are the heroic episodes; and the poetry of symbol is in Moberg a poetry of everyday life, as in the instance of The America Chest, whose sturdy *utility* was its abiding glory:

One day the Nilsa family's old clothes chest — of solid oak painted black — was pulled from its place in a cobweb-infested corner of the attic, and carried down into the kitchen for inspection and dusting. No one knew how old this chest was — the hands which made it were mixed with the earth of the churchyard many hundreds of years ago. It had passed from father to son through numerous generations. More than one young bridegroom had entrusted his finery to it after the wedding feast, more than once had the farm's women fetched winding sheets from it when there was a corpse in the house to shroud. Under the lid of the chest valuable things had been secreted; this lid had been lifted by the shaking hands of old women, and by young, strong, maiden fingers. It had been approached mostly at life's great happenings: baptisms, weddings, and funerals. This enduring piece of furniture had through centuries followed the family, and at last been pushed away into a dark attic corner where it had long remained undisturbed. Now it was pulled out into the daylight once more; it was the roomiest and strongest packing case they could find — five feet long and three feet high, wrought with strong iron bands three fingers wide.

In its old age the Nilsa family clothes chest must go out into the world and travel.

It was tested in its joints, and the still-sound oak boards passed the inspection. It was scrubbed clean inside, and old rust scraped from hinges and escutcheons. After timeless obscurity the heavy, clumsy thing was unexpectedly honored again. From its exile in attic darkness it was now honored with the foremost place in the house. The chest had been half forgotten, years had passed without its lid being lifted; now it became the family's most treasured piece of furniture, the only one to accompany them on the journey.

The four oak walls of this chest were for thousands of miles to enclose and protect their essentials; to these planks would be entrusted most of their belongings. Again the old adage, "Old is reliable and best," was proved. And the ancient clothes chest which was about to pass into an altogether new and eventful epoch of its history was even given a new name in its old age. Through its new name it was set apart from all its equals and from all other belongings. It was called "The America Chest," the first so named in this whole region.

Not often is Moberg moved to such extended symbolistic utterance, sober in spirit and measured in manner though it may in the last analysis be. Much more frequently the mark of his prose style is what may be called *the integrity of the fact*, a stylistic manner nowhere more strikingly reflected in his work than in the quietly severe restraint of the short closing paragraph of *The Emigrants*:

It was on Midsummer Eve, in the year 1850, that the brig Charlotta of Karlshamn tied up at the pier in New York, after ten weeks' sailing from her home port. Precarious, insecure, and unstable were the first steps of the immigrants on American soil.

Here is *simply* a statement of fact, the bare record of an arrival, its date, the name of the ship together with its point of origin, and a few words about the condition of the passengers. Nothing more, strangely enough, despite the fact that Midsummer Eve is the day on the Swedish calendar most calculated to inspire the fantasy and arouse the traditional poetic strain even in the most sluggard of Swedes. But Moberg refuses to be tempted on the occasion by the magic of Midsummer Eve. He remains sober, records only the facts — neither encouraging nor deterring, it should be noted, those of his readers who might wish to read these simple lines with an eye for something more than the simple record of certain simple facts.

That Moberg is capable, however, of adding another dimension to his realism is apparent especially in the last two volumes of his immigrant tetralogy, in which the measured pace of everyday realism is on occasion quickened, rises at times to heroic moments, and manages to create in the person of Karl Oskar Nilsson something of a mythical figure. Not that Moberg seems deliberately to be intending such an effect, but simply by the stubborn earth-bound integrity of his vision he finally comes to create a character who gradually, almost imperceptibly takes on the unforgettable stature of a figure in a mythical or at least half-mythical world. Karl Oskar Nilsson, like Isak in Hamsun's *Growth of the Soil*, is a man in the presence of destiny, though the pattern of fate woven about Moberg's hero is at once more variegated and less optimistic in its final implications. *Growth of the Soil* may be called a realistic idyl despite its epic sweep, Moberg's tetralogy by comparison an extended tale with an undertow of tragedy. Man succeeds in his struggle with the soil in Moberg's world, but at a cost, as in Rølvaag's *Giants in the Earth.*

Though it is as a novelist that Moberg is chiefly known, he has from early in his career been active also as a dramatist. He has tried his hand at a variety of dramatic genres (folk tragedies and comedies, problem plays in the manner of Ibsen, biblical drama, etc.) and succeeded acceptably in all of them without having definitively broken through as a dramatist of high distinction. The Swedish theater and radio have, however, been generous in their recognition of his plays by producing most of them, some with considerable success. A few years ago The Swedish National Radio (Radiotjänst) recognized his contribution to Swedish drama by presenting in a special series no less than eight of his plays. Some of Moberg's plays are dramatized versions of such of his novels as *The Clenched Hands, Ride This Night!*, and *Mans kvinna* (Man's Woman, an English version of which is titled *Fulfillment*). Of these plays *Fulfillment* is certainly the most important. It is also thoroughly typical of the dramatist Moberg, being related both to his early folk tragedy *Hustrun* (The Wife) and to the later social problem plays *Våld* (Violence) and *Vår ofödde son* (Our Unborn Son). As in *The Wife*, the scene of *Fulfillment* is on the Swedish countryside, and it has to do with peasants and their erotic-marital relations. But *Fulfillment* is also a kind of modern problem play in that it deals with basic problems of morality and conscience, raising centrally the question whether one should follow his own inner drives or submit to conventional social standards. *Violence* is a modern family tragedy reminiscent of both Ibsen and Strindberg, of Ibsen in its concern with the problem of the individual's rights, of Strindberg in the precipitate intensity of its mood and action. *Our Unborn Son*, one of the two or three best of Moberg's plays, deals with the theme of abortion. Though it is marred somewhat by the rather arid, pedagogical formulation of theme so often typical of Moberg's problem plays, it manages at points to rise above the level of mere pedagogical moralizing, chiefly by employing certain symbolistic elements such as the half-legendary figure Maria, a fourteen-year-old school child who has strange religious visions related vaguely to the problems of conscience with which the chief characters in the play must struggle. On the whole, however, *Our Unborn Son* does not measure up to the dramatic quality of *The Wife* and *Fulfillment*, the finest of Moberg's folk dramas, a genre which he has cultivated more successfully than any other Swedish dramatist.

During the years in which Moberg was introducing Swedish readers for the first time to one of the less favored social classes, the peasant with small holdings (*småbonden*), a number of other Swedish novelists, commonly referred to as "the *statare* group," were acquainting their often shocked readers with a still less favored rural class — the agricultural laborer, the landless proletariat of the Swedish countryside known as the *statare*. Though the *statare* had scarcely been heard of in Swedish literature before 1930, this class has since become perhaps the most thoroughly treated social class in Swedish literature. The name *statare* as applied to a social class comes from the word *stat*, meaning wages in kind rather than cash. Miserably poor, at the very bottom of the social ladder, this class had for more than a century become progressively more exploited by large landowners, who in most cases housed them in dilapidated huts and ramshackle barracks, squeezed out of them every last ounce of labor, and maintained an almost absolute control over every phase of their existence. Once a year, in October, a *statare* and his family were permitted by law to depart from the estate or farm to which they had been attached, and many did — but to land on another property probably no better than the one from which they had escaped. This ugly cancer on the Swedish economic and social body was removed by law in 1945, certainly in part because of the detailed exposé of *statare* working and living conditions contained in the novels, short stories, and polemic essays of three authors, Ivar Lo-Johansson, Jan Fridegård, and Moa Martinson, each of whom had come directly from *statare* stock and had grown up in the midst of its countless frustrations and miseries.

Illiteracy was taken for granted among the *statare*, a circumstance which made the more hopeless any faint desire that some of them may have had to better their lot, to "get up in the world." Occasionally (as in the case of Ivar Lo-Johansson's father, late in life) they took one step up the social ladder — became cottagers with a tiny plot of their own land. More often their children revolted against the system, escaped to the cities and became with some exceptions swallowed up in the new urban proletariat. Among the most striking exceptions were those who had literary talents and who finally, after years of often bitter struggles, forced their way into the ranks of accepted authors of their day. Their "education" had to be picked up along the way, as it were, and the early products of their literary apprenticeship found such outlets as were available in laboring-class news sheets and journals whose readers were neither fastidious nor discriminating enough to demand literature much above a popular level. But in one way or another the budding *statare* authors came into possession of a literary education of sorts, chiefly by immersing themselves in Russian authors, Tolstoi, Dostoevski, and the prince of Russian proletarians Gorki, together with other novelists of distinct proletarian predilections such as Jack London and Martin Andersen Nexö.

In one case — that of Ivar Lo-Johansson (b. 1901) — years of contact with conditions among the poor on the European Continent also served to "educate" a *statare* author. Among the many moving tales of youthful "hunger for books" on the part of prospective proletarian authors, none is more moving than Ivar Lo-Johansson's. In one of his autobiographical sketches he admits that in his youth he stole in desperation in order to get money for books — an extremity, he assures us, that has never bothered his conscience. "It was society's fault," he comments wryly, "that I found my way so badly in the world of literature that I at times bought worthless books for the stolen money!" His wander-years on the Continent and in England in the late 1920's resulted in the publication of a number of "travel books" dealing with proletarian conditions abroad. These books met with only a mild response on the part of his countrymen. "The only success I had with my travel books," he tells us, "was that a Danish religious publisher had by mistake commissioned a translation of *Nederstigen i dödsriket* (Descended into the Kingdom of the Dead), assuming from the title that the book had to do with religious matters." *Descended into the Kingdom of the Dead* is an account of his experiences in London's East End slums.

The proletariat-oriented travel books gave way presently in Ivar Lo-Johansson's production to the group of works which made his name synonymous with the Swedish *statare* class. Beginning in 1933, and continuing for a full decade, he devoted himself exclusively to the task of acquainting his readers with the conditions of existence of this class and pleading their cause as the most neglected group in the Swedish economic and social structure. No Swedish author has devoted himself more single-mindedly and more systematically to throwing light on every phase of existence of a single social group. Between 1933 and 1943 five stout novels, three volumes of short stories, and innumerable essays and pamphlets — all dealing with *statare* life and the *statare* problem — came from Ivar Lo-Johansson's pen. Though much of the material in these works was drawn from his firsthand contact with the *statare* world, not a little of it was based on extensive investigations into the whole century-and-more history of *statare* developments in Sweden. His thorough familiarity with this *statare* world carries over inevitably into the literary form which his novels and short stories take. It accounts for Ivar Lo-Johansson's naturalistic method of minute documentation, of emphasis on milieu with its unafraid piling up of indelicate detail, and in style and general construction it lends a heavy, factual, earth-bound quality and calls for a deliberate striving on the author's part to realize the proletarian fictional ideal of the "collective novel" (*kollektivroman*). In fact, Ivar Lo-Johansson more than any other Swedish author experiments with the "collective" form, believes that it is the inevitable form for the kind of fiction which concerns itself primarily with the masses rather than with the individual. Two of his novels, *Godnatt, jord* (Good Night, Earth, 1933) and *Traktorn* (The Tractor, 1943), deliberately attempt to employ the diffused focus of the "collective novel," while his three volumes of short stories, *Statarna*, I, II (1936, 1937) and *Jordproletärerna* (The Earth Proletarians, 1941), with their wide-ranging panoramic picture of the *statare* masses in all phases of their existence, are, as their author tells us, "meant to be units in a collective whole."

Of the two "collective novels," *The Tractor* realizes the ideal of mass treatment somewhat better than *Good Night, Earth*, for the latter, being in part autobiographical in its emphasis, strays at times away from mass effects into the less expansive areas of individual portraiture, especially in its treatment of the two young boys Mikael Bister, who is Ivar Lo-Johansson himself as child and youth, and his friend Ture, a gifted young mechanical genius. In the main, however, *Good Night, Earth* is sufficiently "collective" in its over-all form, building up to a massive living fresco of slowly shifting scenes and episodes drawn directly from the daily lives of scores on scores of human beings reduced to the status of abject work horses, each resigned to his or her dumb-beast lot from which the only means of escape appears to be petty gossip and sullen backbiting among the women and occasional drunken bouts among the men. So multitudinous is the total effect that sometimes utter disorder seems about to take over, but by a rather skillful use of symbols and symbolical episodes and by recurrently focusing the otherwise dispersed action on the character of Mikael Bister the danger of complete confusion is avoided.

Ivar Lo-Johansson's interest in people is, in the last analysis, particular and concrete rather than general and abstract, and this enables him even in his deliberately "collective" novels to elude most of the rigid schematic extremes which tend to take possession of novelists who cultivate the mass-effect genre. So genuine, in fact, is his interest in the individual that even in the years when he is attempting to write *the* collective epos he disengages himself from the demands of this genre long enough to write two novels, *Kungsgatan* (King's Street, 1935) and *Bara en mor* (Only a Mother, 1939), neither of which is concerned with motley mass effects. In *King's Street* he turns temporarily away from the *statare* masses in their native rural milieu and occupies himself with the fates of two young people of peasant origins, caught up in the complex mazes of urban life. But in *Only a Mother* we find ourselves again in a geniune *statare* world, and yet this novel — Ivar Lo-Johansson's finest — concerns itself so predominantly with one human fate that its author has admitted somewhat ruefully that he "never was so disappointed" as he was with it. "I didn't want to write individualistic novels but collectivistic ones. But this novel went its own way."

Only a Mother is the magnificently sensitive and understanding story of a *statare* woman, Rya-Rya by name, from the year, her eighteenth, when she scandalizes her neighbors by bathing naked alone in a lake, until as an old woman, worn out by hard work and the bearing of many children, she dies of cancer — "a dirty female bundle that stank." The bathing scandal (incited by narrow *statare* prejudices against unclad bathing, even though solitary) results in the breaking of Rya-Rya's engagement to a cottager's son and her subsequent defiant marriage to a loud-mouthed, lumbering hulk of a man from the *statare* class — a marriage which leads inevitably from one brutal humiliation to another, lighted only by the joys of Rya-Rya's motherhood. The title of the novel is to be read with the accent on the first word: as a wife she fulfills her duty to her husband but is unable to share with him any deep feeling of relationship. Only her own splendid inner vitality carries her, somehow, erect in body and spirit through all the degradation which poverty forces upon her and which petty *statare* neighbors compound by all manner of meanness and spite. Though the life story of Rya-Rya is related with relentless realism, it breathes a spirit of quiet heroism, the heroism of a mother whom only physical death could finally break.

In *King's Street* from 1935, as well as in certain more recent autobiographical works from the early 1950's — *Analfabeten* (The Illiterate), *Gårdfarihandlaren* (The Country Peddler), *Stockholmaren* (The Stockholmer) — Ivar Lo-Johansson finds occasion to take to task those among his literary contemporaries who romanticized the city and the machine and / or sought to escape the complexities of modern life in the dream of vagabondage, the irresponsible individualism of "the road." In *King's Street* the city is presented as far more often evil than good, particularly insofar as its superficial glitter tempts country youth to its destruction, as illustrated in the fates of Marta and Adrian. The title of the novel is taken from Stockholm's busiest thoroughfare, which becomes a symbol of evil when, after darkness takes over, women of the street linger in half-shadowed areas to offer their tawdry wares to not too fastidious males. At times *King's Street* stoops to melodramatic effects both in its rather heavy-handed symbolism and in certain of its episodic sequences, but on the whole it is a solid, hard-hitting novel, tightly constructed and focusing with almost painful effectiveness on the serious problem, very actual in the Swedish 1930's, of precipitate population shifts from rural areas to urban centers. These population shifts carried with them an accentuation of certain social evils, not the least of which was a rapid increase in the number of prostitutes, recruited largely from the ranks of country girls lost in the wilderness of big city life. For documenting in his novel this phenomenon in detail, and providing the reader with a clinically exact and detailed study of an actual case of gonorrhea, Ivar Lo-Johansson was of course violently denounced by some.

While *King's Street* was a product of its author's early polemic period, the series of autobiographical novels beginning with *The Illiterate* (1951) is a fruit of his more temperate maturity, and in consequence these later works are in tone more gentle and restrained, in form much more free and flexible. In fact, there is an element in these late volumes which may be called almost "playful," a vein of sly humor and warm fantasy. The "loaded phrase" and half-bitter irony of Ivar Lo-Johansson's earlier works occur much less frequently in his autobiographical volumes — even in *The Country Peddler* when he takes up the cudgels against Harry Martinson's nomadic "tramp" philosophy. And yet in Ivar Lo-Johansson's retrospective treatment in this volume of his own youthful vagabondage on the Swedish countryside, he is not a little nostalgic in spite of his intention to expose the essential emptiness of the vagabond's world. In *The Illiterate*, too, he is somewhat predisposed toward the idyllic mood, prepared even to look upon the grim *statare* world of his boyhood with some equanimity, especially in the portrait of his father with its finally realized dream of a cottager's bliss. In later volumes of the autobiographical series, however, a less nostalgic mood asserts itself and the combative manner of Ivar Lo-Johansson's earlier work becomes more and more conspicuous, reaching a climax of satiric caricature in the seventh in order of the series, *Soldaten* (The Soldier, 1959), which depicts his experience in Sweden's "preparedness" forces during the Second World War.

There is much of this equanimity of spirit also in the more recent work of Jan Fridegård (b. 1897) though his earlier novels have a hard, brutal, violently defiant quality that makes even Ivar Lo-Johansson's early work pale and relatively inoffensive by comparison. Fridegård's world in his first novels, like Lo-Johansson's, is that of the hopelessly enslaved *statare* population, but Fridegård, unlike his literary colleague, is seldom directly polemic and he does not attempt to write a collective novel. His social criticism is implicit rather than explicit, and his novels deal centrally with individual destinies rather than with the fate of the masses — albeit his individuals more often than not tend to symbolize the struggle of the masses. Fridegård is the finest stylist and the most penetrating psychologist among the *statare* authors, but it took some time before his readers and critics properly appreciated his unobtrusive mastery of word and phrase, his incisive analytical gift, and his remarkable economy of narrative patterns. Where Lo-Johansson overwhelms us with an avalanche of words and scenes and episodes, Fridegård is chary of phrase and constantly on his guard against effects which depend largely upon a massive accumulation of detail. In matters of form his work may be described as a modern refinement of the saga manner — miraculously simple and direct, and factual as is the Icelandic saga at its best, but in Fridegård's case adding a new dimension to the saga, a warm, emotional dimension, broadly humorous or quietly understanding by turn.

The failure of Fridegård's readers to recognize at once the finer sides of his work is perhaps understandable. They were so shocked by what appeared to be the bottomless cynicism of his first important novel that they had no ear for the subtleties of its art or for its ethical implications. The novelists of the 1930's had conditioned their readers to expect a great deal by way of a frank, boldly realistic portrayal of life, but nothing quite like the brutal candor of Fridegård's *Jag, Lars Hård* (I, Lars Hård) had been recorded in Swedish print before 1935, the date of its publication. And before the shock of the first Lars Hård book had spent itself, two more equally candid Lars Hård volumes appeared, *Tack för himlastegen* (Thanks for the Heavenly Ladders) and *Barmhärtighet* (Charity) in 1936, followed in 1942 by a final, somewhat less disquieting volume, *Här är min hand* (Here Is My Hand).

The Lars Hård story is sufficiently coarse and repulsive in its general portrayal of life to disturb even a relatively callous reader, but what was particularly disturbing about it was the almost unbelievably brazen manner in which the title character, Lars Hård, conducts himself — apparently with no consideration for others, with no sense of social responsibility. His family name "Hård" means "hard," and the name is in his case uniquely appropriate. But what many of Fridegård's appalled readers did not at first observe beneath the surface coarseness of his story was that Lars Hård is what he is (a "rascal," a "scoundrel," a "lout" are some of the categories assigned by the critics) because society made him this way. He is asocial to the extreme, defiant to the point of criminality, because life had run roughshod over him. But Lars Hård's defiance, we come ultimately to know, was largely compounded of bravado, his impudent shamelessness a desperate means of proving his own "manliness." Though society may in some ways have been responsible for his brazen immodesty of attitude and deed, Lars Hård himself is scarcely inspired by ideals of a higher order than those of the society whose conventions he defiantly crushes under foot. If society is evil, he himself is empty and false and sterile. In such terms as these the story of Lars Hård becomes at the last an accounting both with society and with the kind of asocial "hero" Lars Hård represents; and it is not therefore surprising that at the end Lars Hård undergoes a kind of change of heart, that he recognizes his own inner sterility and reaches awkwardly out for values which to him dimly suggest concepts that we associate with human solidarity, values that can be caught up in such words as "love" and "understanding" and "selflessness." It should not be assumed from this, however, that the Lars Hård novel ends in an excess of sentiment. It does not. Fridegård can be warm and understanding and gentle, but never sentimental. "A coarse book could not end more beautifully," observes a Swedish critic who is not known for sentimental refinements of feeling.

One should not close even a short commentary on the Lars Hård series without also mentioning the way in which it reflects through its hero Fridegård's extraordinarily fresh and spontaneous response to nature:

It was at the close of April and the joy of the earth was turbulent. I went past some spruces which attempted in vain to retain their sullen dignity. The resin let off its fragrance, and aniline-colored cones in the treetops babbled about their inner gladness. I tried to force my way in and become a party to all of this, but cowardly, sickly apprehensions dragged their dark dregs over everything I felt.

The Lars Hård who could have these feelings was not a callous cynic despite the many outward appearances to the contrary.

The autobiographical materials into which Fridegård had dipped deeply in following the fortunes of Lars Hård were exploited further but somewhat more freely in two other novels, *Offer* (Sacrifice, 1937) and *Äran och hjältarna* (Honor and the Heroes, 1938), as well as in three volumes of *statare* short stories, *Statister* (Supernumeraries, 1939), *Kvarnbudet* (The Message from the Mill, 1944), and *Kvinnoträdet* (The Female Tree, 1950). In these works the contemporary scene, largely on the countryside, is examined with an honest realism that is often softened or relieved by strains of alternately tender and grotesque humor and fantasy. In certain other works — the delightfully juxtaposed companion pieces *Torntuppen* (The Tower Rooster, 1941) and *Porten kallas trång* (The Gate Is Called Narrow, 1952) — religious fantasy combines ingeniously with considerations of basic ethical problems; and in still others, especially the historical trilogy *Trägudars land* (Land of the Wooden Gods, 1940), *Gryningsfolket* (People of the Dawn, 1944), and *Offerrök* (Sacrificial Smoke, 1949), Fridegård examines with considerable learning and imagination the hard conditions of the slave in an ancient Swedish society. His concern with the past has led him even to try his hand, with some success, at a school text for children, *Fäderna* (Our Forefathers, 1947), providing a re-creation of life in the Stone Age.

Though both the *statare* short stories and the historical trilogy beginning with *Land of the Wooden Gods* contain a vein of social criticism, a defense of the enslaved masses of the past and present against their masters, Fridegård is in these works considerably less concerned with the plight of the underprivileged or with social criticism than he was in the Lars Hård books. And more and more as time goes on his concern is with the individual, in the ethical and religious sense, though he manages to avoid a heavy-handed moralizing manner in bringing men before the judgment seat of whatever God or Gods may exist. That Fridegård has even flirted with spiritualism is evident in some of his later work, but this flirtation, as all genuine flirtation, has not gone too deep, with the result that his art has been released rather than tyrannized by his religious preoccupations. In such later novels as *The Tower Rooster* and *The Gate Is Called Narrow* Fridegård's realism and miraculous economy of phrase remain, but to these is added a finely disciplined fantasy together with certain ethical and religious frames of reference which give greater depth and perspective to his work. The corrosive cynicism of his early novels often gives way in his later work to a playfully tender manner without in any way stooping to overidealization or sentimentality. Life's realities remain realities and man's evil remains evil, but seen in larger perspectives these realities and this evil appear to Fridegård less harshly decisive in the determination of man's fate, more capable of manipulation toward the ends of private and social decency. Fridegård's line of development has not made of him a modern Saint Francis, but it has tempered his early Lars Hård mentality to a point where some of the gentle ideals of the Saint are among those virtues which he may be said to embrace.

Though the third of the *statare* novelists, Moa Martinson (b. 1890), is the least important, she is in her way a literary personality of considerable interest. She is with all her faults definitely the most talented among Swedish working-class authors of her sex, and she has added to the proletarian types treated in Swedish literature before her what may be called "the hybrid proletarian," that is to say the proletarian type whose labors and conditions of existence oscillate uncertainly between the countryside and the city. Moa Martinson herself represents this type both in her origins and in her experience of life down to the time that she broke through definitely as a novelist.

An illegitimate child whose father deserted the mother, Moa Martinson first saw the light of day in the gray working-class districts of Norrköping, where her mother toiled in a factory. As a child she had had thrust upon her a stepfather of dubious stability, and at twenty she married a workingman of even less stability, to which union five children were born in as many years. Widowed at twenty-five upon the suicide of her mate, and deprived some years later of two of her children by drowning, she struggled along as best she could, managing to maintain little more than a bare subsistence level of existence by performing menial tasks as a nursemaid and as a hotel drudge in Stockholm and elsewhere. Meanwhile she identified herself with more or less radical labor groups and began writing for their publications. In 1929 she married the then relatively unknown young seaman-poet Harry Martinson (her maiden name was Helga Swartz), a marriage dissolved eleven years later.

The long years which encompassed such a succession of miseries with only occasional compensations would have crushed a woman of less spiritual flexibility than Moa Martinson. She survived somehow — to become in her forties what has been called "misery's cheerful narrator," remaining vigorous, expansive, always impulsive and vital, even in the midst of the daily drudgery and poverty-marked proletarian world which she depicts. Most of her novels fall in terms of their subject matter into either of two groups, those of an essentially autobiographical kind and those which are freely realistic reconstructions of conditions among the lower classes in times past. In the first group she has succeeded best in the trilogy *Mor gifter sig* (Mother Gets Married, 1936), *Kyrk-bröllop* (Church Wedding, 1938), and *Kungens rosor* (The King's Roses, 1939), in which her proletarian childhood is presented with a liveliness, humor, and wealth of gutty — often grotesque — detail that reminds one at times of Gorki and is all but unique in the Swedish proletarian novel. Of the novels which deal with the past the best is *Rågvakt* (Rye Watch, 1935), with its sharply conceived everyday realism giving way at times to certain half-magic dramatic effects; but others — such as *Drottning Grågyllen* (Queen Grågyllen, 1937), and the series which includes *Vägen under stjärnorna* (The Road Under the Stars, 1940), *Brandliljor* (Fire Lilies, 1941), and *Livets fest* (Life's Feast, 1949) — are in some ways equally impressive, particularly in their not unskillful use of tangled patterns of realism and symbolism in depicting the primitive drives and bloody passions of a family's history on the Östergötland countryside in the eighteenth and nineteenth centuries. Fairy tale and folk tale practices join with modern realistic documentation in these novels, often though by no means always happily. Moa Martinson's chief virtues as a novelist are her spontaneity, her lively inventiveness, her warm, direct sense of contact with life's everyday realities. Her chief fault is careless composition, a failure to select and properly distribute the parts in the whole. With few exceptions her novels fail to maintain a central narrative focus.

An infinitely finer literary craftsman than Moa Martinson — in some ways the finest in the contemporary Swedish novel — is Olle Hedberg (b. 1899), whose stylistic precision and neatly arranged narrative sequences reflect at least on the surface the well-ordered conventional world of the upper middle classes who people his numerous novels. What Olle Hedberg does with this well-ordered world is, however, to lay bare its emptiness and egotism, and he does so with both the incisive skill of a master surgeon and the mercilessness of a master satirist. The process is always fascinating to watch, if for no other reason than to enjoy Hedberg's superb artistry, his elegantly efficient narrative craftsmanship. Few Swedish novelists handle the tools of their profession with his unerring touch. Among his contemporaries he stands alone in this respect. One must seek as far back as Hjalmar Söderberg, at the turn of the century, to find a stylistic parallel to Hedberg. Like Söderberg he has learned from the French moralists, but, unlike Söderberg, he does not cushion his satire with a half-lyrical prose or with ironic effects calculated as much to amuse as to instruct. Hedberg's prose is, despite its elegance, relatively bare and lean, sharp, directly to the point. Without employing the voguish Freudian methodology of stream-of-consciousness fiction, he unmasks human motives with devastating effectiveness. No other Swedish author has so persistently probed the empty egotism of the middle class — its shallowness and vanity, its self-deception and self-seeking, and its bottomless spiritual sterility.

Though Hedberg's productivity has been little short of astonishing (a full-length novel every year since 1930), he has maintained throughout his career an extraordinarily even level of distinguished if not great literary quality. That he has attracted an increasingly large number of readers despite what may be considered a monotonously single-minded preoccupation with one highly conventional and therefore presumably dull social class suggests something of the measure of his narrative skill. And that these readers are drawn largely from the very class whom he so persistently pillories is further evidence of the technical finesse with which he manipulates his material.

What disturbs Hedberg chiefly in the conventional world of the middle classes is the way in which all forms of an ideal spontaneous life become choked off by economic concerns, by an exaggerated class consciousness, by cold, calculating procedures of all kinds. This is the theme of his first novel *Rymmare och fasttagare* (Runaways and Captors, 1930) — and the theme which is repeated with an apparently inexhaustible variety of approaches in the steady stream of novels which follow. It has been observed that the method which Hedberg usually employs in developing this theme is to confront the middle classes with their opposite, with human beings who because they are in most cases not of this class are at least in part capable of less calculating behavior, in some cases even capable of a kind of spiritual heroism. This method of developing his theme is particularly apparent in Hedberg's early novels. In *Runaways and Captors* the confrontation results finally in defeat for the one who attempts to defy convention, in this case a sensitive youth of the middle classes who, disillusioned by the cheap self-seeking of his family, runs away and seeks to live his own life, only to capitulate finally to the dictates of his class. He becomes with the years hardened, the process of "growing up" becomes, as so often in Hedberg's novels, the equivalent of spiritual petrification. In the novel *Fria på narri* (Deceptive Proposal, 1933) and its sequel *Iris och löjtnantshjärta* (Iris and the Lieutenant's Heart) the confrontation of differing class mentalities is more sharp, that of a young domestic servant, Iris, against the family which she serves; but the moral of the confrontation loses some of its force and validity when we discover that Iris herself is rather far from being a creature of disinterested idealistic motives. Only in *Får jag be om räkningen* (May I Have the Bill, 1932), Hedberg's finest novel, is the confrontation worked out in a way which satisfies the ethical demands of the situation without dulling the sharp edge of the author's satiric intentions. In this novel an ordinary traveling salesman is found to be a man of quietly heroic sensitivity and consideration for those about him in a world peopled otherwise by self-complacent, money-mad representatives of the middle classes.

Though Olle Hedberg never casts off his bitter antipathy toward characteristic manifestations of middle-class insensitivity and meanness, his novels from the 1940's are less exclusively satiric in their attitudes, more positive in their moralizing strain, even reflecting religious leanings though of a not always clearly defined kind. In *Josefine eller Säg det med blommor* (Josephine, or Say it With Flowers, 1940) the heroine is an incarnation of unassuming kindliness, while in the five-volume Bo Stensson Svenningsson series (1941–45) and in *Bekänna färg* (Confess Color, 1947) a search for moral and religious values is central in the development of theme. In the Bo Stensson Svenningsson series and in *Confess Color* Hedberg's preoccupation with the problem of evil has become less an occasion for social satire and more a serious concern with the possibilities of an embattled young idealist's efforts to triumph over the limitations of the material world. The central character in each of these novels is in search of a way out of the soul-destroying externalities of man's physical existence. In Bo Stensson Svenningsson's case the search takes on rather vague speculative forms and is in the end inconclusive, but in *Confess Color* the central character, who has had to face more than his share of evil at the hands of his fellows, is a Christian who has found his God.

That Hedberg does not, however, find any great (or at least final) comfort in the religious implications of *Confess Color* is apparent from his novels of the 1950's, novels in which he castigates with renewed sharpness, in fact with an almost Strindbergian fury, the hypocrisy and total spiritual sterility of the middle classes. *Dockan dansar klockan slår* (The Doll Dances, the Clock Strikes, 1955) is a worthy companion piece to Strindberg's *Spook Sonata* in its absolute disillusionment and merciless exposure of a middle-class society's pretentious emptiness, and Hedberg's last work to date, *Djur i bur* (Caged Animals, 1959), consists of two prose pieces in stark dialogue form which are so close to Strindberg's bizarre dream-play visions and techniques that one wonders if Hedberg, after thirty years as a novelist, is not on the verge of turning his talents toward the stage. If he does, the Swedish theater may have something new to concern itself with.

In any case his record as a novelist has been sufficiently impressive. Underneath the measured refinements of his prose style lurks always the merciless analyst, the unsparing moralist, acutely aware of that which is false and treacherous in man, and ever prepared to lay bare the evil which seeks to disguise itself in the elegant externals of a conventional world. His strength as a novelist derives largely from his refusal to stray outside the world he really knows, the world of the Swedish middle classes. This world he examines from every angle, with the assistance of every available analytic device, and thanks to the skill of the examination the reader forgets the sharply delimited boundaries of the world being examined. Hedberg is too honest a realist to pretend to know any other world.

Though Arvid Brenner (pseud. of Helge Heerberger, b. 1907) has not attracted the great number of readers who swarm eagerly around Olle Hedberg's accounts of the way of life of the Swedish middle classes of our day, Brenner has written novels on these classes that need not fear comparison with Hedberg's. Brenner has neither the stylistic flair nor the sharp satiric thrust of Hedberg, but he has a more understanding approach to middle-class mentality, and in general a more inclusive creative range, in part certainly because of his international background. Born in Berlin of a German father and a Swedish mother, he experienced at close quarters the breakthrough of Nazism before emigrating to Sweden. Of Brenner's novels on the Swedish middle classes, *Rum för ensam dam* (Room to Let for Single Lady, 1941) and *Vintervägen* (The Winter Way, 1945) are the most notable. *Room to Let for Single Lady* is a satiric exposé of human weakness, a novel of remarkable penetration, which in its sensitive objectivity retains elements of understanding if not actually sympathy for its central character, Magda Nilsson, who struggles as best she can to maintain a decent existence despite the gossip which oozes about her in slimy alternations of admiration and spite. Brenner's most telling satiric blows in this novel fall on Magda Nilsson's neighbors, though he is not prepared to idealize the object of their gossip. *The Winter Way*, Brenner's best novel to date, probes with equal objectivity into the devious ways by which a limited humanity seeks to resolve its tangled interactions, in this instance, however, with a greater degree of understanding and somewhat more satisfactory results than in his previous work. Brenner has also distinguished himself as a short story writer, most satisfactorily in the collection entitled *Stjärnorna ser oss inte* (The Stars Do Not See Us, 1947), in which he operates quietly but with a psychological finesse that maintains the same stylistic and analytic levels as in his best novels.

Though the most extensive, perhaps weightiest, contributions to the Swedish novel of the 1930's, with the exception of Olle Hedberg, were made by such "self-made authors" as Eyvind Johnson, Moberg, Lo-Johansson, and Fridegård, prose fiction during this decade has many other thoroughly competent representatives, some of whom pursue further the characteristic themes and forms of the day while other, more independent, artistic temperaments go their own ways. One of the signs of literary maturity in contemporary Sweden is, in fact, the number of novelists who write with intelligence and fine perceptivity and yet can scarcely be counted among those who have significantly shaped the substance and form of the contemporary Swedish novel. The novel flourishes today in Sweden far more than in any earlier period in the nation's history. So numerous, indeed, are those writers who turn out novels of some distinction that we can here refer to but a fraction of them and give some critical attention only to those among them who have succeeded in distinguishing themselves in one way or another from their fellow novelists.

Among those who have provided a reasonably high quality of fiction for the modern Swedish reader are a number of woman novelists, none of whom is experimental in matters either of theme or form but most of whom are sensible, warmhearted literary craftsmen of taste and considerable talent. Representative figures in this group are Dagmar Edqvist (b. 1903), Eva Berg (b. 1904), Tora Dahl (b. 1886), Gertrud Lilja (b. 1887), and — the most important of them — Irja Browallius (b. 1901). To these may also be added Marika Stiernstedt (1875–1954), who began her literary career a generation or more earlier than the others but who pointed the way toward the kind of prose fiction which most of her successors cultivated. This prose fiction generally is concerned with women in a middle-class professional society of a reasonably high cultural level. The women involved have their "problems," but these problems — unlike those of the feminists of an older tradition in the Swedish novel — are private and marital rather than social and political. Such titles as Dagmar Edqvist's *Kamrathustru* (Companion Wife) and Eva Berg's *Ungt äktenskap* (Young Marriage) and *Ny kvinna* (New Woman) suggest broadly the dominating themes of many of the novels. The manner in which these subjects are handled is usually sufficiently discreet and restrained without being unduly prudish. The "modernity" of these woman novelists, insofar as it exists, is kept for the most part under due control. It is on the whole the limited modernity of a cultured middle-class contemporary society.

But in the work of one of these woman novelists, Irja Browallius, the world we come upon is less cultivated and restrained, is in fact a definitely disquieting world of harsh realities and violent passions far removed from the cultivated environs of a well-ordered urban society. As a depicter of life on the Swedish countryside (specifically peasant life in one of the more primitive areas of the province of Närke) Irja Browallius ranks with Moberg, Lo-Johansson, and Moa Martinson. However, unlike these novelists, Irja Browallius — city-born and formally educated — acquired her knowledge of peasant life during ten years of teaching in a rural school. During those ten years her eyes missed nothing either of the externals of life on the countryside or the inner ways of the peasantry, with the result that at least two of her novels, *Synden på Skruke* (Sin at Skruke, 1937) and *Elida från gårdar* (Elida from the Farms, 1938), are counted among the few really monumental Swedish peasant novels. They rank with the best that Moberg and Lo-Johansson and Fridegård have given us in this genre, and in two respects — in their passionate intensity and their overwhelming sense of fate as the final determinant in life — they rise above almost all that Moberg and Lo-Johansson and Fridegård have written. Over Irja Browallius's world broods a dark, relentless fate, of an ancient, primitive Scandinavian kind. In her novels actions always have their inexorable consequences, more frequently than not brutal and bloody. Man must pay for his evil deeds, with no hope of succor in this world or another. Irja Browallius looks upon her Närke peasant with utter objectivity, admiring his industry and tough-minded individualism, but she is more apt to see in him, as one Swedish critic has put it, "a greedy, crafty, spiteful, vindictive, backward, superstitious, gross, sanctimonious breed." The noble peasantry of Romantic speculation has to her no basis whatsoever in reality. In their almost stylized simplicity and directness, her Närke novels (she has also written about urban life) have been compared with the Icelandic saga.

The university community at Lund out of which came one of the major poets of the 1930's, Hjalmar Gullberg, and the poet-dramatist Karl Ragnar Gierow, has also contributed to contemporary Swedish letters three of the most original masters of prose, Frans G. Bengtsson (1894–1954), Fritiof Nilsson Piraten (b. 1895), and Sigfrid Lindström (1892–1950). Of these three Bengtsson is by far the most versatile, a poet, essayist, and biographer as well as a novelist, while nearly all the work of Nilsson Piraten and Lindström falls into the genres of prose fiction and is basically rather limited and traditional. But each of these authors places the inimitable stamp of his own temperament on conventional literary forms, lending to these forms fresh (if not new) perspectives and turns of thought. Their having been strenuously exposed in formative academic years to the rather special intellectual atmosphere of Lund during and after the First World War has had more than a little to do with their ways of reacting toward life and has influenced sharply the form which their work has taken. The Lund of the 1920's, and for some years earlier, was learned and skeptical and given to a kind of intellectual horseplay which delighted in waggish irony and the spinning of tall tales of whatsoever provenance and variety. Dialectical subtleties, learned discursiveness, challenging irreverences, poetic digressions, burlesque humor, a not exactly modest use of the bottle — these were the motley ingredients of the through-the-night bouts of camaraderie indulged in by some of the more gifted Lund students of the day. Regular attendance at lectures and the systematic pursuit of academic studies were apparently cardinal sins to such students. Bengtsson is perhaps not unduly exaggerating when, in an autobiographical essay entitled "How I Became an Author," he tells us that during "four years at the University . . . I heard ten lectures, wrote a great deal of bad verse, and played three or four games of chess which were good enough to be published." But this offhand attitude toward formal studies led in later years neither to nonscholarly habits of mind nor to professional ineptitude nor to literary sterility on the part of those who, like Bengtsson, may seem to have idled away their university years. Bengtsson himself became with time an amazingly learned man, Nilsson Piraten a highly regarded lawyer, Lindström a competent journalist whose literary production was worlds removed from the superficialities of the daily pursuits of journalism.

Frans G. Bengtsson's learning became, in fact, legendary, and is reflected everywhere in his poetry and prose. But this learning never weighs down his literary work, rather gives to it a rare, venturesome flavor, in part because he handles it with such vigorous zest and in part because his intellectual bent is always on the lookout for strange and exotic phenomena, for unusual and colorful characters and episodes, often out of the distant past and far-flung climes. Bengtsson has been called "the last troubadour," and the label fits him in almost every respect. In a period when Swedish poets sang by preference in restrained, unadorned phrases or experimented with advanced modernistic forms, Bengtsson in his two volumes of verse — *Tärningskast* (Throw of the Dice, 1923) and *Legenden om Babel* (The Legend of Babel, 1925) — deliberately cultivated ornately overwrought effects and sweeping sonorous cadences. In a sense he was just as traditional in his choice of subject matter, ransacking the corridors of legend and history for colorful and finely toothsome motifs and themes, motifs and themes worthy of a learned modern troubadour's lute. When he turned to prose (which he did early) he was just as belligerently traditional in taste, his essays resembling in form the informal essays of such English Romantics as Lamb and Hazlitt, and his two arresting ventures in extended prose forms — the two-volume biography of Charles XII (tr. *The Life of Charles XII King of Sweden 1697–1718*, 1935, 1936) and the novel *Röde Orm* (tr. *The Long Ships*, 1941, 1945) — being conceived and executed in respectively heroic-romantic and burlesque-romantic veins.

Bengtsson's poetry is competent but somewhat strained in its effects, and on the whole it has not worn well. It was as an essayist that he first attracted a host of admirers, a host which increased rapidly in numbers with each successive volume. His first collection of essays bore the title *Litterörer och militärer* (Literary and Military Figures, 1929), followed in

Bengtsson's lifetime by *Silverskölderna* (The Silver Shields, 1931), *De långhåriga merovingerna* (The Longhaired Merovingians, 1933), and *Sällskap för en eremit* (Company for a Hermit, 1938). A posthumous collection, *Folk som sjöng och andra essayer* (People Who Sang and Other Essays), appeared in 1955. One of the reasons for Bengtsson's smashing success as an essayist was that the informal essay as a respectable literary genre was before his appearance practically nonexistent in Swedish literature. His success in the genre was partly the success of novelty. Swedish poets and novelists of distinction could be numbered in the dozens if not scores, but no essayists of real distinction had appeared before Bengtsson in 1929. But Bengtsson's success as an essayist derives even more from the fact that he was really a master of the genre, a natural purveyor of informal prose which need not fear comparison with some of the greatest French and English essayists.

He invariably writes about what he likes, as all great informal essayists have done. Many of his essays are on literary or historical subjects, but he tosses off with equal facility and comprehension delightful and often pungent observations on such diverse subjects as ghost stories and the difficulty of maintaining an optimistic view of human existence; popular ditties and man's relation to nature; the mysteries of the ant world and the fine art of lying. Adventurers from all times and climes and military heroes from the earliest ages down to the American Civil War especially attract him, as do great literary individualists such as Byron, Carlyle, and Henry David Thoreau, whose *Walden* he has rendered into Swedish. Among his other notable translations have been those of *The Song of Roland* and *Paradise Lost*. Fabulous erudition vies with offhand whimsicalities in nearly all of Bengtsson's essays, as in the famous one on Villon in which he notes in passing, without batting an eyelash: "He was at this time twenty-five years old and had just committed his first murder and written his first longer poem, fairly innocuous things both." At times whimsicality takes over completely, as when he writes about his curious vagaries in matters of literary taste ("Before a Bookshelf") or provides the reader with an inventory of the physical and mental habits of semi-domesticated cats, rats, and bats ("My Closest Companions"). A reasonably representative selection of Bengtsson's essays is available in English under the title *A Walk to the Ant Hill and Other Essays*. All in all Bengtsson may be said to combine in his essays the whimsicalities of Charles Lamb, the vigor and independence of spirit of William Hazlitt, and the heroic-romantic idealism of Robert Louis

Stevenson. The only flaw which mars his essays is an occasional bit of stylistic coquetry.

Bengtsson's frequent preoccupation in his essays with past heroic ages and their representative personalities carries over into his two larger works, on Charles XII and on the Viking period. In his biography of Charles XII he is at his brilliant best in the serious reconstruction of history; in *The Long Ships* he is at his zestful best in a burlesque treatment of the Viking age. In both of these works he shoulders his learning effortlessly, with the skill of a scholar who defies the dust of learning and recaptures those vital realities of life in the past which have too often been written about in heavy, measured, lifeless periods. Which of these two works is his best is a matter of taste. Each of them is in its kind a masterpiece, the Charles XII biography majestic and monumental in line, *The Long Ships* gutty and sly in its human portraiture, madly comic in its handling of episode and narrative movement. Perhaps the Charles XII work will weigh heavier in the judgment of future generations, especially because in the presence of the final fate of Sweden's hero king Bengtsson dispenses with his usual freewheeling style and faces the tragic dilemma of human life on a level of utterance worthy of his elevated subject. Bengtsson's motto as an artist was, "I paint thus, donna Bianca, because it amuses me to paint this way," but in the Charles XII book he painted for this and *other* reasons.

The far-ranging erudition of Frans G. Bengtsson is not a part of the literary equipment of his Skåne colleague Fritiof Nilsson Piraten, but the latter shares Bengtsson's whimsicality and his taste for tall tales, the *skepparhistorier* (seamen's tales) of Swedish folk tradition. Even Nilsson Piraten's second surname (he was born Fritiof Nilsson) seems to have become attached to him in consequence of a fantastic prank of the tall-tale type that he wishes us to believe he had actually committed in his youth. We have it on his own word that as a naval seaman he once, in an alcoholic state, occupied with a squad under his command a whole island — to the angered consternation of his superiors, who had been totally unaware of the "piratical" activities that were taking place under Seaman Nilsson's "command." However true this tale may be, Fritiof Nilsson seems to have convinced his hearers of its truth when among his fellow students at Lund he became the most listened-to teller of tall tales in a circle that included a no less redoubtable competitor than Frans G. Bengtsson, who in later years was to spin a fabulous succession of episodes in *The Long Ships*. A long time passed before Nilsson Piraten's oral narrative talents found their way into written form and ultimately into publication. He was thirty-seven when his first book appeared — *Bombi Bitt och jag* (tr. *Bombi Bitt*, 1932), with its mischievous boyish pranks and grotesque high jinks, a worthy Swedish counterpart to *Tom Sawyer* and *The Adventurers of Huckleberry Finn*. Since 1932 Nilsson Piraten has written a half dozen more books, but (except for a tentative return to the Bombi Bitt world in *Bombi Bitt och Nick Carter*, 1946) they did not contain exactly what the delighted readers of *Bombi Bitt and I* may have had the right to expect, i.e., a series of picturesque, carefree, fantastically impish exploits on the part of two irresponsible boys on a peaceful Swedish countryside. And exploits couched in a comic style loaded with unexpected turns of phrase and waggish verbal anachronisms. Not that festive narrative fare has not continued to be dished up with unstinted energy by Nilsson Piraten since *Bombi and I*. But in his later novels and short stories irresponsible juveniles are largely absent, and merely picturesque elements are decreasingly employed. The harmlessly grotesque ingredients of his early work not infrequently take on in later years bizarre and harshly macabre forms — until in such grimly tragicomic character studies as are contained in *Småländsk tragedi* (Småland Tragedy, 1936), *Bokhandlaren som slutade bada* (The Book Dealer Who Ceased Bathing, 1937), *Historier från Färs* (Tales from Färs, 1940), and *Vänner emellan* (Among Friends, 1955), Piraten's world assumes many of the qualities of Hjalmar Bergman's ominous portraits of human vagaries carried to the point of deadly decay and total character disintegration. In fact, Nilsson Piraten reminds one constantly of Bergman despite the undeniable originality of his own work. He is far less prolific than Bergman, and his comic vein is less rich and luxuriant. But on a more limited scale his narrative vein is equally inventive, his verbal skill equally fresh and concretely alive, his awareness of the tragic drift of life equally perceptive and profound, and his sympathy for erring humanity equally warm and understanding.

Sigfrid Lindström's narrative vein is by comparison with Nilsson Piraten's spare and lean and essentially ascetic. In the academic circle at Lund, Lindström served as a wry and quizzical kind of "conscience" amidst its otherwise relatively expansive, lighthearted comic spirit, and his ironic commentary on the ways of the world was highly regarded. This commentary bordered frequently on the painfully grim, but it was always accompanied by a glint of canny humor which provided a special fillip to the flashing intellectual bouts indulged in by him and his fellows in the southern Swedish academic community. His literary productivity was as spare and self-critical as was his emaciated monk-like person, consisting of a single volume of verse, *De besegrade* (The Conquered, 1927), and three relatively small collections of strangely original fairy tales, two of which, *Leksaksballonger* (Toy Balloons, 1931) and *Vindsröjning* (Clearing the Attic, 1939), are especially impressive. His poetry lacks the subtlety and penetration of his prose though it gives at times a finely modulated expression to his sympathy for those in life who have been "conquered," i.e., those who have been run over roughshod by the brutalities of existence — and been forgotten. His prose also reflects these feelings, but in a more sharply original and arresting form than in his verse. In Lindström's prose, myth and fairy tale are employed to provide a quietly bitter commentary on life. Like Pär Lagerkvist, he uses mythical motifs and fairy tale fantasies in his own way, particularly to suggest a mood of astringent modern disillusionment. Though one often comes upon idyllic elements in Lindström's prose, landscape scenes of exquisite beauty, such elements are seldom allowed to take over, but are employed usually to provide grimly restrained contrasts to the quietly corrosive implications of the tales. On the surface the tales are often disarmingly delightful, but this serves largely to intensify the author's incisive ironic mockery — a mockery which not infrequently is as devastating as Voltaire's or Swift's, without the heartlessness of these incomparable masters of the derisive mood. Lindström's ability to cast a blinding searchlight of satire over human foibles borders at times on surrealistic effects without in any way deliberately affecting surrealistic techniques. He remains essentially a traditionalist in matters of form though traditional patterns undergo in his hands a partial metamorphosis that at times amounts almost to the creation of a new form. Without pretending to be a "modern," Lindström in some ways is one.

The same cannot be said of three of Lindström's contemporaries who in the course of the 1930's and since have each in his own way followed the lead of Eyvind Johnson in breaking sharply with tradition and cultivating highly modern fictional forms. Two of the three, Walter Ljungquist (b. 1900) and Thorsten Jonsson (1910–50), find their models primarily in American fiction, Ljungquist in Hemingway and probably Faulkner, Jonsson more exclusively in Hemingway, while the third, Tage Aurell (b. 1895), who spent a decade after the First World War in Paris, is oriented largely in French culture. All three of these figures eschew the realistic documentary novel of the Swedish 1930's, Jonsson and Aurell becoming masters of the highly concentrated forms of fiction, Ljungquist beginning with short, tightly integrated patterns but later forsaking such rigidity in favor of a more expansive and diffuse form. The advanced experimental art of Ljungquist, Jonsson, and Aurell is always arresting and not infrequently exciting, but it is an art which has not always attracted large numbers of readers and has not been conducive, except in the case of Ljungquist, to a high rate of productivity. Aurell has published but a half dozen small books during a quarter century of intensive literary labors. Jonsson might conceivably have added considerably to the amount of his prose fiction had he not died at the early age of forty and had he devoted less energy than he did to literary criticism. As it is, he has left us only two collections of short stories and one novel in addition to his two early volumes of verse and some excellent critical work.

Ljungquist distinguished himself early by winning a literary prize with the novel *Ombyte av tåg* (Change of Trains, 1933). This work was in an unhappy sense his fate for a full decade and a half, for it had, as the first Swedish novel in the manner of Hemingway, engaged its author so deeply in Hemingway's world that he had great difficulty in extricating himself from this world and finding a new form which was essentially his own. During the 1930's only Ljungquist's short story collection *En dörr står på glänt* (A Door Stands Ajar) is worthy of the author who wrote *Change of Trains*. In the larger form of the novel neither his *Släkten står på trappan* (The Family Stands on the Steps) nor *Resande med okänt bagage* (Traveler with Unknown Baggage) from the 1930's, nor *Vägskäl* (Fork of the Road) from the mid-1940's, manages finally to impress us, though each of them has its fine moments and the last of them suggests that Ljungquist is not far from bringing under satisfactory literary control his complex vision of man and the world in which man must live. On the whole, however, these novels interest us chiefly as ambitious *efforts* on the author's part to find a form and depict a world which is uniquely Ljungquist's own.

Not until 1948, in the arresting work *Azalea*, does Ljungquist finally break through with a novel in which he is in complete command of his material, and since this date his work — as represented in what may loosely be called "the Jerk Dandelin series," which includes *Revolt i grönska* (Revolt in Verdure, 1951), *Liljor i Saron* (Lilies in Sharon, 1952), and *Kammarorgel* (Chamber Organ, 1954) — has progressively improved in originality of conception, sensitivity of feeling, analytical penetration, and firmness of control of complex narrative patterns. There are in these novels from Ljungquist's maturity some of Hemingway's stylistic mannerisms (the and-and-and constructions, for instance), but Hemingway's spare world of action and "hard-boiled" pose are entirely absent. Instead, Ljungquist conjures up a fantastically luxuriant Swedish countryside, heavily decadent in most of its manifestations, but subtly instinct with evasively persistent "meanings" propounded by the author's alter ego, Jerk Dandelin, who alternately observes and becomes engaged in the mysterious ebb and flow of life around him. There is much of Faulkner's tropical luxuriance of landscape and phrase in these novels, but relatively little of Faulkner's "sound and fury," for Ljungquist's talent is essentially vegetative, passive, with a careful eye for the externals of quiet stagnation and decay, a perceptive ear for the inner essences which life may yield to those who do not try to force it. Ljungquist himself prefers his readers to think of his recent novels as mystery plays. In them he is an intimist-visionary.

Unlike Walter Ljungquist, Tage Aurell and Thorsten Jonsson are neither Faulkner-like nor intimist-visionaries, though a critical essay by Jonsson on Faulkner reflects both understanding and admiration for the American novelist. Both Aurell and Jonsson are among the most highly conscious of Swedish literary artists. Aurell, in fact, is so highly conscious, so utterly refined in his fictional craftsmanship that the reader's attention is at times strained almost to the breaking point in following the narrative pattern and the development of theme. And this despite the fact that Aurell's tales are simple in outline and are concerned with quite ordinary people in relatively ordinary situations. All of his stories deal with rural and small-town life in western Värmland, in which region he settled down after his return from Paris in 1931. None of his books runs to much more than a hundred pages in length, and yet they manage to provide the reader with a treatment of certain situations in life which in both breadth and depth of treatment is not often attained in works of much greater length. In his first book, the little novel *Tybergs gård* (Tyberg's Tenement, 1932), he manages to give us a vividly alive impression of a whole group of inhabitants of the ramshackle structure in which they carry on their tawdry, limited existences. In his other works, the most important of which are *Martina* (1937) and *Skillingtryck* (Pamphlet, 1943), he centers his attention on certain individual fates but by no means neglects the total environmental set of circumstances in which these fates play out their tragic roles.

In order to effect such fullness of treatment in books of scarcely more than a hundred pages Aurell must subject his prose to the severest possible disciplines, employing an absolute minimum of words (by preference unobtrusively expressive words), sketching in the barest outlines his narrative sequences, indulging in hints and verbal indirections of all kinds, leaving a multitude of lacunae which the alert reader is expected to fill in. At times such fanatical narrative concentration goes almost too far, as in the case of the heroine in *Martina* who remains rather too shadowy in outline because of the author's firm distaste for anything remotely resembling direct and exhaustive treatment. But Aurell's spare narrative method at its best, and it seldom falls below this best, creates an illusion of reality which holds the reader spellbound, not least because the author never comments directly on the action, allowing instead his objectively conceived material to suggest by a kind of magic indirection whatever "meanings" his tales may have. But perfect as is Aurell's narrative art, it has to date been rather too limited in the tasks which it has attempted. Aurell's books are, in consequence, sketch-like studies, skillful, even profound finger exercises, rather than larger compositions with wide, inclusive perspectives. One wishes that a talent of his impressive integrity might in the future attempt larger tasks, come more sharply to grips with the world of reality which he knows so well. But perhaps his very artistic integrity forbids attempts which it feels cannot be realized. Perhaps Aurell feels that the world of reality is so complex that an art which attempts to encompass it on a larger scale would be a futile and therefore false art.

Thorsten Jonsson has a great deal of Aurell's stylistic concentration and narrative objectivity, but his objectivity is not always so absolute — it does not succeed in retaining its apparently unengaged attitude as does Aurell's even when in Jonsson's case this objectivity becomes most "hard-boiled." In fact, its "hard-boiled" quality betrays by its very excess of hardness a latent fellow-feeling for his characters, which amounts in the last analysis to understanding, if not actually sympathy, for at least some of them. Jonsson, like his master Hemingway, is really incapable of the absolute objectivity which he affects. His "hard-boiled" stylistic surfaces should deceive no one. It is true that in his best creative work he does not permit himself the luxury of overt commiseration for his fellows, but he has in his best literary criticism responded with enthusiasm to those authors who do, and this enthusiasm does not fail to leave its mark on his own creative work though it admittedly does so in such restrained forms as are not always immediately apparent. In two of his literary-critical works, *Stor-Norrland och litteraturen* (Great-Norrland and Literature, 1938) and *Martin Koch* (1941), he writes with profound understanding of some of those Swedish authors who first championed the cause of the masses, and in the posthumously published *Dimman från havet* (Fog from the Sea) he sketches with sensitivity and understanding the life stories of a number of odd human types with whom he had come in close contact during the years 1943–46 when he served as the New York correspondent for the Stockholm newspaper *Dagens Nyheter*. Before his America sojourn he had attracted very favorable critical attention with two volumes of short stories, *Som det brukar vara* (As It Usually Is, 1939) and *Fly till Vatten och morgon* (Flee to Water and Morning, 1941), and with his work on the contemporary American novelists, which included brilliant translations of Hemingway and Steinbeck and a collection of incisive critical essays (*Sex amerikaner* [Six Americans], 1942) on these two novelists and four others, Faulkner, Erskine Caldwell, James T. Farrell, and Saroyan. It is characteristic of Jonsson that despite his admiration for Faulkner and Steinbeck he reacts rather strongly, on the one hand, against the former's violent inhumanity and, on the other, against the latter's oversimplified psychological idealization of the folk in such a novel as *Grapes of Wrath*.

After his years in America Jonsson served as cultural editor of *Dagens Nyheter* and published *Sidor av Amerika* (Aspects of America, 1946), an excellent personal report on the United States, and *Konvoj* (1947), a kind of collective novel, in which the tension-filled life aboard a small freighter in a huge wartime convoy on a dangerous North Atlantic crossing is described with a fascinating but somewhat melodramatic sense both for its dramatic effects and its inner human values. Jonsson is at his best, however, in the short story. He is, in fact, perhaps more responsible than any other contemporary Swedish author for revitalizing this genre and for pointing the way, for the new generation of authors in the 1940's, to an awareness of the artistic possibilities of the genre. His two collections of short stories *As It Usually Is* and *Flee to Water and Morning*, hailed on their first appearance as masterpieces of their kind, are Jonsson's chief claim to literary fame. The first of them deals with aspects of provincial life in Jonsson's native Norrland, the second with the pathology of certain criminal types. The sharpness of observation and the scientific precision of these carefully documented tales are enormously impressive, but even more impressive is the narrative form

538

in which they are cast, a form which at times approaches the miraculous in stylistic finesse and story-telling skill. Jonsson had not acquainted himself in vain with the entire gamut of modern narrative techniques as practiced by the masters of his day. He learned from the surrealists and from Hemingway as well as from Joyce and Faulkner and from his Swedish countryman Eyvind Johnson, but he has not copied them, especially the tendency of some of them to indulge in wordiness and a looseness of over-all form. He demonstrates how the inner monologue of Joyce can be employed in sharply spare, explosively fragmented patterns, and he uses Faulkner's italicized line to point up half-conscious inner emotions or drives, but he does so with an economy and precision of phrase not particularly characteristic of Faulkner. And Jonsson is as skillful as Hemingway in the use of an apparently casual but actually highly suggestive detail to build up dramatic suspense. All in all his tales *are* often little dramas, concentrated, tense, sharply explosive in effect. Jonsson's early death has deprived contemporary Sweden of one of its finest critical minds and its most expert manipulator in the short story of the technical attainments represented in the more advanced forms of contemporary prose fiction. Fortunately his successors have appreciated his modernity and have experimented further in the directions suggested by his example.

The sharp drift toward new fictional forms characteristic of Ljungquist, Aurell, and Jonsson is almost completely absent in the work of Gösta Carlberg (b. 1909), though his first novel, the prize-winning three-volume *Bären varandras bördor* (Bear One Another's Burdens, 1937), with its frenzied preoccupation with the psychology of puberty and its predilection for complex symbolistic patterns, might well have suggested to its early readers that Carlberg also was moving in the direction of literary modernism. But his psychological concerns soon came to be in part subordinated to moral and religious considerations of a cultural-anthropological kind, and his symbolism had from the beginning none of the literary stringency of much modern fiction. Though he has serious musical and artistic interests, he has found time to write more than a dozen novels and collections of legends, four volumes of verse, and three expository works concerned with sociological problems.

Carlberg's prose is markedly superior to his verse without ever being quite distinguished, weighed down as it so often is by wordiness and a rather involved discursiveness. With few exceptions his novels deal with the legendary and mythical lore of the biblical East and ancient Greece. His approach to these materials combines the imaginative freedom of the poet and the disciplines of the modern scholar, employing the most recent psychological speculation to explain legendary material and seeking always to lay bare the realistic backgrounds of ancient myth. Typical of his novels are *Vi vilja se Jesus* (We Would See Jesus, 1938), in which with no intention of religious offense the case of Jesus is accounted for in terms of an overcompensated inferiority complex, and *Den sparade ynglingen* (The Spared Youth, 1954), which with delicately manipulated psychological insights traces the roots of homosexuality back to certain conditioning factors in primitive Greek society. Those of Carl-berg's readers who are prepared to follow his speculative excursions into cultural-anthropological areas may be referred to *Svensk landsbygd som kulturmiljö* (The Swedish Countryside as a Cultural Milieu, 1949), *Om människans behov och värden* (On Man's Needs and Values, 1950), and *Kultur och religion* (Culture and Religion, 1951), which works reflect the extraordinary range of his psychological interests and anthropological learning and throw considerable light on related matters in his novels. All in all Carlberg is an arresting figure in contemporary Swedish literature, bringing to this literature a restlessly inquiring mind but caring little for the finesses of literary craftsmanship, for those formal literary requisites which are of central concern to so many poets and novelists of his generation. He is in consequence an isolated though scarcely a negligible figure among his literary contemporaries.

Modernism Triumphant and Its Aftermath

THE LAST GENERATION of Swedish authors, those who have most recently come upon the literary scene, usually consort under the labels *40-talister* and *50-talister* because their representative works first appeared in the 1940's and 1950's respectively. The labels are chronologically convenient but somewhat misleading, for they suggest lines of demarcation between the 1930's and the 1940's on the one hand, and between the 1940's and the 1950's on the other, which are not in reality nearly as clear-cut as the terms *40-talister* and *50-talister* imply. No really revolutionary changes took place during the 1940's, despite the claims of special status which the literary generation of this decade sometimes made. And whether the 1950's, so recently come to an end, succeeded in significantly breaking its own way remains to be seen, for we ourselves are part and parcel of this decade and can scarcely look upon it with anything resembling historical perspective or objectivity. Even the 1940's poses problems of perspective that are difficult of critical and historical resolution, but the record of those ten years seems to suggest that the 1940's was more a continuator and consummator of certain of the more advanced trends in the literature of the 1930's than a point of departure for new developments. It is true that the generation of the 1940's had little of the social and political interests of the 1930's and was prepared to discard as a worn-out garment the minutely documented autobiographical novel of its immediate predecessors, but otherwise it may be said that the authors of the 1940's for the most part pursued themes and experimented with forms in much the same spirit of literary modernism as had such poets and prose writers of the 1930's as Harry Martinson, Artur Lundkvist, and Gunnar Ekelöf, Eyvind Johnson, Tage Aurell, and Thorsten Jonsson. The 1940's simply witnessed a more advanced — and perhaps final — *phase* of this earlier literary modernism, a phase in which the literary internationalization of the 1930's became more marked and in which formal experimentation in the direction of the "difficult" and the "unintelligible" became more pronounced. It is in consequence symptomatic of the more "advanced" modernism of the 1940's that in its contacts with foreign literatures it preferred Faulkner to Hemingway, Eliot to Lawrence, and Kafka to Proust or Gide.

If in most respects the literature of the 1940's simply developed further some of the patterns of idea and form of the 1930's, it may be said that in at least one respect — in the special quality of its disillusionment — it tended to distinguish itself rather sharply from the 1930's. While the disillusionment of the 1930's tended to be emotional and apocalyptic in its vision of life, the disillusionment of the 1940's was in the main clearheaded and relatively sober, expecting no great things of life and prepared to accept the conditions — admittedly the harshly limited conditions — under which life must be lived. Especially suspicious was the generation of the 1940's of any and all of the "ways of salvation" (Marxism, Freudianism, primitivism, humanism, and so on) cultivated by the literary representatives of the 1930's. The new generation of the 1940's insisted that man will be saved from his anguish and terror only if he refuses to expect much of life and is prepared to assume that no "truth," whatever its origins, has any final and universal validity. The most paradoxical forms which this sober disillusionment took among the *40-talister* are to be found in the work of Stig Dagerman and Karl Vennberg, the former having derived his theories as to man's possible salvation from association with Syndicalist political thought, the latter having fed on the arresting investigations into the nature of knowledge and the concept of justice of the Uppsala philosopher Axel Hägerström (1868–1939). To admit one's terror, Dagerman insisted, is the first step in gaining a victory over it. And with the Syndicalists he reacted sharply against the practical cynicism that politics is the art of the possible. Dagerman suggests, rather, that only in patiently attempting the impossible may the possible — peace and a measure of happiness for man — be conceivably attained. Vennberg's position with regard to the possibilities of existence is more grimly extreme than Dagerman's. He can but postulate that mankind lives, and

To live is to choose
O blessed choice

between the indifferent
and the impossible.

Agnostic sobriety can hardly be formulated more paradoxically, but such paradoxes enabled the authors of the new generation to view life with an emotional restraint — some would say with a cerebral cold-bloodedness — not characteristic of the apocalyptic pessimism of the generation which preceded them.

Whether such paradoxes are in the last analysis, however, a sign of maturity or an evidence of spiritual sterility is not easy to say. Dagerman's death by his own hand shortly after he passed his thirtieth year need not necessarily belie the general efficacy of his Syndicalist theories, but it provides some evidence at least that he himself found no final source of comfort in these theories. But Vennberg's sharply relativistic agnosticism has led to no serious personal crisis for him, and in somewhat less extreme forms this agnosticism came to permeate the thought of a whole generation of young Swedish authors with no catastrophic results. In fact, it provided a basic point of departure, if not actually a means of survival, for what might otherwise have been a completely confused literary generation buffeted by a thousand winds of doctrine in a dark and desperate postwar age. Under the circumstances a clear-headed skepticism seemed to many of the new literary generation but common sense, the only honest way of facing life's realities. For a poet or a novelist or a dramatist to assume that life is good and to offer to man a simple way of salvation would be to falsify, to lead man, in fact, to his destruction while ostensibly comforting him. Literature must rather function in the direction of awakening man to a sense of his fearful dilemma in the hope that he may somehow — because of this awakening — survive. Dagerman's words put the point succinctly: "Consciousness, open eyes which fearlessly observe their terrifying position, must be the ego's star, our only compass, a compass that determines the direction — for when there is no compass there is no direction. We must therefore keep fear living in us like a permanently ice-free harbor which helps us to survive the winters, the deep-flowing stream under the winter floods."

Despite the diversity of talent represented in the new literary generation, a relatively solid front was maintained by them as evidenced in such enterprises as the two short-lived but important-for-their-time literary journals *40-tal* and *Utsikt* as well as in the representative collection of verse *40-tals lyrik* (1947) and the critical anthology *Kritiskt 40-tal* (1948). In such publications as these, which deliberately sought to re-

543

flect a broadly common literary ideal among the collaborating poets and critics, as well as in the novels and short stories, dramas and volumes of verse bearing the signatures of individual authors, the *40-talister* made their voices heard — sometimes to the consternation of Swedish readers, at other times to their delight. Among the score or more representatives of the new literary generation, the most arresting figures, aside from Dagerman and Vennberg, are the poet Erik Lindegren and the novelists Lars Ahlin, Sivar Arnér, and Björn-Erik Höijer.

Whether two other novelists of some distinction, Folke Fridell (b. 1904) and Stina Aronson (1892–1956), should be counted among the characteristic authors of the 1940's is problematical, for the former is no radical experimenter in matters of literary form and the latter had a long career behind her before she finally managed to gain serious literary recognition late in the 1940's. Folke Fridell, whose first novel *Död mans hand* (Dead Man's Hand) appeared early in the 1940's when he was forty-two, after he had labored thirty years in a textile factory, has with some success revitalized the proletarian novel by concentrating on the problem of the workingman of today, who, having finally gained economic independence and political power, is in the process of losing his spiritual freedom, his dignity as an individual. The workingman's outward success, Fridell points out, often spells inner failure, to the detriment of both himself and society. Fridell's view of the possibility of man maintaining his dignity as an individual in an increasingly mechanized society becomes more and more pessimistic with the years, until in his most recent novel, *Äldst i världen* (Eldest in the World, 1959), his nausea in the presence of modern man's plight breeds a loathing and bitterness which approaches the absolute. Stina Aronson's recent books about daily life in the primitive reaches of Norrland are distinguished on the one hand by a profound understanding of the folk of this region and on the other by a use of language ever subtly aware of the unobtrusively expressive speech of the folk. She first attracted the serious attention of the critics with two gripping tales from the volume *Hitom himlen* (On This Side of Heaven) in 1946, and has since added a number of equally gripping works in which she digs deeply into the psychology of isolated humans struggling more or less hopelessly for existence in brutally inhospitable semi-Arctic regions.

For a brief and brilliant period before his early death Stig Dagerman (1923–54) was the wonderchild in contemporary Swedish literature.

When he was but twenty-three his first novel, *Ormen* (The Serpent), became the sensation of the autumn book season, and in the immediately following years he wrote two more novels, *De dömdas ö* (The Isle of the Damned, 1946) and *Bränt barn* (tr. *Burnt Child*, 1948), a collection of short stories entitled *Nattens lekar* (tr. *The Games of Night*, 1947), an incisive travel book on postwar Germany *Tysk höst* (German Autumn, 1947), and a number of fascinating plays, most of which have been performed on the Swedish stage with considerable success. In its bulk and its over-all quality this production by such a young author during a brief span of less than ten years is without a Swedish parallel and is the more astonishing because of the originality of its conception and the variety and range of its form. Dagerman is at his most impressive in the symbolistic and expressionistic forms employed in the two novels *The Serpent* and *The Isle of the Damned* and in the drama *Den dödsdömde* (perf. 1947, pub. 1948, tr. *The Condemned*). But he has written a gripping psychological study in *Burnt Child* and a number of brilliant realistic short stories, and in *Streber* (perf. 1948) he has tried his hand with limited success in a traditional problem drama. Whether Dagerman employs symbolistic or expressionistic or realistic forms, or some combination of these, he employs the form which he feels might best express his ideas, his central theme in the work in question. That which is recurrent in nearly all of his work is the terror theme, or, rather, the necessity of overcoming our terror by facing it, grappling with it, and conquering it. This theme is most central in *The Serpent*, but it figures more or less consciously in most of Dagerman's other work, frequently — as in *The Isle of the Damned* and *The Condemned* — in bizarre tragic variations, in situations where the element of terror is so overwhelming that a victory over it seems quite out of the question.

Among those of his generation who wrote in dramatic form Dagerman is on the whole the most notable, particularly in *The Condemned*, his first play. In this play he is dealing with a basic moral problem — the problem of the limitations of human justice. The events which at the beginning of the play provide the point of departure for a consideration of its central moral problem are ordinary enough: a husband has been condemned to death for the murder of his wife, though his wife's lover rather than he is the murderer. But then a queer twist of events occurs: the innocently condemned husband escapes the death penalty when the executioner becomes suddenly ill, and immediately thereafter the real murderer confesses and the hitherto presumed murderer is set free. In the tragic interplay in the drama between the condemned man and various representatives of society, the author is treating symbolically the essentially tragic nature of life itself. We are often condemned through imperfect instruments of so-called justice, Dagerman would say — not because of what we have done or what we are, but rather because of other people's notions of what we have done or what we are, notions frequently based on the thinnest kind of evidence and nurtured by human callousness and the primitive sadistic instincts of the mass eager for "the kill." Though the condemned man in this instance was morally the same man during his imprisonment awaiting execution and after his release, a stupid and fatuous public, alternately sensation-ridden and callously apathetic to human suffering, finds this man at first repulsive but later a sentimental object of pity, even a creature worthy of at least partial admiration. The condemned man comes to have nothing but scorn for a humanity which finds its pleasure in such an indiscriminate medley of contradictory feelings toward him — "to hate and detest a man one second and the next to pour your sympathy over him without the man having changed in the least. How do you think one could depend on your kindheartedness when one cannot even depend on your hardheartedness?" And a bit later:

I can do without your kindheartedness. I do not need it at all. The second week I was in prison I found out that sympathy really only makes it harder to live, and, above all, harder to die. I have learned to do without everything because I have been in a place where one *must* do without everything. I have been in a place where life reveals itself as a series of misconceptions, misconceptions of what one ought to have done and of what one ought not to have done. I have been in a place where it does not serve any purpose to curse, to rebel, to hope, because the law takes its course and nothing can be changed.

In these words Dagerman gives explosive dramatic expression to the theme constantly recurring in his work, the idea that we shall never overcome evil without facing it squarely, without drinking it to the very dregs.

And in the over-all structure of the play the theme is developed with an astonishing virtuosity and piling-up of dramatic effects: in the first act in a controlled pianissimo with certain restrained grotesque overtones; in the second with a complex obbligato, bizarre and cumulatively furioso; in the third act with a grim, starkly intense intermezzo formulation; and in the fourth with a haunting diminuendo in which the harsh patterns of the thematic development stalk quietly but inexorably toward the tragic denouement. The controlled pianissimo of the opening act introduces the theme of human callousness in the apathetic indifference of the prison doorkeeper, while a half-developed grotesque counterpoint is provided by the moronic newsmongering representatives of a maudlin, sensation-exploiting daily press. The complex obbligato of the second act, rising to a furioso at the end, is developed (with a Satanic fury reminiscent of the Strindberg of the "Chamber Plays") by means of probing grimly the weird motivations of a bizarre group of characters who call themselves The Rescued-Men's Club and who have arranged an evening's fantastic "Symposium" in honor of the recently freed condemned man. The stark intensity of the third-act intermezzo provides a kind of torture-chamber study in the condemned man's impotence, resulting from the terror of his four months' imprisonment. And the starkly haunting diminuendo of the fourth act reintroduces us to the restrained tone of the opening act, recapitulating the theme of the play with a mercilessly quiet note of tragic inevitability.

Despite the general critical acclaim accorded *The Condemned* on its first performance in Stockholm, some critics expressed their enthusiasm with reservations, suggesting particularly that its preoccupation with an ethical problem drove the psychological problem too far into the background, and that the symbolistic form of the play was so rigidly schematic that it tended to force the drama too far in the direction of the abstract and the near-esoteric. That Dagerman himself was aware of these dangers would seem to be clear from an examination of his subsequent plays, each of which in its way apparently seeks to reduce the dangers inherent in the type of symbolistic drama represented in *The Condemned*. Unfortunately, however, Dagerman did not in these later plays succeed in making an entirely satisfactory shift toward either the modern psychological play, which he attempted in *Skuggan av Mart* (The Shadow of Mart, 1948) and *Ingen går fri* (No One Is Free, 1949), or the realistic play with a carefully observed milieu, which he tried in *Streber* (The Climber, 1949). The last of these plays, despite its having captured with absolute fidelity the exact quality of everyday living among certain working-class groups, fails finally to impress us on the whole because of certain of its propagandistic excesses, its tendency to depict human character in terms of naïve contrasts, in white and black, good and evil. In developing its plot — the disintegration of an ideally conceived cooperative business venture on the part of a small group of workingmen, in which the vulgar "climber" egotism of one of the partners finally suc-

547

ceeds in destroying the venture — Dagerman satirically trains his Syndicalist sights too obviously on the renegade climber, who becomes reduced simply to the status of the villain in an old-fashioned melodrama with social reform purposes. In *The Shadow of Mart* and *No One Is Free*, on the other hand, where Dagerman joins psychological insights of considerable penetration with a dramatic form which maintains a nice balance between its realistic and symbolistic elements, he is more successful. The former of these plays is a study in the tragic frustrations of a young man who must drag on his existence in the shadow of a brother who had attained the legendary distinction of martyrdom as an underground fighter in a recent war, while in the latter play Dagerman adapts to the stage his novel *Burnt Child*, a complex modern study of a young man's brooding mother fixation.

It is not possible for us yet to disentangle the confused skein of circumstances which led to Dagerman's early death, but it is probable that literary frustrations, his momentary inability to quickly fulfill his youthful promise, had something to do with it. His very last years were creatively sterile in comparison with the few short years which had catapulted him to fame. It may be said that he ripened too rapidly, that his reading public came to expect too much of him, and that he could not meet his public's demands. Had circumstances permitted him to lie fallow for a few years before again taking up the pen he might finally have produced with the fullness and maturity which his early brilliance had promised.

If the involved symbolism of some of Dagerman's novels and plays impressed but often simultaneously confused his reading public, the poetry of Erik Lindegren and Karl Vennberg (both born in 1910) was by comparison even more confusing to its readers on its first appearance. In fact, even today not many Swedish readers feel entirely at home in the verse of either Lindegren or Vennberg or their poetic fellows, though an increasing number of critics bow respectfully in their presence and seek as best they can to decipher their often cryptic poetic language. It is not easy to decipher this language, for the poets who cultivate it are prepared to push the cult of verbal unintelligibility to a point which at times seems to be flirting with absurdity. Dagerman's allegorical symbolism with its attendant expository digressions is considerably more comprehensible. But once one has penetrated the levels of consciousness of this poetry and submitted to the patterns of its world of mood and idea, one is not infrequently apt to find it both intelligible and reasonable.

And — it should be added — this poetry grows more intelligible with time, some of its earlier examples yielding to critical analysis though offering extraordinarily stubborn resistance to the process, while later poems by the same authors are more often than not considerably less confusing. It should not be assumed, however, that the relatively greater intelligibility of the later poems reflects fundamental changes in any of these poets' conceptions of the nature and function of poetry. It represents rather, in most cases, simply a maturing of the poet's art, a greater refinement in his handling of the poetic instrument, a less agitated vision of the stupidities and horrors of the contemporary human scene.

The year 1946 witnessed the definitive breakthrough of the poetry of the 1940's with the appearance of Lindegren's *mannen utan vag* (the man without a way), followed in 1947 by the anthology *40-talslyrik* (Poetry of the 1940's), edited by Lindegren and Vennberg and including verse from more than a score of young poets whose work more or less consciously reflected characteristic ideas and moods of the decade. In 1942 Lindegren had privately printed *the man without a way*, and in the years between the first and second printing of this work Vennberg had become a literary power to reckon with both as a critic and as the author of the two volumes of verse *Halmfackla* (Straw Torch) and *Tideräkning* (Reckoning of Time).

All things considered, the importance to the poetry of the 1940's of Lindegren's *the man without a way* cannot be overestimated. It was the first book to announce in unequivocal terms the advent of the new poetry. Written in the years 1939–40, it reflects in a startlingly original but wholly apropos form the poet's horror and confusion in the presence of the catastrophic world developments of the day. To Lindegren the Second World War was simply the last ghastly fatuity of man, the ultimate evidence of a total breakdown in society's efforts to maintain order and decency in the world. With the world erupting in explosive fragments around him he sought a literary form appropriate to the burden of his poetry, whose central symbol in *the man without a way* is a man gazing in fascinated horror at a crossroads signpost which gives no final directions — or rather gives a dozen directions at once, each equally indecisive. Aside from this central symbolism, the general mood of the volume reflects a sense of constant and violent tension between the rigidity of its form and the dissolving fragmented patterns of its thematic detail.

Each of the forty poems in the volume has an identical form, seven non-rhyming couplets comprising a kind of modern sonnet. And each poem is numbered rather than given a title, suggesting the impersonality in point of view and the organic relation of each poem to the entire sequence. But in conflict with these rigidities of general structural form is the eccentric manner of handling detail — the omission of capital letters and punctuation, the refusal to employ normal syntactical forms, and, most important, the explosive concentration of a starkly fragmented imagery. How a soldier, for instance, might look upon his role in the conduct of modern war is expressed thus:

> to shoot the enemy and roll a cigarette
> to flame up and die out like a beacon in a storm
>
> to sit like a fly in the web of interested parties
> to believe oneself born unlucky though one is merely born
>
> to be a functionary in that which does not function
> to be something else or not to be at all
>
> to be fitted as the grey stone into the wall of hatred
> and yet to feel contact like the joy of heather
>
> to feel all that is neglected in the steaming rain
> to enjoy the excitement of the smouldering pyre
>
> to doubt that this must be the last time
> to affirm everything if only not repeated
>
> to break through and attain a lookout
> where lightning stalks to avenge humanity

Verse can scarcely be more naked, more compressed in phrasing, more stubbornly angular, more explosively fragmented; and it is therefore that the poems in *the man without a way* have been called "exploded sonnets," i.e., sonnets which disdain all dulcet harmonies and scorn any indulgence in the traditional luxuries of the well-rounded phrase and the lovely image. Such "sonnets" are modern with a vengeance, fiercely aware of the splintered cacophonies of modern existence and grimly determined to pile up such discords as might best give expression to these cacophonies.

That verse of this kind could be successfully maintained throughout a sequence of forty "sonnets" suggests the measure of Lindegren's artistic attainment in *the man without a way*. But the extremity of the performance could not safely be repeated, and in the two volumes of Lindegren's poetry which have since appeared, *Sviter* (Suites, 1947) and *Vinteroffer* (Winter Sacrifice, 1954), he wisely refrains from pursuing further the mad discords of his earlier verse but without surrendering anything essential in his poetic modernism. The fragmented images and grim view of life remain, but the imagery is less abrupt in line, more subtle and sinuous in design, more adapted to the finely *musical* modernism which is especially characteristic of Lindegren's later verse. Even in *the man without a way* the deliberate angularities of Lindegren's verse had not excluded a certain musical quality, and in *Suites* this musical quality is dominant if not actually supreme. The rigidities of the early poetry give way here to delicate associative patterns and involved symbolical sequences of haunting power, and the mood of this later verse, though somber, is seldom violent or forbidding. Torso-like fragmentary details of love and of memory, combined with glimpses of nature's magic play with line and color, provide in *Suites* — and to a lesser extent in *Winter Sacrifice* — visions of a somewhat better world than the one we come upon in *the man without a way*. But these visions, it should be emphasized, are to Lindegren fleeting, fragile, and beyond substantial recall. They offer but the slenderest of solaces to man.

While Lindegren thinks largely in terms of images, within the splintered folds of a visual poetic design, his colleague and close friend Karl Vennberg thinks abstractly, tends to reduce poetry to a series of pronouncements, definitions, and syllogisms — pursuing and seeking to perfect what has been called "the critical-analytical line" in modern Swedish poetry. Like one of his literary masters T. S. Eliot, whom he has translated, Vennberg is as distinguished and influential a critic as he is a poet. His intelligent, hard-hitting book reviews and critical essays spearheaded the radical fighting cause of the *40-talister* and gave to their program substance and a solid rationale. Moreover, his three volumes of poetry from the 1940's provided, together with Lindegren's two collections from these years, the sacred canonical works of the new poetry. And in the 1950's Vennberg's poetic vein continued to yield richly — a book each year between 1952 and 1955. None of these volumes reflects any appreciable lag in poetic quality.

Vennberg's familiarity with the most advanced trends in European literature was phenomenal from the beginning of his career and has had a marked influence especially on his early verse. Besides Eliot, his chief master is Franz Kafka, whose speculative skepticism and ironical manner are echoed with new variations in the Swedish poet's verse. Vennberg's skeptical dialectic is by contrast with Kafka's more dry and matter-of-fact, less given to symbolistic fantasy and emotion-freighted effects. And Vennberg's irony has more immediate targets, especially in his early verse, in which he waylays and murderously exposes all manner of contemporary deception and self-deception whether parading under political, religious, or cultural banners. How playfully devastating this irony can be is illustrated in the title poem of *Reckoning of Time* (1945):

> Some people have got the idea
> that I, in pure defiance
> and out of youthful desire to rebel,
> would deny the usual chronometries
>
> but I have the greatest respect for chronometries:
> Julian, Jewish, Gregorian, Mohammedan
> and never embark on any of my important enterprises
> without establishing their place in time
> their position in relation to the world's creation
> the founding of Rome
> the flight to Medina and so forth
>
> Those who charge
> that I have blasphemously
> violated the chronological sense
> presumably suffer from personal ill-will
> Who could seriously wish to do away with
> these threadbare calendars
> with all their domesticated swindle
> who would dare meet
> without time's masks and concatenations
> all the silent stipulations of history
> in the dark's hollowed stairs
>
> There really isn't much
> that in itself is worth loving
> and contrary traits
> can as a rule shake hands with each other
> Even truth
> can be bisexual
> and beget monstrous children with itself
> And how moreover can the hunter's truth
> be reconciled with the quarry's
> Conscience and sense of justice
> can dupe us with the simplest fits of ague
>
> *Translated by Richard B. Vowles*

What makes Vennberg's irony the more acceptable is that he is honest enough — especially in his later verse — to turn it in upon himself, to admit as possible, even probable, the shortcomings of his own dialectic, the shabbiness of his own spirit.

This honesty is in part certainly a logical result of his skepticism, but it is almost certainly related in some way to his paradoxical desire to know, in spite of all, the unknowable truth and to break out of the isolation of his irony into some kind of fruitful relation with society and his fellows. Self-deception — he senses vaguely — may haunt the world of the skeptic even while he luxuriates in his superior intelligence and lets fly the barbs of his irony. But like the Kafka whose work he so much admires, Vennberg does not succeed in breaking out of his isolation. "Some of us must remain alone," as he puts it in the grimly restrained poem "October" in *Gatukorsning* (Crossing the Street, 1952). And in Vennberg's poetry from the 1950's — perhaps most strikingly in *Synfält* (Points of View, 1954) — we find what would seem to be his final and definitive position, a position which retains much of his early scorn for political pretentiousness and his refusal to believe in either God or man, but a position which finds some solace in life's fleeting visions of beauty and man's open-eyed determination to endure and, when possible, to enjoy.

> Never has life had the circle's
> restful circumambience.
> A searching flight it's been
> close to the earth,
> like the bumble-bee's on its first spring day.
>
> Never has man's hand
> found its rite and its jewel.
>
> Always salvation uncertain
> and life's return tardy.
>
> But here we still remain.
> With seeing eyes.
> With life's
> consuming
> sweetness on our tongue.
>
> Here we still remain
> Like a garment of light.
> Like a promise.
> On searching flight
> like the bumble-bee's on its first spring day.

These lines brook neither bitterness nor defiance. In their quiet disillusionment they harbor a half-uttered sense of the mystery of existence together with a restrained readiness to accept the unhappy conditions of life.

The sophisticated cerebral quality of Vennberg's verse, and, for that matter, of much of the poetry of the 1940's, left its mark also on the prose of the time though not so sharply and pervasively as one might expect. The novel of the 1940's, as represented in such figures as Lars Ahlin (b. 1915), Sivar Arnér (b. 1909), and Björn-Erik Höijer (b. 1907), experimented freely with fictional forms and reflected in its constant search for ultimate spiritual values a strong speculative quality, but in its technical experimentation it was somewhat less radical than the poetry, and its speculative vein retained a more manifest sense of relation to the actual conditions of man's everyday existence than did the poetry. By comparison with the realistic problem novel of preceding decades, however, the novel of the 1940's was far less concerned with man as a social creature, far more concerned with him in the more purely psychological and ethical aspects of his being. Even when — as especially in some of the early work of Ahlin and Höijer — labor conflicts and related matters provide the material of action in the novel, the emphasis is placed in the last analysis on inner conflicts, the struggle of the individual with himself, with a "value" or a "truth" compulsively pursued, with in some cases an awareness of a divine principle or presence. While the disillusioned skepticism which had taken possession of the representative poets of the day permitted only the most tentative, hesitant, and highly qualified of approaches to a religious or mystical view of life, the search for values on the part of the novelists was persistent, a central — if not actually *the* central — preoccupation of the author. This search does not, however, reduce these novelists to the status of literary purveyors of pious devotional prose far removed from the actualities of existence. On the contrary the search invariably takes place in a world of reality, of an oftentimes crass and brutal and malevolent reality, the profoundly disquieting reality of modern life.

None of the Swedish novelists of our day is as unabashedly in search of ultimate spiritual values as Lars Ahlin, and none is more unafraid of pursuing forms of human weakness and self-deception and depravation into their uttermost labyrinthine lairs. Among the novelists of the generation of the 1940's he is perhaps the profoundest and certainly the least disciplined talent. He reminds one of both Gorki and Dostoevski, having something of the total appetite for life of the former and not a little of the psychological penetration and the unconventional religious ardor of the latter. Like Gorki, too, his formative years were poverty-marked and chaotic. Among Swedish authors he reminds one of Hjalmar Bergman, whose fabulous narrative fantasy and taste for the bizarre and the macabre recur in Ahlin. But he does not have the instinctive artistry of Bergman, the ability to pursue a complex narrative pattern with a fine sense of balance among its various parts. Ahlin's artistry is untidy, given to wordiness and not infrequently to repulsive effects, and in his speculative predilections he often bites off considerably more than he can chew. This artistic untidiness and intellectual overextension results in part from his unhappy backgrounds and in part from the fierce directness of his engagement with the materials of his novels. He seldom allows his characters to live their own lives. They must illustrate one of their creator's theories, function as links in his ethical and/or religious demonstrations. Considering himself primarily a "mediator" (*förbedjare*) between man and God, Ahlin often ignores the demands of narrative action and tends to reduce his novels to moral discourse, to religious commentary on the part of the author. This is especially true of one of his most arresting novels, *Om* (If, 1946). And yet, somehow, Ahlin's novels have a fantastic vitality, a vitality which often communicates itself to the reader with an eerie, at times almost volcanic, force. This vitality derives from primitive creative resources of a constitutive kind which cannot finally be dissipated by Ahlin's predilection toward excessive narrative meandering or by his at times curious theorizing about the nature of man and his relation to God.

The appearance in 1943 of *Tåbb och manifestet* (Tåbb and the Manifesto) first startled the Swedish reading public into an awareness of a new and highly original literary personality, and since this date scarcely a year has passed without Ahlin's adding a volume to his literary output. Among his most striking (and, it may be said, most hotly attacked and defended) novels besides *If* are *Min död är min* (My Death Is Mine, 1945), *Fromma mord* (Pious Murders, 1952), and *Kvinna, kvinna* (Woman, Woman, 1955). Artistically he is at his best in the novel *Kanelbiten* (The Cinnamon Stick, 1953), in the fascinating autobiographical sketches of *Stora glömskan* (The Great Forgetfulness, 1954) together with its sequel *Natt i marknadstältet* (Night in the Market Tent, 1957), and in some of his short stories, in all of which works he manages to bridle his speculative penchant and create human situations relatively free from the tyranny of his theorizing. Though Ahlin's work is so many-faceted that even the most ingenious of critics are not usually sure as to just how one is to interpret a given novel, it is clear enough that in general his work is centrally concerned with the vagaries of human consciousness and the necessity of seeking a way out of these vagaries in terms of some kind of divine guidance. What is most impressive about his work is its unflinching psychological realism and its seething variety of narrative forms. He probes the devious ways of the human consciousness with no concern for a shocked reader's more fastidious feelings, and he employs in his best novels realistic or dream techniques by turn or simultaneously, fitting form to idea and mood with amazing virtuosity and considerable effectiveness. Ahlin's literary resources seem quite inexhaustible, his appetite for life Gargantuan, his language a constant source of delighted amazement to the reader. But despite Ahlin's attainments to date one has the feeling that his very best work is ahead of him. If — and when — he succeeds in combining in a single novel the artistic discipline of *The Cinnamon Stick* with the overwhelming creative fertility of *My Death is Mine* or *Woman, Woman*, he will have written one of the really great Swedish novels.

Though Sivar Arnér shares Ahlin's interest in moral and religious problems and has something of Ahlin's brutal frenzy in depicting human evil, he is in most other respects Ahlin's absolute antipodes. Arnér, unlike Ahlin, is an intellectual both by training and temperament, and his work on the whole reflects an artistic self-discipline of remarkable firmness and integrity. His style is sober, measured, always to the point. His general manner of procedure is cool, controlled, analytical, even when his feelings may be most sharply engaged. His "plots" are at times rather too schematic, having the ridigity and intricacy of a complex mathematical equation. But he manages to manipulate and finally resolve such equations with impeccable skill, and in the process manages with equal skill to employ certain of the more advanced techniques of modern fiction. Usually his advanced techniques are inserted incidentally into narrative structural patterns which are otherwise relatively conventional, but in some cases the basic structural pattern itself is aggressively modern. This is particularly true of the novel *Egil* (1948), which like James Joyce's *Ulysses* ransacks the stream of consciousness of its hero during a single day of the hero's life. And in *Fyra som var bröder* (Four Who Were Brothers, 1955) we seem to have a modern semi-apocalyptic fable partly in the grim future-seeing manner of Orwell's *1984* or Karin Boye's *Kallocain*. In neither of these novels, however, is Arnér quite at his best. He moves more surely in what may be called his own special form, the novel which within a rigid structural frame manipulates a small group of characters in a tight realistic conflict that has moral implications far beyond the immediate realities of the conflict. Among the subtlest and most complex of these novels is *Han — Hon — Ingen* (He — She — No One, 1951). Not infrequently the moral implications of these novels operate on mystical planes. Arnér's realism is decidedly a four-dimensional realism, though the fourth — the mystical — dimension is more often hinted at than mentioned, more often an organic accompaniment to the action than a direct commentary on it.

In his treatment of the relation between the sexes, marital or otherwise, Arnér has none of the naïve erotic optimism of the primitivists of the 1930's. Especially in his earlier novels and short stories — those from the 1940's such as *Du själv* (You Yourself) and *Verandan* (The Veranda) — marital relations tend rapidly to degenerate into a love-hate complex of Strindbergian bitterness and intensity. In 1950, on the appearance of *Vackert väder* (Lovely Weather), some critics were prepared to announce with considerable confidence the arrival of a "new Arnér," an Arnér who could envision love relations in less grim and splintered forms than before, an Arnér in whom the mystical strain had become more positive and optimistic. And undeniably *Lovely Weather* both in its form and substance seemed to justify the assumption that the harsh analyst was yielding finally to a reasonably tempered if not complaisant observer of the human scene. But — except for the collection of short stories *Säkert till sommaren* (Certainly When Summer Comes, 1954), which contains a number of marital studies in the possibilities of submissiveness and understanding — there is not much in Arnér's later work that suggests a "new Arnér." His style in *Som svalorna* (Like the Swallows, 1956) is more light and flexible than before, and the sense of tension between the world of reality and another mystical world becomes more marked, but this tension is seldom satisfactorily resolved, chiefly because Arnér's analytical method becomes with the years increasingly intricate and subtle. One can be impressed by the fine integrity of this analytical method without being convinced that it leads either to literary distinction of the highest order or to ethical and religious values which man actually can live by.

The novels and plays of Björn-Erik Höijer have little of the daemonic fury of Ahlin and less of the razor-sharp, oversubtle intelligence of Arnér, but in its relatively undistinguished way Höijer's work is sufficiently representative of the literature of the 1940's. He attempts, not always very successfully, to approximate some of the best examples of current experimental forms, and joins the novelists of his generation in their preoccupation with psychological problems and their search for moral and religious values. His distinguishing mark among his fellows of the 1940's is that he has localized the action of much of his work in an immediately identifiable milieu, the Malmberg mining area in Norrbotten, just above the Polar Circle, a point on the Swedish map where he was born and raised and where for years before breaking through finally as an author he had functioned as a teacher of manual training. But Höijer only somewhat more than other representative authors of his day allows milieu to occupy a relatively central role in his work, as can be seen in his first more important novel *Se din bild* (Look at Yourself, 1946), which begins with externals of scene and labor conflicts in the manner of the conventional proletarian novel but concerns itself finally with the inner world of the chief protagonists in these conflicts. It is in one sense unfortunate that Höijer yields to the literary taste of the 1940's and in his later novels allows psychological and religious concerns to blunt the sharp edge of his immediate physical responses, for he has sensory gifts of rather extraordinary sharpness and range. By no means, however, has he allowed "higher concerns" to displace completely his genius for catching up the exact quality of a given limited milieu. Even in his dramas this quality is present, so much so, indeed, that one of his delighted critics in reviewing the play *Dans på bryggan* (Dance on the Pier) insists that "he has to a higher degree than any other Swedish dramatist: *stuglukten* (literally 'the cabin odor')." And the critic goes on to elaborate on the play's realism of scene and action: "through the clamor and the clawing and the hearty boozing (*ölgemytligheten*) and the shabbiness of his characters' life together *stuglukten* forces its way upon us — that indescribable odor of coffee and unaired bedding, cat-leavings (*kattsnusk*) and clumsy old boots." Despite the critic's protestations that he was not being ironic in his observations, Höijer — whose literary ambitions lie on a higher plane than merely rendering with exactness olfactory sensations — was offended.

Aside from a group of excellent sketches of his childhood in a series of volumes beginning with *Martin går i gräset* (Martin Walks in the Grass,1950), Höijer has devoted his literary energies about equally to three genres, the short story, the novel, and the drama. Of his three more important novels — *Trettio silverpengar* (Thirty Pieces of Silver, 1949), *Innan änkorna kom* (Before the Widows Came, 1951), and *Rosenkransen* (The Crown of Roses,1953) — the first two are on the whole superior to the last, which suffers among other things from a rather confusing excess of symbolism. Both *Thirty Pieces of Silver* and *Before the Widows Came* are somewhat schematic but nevertheless enthralling tales, centering their attention on psychological-moral problems and manipulating their narrative material with considerable finesse and ingenuity. *Thirty Pieces of Silver* is a kind of detective tale, in which the unraveling of a mystery (who has stolen the missing three hundred crowns from the strong box of an isolated far-northern church?) provides the occasion for a minute examination of the varieties of more or less dubious "spirituality" represented in the pastor of the church and its six elders. *Before the Widows Came* focuses its attention on *one* character, a years-long-bedridden old man who finds himself helplessly snowbound alone with the corpse of his wife in an isolated cottage for two terrifying days and nights before the arrival of some neighboring widows. Out of the forty-eight hours of terror Höijer constructs a fascinating stream-of-consciousness novel, one in which the old man ransacks his past, particularly his relations with his wife and his only son, a process which amounts to a searching moral accounting with himself. The false, inhuman rigidity of the old man's "idealism," with its unhappy consequences for wife and son, is a theme which reappears in one of Höijer's most important plays, *Isak Juntti hade många söner* (Isak Juntti Had Many Sons), though the play, concerned as it is with the primitive religious sectarianism of the Far North, has an imaginative intensity and range of a much higher order than the novel. Höijer's strength in general as a dramatist lies in his use of telling atmospheric effects and in a dialogue often punctuated with vigorous repartee; his weakness is a tendency toward lurid melodramatic excesses of one kind or other. Among the literary generation of the 1940's he has none of the elegant artistic fastidiousness of some of his colleagues, but in sharing their absorbing preoccupation with psychological and moral problems he brings to a consideration of these problems a quality of freshness and vigor and of dramatic concretion that is not common in his literary generation.

In the spring of 1953 one of Sweden's more discriminating critics began a review of a new novel with the categorical assertion: "It is just as well to say immediately — *Tjärdalen* (The Tar Still) is a remarkable book, not only relatively speaking, or as a debut novel, but in the absolute sense, that is to say considered in the larger contexts of literary achievement." *The Tar Still* is the first novel by Sara Lidman (b. 1923), Sweden's only author of the youngest generation (those appearing around

1950 and after) whose work from the outset has won the universal acclaim of critics and a wide reading public. That her second novel *Hjortronlandet* (Cloudberry Land, 1955) received an equally enthusiastic reception indicates that Sara Lidman is presently on the way to becoming one of the two or three really distinguished Swedish women novelists. Her two plays to date, *Job Klockmakares dotter* (Job the Clockmaker's Daughter) and *Aina*, have not received more than respectful attention by theatergoers, but her two first novels easily rank with the best work of Selma Lagerlöf's brilliant early years. In fact, they rank in certain ways considerably higher in the judgment of some critics today. Their style is marked by a subtly controlled spontaneity, their humor is sly but warm and profound, their narrative flow is easy, unhurried, quietly lively, their psychological penetration and moral seriousness satisfy every demand of a sophisticated modern reader. Though her third, and most recent novel, *Regnspiran* (1958), does not quite attain the high distinction of *The Tar Still* and *Cloudberry Land*, it is clearly the work of a mature and sensitive artist. Sara Lidman's talent is so balanced and genuine, so deeply rooted in the realities of existence, that one has no reason to believe that she will not in the future continue to produce distinguished work in the narrative genres.

Both *The Tar Still* and *Cloudberry Land* deal with rural life in Västerbotten, the southeastern area of far-northern Sweden where Sara Lidman spent her childhood and young womanhood. While pursuing studies (interrupted for long periods by a stubborn tubercular condition) she wrote conventional short stories — until, we are told, under the impact of Dostoevski and the Swedish "moderns" Tage Aurell, Thorsten Jonsson, and Stina Aronson, she found her own form and area of interest. The locality Eckträsk of *The Tar Still* is in reality the parish of Missenträsk of Sara Lidman's early years, where not much more than a bare existence rewarded the heavy farm labors of its inhabitants. But outwardly limited and dreary as the conditions of existence in this region seem to be, Sara Lidman manages to bring these conditions intensely alive, not by superimposing on the inhabitants of Eckträsk false heroic qualities, but by allowing them to live their own lives and respond in their own ways to the daily drift of events on the countryside. Neither the series of episodes (the wrecking of the tar-distilling structure and its aftermath) which gives dramatic concentration and drive to the novel, nor the manner in which the "moral" of the story is developed, obtrudes unduly on the reader's feeling of sheer delight in simply sharing the daily life of Sara Lidman's Eckträsk natives. She *lives herself* so deeply into the world of her characters that whatever moral problems come to concern them and the author do so naturally, with none of the dialectic rigidity and sense of finality which at times attend the development of theme in modern fiction. Sara Lidman's analysis of human failings cuts deep, particularly in her examination of the loose moral fiber of Petrus Andersson, the "spiritual leader" of the Eckträsk community; but she does not "preach" or press judgment. She merely relates and reveals, and this is enough. The fairly tight structure of *The Tar Still* gives way to a looser narrative form in *Cloudberry Land*, a novel which also differs from *The Tar Still* in its less pronounced use of a picturesque local dialect and in its essentially "collective" concern with a kind of rural proletariat, the outlander marsh dwellers called Öare. Otherwise we are moving in *The Tar Still* and *Cloudberry Land* in much the same world, concerned with broadly similar conditions of existence and related ethical problems. But the author's touch in *Cloudberry Land* is on the whole lighter, somewhat less earth-bound, moving more freely, with a greater assurance of its control over the materials of the world which it unfolds for us. Possibly the fact that women play a more important role in *Cloudberry Land* than in *The Tar Still* may account in part for Sara Lidman's greater sense of artistic assurance in her second novel. Certainly the encouragement given her authorship by the enthusiastic reception of *The Tar Still* dispersed any doubts she may have had about her literary competence and allowed her in *Cloudberry Land* to create on a larger scale and with greater finesse and flexibility.

No such encouragement has been heaped upon other Swedish authors of Sara Lidman's generation, in part, one should hasten to say, because they are apparently not deserving of it. That the literary generation of the 1950's has in its ranks not a few interesting talents is undeniable, but with the single exception of Sara Lidman none of these talents has as yet attained any real measure of intellectual and artistic maturity. This lack of maturity cannot alone be accounted for by the fact that the last generation of Swedish authors is very young — most of them still in their twenties. A perhaps deeper-lying reason is that they are too precocious and too prolific. Nearly all of them published their first work at the age of twenty or shortly thereafter, and the average number of books each has been responsible for by the mid-1950's is four to five. The most precocious of them, Per Wästberg, published a first novel when he was fifteen, while the most prolific, Bo Setterlind, has turned out more than a score of books in less than a decade! Such precocious productivity suggests astonishing verbal facility rather than disciplined art, and it is clear that many of the works of these young authors were — if not actually stillborn on appearance — of minimal importance in the larger contexts of Swedish literary developments.

Unlike the literature of the 1940's that of the 1950's seems at most points incapable of coming significantly to grips with the enormous complexities of life in the mid-twentieth century, and not infrequently takes the easy way out of its plight by escaping into various Romantic moods and frames of reference. The poetry of the generation of the 1950's not infrequently cultivates vaguely nationalistic and religious strains more or less directly reminiscent of such Swedish Romantics of more than a century ago as Stagnelius and C. J. L. Almqvist, and in matters of form this poetry is often deliberately naïvistic and affects such genres as the ballad and the folk song. At times genuine-enough poetry has resulted from this modern experimenting with apparently outmoded Romantic moods and forms. But much more often the result is coquettish pretentiousness and poetic twaddle. How pretentiously confused in its thinking the younger generation of poets can become is apparent in Bengt Nordenborg's proposal that Schelling's speculative mysticism be resurrected as *the* means of attaining a revolutionary new modernism in poetry, or in Bo Setterlind's bombastic pronouncement of a few years ago on what he calls "the new realism": "Here is the most radiant of all the poet's methods, the new realism, out of a language which has its roots in reality. It grows up in The Tree which belongs to the heavenly knowledge. I call it something of a revelation, a new testament. What becomes then of surrealism? Weak delirium. And naturalism? The day after."

There can be little doubt that along such childishly assertive lines as these lies poetic sterility and that those who persist in pursuing such fatuous paths are doomed ultimately to literary obscurity no matter how talented they may seem to be. Fortunately, some of the younger Swedish authors of today are less infantile in their attitudes and seek in part at least to fashion their work in terms of the realities of modern life. Indeed in some instances, most notably in the fascinating psychological-political problem novels of Arne Sand, a backward-looking Romantic mentality is banished completely, in favor of a realistic modernism of an advanced kind. In most cases, however — even when the younger generation is prepared to seek contact with the world of reality about them — they do so only hesitantly and half way, with the consequence that their work has a dangerously ambivalent quality, fluctuating precariously between the extremes of an imitative (or at least a derivative) Romanticism and a forced, at times rather hysterical modernism. In the poetry of Paul Andersson, for instance, purely visionary Romantic elements rub shoulders with a Rimbaud-inspired modernism, and in some of the work of Lars Forsell one comes upon experiments in the direction of transforming folk song naïvisms into popular ditties for today's radio audiences. In his more important work, however, Lars Forsell has learned from Ezra Pound and other American and English poets, and he is one of that small number among the younger generation of poets who have inherited some of the grim disillusionment and critical intellectualism of the Swedish 1940's. Forsell's "Lycidas," in *Ryttaren* (The Equestrian, 1949), provides a subtle variation on Milton's elegy of the same title, and some of his verse in *Narren* (The Fool, 1952) has obvious points of contact with T. S. Eliot's *Sweeney Agonistes*. Lars Forsell's relation to the 1940's is to date, however, very ambivalent, how much so can be seen most clearly in the volume *F. C. Tietjens* (1954), in which the poet's precociously waggish intellectualism pokes airy fun at the more mature and serious intellectualism of his immediate Swedish predecessors. The irony of the verse in *F. C. Tietjens* both derives *from* the intellectualism of the 1940's and is employed as a means of attack *upon* this intellectualism.

Whether the youngest generation of Swedish authors will come in the future to fulfill in really significant ways whatever promise some of them have shown, remains to be seen. At the moment they are feeling their way forward, for the most part with uncertain steps along rather confused but not necessarily hopeless ways. When — and if — they come to recognize literary blind alleys for what they are, and succeed in avoiding them, some of the most recent additions to the ranks of the Swedish writing fraternity may in time establish for themselves a firmer position in Swedish literature than they hitherto have done. But whether they do so or not we need have no fear of any lack of creative vitality in Swedish literature today, for what the youngest generation at the moment may lack is provided in sufficient abundance by the continued productivity of the elder generations. Not only are such key representatives of the 1940's as Erik Lindegren and Karl Vennberg still writing poetry on a high level of excellence; many of the poets and novelists whose early work brought high distinction to the literature of the 1930's have in later years shown few signs of a diminishing creative vitality. Indeed some of the best work of those who emerged in the 1930's has been written in the last decade or two. Harry Martinson, Eyvind Johnson, Vilhelm Moberg, and a half dozen others are cases in point. And even Pär Lagerkvist, whose initial literary efforts antedate the First World War, is still today adding to the dozens of works which have come from his pen and which came early to mark him as the central portal figure in twentieth-century Swedish literature. Beginning with *Barabbas* in 1951 Lagerkvist has published at three-year intervals two of his most important prose works and a distinguished volume of verse. When some Swedish critics talk about a "lull" (*stiltje*) in literary developments in the 1950's they can be said to be justified in doing so only if what they mean by the literature of the 1950's is that written by the youngest generation of Swedish authors, those who up to the present moment have scarcely more than cut their literary eyeteeth.

BIBLIOGRAPHY, LIST OF TRANSLATIONS, NOTE ON
PRONUNCIATION, AND INDEX

A Bibliographical Guide for Additional Readings and Studies

ALTHOUGH the bibliography which follows is selective, it does not restrict itself rigidly to books and articles in English, chiefly because a bibliography thus limited would leave all too many unfortunate gaps in the over-all picture of Swedish literature which the present book attempts to provide. Important as are some English and American studies on a given Swedish author or phase of Swedish literature, the fact remains that no period in Swedish literature has been cultivated intensively by competent English and American critics and scholars, and most periods have been neglected entirely except for an occasional study of greater or lesser worth. It would therefore seem desirable, if not imperative, to include even in a selective bibliography aimed primarily at English-speaking readers a reasonable sampling of representative studies in languages other than English — in the first instance, of course, basic books and shorter studies in Swedish, but also works in French and German. Such inclusions should be of assistance to the more serious student without in any way neglecting the needs of the general reader or those who must pursue their interest in Swedish literature in a language or languages other than Swedish itself. Because of the relatively limited number of studies in languages other than Swedish, I have included in the selections made here some studies in English, French, and German which leave something to be desired in critical penetration or thoroughness of treatment. I have not hesitated, however, to ignore items appearing in these non-Scandinavian languages which in my judgment are distinctly mediocre, misleading, or worthless.

In order to enlarge the possible range of readings for those who must restrict themselves to sources in English, I have on occasion included in the present bibliography certain English translations of Swedish novels and plays which are concerned with Swedish political and/or cultural history. Though free literary re-creations of history not infrequently distort historical fact in one way or other, they often serve to arouse in the reader a vivid sense of the pulsing reality of the past, and in some cases they may actually come closer to that reality than history itself.

I have deliberately excluded from this bibliography any listing of critical (or other) editions of the works of the authors with whom my book is concerned. The reader who may be interested in such purely textual matters will find information of this kind in the exhaustive Swedish bibliographical sources referred to below.

A reasonably full listing of English translations of Swedish literary works is separately provided immediately following the present bibliography.

When the place of publication is Stockholm, only the date of publication is given. Otherwise both the date and place of publication are indicated.

The following abbreviations are used for certain periodical publications of most frequent occurrence:

ASR   The American-Scandinavian Review
BLM   Bonniers Litterära Magasin
FT   Finsk Tidskrift
MFÅ   Årsskrift för modersmålslärarnas förening
NS   Nysvenska Studier
OoB   Ord och Bild
S   Samlaren [the letters "n.f." after S refer to Ny Följd (New Series)]
SLT   Svensk Litteraturtidskrift
SS   Scandinavian Studies

General Works

In English two helpful bibliographical lists exist, Nils Afzelius's *Books in English on Sweden* (1951) and Naboth Hedin's *Guide to Information About Sweden* (New York, 1947). In Swedish the standard bibliographical source is the annual bibliography appearing in the literary-historical journal *Samlaren* (1880ff.), from which has been compiled the indispensable *Svensk litteraturhistorisk bibliografi 1900–1935* (1939ff.). With the exception of the present book and the sketchy but essentially sound sections on Swedish literature in *An Introduction to Scandinavian Literature* (Cambridge, 1951) by Elias Bredsdorff, Brita Mortensen, and Ronald Popperwell, no general treatment of the whole of Swedish literature has appeared from an English or American pen in our century. The Bach-Blankner *History of the Scandinavian Literatures* (New York, 1938) is a badly edited compilation of extremely uneven quality based originally on a very dubious book of Italian provenance. (See my review in *The Journal of English and Germanic Philology*, xxxviii (1939), 628–32). A couple of earlier, outdated works which may be mentioned are William and Mary Howitt's *The Literature and Romance of Northern Europe* (London, 1852) and Frederik Winkel Horn's *History of the Literature of the Scandinavian North from the Most Ancient Times to the Present* (Chicago, 1884). Early critics of some consequence writing in English about Scandinavian literature are Edmund Gosse and H. H. Boyesen. Gosse's *Studies in the Literature of Northern Europe* (London, 1879) and *Portraits and Sketches* (New York, 1913) contain respectively an essay on Runeberg and a section entitled "Carl Snoilsky and Some Recent Swedish Poets [Fröding, Levertin, Heidenstam]." Boyesen's *Essays on Scandinavian Literature* (New York, 1925) includes an essay on Esaias Tegnér. A relatively recent handbook, H. G. Topsöe-Jensen's *Scandinavian Literature from Brandes to Our Day* (New York, 1929), deals with the literature of Denmark, Norway, and Sweden from the 1870's to the 1920's. Many short articles on Swedish authors since the 1870's, as well as a brief sketch of Swedish literature as a whole during the same period, are available in the *Columbia Dictionary of Modern European Literature* (New York, 1947). In the *Columbia Dictionary* the present writer has been responsible for most of the articles on individual Swedish authors while Adolph B. Benson has written the general sketch on modern Swedish literature. In French we have two general histories of Swedish literature, the distinguished Swedish scholar Henrik Schück's *Histoire de la littérature suédoise*, tr. with an *avant-propos* by Lucien Maury (Paris, 1923) and Ingvar Holm and Magnus von Platen's *La Littérature suédoise* (Stockholm, 1957), and two helpful books which treat representative Swedish authors of the nineteenth and twentieth centuries, Lucien Maury's *L'Imagination scandinave* (Paris, 1929) and *Panorama de la littérature suédoise contemporaine* (Paris, 1940). Students broadly concerned with the impact of one national literary culture on another, specifically French on Swedish, will find much of interest in Anton Blanck's brilliant survey "Sverige och den franska litteraturen" in *Bellman vid skiljovägen och andra studier* (1941), pp.60–108, which has also appeared in Lucien Maury's translation *La Suède et la littérature française des origines à nous jours* (Paris, 1947).

The standard general history of Swedish literature is the five-volume recently published *Ny illustrerad svensk litteraturhistoria* (1955–58), which carries literary developments down through the 1890's. This work is meant to supersede the out-of-print and somewhat dated Schück and Warburg's *Illustrerad svensk litteraturhistoria* (latest edition 1926ff.), the seventh, and last, volume of which, Erik Hj. Linder's *Fyra decennier av nittonhundratalet* (1952) – also included as the fifth volume (1958) of *Ny illustrerad svensk litteraturhistoria* – is the definitive work on Swedish literature in our century. A work which in its way is of parallel importance to Schück and Warburg is the three-volume *Svenska litteraturens historia* (new and rev. ed. 1929) ed. by Otto Sylwan. A lively, highly stimulating single-volume work is E. N. Tigerstedt's *Svensk litteraturhistoria* (1948). All of these general literary histories in Swedish contain valuable bibliographical sections, that of Tigerstedt offering illuminating critical commentary in addition to simply listing titles.

On the theater and drama from the beginnings down to relatively modern times the Swedish works which should be mentioned are G. E. Klemming's bibliographical listings *Sveriges dramatiska litteratur till och med 1875* (1863–75), Gustaf Ljunggren's old but still valuable *Svenska dramat intill slutet af sjuttonde århundradet* (Lund and Copenhagen, 1864), Nils Personne's *Svenska teatern under Gustavianska tidehvarfvet jämte en återblick på dess tidigare öden* (1913, 1914), and Georg Nordensvan's *Svensk teater och svenska skådespelare från Gustaf III till våra dagar* (1917). On the theater and drama largely of the last hundred years see Gustaf Hilleström's brief *Theatre and Ballet in Sweden* (1953) and Alrik Gustafson's "The Scandinavian Countries" in *A History of Modern Drama*, ed. by B. H. Clark and G. Freedley (New York and London, 1947), pp.1–75.

Otto Sylwan has investigated the fortunes of Swedish prosody down through the centuries in two works, the short survey *Svensk verskonst från Wivallius till Karlfeldt* (1934) and the much more detailed three-volume *Den svenska versen från 1600-talets början* (Göteborg, 1926–34). Though no equally exhaustive general study of Swedish prose fiction has been made, Fredrik Böök's *Romanens och prosaberättelsens historia i Sverige intill 1809* (1907) covers roughly the same period for the novel and the tale that Sylwan's three-volume study does for lyric poetry. Olle Holmberg's *Lovtal över svenska romaner* (1957) offers short informal essays on representative Swedish novels of the last century and a half, while Staffan Björck's *Romanens formvärld* (4th ed. 1957) provides a penetrating investigation of the formal, technical side of prose fiction as reflected especially in the twentieth-century Swedish novel. Alrik Gustafson's *Six Scandinavian Novelists* (Princeton and New York, 1940) contains chapters on two Swedish novelists and provides in passing a general orientation in modern Scandinavian prose fiction. For those interested in the various phases of development of the Swedish language Gösta Bergman's *A Short History of the Swedish Language* (1947) is recommended. Of the available general histories of Sweden in English the most recent and the best is Ingvar Andersson's brilliant *A History of Sweden* (London, 1956). Equally satisfactory on economic history is Eli F. Heckscher's *An Economic History of Sweden* (Cambridge, Mass., 1954). An able account of the rise of the Swedish middle classes to economic and political power is provided in Bryn Hovde's *The Scandinavian Countries 1720–1865* (Ithaca, N.Y., 1948). On modern industrial developments the standard work is Arthur Montgomery's *The Rise of Modern Industry in Sweden* (London, 1939).

Aside from these general works the English-speaking reader will find items of interest by thumbing through the volumes of such American and English periodical publications as *The American-Scandinavian Review* (1913ff.), *Scandinavian Studies* (1911ff.), *The Norseman* (1943ff.), *The American-Swedish Monthly* (1934ff., earlier *The Swedish-American Trade Journal*), and *The Anglo-Swedish Review* (1934ff., earlier under various titles). The bibliographical entries under the separate chapter sections which follow will from time to time have occasion to refer to the more competent articles appearing in these American and English periodical sources. Three *quite indispensable* journals for the really serious student of Swedish literature are *Samlaren* (188off.), the standard journal concerned with all periods of Swedish literature, and *Svensk Litteraturtidskrift* (1938ff.) and *Bonniers Litterära Magasin* (1932ff.), both of which concentrate largely on contemporary literary developments. Other Swedish journals of value to the student of literature are *Ord och Bild* (1892ff.), *Tiden* (1908ff.), *Svensk Tidskrift* (1911–32, 1936ff.), *Nysvenska Studier* (1921ff., a continuation of *Språk och Stil*, 1901–20), *Nordisk Tidskrift* (1878ff.), and *Samtid och Framtid* (1944ff.). The publications of Svenska Litteratursällskapet i Finland (*Förhandlingar och uppsatser*, 1886–1924, continued as *Historiska och litteraturhistoriska studier*, 1925ff.) also contain important material. A popular but within its limits highly authoritative collaborative work on all aspects of Swedish life and culture from the most ancient times to the present is the thirteen-volume, richly illustrated *Svenska folket genom tiderna* (Malmö, 1938ff.).

Anthologies which include representative works or parts of works from the whole range of Swedish literature are available only in Swedish. Three of these are especially worthy of mention: *Sveriges national-litteratur 1500–1900*, ed. by Henrik Schück, Ruben G:son Berg, and Fredrik Böök (2nd ed. 1921–22), 30 volumes; *Svenska mästare*, ed. by Bernhard Risberg (1934–35), 15 volumes; and *Levande svensk litteratur från äldsta tider till våra dagar*, ed. by Sten Selander (1936–38), 24 volumes. Many shorter anthologies designed for Swedish school use are, of course, also available. In English the closest approximations to the broadly inclusive Swedish anthologies are a number of collections in translation of Swedish poetry and of the shorter forms of prose fiction. Of the collections of poetry in translation, two, C. W. Stork's *Anthology of Swedish Lyrics from 1750 to 1925* (New York and London, 1930) and M. S. Allwood's slighter *Swedish Songs and Ballads* (New York, 1950), cover the longest time range, while two others, C. D. Locock's *A Selection from Modern Swedish Poetry* (New York, 1930) and a volume entitled *Twentieth Century Scandinavian Poetry*, with M. S. Allwood as its General Editor, concentrate exclusively on modern poetry. Representative collections of Swedish short stories are to be found in *Modern Swedish Masterpieces* (New York, 1923) and *Sweden's Best Stories* (New York, 1928), both translated by C. W. Stork, and *Modern Swedish Short Stories* (London, 1934), published under the auspices of the Anglo-Swedish Literary Foundation. Mention may also be made here of *Scandinavian Plays of the Twentieth Century* (Princeton and New York, 1944, 1951), two of the three volumes of which are devoted to the contemporary Swedish drama.

Chapter 1. The Origins

On the physical, historical, and cultural backgrounds and on literary developments in Scandinavia in general consult such works in English as Sven Axel Anderson, *Viking Enterprise* (New York, 1936); W. A. Craigie, *The Religion of Ancient Scandinavia* (London, 1906) and *The Icelandic Sagas* (Cambridge, 1913); T. D. Kendrick, *A History of the Vikings* (New York, 1930); Halvdan Koht, "The Scandinavian Kingdoms until the End of the Thirteenth Century" in the *Cambridge Medieval History* (Cambridge, 1929), vi, 362–92, and *The Old Norse Sagas* (New York, 1931); Axel Olrik, *Viking Civilization*, revised after the author's death by Hans Ellekilde (New York, 1930); Bertha S. Phillpotts, *Kindred and Clan in the Middle Ages and After* (Cambridge, 1913) and *Edda and Saga* (New York and London, 1931); William Roos, "The Swedish Part in the Viking Expeditions," *English Historical Review*, vii (1892), 209–23; Haakon Shetelig and Hjalmar Falk, *Scandinavian Archaeology*, tr. by E. V. Gordon (Oxford, 1937); Vilhelm Thomsen, *The Relations between Ancient Russia and Scandinavia* (Oxford and London, 1877); G. Turville-Petre, *The Heroic Age of Scandinavia* (London, 1951); Mary W. Williams, *Social Scandinavia in the Viking Age* (New York, 1920); J. J. A. Worsaae, *The Pre-History of the North*, tr. by H. F. Morland Simpson (London, 1886); and *A Pageant of Old Scandinavia*, ed. by Henry Goddard Leach (New York, 1946). Frans G. Bengtsson's lively, slyly knowing novel *Röde Orm* (tr. *The Long Ships*, 1941, 1945) insists — not without reason — on reducing the "heroic" qualities to somewhat more ordinary and believable proportions than is usually the case in historical novels and popular accounts of the Vikings.

The standard general work on all aspects of Scandinavian life and culture from the beginnings down through the Middle Ages and somewhat beyond is the recently completed *Nordisk kultur*, ed. by J. Brøndum-Nielsen, Sigurd Erixon, Otto von Friesen, and Magnus Olson (Copenhagen, Oslo, and Stockholm, 1931ff.), 30 volumes. In German an excellent work on all of the early Germanic literatures is Andreas Heusler's *Die altgermanische Dichtung* (1923; 2nd ed. 1943).

Translations from the Icelandic of the *The Prose Edda* and *The Poetic Edda* have been rendered respectively by Arthur G. Brodeur (New York, 1916) and Henry Adams Bellows (New York, 1923; new ed. 1957). P. A. Munch and Magnus Olsen's *Norse Mythology* (New York, 1926) is a standard work on mythological lore. Tacitus's notes on the Germanic tribes may be consulted conveniently in English in *The Complete Works of Tacitus*, tr. by A. J. Church and W. J. Brodribb (New York, 1942), and Jordanes's on the Goths in *The Origins and Deeds of the Goths*, tr. by Charles C. Mierow (Princeton, 1908). Of interest on the Swedes in Russia is *The Russian Primary Chronicle*, tr. by Samuel H. Cross (*Harvard Studies in Philology and Literature*, xii [1930], 121ff. *et passim*). English versions of *Heimskringla*, whose opening section, "Ynglingatal," provides a largely legendary account of the famous Ynglinga dynasty at Uppsala, are those by Samuel Laing (1844; available in the Everyman's Library, nrs. 717, 847), William Morris and E. Magnússon, *The Stories of the Kings of Norway* (London, 1893–1905), and Erling Monsen (London and New York, 1932).

For the results of archaeological investigation concerned primarily with Sweden see Oscar Montelius, *The Civilization of Sweden in Heathen Times*, tr. by F. H. Woods (London and New York, 1888) and *Swedish Antiquities Arranged and Described* (1922–30), and for Norway and Sweden H. Hildebrand, *The Industrial Arts of Scandinavia in the Pagan Time* (London, 1883). Geoffrey Bibby's broadly inclusive history of archaeological investigation in Europe *The Testimony of the*

Spade (New York, 1945) concerns itself not infrequently with Scandinavian matters — with, for instance, the brilliant work in archaeological dating by the three Swedes Oscar Montelius, Gerard de Geer, and Lennart Post, and with the ancient Scandinavian rock tracings. Montelius's *Sur les sculptures de rochers de la Suède* (in Compte rendu du congrès internationale d'Anthropologie, Stockholm, 1874) provides an expert early treatment of the rock tracings, and George T. Flom, "South Scandinavian Rock-tracings," *SS*, vii (1921), 1–23, offers some observations in English. A popular but entirely adequate account of research on the rock tracings is Åke Fredsjö, Sverker Janson, and Carl-Axel Moberg's *Hällristningar i Sverige* (1957). The Royal Swedish Embassy in Washington has recently made available for temporary exhibit in American museums a magnificent collection of photographs of these tracings together with an illustrated catalog of the collection.

On the runes there is no up-to-date book in English, but Elias Wessén's article "Swedish Rune Stones," *ASR*, xxi (1933), 208–17, provides a thoroughly authoritative brief treatment of the subject. Early works in English that may be examined are three by G. Stephens: *The Old-Northern Runic Monuments of Scandinavia and England* (London and Copenhagen, 1866–1901), *Handbook of the Old Northern Runic Monuments of Scandinavia and England* (London, 1884), and *The Runes, Whence They Came* (London and Copenhagen, 1894). Standard general works in Swedish on the runes are Erik Brate's *Sveriges runinskrifter* (2nd ed. 1928) and Otto von Friesen's *Runorna i Sverige, en kortfattad översikt* (Uppsala, 3rd ed. 1928). To those interested in *Beowulf* and its partly Swedish backgrounds Knut Stjerna's early archaeological investigations in *Essays on Questions Concerned with the Old English Poem of Beowulf*, ed. and tr. by John Clark Hall (London, 1912) should be checked against later findings in Beowulf scholarship as reflected in such works as W. W. Lawrence's *Beowulf and the Epic Tradition* (Cambridge, Mass., 1928) and R. W. Chambers' *Beowulf. An Introduction to the Study of the Poem* (Cambridge, 2nd ed. 1932; 3rd ed., with a Supplement by C. L. Wrenn, 1959).

Efforts to reconstruct a hypothetical ("lost") Swedish literature from ancient times have been made by Henrik Schück in the first volume of Schück and Warburg's *Illustrerad svensk litteraturhistoria* (1926), by Birger Nerman, *Studier i Svärges hedna litteratur* (Uppsala, 1913), and by Ture Hederström, *Fornsagor och eddakväden* (1917–27). Two definitive books on ancient Sweden are Sune Lindqvist's *Svensk forntidsliv* (1944) and *Uppsala högar och Otharshögen* (1936), the former treating all aspects of Swedish life in the period immediately preceding the Middle Ages, the latter (which includes a rather full English summary) dealing with certain famous burial mounds from prehistoric times. Thede Palme has investigated exhaustively the Old Uppsala religious traditions in *Uppsalalunden och Uppsalatemplet* (Lund, 1941), and Birger Nerman has written in more popular form of related matters in *Gamla Uppsala — svearikets hjärtpunkt* (1943). For a sketchy, highly popular account of the Uppsala burial mounds and related matters see Birgit Magnusdotter-Hedström's article "Old Uppsala," *ASR*, xx (1932), 492–500.

Chapter 2. The Middle Ages

The standard general work as mentioned above is *Nordisk kultur*, i–xxx. A "lexicon" on the Scandinavian Middle Ages, *Kulturhistoriskt lexikon för nordisk medeltid från vikingatiden till reformationstid*, is now being issued, the fourth volume (*Epistolarium — Frälsebonde*) having appeared in 1959. Erik Lönnroth's *Från svensk medeltid* (1959), the most recent general work on the Swedish Middle Ages, is a lively and authoritative treatment of religious, political, and economic cross currents from Viking times to Gustav Vasa. In French, Lucien Musset's *Les Peuples scandinaves au Moyen Age* (Paris, 1951) provides a dependable historical survey. Items in English on the Swedish Middle Ages strictly speaking are rare, and those of importance rarer. Except for C. H. R. Steenstrup's *The Medieval Popular Ballad*, tr. by E. G. Cox (Boston, 1914), and Henry Goddard Leach's *Angevin Britain and Scandinavia* (Cambridge, Mass., 1921), the English-speaking reader with no familiarity with Swedish must confine himself almost exclusively for his knowledge of the Swedish Middle Ages and its literature to general histories such as Ingvar Andersson's *A History of Sweden* (London, 1956), to certain chapters in works concerned primarily with pre-medieval periods listed above under "The Origins" (Olrik's chapter on the ballad in *Viking Civilization*, for instance), to a number of hardly satisfactory biographies of Saint Birgitta, and to a scattering of articles popular or learned in English and American journals. Even Steenstrup and Leach are concerned only in part with Sweden, Steenstrup's book dealing primarily with the Danish ballad and Leach's work including Swedish material in larger Scandinavian contexts.

The famous work by Adam of Bremen which provides us with an early account of the coming of Christianity to Sweden has recently appeared in English under the title *History of the Archbishops of Hamburg-Bremen*, tr. with an Introduction and Notes by Francis J. Tschan (New York, 1959). C. J. A. Oppermann's *The English Missionaries in Sweden and Finland* (London, 1937) handles its sources so uncritically that it can hardly be depended upon in matters of detail. Much more satisfactory in these religious contexts are a number of books in Swedish such as Helge Ljungberg's *Den nordiska religionen och kristendomen* (Uppsala, 1938) and K. B. Westman's *Den svenska kyrkans utveckling från S:t Bernhards tidevarv till Innocentius III:s* (1915), and four reasonably sound though relatively popular works, Toni Schmid's *Sveriges kristnande* (1934), Birger Nerman's *När Sverige kristnades* (1945), Helge Ljungberg's *Hur kristendomen kom till Sverige* (1946), and Sven Ulric Palme's *Kristendomens genombrott i Sverige* (1959), the last of which combines stylistic facility and interpretative skill with a sober awareness of the latest scholarly findings in a field of investigation where too often in the past legend and myth have tended to take over.

On medieval literature in Sweden exclusive of the ballads see Rolf Pipping's "Den fornsvenska litteraturen" in *Nordisk kultur*, VIII:A. ¶ In France, Ernest Renan's lively critical intelligence has been fascinated by Petrus de Dacia, "Sweden's first author" (cf. *Revue des deux Mondes*, 1880, and *Hist. litt. de la France*, 1881). Among Swedish treatments of Petrus de Dacia are Henrik Schück's *Vår förste författare* (1916), Harald Schiller's "Petrus de Dacias helgonbiografi," *OoB*, XXXV (1936), 257–67, and Margit Abenius's review article "Kärlek i trettonde seklet," *BLM*, XIX (1950), 360–65. ¶ Of the three biographies of Saint Birgitta which have appeared in English in the last quarter century — Edith Peacey's *Saint Birgitta of Sweden* (London, 1934), Helen M. D. Redpath's *God's Ambassadress, Saint Bridget of Sweden* (Milwaukee, Wisc., 1947), and Johannes Jørgensen's *Saint Bridget of Sweden*, tr. by Ingeborg Lund (London and New York, 1954) — only the last is of some distinction though for literary rather than strictly historical reasons. As a product of the most distinguished Catholic convert among modern Danish literary figures, Jørgensen's book is naturally somewhat slanted and uncritical. Jørgensen's countryman of a century ago, Fr. Hammerich, has in *Den hellige Birgitta og Kirken i Norden* (Copenhagen, 1863) produced a work on Birgitta which for its day was of first importance and still today is among the best works on the Swedish saint. In French, C. de Flavigny's *Sainte Birgitte de Suède* (Paris, 1892; 3rd ed. 1912) has provided orthodox Catholics with a satisfactory Birgitta book. A more recent French item is F. Vernet's "Birgitte de Suède" in *Dictionnaire de spiritualité ascétique et mystique*, I (Paris, 1937). Among the more sound Birgitta studies in Swedish are K. B. Westman's *Birgitta-studier*: I (Uppsala, 1911), Toni Schmid's *Birgitta och hennes uppenbarelser* (Lund, 1940), Erik Noreen's "Heliga Birgitta som svensk författare," *OoB*, L (1941), 289–97, and a number of studies by Emilia Fogelklou, two of which are chiefly of general interest, a book entitled simply *Birgitta* (1919; new ed. 1955) and an article in *OoB*, LIV (1945), 49–59, which examines in some detail Birgitta in modern Swedish literature, especially in Strindberg's dramatic production and Heidenstam's prose fiction. Strindberg's chief portrait of Birgitta is to be found in *Folkungasagan* (1899; tr. *The Saga of the Folkungs*, 1929), Heidenstam's in a novel, *Heliga Birgittas pilgrimsfärd* (Saint Birgitta's Pilgrimage, 1901). Both Strindberg's *Saga of the Folkungs* and Heidenstam's novel *Folkungaträdet* (1905, 1907; tr. *The Tree of the Folkungs*, 1925) provide vivid though not always trustworthy glimpses into general political and religious conditions in the Swedish Middle Ages, Strindberg's drama being concerned with the last fateful years of the Folkung dynasty, Heidenstam's novel with the half-legendary, half-historical backgrounds of the rise of the first Folkungs to political power.

Secular literature in the Swedish Middle Ages has been the subject of considerable research by Swedish experts and has engaged the occasional attention of some English and American scholars. The provincial laws have recently been rendered into modern Swedish (*Svenska landskapslagar*. Tolkade och förklarade av Åke Holmbäck och Elias Wessén, I–V, 1933–46) and have been subjected to very satisfactory literary analysis by the editor-translators of this modern Swedish edition as well as by Carl Ivar Ståhle in *Ny illustrerad svensk litteraturhistoria*, I, 39–52. It would serve no useful purpose here to enter into the intricacies of scholarly literature on the medieval chronicles and the so-called *Eufemiavisor*. This scholarship concerns itself largely with knotty problems of authorship and dating and reflects considerable disagreement among the scholars involved. Those who may be interested in sampling the subject matter of the *Eufemiavisor* and related tales in a popular English version are referred to a retelling of some of this narrative material in Henrik Schück's *Medieval Stories*, tr. by W. F. Harvey (London, 1902).

Of much greater interest to the general reader than the literature on the chronicles and the *Eufemiavisor* is the relatively rich body of material on "folk literature" of various kinds – the ballad, the folk tale, folk sayings, and proverbs. C. W. von Sydow's *Våra folkminnen* (Lund, 1913) provides an excellent popular introduction to the whole range of folk literature together with practical suggestions for those engaged in collecting the various kinds of folk material. Though work published in English on Swedish folk literature is not extensive in amount, it is sufficiently substantial in quality. It is, however, restricted almost entirely to the ballad, and with an exception or two (see Per G. Stensland's sketchy survey "Medieval Swedish Folk Songs," *Germanic Review*, XX [1945], 287–98) it treats the specifically Swedish ballad only in passing, as providing interesting parallels to the more extensive ballad survivals of Denmark. But this is not as unfortunate as it might seem, for the ballad, like all folk literature, is international in its ramifications and interrelations, and the interrelations among ballads of the various Scandinavian countries are often particularly close. The most authoritative surveys available in English on the Scandinavian ballad are C. H. R. Steenstrup's *The Medieval Popular*

Ballad (Boston, 1914) and Axel Olrik's chapter on the ballad in his *Viking Civiliza-tion* (New York, 1930). Olrik has also provided an Introduction to *A Book of Danish Ballads*, tr. by E. M. Smith-Dampier (Princeton and New York, 1939). Other works of value in English are W. J. Entwistle's *European Balladry* (Oxford, 1939) and E. K. Chambers' *English Literature at the Close of the Middle Ages* (Ox-ford, 1945), the first of which places the Scandinavian ballad tradition in its larger European contexts, the second in its more narrowly British world of relations. B. S. Hustvedt's *Ballad Criticism in Scandinavia and Great Britain* (New York, 1916) and *Ballad Books and Ballad Men* (Cambridge, Mass., 1930) concentrate primarily on the antiquarian and scholarly activities of ballad enthusiasts since the Middle Ages. There is unfortunately no Swedish equivalent to the English version of Dan-ish ballads translated by Smith-Dampier, but some acceptable French renderings of Swedish ballads are included in L. Pineau's *Le Romancero scandinave* (Collection de contes et chansons populaires: xxx, Paris, 1906). Though the scholarly methods and conclusions of Sverker Ek, one of the chief Swedish balladists, have not always been accepted by the experts, his general surveys of the Swedish ballad (*Den svenska folkvisan*, 1924, and a section on the ballad in *Nordisk kultur*, IX, 38–54) remain on the whole quite satisfactory. Ek is together with Erik Blomberg responsible for the popular ballad anthology *Svenska folkvisor i urval* (Stockholm, 1939). On the political ballads of the late Middle Ages see Karl-Ivar Hildeman, *Politiska visor från Sveriges semmedeltid* (Uppsala, 1950). Hildeman has also contributed an ex-cellent chapter on Swedish ballads generally to *Ny illustrerad svensk litteratur-historia*, I, 223–72.

The Swedish folk tale in its various manifestations has been subjected to exten-sive investigation particularly by C. W. von Sydow, whose general surveys in *Nordisk kultur*, VI, 211–39, IX, 96–139, 199–239, and in *Våra folksagor* (1941) are of first importance. Because of the international ramifications of folk-tale motifs and traditions, the serious student of the Swedish folk tale should acquaint himself with *Folk-lore Fellows Communications* (1910ff.), a journal-series originating in Fin-land but conceived from its beginnings as an international scholarly venture con-cerned with folkloristic materials of the entire world. Stith Thompson's *The Folk-tale* (New York, 1946) is by far the most solid work in English on its subject. On Swedish folk sayings, proverbs, and riddles Fredrik Ström's three books *Svenskarna i sina ordspråk* (1926), *Svenska ordstäv* (1929), and *Svenska folkgåtor* (1937) are of considerable value despite the author's failure to observe strict scholarly procedures in the collecting and analysis of the materials involved. A Swedish study which stresses the "literary" as distinguished from the "folk" origins of the medieval rid-dle is Åke Campbell's "Om litterärt och folkligt i svenska gåtsamlingar från medeltiden till 1900," *Saga och Sed* (1942), pp.27–42. Erik Wahlgren's article "A Swedish-Latin Parallel to the *Joca Monacorum*," *Modern Philology*, XXXVI (1938–39), 239–45, offers some notes on an early riddle list of a religious-catechetical kind.

Chapter 3. Religious Reformation and Cultural Decline

Very little reliable material is available in English on the Swedish Reformation, and what little we have is restricted almost entirely to political and religious rather than literary considerations. In the absence of any adequate up-to-date English treatment of the political scene in Sweden in the first decades of the sixteenth cen-tury, the English-speaking reader may be referred to the English version (1843) of J. W. von Archenholz's *Geschichte Gustaf Vasa, König von Schweden* (Tübingen, 1801) and to P. B. Watson's account of the early career of the King in *The Swedish*

Revolution under Gustaf Vasa (London, 1889). An old but liberal and humane history of the Swedish Reformation from a distinguished Swedish pen is L. A. Anjou's *The History of the Reformation in Sweden*, tr. by Henry M. Mason (New York, 1859). See also for this and later periods the far less satisfactory J. Wordsworth's *The National Church in Sweden* (London, 1911). Michael Roberts, *Gustavus Adolphus, a History of Sweden, 1611–1632* (London, New York, and Toronto, 1953, 1958), I, 350ff., provides an excellent general treatment of the Swedish Church in the sixteenth century.

In consequence of the spotty non-Swedish coverage, the student who wishes to get much beyond the threshold of the literary scene in Sweden in the sixteenth century must turn to Swedish sources, of which there is a sufficiency, first, in the standard literary histories, second, in scattered passages in biographical works, and third, in special literary studies of one kind or other. Two brilliant books by Ingvar Andersson, the biography *Erik XIV* (4th ed. 1951) and a collection of essays entitled *Svenskt och europeiskt femtonhundratal* (Lund, 1943), provide penetrating glimpses into various aspects of sixteenth-century cultural life. Knut Hagberg's collection of royal vignettes *Av Vasarnas ätt* (2nd ed. 1929) is, though historical and psychological in primary emphasis, also constantly aware of the literary and artistic sensitivities of certain members of the famous dynasty established by Gustav Vasa. ¶ Though no definitive biographies of either Gustav Vasa or Olaus Petri exist, we have a number of more or less popular Swedish "lives," the most recent of which are Sven Wikberg's two-volume *Gustaf Vasa* (1944, 1945) and Robert Murray's *Olaus Petri* (1952). On Olaus Petri as a historian there are two works, L. Stavenow's early, relatively popular *Olaus Petri som historieskrivare* (Göteborg, 1898) and Gunnar T. Westin's definitive *Historieskrivaren Olaus Petri* (Lund, 1946). On Olaus Petri as a religious thinker and reformer we have a number of works, among which may be mentioned two books in English, C. J. I. Bergendoff's *Olaus Petri and the Ecclesiastical Transformation in Sweden* (New York, 1928) and Eric E. Yelverton's *The Manual of Olaus Petri* (London, 1953). Though some of the problems raised in connection with the formidable accumulation of scholarship on the first Swedish translations of the Bible (see *Ny illustrerad svensk litteraturhistoria*, I, 392–93, and Tigerstedt, *Svensk litteraturhistoria*, p.517) are of only peripheral interest to the student of literature, where this scholarship is concerned with stylistic matters in general and with Olaus Petri's part in the translations in particular these scholarly investigations are of basic literary importance. We have nothing in English on either Gustav Vasa or Olaus Petri as important prose stylists. ¶ With the brothers Magnus and such seventeenth-century writers as Messenius and Wivallius, however, Michael Roberts is concerned in passing in his section on literature in *Gustavus Adolphus 1611–1626* (1953). Edward Lynam's *Carta marina of Olaus Magnus* (Jenkintown, 1949) is an authoritative work in English on Olaus Magnus as a cartographer. The brothers Magnus have also been the subject of a brief French study, Jules Martin's "Deux confesseurs de la foi au XVIᵉ siècle" in *L'Université catholique* (1932). An important Swedish work on the period, J. Nordström's brilliant *De yverbornes ö* (1934), fits Johannes Magnus into the general intellectual contexts of his day and later. ¶ On Messenius and Wivallius the following studies are of chief general value: Henrik Schück's biography *Messenius* (1920), Hilding Lidell's *Studier i Johannes Messenius' dramer* (Uppsala, 1935), Henrik Schück's *Lars Wivallius, hans lif och dikter* (1893–95), and Sverker Ek's two works *Studier i Wivalliusvisornas kronologi* (Uppsala, 1921) and *Lars Wivallius' visdiktning* (1930). Schück has in addition written a popular fictionalized account of Wivallius's fantastic escapades in various parts of Europe, entitled *En äfventyrare: värklighetsroman från det trettioåriga krigets tid* (1918).

Strindberg's interest in the fifteenth and sixteenth centuries bore fruit in his dramatic production throughout his life, to begin with in the vigorous Reformation drama *Mäster Olof* (1872), continued in *Gustaf Vasa* (1899) and *Erik XIV* (1899), and concluded in *The Last of the Knights* (1908) and *The Regent* (1909). Some of Strindberg's historical short stories *Svenska öden och äfventyr* (1883ff.) deal with certain of the economic and social effects of the political and religious upheaval of the time.

Chapter 4. Political Expansion and Literary Renaissance

The seventeenth century in Sweden is considerably more accessible to those who do not read Swedish than is the preceding century, thanks to the world role which Sweden temporarily came to play in the new century and the fascination which three of her monarchs, Gustavus Adolphus, his daughter Christina, and Charles XII, have exercised over their contemporaries and those who came after. Since their time scarcely a generation has passed in which one or more French or German or English or Swedish biographies of these monarchs have not appeared. Gustavus Adolphus was already in his day a legendary "folk hero" among Protestant peoples everywhere in Europe, and he has never ceased to occupy the attention of historians. Christina's enigmatic personality and her renouncement of the throne in consequence of her conversion to Catholicism have again and again intrigued biographical practitioners of various competences and skills. And Charles XII's equally enigmatic character and tragic-heroic career have fascinated no less critical eighteenth-century intelligences than those of Voltaire and Samuel Johnson, and since their day the hero-king has engaged the labors of a dozen or more biographers and has been in Sweden the subject of an enormous amount of scholarly investigation. Most of the concern of the biographers of these Swedish monarchs has naturally been with political and military matters and with the psychological problems which Christina and Charles XII in particular pose, but the cultural interests of Gustavus Adolphus and Christina were such that no competent biographer could ignore what was taking place in general cultural and literary matters during their reigns.

Of the numerous biographical works on Gustavus Adolphus two may be mentioned here, Nils Ahnlund's *Gustaf Adolf the Great* (New York, 1940), an English version of the standard Swedish biography, and Michael Roberts' impressive two-volume *Gustavus Adolphus, a History of Sweden, 1611–1632* (London, New York, and Toronto, 1953, 1958), the latter work including excellent summary sections on education, the arts, and literature in fifteenth- and sixteenth-century Sweden. See also Lydia Wahlström's "Gustavus Adolphus: a tercentenary," *ASR*, xx (1932), 537–45, 571–78.

Works on Christina are on the whole less satisfactory, partly because her personality is so baffling and partly because her conversion to Catholicism has too often made her the object of partisan judgments. Especially unsatisfactory are the numerous biographies of Christina in English, and the English-speaking reader's concern with the Queen can therefore best be served by Ruth Stephan's distinguished novel *The Flight* (New York, 1956). A brief popular sketch is contained in the Swedish historian Carl Grimberg's "Kristina, Daughter of Gustavus Adolphus," *ASR*, xv (1927), 525–35. Some interesting though often stuffy and prejudiced contemporary observations on Christina's court and on Swedish life in general in the mid-seventeenth century are to be found in B. Whitelocke's *A Journal* of the Swedish Embassy in the Years 1653 and 1654 from the Commonwealth of England, Scotland and Ireland (London, 1772; new ed. 1855). Representative of the better longer studies in Swedish are Curt Weibull's Drottning Kristina: studier och forskningar (1931; 2nd ed. 1934), Elis Essen-Möller's Drottning Christina: en människostudie ur läkaresynpunkt (Lund, 1937), and Ernst Cassirer's Drottning Christina och Descartes: ett bidrag till 1600-talets idéhistoria (1940). Brief contributions of particular interest are two items by Johan Nordström, "Cartesius och drottning Kristinas omvändelse" (Lychnos, 1941, pp.248–90), which takes issue with Cassirer on some points, and "Några notiser om drottning Kristinas akademier" (Lychnos, 1944, pp.333–41), which adds to our previous knowledge about the learned academies at Christina's court. On the court as a center for the arts and sciences one may consult, besides Nordström's note in Lychnos, 1940, Harald Wieselgren, "Drottning Kristinas bibliotek och bibliotekarier," Vitterhetsakademiens handlingar, XXXIII (1901), Gustaf Ljunggren, Svenska dramat intill slutet af sjuttonde århundradet (Lund and Copenhagen, 1864) and Agne Beijer, Slottsteatrarna på Drottningholm och Gripsholm, I (1937) on the court ballets, and Karl Erik Steneberg, Kristinatidens måleri (1955) on painting and the aesthetic interests generally of Christina's court. A short but stimulating and authoritative general item on Christina is available in Knut Hagberg's Av Vasarnas ätt (1927). The most recent Swedish studies on Christina are Sven Stolpe's two works, the dissertation Från stoicism till mystik: studier i drottning Kristinas maximer and Kristinastudier, both from 1959.

Voltaire's frequently reprinted L'Histoire de Charles XII (1731) is most conveniently available in English in Everyman's Library, nr. 270 (1925). A more recent but still outdated and sketchy "life" is R. N. Bain's Charles XII and the Collapse of the Swedish Empire 1682–1718 (New York and London, 1895). The two most recent biographies are Otto Heintz's three-volume König Karl XII von Schweden (Berlin, 1958) and the brilliant Swedish essayist Frans G. Bengtsson's Karl XII:s levnad (1935, 1936), tr. into German by Konstantin Reichardt. Heintz's study is the standard work on Charles XII. After this bibliography went to press, Bengtsson's biography appeared in English under the title The Life of Charles XII, King of Sweden 1697–1718 (Stockholm, 1960).

For a meticulous scholarly account of economic conditions during the Great Power period see Heckscher's An Economic History of Sweden, and for a stimulating but perhaps somewhat exaggerated account of the unhappy condition of the Swedish peasantry during the period Axel Strindberg's Bondenöd och stormaktsdröm (1937). See also in these contexts Bertil Walden, "Vardagsliv och lyx under stormaktstidevarvet" in Svenska folket genom tiderna (Malmö, 1939), v, 267–300.

Among the Swedish poets who have celebrated the memory of Charles XII and his people in verse are Geijer, Tegnér, and Snoilsky, while Heidenstam has retold the story of the nation at home and the King and his armies abroad in the stirring prose of Karolinerna (tr. The Charles Men, 1897–98). For a detailed treatment of Charles XII in Swedish literature down through the first decades of the nineteenth century see Olov Westerlund's dissertation Karl XII i svensk litteratur från Dahlstierna till Tegnér (Lund, 1951). The Sweden of Viktor Rydberg's historical novel Fribytaren på Östersjön (tr. The Freebooter of the Baltic, 1857) is that of Charles XII's father, while the backgrounds of Vilhelm Moberg's anti-Nazi propaganda novel Rid i natt! (tr. Ride This Night!, 1941) are those of Christina's day, as seen partly, it would seem, through the eyes of Axel Strindberg in his above-mentioned book. Except for the period leading up to and including Gustav Vasa's and his sons' occupation of the throne, no era in Swedish history has received such extensive coverage in August Strindberg's dramas as the Great Power period, though professional historians have been on the whole more critical of Strindberg's reconstruction of history in the plays *Gustaf Adolf* (1900), *Karl XII* (1901), and *Kristina* (1903) than with regard to the earlier Vasa cycle. That Strindberg partly for purely theatrical reasons took liberties particularly with the historical figure of Christina is undeniable, but it is also undeniable that he has made Christina as well as Gustavus Adolphus and Charles XII *live* as they never before had lived in literature or the theater. Of these three figures Strindberg personally has been most fascinated (usually antipathetically) by Charles XII, who appears with recurrent regularity in Strindberg's work, most interestingly outside the drama *Karl XII* in the historical tale "Vid likvakan i Tistedalen" (At the Deathwatch in Tistedalen, 1890).

The most recent general treatments of literary developments in the Great Power period are parts of Sten Lindroth's "Reformation och humanism" and Carl Fehrman's "Karolinsk barock och klassicism" in *Ny illustrerad svensk litteraturhistoria*, I, 275–364, and II, 3–81. Especially worthy of mention among the earlier inclusive treatments of the literature of the period are Gunnar Castrén's *Stormaktstidens diktning* (Helsingfors, 1907) and the same scholar's section on the period in the first volume of *Svenska litteraturens historia* (new rev. ed. 1929). An old but still illuminating study of the comic strain in this literature is E. Wrangel's *Det carolinska tidehvarfvets komiska diktning* (Lund, 1888). On the technical features of verse see Otto Sylwan's *Den svenska versen från 1600-talets början* (Göteborg, 1926–34), on the drama Gustaf Ljunggren's *Svenska dramat intill slutet på sjuttonde århundradet* (Lund, 1864), and on the beginnings of prose fiction Fredrik Böök's *Romanens och prosaberättelsens historia i Sverige till 1809* (1907). On the increasing cultural contacts with Holland and Germany see E. Wrangel's investigations in *Lunds Universitets Årsskrift*, XXXIII, XXXV (1897, 1899), with England Tönnes Kleberg's two studies in *Lychnos* (Uppsala, 1942, 1943), K. M. Lea's note "English Players at the Swedish Court," *Modern Language Review*, XXVI (1931), 78–80, and Ethel Seaton's encyclopedic investigations in *Literary Relations of England and Scandinavia in the Seventeenth Century* (Oxford, 1935).

Though such early Stiernhielm studies as Birger Swartling's biography (Uppsala dissertation, 1909) and Hjalmar Lindroth's *Stiernhielms Hercules* (1913) remain valuable to the student of Georg Stiernhielm, recent Stiernhielm scholarship as represented in Johan Nordström's Introduction to his edition of Stiernhielm's *Filosofiska fragment* (1924), Axel Friberg's *Den svenske Herkules* (1945), and various studies by Per Wieselgren has thrown a great deal of new light especially over Stiernhielm's idea world. Per Wieselgren has also written the short biography *Georg Stiernhielm* (1948), which in brief form brings us up to date on the findings of recent investigators. On Stiernhielm's activities as a Court poet in the composition of so-called *upptåg*, dramatic spectacles with elaborate allegorical implications, widely popular in European court life of the time, see Mårten Liljegren's very illuminating "Stiernhielms riddarspel," *OoB*, LX (1951), 547–56.

The fundamental work on the fantastic "Gothic" speculations of Olaus Rudbeck and his predecessors is Johan Nordström's *De yverbornes ö* (Stockholm, 1934). In his Gustavus Adolphus biography Michael Roberts provides in English an excellent survey of the philological, historiographical, and runological ramifications of the Gothic speculations prior to their final extravagant apotheosis in Rudbeck's *Atland eller Manheim* (1679ff.). In volume five of *Svenska folket genom tiderna* Eskil Källquist has contributed a brief sketch of Rudbeck's speculations together with a general survey of the intellectual and literary world of the day in Sweden. On Olaus Rudbeck as a scientist Nils von Hofsten has provided an excellent short account in *Swedish Men of Science 1650-1940* (1952).

On the poets of the period mention should be made of Erik Axel Karlfeldt's *Skalden Lucidor* (1914), Magnus von Platen's *Johan Runius: en biografi* (1954), Fredrik Böök's "Runius" in *Stridsmän och sångare* (1910), Martin Lamm's *Gunno Dahlstierna* (1946), and Lamm's chapter on Jacob Frese's pietistic inclinations in *Upplysningstidens romantik* (1918), I, 140-46. As a modern poet's portrait of a fellow poet of three hundred years ago, Karlfeldt's study of Lucidor is as sensitive in its treatment of the earlier poet as it is rich and penetrating in its account of the Renaissance world of which Lucidor was a part.

Two items should finally be noted on the dramatist-scientist Urban Hiärne, Olof Strandberg's *Urban Hjärnes ungdom och diktning* (1942) and Sten Lindroth's "Urban Hjärne" in *Swedish Men of Science 1650-1940*.

Chapter 5. The Period of the Enlightenment

Except for the considerable body of material in English on Swedenborg and Linné, and on other scientists of their day, published work in English on the Swedish eighteenth century is very limited, consisting of a single larger literary study (W. G. Johnson's dissertation, *James Thomson's Influence on Swedish Literature in the Eighteenth Century*, Urbana, Ill., 1936), some reasonably extensive biographical records on Gustaf III, a number of brochures, journal articles, and brief notices on the Gustavian theater, and an item or two of no particular importance on the major poet of the century, Carl Michael Bellman. For secondary sources in matters *strictly literary* we must therefore turn very largely to Swedish items. An old but essentially sound historical and cultural survey which covers the period down to Gustaf III's *coup d'état* in 1772 is Ludvig Stavenow's *Frihetstiden: dess epoker och kulturliv* (Göteborg, 2nd ed. 1907). Shorter popular literary surveys have appeared in *Svenska folket genom tiderna*, VI and VII, which volumes also contain survey articles on many other aspects of eighteenth-century Swedish life and culture.

Of the more solid specialized works Sylwan's *Den svenska versen från 1600-talets början* is especially full in its treatment of poetic developments in the eighteenth century, as is Böök's *Romanens och prosaberättelsens historia i Sverige intill 1809* on prose fiction. Elof Ehnmark's *Studier i svensk realism: 1700-talstradition och Fredrik Cederborgh* (Uppsala, 1930) is also valuable, particularly on realistic comic and satiric trends in eighteenth-century prose. Two monumental works which examine with exemplary skill and learning the persistence of what may be called Romantic elements in a period otherwise largely dominated by the ideas and attitudes of the Enlightenment are Anton Blanck's *Den nordiska renässansen i sjuttonhundratalets litteratur* (1911), a wide-ranging comparative investigation of "Gothic" enthusiasms in England, France, and Germany as well as in Denmark and Sweden, and Martin Lamm's *Upplysningstidens romantik* (1918, 1920), I-II, an exhaustive study of, as its subtitle indicates, "the mystical-sentimental strain" in the Sweden of the eighteenth century. A popular sketch of the Swedish theater in the eighteenth century is provided by Lennart Breitholtz in a collective work *Det glada Sverige: våra fester och högtider genom tiderna* (1947), II, 935-1028, and a magnificent, richly illustrated monograph on the famous Swedish court theaters at Drottningholm and Gripsholm is available in Agne Beijer's *Slottsteatrarna på Drottningholm och Gripsholm*, I (1937), which provides also an excellent retrospective examination of Swedish theater history, tracing the relations between an earlier baroque style and the later French-classical tradition represented in the Swedish Gustavian theater. Socio-logical aspects of Swedish literature in the late eighteenth and early nineteenth cen-turies are subjected to searching examination in Victor Svanberg's "Medelklass-realism, 1–3," *S*, n.f. xxiv (1943), 111–73, xxv (1944), 1–99, and xxvii (1946), 102–39. The relatively unimportant Swedish ballad criticism of the century is placed in its larger and richer Danish and British contexts in S. B. Hustvedt's *Ballad Criticism in Scandinavia and Great Britain during the Eighteenth Century* (New York, 1916).

Studies on the impact of ideas and literary trends from abroad, especially from France and England, are rather numerous, at times being incorporated into works not primarily comparative in emphasis (like Lamm's *Upplysningstidens romantik* and his *Olof Dalin*), at other times taking on the form more or less exclusively of influence studies. Representative of the latter are (in addition to W. G. Johnson's work previously mentioned) E. Wrangel's "Tysklands litteratur under 1700-talet före Klopstock och dess förhållande till den svenska," *S*, xxii (1901), 47–64, Anton Blanck's "Sverige och den franska litteraturen" in *Bellman vid skiljovägen och andra studier* (1941), T. Hasselqvist's *'Ossian' i den svenska dikten och litteraturen* (Malmö, 1895), Harald Elovson's *Amerika i svensk litteratur 1750–1820* (Lund, 1930), Nils Molin's *Shakespeare och Sverige intill 1800-talets mitt* (Göteborg, 1931), and Carl Fehrman's *Kyrkogårdsromantik från Thomas Gray till Carl Michael Bellman* (Lund, 1954). Carl Fehrman devotes also considerable space to the eighteenth century in his fascinating comparative study of prevailing symbols of death in *Liemannen, Thanatos och Dödens Ängel: studier i 1700- och 1800-talens litterära ikonologi* (Lund, 1957). Both of Fehrman's works include English summaries.

The artistically most sensitive, though not always the soundest, interpreter of Swedish cultural life of the second half of the eighteenth century is the poet-critic of a century and more later, Oscar Levertin, whose early academic training led him into investigations of the Gustavian theater (*Teater och drama under Gustaf III*, dissertation 1889) and whose later critical work resulted in the publication of two monographs (*Gustaf III som dramatisk författare*, 1894, and *Från Gustaf III:s dagar*, 1896) as well as a number of brilliant critical essays on such representative figures of the day as fru Nordenflycht, Gyllenborg, Creutz, and Bellman (see L's *Samlade skrifter*, 1907ff.). An unfinished manuscript on Linné was published after Levertin's death. Among the most delightful prose pieces from Levertin's pen which have to do with the eighteenth century are his *Rococonoveller* (1899), delicately sensitive rococo pastiches at once subtly critical and playfully creative. Strindberg, who has also tried his hand at a literary re-creation of the late eighteenth-century world in the play *Gustaf III* (1903), reveals himself in this play as a far less initiated student of Gustavian preciosities than Levertin, but he is much more aware than is Levertin of the realistic sides of the life of the day and succeeds on the whole well in depict-ing the King in his dual historical role as monarch and theatrical enthusiast.

Since Swedenborg and Linné (Linnaeus) belong to the world outside Sweden almost as much as to their native land, the vast accumulation of books and articles which have been written about them comes from non-Swedish pens as often as from Swedish. In fact, so much has been published in English alone on Swedenborg and Linné that only the advanced student need pursue his Swedenborgian or Lin-néan studies outside English sources. While no broadly inclusive bibliography on works about Swedenborg exists, A. H. Stroh and Greta Ekelöf's *An Abridged Chronological List of the Works of Emanuel Swedenborg* (Uppsala and Stock-holm, 1910) accounts for the works by Swedenborg written or published during his life-time, and James Hyde's *A Bibliography of the Works of Emanuel Sweden-*

borg (London, 1906) provides exhaustive listings of editions of Swedenborg's works in all languages down to the early twentieth century. More up-to-date bibliographical material of various kinds is available in the more recent biographical studies. Though the most penetrating general study on Swedenborg is perhaps his countryman Martin Lamm's *Swedenborg: en studie öfver hans utveckling till mystiker och andeskådare* (1915), a number of adequate general works in English have appeared, the most recent and among the best being Signe Toksvig's *Emanuel Swedenborg, Scientist and Mystic* (New Haven, 1948) and Cyriel O. Sigstedt's *The Swedenborg Epic* (New York, 1952). Signe Toksvig has also written a brief essay "Emmanuel Swedenborg, Stockholmer," *ASR*, xxxvi (1948), 31–36, and Marguerite Block a popular review of Swedenborg's Swedish backgrounds and reputation, "A Prophet in His Own Country," *ASR*, xxiv (1936), 24–38. A lively, informative item in English on Swedenborg by the Swedish critic Magnus von Platen has appeared in *Industria International 1959–60* (1959), pp.114, 148, 150.

Some interesting notes on Swedenborg's impact on early nineteenth-century New England culture together with a rapid survey of Swedenborg's life and work based on Martin Lamm's book are provided by David F. Swenson in *Swedes in America 1638–1938* (New Haven, 1938), pp.262–78. In German a sound general work is *Emanuel Swedenborg: Naturforscher und Seher* (Munich, 1948) by Ernst Benz, who has also published the special study *Swedenborg in Deutschland* (Frankfurt-am-Main, 1947). Among the literary men and artists who have been fascinated by Swedenborg are Blake, who was strongly influenced by the Swedish mystic; Emerson, who devotes to him an essay, "Swedenborg, or the Mystic," in *Representative Men* (1850); Balzac, whose novel *Seraphita* (1835) derives directly out of Swedenborgian speculations; William Butler Yeats, who includes a piece entitled "Swedenborg, Mediums, and the Desolate Places," dated 1914, published in *If I Were Four and Twenty* (Dublin, 1940); and Strindberg, who not only dedicated the famous "Blue Books" (Blå Böckerna, 1907ff.) "To Emanuel Swedenborg, Teacher and Leader" but refers constantly to Swedenborg's ideas and teachings in the pages of the "Blue Books." Among the studies on Swedenborg's influence on literary men and literary and artistic trends outside Sweden are Waldo C. Peebles, "Swedenborg's Influence on Goethe," *Germanic Review*, viii (1933), 147–56, two articles on Swedenborg and Blake, one by Mark Schorer in *Modern Philology*, xxxvi (1938–39), 157–78, the other by David V. Erdman in *Comparative Literature*, v (1953), 247–57, a lengthy study by Pauline Bernheim entitled *Balzac und Swedenborg* (Berlin, 1914), and a broadly inclusive examination of Swedenborg's impact on pre-Romantic European literary trends in Jacques Roos' *Aspects littéraires du mysticisme philosophique et l'influence de Boehme et de Swedenborg au début du romantisme: Blake, Novalis, Ballanche* (Strasbourg, 1951). One of the antirationalistic strains in eighteenth-century Sweden examined by Martin Lamm in *Upplysningstidens romantik* is Swedenborgianism and related phenomena, a subject earlier investigated in narrower contexts by R. Sundelin in *Swedenborgianismens historia i Sverige* (Uppsala, 1886). An early but in its way excellent account of Swedenborg, especially interesting as an evidence of a Swedish Romantic's sensitive understanding of a misunderstood countryman, is P. D. A. Atterbom's study on Swedenborg in *Svenska siare och skalder* (1841–55).

Items on Swedenborg as a scientist range from learned professional articles on his scientific discoveries and theories to acceptable non-technical accounts of these matters. Examples in English of the former are A. G. Nathorst's "Emanuel Swedenborg as a Geologist," Svante Arrhenius's "Emanuel Swedenborg as a Cosmologist," and A. H. Stroh's "The Sources of Swedenborg's Early Philosophy of Nature," all printed in the definitive Latin edition of Swedenborg's scientific works *Opera quaedam aut inedita aut obsoleta de rebus naturalibus* (publ. under the auspices of the Swedish Academy of Science, 1907-11), 3 vols. Designed primarily for a general reading public are Sten Lindroth's excellent article on Swedenborg in *Swedish Men of Science 1650–1940* and Adolph B. Benson's survey "Swedenborg as a Scientist" in *Bulletin, The American-Swedish Institute* (Minneapolis, June 1951), pp.16–30. Benson's Swedenborg item is the last in a series of three popular articles covering Swedish scientific developments from Olaus Rudbeck through Christopher Polhem to Swedenborg.

Vast as is the literature on Swedenborg, books and articles on Linné (Linnaeus) are even more numerous — and they are on the whole more uniformly sound, chiefly because so much of what has been written about Swedenborg bears the stamp of his followers' religious enthusiasm rather than the mark of a disinterested, objective scholarship. Fortunately for those who desire bibliographical guidance on Linné beyond what can be provided here, B. H. Soulsby's *A Catalog of the Works of Linnaeus . . . preserved in the Libraries of the British Museum* (London, 2nd ed. 1933) includes a well-nigh exhaustive listing of works by and about the famous Swedish naturalist. Fortunately also for the English-speaking reader in particular is the fact that a number of the better general works on Linné are available in English, including Norah Gourlie's recent and quite competent *The Prince of Botanists, Carl Linnaeus* (London, 1953) as well as such works of non-English origins as D. H. Stöver's *Leben des Ritters Carl von Linné* (Eng. version *The Life of Sir Charles Linnaeus*, London, 1794) and the two Swedish works Th. M. Fries's monumental *Linné: lefnadsteckning* (translated and adapted for the English reader by B. D. Jackson under the title *Linnaeus. The Story of His Life*, London, 1923) and Knut Hagberg's *Carl Linnaeus* (Eng. version under the same title, London, 1952). Fries's work, though first published more than fifty years ago, still remains the standard biography, while Hagberg's book is a brilliant biographical portrait in which are gracefully and skillfully blended solid learning and psychological penetration together with a large awareness of Linné as a complex cultural personality and a born prose stylist.

Other items from Swedish pens which stress Linné's cultural and literary importance as distinguished from his purely scientific contributions are Oscar Levertin's unfinished *Carl von Linné: några kapitel ur ett oavslutat arbete* (1906), Elis Malmeström's two books *Linné som kulturpersonlighet* (Uppsala, 1925) and *Carl von Linnés religiösa åskådning* (1926), Erland Ehnmark's "Linnaeus and the Problem of Immortality," *Hum. Vet.-samf. i Lund Årsber.* 1951/52, pp.63–93, and Knut Hagberg's wide-ranging observations on the Linnaean "tradition" in Sweden in *Carl Linnaeus: den linnéanska traditionen* (1951). In various issues of the Swedish Linnaean Society's official organ, *Svenska Linnésällskapets årsskrift* (1918ff.), competent analyses of Linné's literary style have appeared. The world outside Sweden has largely had to forego cultural and literary considerations in its concern with Linné in favor of the more limited though central scientific considerations, but not a little of Linné's personal charm (and with it by indirection something of his cultural impact) breaks through in the biographical works by foreign pens.

On Linné as a scientist the fundamental Swedish work is *Carl von Linnés betydelse som naturforskare och läkare* (Uppsala, 1907), a formidable tome issued by the Royal Academy of Sciences on the occasion of the two hundredth anniversary of Linné's birth and containing lengthy analyses of his contributions as medical man and zoologist, botanist, and geologist. A German version of the entire bicentenary volume appeared in 1909, and the essay from the volume on Linné as a geologist appeared in English in *The Smithsonian Institution Annual Report, 1908* (Washington, 1909), pp.711–43. On the same occasion E. O. Hovey contributed "The Bicentenary of the Birth of Carolus Linnaeus" to the *New York Academy of Science Annals*, XVIII (1908), 1–90, and a generation later B. Hj. Larsson wrote on "Carolus Linnaeus, Physician and Botanist" in the *Annals of Medical History*, x (1938), 197–214. Adolph B. Benson includes an article entitled "The Beginnings of American Interest in Linnaeus" in his *American Scandinavian Studies* (New York, 1952), pp.63–70, and John L. Heller has provided a study on "Classical Mythology in the *Systema Naturae*," *Transactions of the American Philological Association*, LXXVI (1945), 333–57. The two hundred fiftieth anniversary spawned a number of popular accounts by experts, including "Carl Linnaeus and His Place in the Evolution of Modern Botany," *The Anglo-Swedish Review* (May 1957), pp.305–12, originally delivered as an address by H. Hamshaw Thomas, President of the Linnaean Society of London, and a little brochure entitled simply *Linnaeus* (The Swedish Institute, Stockholm, 1957) by Arvid Hj. Uggla, a leading Swedish authority on Linné, who is also responsible for the excellent chapter on Linné and his disciples in *Ny illustrerad svensk litteraturhistoria*, II, 200–48. Worthy of mention in these anniversary contexts are Dag Hammarskjöld's address before the Swedish Academy entitled *The Linnaeus Tradition and Our Time* (1957) and two items of bibliographical importance, the very valuable *Catalogue of the Works of Linnaeus*, issued by Sandbergs Bokhandel, Stockholm (1957) and Thomas R. Buckman's illustrated *Catalog of an Exhibition Commemorating the 250th Anniversary of the Birth of Carolus Linnaeus* . . . (University of Kansas Libraries, 1957). Other important short accounts of Linné as a scientist are three chapters in D. C. Peattie's *Green Laurels: The Lives and Achievements of the Great Naturalists* (New York, 1936) and Sten Lindroth's chapter on Linné in *Swedish Men of Science 1650–1940*.

Among the many disciples of Linné who traveled to all corners of the globe in search of scientific information was one Petrus Kalm, who came to America in 1750 and upon returning to his homeland published a detailed account of his observations, an account which has been rendered into English by A. B. Benson in *America in 1750: Peter Kalm's Travels in North America* (Elmira, N.Y., 1937). Benson had earlier contributed a short article "Pehr Kalm's Journey to North America" to *ASR*, x (1922), 350–55, and more recently the English geographer W. R. Mead has written a longer and more inclusive study entitled "A Northern Naturalist: Pehr Kalm, Disciple of Carl Linnaeus," *The Norseman*, XII (1954), 98–105, 182–88.

Among the general popular accounts in English of Linné and his work which may finally be mentioned is one by Elof Förberg in *ASR*, x (1922), 595–602, and two by Louis H. Roddis in the same journal, XXXII (1944), 32–47, and XLIII (1955), 369–75. It should perhaps also be noted as a curiosity if nothing more that Linné even "made" *The Reader's Digest* in 1952!

On Swedish eighteenth-century literary figures strictly speaking we must turn almost entirely, as has been noted, to Swedish critical and scholarly sources. ¶ On Olof Dalin, the figure of chief importance during the first half of the century, two early but still basic works are Karl Warburg's *Olof Dalin: hans lif och gerning* (1884) and Martin Lamm's *Olof Dalin: en litteraturhistorisk undersökning af hans verk* (Uppsala, 1908), the latter being especially rich in its ferreting out details of Dalin's dependence on foreign literary practices, among which of special interest to the English reader are those of Swift, Addison, and Steele. Two important recent studies are Nils-Olof Dyberg's monograph *Olof Dalin och tidsidéerna: en komparativ undersökning av hans diktning till omkring 1750* (Uppsala, 1946) and Magnus von Platen's "Dalins politiska satirer," *S*, n.f. xxxviii (1957), 5–45. Fredrik Böök has included a couple of shorter Dalin studies in his *Stridsmän och sångare* (1910), and Otto Sylwan has provided a competent biography together with a useful bibliographical listing of Dalin's published works and manuscripts in *Svenskt biografiskt lexikon*, x (1931). ¶ To fru Nordenflycht, central figure in the mid-century "Tankebyggare" group, has been devoted one of Oscar Levertin's finest critical essays in his *Svenska gestalter* (1903), a volume which also includes essays on Gyllenborg and Creutz, the other two genuine poets of the group. Gyllenborg's *Mitt leverne: 1731–1775: självbiografiska anteckningar*, utg. af Gudmund Frunck (1885) throws much light both on Gyllenborg himself and on his circle of colleagues and friends. The basic general works on Gyllenborg and Creutz are Gardar Sahlberg's *Gustaf Fredrik Gyllenborg: hans liv och diktning under frihetstiden* (1943) and two works by Gunnar Castrén, the solid, detailed early monograph *Gustav Philip Creutz* (Stockholm and Helsingfors, 1917) and the brilliant little later work bearing the same title (1949). The section on Creutz in Martin Lamm's *Upplysningstidens romantik*, i (1918) is also of first importance.

The literature on Bellman is naturally very extensive and concerns itself with every conceivable aspect of the poet's life and work. Of the earlier Bellman studies four in particular are of importance, P. D. A. Atterbom's essay in *Svenska siare och skalder* (1841–55), G. Ljunggren's *Bellman och Fredman's epistlar* (1867), Oscar Levertin's three Bellman essays from 1896, 1903, and 1905 (most conveniently available in his *Samlade skrifter*, vii, ix, and xix), and Richard Steffen's investigations into the chronology of Bellman's poems "Anteckningar till Bellmansdiktens historia," *S*, xvi (1895), 150–71, and xvii (1896), 113–64. With the two striking exceptions of Otto Sylwan's *Bellman och Fredmans epistlar* (Lund, 1943) and Anton Blanck's *Carl Michael Bellman* (1948) most of the more recent Bellman scholarship is concerned with other than aesthetic or purely literary considerations, but within its limitations this scholarship has turned up a wealth of new material on biographical and textual detail, the dating and interpretation of individual poems, Bellman's immediate milieu, his relations with contemporaries and fortunes at the hands of later critics, literary and musical influences on him, etc. Much of this scholarship has appeared in the dozen volumes of *Bellmansstudier* (1924ff.), the official organ of Bellmanssällskapet. Some of the more important recent works on Bellman exclusive of the items in *Bellmansstudier* are Nils Afzelius's *Myt och bild: studier i Bellmans dikt* (1945), which among other things serves as a partial corrective to those who insist upon emphasizing Bellman's "realism" at the expense of his more conventional "literary" qualities, Anton Blanck's *Bellman vid skiljovägen och andra studier* (1945), whose title-essay attempts to demonstrate (probably somewhat too sharply) that Bellman's later poetry reflects a marked difference from the earlier in stylistic and moral refinements, and Olof Byströms *Kring Fredmans epistlar: deras tillkomst och utgivning* (1945), which together with a Supplement (1946) alters in many details the dates earlier ascribed to the individual "epistles" by Steffen. Strangely enough we do not have an adequate, relatively exhaustive biography of Bellman, and must in consequence use the best available short biographical essay, that by Richard Steffen in *Svenskt biografiskt lexikon*, iii (1921). An autobiographical fragment from Bellman's own hand has been edited and published by Olof Byström — *Levernesbeskrivning* (1947). Henrik Schück's chapter in *Illustrerad svensk litteraturhistoria*, iii (3rd rev. ed. 1927) has been considered by some the best short treatment of the poet and his work. Excellent popular sketches are provided by Nils

Afzelius in *Svenska folket genom tiderna*, VII, 163–96, and by Olof Byström in *Svenska män och kvinnor*, I, 201–3. On the musical aspects of Bellman's work see especially the Danish study by Torben Krogh *Bellman som musikalsk Digter* (Copenhagen, 1945). It is highly unfortunate that in English we have only one reasonably competent sketch, C. W. Stork's "Bellman the Incomparable," *ASR*, xv (1927), 220–30. Hendrik Willem van Loon's chatty Introduction to *The Last of the Troubadours* (New York, 1939) can appeal only to the utterly uncritical mind, but the book may be said to serve one purpose, being so far as I know the only work in English which provides both the music and the text of a substantial number of Bellman's songs.

On Jacob Wallenberg, whose claim to fame rests on the authorship of a single comic travel book, the following studies may be mentioned: Oscar Levertin, "Min son på galejan och dess författare" in *Essayer* (1907), I, 44–48, two studies by Nils Afzelius, "Min son på galejan och den komiska resebeskrivningen," *S*, n.f. v (1924), 198–224, and "Jacob Wallenberg," *OoB*, XXXIX (1930), 141–56, Sigfrid Siwertz, "Minne av Jacob Wallenberg," *Svenska Akademiens handlingar från 1886*, XLVIII (1937), 29–104, reprinted in Siwertz's *Den goda trätan* (1956), pp.154–210, and Sven Rydberg, "Jacob Wallenberg i England," *OoB*, LIII (1944), 145–57, the last being an account of a two-months visit to England by Wallenberg in the late summer of 1769. For an exhaustive bibliography of the works on and by Wallenberg see Nils Afzelius's edition of Wallenberg's collected works in *Svenska författare utgivna av Svenska vitterhetssamfundet*, I–II (1929–41).

Though most of the general works on late eighteenth-century Swedish literature reflect in one way or other the cultural role played by Gustaf III during the last decades of the century, the student of these decades must be referred also to those works which focus more exclusively on the person of the King and his central importance in furthering the arts, particularly those of the theater. Three types of works illuminate clearly the King's active cultural role: biographical studies like Knut Hagberg's portrait of Gustaf III in *Av Vasarnas ätt* (2nd ed. 1929) and Beth Hennings' full-length biography *Gustaf III* (1957), works on the Gustavian theater in all its ramifications such as Oscar Levertin's *Teater och drama under Gustaf III* (1889) and *Gustaf III som dramatisk författare* (1894) and Agne Beijer's *Slottsteatrarna på Drottningholm och Gripsholm*, I (1937), and investigations of the King's personal working relations with literary figures and artists of his day, like Sverker Ek's "Kellgren och Gustaf III," *OoB*, XLII (1933), 1–16, Olof Byström's "Bellman som Gustaf III:s medarbetare," *Bellmansstudier*, VII (1938), 66–77, and Olle Holmberg's *Leopold och Gustaf III 1786–1792* (1954). On Kellgren's reactions toward Gustaf III's politics see Verner Ekenvall's "Kellgrens inställning till Gustaf III och hans politik före 1789," *S*, n.f. xx (1939), 58–92. G. Landberg's *Gustav III i eftervärldens dom* (1945) provides an over-all account of the King in the eyes of the world of his time. Such English and French biographies of Gustaf III as R. N. Bain's *Gustavus III and His Contemporaries 1746–1792* (London, 1894) and Pierre Henri de La Blanchetai's (pseud. Pierre de Luz) *Gustave III* (Paris, 1949; Swedish version also 1949) have general value but are of little assistance in tracing the King's cultural interests and activities, Bain's work being largely political in point of view and La Blanchetai's primarily psychological in emphasis. In order to gain an overall view of the Gustavian drama and theater in relation to the whole Swedish theatrical tradition the student should consult — in addition to Agne Beijer's monumental *Slottsteatrarna på Drottningholm och Gripsholm*, I (1937) — the appropriate sections in the standard works on Swedish drama and theater by Gustaf Ljunggren

(1864) and Georg Nordensvan (1917-18). The most recent book by an expert on the Drottningholm Theatre is Gustaf Hilleström's *Drottningholmsteatern förr och nu* (1957). Those who may be interested in the exact nature of Gustaf III's collaboration with one of his "court poets" in the preparation of an opera libretto should examine Lennart Breitholtz's *Studier i operan Gustaf Wasa* (Uppsala universitets årsskrift, 1954), which includes a brief summary in French. Popular but expert accounts of Gustavian literature in general and of the Gustavian theater in particular are provided by Fr. Vetterlund and Agne Beijer in a couple of chapters entitled respectively "Den litterära bildningen" and "Teaterlynnet" in *Svenska folket genom tiderna*, VII, 197-230, 231-62. Among the rather numerous items in English of greater or lesser popular value on the famous Drottningholm Theatre are the following: John Mason Brown's "An Eighteenth Century Theatre," *Theatre Arts*, VIII (1924), 243-58, Monica Ewer's "The Player King and the Theatre at Drottningholm," *Theatre Arts*, XV (1931), 228-32, Agne Beijer's two articles "Gustaf III's Theatre Restored," *ASR*, XX (1932), 32-35, and "The Drottningholm Theatre Museum," *Theatre Arts*, XVIII (1934), 193-205, Holger Lundbergh's "An Eighteenth Century Theatre," *ASR*, XXXVI (1948), 313-18, and Philip C. Lorraine's *Drottningholm Court Theatre* (1956).

On Carl Gustaf Leopold, the Gustavian literary figure who stood closest to the King, Olle Holmberg's massive and scholarly though often wittily written biography will be, when completed, the standard work. To date three volumes have appeared, *Den unge Leopold, 1756-1785* (1953), *Leopold och Gustaf III* (1954), and *Leopold och Reuterholmska tiden: 1792-1796* (1957). Of first importance also is Allan Sjöding's *Leopold, den gustavianska smakdomaren* (Vesterås, 1931). Much of the other scholarly work on Leopold is concerned with detail problems of interest chiefly to the Swedish specialist — with the possible exception of Kjell Strömberg's "La tragédie voltairienne en Suède," *Revue d'histoire littéraire de la France*, XXIII (1916), 107-19, which because of its treatment of the French precursors of Gustavian tragedy as represented in Leopold's *Oden* should be of some interest to students of comparative literature. ¶ On Johan Henric Kellgren, scholarship has been very active, with in not a few cases impressive results. Aside from the two items on Kellgren and Gustaf III noted above, special mention should be made of such general works as Otto Sylwan's *Johan Henrik Kellgren: en översikt av hans levnad och författarskap* (1912, new and rev. ed. 1939), Lennart Josephson's *Kellgren och samhället: Kritik och satir till mitten av 1780-talet* (Uppsala, 1942), E. N. Tigerstedt's short but excellent *Johan Henric Kellgren* (1954), and the little Verdandi book by Allan E. Sjöding, *Johan Henrik Kellgren* (1948). To these may be added A. Forsström's study in Kellgren and Horace (*Förhandlingar och uppsatser utg. av Svenska Litteratursällskapet i Finland*, XXXIII (1919), a couple of items on Kellgren's style, Margit Abenius's *Stilstudier i Kellgrens prosa* (Uppsala, 1931) and S. Belfrage's *Gustavianska dikter i stilhistorisk belysning* (1923; new and rev. ed. 1950), and four treatments of Kellgren as a journalist, Otto Sylwan's "Stockholms-Posten och Kellgren," *S*, XXX (1909), 1-31, Fredrik Böök's "Stockholms-Posten, Kellgren och fru Lenngren" in *Stridsmän och sångare* (1910), pp.119-57, Gunhild Berg's chapter on Kellgren in *Litterär kritik i Sverige under 1600- och 1700-talen* (1916), and Elof Ehnmark's chapter "Stockholms-postens satir och novellistik" in *Studier i svensk realism* (Uppsala, 1930), pp.73-173. Of interest chiefly to the specialist is the extensive debate which has been conducted with learning and ingenuity by a dozen or more scholars for nearly a half century on the questions connected with Kellgren's last great poem "Den nya skapelsen." ¶ Anna Maria Lenngren, a far less complex literary figure than Kellgren, has posed few knotty problems for critics and scholars. In fact, the only really knotty problem which her work poses involves the extent of her contributions to *Stockholms-Posten*. Debate on this subject has been lively but on the whole inconclusive. Of the not very considerable number of items of general importance on fru Lenngren only four need be mentioned here, Karl Warburg's biography *Anna Maria Lenngren* (2nd ed. 1917), Anton Blanck's lengthy title-essay in *Anna Maria Lenngren poet och pennskaft jämte andra studier* (1922), Blanck's short recent biography *Anna Maria Lenngren* (1948), and Henry Olsson's sensitive psychological analysis of fru Lenngren in *Törnrosdiktaren och andra porträtt* (1956), pp.9–33. Of some interest particularly to specialists in English literature of the eighteenth century is K. F. Freudenthal's "Motiv ur The Spectator i Anna Maria Lenngrens Portraiterne," *S*, n.f. xxviii (1947), 101–4.

The complex of mood and idea which accounts for the break late in the eighteenth century between Gustavian classicism and certain "Romantic" or "pre-Romantic" trends reflects, in part, simply an intensification of moods and ideas which had maintained throughout the earlier decades of the century a relatively submerged existence, and, in part, certain later related developments. In their broader contexts these moods and ideas have been investigated brilliantly in Martin Lamm's *Upplysningstidens romantik*, i–ii (1918, 1920), in Anton Blanck's *Den nordiska renässansen i sjuttonhundratalets litteratur* (1911), and in a number of studies which concentrate particularly on English influences and parallels of a pre-Romantic kind, Theodor Hasselqvist's *"Ossian" i den svenska dikten och litteraturen* (Malmö, 1895), Nils Molin's *Shakespeare och Sverige intill 1800-talets mitt* (Göteborg, 1931), T. T. Segerstedt's *Moral sense-skolan och dess inflytande på svensk filosofi* (Lund, 1937), and Carl Fehrman's *Kyrkogårdsromantik från Thomas Gray till Carl Michael Bellman* (Lund, 1954). Martin Lamm's *Johan Gabriel Oxenstierna: en gustaviansk natursvärmares lif och dikt* (1911) is concerned, as the subtitle indicates, with nature moods as reflected in a typical late eighteenth-century Swedish poet. ¶ With few exceptions the more important critical and scholarly literature on Thomas Thorild (who together with Bengt Lidner most sharply reflects the break with Gustavian classicism) is restricted to an examination of his ideas and his philosophical significance rather than his literary importance strictly speaking. Whether Thorild was a systematic rationalist or a Classical stoic or a Romantic in any one or more of their usual meanings has been the subject of vigorous controversy among scholars and has resulted in a considerable accumulation of books and articles which need not be listed here. Of more interest to the student of literature are two studies by Ernst Cassirer on Thorild's Sturm und Drang propensities, *Thorilds Stellung in der Geistesgeschichte des achtzehnten Jahrhunderts* (Vitterhetsakademiens handlingar, 1941) and "Thorild och Herder," *Theoria*, vii (1941), 75–92, and an article by Alfred Forsvall, "Thorild och [Edward] Young," *Lunds universitets årsskrift* (1908), 27–36. Critical literary analyses of Thorild's famous poem *Passionerna* have been made by C. D. Marcus (in *Göteborgs Vetenskaps- och Vitterhetssamhälles handlingar*, Series 4, xv, 1913), by R. Brieskorn (in *NS*, v [1925], 93–146), by Harald Elovson (in *S*, n.f. xiii [1932], 106–23), and by G. Fredén (in *S*, n.f. xxxiii [1952], 88–98). ¶ Aside from Karl Warburg's early biography *Lidner* (1889), Martin Lamm's "Lidnerstudier," *S*, xxx (1909), 69–170, and his section on Lidner in *Upplysningstidens romantik*, ii (1920), and Lennart Josephson's short but able recent work *Bengt Lidner* (1947), Lidner studies have been concerned about equally with textual matters, with the turning up of new biographical details, and with providing critical interpretations of Lidner's poetry. Of chief literary interest are Lamm's Lidner studies mentioned above, Mathias Feuk's dissertation *Lidners poetiska språk* (Lund, 1912), and Sixten Belfrage's *Gustavianska dikter i stilhistorisk belysning* (1950). Nils Molin calls attention to a Shakespeare influence on Lidner in *Shakespeare i Sverige intill 1800-talets mitt* (1931), and Carl Fehrman has investigated Lidner's relation to eighteenth-century "graveyard poetry" in *Kyrkogårdsromantik från Thomas Gray till Carl Michael Bellman* (1954).

Chapter 6. Romanticism

Because of its high poetic eminence and its plenitude of distinguished cultural personalities Swedish Romantic literature of the early nineteenth century has naturally been a major preoccupation of critics and literary historians in Sweden, and it has occasionally engaged the attention of scholars elsewhere, especially brilliantly in the hands of the Danish critic Valdemar Vedel, whose *Svensk romantik* (Copenhagen, 1894) is a little classic of its kind and is still highly stimulating reading though published more than half a century ago. In America a number of investigations and surveys of some importance have been made, those of general interest being Adolph B. Benson's *The Old Norse Element in Swedish Romanticism* (New York, 1914) and "The English Element in Swedish Romanticism," *SS*, v (1918–19), 47–71, Otto Springer's *Die nordische Renaissance in Skandinavien* (University of Kansas dissertation publ. in *Tübinger germanistische Arbeiten*, xxII, 1936), and S. B. Hustvedt's *Ballad Books and Ballad Men: Raids and Rescues in Britain, America, and the Scandinavian North since 1800* (Cambridge, Mass., 1930). See below for American studies on particular Romantic poets.

The only detailed surveys of Swedish Romanticism are those included in the standard literary histories in Swedish. Of general interest, too, are Fr. Vetterlund's *Romantik* (Helsingfors, 1920), a selection of sensitive essays on various facets of Romantic literature, Albert Nilsson's *Svensk romantik* (Lund, 1916), which traces the Platonic strain in a half dozen Romantic poets, J. Victor Johansson's *Den förromantiska balladen i Sverige* and Karl J. Samuelson's *Fosforisternas ballader och romanser 1810–13* (both in *Göteborgs högskolas årsskrift*, xvIII, 1912) and Fritz Andersson's "Nyromantikernas folkmytologiska diktning," *S*, n.f. xIX (1938), 105–28, which examine the origin and nature (essentially *literary* rather than directly folk-inspired as Andersson points out) of Romantic ballad traditions, and Erik Wallén's *Nordisk mytologi i svensk romantik* (1918) and *Studier över romantisk mytologi i svensk litteratur* (Malmö, 1923), both of which penetrate rather deeply into the uses of Nordic mythology in Swedish Romantic literature. The third volume of Otto Sylwan's *Den svenska versen från 1600-talets början* (1934) deals in detail with the prosody of the Romantics. The broader aspects of foreign literary influences, particularly those of England and Germany, have been sketched in Adolph B. Benson's previously mentioned survey and investigated in more detail in such special studies as Theodor Hasselqvist's *"Ossian" i den svenska litteraturen* (1895), Gunnar Biller's "Byron i den svenska litteraturen före Strandberg," *S*, xxxIII (1912), 123–65, Erik Lindström's *Walter Scott och den historiska romanen och novellen i Sverige* (Göteborgs högskolas årsskrift, xxxI, 1925), Nils Molin's *Shakespeare och Sverige intill 1800-talets mitt* (Göteborg, 1931), Ruben G:son Berg's "Novalis och Fouqué i Sverige," *Studier i modern språkvetenskap*, iv (1908), 165–85, V. Ljungdorff's "E. T. A. Hoffmann och Sverige," *Edda*, x (1918), 96–140, 249–95, and a dissertation by Sigvard Magnusson, *Det romantiska genombrottet i Auroraförbundet* (1936), which emphasizes more than had been the practice among earlier scholars the intellectual impact on the New Romantics of Schelling. Of great value also in these contexts are Anton Blanck's general sketch of French-Swedish interrelations in *Bellman vid skiljovägen och andra studier* and Harald Elovson's *Amerika i svensk litteratur 1750–1820* (Lund, 1930). Of interest as evidence of an early, largely abortive English concern with Swedish Romantic literature is Hedvig af Petersens' "Robert Pearse Gillies, Foreign Quarterly Review och den svenska litteraturen," *S*, n.f. xiv (1933), 55–106.

Early scholarly treatment of the so-called "New Romantics" (*nyromantikerna*) was largely partisan in tone though not always negligible in quality, while in our century a more judicious examination and evaluation of the literary contribution of the "New Romantics" has been possible. Most of the mature scholarship on the group has naturally been concerned with its chief figure P. D. A. Atterbom, and on the whole more with the poet than the man, though psychological and biographical approaches — notably Gunnar Axberger's *Den unge Atterbom: psykologiska problem i hans liv och diktning 1806–1819* (Uppsala, 1936) and Elisabeth Tykesson's *Atterbom, en levnadsteckning* (1954) — have not been wanting. A very large portion of the significant work on Atterbom's poetry is occupied with his two larger central works *Fågel Blå* and *Lycksalighetens ö*, whose backgrounds and ideas have been subjected to repeated and often penetrating analyses, particularly at the hands of Fredrik Vetterlund and Carl Santesson. Among Vetterlund's more important studies are *Atterboms sagospel 'Lycksalighetens ö': en estetisk och litteraturhistorisk undersökning* (1924) and "Atterboms sagospel Fågel Blå" in *Bortom de blå bergen* (1942), pp.11–70. Among Santesson's, *Atterboms ungdomsdiktning* (1920), a number of investigations in *Samlaren* (1923, 1925, 1947–49), and *Mot Lycksalighetens ö* (1956). Other important special studies are Holger Frykenstedt's *Atterboms sagospel Lycksalighetens ö* (1951), which combines sharp psychological analysis with an examination of the intellectual backgrounds of Atterbom's chief work, and Jacob Kulling's *Atterboms 'Svenska siare och skalder'* (1931), which is concerned with Atterbom as a literary historian, a subject pursued further by Henry Olsson in "Den svenska romantikens litteraturforskning," *FT*, cxiii (1932), 51–75, an article which uses Kulling's book as a point of departure for certain more inclusive observations on literary history as practiced by the Swedish Romantics. Byron's tentative and fragmentary impact on Atterbom has been examined in passing in Carl Santesson's chapter "Italien och Fågel Blå" in *Atterbomstudier* (1932), pp.132–71, and in the same author's article "Atterboms Byron-dikt," *S*, n.f. xiv (1933), 122–50. For those who wish a brief introduction to Atterbom a helpful little work is Elisabet Hellsten-Wallin and Isak Wallin's *Den unge Atterbom och romantiken: genombrottsåren* (1954), an anthology which provides representative selections from Atterbom's early work together with a running commentary based on the latest findings in Atterbom scholarship. A continuation of this work is *Den unge Atterbom och romantiken: från Urania och Fågel Blå till Pilgrimshälsning* (1957).

Few Swedish literary figures have been as intensively subjected to critical investigation from all possible points of view as Erik Gustaf Geijer, and in consequence the present selective bibliography can take note of but a small fraction of even the more important literature on Geijer. A chief reason for the abundance of these studies is that Geijer's personality and work are so many-faceted. He interests us not merely as a man and a poet but as a thinker of strong philosophical bent, as a leading figure in the Gothic Society, as a historian of high distinction, and as a social and political theorist who played an active role in the public life of his day. John Landquist's recent *Geijer, en levnadsteckning* (1954) has superseded all earlier biographical works, including Landquist's own work of a generation ago, *Erik Gustaf Geijer: hans levnad och verk* (1924). Primary sources of first importance on Geijer's early life are the fascinating autobiographical sketch *Minnen* (1834) and the collection of letters edited with commentary by Anton Blanck under the title *Geijer i England 1809–10* (1914). The latter work has been issued in somewhat revised form in English as *Impressions of England 1809–10* (London, 1932). Of the overwhelmingly rich memoir material of greater or lesser dependability on Geijer, his backgrounds and circle of friends, only two items can be mentioned here, Malla Montgomery-Silfverstolpe's very important *Memoarer*, I–IV (1908–11) and Anna Hamilton-Geete's highly popular, of dubious historical value, *I solnedgången*, I–IV (1910–14). The latter has served as a point of departure for a sensitive though somewhat overidealized chapter on Geijer in Uppsala in the French critic Lucien Maury's *L'Imagination scandinave* (Paris, 1929).

On Geijer as a poet and his activities in the Gothic Society space permits us to list only some of the more inclusive studies such as C. D. Marcus's *Erik Gustaf Geijers lyrik* (1909), Anton Blanck's *Geijers götiska diktning* (1918), Jacob Kulling's "Geijers senare lyrik," *OoB*, XLV (1936), 225–38, Sven Cederblad's "Geijer och götiska förbundet," *S*, n.f. XXXVI (1955), 28–37, Erik Wallén's two works on Nordic mythology among the Romantics referred to above under Atterbom, and parts of Elsa Norberg's *Geijers väg från romantik till realism* (1944), which otherwise, and in the main, is a thoroughgoing investigation of the philosophical bases of Geijer's shift from an early romanticism to a later realism. For those who do not read Swedish Viola H. Spongberg's New York University dissertation *The Philosophy of Erik Gustaf Geijer* (Rock Island, Ill., 1945) provides a sketchy general introduction to Geijer as a thinker.

The social and political liberalism which became the practical consequence of Geijer's later philosophical realism has been investigated in a number of studies, the most exhaustive of which, C. A. Hessler's *Geijer som politiker*, I–II (1939–47), should be read in conjunction with two less fundamental but in their way equally interesting investigations, the Geijer chapter in Alf Kjellén's *Sociala idéer och motiv hos svenska författare under 1830- och 1840-talen*, I (1937) and Edvard Rodhe's *Geijer och samhället* (1942). Kjellén's investigations reveal among other things how intensely interested Geijer was in his last years in certain contemporary English reform trends. Geijer's concern with specifically economic aspects of modern society is traced in detail down to 1830 in Ingemar Olofsson's *Geijer och samhällsekonomin* (1959).

Two relatively popular general books which trace Geijer's development by means of skillfully selected and arranged material from Geijer's own writings are Greta Hedin's *Arvet efter Geijer: en bild av Erik Gustav Geijer sammanställd ur hans skrifter* (Lund, 1942) and Alf Kjellén's *Den levande Geijer: ett prosaurval belysande den andliga linjen i Geijers författarskap* (1947). Because the only competent general treatment of Geijer in English is the short article by John Landquist, "Erik Gustaf Geijer: Swedish Poet and Historian," *ASR*, XVI (1928), 589–601, the English or American student who has no command of Swedish must as best he can fill in details of the Geijer portrait through reading translations of his work, of which we have, in addition to some of his poems, three representative prose works, the *Impressions of England 1809–10* already mentioned, *The History of the Swedes*, tr. by J. H. Turner (London, 1845), and *The Poor Laws and Their Bearing on Society: A Series of Political and Historical Essays* (1840).

In contrast to the almost nonexistent critical and scholarly material in English on Geijer, material in English on Esaias Tegnér is fairly rich in amount if not often particularly solid in quality. Of first importance is Georg Brandes's famous Tegnér essay (1876), which appeared in an English translation by R. B. Anderson as early as 1886 and has been most recently reprinted in Georg Brandes, *Creative Spirits of the Nineteenth Century* (New York, 1923), pp.106–83. Two lesser but in their way helpful general essays are H. H. Boyesen's "Esaias Tegnér" in *Essays on Scandinavian Literature* (New York, 1895, reprinted 1925), pp.219–88, and Fredrik Böök's brief "Esaias Tegnér," *ASR*, xiv (1926), 653–59. A number of odds and ends of decidedly uneven quality on Tegnér have been contributed to *SS* over a period of years (1911, 1916, 1918, 1920, 1921, 1926, and 1948) by A. M. Sturtevant. The bulk of American studies on Tegnér has been concerned with Longfellow's relation to the Swedish poet and with English and American translations of Tegnér, particularly translations of *Fritiofs saga*. Andrew Hilen has investigated the Longfellow-Tegnér relations in their broadly Scandinavian contexts in *Longfellow and Scandinavia: A Study of the Poet's Relationship with the Northern Languages and Literatures* (New Haven, Conn., 1947), while other Americans have concerned themselves only more or less satisfactorily with the quality of Longfellow's translations of Tegnér or with possible influences of the Swedish poet on Longfellow (see *SS*, 1915, 1920, 1949). Of bibliographical interest are an article by Gustaf N. Swan, "The English Versions of Tegnér's *Axel*," *SS*, I (1911–14), 179–84, and one by Adolph B. Benson, "A List of the English Translations of the *Frithjofs Saga*," *Germanic Review*, I (1926), 142–67 (reprinted in Benson, *American Scandinavian Studies* [New York, 1952], pp.277–98). Benson's article seems to have settled for all time the question of the number of English versions of Tegnér's most famous poem.

From the enormous accumulation of Swedish studies on Tegnér it is exceedingly difficult to make a representative selection, not only because the *number* of such studies is so great but also because there has been considerable disagreement among Swedish scholars in such basic areas of investigation as the diagnosis of Tegnér's mental illness and the central features of his religious and philosophical position. There is less disposition among the experts to challenge one another on matters of a purely literary kind, but the relative paucity of more broadly inclusive investigations of the formal aspects of Tegnér's poetry forces the student almost from the start into the often confusing maze of special studies of individual poems or clusters of intimately related poems. We can here call attention to but an absolute minimum of the more important studies in Swedish, and refer the reader who seeks further guidance to the excellent bibliographical section on Tegnér in *Ny illustrerad svensk litteraturhistoria*, III, and to Carl Fehrman's illuminating review article "Tegnérbilden: en översikt över litteraturen till hundraårsjubileet," *OoB*, LVI (1947), 106–16. The standard biography is Fredrik Böök's *Esaias Tegnér: en levnadsteckning*, I–II (1946), which is not to be confused with Böök's much less satisfactory book on Tegnér from 1917. Brandes's brilliant essay of 1878 destroyed the early traditional and overidealized picture of Tegnér and opened the way to honest biographical research, which, however, proceeded rather slowly to begin with. Of Ewert Wrangel's seven detailed biographical studies the one of chief general value is *Tegnér i Lund*, I–II (1932), while the others are primarily of interest for the light they throw on Tegnér's early Värmland backgrounds and the much discussed problem of the women in Tegnér's life. Among the more recent items on the latter subject are Henry Olsson's "Esaias Tegnér, Euphrosyne Palm och Emili Selldén," *SLT*, IX (1946), 153–68, Hedvig af Petersens' two studies "Martina von Schwerin och Tegnér," *SLT*, IX (1946), 169–85, and "Legenden om Martinas 'rymning'," *SLT*,

XVII (1954), 65–80, and Richard Steffen's title-essay in *Kvinnorna kring Tegnér och andra studier* (1947). Algot Werin has devoted some pages to Tegnér as a bishop in Växjö in *Svensk idealism* (Lund, 1938), a subject taken up in great detail and with some impressive results in Carl E. Göransson's *Biskop Tegnér i traditionen och i verkligheten* (1959). Tegnér's mental illness has been examined in considerable detail and with conflicting results by a number of Swedish psychiatrists and psychologists, beginning with Bror Gadelius, *Skapande fantasi och sjuka skalder* (1927), and continuing with Torsten Sondén, *Tegnérs psykiska ohälsa* (in *Lunds universitets årsskrift*, 1946), and Philip Sandblom, "Tegnérs kroppsliga ohälsa," *Tegnérstudier 1951* (Lund, 1951). For pointed reflections by literary historians on these diagnoses see Carl Fehrman, "Tegnérbilden," *OoB*, LVI (1947), 109–13, and Algot Werin, "Tegnérs mjältsjuka" in *Den svenske Faust och andra essayer* (Malmö, 1950), pp.120–32.

Tegnér's intellectual world was first examined with critical precision in Albert Nilsson's lengthy Introduction to *Esaias Tegnér: Filosofiska och estetiska skrifter* (1913) and in the same scholar's Tegnér section in *Svensk romantik* (Lund, 1916). Albert Nilsson's emphasis on the primary importance of German philosophical idealism and of Platonism in Tegnér's thinking has been challenged in Svante Bohman's dissertation *Esaias Tegnérs tänkesätt och idéer* (Uppsala, 1933), which finds in Tegnér's thinking a less theoretical and speculative, an essentially empirical bent. Albert Nilsson defended his position in *Tegnér och Uppsalafilosofien* (1934). Though Bohman's work lacks at points analytical precision and adequate documentation, Elsa Norberg's "Diskussionen om den unge Tegnérs filosofiska åskådning," *Studier tillägnade Anton Blanck* (Uppsala, 1946), makes clear that the position of Bohman is far from being indefensible. Of the many brief articles on Tegnér and religion Algot Werin's comparative study of Tegnér, Runeberg, and Rydberg "Nu står parnassen i den kristna kyrkan" in *Svensk idealism* is especially illuminating. Among the more recent longer studies which may be mentioned are Johannes Lindblom's *Tegnér och bibeln* and Ernst Newman's *Tegnér inför brytningarna inom tidens teologi och fromhetsliv* (both in *Lunds universitets årsskrift*, 1946) and Thure P:son Wärendh's somewhat biased but otherwise satisfactory dissertation *Tegnér och teologien* (1939). Tegnér's shifting position with reference to Classical and Romantic literary ideals has been examined in some detail in Greta Hedin's *Tegnérs uppfattning av klassiskt och romantiskt* (in *Göteborgs högskolas årsskrift*, XLI, 1935, Part 4). See also on this subject the fourth chapter of Albert Nilsson's Introduction to Tegnér's *Filosofiska och estetiska skrifter* (1913), pp.94–114. Though Tegnér's relation to Classical antiquity has not been exhaustively studied, a couple of approaches to the subject are provided in Gunnar Rudberg's *Esaias Tegnér, humanisten och hellenen* (1930) and Paul Nissen's "Die Griechische Formung Tegnérs," *Edda*, XXXIX (1939), 452–78.

On Tegnér as a poet only Brandes's essay, J. Mjöberg's *Stilstudier i Tegnérs ungdomsdiktning* (*Göteborgs högskolas årsskrift*, 1912), Carl Santesson's two studies, *Tegnérs reflexionsdiktning 1801–1805* (in *Uppsala universitets årsskrift*, 1913) and "Något om Tegnérs sista diktning," *Studier tillägnade Anton Blanck* (1946), and Algot Werin's *Esaias Tegnér: från Det eviga till Mjältsjukan* (Lund, 1934) attempt relatively inclusive and somewhat detailed analyses of the whole or part of his production. Most of the literary studies (they run into the scores if not the hundreds) are concerned with special topics and more often than not limit their attention to a particular poem. The most many-sided analysis of *Fritiofs saga* is a collective work by Greta Hedin, Erik Wallen, Otto Sylwan, and Elof Hellquist entitled *Tegnérs Fritjofs saga: fyra studier* (1931), which, besides a lengthy general study of *Fritiofs saga*, includes essays on the poem's mythological concepts, its verse forms, and its language. Albert Nilsson's *Tre fornnordiska gestalter* (Lund, 1928) provides a penetrating comparative investigation of *Fritiofs saga*, Oehlenschläger's *Helge*, and Runeberg's *Kung Fjalar*. Aside from the impact of Classical culture on Tegnér to which we have already referred, English, German, and French influences on the Swedish poet have been examined in a rather large number of studies, some of the more important of which are Fredrik Böök's "Tegnér och Ossian," *S*, xxxvii (1916), 133–61, Albert Nilsson's "Schillers inflytande på Tegnér och Tegnérs samtida," *S*, xxvi (1905), 9–60, Maurice Gravier's *Tegnér et la France* (Paris, 1943), and Algot Werin's essays "Goethe och Tegnér," *OoB*, xli (1932), 575–86 (reprinted in *Svensk idealism*, 1938), "Tegnér och Rousseau" in *Festskrift til Paul V. Rubow* (Copenhagen, 1956), and *Tegnérs Byronism* (in *Lunds universitets årsskrift*, 1946). Attitudes toward Tegnér as reflected among his contemporaries have been brought together in *Esaias Tegnér sedd av sina samtida*, ed. by Nils Palmberg (1958). Many articles of value are to be found in *Tegnérstudier*, published by Tegnérsamfundet, 1948ff. Attention should finally be called also to the edition of Tegnér's *Brev*, ed. by Nils Palmberg (six volumes of which have appeared to date). Tegnér's letters, together with Strindberg's, are the most fascinating, and revealing, in Swedish literature.

On the centenary of Johan Olof Wallin's death in 1939 a miscellany of studies was issued by Hilmer Wentz under the title *Johan Olof Wallin: till hundraårsminnet*. Other recent items from the rather limited Wallin literature are Emil Liedgren's *Johan Olof Wallin i yngre år* (1929), Henry Olsson's "Wallins oro och 'krisen' i hans liv," *S*, n.f. xviii (1937), 35–52, and "Korta kommentarer," *S*, n.f. xxi (1940), 149–156, Erik Hörnström's "Wallins utvecklingsgång, sådan den framträder i hans psalmer" in *Studier tillägnade Anton Blanck* (1946), pp.172–95, Knud Koch's *Johan Olof Wallin, Sveriges store salmedigter* (Copenhagen, 1946), Daniel Almqvist's "Från Wallins barndom," *OoB*, lvii (1948), 57–61, Tor Persson's dissertation *Studier i J. O. Wallins predikostil* (1950). Daniel Andreae's *Johan Olof Wallin* (1956), and Robert Murray's *Johan Olof Wallin* (1958). Incisive observations on Wallin's treatment of the theme of death in his famous poem "Dödens Engel" are to be found in Carl Fehrman's *Liemannen, Thanatos och Dödens Ängel* (Lund, 1957).

Only a dozen or so Swedish scholars have concerned themselves seriously with Erik Johan Stagnelius, and two of them, Fredrik Böök and Sven Cederblad, have borne most of the scholarly burden. Besides being responsible for the critical edition of Stagnelius's works (1911–19), Böök has published two monographs, *Erik Johan Stagnelius* (1919) and *Erik Johan Stagnelius: liv och dikt* (1954), has contributed a number of shorter Stagnelius studies (in *Samlaren*, in *Svenska Studier i Litteraturvetenskap*, and elsewhere), has written the little book *Stagnelius än en gång* (1942) in which he defines his position with regard to the central problems of Stagnelius scholarship, and, most recently, has published *Kreaturens suckan och andra Stagneliusstudier* (Malmö, 1957). Cederblad has been almost as active, having issued two major works, *Studier i Stagnelii romantik* (Uppsala, 1923) and *Stagnelius och hans omgivning* (1936), and contributed to *S* (1917, 1923, 1925) a series of basic Stagnelius investigations. Others who have contributed repeatedly and authoritatively to the clarification of various problems in Stagnelius are Albert Nilsson, with a chapter on Stagnelius in *Svensk romantik* (Lund, 1916) and with *Kronologien i Stagnelius diktning* (Uppsala, 1926), Olle Holmberg, who has also taken up problems of dating (*S*, 1939), and has written the challenging book *Sex kapitel om Stagnelius* (1941), Henry Olsson, whose particular concern has been with biographical detail (*S*, 1925, 1927, 1933), and B. Risberg, who has contributed a number of textual studies (*Nysvenska studier*, 1921–23, 1925, 1943). For an under-standing of Stagnelius's strange idea world, G. Widengren's "Gnostikern Stag-nelius," *S*, n.f. xxv (1944), 115–78, is of considerable interest. For a thorough review of French influences, see Pierre Brachin's *Les Influences françaises dans l'oeuvre de E. J. Stagnelius* (Paris, 1953). Among the most recent books on Stagnelius is Daniel Andreae's *Erik Johan Stagnelius* (1955), which provides a fresh but questionably acceptable approach to the poet's psyche and his work.

Chapter 7. Mid-Century Ferment

In addition to the material in the general Swedish literary histories, two special surveys of the mid-nineteenth-century literary ferment are available, Otto Sylwan's *Svensk litteratur vid adertonhundratalets midt* (Göteborg, 1903) and Johan Mor-tensen's *Från Aftonbladet till Röda rummet* (1905; 2nd ed. 1913). Examinations of certain antiromantic trends are made in Karl Warburg's "Den börjande reaktionen mot nyromantiken," *S*, xxiv (1903), 71–123, and in Jacob Kulling's "Hegel och reaktionen mot romantiken i Sverige," *Edda*, xxxviii (1938), 494–509, while studies of more broadly inclusive value are Alf Kjellén's *Sociala idéer och motiv hos svenska författare under 1830- och 1840-talen*, i (1937) and two items by Victor Svanberg, a popular survey of middle-class prose fiction during the period in *Svenska folket genom tiderna* (Malmö, 1939), ix, 281–322, and the penetrating social-oriented in-vestigations in "Medelklassrealism, i–iii," *S*, n.f. xxiv (1943), 111–73, xxv (1944), 1–99, xxvii (1946), 102–39. Early "realistic" developments in Swedish prose fiction are ex-amined in Nils Sylwan's *Svensk realistisk roman 1795–1830* (1942). Nineteenth-century Swedish liberalism is examined in considerable detail in Valfrid Spångberg's *Liberalismen i svensk politik*, i–ii (1927). The political journalism of the mid-century is investigated in certain limited contexts in Jean Göransson's *Aftonbladet som politisk tidning 1830–1835* (Uppsala, 1937), liberal literary criticism in Daniel An-dreae's *Liberal litteraturkritik: J. P. Theorell. C. F. Bergstedt* (1940), and new re-ligious trends in Edvard Rodhe's *Den religiösa liberalismen: Nils Ignell, Victor Rydberg, Pontus Vikner* (1935) and Gunnar Westin's *George Scott och hans verk-samhet i Sverige* (1928–29). In English Bryn J. Hovde's *The Scandinavian Coun-tries 1720–1865* (Boston, 1943) provides a detailed examination of the rising impor-tance of the middle classes while Eli F. Heckscher's *An Economic History of Sweden* (Cambridge, Mass., 1954) and G. A. Montgomery's *The Rise of Modern Industry in Sweden* (London, 1939) offer authoritative examinations of economic and industrial developments during the period.

The enigmatic personality and arresting work of C. J. L. Almqvist have been the subject of a number of distinguished monographs, the more inclusive of which are Olle Holmberg's *C. J. L. Almquist från 'Amorina' till 'Columbine'* (1922) and Algot Werin's *C. J. L. Almquist: realisten och liberalen* (1923), which deal respec-tively with Almqvist's early and later periods, and Henry Olsson's two works *C. J. L. Almquist före Törnrosens bok* (1927) and *Carl Jonas Love Almquist till 1836* (1937), the latter of which in addition to analyzing Almqvist's literary pro-duction down to 1836 provides a brilliant diagnosis of his complex psyche. Henry Olsson has also provided by far the best general introduction to the life and total work of Almqvist in the extended critical essay "Törnrosdiktaren" (in *Törnros-diktaren och andra porträtt* [1956], pp.35–213), a considerably enlarged version of his chapter on Almqvist in *Ny Illustrerad svensk litteraturhistoria*, iii. Almqvist's fugitive existence in the United States from 1851 to 1865 and the catastrophic series of events which led up to it have been thoroughly investigated by Ruben G:son

Berg in *C. J. L. Almquist i landsflykten* (1928) and A. Hemming-Sjöberg in *Rätte-gången mot C. J. L. Almquist* (1929). The latter work has appeared in an English version entitled *A Poet's Tragedy: The Trial of C. J. L. Almqvist* (London, 1932). In the now century-long debate as to whether Almqvist was guilty of the criminal charges against him Ruben G:son Berg, a literary historian, maintains a qualified "no" while A. Hemming-Sjöberg, a lawyer, counters with an unqualified "yes." Two of the more recent contributions to the subject of Almqvist's "guilt" are Knut Jaensson's in *Dagens Nyheter*, August 14, 16, and 18, 1949, and Algot Werin's "Brotts-lingen Almquist" in *Den svenske Faust och andra essayer* (Malmö, 1950), pp.133–52. Representative of the many special shorter studies which throw light on one side or other of Almqvist's personality and work are Oscar Levertin's "Stockholmsnaturen i svensk dikt," *Samlade Skrifter*, xix (1923), 157–255, Fredrik Vetterlund's "Love Almqvists poetiska exotism" in *Romantiskt 1800-tal* (1934), pp.9–64, Nils Staf's "C. J. L. Almquist och Aftonbladet," *S*, n.f. xxi (1940), 162–69, Torsten Bohlin's "Fromhet och religiös spekulation hos C. J. L. Almqvist" in *Profiler* (1946), pp.96–146, and Gustaf Fredén's "Balzac dans la littérature suédoise" in *Hommage à Balzac* (Paris, 1950), pp.239–65. Mention should finally be made of Roland Fridholm's "Almquists marivaudage," *S*, n.f. xxv (1944), 179–202, which contributes significantly to the analysis of Almqvist's personality in terms of modern psychological concepts, Alf Kjellén's Almqvist chapter in *Sociala idéer och motiv hos svenska författare under 1830- och 1840-talen*, i (1937), 171–229, which examines the liberal-revolu-tionary ideas that inspire the social reform trends in Almqvist's prose fiction, Karl Warburg's "Det går an" in *Essayer* (Uppsala, 1918), pp.146–207, which investigates the ideational backgrounds of *Det går an* and documents in some detail the uproar which the novel aroused upon its publication in 1838, and — of interest especially to those concerned with Sir Walter Scott's impact on Almqvist and his Swedish contemporaries — Erik Lindström's *Walter Scott och den historiska romanen och novellen i Sverige intill 1850* (Göteborg, 1925).

Though Fredrika Bremer has quite appropriately received far more attention than have her feminine contemporaries and literary rivals Sophie von Knorring and Emilie Flygare-Carlén from those concerned with literature and allied matters, the quality of the Fredrika Bremer studies has until relatively recent years been rather pedestrian and uneven, chiefly because the many earlier books and articles about her were with some exceptions more or less uncritical, if not actually partisan, accounts of her work as a feminist and social idealist. This is to a certain degree (though not fatally) true even of the standard biography, S. L-d Adlersparre and Sigrid Leijonhufvud's *Fredrika Bremer*, i–ii (1896), and considerably more true of other early books and articles on Fredrika Bremer. A more mature but not entirely disinterested work is Ellen Kleman's *Fredrika Bremer* (Uppsala, 1925). It may, in-deed, be said that Fredrika Bremer scholarship did not really come of age until our generation — in the hands of Alf Kjellén, whose *Sociala idéer och motiv hos svenska författare under 1830- och 1840-talen*, i (1937) defined Fredrika Bremer's place in the contexts of early nineteenth-century social and political liberalism, of Victor Svanberg, whose notes on Fredrika Bremer's upper middle-class origins ("Medel-klassrealism: ii," *S*, n.f. xxv [1944], 87ff.) offer a new perspective on her authorship, of Gunnar Axberger, whose *Jaget och skuggorna: Fredrika Bremer studier* (1951) provides us with the first penetrating modern psychological study of her person as reflected in her work, and of Elof Ehnmark, whose detailed analyses of her early Sketches and Tales and of her first novel, *Familjen H...* (see *S*, 1938, 1939–40), have concentrated our attention as no one before him on the more purely literary side of Fredrika Bremer's work. Kjellén has also (in "Fredrika Bremers Syskonlif," *S*, n.f. xxvii [1946], 31–51) subjected one of Fredrika Bremer's novels to a close examination, and Ehnmark has recently written the short up-to-date general study *Fredrika Bremer* (1955). The only items that need be added to the present listing of Swedish studies are an essay by Algot Werin, "Fredrika Bremer" in *Svenskt 1800-tal* (Lund, 1948), pp.7–49, a popular but sensitively conceived and well-executed biographical study by Gustaf Fredén entitled *Arvet från Fredrika Bremer* (Lund, 1951), and the unfinished Swedish Academy "Minnesteckning" by Elin Wägner *Fredrika Bremer* (1949).

In the Anglo-American world much has been written about Fredrika Bremer, in part because her novels were extensively translated into English and in part because of her travel-residence in the United States and England. But aside from the early reviews of the English versions of her books and one later study (Alrik Gustafson's "English Influences in Fredrika Bremer, i–iii," *The Journal of English and Germanic Philology*, xxx, xxxi, xxxii [1931, 1932, 1933], 223–35, 92–123, 373–91), practically all of the material in English on Fredrika Bremer is concerned with biographical matters or has to do with her travels and social-philanthropical interests rather than with her literary activities. The first general "life" in Swedish appeared as early as 1868 in an English version entitled *Life, Letters, and Posthumous Works of Fredrika Bremer*, ed. by Charlotte Bremer. Two years earlier Margaret Howitt's two-volume *Twelve Months with Fredrika Bremer in Sweden* had appeared in London. Many hands, including Fredrika Bremer's own (see the list of English translations of Swedish books following the present bibliography), have recorded and commented on her English and American travels, particularly the latter. On the American reception of her work see two articles in Adolph B. Benson's *American Scandinavian Studies* (New York, 1952), pp.196–213, 214–21.

By far the most ambitious of the studies on Fredrika Bremer in America is Signe A. Rooth's *Seeress of the Northland: Fredrika Bremer's American Journey 1849–1851* (Philadelphia, 1955), a somewhat popularized version of a dissertation submitted at the University of Chicago in 1953. Besides providing a rather detailed account of Fredrika Bremer's travels in the United States, this book contains seventy-three previously unpublished Bremer letters (almost all addressed to American friends) and a bibliography which scarcely leaves a stone unturned in its search for bibliographical minutiae of all kinds. The student of Fredrika Bremer in America will find this bibliography invaluable, but he may be irritated by its mechanical, rather meaningless organization and by its mere *listing* of titles with no indication of the relative value of the items included.

Among the few studies of value on Sophie von Knorring and Emilie Flygare-Carlén only the following need be mentioned here: Barbro Nelson, *Sophie von Knorring: en svensk romanförfattarinnas liv och dikt* (1927), Fredrik Böök, "Sophie von Knorring" in *Fem porträtt* (1929), Alf Kjellén, *Emilie Flygare-Carlén* (1932), Assar Janzén, *Emilie Flygare-Carlén: en studie i 1800-talets romandialog* (in *Göteborgs Vetenskaps- och Vitterhetssamhälles handlingar*, vi, ser. A, vol. 3, n:r 4), and Victor Svanberg, "Medelklassrealism, iii," *S*, n.f. xxvii (1946), 102–12. ¶ On C. A. Wetterbergh, August Blanche, and Fredrik Cederborgh, who contemporaneously with their female literary counterparts Sophie von Knorring and Emilie Flygare-Carlén dispensed light prose fiction to a popular Swedish reading public, see Hilding Lundberg's dissertation *C. A. Wetterberghs sociala författarskap* (Uppsala, 1943), Martin Lamm's monograph *August Blanche som Stockholmsskildrare* (1931), and Fredrik Böök's *Fredrik Cederborgh: Minnesteckning* (1925).

Of the two major mid-nineteenth-century literary figures Johan Ludvig Rune-berg and Viktor Rydberg, Runeberg in particular has been worked over with a fine-tooth comb, chiefly but by no means exclusively in the hands of Swedo-Finnish scholars. Werner Söderhjelm's *Johan Ludvig Runeberg: hans lif och diktning* (Helsingfors, 1904–6; new rev. ed. 1929) laid the solid groundwork for all bio-graphical studies to follow and has not been made superfluous even by Lauri Viljanen's monumental two-volume work in Finnish (1944, 1948), the first volume of which, covering the years 1804–37, has been published in Swedish (1947). Vil-janen's work has incorporated all of the findings of Runeberg scholarship of the last generation or two, a scholarship which from various points of view has man-aged to divest the poet of many of the purely legendary attributes which had earlier attached themselves to his person and work as the great *national* poet of Finland. How far the older scholarly and semi-scholarly literature on Runeberg had gone in its uncritical worship of "the master" has been brilliantly investigated in *Rune-bergskulten* (1935) by Yrjö Hirn, who has also in *Runeberg-gestalten: strödda studier* (1942) given us some of the finest fruits of his extensive Runeberg investi-gations. Without seeking in any way to deny Runeberg's greatness, a latter-day scholarship has brought the poet down to earth, has humanized him, and has dem-onstrated conclusively that he was far more dependent on the general thought trends of his time, especially on German Romantic idealism, than his earlier cultish ad-mirers had been ready to admit. Those who are interested in the details of the more recent Runeberg scholarship may be referred to the review-article by E. N. Tiger-stedt, "Modern Runebergforskning," *Nordisk Tidskrift*, xix (1943), 364–70, and to Lauri Viljanen's bibliographical notes "En blick på Runeberg-forskningen" at the close of his work *Runeberg och hans diktning 1804–1837* (Lund, 1947).

Though some arresting efforts to identify Runeberg's relations to a larger world of idea and literary form than the contemporary scene in Finland were made in the first decade of our century (see especially Johan Mortensen's "Till Runebergs förebilder," *S*, 1904, 1908), it was not until the following decade that this approach celebrated its first great triumphs – in such studies as Ruth Hedvall's dissertation *Runebergs poetiska stil* (Helsingfors, 1915), in Martin Lamm's "Ödesuppfattningen i Runebergs 'Kung Fjalar'," *Festskrift till Gerhard Gran 1916* (Kristiania, 1916), and in Sixten Belfrage's *Johan Ludvig Runeberg i sin religiösa utveckling* (Uppsala, 1917). Other studies of a similar kind have followed, the most brilliant and thor-ough being Gunnar Tideström's *Runeberg som estetiker: litterära och filosofiska idéer i den unge Runebergs författarskap* (Helsingfors, 1941). Of interest to students of English Romanticism is also a section on Sir Walter Scott's impact on Runeberg in Erik Lindström's *Walter Scott och den historiska romanen i Sverige* (Göteborg, 1925), pp.256–74. Among the many studies which have been concerned with rede-fining Runeberg's "realism" is the work *Idealism och realism i Runebergs diktning* (Helsingfors, 1931) by Eirik Hornborg, who has also in *Fänrik Ståls sägner och verkligheten* (Helsingfors, 1954) published a valuable investigation of the extent to which Runeberg departed from the military realities of the Finno-Russian War of 1808–9 in his highly popular narrative sequence dealing with the War. Books and articles on limited aspects of Runeberg's life and investigations of his specifically Finnish backgrounds are so numerous that I must here refer the interested reader to the bibliographical listings in *Ny illustrerad svensk litteraturhistoria*, iii, 608–13. Among the works of a more general kind which should be mentioned in addition to the Söderhjelm and Viljanen biographies are Ruth Hedvall's lively and often penetrating but not always reliable *Runeberg och hans diktning* (1931, 2nd ed.

1941), Gunnar Castrén's brief but excellent *Johan Ludvig Runeberg* (1950), and Yrjö and Marta Hirn's richly illustrated book *Runeberg och hans värld* (Helsingfors, 1937), which brings magnificently to life the various Finnish milieus in which the poet passed his life.

The fortunes of Runeberg at the hands of German, French, and English translators and critics were quite early examined in Werner Söderhjelm's "Runeberg inför utlandet" in *Profiler ur finskt kulturliv* (Helsingfors, 1913), the findings of which have recently been considerably supplemented so far as English translators and critics are concerned in Nils Erik Enkvist's "Samtida engelska omdömen om Runeberg," *FT*, CLXI–CLXII (1957), 7–18. The only readily available items of value in English on Runeberg are Edmund Gosse's early essay on the poet in *Studies in the Literature of Northern Europe* (London, 1879, reprinted under the title *Northern Studies*, 1890) and two items of Finnish origin, the poet Bertel Gripenberg's nostalgic essay "A Poet's Town: Borgå, Where Runeberg's Memory Is Enshrined," *ASR*, XXI (1933), 81–88, and the scholar Yrjö Hirn's little survey of the origins and popularity of *Fänrik Ståls sägner* which provides the Introduction to *The Tales of Ensign Stål* (New York and Princeton, 1938), C. W. Stork's translation of Runeberg's famous work. In French a section on Runeberg has been included in Lucien Maury's *L'imagination scandinave* (Paris, 1929), pp.31–63.

Though Rydberg criticism and scholarship is not as extensive as that about Runeberg, it maintains at least as high an interpretative level and has not become entangled, as so often in the case of Runeberg, in a cultish confusion of interpretative undergrowth. But literary historians of the last generation have had to revise certain earlier assumptions as to the relative mildness of Rydberg's liberalism. The central importance for Rydberg of nineteenth-century liberalism and its persistence in his thinking has been emphasized by two scholars in particular, Victor Svanberg and Örjan Lindberger, Svanberg especially in *Novantiken i Den siste athenaren* (Uppsala, 1928) and "Viktor Rydbergs lyriska genombrott," *S*, n.f. XVIII (1937), 53–177, and Lindberger in the impressive, far-ranging monograph *Prometeustanken hos Viktor Rydberg*, I–II (1938). On Rydberg's religious liberalism the basic work is Isak Krook's *Viktor Rydbergs lära om Kristus* (1935), which may be read in conjunction with Edvard Rodhe's *Den religiösa liberalismen: Nils Ignell, Viktor Rydberg, Pontus Wikner* (1935).

No general biographical work on Rydberg has appeared since Karl Warburg's two-volume *Viktor Rydberg, en levnadsteckning* (1900), but biographical research during the last half century on particular episodes or periods in Rydberg's life has turned up much new material. Representative of this biographical research are Axel Forsström's *Viktor Rydbergs barndom och skolår i Jönköping och Växjö* and H. Hedlund's *Viktor Rydberg som tidningsman och andra Rydbergsminnen* (both in *Viktor Rydberg, Minnesskrift*, utg. av Göteborgs högskolas studentkår 1928), two items by Olle Holmberg, "Viktor Rydberg i Lund" in *Gud som haver* (1939), pp. 125–46, and "Viktor Rydberg och kvinnorna," *SLT*, XI (1948), 185–92, Axel Forsström's "Svårmodskrisen i Viktor Rydbergs liv," *SLT*, XIV (1951), 41–48, and Örjan Lindberger's "Rydberg och nordstjärnan," *SLT*, XIV (1951), 112–27. Two short general works of some value representing respectively a conservative and a liberal point of view are Knut Hagberg's *Viktor Rydberg* (1928) and Torsten Fogelkvist's *Till Viktor Rydbergs minne* (1928).

Of general interest on Rydberg's impact upon Swedish thought is Harald Elovson's popular survey "Rydberg och hans inflytande på tänkesättet," *Svenska folket genom tiderna*, IX, 93–116. Paul Gemer has examined the whole of Rydberg's literary production down to and including *Den siste athenaren* (1859) in the dissertation *Viktor Rydbergs ungdomsdiktning* (1931), while Olle Holmberg has written the standard work on Rydberg's poetry in *Viktor Rydbergs lyrik* (1935). See also Sverker Ek's *Viktor Rydbergs lyriska diktning* (in *Viktor Rydberg, Minnesskrift*, 1928, pp.76–175). Among the more arresting shorter general items in Swedish which may finally be mentioned are Oscar Levertin's necrology in *Diktare och drömmare* (1898), Algot Werin's essay in *Svensk idealism* (Lund, 1938; orig. publ. in *OoB*, 1928), and the investigation of Rydberg's Platonism by Albert Nilsson in *Svensk romantik* (Lund, 1916). In French Maurice Gravier has contributed a study on Rydberg's puristic theories and practices in the article "Un puriste suédois: Viktor Rydberg" in *Mélanges de linguistique et de philologie: Fernand Mossé in memoriam* (Paris, 1960), pp.185–96. In German Hermann Büssow's *Viktor Rydbergs historische Romane* (Braunschweig, Berlin, Hamburg, 1929) may be consulted.

We need here take note of only a few of the studies on the literary ramifications of mid-nineteenth-century pan-Scandinavianism and on the so-called "Signature" group of poets exclusive of Carl Snoilsky. On the poetry of the period in general see Gudmar Hasselberg's *Realistisk lyrik* (Lund, 1923). The pan-Scandinavianism of the mid-nineteenth century has been examined in detail in Åke Holmberg's dissertation *Skandinavismen i Sverige vid 1800-talets mitt* (Göteborg, 1946) and in brief, popular form by Edvard Thermaenius in *Svenska folket genom tiderna*, ix, 11–36. The popularity of this pan-Scandinavianism among university students has been treated at some length in Otto Sylwan's *Fyrtiotalets student* (1914) and briefly by the same scholar in *Svenska folket genom tiderna*, ix, 359–84. Modern pan-Scandinavianism in Sweden has been placed in its larger historical contexts from the early Middle Ages down to and including the nineteenth century in Hans Lennart Lundh's little book *Skandinavismen i Sverige* (1951). ¶ Bernhard Tarschy's dissertation *Talis Qualis, studentpoeten* (1949) is concerned with C. V. A. Strandberg, the chief Swedish poet among the pan-Scandinavianists of the 1840's. See also Algot Werin's "Student på 1840-talet" in *Den svenske Faust* (Lund, 1950), a review-article occasioned by Tarschy's book. ¶ On the "Signature poets" as a group see Lorentz Dietrichson's memoirs *Svunne tider*, ii–iii (Kristiania, 1899, 1901) and Holger Nyblom's "Namnlösa sällskapet," *SLT*, x (1947), 145–60. On Edvard Bäckström see Stig Torsslow's *Edvard Bäckström och hans dramatiska diktning* (Göteborg, 1947). ¶ The only really sympathetic effort to "explain" C. D. af Wirsén and his work has been at the hands of Fr. Vetterlund, who in various places (in the books *Romantik*, 1920, and *Ur portföljen*, 1927, and in the journals *S*, 1936, and *Svensk Tidskrift*, 1942) has sought not very impressively to rehabilitate the memory of Wirsén. Two earlier commentaries of interest on Wirsén are Levertin's exposé (1900) of his critical attitudes and methods (L's *Samlade skrifter*, xxiv [1910], 167–81) and Heidenstam's diplomatically courteous Swedish Academy necrology (H's *Samlade verk*, xxiii). ¶ The most distinguished work on Snoilsky has been done by Henry Olsson, whose early investigations, reflected in "Snoilskys tidigare sociala diktning," *S*, n.f. xii (1931), 5–96, and "Snoilskys Svenska bilder," *OoB*, xliv (1935), 11–28, have culminated in the solid monograph *Den unge Snoilsky* (1941) and the sensitive extended essay "Snoilskygestalten" in *Törnrosdiktaren och andra porträtt* (1956). Karl Warburg's early work *Carl Snoilsky: hans levnad och skaldskap* (1905) suffers from having had to be too circumspect in its use of sources. Snoilsky has repeatedly engaged Oscar Levertin's critical attention (see L's *Svenska gestalter*, 1903, pp.253–66, *Essayer*, i, 1907, pp.233–42, *Diktare och drömmare*, 1908, pp.217–24, and *Svensk litteratur*, ii, 1909, pp.28–32). Fredrik Böök has devoted two studies to Snoilsky,

"Snoilskys sociala diktning," *Svenska studier i litteraturvetenskap*, 1913, and "Snoilsky och åttiotalet," *OoB*, xxx (1921), 17–32, both of which have been reprinted in Böök's *Från åttiotalet* (Stockholm, 1926). The first of these studies has been sharply challenged by Hans Larsson in "Snoilskys sociala diktning, en anti-kommentar," *Forum*, iii (1916), 51–55, reprinted in revised form in Hans Larsson's *Litteraturintryck* (Stockholm, 1926). Other Snoilsky items of value are Nils Svanberg's "Uttrycksfulla metriska former hos Snoilsky och Rydberg," *NS*, xviii (1938), 37–85, Paul Gemer's "Svenska Bilders förebilder," *OoB*, xxxix (1930), 543–46, and Hugo Valentin's "Snoilskys 'demokratiska' historieuppfattning," *OoB*, lvi (1947), 201–9. Edmund Gosse's "Carl Snoilsky and Some Recent Swedish Poets" in *Portraits and Sketches* (New York, 1913), pp.229–40, touches *merely* the surface of its subject.

Chapter 8. Strindberg and the Realistic Breakthrough

Works of general survey importance on the realistic breakthrough in the 1880's are, in addition to the standard literary histories previously mentioned, David Sprengel's prejudiced but stimulating *De nya poeterna* (1902), Johan Mortensen's *Från Röda rummet till sekelskiftet*, i–ii (1918, 1919), and the early portions of Kjell Strömberg's little book *Modern svensk litteratur* (1932). Though Melker Johnsson's *En åttitalist: Gustaf af Geijerstam 1858–1895* (Göteborg, 1934) is concerned primarily with one representative figure of the 1880's, its broadly inclusive approach to Geijerstam's total intellectual and literary environment provides the reader incidentally with a host of insights into the mentality of the 1880's in general. Fredrik Böök's *Från åttiotalet* (1926) includes essays on a number of key figures of the decade. Important on general economic, social, and political conditions during the period as well as on literary matters is *Sverige i dikt och data 1865–1940* (1941), a collective work consisting of a series of radio lectures by a number of experts in the various fields represented. Gunnar Ahlström's arresting monograph *Det moderna genombrottet i Nordens litteratur* (1947) covers the Scandinavian literatures in general from an essentially sociological point of view.

Other studies which illuminate less broadly than Ahlström's work the interrelations among the literatures of Denmark, Norway, and Sweden during the period are Holger Ahlenius's *Georg Brandes i svensk litteratur till och med 1890* (1932), Nils Åke Sjöstedt's *Sören Kierkegaard och svensk litteratur: från Fredrika Bremer till Hjalmar Söderberg* (Göteborg, 1950), Arne Lidén's *Den norska strömningen i svensk litteratur under 1800-talet* (Uppsala, 1926), and Torsten Svedfelt's "Alexander Kielland och det svenska åttitalet," *Edda*, xxxi (1931), 287–312. Of great value as basic source material are *När vi började* (1902), which includes autobiographical contributions from a number of Swedish authors, chiefly the generation of the 1880's, and *Bonniers, en bokhandlarfamilj*, iv, v (Stockholm, 1931, 1956), which provides a rich dossier on many authors of the period insofar as they had relations with the great publishing house of Bonniers. On the academic radicalism of the day as represented in the Verdandi Society at Uppsala see *Verdandi genom femtio år* (Stockholm, 1932). The journal *1885. Revy i litterära och sociala ämnen*, with a second, and last, volume, *1886*, reflects in various ways the mentality of the 1880's in Swedish literature.

In English some notes are provided in the Introduction to my book *Six Scandinavian Novelists* (Princeton and New York, 1940) on the major role played by Georg Brandes in the Scandinavian literary developments of the 1870's and 1880's, while an essay on Brandes by Oscar Seidlin in the *Journal of the History of Ideas*, iii (1942), 415–42, offers an adequate analysis and summation of the famous Danish critic's thought. For a general survey of the literature of the period see H. G. Topsöe-Jensen's somewhat sketchy handbook *Scandinavian Literature from Brandes to Our Day* (New York, 1929), and for thumbnail sketches of most of the Swedish authors of the day see the *Columbia Dictionary of Modern European Literature* (New York, 1947). The new economic forces which triggered demands for social reform and political change in late nineteenth-century Sweden may be examined in such standard works as Eli F. Heckscher's *An Economic History of Sweden* (Cambridge, Mass., 1954) and G. A. Montgomery's *The Rise of Modern Industry in Sweden* (London, 1939), and the changing political patterns resulting from the new economic conditions can be studied in such recent books as Dankwart A. Rustow's excellent work *The Politics of Compromise: A Study of Parties and Cabinet Government in Sweden* (Princeton, 1955) and Douglas V. Verney's less satisfactory *Parliamentary Reform in Sweden, 1866–1921* (New York, 1957).

Though Strindberg has over an extended period of time attracted more international attention than any other Swedish author, only in Sweden, quite naturally, has his person and work engaged the finest energies of a large number of highly competent critics and scholars. Elsewhere he has only sporadically met with understanding and adequate critical appraisal. Most of the more superficial or merely wrong-headed studies of non-Swedish origin on Strindberg can be ignored in the present contexts, but what of greater or lesser value remains after such exclusions is still so extensive that it makes difficult the efforts of one who labors under the necessity of being reasonably selective in his inclusions.

The rather numerous serious studies on Strindberg in German have been concerned largely with the pathological sides of his genius, with his world of ideas, and with the radical experimental aspects of his dramaturgy. The best of the half dozen or more German efforts to diagnose his psychic illness is perhaps Karl Jaspers' *Strindberg und van Gogh* (Berlin, 2nd ed. 1926), a work which suffers, however, from an oversimplification in its diagnosis and a rather careless handling of chronology. Representative of a number of German efforts to place Strindberg in the intellectual currents of his day is Arthur Liebert's little study *August Strindberg, seine Weltanschauung und seine Kunst* (Berlin, 1920). One-sided as Liebert's rigid neo-Kantian approach to Strindberg is, it succeeds in throwing considerable light over Strindberg's relation to the interplay between a naturalistic determinism and new mystical and semi-mystical tendencies in modern thought. An interesting but rather too polemic treatment of Strindberg's impact on German expressionistic drama and theater is provided in Bernhard Diebold's *Anarchie im Drama* (Berlin, 4th ed. 1928). A popular but inclusive and generally adequate book on Strindberg's total dramatic production is C. D. Marcus's *Strindbergs Dramatik* (Munich, 1918). In German there is also available an interesting analysis of Strindberg's "dream play" propensities in H. Taub's *Strindberg als Traumdichter* (in *Göteborgs Vetenskaps- och Vitterhetssamhälles handlingar*, 1945) and also a dissertation by E. Peukert, *Strindbergs religiöse Dramatik* (Hamburg, 1929). Of biographical interest two Swedish "lives" of Strindberg have appeared in German versions, Nils Erdmann's rather superficial *August Strindberg. Die Geschichte einer kämpfenden und leidenden Seele* (Leipzig, 1924) and Erik Hedén's excellent *Strindberg. Leben und Dichtung* (Munich, 1926), and three more or less untrustworthy memoir volumes, those by the Finns Adolf Paul (*Strindberg-Erinnerungen und -Briefe* [Munich, 1924; also a number of Swedish editions]) and Wettenhovi-Aspa (*August Strindberg intim* [Helsingfors, 1936]) and the German physician Carl Ludwig Schleich's *Strindberg-Erinnerungen* (*Vossische Zeitung*, 1917; tr. into Swedish as *Hågkomster om Strindberg* [Stockholm, 1917]), reprinted in Schleich's inclusive memoirs *Besonnte Vergangenheit* (1921) and in its Swedish and American editions, 1937 and 1936 respectively. The title of the American edition is *Those Were Good Days!* Of great value for the post-Inferno period are Strindberg's *Briefe an Emil Schering* (Munich, 1924). Mention should also be made in passing here of the German scholar Walter Berendsohn, to whose more important Strindberg investigations we shall, however, refer below inasmuch as they have nearly all appeared in Swedish because of Berendsohn's permanent residence in Sweden since the middle 1930's. A popular little book by Berendsohn in German is the recent *August Strindberg ein geborener Dramatiker* (Munich, 1956).

In French, Strindberg studies are not nearly so numerous as in German, but they are less speculative and more solid and palatable, particularly those by A. Jolivet and Maurice Gravier, both of whom are thoroughly familiar with Strindberg and Strindberg scholarship. Jolivet has contributed, in addition to his major Strindberg work *Le Théâtre de Strindberg* (Paris, 1931), an article on Rousseau and Strindberg and another on Nietzsche and Strindberg (*Revue de littérature comparée*, 1933, 1939). Gravier, who as a Strindberg scholar has to date concerned himself chiefly with Strindberg and German literature – see especially his *Strindberg et le théâtre modern, I: L'Allemagne* (Paris, 1949) and "Strindberg et Kafka," *Études germaniques*, XXXI (1953), 208-28 – proposes to add to his comparative investigation of Strindberg's influence on the German drama and theater similar studies of Strindberg's impact on the drama and theater of the Scandinavian, Anglo-Saxon, and the Latin countries. Of considerable interest also are Gravier's articles "Skandinaviske författare i eksil [on Snoilsky, Ibsen, and Strindberg]," *Edda*, LVIII (1957), 301-16, "Mises en scène de Strindberg," *La Mise en scène des oeuvres du passé* (Paris, n.d.), pp.41-51, and "Strindberg traducteur de lui-même" in *Mélanges de philologie romane offerts à M. Karl Michaëlsson* (Göteborg, 1952), pp.217-24. Other items in French of greater or lesser value are L. Lagriffe's "La Psychologie d'Auguste Strindberg," *Journal de Psychologie*, IX (1912), 481-500, Lucien Maury's miscellany of short articles on Strindberg in *L'Imagination scandinave* (Paris, 1929), pp.114-53, and two chapters in *Panorama de la littérature suédoise contemporaine* (Paris, 1940), pp.65-81, 155-63, Martin Lamm's "Quelques influences françaises sur l'autobiographie de Strindberg," *Mélanges . . . offerts à F. Baldensperger*, II (Paris, 1930), pp.22-27, A. Dikka Reque's *Trois auteurs dramatiques scandinaves: Ibsen, Björnson, Strindberg devant la critique française* (Paris, 1930), Gustaf Fredén's notes on Balzac and Strindberg in "Balzac dans la littérature suédoise," *Hommage à Balzac* (Paris, 1950), and Élie Poulenard's dissertation *Strindberg, romancier et nouvelliste* (Paris, 1957). On French theater directors and actors who have been attracted to Strindberg consult, besides André Antoine's *Souvenirs sur le Théâtre-Libre*, Jacques Robichez's *Le Symbolisme au théâtre: Lugné-Poe et les débuts de L'Œuvre* (Paris, 1957), and Arthur Adamov's *Auguste Strindberg dramaturge* (Paris, 1955). See also the eighteen-page résumé in French at the close of Stellan Ahlstrom's *Strindbergs erövring av Paris* (Stockholm, 1956), a study on Strindberg's relations to France from his youth down to the Inferno experience.

Though the commentary on and the excerpting from the books, articles, and reviews included in Esther H. Rapp's bibliography on Strindberg in England and America (*SS*, XXIII [1951], 1-22, 49-59, 109-37) are not very satisfactory, her ferreting out and recording of practically every mention of Strindberg in English and American sources is of considerable value to those interested in Strindberg's fortunes outside Sweden. A reasonably detailed survey of the opinions expressed in

Anglo-American periodical criticism for two decades after 1892 is provided in my article "Some Early English and American Strindberg Criticism," *Scandinavian Studies Presented to George T. Flom* (Urbana, Ill., 1942). Of the more prominent early English and American treatments of Strindberg three may be mentioned here, Justin McCarthy's enthusiastic introduction of Strindberg to English readers in the columns of *The Gentleman's Magazine* and *The Fortnightly Review* in the years 1892–93, James Huneker's freewheeling and enthusiastic but often inaccurate accounts of Strindberg in the periodicals *The Lamp* (January 1905) and *Harper's Weekly* (July 27, 1912), and Edwin Björkman's less expansive but generally sound articles in *The Forum* (February and March, 1912). The notes on Strindberg in *The Lamp* were reprinted in revised and somewhat extended form in Huneker's *Iconoclasts* (New York, 1905), and Björkman's articles in *The Forum* reappeared in greatly expanded form in the author's *Voices of Tomorrow* (New York and London, 1913). Björkman was also busy during the years around 1912 with his translations of Strindberg's plays, each of the five volumes of which included Introductions of no little value at the time.

Since the first two decades of Anglo-American Strindberg criticism, American critics and scholars have busied themselves somewhat more with Strindberg than their English colleagues. Nevertheless, work of English origin on Strindberg has provided the only reasonably adequate biography in English in Elizabeth Sprigge's *The Strange Life of August Strindberg* (London, 1949), the only satisfactory survey in English of the total literary production of Strindberg in Brita M. E. Mortensen's contribution to Mortensen and Downs's *Strindberg: An Introduction to His Life and Work* (Cambridge, 1949), and the only extended study in a major literary influence on Strindberg in Joan Bulman's *Strindberg and Shakespeare* (London, 1933). No book exclusively concerned with and covering the whole range of Strindberg's drama has as yet appeared either in England or America, but more or less satisfactory surveys and/or critical treatments of particular aspects of Strindberg's drama are included in such general works on the drama as Ludwig Lewisohn's *The Modern Drama* (New York, 1915), Storm Jameson's *The Modern Drama in Europe* (London and New York, 1920), Eric Bentley's *The Playwright as Thinker* (New York, 1946), Joseph Wood Krutch's *'Modernism' in Modern Drama* (Ithaca, N.Y., 1953), Raymond Williams' *Drama from Ibsen to Eliot* (London and New York, 1953), John Gassner's *Masters of the Drama* (New York, 3rd rev. and enl. ed. 1954), and the section by Alrik Gustafson entitled "The Scandinavian Countries" in *A History of Modern Drama* (New York and London, 1947), ed. by B. H. Clark and G. Freedley. To these general works of English and American origin should be added the greatest of Strindberg scholars Martin Lamm's *Modern Drama*, tr. by Karin Elliott (Oxford, 1952). Of less interest to the general reader are a number of works reflecting on the whole more the weaknesses than the strengths of the American doctoral dissertation – A. J. Uppvall's *August Strindberg. A Psychoanalytic Study with Special Reference to the Oedipus Complex* (Boston, 1920), C. A. Helmecke's *Buckle's Influence on Strindberg* (Philadelphia, 1924), Harry V. E. Palmblad's *Strindberg's Conception of History* (New York, 1927), and C. E. W. L. Dahlström's *Strindberg's Dramatic Expressionism* (Ann Arbor, 1930). Dahlström has also been responsible for a rather large number of ingenious and sometimes stimulating but one-sided and overly dogmatic shorter studies dealing particularly with Strindberg's relation to naturalism (see especially SS, xv, 257–65, xvi, 83–94, 212–19, XVII, 121–32, 269–81, XVIII, 14–36, 41–60, 98–114, 138–55, 183–94). On Strindberg's naturalism see also Børge Madsen's unpublished dissertation *The Im-*

pact of *French Naturalists and Psychologists on August Strindberg's Plays of the 1880's and Early 1890's* (University of Minnesota, 1957). On Strindberg's historical plays see J. G. Robertson's sketchy but stimulating generalizations in the Introduction to *Master Olof and Other Plays* (London, 1931) and Walter Johnson's rather full and informative Introductions and Notes to his five volumes of translations, *Queen Christina, Charles XII, Gustav III* (Seattle and New York, 1955), *The Last of the Knights, The Regent, Earl Birger of Bjälbo* (Seattle, 1956), *Gustav Adolf* (Seattle, 1957), *The Vasa Trilogy: Master Olof, Gustav Vasa, Erik XIV* (Seattle, 1959), and *The Saga of the Folkungs, Engelbrekt* (Seattle, 1959).

Two scarcely dependable books (originally appearing in Swedish and German) are Gustaf Uddgren's *Strindberg the Man* (Boston, 1920) and the sharply condensed English version of Strindberg's second wife Frieda Uhl's *Marriage with Genius* (London and Toronto, 1937, 2nd ed. 1940). The letters to Harriet Bosse, Strindberg's third wife, have been translated and edited by Arvid Paulson in *Letters of Strindberg to Harriet Bosse* (New York, 1959). Sound and reliable brief general essays of Swedish origin on Strindberg are Johan Mortensen's "Strindberg's Personality," *ASR*, x (1922), 289–95, and Helge Åkerhielm's "August Strindberg," *ASR*, xxvi (1938), 312–17. Strindberg's brief and hectic Nietzschean interlude has been examined in detail in Harold H. Borland's *Nietzsche's Influence on Swedish Literature* (Göteborg, 1956), pp.17–46.

Representative, finally, of the many items in English on various relatively limited aspects of Strindberg's many-faceted personality and work are three studies on Shakespeare and Strindberg, H. V. E. Palmblad's "Shakespeare and Strindberg," *Germanic Review*, iii (1928), 71–79, 168–77, Hans Andersson's *Strindberg's 'Master Olof' and Shakespeare* (Uppsala, 1952; cf. my review in *Bulletin de la Société Néophilologique de Helsinki. Neuphilologische Mitteilungen*, lvi, 1–2, pp.74–76), and Birgitta Steene's "Shakespearean Elements in the Historical Plays of Strindberg," *Comparative Literature*, xi (1959), 209–20; one on Strindberg's religious "conversion" as reflected in his later plays, Einar Haugen's "Strindberg the Regenerated," *Journal of English and Germanic Philology*, xxix (1930), 257–70; another on Strindberg's comic vein, A. B. Benson's "Humor and Satire in Strindberg's 'The Island of Paradise'," *SS*, xxvi (1954), 17–24; one on Strindberg and women, Jules Mauritzson's "August Strindberg and the Woman Question," *SS*, i (1911–14), 207–15; two on Strindberg's pathological condition, Axel Brett's "Psychological Abnormalities in August Strindberg," *Journal of English and Germanic Philology*, xx (1921), 47–98, and A. J. Uppvall's "Strindberg in the Light of Psychoanalysis," *SS*, xxi (1949), 135–50; one purely textual investigation, H. Bergholz's "Toward an Authentic Text of Strindberg's *Fröken Julie*," *Orbis Litterarum*, ix (1954), 167–92; one on Strindberg and naturalism, Børge G. Madsen's "Strindberg as a Naturalistic Theorist," *SS*, xxx (1958), 85–92; another, by John Milton, "The Esthetic Fault of Strindberg's 'Dream Plays'," *The Tulane Drama Review*, iv (Spring 1960), 108–16; three on Strindberg and the arts, E. M. Grew's "Strindberg and Music," *The Musical Quarterly*, xix (1933), 59–73, Paul Arnold's "From Aeschylos to Surrealist Theater," *Journal of Aesthetics and Art Criticism*, vii (1949), 349–54, and Paul Wescher's "Strindberg and the Chance-images of Surrealism," *The Art Quarterly*, xvi (1953), 93–105; one on Strindberg and Huysmans, Janko Lavrin's *Studies in European Literature* (London, 1929), pp.118–30; four on Strindberg's impact on American drama, Ira N. Hayward's "Strindberg's Influence on Eugene O'Neill," *Poet Lore*, xxxix (1928), 596–604, Frederic Fleisher, "Strindberg and O'Neill," *Symposium*, x (1956), 84–94, S. K. Winther's "Strindberg and O'Neill: A Study in Influence," *SS*,

XXXI (1959), 103-20, and William Beyer's notes on Lillian Hellman in "The State of the Theatre: The Strindberg Heritage," *School and Society*, LXXI (1950), nr. 1830, pp.23–28; four on Strindberg in broader world contexts, J. G. Robertson's "Strindberg's Position in European Literature" in *Essays and Addresses on Literature* (London, 1935), Arthur Burkhard's "August Strindberg and Modern German Drama," *The German Quarterly*, VI (1933), 163–74, Eric Bentley's "Strindberg in Europe," *Theatre Arts*, XXXIV (1950, nr. 2), 20–25, and John Gassner's "Strindberg in America," *Theatre Arts*, XXXIII (1949, nr. 4), 49–52; and one on the Centennial celebration in Stockholm of Strindberg's birth, Alrik Gustafson's "August Strindberg 1849–1949," *ASR*, XXXVII (1949), 125–31. The Centennial occasion resulted also in an effort on the part of C. E. W. L. Dahlström to define the significance of Strindberg for a modern frustrated world (see *SS*, XXI [1949], 1–18) and in the publication in America of a "Strindberg Issue" of the *Bulletin of the American Institute of Swedish Arts, Literature, and Science* (Minneapolis, 1949), which contains a number of popular articles in English on Strindberg by Swedish scholars. Theodore Jorgenson's "August Strindberg," *Christian Liberty*, I:2 (March 1953), 45–64, is a general lecture on Strindberg delivered at the University of Southern California in 1949.

Those who may be interested in a critical appraisal of certain basic Strindberg studies from Scandinavian pens are referred to my two review-articles "Recent Developments and Future Prospects in Strindberg Studies" and "Six Recent Doctoral Dissertations on Strindberg," *Modern Philology*, XLVI (1948), 49–62, and LII (1954), 52–56. The works I have considered in these two review-articles are, with an exception or two, representative of the best in Strindberg scholarship. Aside from Martin Lamm's two fundamental monographs on the dramas and the literary production generally, *Strindbergs dramer*, I–II (1924, 1926) and *August Strindberg*, I–II (1940, 1942), Torsten Eklund's penetrating study in Strindberg's psyche *Tjänstekvinnans son: en psykologisk Strindbergsstudie* (1948), and Walter Berendsohn's stimulating miscellany *Strindbergsproblem* (1946), the works dealt with in my review-articles are concerned with certain special periods and/or problems in Strindberg's development: Harry Jacobsen's *Digteren og Fantasten* (Copenhagen, 1945) and Allan Hagsten's *Den unge Strindberg* (1951) primarily with biographical matters; Nils Norman's *Den unge Strindberg och väckelserörelsen* (Malmö, 1953), Martin Lamm's *Strindberg och makterna* (1936), and Gunnar Brandell's *Strindbergs Infernokris* (1950) with two phases of Strindberg's religious experience; and Gunnar Ollén's *Strindbergs 1900-talslyrik* (1941), Hans Lindström's *Hjärnornas kamp* (Uppsala, 1952), Carl Reinhold Smedmark's *Mäster Olof och Röda Rummet* (1952), and Vagn Børge's rather abortive *Strindbergs mystiske Teater* (Copenhagen, 1942) with diverse problems of motif and form in Strindberg's poetry, prose fiction, and drama.

Among the dozens of other books and hundreds of more or less valuable articles on Strindberg in Swedish I can here but list some of the more important. Erik Hedén's *Strindberg: en ledtråd vid studiet av hans verk* (1921; 2nd Swedish ed. and German ed. 1926) still remains the best biography though it appeared well over three decades ago. Besides Hagsten's, Norman's, Jacobsen's, and Brandell's works mentioned above, a number of other special studies deepen our understanding of Strindberg's personality and add valuable biographical detail. Chief among these are Strindberg's first daughter Karin Smirnoff's *Strindbergs första hustru* (1925) and Harry Jacobsen's *Digteren og Fantasten* (Copenhagen, 1945), *Strindberg og hans første Hustru* (Copenhagen, 1946), and *Strindberg i Firsernes København*

(Copenhagen, 1948), which examine in great detail the crisis in Strindberg's life which led to his first divorce together with certain other matters of biographical concern for the period involved. Of some interest in these contexts is also David Norrman's *Strindbergs skilsmässa från Siri von Essen* (1953), which occasioned a book from an indignant Karin Smirnoff entitled *Så var det i verkligheten* (1956).

Other items of biographical value are a number of special studies of particular episodes or phases of development in Strindberg's life such as Torsten Eklund's "Förbundet Runas protokoll," *S*, n.f. vi (1925), 131–68, and "Strindbergs verksamhet som publicist 1869–80," *S*, n.f. xi (1930), 142–92; E. Vendelfelt's "Bengt Lidforss och Strindberg under Infernokrisen," *OoB*, lxiii (1954), 633–39; Göran Lindström's "Edvard Munch i Strindbergs Inferno," *OoB*, lxiv (1955), 129–43; Stellan Ahlström's essay "Kommunarden Strindberg," *OoB*, lx (1951), 453–58, and Ahlström's dissertation *Strindbergs erövring av Paris* (1956); and Walter Berendsohn's *Strindbergs sista levnadsår* (1948). Typical of the numerous volumes of memoirs on Strindberg are Axel Lundegård's *Några Strindbergsminnen knutna till en handfull brev* (1920), Birger Mörner's *Den Strindberg jag känt* (1924), Johan Mortensen's *Strindberg som jag minnes honom* (1931), Anna von Philp and Nora Hartzell's *Strindbergs systrar berätta* (1926), and Fanny Falkner's *August Strindberg i Blå tornet* (1921).

Strindberg as seen generally by his contemporaries is presented in the observations of *ögonvittnen* (eye witnesses) in *Samtida om Strindberg*, ed. by Stellan Ahlström (1959), the first of two volumes to be devoted to Strindberg in a series which proposes similar books on other famous Swedish personalities. On Strindberg's relation to Nietzsche see Harold H. Borland's doctoral dissertation, *Nietzsche's Influence on Swedish Literature with Special Reference to Strindberg, Ola Hansson, Heidenstam, and Fröding* (Göteborg, 1957). The rather numerous collections of Strindberg letters to various correspondents (J. O. Strindberg, Ola Hansson, Harriet Bosse, and others) which have appeared from time to time will ultimately become incorporated in the complete *Brev* (1948ff., six volumes to date), expertly edited by Torsten Eklund, who has also issued under the title *Från Fjärdingen till Blå tornet* (1946) an excellent selection of the correspondence with an illuminating commentary linking successive groups of letters into an organic sequence which amounts to a kind of biography.

Though there is less concern with purely literary than with broadly biographical matters in the vast accumulation of Swedish scholarship on Strindberg, there is much more on his drama, prose fiction, poetry, and miscellaneous work than we can account for here. Lamm's two works, *Strindbergs dramer* and *August Strindberg*, are by far the most inclusive of the literary studies, the former dealing exhaustively with Strindberg's drama, the latter covering in less detail the whole of the literary production, with somewhat more emphasis on the prose fiction and the drama than on the other literary genres cultivated by Strindberg. An exemplary brief treatment of Strindberg's post-Inferno drama is provided in passing in Agne Beijer's Introduction to his *Teaterrecensioner 1925–1949* (1954). Few scholars have concerned themselves with Strindberg's poetry. In addition to Gunnar Ollén's basic work, *Strindbergs 1900-talslyrik* (1941), only Henry Olsson's "Strindbergs Sömngångarnätter," *Nordisk Tidskrift*, n.s. vii (1931), 329–50 [reprinted in O's *Från Wallin till Fröding*, 1939] and Teddy Brunius's "Studier i August Strindbergs ungdomslyrik," *S*, n.f. xxxi (1950), 102–9, need here be mentioned. On the backgrounds of the autobiographical works see (in addition to the above mentioned books by Hagsten, Smirnoff, Jacobsen, Brandell, and Ahlström) Hans Lindström's "Strindberg, Pehr Staaff och En dåres försvarstal," *OoB*, lviii (1949), 13–18. On the prose fiction the first lengthier study is Göran Lindblad's *August Strindberg som berättare* (1924), some of the findings of which have been rather sharply challenged in various contexts by Martin Lamm. Carl Reinhold Smedmark's *Mäster Olof och Röda Rummet* (1952) provides the most thorough analysis of Strindberg's first important novel, while two other novels, *Hemsöborna* and *I havsbandet*, have attracted some rather intensive critical attention: *Hemsöborna* at the hands of Martin Lamm, "Förhistorien till Strindbergs Hemsöborna," *SLT*, 1 (1938), 41–46, Knut Lundmark, "Strindbergs *Hemsöborna*, dess tillkomst och förhistoria," *Edda*, XLI (1941), 81–112, R. Jirlow, "Hemsöborna och verkligheten," *Fataburen* (1945), pp.21–40, and Staffan Björck, "I marginalen till Hemsöborna," *MFÅ* (1950); and *I havsbandet* at the hands of Torsten Eklund, "Strindbergs I havsbandet," *Edda*, XXIX (1929), 113–44, Olle Holmberg, "Fiskeriintendenten Borg" in *Gud som haver* (1939), pp.125–46, and Walter Berendsohn, "August Strindbergs I havsbandet," *S*, n.f. XXVI (1945), 101–16. Some attention has been paid to the shorter fictional forms in such studies as Fredrik Böök's "Tre noveller ur Svenska öden och äventyr," *Skrifter utgivna av Modersmålslärarnas förening* (1915), Martin Lamm's "Strindbergs *Från Fjärdingen och Svartbäcken*," *Vår Tid*, XI (1930), 113–28, Arne Häggqvist's "Strindbergs *Samvetskval*," *Edda*, XXXIX (1939), 257–307, and Harry Jacobsen's background investigations of *Tschandala* in *Digteren og Fantasten* (1945).

Though Strindberg's contemporaries hardly responded with great enthusiasm to his so-called expressionistic dramas, Pär Lagerkvist, in an extended critical essay "Modern teater: synpunkter och angrepp" (1918), and Martin Lamm, in the second volume of *Strindbergs dramer* (1926), sharply stressed their central importance, and for a generation or more now Scandinavian critical and scholarly attention has been at least as much concerned with the post-Inferno plays as with the earlier naturalistic dramas. Among the more arresting recent studies in Strindberg's post-Inferno drama are Ejnar Thomsen's "Bidrag till tolkningen av Ett drömspel," *Orbis litterarum*, 1 (1943), 81–110, and Göran Lindström's "Strindberg contra Ibsen: något om Vildanden och Spöksonaten," *Ibsen-Årbok 1955–56* (Skien, 1956), pp.77–98. Vagn Børge's previously mentioned *Strindbergs mystiske Teater* (1942) and Aage Kabell's "Påsk och det mystiske teater," *Edda*, LIV (1954), 158–235, are interesting but often vague and confused efforts to penetrate the mazes of the post-Inferno mood and mentality of Strindberg's later dramas. A not misleading popular treatment of the Chamber Plays is C. J. Elmquist's *Strindbergs Kammerspil* (Copenhagen, 1949). Of primary source importance on the Chamber Plays and Strindberg's Intimate Theater for which these plays were written are August Falck's *Fem år med Strindberg* (1935) and the facsimile collection of letters *Strindberg och teater: bref till medlemmar af gamla Intima teatern från August Strindberg* (1918). Gunnar Ollén's excellent handbook *Strindbergs dramatik* (1948) provides a very sound introduction to Strindberg's total dramatic production together with its fortunes both in the Swedish theater and abroad. Yngve Hedvall's *Strindberg på Stockholmsscenen 1870–1922* (1923) provides a survey of theater criticism of Stockholm performances of Strindberg plays over half a century. Among the more interesting reminiscences and serious studies in what is usually called "the naturalistic dramas" are Axel Lundegård's notes on the world *première* of *Fadren* and the revisions of *Kamraterna* in Lundegård's *Några Strindbergsminnen knutna till en handfull brev* (1920), Harald Schiller's essay on *Fadren* in *Diktare och idealister* (1928; orig. publ. in *Edda*, 1927), pp.33–69, and John Landquist's "Litteraturen och psykologien" in *Dikten, diktaren och samhället* (1935), pp.73–93. Of the historical plays *Mäster Olof* has to date received major scholarly attention, including – in addition to Lamm's masterly analysis

A BIBLIOGRAPHICAL GUIDE

in *Strindbergs dramer*, I (1924) – two early studies, Per Lindberg's *Tillkomsten av Strindbergs 'Mäster Olof'* and Hanna Rydh's *De historiska källorna till Strindbergs 'Mäster Olof'* (both publ. in *Skr. från Stockholms högskolas litteraturhistoriska seminarium*, 1915), and the first section of Carl Reinhold Smedmark's dissertation *Mäster Olof och Röda Rummet* (1952). Of general importance on Strindberg may finally be mentioned an arresting comparative study "Ibsen och Strindberg: en litteratur-psykologisk parallell" in *Ibsen, Strindberg och andra* (1936) by Sten Linder, who has also written the knowing little Verdandi volume *August Strindberg* (1942). More than a score of the great and near great of the contemporary literary world paid tribute to Strindberg on the hundredth anniversary of his birth in *SLT*, XII (1949), 1–71. In addition to being responsible for the publication of some rare Strindbergiana and the critical edition of Strindberg's letters, Strindbergssällskapet has issued from time to time since 1945 *Meddelanden från Strindbergssällskapet*, which provides short articles and reviews, notes on current Strindberg performances, and miscellanea of one kind or other.

Though essays and shorter critical articles in sufficient numbers have been devoted to each of the half dozen or so authors of the 1880's exclusive of Strindberg, only three of them, Gustaf af Geijerstam, Ola Hansson, and Victoria Benedictsson, have been subjected to any very thorough scholarly investigation. And in the case of Geijerstam only Melker Johnsson's excellent monograph *En åttitalist: Gustaf af Geijerstam 1858–1890* (Göteborg, 1934) is a work of serious pretensions and solid attainments. Otherwise in Swedish Nils Erdmann's "Gustaf af Geijerstam," *OoB*, XVIII (1909), 221–39, and Torsten Husén's "Strindberg, Geijerstam och förbryteriet," *SLT*, III (1940), 187–96, may be consulted. The enthusiasm engendered in Lucien Maury (*L'Imagination scandinave*, pp.154–61) and Esther H. Rapp ("Gustaf af Geijerstam in the Field of the Psychological Novel," *SS*, VIII [1925], 239–48) by such of Geijerstam's works as *Boken om lille-bror* and *Kvinnomakt* is not shared by competent Swedish critics, who look upon these novels as sentimental and pretentiously profound, a definitive evidence of literary decay. ¶ On Ola Hansson we have three respectable dissertations, Erik Ekelund's *Ola Hanssons ungdomsdiktning* (Helsingfors, 1930), Ingvar Holm's *Ola Hansson, en studie i åttiotalsromantik* (Lund, 1957), and Hans Levander's *Sensitiva amorosa: Ola Hanssons ungdomsverk och dess betydelse för åttiotalets litterära brytningar* (1944). Cf. in connection with the latter work some notes on Hansson and Baudelaire in Örjan Lindberger's review, *S*, n.f. xxv (1944), 286–88. Harold H. Borland has investigated thoroughly the impact of Nietzsche on Hansson in *Nietzsche's Influence on Swedish Literature* (Göteborg, 1956), pp.47–81, and Fredrik Vetterlund has made some interesting observations on Hansson's relations to a later surrealism in "Svensk modern poetisk drömsymbolik – och fransk" in *Bortom de blå bergen* (1942), pp.90–102. Among the other more important shorter studies are Hjalmar Gullberg's Introduction to Hansson's *Efterlämnade skrifter i urval*, I (Hälsingborg, 1928), Fredrik Böök's "Åttiotalslyrik, I: Ola Hansson" in *Från åttiotalet* (1926), pp.35–53, S. G. Strand's "Ung Ofeg som nietzschean," *Tiden*, XVIII (1926), Ivar Harrie's "Européen från Hönsinge" in *Orientering* (1932), pp.11–24, and Algot Werin's "Ola Hansson," *OoB*, xxxv (1926), 33–39, reprinted in Werin's *Svensk 1800-tal* (Lund, 1948), pp.162–79. A couple of revealing letters from Hansson to a Swedish-American critic have been published for the first time in my "Några brev från det litterära Sverige till en svensk-amerikansk kritiker på 90-talet," *SLT*, XIX (1956), 84–92, an article which also includes letters to the same addressee from Geijerstam and a short note from Strindberg. Stellan Ahlström's *Ola Hansson* (1958) is the most recent extended study. ¶ Though

609

most of what has been written about Victoria Benedictsson is concerned with her personality and her tragic life story, Sten Linder's *Ernst Ahlgren i hennes romaner: ett bidrag till det litterära åttitalets karakteristik* (1930) remains the most solid and illuminating monograph. Of the more recent biographical works such as Axel Lundegård's *Victoria Benedictsson: dagboksblad och brev samlade till en levnadsteckning* (1928; two earlier, less extensive eds. 1890, 1908), Tora Sandström's *En psykoanalytisk kvinnostudie* (1935), and Fredrik Böök's two books *Victoria Benedictsson och Georg Brandes* (1949) and *Victoria Benedictsson* (1950), Tora Sandström's is the most controversial, chiefly because of the schematic rigidity with which it applies Freudian concepts and terminology to its subject. The most impressive corrective to Tora Sandström's excessively Freudian approach has been provided by Sten Linder in *Ibsen, Strindberg och andra* (1936), pp.272–99, a book in which Linder has also written with penetration and understanding on the knotty problem of Victoria Benedictsson's relations with Georg Brandes. Questions concerned with the scholar's discretion in the use of certain materials were raised (by Örjan Lindberger in *Prisma*, 1950, and Axel Olsson in *Försvar för död kvinna*, 1950, among others) on the publication of Böök's *Victoria Benedictsson och Georg Brandes*. The correspondence between Victoria Benedictsson and Georg Brandes has been published in *Georg och Edvard Brandes brevväxling med svenska och finska författare och vetenskapsmän* (Copenhagen, 1939), I, 183–288. Among the shorter studies of general value which may be mentioned are John Landquist's "Victoria Benedictsson" in *Essayer* (1913), Erik Kihlman's "Victoria Benedictsson," *Edda*, XIV (1920), 1–38, Fredrik Böök's "Ernst Ahlgren" in *Från åttiotalet* (1926), pp.206–41, Olle Holmberg's "Ernst Ahlgren-konturen" in *På jakt efter en världsåskådning* (1932), pp.89–107, and Algot Wern Werin's two studies "Ernst Ahlgren i Stockholm och Köpenhamn" and "Den bergtagna" in *Svensk 1800-tal* (Lund, 1948), pp.110–61. Aside from my review of Linder's book *Ernst Ahlgren i hennes romaner* (*SS*, XII, 1932, 45–50) and my brief article in the *Columbia Dictionary of Modern European Literature*, I know of no items in English on Victoria Benedictsson and her work. In French Lucien Maury's *L'Amour et la mort d'Ernst Ahlgrén* (Paris, 1945) is a freely handled but not misleading version of Victoria Benedictsson's tragic life story. ¶ Competent surveys of the work of both Tor Hedberg and Axel Lundegård are provided by Sten Linder on the occasion of their deaths in *OoB*, XL (1931), 625–41, 482–90 [both reprinted in substantially unaltered form in Linder's *Ibsen, Strindberg och andra*, 1936]. See on Hedberg also Sten Selander, "Tor Hedberg," *OoB*, XXXI (1922), 149–57, and Gunnar Ollén, "Tor Hedbergs dramatik," *SLT*, VIII (1945), 75–89, and on Lundegård my brief article in the *Columbia Dictionary of Modern European Literature*. ¶ On A. U. Bååth there are a couple of rather pedestrian monographs, Emma Bendz's *A. U. Bååth och hans krets* (1926) and Bengt Bolin's *A. U. Bååth* (Hallsberg, 1946), a sensitive general study by a fellow-poet from Skåne, Anders Österling's *A. U. Bååth* (1959), and a number of rather distinguished shorter studies, among which may be mentioned Hans Larsson's "A. U. Bååth 1879" in *Litteraturintryck* (1926), Fredrik Böök's "Åttiotalslyrik, II: A. U. Bååth" in *Från åttiotalet* (1926), pp.18–34, and Anders Österling's "Skånes första skald" in *Horisonter* (1939), pp.51–59.

Chapter 9. The Poetic Renaissance of the 1890's

The second volume of Johan Mortensen's *Från Röda rummet till sekelskiftet* (1919) deals exclusively with the literary figures of the 1890's, as do a collection of essays by Ruben G:son Berg, *Svenska skalder från nittiotalet* (1906), and the scholarly miscellany *Nittiotalsstudier tillägnade Olle Holmberg den 20 oktober 1943* (Lund, 1943). Short surveys of fairly recent date on the period are the first three chapters in Kjell Strömberg's *Modern svensk litteratur* (1932) and Harald Elovson's "Den skönlitterära förnyelsen," *Svenska folket genom tiderna* (Malmö, 1939), XII, 93–124. On the political and religious tendencies of the decade see such studies as Emil Liedgren's "Nationellt och religiöst i 1890-talets litterära renässans" in *Kyrka och dikt* (1917), pp.90–127, and Helge Gullberg's "Unionskrisen 1905 återspeglad hos några samtida diktare," *S*, n.f. XXV (1944), 100–14. On the treatment of folk life in the literature of the 1890's see Erik Lindström's *Nordisk folklivsskildring* (1932), pp.147–91, and on the broadly cultural ramifications of the renewed interest in the "folk" see the references below under Erik Axel Karlfeldt, the poet who most profoundly represents these cultural developments in the 1890's and later.

The tendency reflected in the two older standard literary histories by Schück and Warburg and by Böök, Castrén, Steffen, and Sylwan to emphasize rather sharply the points of conflict between the 1880's and the 1890's have of late been less marked. In fact, in the most recent literary histories, E. N. Tigerstedt's *Svensk litteraturhistoria* (1948) and the fourth volume of *Ny illustrerad svensk litteraturhistoria* (1957), the very chapter divisions ignore the differences between the two decades, and the treatment of the 1880's and the 1890's seeks deliberately to modify earlier held views as to their essentially antipathetic relations. Whether there is sufficient reason for thus radically all but "joining" the two decades is in the last analysis debatable, but such studies as Harald Elovson's "Livsglädje och levnadsglädje: en litteraturhistorisk ordstudie" and "Studier i brytningarna i nordisk litteratur omkring 1890," *Edda*, XXX (1930), 48–59, and XXXVI (1936), 369–449, and Karl-Erik Lundevall's *Från åttital till nittital: om åttitalslitteraturen och Heidenstams debut och program* (1953) make an impressive case for a reconsideration of the complex problem of the interrelations of the 1880's and the 1890's. The point is developed incidentally also in Holger Ahlenius's *Georg Brandes i svensk litteratur till och med 1890* (1932) and in Gunnar Ollén's *Strindbergs 1900-talslyrik* (1941). Of less importance but certainly not negligible is Bertil Malmberg's suggestion (in *Förklädda memoarer* [1956], pp.221–27) that the 1890's has placed its mark on the Swedish poetic modernism of the last two or three decades, a view maintained *passim* also in Olof Lagercrantz's Karlfeldt study, *Jungfrun och demonerna* (1938). Among the autobiographical and memoir materials of general importance for the 1890's are the two volumes *När vi började* (1902) and *Innan vi började* (1921), with contributions from many hands, and Valfrid Spångberg's *När tiden byter skinn* (1932), which is illuminating on the transition from the 1880's to the 1890's. Those interested in memoirs of the more indiscreet kind may wish to read Erik Norling's *Mänskligt* (1930). Holger Ahlenius has provided a running account of books and ideas in the Swedish 1890's in the earlier pages of his contribution "Svensk dikt och debatt" to *Den svenska boken under 50 år* (1943).

On Heidenstam five recent monographs are of chief importance, Hugo Kamras's *Den unge Heidenstam* (1942), Staffan Björck's *Heidenstam och sekelskiftets Sverige: studier i hans nationella och sociala författarskap* (1946), Karl-Erik Lundevall's previously mentioned *Från åttital till nittital* (1953), Fredrik Böök's brilliant but scarcely definitive two-volume *Verner von Heidenstam* (1945, 1946; new, somewhat revised ed. 1959), and Gunnar Axberger's interesting examination of the fire motif in Heidenstam's early work in *Diktaren och elden* (1959). Of these the most penetrating is the book by Björck, who has also given us the short general study *Verner von Heidenstam* (1947). Among the earlier general studies are the popular surveys

611

by John Landquist (1909) and Göran Lindblad (1913), and Ruben G:son Berg's more detailed *Före Vallfarts- och vandringsår: ur Verner von Heidenstams ung-domsdiktning* (1919). Of biographical importance are *Mårbacka och Övralid* (Uppsala, 1940, 1941), Heidenstam's *När kastanjerna blommade: minnen från Olshammar samlade och redigerade av Kate Bang och Fredrik Böök* (1941), and Kate Bang's two books on Heidenstam's later years, *Vägen till Övralid* (1945) and *Övralid* (1946). Representative items of chiefly literary importance from the rather large number of Heidenstam studies are Nils Svanberg's *Verner von Heidenstam och Gustaf Fröding: två kapitel om nittiotalets stil* (1934), Karl-Erik Lundevall's "Heidenstams Vallfart i åttiotalets idévärld," *Edda*, XLVII (1947), 1–38, Olle Holmberg's "Kring Heidenstam" in *Litterärt* (1924), pp.225–42, C. D. Marcus's "Hans Alienus" in *Nordiska essayer* (Helsingfors, 1923), pp.9–53, Ingrid Brilioth's "Heidenstams Birgittaroman: några notiser," *SLT*, VI (1943), 122–30, Torsten Ljunggren's "De nordiska motiven i Heidenstams Nya Dikter" and Evald Elveson's "Heidenstams och Rydbergs brevväxling," both in *Nittiotalsstudier tillägnade Olle Holmberg* (Lund, 1943), pp.28–39, Arne Lidén's "Visioner hos Heidenstam," *S*, n.f. XXIII (1942), 1–42, Gunnar Svanfeldt's "Den gamla och världsmodern" in *Studier tillägnade Anton Blanck* (Uppsala, 1946), pp.332–50, and Harald Elovson's "Heidenstam och Amerika," *Edda*, XXXIII (1933), 93–102. Among the Swedish poets who have paid their tributes to Heidenstam are Oscar Levertin (in *Diktare och drömmare*, 1898), Sten Selander (*OoB*, XXXVIII [1929], 289–302), Bertil Malmberg (in *Värderingar*, 1937), Erik Blomberg (in *Mosaik*, 1940), and Pär Lagerkvist (Inträdestal i Svenska Akademien 1940). In English see Ruben G:son Berg's brief sketch "Verner von Heiden-stam," *ASR*, V (1917), 160–68, G. C. Schoolfield's study in a Heidenstam influence on Rilke "Charles XII Rides in Worpswede," *Modern Language Quarterly*, XVI (1955), 258–67, Alrik Gustafson's extended essay "Nationalism Reinterpreted: Verner von Heidenstam" in *Six Scandinavian Novelists* (Princeton and New York, 1940), pp.123–76, and Harold Borland's "Heidenstam and Nietzsche" in *Nietzsche's Influence on Swedish Literature* (Göteborg, 1956), pp.82–111. An excellent popular introduction to Heidenstam's work by Staffan Björck and issued by The Swedish Institute, Stockholm, has appeared in *Vasastjärnan*, LII, nr. 10 (October 1959), 6–8. W. Gore Allen's section on Heidenstam (as well as the one on Selma Lagerlöf) in *Renaissance in the North* (New York, 1946) is superficial, opinionated, and inac-curate, the popular lecture type of "criticism" at its worst.

Despite the rich accumulation of books and shorter studies in Swedish on Selma Lagerlöf, there is no entirely satisfactory biographical work among them, and no definitive broadly inclusive study on her prose fiction. Elin Wägner's *Selma Lager-löf*, I–II (1943) is in its way a sensitive and distinguished work, but one puts it aside after a reading with the feeling that its author hasn't *quite* measured up to the task of penetrating with critical finality the canny, complex personality which lay behind Selma Lagerlöf's deceptively simple surface mask. Some light has been thrown on certain of the more curious facets of this personality by the psychoanalytical probings of Jørgen Ravn (*Gösta Berlings saga i psykiatrisk belysning*, Copenhagen, 1952, and "Selma Lagerlöfs psykiske konstitution," *BLM*, XXIV [1955], 432–36), and in such efforts to penetrate her "mysticism" and related matters as Jacob Kulling's *Selma Lagerlöfs religiositet* (1933), Ida Bäckmann's *Mitt liv med Selma Lagerlöf*, I–II (Malmö, 1944), Sven Stolpe's "Selma Lagerlöfs mystik," *BLM*, XIV (1945), 132–40, Harald Schiller's " 'Körkarlens' budskap" in *Tomma hövdingahus och andra minnen* (1945), and Erik Eliasson's "Om Selma Lagerlöf och teosofien," *OoB*, LX

(1951), 263–77, but none of these studies provides anything like a definitive picture of Selma Lagerlöf's personality or the sources of her literary power.

Of the longer Swedish studies (aside from those appearing in the centennial year 1958, cf. below) on Selma Lagerlöf's literary production, Stellan Arvidson's *Selma Lagerlöf* (1932) examines the "problem novel" element in her early work, including *Gösta Berling's Saga*; Gunnar Ahlström's *Den underbara resan* (Lund, 1942; new ed., 1958) is a classic study on *The Wonderful Adventures of Nils*; Bengt Ek's *Selma Lagerlöf efter Gösta Berlings saga* (1951) deals with the literary production immediately following the publication of *Gösta Berling's Saga*; Lars Ulvenstam's *Den åldrade Selma Lagerlöf* (1955) with the Löwensköld trilogy, the last extended literary work; Erland Lagerroth's *Landskap och natur i Gösta Berlings saga och Nils Holgersson* (1959) with the use of "landscape and nature" in two of Selma Lagerlöf's major works; and Gunnar Ahlström's *Kring Gösta Berlings saga* (1959) examines Selma Lagerlöf's first novel from fresh and stimulating points of view. Both Ulvenstam's and Lagerroth's books contain English summaries. Not a few of the shorter studies take up special problems posed by *Gösta Berling's Saga* and *Jerusalem*. A. L. Elmquist (*Språk och stil*, 1909), T. Lindstedt (*Nysvenska studier*, 1922), and Helge Gullberg (*Göteborgs Vetenskaps- och Vitterhets Samhälles Handlingar*, 1948) have examined in some detail the prose style of *Gösta Berling's Saga*, while Arvid Noreen (*Personhistorisk tidskrift*, 1917), Axel Strindberg (*Edda*, 1937), and Linus Brodin (in his book *Kavata kvinnfolk och kavaljerer*, 1933) have speculated more or less soundly about the real persons who may have been originals of the characters in Selma Lagerlöf's first novel. Much attention is paid to the general Värmland backgrounds of *Gösta Berling's Saga* in the detailed study of the novel in C. D. Marcus's *Nordiska essayer* (Helsingfors, 1923), pp.54–136. Literary influences and folk traditions in the novel *Jerusalem* have been examined by Hilding Celander (*MFÅ*, 1944), while Arne Häggqvist (*BLM*, 1946) has investigated the realities behind the novel, and Nils Nihlén (*S*, 1951) has studied its relations to the Icelandic saga. Other items of special importance are Arvid Novallius's examination of the Carlyle influence in "Selma Lagerlöf i jättens fotspår, I–II" (*BLM*, 1941), Erik Eliasson's "Selma Lagerlöf och folkdiktningen" (*S*, 1950), Jacob Kulling's "Försynstanken i Gösta Berlings saga" (*FT*, 1937), Ying Toijer-Nilsson's two studies "Naturens förbannelse: en studie i Selma Lagerlöfs naturuppfattning" (*S*, 1954) and "Kristendom och hedendom: en studie i Selma Lagerlöfs fornnordiska noveller" (*BLM*, 1954), and – among the general appreciations – Johan Mortensen's *Selma Lagerlöf* (1908) and Algot Werin's "Selma Lagerlöf," *OoB*, xxxvii (1928), 599–610 (reprinted in W's *Svensk idealism*, 1938). The collective memoir volumes *Mårbacka och Övralid* (Uppsala, 1940–41) provide miscellaneous detail often of biographical value. Of essentially popular general interest are Linus Brodin's *Fröken på Mårbacka: en bok om människan Selma Lagerlöf* (Uppsala, 1940), an account of Selma Lagerlöf's later years of fame at Mårbacka, and Erik Lindorm's *Selma Lagerlöf* (1933), a so-called "bok-film," containing a rich variety of contemporary illustrative material with a lively running commentary.

The centenary in 1958 of Selma Lagerlöf's birth encouraged a rash of books, including – in addition to *Lagerlöfstudier 1958*, a volume published by the recently established Selma Lagerlöf-sällskapet – a revised version of Elin Wägner's *Selma Lagerlöf* by Bengt Ek; a work by the Danish psychiatrist Jørgen Ravn, *Menneskekenderen Selma Lagerlöf*; the little book by Arne Eklund on one of the originals of Gösta Berling, *Calle Frykstedt: till Gösta Berling's gestaltens bakgrund och utformning*; the monograph *Fact and Fiction in the Autobiographical Works of Selma*

Lagerlöf by the Dutch scholar F. S. de Vrieze; and such popular books as K. O. Zamore's little sketch *Selma Lagerlöf* and Maja Petré's chronicle in pictures *Selma Lagerlöf och Mårbacka*, which is also available in an English edition. In 1959 Jacob Kulling added to the growing number of Swedish studies *Huvudgestalten i Selma Lagerlöfs författarskap*, concerned with the religious strain in Selma Lagerlöf's work.

Selma Lagerlöf's great world popularity has been documented by Nils Afzelius (*Nordisk familjeboks månadskrönika*, 1938). In German the basic book is Walter Berendsohn's *Selma Lagerlöf* (Munich, 1927), a work which has appeared also in Swedish and Danish, and in a drastically abridged English version. Among the more scholarly recent studies in German is Theodor Nissen's "Die Quellen von Selma Lagerlöfs Erzählung *Herr Arnes penningar*," *Germanisch-romanische Monatsschrift*, XXV (1937), 431–37. In French see A. Jolivet's comparative study "La Winter-ballade de Gerhart Hauptmann et Herr Arnes Penningar de Selma Lagerlöf" in *Mélanges offerts à M. Charles Andler. . . .* (Strasbourg, 1924), pp.164–70, and Lucien Maury's lively notes on *Nils Holgerssons underbara resa* and some of the novels and tales in *L'Imagination scandinave* (Paris, 1929), pp.195–220, as well as in his *Panorama de la littérature suédoise contemporaine* (Paris, 1940), pp.119–28. In the United States, as elsewhere throughout the world, interest in Selma Lagerlöf has been reflected in scores of notes and shorter or longer essays and in one well-balanced and enthusiastic book, Hanna Astrup Larsen's *Selma Lagerlöf* (New York, 1936; originally published serially in *ASR*, XXIII, 1935, pp.7–19, 113–28, 207–22, 309–26). Of the longer essays and studies in English three especially are of value, Edwin Björkman's "The Story of Selma Lagerlöf" in *Voices of Tomorrow* (New York and London, 1913), pp.139–53, Elizabeth Monroe's "Provincial Art in Selma Lagerlöf" in *The Novel and Society* (Chapel Hill, N.C., 1941), pp.88–110, and Alrik Gustafson's "Saga and Legend of a Province: Selma Lagerlöf" in *Six Scandinavian Novelists* (Princeton and New York, 1940), pp.177–225. See also the rather brief but knowing examination of Selma Lagerlöf's genius by the Swedish critic Lars Ulvenstam in *The American-Swedish Monthly*, December 1958. Elsa Pehrson's "Glimpses from the Hidden Workshop of Selma Lagerlöf," *ASR*, XXXIII (1945), 41–44, is an informed review of Elin Wägner's biography of the Swedish novelist. Selma Lagerlöf's own account of her early life is available in English in the three autobiographical volumes *Mårbacka*, *Memories of My Childhood*, and *The Diary of Selma Lagerlöf*. The little book by Harry E. Maule entitled *Selma Lagerlöf: The Woman, Her Work, Her Message* (Garden City, N.Y., 1917) is a disguised publisher's blurb of no value.

It is deplorable though perhaps not surprising that we have but the merest handful of competent items on Gustaf Fröding in English, only four of which may be mentioned here: Sten G. Flygt's "Fröding's Conception of Eros," *Germanic Review*, XXV (1950), 109–23, Walter Johnson's "Fröding and the Dramatic Monologue," *SS*, XXIV (1952), 141–48, my "Two Early Fröding Imitations: Vilhelm Ekelund's 'Skördefest' (1900) and 'I pilhäcken' (1901)," *Journal of English and Germanic Philology*, XXXV (1936), 566–80, and especially Harold H. Borland's chapter on "Fröding and Nietzsche" in his *Nietzsche's Influence on Swedish Literature* (Göteborg, 1956), pp.112–48. In French Lucien Maury has provided some brief notes on Fröding in *L'Imagination scandinave* (Paris, 1929) and *Panorama de la littérature suédoise contemporaine* (Paris, 1940), and in German G. Krumm has made a rather thorough investigation of Fröding's relations to Germany in *Gustaf Frödings Verbindungen mit der deutschen Literatur: ein Beitrag zur Geschichte der geistigen Wechselbeziehungen zwischen Deutschland und Skandinavien* (Greifs-wald, 1934). So scattered and on the whole so fragmentary are the Fröding items in English, French, and German that the student must turn to Swedish studies if he is to gain an adequate understanding of the man and his work.

Though no strictly biographical work of a more inclusive kind exists, much valuable memorabilia has seen print and two of the more weighty monographs on Fröding's poetry, Henry Olsson's *Fröding: ett diktarporträtt* (1950) and John Landquist's most recent Fröding book *Gustaf Fröding* (1956) meet the reader's biographical interests without at all neglecting the demands of literary analysis. The Fröding correspondence published in his *Samlade skrifter* (1918ff.) has been supplemented by material appearing in various periodical publications (*OoB*, 1953, *Vår tid*, 1930, *SLT*, 1939, 1951, et al.) and in two invaluable memoir volumes, Mauritz Hellberg's often reprinted *Frödingsminnen* (Stockholm, 1925) and Hjalmar Wall-gren's *Gustaf Fröding och hans tankeliv: hågkomster och intryck hos en gammal kamrat från skoltiden* (1936). Ida Bäckmann's two highly controversial books *Gustaf Fröding skildrad* (Göteborg, 1913) and *Gralsökaren: Med företal av Selma Lager-löf* (1940) have provided the point of departure for a recent investigation, Germund Michanek's *Gustaf Fröding och Ida Bäckmann* (1955). Fröding's tragic mental crisis together with its effect on his poetry has naturally interested a number of specialists in mental disorders, including Frey Svensson (*Gustaf Frödings diktning: bidrag till dess psykologi*, 1916), Bror Gadelius (*Skapande fantasi och sjuka skalder*, 1927), Nils von Hofsten (*Ärftlighetsproblemet i Frödings diktning*, 1921), and Georg Brandell (*Gustaf Fröding: psykologiska studier*, 1933). Related problems are dealt with in Stig Sjöholm's dissertation on Fröding's Nietzschean phase *Övermän-niskotanken i Gustaf Frödings diktning* (1940), which occasioned Sven Cederblad's "Fröding ur psykiatrisk och litteraturhistorisk synvinkel," *S*, n.f. XXII (1941), 97–116. The impact upon Fröding of Heidenstam, Burns, Byron, Heine, and Tolstoi respectively has been examined in the following articles: Johannes Edfelt, "Heiden-stams betydelse för Frödings genombrott," *Edda*, xxx (1930), 497–540; Gunnar Svanfeldt, "Frödings exemplar av Burns' och Björnsons dikter," *S*, n.f. XXIII (1942), 139–41; Stig Sjöholm, "Fröding och Byron," *Edda*, xxxix (1939), 145–214; Sven Hellner, "Några Byroninfluerade Frödingsdikter," *MFA* (1949); Otto Sylwan, "Fröding-Heine," *Språk och stil*, xviii (1918), 164; Nils Svanberg, "Fröding och Heine," *NS*, i (1921), 1–78; and Gunnar Ahlström, "Fröding och Tolstoi," *Edda*, xxx (1930), 637–66.

The stir occasioned by Levertin's critical reaction against what he considered the merely "folksy" element in some of Fröding's poetry has been examined in a number of studies, among which are Bernhard Tarschy's "Fröding och Levertin," *Edda*, xxvii (1927), 265–302, and Olof Gjerdman's "Frödings svar på Levertins an-grepp," *S*, n.f. xiv (1933), 191–226. The formal side of Fröding's poetry has been examined in Nils Svanberg's comparative study *Verner von Heidenstam och Gustaf Fröding: två kapitel om nittiotalets stil* (1934) and in such short specialized studies as M. Feuk's "Nybildade adjectiv (och adverb) hos Fröding," *Språk och stil*, xiii (1913), 124–37, R. Saxén's "Participerna hos Fröding," *Tidskrift utg. av Pedagog-iska Föreningen i Finland*, vi, part i, 245–62, vii, part 2 (1927), 325–41, Sven Rin-man's "Några jämförelser mellan Frödings prosa och vers," *NS*, viii (1928), 97–134, Bernhard Risberg's "Om versmåttet i Frödings 'Ur Anabasis'," *NS*, xiii (1933), 221–36, Charlotte Pfeffer's "Det musikaliska i Frödings diktning," *Edda*, xxxiv (1934), 53–60, and Karl-Hampus Dahlstedt's "Alliteration och assonans i Frödings Stänk och flikar," *NS*, xviii (1938), 143–89. Individual poems or groups of poems have been examined from various points of view by Fredrik Böök in diverse places (in his *Essayer och kritiker 1913–14*, *Essayer och kritiker 1915–16*, and *Från åttiotalet*, 1926, and in *Edda*, 1915, 1916), by Henry Olsson in *Från Wallin till Fröding* (1939), pp.130–249, by M. Feuk (*Språk och stil*, 1914, 1915), Ruben G:son Berg (*OoB*, 1916), Ruth Hedvall (*FT*, 1917), Johan Mortensen (*Edda*, 1918), Sverker Ek (*Festskrift tillägnad Werner Söderhjelm 1919*), S. Segerström (*Edda*, 1926), Erland Lindbäck (*MFÅ*, 1949), Karl-Ivar Hildeman (*BLM*, 1955), and Victor Svanberg (*Festskrift tillägnad Gunnar Castrén 1938*). Three basic books which investigate from different angles of vision Fröding's poetry as a whole are John Landquist's *Gustaf Fröding: en psykologisk och litteraturhistorisk studie* (1916), Olle Holmberg's *Frödings mystik: några grundlinjer* (1921), and Arne Munthe's *Frödings sociala diktning* (1929). The Fröding centennial 1960 has provided two books of considerable importance, *Och minns du Ali Baba . . . : Cecilia Fröding berättar om sin bror*. Med inledning och kommentarer av Henry Olsson, and *Så minns vi Gustaf Fröding*. Sammanställd av Germund Michanek.

The upsurge of interest in the Swedish countryside which is so central in the literature of the 1890's and whose chief poetic representative was Erik Axel Karlfeldt has been dealt with in a number of works of broadly cultural rather than narrowly literary interest – in such works, for instance, as Fredrik Böök's *Artur Hazelius* (1923) and Gustaf Näsström's *Dalarna som svenskt ideal* (1937), Böök's book being a biography of Hazelius, the inspired collector of ethnographical materials of all kinds and the founder of the famous ethnographical museum Nordiska Museet and its out-of-doors counterpart Skansen, while Näsström's work provides an account of the role which Dalarna came to play in the Swedish national consciousness as the province which had most perfectly preserved a traditional Swedish way of life. Iona Plath's *The Decorative Arts of Sweden* (New York and London, 1948) and Mats Rehnberg's *The Nordiska Museet and Skansen* (Stockholm, 1957) provide the English-speaking reader with two richly illustrated sketches of the Swedish folk arts and the ethnographical institutions which have preserved these arts together with related matters. The cultural regionalism explicit or implicit everywhere in Karlfeldt's poetry has forced those who have been concerned with him and his work to investigate in detail his Dalarna backgrounds. What has been called "the classical Karlfeldt book," Torsten Fogelkvist's *Erik Axel Karlfeldt: en minnesteckning* (1931; 2nd rev. and enl. ed. 1941) constantly calls the reader's attention to these backgrounds, while a study like Jöran Mjöberg's *Det folkliga och det förgångna i Karlfeldts lyrik* (1945) is concerned exclusively with the folk-cultural foundations of Karlfeldt's poetry, and Klas Wennerberg's *Vårgiga och hösthorn* (Uppsala, 1944) recognizes the necessity of elucidating for a later generation of Swedes the many older words and turns of phrase and the local folkways and folk-beliefs which abound in Karlfeldt's verse. Volume twelve of *Hågkomster och livsintryck av svenska män och kvinnor* (Uppsala, 1931) contains Dalarna reminiscences among other items on Karlfeldt, while Carl Mangård's *En bok om Karlfeldt* (1931) dishes out in uncritical confusion a miscellany of observations on Karlfeldt and his Dalarna backgrounds. Karlfeldt's not-easy-to-define religious position, especially as it involves his relation to Christianity, has been variously interpreted by Erik Fries, *Karlfeldt och fädernas tro* (Uppsala, 1942), Jacob Kulling, *Karlfeldts livsproblem* (1943), and Ingvar Högman, *Lejonets barn: gudstro och människouppfattning i Karlfeldts diktning* (1945).

A magnificently illustrated monograph on the peasant wall paintings of Dalarna has been provided by Svante Svärdström (*Dalmålningar*, 1944), who has also contributed to our understanding of Karlfeldt's relations to these paintings in "Karl-feldt och dalmålningarna," *Gammalt och nytt från Dalarne*, x (1948), 1–3, and "Dik-tens dalmåleri och verklighetens," *Paletten*, x (1949). Svärdström's *Dalmålningar i urval* (1957; also in an English edition) is a sharply reduced, though valuable, version of *Dalmålningar* (1944). Those who may be interested in the folk *musical* side of the ancient Dalarna culture should consult Otto Andersson's *Spel opp i spelmänner* (1958). Jöran Mjöberg's above-mentioned monograph includes folk-cultural motif studies in Karlfeldt's poetry. More limited Dalarna motif studies of various kinds are Torsten Thunman's "Växtmotiv i Karlfeldts dikter," *MFÅ* (1937), 257–68, Karl Hedlund's "Leksandsmotivet i Erik Axel Karlfeldts diktning," *Vår socken* (1948), 128–39, Evert Salberger's "Linets blomning i Karlfeldts Trä-slottet," *Nordisk tidskrift*, xxvii (1951), 117–23, and Peter Hallberg, "Dalälven i Karlfeldts diktning," *Nordisk tidskrift*, xxviii (1952), 327–37. Stylistic detail is ex-amined in Arne Häggqvist's "Stil och stilistik: arkaismer i Hösthorn," *Presens*, i (1934), 132–38, Nils Gobom's "Rimmen hos Karlfeldt," *Uppsala universitets års-skrift*, 1911, bd. i, 1–75, and Eskil Hummelstedt's "Karlfeldts bildspråk: några stil-drag," *FT*, cxxiv (1938), 326–39. Some English echoes are noted in Karlfeldt's verse in Nils Uthorn's "Engelska [Kipling] reminiscenser hos Karlfeldt," *SLT*, xvi (1953), 177–78, and in Nils Molin's "Kiplingrytmer hos Karlfeldt," *Göteborgs högskolas årsskrift*, lvi (1950:3), 171–78. Individual poems have been subjected to analysis most recently by C. E. af Geijerstam and Gunnar Tideström in *Lyrisk tidsspegel* (Lund, 1947) and by Örjan Lindberger and Reidar Ekner in *Att läsa poesi* (Ver-dandis skriftserie, 4, 1955).

Of the more general, relatively inclusive studies in Karlfeldt's poetry Olof Lager-crantz's *Jungfrun och demonerna* (1938) is the most arresting and sensitive. Of considerable importance also is Roland Fridholm's *Sångmön av Pungmakarbo: en studie över Karlfeldts diktning* (1950), which provides the most sharp and detailed arraignment of some of Karlfeldt's poetry since Victor Svanberg in *Poesi och politik* (1931) coined the expression "Karlfeldtsfaran" in reaction against what the moderns consider the Romantic escapism of Karlfeldt. Short earlier general treatments of Karlfeldt such as those by Sten Selander and Ruben G:son Berg (*OoB*, 1924, 1931) had been uniformly admiring and appreciative.

Though we have in English no great amount of material on Karlfeldt, we are better provided with general survey matter on him and his backgrounds than we are on his contemporary Fröding. In addition to C. W. Stork's essay "Erik Axel Karlfeldt," *ASR*, xix (1931), 581–94, and the Introduction to his volume of Karl-feldt translations entitled *Arcadia Borealis* (Minneapolis, 1938), we have a short background article from a Swedish pen, Carl Larsson i By's "Erik Axel Karlfeldt: a poet of Dalecarlia," *ASR*, xiii (1925), 15–20, A. J. Uppvall's rather heavy-handed but reasonably accurate article "The Poetic Art of Erik Axel Karlfeldt," *Germanic Review*, ii (1927), 244–61, and the Swedish scholar Karl-Ivar Hildeman's excellent study "The Evolution of 'Längtan heter min arvedel'," *SS*, xxxi (1959), 47–64. On the broadly national as well as on the more narrowly regional folk-cultural backgrounds of Karlfeldt's poetry we have such popular articles as Ann Margret Holmgren's "Artur Hazelius," *ASR*, xxi (1933), 494–97, Betty Burnett's "Skansen," *ASR*, xliii (1955), 151–59, and two items on the peasant wall paintings of Dalarna, Marie Olsen's "A Homely Form of Art," *ASR*, xix (1931), 595–98, and Ellen Johnson's "Swedish Peasant 'Bonader'," *ASR*, xxxi (1943), 220–30, the latter being in every way a competent general account of the primitive art form which inspired the crea-tion of one of the most arresting groups of Karlfeldt's poems.

On such figures as the feminist Ellen Key and the philosopher Hans Larsson, whose literary importance is more obliquely pervasive than directly creative, see — in addition to my brief articles on them in the *Columbia Dictionary of Modern European Literature* — Mia Leche-Löfgren's *Ellen Key: hennes liv och verk* (1930), Axel Forsström's *Om Ellen Key* (Malmö, 1949), Ulf Wittrock's *Ellen Keys väg från kristendom till livstro* (Uppsala, 1953), Ivar Harrie's essay on Larsson, "Hembygdens lärodiktare" in *Orientering* (1932), pp.42–58, and contributions from various hands in *En bok om Hans Larsson* (Lund, 1945). ¶ On Pelle Molin see Gösta Attorp's dissertation *Pelle Molin: hans liv och diktning* (1930) and Henry Olsson's "Pelle Molin och Norrlandsskildringen" in *Från Wallin till Fröding* (1939), pp.108–29. ¶ And on Albert Engström see the miscellany volume *Mest om Albert Engström* (Uppsala, 1941), Gunnar Mascoll Silfverstolpe's address (*Svenska Akademiens handlingar ifrån 1886*, LII [1941], 19–36), and Erik Noreen's "Albert Engström som stilist" in *Från Birgitta till Piraten* (1942), pp.162–66.

Werner Söderhjelm has laid the foundations for all serious Levertin studies in his two-volume monograph *Oscar Levertin: en minnesteckning* (1914, 1917). Fredrik Böök's *Oscar Levertin* (1944) and Anna Levertin's *Den unge Levertin* (1947) have added critical and biographical detail. An interesting sketch of Levertin by a friend and admirer is available in Carl G. Laurin's *Människor* (2nd ed. 1912), pp.63–78. A somewhat slanted but otherwise penetrating and sensitive study in Levertin's thinking has been provided by Holger Ahlenius in *Oscar Levertin: en studie i hans tankevärld* (1934). Carl Fehrman has in recent years not only given us in *Levertins lyrik* (Lund, 1945) a brilliant study of Levertin's verse partly with reference to its Continental backgrounds, but has also published the brief though excellent general book *Oscar Levertin* (1947) and the article "Den 'sympatiske' kritikern: en studie i Levertins kritik," *Nittiotalsstudier tillägnade Olle Holmberg 1943* (Lund, 1943), pp.40–46. Levertin's work as a literary critic became the subject of a sharp controversy in connection with the famous "Strindbergsfejden" in the years shortly after Levertin's death. Among the contributors to this controversy were Bengt Lidforss, *Levertinkultens apologet* (1910); Fredrik Böök, *Oscar Levertin och professor Lidforss* (1910) and "Oscar Levertin som litteraturhistoriker och kritiker" in *Studier och strövtåg* (1911), pp.1–20; John Landquist, "Oscar Levertin: litteraturhistorikern och kritikern" in *Essayer*. Ny saml. (1913), pp.351–83; and Erik Hedén, "Oscar Levertin som litteraturkritiker: en efterskrift till 1910 års Strindbergsstrid" in *Valda skrifter* (1927), I, 198–210. Less heated later analyses of Levertin's contribution as a critic are Olof Byström's "Levertins Bellmansuppfattning," *Bellmansstudier*, I (1924), 72–110, Karin Beskow's "Levertins Linnéuppfattning," *Svenska Linnésällskapets årsskrift*, XVII (1934), 91–117, and Sven Gunnard's "Levertins Gustav III-uppfattning," *Bellmansstudier*, X (1944), 105–55. In English Eleanor E. Murdock's "Oscar Levertin: Swedish Critic of French Realism," *Comparative Literature*, V (1953), 137–50, is a competent investigation of Levertin's life-long critical preoccupation with French culture.

The basic work on Per Hallström is the dissertation *Berättarkonst och stil i Per Hallströms prosa* (Göteborg, 1939) by Helge Gullberg, who has also contributed a number of special studies — "Per Hallströms Norrlandsskildring," "Stoffstudier till Hallströms 'Det stumma' och 'Phocas'," and "Humor och satir hos Per Hallström" (*MFÅ*, 1941, 1948, 1951 respectively), "Källor till Per Hallströms 'Döda fallet'" and "Källstudier till Per Hallströms 'Thanatos'" (*S*, 1942, 1948) — and the general appreciative essay "Den bortglömde diktaren: till Per Hallströms åttioårsdag," *OoB*, LV (1946), 411–18. Other appreciations and general critical appraisals are those by Ruben G:son Berg in *Svenska skalder från nittiotalet* (1906), C. D. Marcus in *Nordiska essayer* (1923), Algot Werin (*OoB*, 1926), and two by Bertil Malmberg, one in *Värderingar* (1937; orig. publ. in *OoB*, 1936), the other in *Förklädda memoarer* (1956). Petrus Bogren has contributed three studies on special aspects of Hallström's prose fiction (*SLT*, 1944, *MFA*, 1945, 1948), Henry Olsson has examined his danicisms (*Språk och stil*, 1916), Anna-Greta Johansson has analyzed stylistic detail (*NS*, 1936), Rolf Arvidsson relations with Obstfelder (*SLT*, 1956), and Ingalill Mossberg the impact of Schopenhauer on Hallström (*S*, 1944). Representative contemporary reviews of Hallström's work are gathered together in Oscar Levertin's *Svensk litteratur* (1908), I, 243–75, and in Erik Hedén's *Eros och Polemos* (1916; reprinted with additions in *Valda skrifter*, IV, 1927), pp.115–24. Of considerable literary-autobiographical significance is Hallström's "En sparf i tranedans," *När vi började* (1902), pp.194–212. C. E. W. L. Dahlström has contributed the article "Hallström's Impressionism as Illustrated in *A Secret Idyll*," *Publications of the Modern Language Association of America*, XLVI (1931), 930–39, and C. W. Stork has a few paragraphs on Hallström in the *Columbia Dictionary of Modern European Literature* (1947).

Chapter 10. Realism Renewed and Challenged

In the final – twentieth-century – sections of the present bibliographical guide I shall be more rigorously selective than hitherto in the inclusion of titles. I am forced to do so in part because the number of competent authors together with their interpreters and critics has multiplied so rapidly in our century that a less selective procedure than the one adopted here would result in an all but unmanageable listing of titles, and in part because critical analyses of the literature of our century are not infrequently lacking in the kind of objectivity which is the ideal of the literary historian. The twentieth century in Sweden, as elsewhere, is a period characterized by so many sharply conflicting critical points of view that even the discerning reader has difficulty at times in distinguishing slanted literary judgments based on one or another credo of critical allegiance. Considerations of space permit me to record here only on occasion some of the relatively more flagrant examples of slanted literary judgments. I can but hope that the reader will have been warned by these examples and that he will in consequence use the secondary sources cited below with due care and circumspection. The very brilliance of some of the Swedish critics of our day can mislead the unwary reader into adopting a given critic's point of view and accepting with little if any question his judgments. Of some value by way of orienting the beginner in these matters is Ragnar Oldberg's "Några vägvisare och smakdomare" in *Några moderna svenska författare* (1944), pp.196–204.

Inasmuch as a great deal of the scholarship and criticism dealing with Swedish literature after 1900 is concerned with this literature in a rather general and inclusive sense rather than with particular developmental phases, I am providing immediately herewith a listing of such broadly inclusive books and shorter items, followed by a listing of items specifically on the first developmental phase (Realism Renewed and Challenged) as conceived in the body of the present book, and followed in turn by bibliographical sections covering each of the two later developmental phases (The Modernistic Ground Swell and Attendant Social Criticism, and Modernism Triumphant and Its Aftermath). This procedure seems desirable even though on occasion it will inevitably result in some repetitiousness and overlapping.

Of indispensable reference value on Swedish literature in our century is Bengt Åhlén's three-volume *Svenskt författarlexikon* (1942), brought down nearly to date in a new five-volume edition in 1959. The basic literary history of the period is Erik Hjalmer Linder's *Fyra decennier av nittonhundratalet* (3rd ed. 1958). Other much shorter but certainly not negligible literary surveys are Kjell Strömberg's *Modern svensk litteratur* (1932), Alf Henriques's *Svensk litteratur efter 1900* (1944; orig. publ. in Danish, 1942), Ragnar Oldberg's *Nutidsförfattare* (1949), and Gudmar Hasselberg's little book for secondary and folk schools, *Svensk nittonhundratalslitteratur* (Lund, 2nd ed. 1945). Linder and Henriques provide rather extensive bibliographical material, which can be supplemented by the standard Swedish bibliographical guide, *Svensk litteraturhistorisk bibliografi 1900–1935* (1939ff.), together with the later numbers of the annual bibliography in *Samlaren*.

The most recent surveys of the Swedish literary scene in our century are Gunnar Brandell's *Svensk litteratur 1900–1950: realism och symbolism* (1958) and Åke Runnquist's *Moderna svenska författare* (1959), the former conceived in broad, frequently illuminating perspectives which in many ways provide points of departure for fresh and stimulating interpretative formulations, the latter (essentially a handbook, though an excellent one) providing – in addition to individual critical sketches of a hundred and forty authors – a section on general backgrounds together with helpful notes on general literary developments in the 1930's, the 1940's, and the 1950's. Stimulating also are Axel Strindberg's lively and often telling Leftist-inspired evaluations in *Människor mellan krig* (1941). Briefer less inclusive items of considerable value in one way or other are Olle Holmberg's "Från Hjalmar Söderberg till Pär Lagerkvist" in *På jakt efter en världsåskådning* (1932), pp.203–73, Ivar Harrie's "Gustaviansk litteratur," *Med folket för fosterlandet* (1938), I, 487–502, Elof Ehnmark's "Litterära strömningar under 1900-talet," *Svenska folket genom tiderna* (Malmö, 1939), XII, 169–92, Holger Ahlenius's "Svensk dikt och debatt 1893–1943: en bokkavalkad" in *Den svenska boken under 50 år* (1943), pp. 111–265, and Erik Hjalmar Linder's "Gemytet som kom bort: blick på fyrtio års svensk litteraturhistoria," *Samtid och framtid*, VI (1949), 115–19. Sven Linnér's dissertation with an English summary *Livsförsoning och idyll* (Uppsala, 1954) traces the ramifications of "idyllicism" and related matters in a representative number of the more important Swedish authors during the decade 1915–25. Other survey studies, which cover only limited periods within the literature of our century, will be cited below in their immediate chronological or subject matter contexts. Essay collections and related critical material reflecting various points of view and ranging more or less widely in twentieth-century Swedish literature are represented in such works as Margit Abenius's *Kontakter* (1944), Stig Ahlgren's *Obehagliga stycken* (1944) and *Orpheus i folkhemmet* (1948), P. O. Barck's *Dikt och förkunnelse* (1936), Erik Blomberg's *Tidens romantik* (1931), *Stadens fångar* (1933), and *Mosaik* (1940), Torsten Fogelqvist's *Typer och tänkesätt* (1927) and *Bok och svärd* (1930), Ivar Harrie's *Orientering* (1932), Knut Jaensson's *Essayer* (1946), N. Johnson's *Profiler i svensk nutidsdiktning* (Uppsala, 1936), Thorsten Jonsson's *Stor-Norrland och litteraturen* (1938), Erik Kihlman's *Nordiska profiler* (Helsingfors, 1935), Alma Söderhjelm's *Mina sju magra år* (1932), Henning Söderhjelm's *Författareprofiler* (1938), Elisabeth Tykesson's *Tolv essayer* (1945), and the freewheeling rash of polemical volumes from Sven Stolpe's hand, beginning with such youthful encomiums to all manner of literary modernity as *Två generationer* (1929) and *Livsdyrkare* (1931), and issuing later in such religious-inspired works as *Själar i brand* (1938) and *I människodjungeln* (1944). Of special value to those interested in the reflection in literature of economic and social change is the series of radio lectures published under the title *Sverige i dikt och data 1865–1940* (1941). Contemporary reviews and review-articles not included in the above titles have been collected in volumes from a number of pens, Erik Hedén (*Litteraturkritik*, I–II, 1927), Tor Hedberg (*Ett decennium*, I, 1912), Axel Strindberg (*Genom denna ruta*, 1943, and *Stick och stånd-punkter*, 1947), Anders Österling (*Dagens gärning*, I–III, 1921–31, and *Horisonter*, 1939), etc. Particular literary genres have been treated in brief surveys: prose fiction in Ivar Harrie's "Svensk roman 1837–1937," *BLM*, VI (1937), 600–5, and in Örjan Lindberger's "Berättarteknikens utveckling från Hjalmar Söderberg till Eyvind Johnson," *MFA* (1939), 94–116; lyric poetry in Johannes Edfelt's "Svensk lyrik 1837–1937," *BLM*, VI (1937), 593–99, and "Lyrisk stil," *Tiden*, XXXIII (1941), 303–11; drama and the theater in *En bok om Per Lindberg* (1944) and Per Lindberg's brief survey "Teater och film" in *Svenska folket genom tiderna* (Malmö, 1939), XII, 341–60, in Gunnar Brandell's "Ett halvsekel dramatik" in *Svensk litteratur 1900–1950* (1958), pp.377–402, and in Agne Beijer's brilliant "Dramatik och teater" in *Teaterrecensioner 1925–1949* (1954; orig. publ. in *Vår tids kunst og diktning i Skandinavia*, III, Oslo, 1948), pp.1–65. Reviews by Beijer of theatrical performances have been collected in the volume just mentioned and by such other critics as Tor Hedberg (*Ett decennium*, III, 1913), Carl G. Laurin (*Ros och ris från Stockholms teatrar*, I–V, 1918–1933), Anders Österling (*Tio års teater*, 1936), Herbert Grevenius (*I afton kl. 8*, 1940, *Offentliga nöjen*, 1947, and *Dagen efter*, 1951), Nils Beyer (*Teaterkvällar 1940–1953*, 1953), and Holger Ahlenius (*Fem år med Thalia*, 1954).

The changing social scene of the twentieth century as it affects the relationship of the working classes to literary developments is touched upon in passing in Fredrik Ström's *Rebellerna* (1930) and *Min ungdoms strider* (1940), and has been examined more deliberately in Ström's sketchy *Arbetardikt i kamptid* (1941) as well as in two important surveys, Holger Ahlenius's two chapters "Radikalism, naturalism, socialism" and "Efter storstrejken" in *Arbetaren i svensk diktning* (1934), pp.100–263, and Åke Runnquist's *Arbetarskildrare från Hedenvind till Fridell* (1952). Rural folk life in the literature of the first three decades of our century has been subjected to a less detailed treatment in Erik Lindström's *Nordisk folklivsskildring* (1932), pp. 192–246.

Of great general value, finally, to the student of contemporary Swedish literature are a number of periodical publications, particularly *Ord och Bild* (1892ff.), *Bonniers Litterära Magasin* (1932ff.), and *Svensk Litteraturtidskrift* (1938ff.), each of which provides in its way a rich repository of literary documents for our century. *Ord och Bild* is broadly cultural in its coverage, while *Bonniers Litterära Magasin*, primarily literary in its emphasis, provides examples of original creative work as well as critical essays and reviews, and *Svensk Litteraturtidskrift* limits itself to the publication of essays and studies, largely on Swedish literature of the last seven or eight decades. Both *Ord och Bild* and *Bonniers Litterära Magasin* also publish reviews of current theater productions, and *Ord och Bild* provides periodic review-articles on current productivity in particular literary genres such as lyric poetry and prose fiction. A journal of more recent appearance, *Perspektiv* (1950ff.), encourages cultural debate and covers current literary developments in relatively brief articles, reviews, and news items. Other journals less narrowly cultural in their interests but which not infrequently contain critical articles of considerable value on literature are *Nordisk Tidskrift* (1878ff.), *Tiden* (1908ff.), *Svensk Tidskrift* (1911–32, 1936ff.), and *Samtid och Framtid* (1944ff.). The bibliographical entries provided below on given literary trends or on individual authors include a representative sampling rather than an exhaustive listing of the studies appearing in the rich Swedish periodical literature of our century. Because few if any of my English-speaking readers are apt to have convenient access to Swedish newspaper files, I feel justified in ignoring generally in the present bibliography those often excellent literary articles and reviews appearing regularly in the "cultural sections" of the leading daily newspapers. Fortunately, many of the best of these articles and reviews have been reprinted in the general essay collections cited above.

In French we have two convenient surveys of contemporary Swedish literature, the last six chapters of Lucien Maury's *Panorama de la littérature suédoise con-temporaine* (Paris, 1940) and a 1953 issue of *L'Age nouveau* entitled *Panorama de la Suède*, the latter happily combining critical articles on the arts of Sweden today with translations of representative contemporary Swedish authors. Except for the portions which deal with Swedish literature in our century in H. G. Topsöe-Jensen's *Scandinavian Literature from Brandes to Our Day* (New York, 1929) and Adolph B. Benson's article in the *Columbia Dictionary of Modern European Literature* (New York, 1947), we owe to Swedish pens the only two general surveys in English of contemporary Swedish literature. American critics, scholars, and journalists have accounted for most of the special studies in English on particular authors and for some of the better books and articles in English on the arts in general in present-day Sweden as well as on social and economic aspects of contemporary Swedish life. The two general surveys in English to which I refer above are Gunnar Ahlström's "Swedish Literature of Our Century" in the October 1949 issue of *Life and Letters* (a continuation of *The London Mercury*), an issue which also includes translations from the work of eight Swedish authors of our century, and Gunnar Brandell's "A Quarter Century of Scandinavian Literature," *Books Abroad*, XXVIII (1954), 407–22, which, as the title of the article indicates, considers Swedish literature in its larger Scandinavian contexts. Of considerable importance to those interested in the American impact on Swedish literature of the last generation or so is Carl L. Anderson's *The Swedish Acceptance of American Literature* (Philadelphia, 1957), the findings of which should be checked in the light of Sven Linnér's review (*S*, n.f. XXXVIII [1957], 230–33) and supplemented by the material in Stephen E. Whicher's "Swedish Knowledge of American Literature, 1920–1952," *Journal of English and Germanic Philology*, LVIII (1959), 666–71. On cultural relations generally between England and Sweden in the twentieth century see Gunnar Ahlström's "Fifty Years of Anglo-Swedish Cultural Relations," *The Anglo-Swedish Review*, April 1957, pp.121–24.

While we have no books in English devoted broadly to contemporary Swedish literature, certain of the other Swedish arts have interested those who have produced books on them, and various aspects of Swedish economic, social, and political life have attracted English-speaking scholars and competent journalists who have turned out a number of acceptable volumes. Unfortunately, there has also been dumped upon an unsuspecting English and American public a fairly large number of general books on contemporary Sweden which are for the most part simply glorified travel books, which in their uncritical enthusiasm either for the "quaint" and "interesting" or for the "streamlined" and "modern" have offered commentaries on present-day Sweden which are as frequently misleading to the average English and American reader as they are distasteful to the discriminating Swede. Representative of the better books in English on the Swedish arts today, exclusive of literature and the theater, are *Swedish Modern: A Movement Towards Sanity in Design* (The Royal Swedish Commission, New York World's Fair, 1939), Maj Sterner's *Home Crafts in Sweden*, tr. by Alice Stael von Holstein (1939), and G. E. Kidder-Smith's *Sweden Builds* (New York and Stockholm, 1950). Professional English and American art journals such as *The Studio* and *Architectural Forum* and the general cultural journal

The American-Scandinavian Review have not infrequently been concerned with the Swedish arts, *The Studio*, for instance, having devoted its entire July 1952 issue to Swedish art today and yesterday. See below (p.634) additional items on modern trends in the Swedish arts and crafts of our century, particularly those of the last three decades.

Works of value in English on the contemporary Swedish social, economic, and political scene range from competent on-the-scene studies by distinguished journalists to expert surveys or monographic investigations by professional functionaries and scholars. Marquis W. Childs' books of two decades ago *Sweden the Middle Way* (New Haven, Conn., 1936; new rev. and enl. ed. 1947) and *This Is Democracy: Collective Bargaining in Scandinavia* (New Haven, 1938) set a standard for journalistic work of this kind which has not been maintained even in William L. Shirer's section on Sweden in *The Challenge of Scandinavia* (Boston and Toronto, 1955). Shirer's book, though sufficiently distinguished in its way, suffers by comparison with Childs' books from a lack of focus, a tendency to distribute its attention on too many problems at one time. The most recent of the reasonably satisfactory attempts on the part of American journalists to introduce an English-speaking reader to contemporary Sweden is Wilfrid Fleisher's *Sweden: The Welfare State* (New York, 1956). Among the more enlightening surveys and scholarly investigations in English of contemporary Swedish society by Scandinavian experts on this side of the Atlantic and the other are Alva Myrdal's "Can Sweden Evolve a Population Policy?" *ASR*, xxv (1937), 114–17, and *Nation and Family: The Swedish Experiment in Democratic Family and Population Policy* (New York and London, 1941), Nils Herlitz's *Sweden: A Modern Democracy on Ancient Foundations* (Minneapolis, 1939), G. A. Montgomery's *The Rise of Modern Industry in Sweden* (London, 1939), Herman Stolpe's *Cog or Collaborator: Democracy in Cooperative Education* (1946), D. A. Rustow's *The Politics of Compromise: A Study of Parties and Cabinet Government in Sweden* (Princeton, 1955), Eli F. Heckscher's *An Economic History of Sweden* (Cambridge, Mass., 1956), Erik Höök's *The Economic Life of Sweden* (1956), Göran Tegnér's *Social Security in Sweden* (Uppsala, 1956), Douglas V. Verney's *Parliamentary Reform in Sweden 1866–1921* (New York, 1957), O. Fritiof Ander's *The Building of Modern Sweden* (Rock Island, 1958), Raymond E. Lindgren's *Norway-Sweden: Union, Disunion, and Scandinavian Integration* (Princeton, 1959), and four works, each by various contributors, *Scandinavia between East and West* (Ithaca, N.Y., 1950), *Social Sweden: Published by the Social Welfare Board* (1952), and the mimeographed record of lectures delivered at two Institutes under the auspices of the University of Minnesota Program in Scandinavian Area Studies — *Scandinavia in a Divided World* (1950) and *Democratic Folk Movements in Scandinavia* (1951). A convenient survey by a Swedish scholar of historical developments in our century is Elis Håstad's *Sveriges historia under 1900-talet* (1958).

Aside from the two literary surveys in English by Ahlström and Brandell noted above, mention should be made here of other literary items of general though more limited inclusiveness. On Swedish prose fiction and lyric poetry of our century, we have in English by way of general surveys or sketches only such rather slight items as Olle Holmberg's Introduction to *Modern Swedish Short Stories* (London, 1934), pp.11–21, C. W. Stork's "Contemporary Swedish Poetry," *ASR*, v (1917), 343–47, and Johannes Edfelt's "Modern Swedish Poetry," *The Norseman*, xi (1953), 396–402. We have fortunately, however, been promised a book on modern Swedish verse by Richard B. Vowles, whose brilliant translations of and critical essays on contemporary Swedish poets have appeared in various American journals (see under individual poets below). On the dramatic arts see Alrik Gustafson's "The Scandinavian Countries" in *A History of Modern Drama* (New York and London, 1947) and his Introductions to *Scandinavian Plays of the Twentieth Century*, First and Third Series (Princeton and New York, 1944, 1951), August Brunius's "The Modern Drama in Sweden" (*ASR*, 1921), Yngve Hedvall's "The Swedish Theatre of Today" and "Anders de Wahl" (both in *ASR*, 1922), Gösta M. Bergman's "Modernism in Stage Designing" (*ASR*, 1932), Anders Österling's "Gösta Ekman" and an unsigned item "A Modern Theatre Opened in Gothenburg" (both in *ASR*, 1934), Märta Lindqvist's "Pauline Brunius: Director of the Dramatic Theatre in Stockholm" (*ASR*, 1938), Helge Kökeritz's "Thalia in Sweden" (*ASR*, 1945), Birgit Wadin-Qvarnström, "The Traveling State Theatre of Sweden" (*ASR*, March 1960), Gösta M. Bergman's "Riksteatern," *The Anglo-Swedish Review* (April 1956), Gustaf Hilleström's *Theatre and Ballet in Sweden* (1953), the Swedish theater issues of *Theatre Arts*, XXIV (August 1940) and of *World Theatre*, IV, nr. 2, Hans Ahlin's "The 'Movies' Won for Literature" (*ASR*, 1923), Elsa B. Marcussen's "The Swedish Film Today" (*ASR*, 1954), and Vernon Young's enthusiastic review-analysis of Alf Sjöberg's adaptation of Strindberg's *Miss Julia* for the film "The History of Miss Julia," *The Hudson Review*, VIII (1955), 123–30.

Ingmar Bergman's rising international fame as a boldly original and inventive film director has resulted in a rash of recent American articles and film reviews; most of them, like the generous cover story in *Time*, March 14, 1960, pp.60–62, 65–66, scarcely rise above the level of the chattily informative. Swedish critics, even when they may seem to be carping, manage to *say something* about Bergman's work in the film. Among items in English on Bergman exclusive of newspaper reviews and surveys (such as those in the theater section of the *New York Herald-Tribune*, October 25 and November 1, 1959, and *The New York Times Magazine* section of December 20, 1959) are Edward Maze's "There Is a Renaissance for the Swedish Film," *The American-Swedish Monthly* (March 1959), Paul Britten Austin's "Ingmar Bergman — Magician of Swedish Cinema," *The Anglo-Swedish Review* (April 1959), and Hollis Alpert's "The Other Bergman," *Saturday Review* (March 21, 1959). Less than overwhelmed by Bergman's cinematic brilliance is Stanley Kauffmann in a partly critical but finely perceptive review of *The Magician* in *The New Republic* (October 12, 1959). Though Bergman insists that he has no literary ambitions, that "film has nothing to do with literature," *Four Screenplays of Ingmar Bergman* (New York, 1960), English versions of four distinguished films, gives evidence that he is no mean practitioner of the difficult art of dramatic dialogue.

Of considerable interest on Ingmar Bergman as well as on the Swedish film generally are Forsyth Hardy's *Scandinavian Film* (London, 1952), Steve Hopkins' "The Celluloid Cell of Ingmar Bergman, and Selected Short Subjects Concerning the Swedish Film," *Industria 1958/1959* (1958), pp.33–36, 108–14, 117, and Rune Waldekranz's richly illustrated *Swedish Cinema*, issued in 1959 by The Swedish Institute in Stockholm. ¶ Of general literary interest, finally, are two series of review-articles on Swedish books appearing in the 1920's, one by Johan Mortensen (*ASR*, January 1920, November 1920, November 1921, and November 1922), the other by Yngve Hedvall (*ASR*, November 1925, May 1927, and June 1928), and an unsigned item "Current Swedish Books" (*ASR*, September 1936).

Items on particular authors are listed under their names as they appear below with the exception of those items included in the *Columbia Dictionary of Modern European Literature* (1947), which are of necessity so brief that, with a few exceptions, they add little or nothing to what has been provided on the authors concerned in the last chapter of the present book. But for those who may wish to consult these items I list them here and shall not repeat them later under the authors concerned: by C. W. Stork the items on Bo Bergman, Hjalmar Bergman, Erik Blomberg, Albert Engström, Karl-Erik Forsslund, Bertil Malmberg, Sten Selander, Sigfrid Siwertz, Birger Sjöberg, and Hjalmar Söderberg; by Alrik Gustafson the items on Dan Andersson, Frans G. Bengtsson, Harry Blomberg, Karin Boye, Ernst Didring, Vilhelm Ekelund, Torsten Fogelqvist, Hjalmar Gullberg, Gustaf Hellström, Olof Högberg, Ragnar Jändel, Martin Koch, Agnes von Krusenstjerna, Pär Lagerkvist, Sven Lidman, Harry Martinson, Moa Martinson, Vilhelm Moberg, Ture Nerman, Ludvig Nordström, Gunnar Mascoll Silfverstolpe, Marika Stjernstedt, Gustaf Ullman, Elin Wägner, and Anders Österling; by C. E. W. L. Dahlström an item on Henning Berger; and by Albin Wédin an item on Carl Larsson i By.

In addition to the general works on twentieth-century Swedish literature cited above, the student of the first two decades of this period should consult C. D. Marcus's *Den nya litteraturen* (1911), Fredrik Böök's *Resa kring svenska Parnassen 1926* (1926), and John Landquist's *Som jag minns dem* (1949), Marcus's book being an early effort to interpret the literature of the new century, Böök's providing critical essays on each of a dozen representative figures of the period, Landquist's offering personal reminiscences about many of these writers. ¶ On the two representative turn-of-the-century figures Hjalmar Söderberg and Bo Bergman, see, on Söderberg, Oscar Levertin's contemporary reviews reprinted in *Svensk litteratur* (1908), I, 334–63; C. G. Laurin's friendly sketch in *Människor* (1919), pp.42–62; two interpretative essays, one by Knut Jaensson, "Hjalmar Söderberg," *BLM*, x (1941), 695–705 (reprinted in J's *Essayer*, 1946), the other by Herbert Friedländer, "Hjalmar Söderberg som Stockholmsskildrare," *SLT*, xv (1952), 158–84; and two books, the little Verdandi study by Sven Stolpe, *Hjalmar Söderberg* (1934), and the more detailed work by Bo Bergman, *Hjalmar Söderberg* (1951). Two brief items on Söderberg are available in English, C. W. Stork's Preface to his translation of *Martin Birck's Youth* (New York and London, 1930) and Eugenie Söderberg's article "Hjalmar Söderberg," *ASR*, xxix (1941), 334–37. ¶ On Bo Bergman consult Sten Linder's little book *Bo Bergman* (1940) together with Linder's two articles "Marionetten och människan: en studie över Bo Bergmans lyrik," *OoB*, xxxiv (1925), 224–32, and "Bo Bergmans 'Gamla gudar'," *OoB*, xlviii (1939), 667–69; Stellan Arvidson's *Bo Bergman* (1945); and Ulla Lundström's "Bo Bergmans befrielse," *SLT*, x (1947), 187–92. ¶ On the two poets from Skåne, Vilhelm Ekelund and Anders Österling, see, on Ekelund, Ivar Harrie's "Apollons präst" in *Orientering* (1932), pp.25–41, Hans Larsson's "Vilhelm Ekelund," *SLT*, I (1938), 1–14, Stellan Ahlström's *Vilhelm Ekelund* (1940), K. A. Svensson's *Vilhelm Ekelund, moralisten–kulturkritikern* (1946) and *Vilhelm Ekelund i samtal och brev* (Lund, 1958), Algot Werin's "Vilhelm Ekelund" in *Den svenske Faust och andra essayer* (Lund, 1950), pp.200–8, Rolf Ekman's "Den andra eros: en studie över erosattityden i Vilhelm Ekelunds författarskap," *OoB*, liv (1955), 443–55, and Alrik Gustafson's "Two Early Fröding Imitations: Vilhelm Ekelund's 'Skördefest' and 'I pilhäcken'," *Journal of English and Germanic Philology*, xxxv (1936), 566–80. ¶ On Österling consult Sten Selander's "Anders Österlings lyrik," *OoB*, xxv (1926), 481–96, Victor Svanberg's "Idyllernas tid" in *Poesi och politik* (1931), pp.21ff., Gunnar Mascoll Silfverstolpe's "Anders Österlings lyrik," *SLT*, iv (1941), 1–22, Johannes Edfelt's "Den skapande oron: några linjer och motiv i Anders Österlings senare lyrik," *OoB*, lxvi (1957), 179–92, and Alrik Gustafson's comparative study *Österling's 'Arrival' as Landskapsdiktare: from*

"*Årets visor*" (*1907*) to "*Blommande träd*" (*1910*) [a phototype publication, Chicago, 1938, of a portion of a dissertation on Österling's early poetic development submitted, 1935, in partial fulfillment for the doctor's degree at the University of Chicago]. ¶ To Sven Lidman has been devoted a reasonably full and understanding critical essay by John Landquist in *SLT*, VI (1943), 68–93. On his seventy-fifth anniversary a volume was dedicated to Lidman, *Boken om Sven Lidman*, ed. by Roland Hentzell, containing literary analyses, personal reminiscences, and a rather full bibliography.

The realistic, social-conscious prose fiction of the first decades of our century as represented in its four chief practitioners, Sigfrid Siwertz, Ludvig Nordström, Elin Wägner, and Gustaf Hellström, has attracted considerable critical attention though we have no broadly inclusive surveys. In French, however, we have in Lucien Maury's *Panorama de la littérature suédoise contemporaine* (Paris, 1940) a few pages devoted to each of these novelists, and in Swedish Fredrik Böök's *Resa kring svenska Parnassen* (1926) includes separate essays on Siwertz, Nordström, and Elin Wägner. Maury also provides some notes on Siwertz in *L'Imagination scandinave* (Paris, 1929). ¶ Among the Swedish items on Siwertz which should in addition be consulted are two on his novel *Selambs* (*Downstream*), Erik Hedén's in *Litteraturkritik* (1927), II, 136–40, and Olle Holmberg's in *Lovtal över svenska romaner* (1957), pp.98–107, and four general appraisals of Siwertz's work, Victor Svanberg's "Sigfrid Siwertz" in *Poesi och politik* (1931), pp.62–73, John Landquist's "Sigfrid Siwertz femtio år," *BLM*, I (1932), 5–12, Erik Hjalmar Linder's "Sigfrid Siwertz och vattenandarna," *SLT*, VIII (1945), 97–113, and Sven Stolpe's little book *Sigfrid Siwertz* (1933). By indirection Siwertz throws considerable light on his own fictional techniques in an article critical of "the inner monologue" in his essay collection *Den goda trätan* (1956), pp.137–45. ¶ The relation of the work of Ludvig Nordström to Swedish industrial expansion in the twentieth century has been sketched in *Stor-Norrland och litteraturen* (1938) by Thorsten Jonsson, who has also contributed an excellent analysis of Nordström as a short-story writer to *SLT*, V (1942), 31–48. Gunnar Qvarnström's *Från Öbacka till Urbs: Ludvig Nordströms småstad och världsstadsdröm* (1954) is a sensitive, original, and broadly inclusive study of Nordström's work as determined by certain psychological conditions. On Nordström's early background and "totalist" speculations consult Giovanni Lindeberg's *Ludvig Nordströms utvecklings-historia: vägen till totalism* (1933) and Örjan Lindberger's "Rötterna till Ludvig Nordströms totalism," *Till Axel Gjöres 11-XI-1949* (1949), pp.1–15. Of general importance are Tore Hallén's little Verdandi book *Ludvig Nordström* (1952), Mauritz A. Persson's "Två författare och samhället," *SLT*, VIII (1945), 114–28, and Marika Stiernstedt's "Ludvig Nordströms Fata Morgana," *BLM*, XX (1951), 17–39. Ulf Wittrock's *Marika Stiernstedt* (1959) is concerned among other things with a detailed account of the marital relations between Marika Stiernstedt and Ludvig Nordström, a subject which has been aired in no less than three other books. Gustaf Näsström's *Ord och Bild* article of 1938 is so sketchy as to be of little if any value. ¶ Of the early review-criticism on Elin Wägner, Erik Hedén's (*Litteraturkritik*, 1927, II, 85–101) is as sound as any. Later, more detailed studies have been made in Holger Ahlenius's brief book *Elin Wägner* (1936), in John Landquist's "Några drag av Elin Wägners berättarkonst," *SLT*, XII (1949), 73–102 (reprinted in L's *Som jag minns dem*), in Örjan Lindberger's two articles "Elin Wägner: Pennskaftet," *BLM*, XII (1943), 658–59, and "Hjärtat och nycklarna," *BLM*, XVIII (1949), 271–78, in Ivar Harrie's "Elin Wägner (Hertha)" in *In i fyrtiotalet* (1944), pp.288–92, and in Harry Martinson's brochure *Elin Wägner* (1949).

See also *Bergsluft, Elin Wägner 1882 16/5 1932* (1932), issued in EW's honor on her fiftieth birthday. ¶ Algot Werin's "Gustaf Hellström som berättare," *SLT*, VI (1943), 97–115, is the best general treatment of the prose fiction of Gustaf Hellström, while Holger Ahlenius's little book *Gustaf Hellström* (1934) is a competent general survey. On Hellström's most important novel, *Snörmakare Lekholm får en idé*, see especially Ingvar Andersson's "Snörmakare Lekholm och sekelskiftets Sverige" in *Sverige i dikt och data 1865–1940* (1941), pp.79–94, and Bengt Tomson's "Gustaf Hellström får en idé: några anteckningar kring snörmakare Lekholm" in *Studier tillägnade Henry Olsson 18.4.1956* (1956), pp.259–76. Other items of some importance are Ivar Harrie's "Fullvuxen gentleman" in *In i fyrtiotalet* (1944), pp.296–300, Jan Olof Olsson's "Gustaf Hellström, reporter," *BLM*, XXIII (1954), 622–34, and Bengt Tomson's " 'Skarpskytten': essay om Gustaf Hellströms tidiga författarskap," *BLM*, XXIII (1954), 635–42.

The first to appear of the three portal figures in contemporary Swedish literature – Hjalmar Bergman – has attracted considerable critical attention, studies on him to date including no less than seven books and a rather rich harvest of articles and critical essays. Ruben G:son Berg's *Hjalmar Bergman* (1935) is slight but not negligible, Erik Hjalmar Linder's *Hjalmar Bergman: en profilteckning* (1940) and *Hjalmar Bergmans ungdom: liv och diktning till 1910* (1942) are works of the first importance, and Hans Levander's recent *Hjalmar Bergman* (1957) has provided some new and stimulating critical approaches to Bergman's work. The volume by various hands entitled *Hjalmar Bergman: minnen och biografiskt* (Lund, 1940) is of considerable value. Among the Swedish essays and shorter studies of importance are Kjell Strömberg's "Hjalmar Bergman," *OoB*, XL (1931), 49–61, Hans Larsson's "Hjalmar Bergman" in *Gemenskap* (1932), pp.251–72, Torsten Klackenberg's "Bidrag till Hjalmar Bergmans psykologi," *Edda*, XXXIII (1933), 409–36, Knut Jaensson's "Hjalmar Bergmans diktning," *BLM*, IX (1940), 532–49 (reprinted in J's *Essayer*, 1946), Per Lindberg's two articles "Clownen Jac," *BLM*, X (1941), 24–36, and "Hjalmar Bergman, dramatikern: synpunkter och data från hans ungdomstid," *SLT*, V (1942), 12–30, Staffan Björck's "Komedier i Bergslagen," *S*, XXX n.f. (1949), 69–100, Vilgot Sjöman's "Leonard Loewen och verkligheten," *BLM*, XX (1951), 109–25, and "Overklighetsproblemet hos Hjalmar Bergman," XX (1951), 436–52, and Örjan Lindberger's "Herr Markurell och livslögnen" and Johannes Edfelt's "Hjalmar Bergmans dialogue med döden," both in *Studier tillägnade Henry Olsson 18.4.1956* (1956). Johannes Edfelt's notes and commentary in Bergman's *Samlade Skrifter* (1949ff.) are of great value.

Fru Stina Bergman, Hjalmar Bergman's widow, has in many ways been of invaluable assistance to those who have occupied themselves with Bergman studies and has from time to time contributed articles of her own, among which are the two items on Bergman's frustrating, short-lived experiences as a Hollywood script writer, "Hur Hjalmar Bergman kom till filmen," *Samtid och Framtid*, January 1946, pp.42–51, and "Hjalmar Bergman i Hollywood," *Folket i Bild*, Christmas issue 1948, nr. 50–51, pp.11–13, 72–73.

Of recent appearance are Gunnar Qvarnström's studies, *I lejonets tecken* (Lund, 1960) and *Den brinnande skogen* (1960), and the first annual volume issued by the newly established Hjalmar Bergman Society, *Hjalmar Bergman Samfundet: Årsbok 1959*, the latter containing among other things a Hjalmar Bergman bibliography 1938–1958, which brings down to date Edgar Lund's *Korta bibliografier: 2. Hjalmar Bergman* (1939). In English I have contributed a study in Bergman's prose fiction, "Hjalmar Bergman's 'Accounting' with the Swedish Middle-Classes," *Sam-*

627

laren, XXXVI (1955), 64-76, and in several other contexts have analyzed in some detail Bergman's dramatic production — in, for instance, my Introductions to *Scandinavian Plays of the Twentieth Century*, First and Third Series (Princeton and New York, 1944, 1951) and in *A History of Modern Drama*, ed. by B. H. Clark and G. Freedley (New York and London, 1947). See also Ruben G:son Berg's brief introductory notes to Bergman's *The Head of the Firm* (London, 1936), a translation of *Chefen fru Ingeborg*. Of interest to students of the theater particularly is a little brochure issued by the Swedish Institute at Stockholm in 1959 and containing, together with a brief sketch (in French, English, and German) on Bergman, nearly two score illustrations from productions of Bergman's plays in various parts of the world.

The time has not yet come for any really definitive studies in the work of Pär Lagerkvist, who is still significantly productive after nearly a half century of distinguished work in an advanced modern vein. The general surveys on Lagerkvist that we have in the Scandinavian languages are Gustaf Fredén's two small but reasonably satisfactory books, *Pär Lagerkvist* (1934) and *Pär Lagerkvist: från Gudstanken till Barrabas* (1954) and Ragnhild Fearnley's more full but rather uncritical *Pär Lagerkvist* (Oslo, 1950). Three less inclusive but more substantial studies are Erik Hörnström's *Pär Lagerkvist: från den röda tiden till Det eviga leendet* (1946), an examination of Lagerkvist's poetry and prose down to 1920, Gösta M. Bergman's *Pär Lagerkvists dramatik* (1928), a critical analysis of the drama of the 1920's, and Jöran Mjöberg's *Livsproblemet hos Lagerkvist* (1951), an investigation of one of the central metaphysical problems in Lagerkvist's total production. Sven Linnér's dissertation *Livsförsoning och idyll* (Uppsala, 1954) deals in part with Pär Lagerkvist's drift toward what is called "idyllicism" in the 1920's.

Shorter studies in essay or article form are numerous and of varying quality. Among the more arresting is Erik Blomberg's extended essay "Det besegrade livet: en studie i Pär Lagerkvists författarskap," *OoB*, XLII (1933), 201–14, 267–78, 325–332 (reprinted in Blomberg's *Stadens fångar*, 1933, and *Från öst och väst*, 1951), in which he expresses a strong reaction against Lagerkvist's early anti-realistic metaphysical position. Blomberg's view has been challenged by P. O. Barck in *Dikt och förkunnelse* (1936), and Blomberg has in *Mosaik* (1940) partly qualified his early position in the light of later developments in Lagerkvist's authorship as reflected in *Bödeln* and *I den tiden*. Other Swedish studies of greater or lesser value are Sverker Ek's "Pär Lagerkvist. En svensk expressionistisk diktare," *Litteraturen*, I (1918), 355–63, Victor Svanberg's "Pär Lagerkvists livstro," *Dikt och studie* (Uppsala, 1922), pp.134–43, Sven Stolpe's "Den fångne guden: 5" in *Två generationer* (Stockholm, 1929), pp.90–113, Holger Ahlenius's "Pär Lagerkvist," *BLM*, I, nr. 7 (1932), 14–21, Artur Lundkvist's "Profiler: 2" in *Atlantvind* (1932), pp.200–6, Hilmer Gillqvist's "Pär Lagerkvists Mannen utan själ," *Nordisk Tidskrift*, XIV (1938), 121–31, Algot Werin's "Kämpande ande" in *Svensk idealism* (1938), pp.190–96, and "Det onda är odödligt" in *Svensk 1800-tal* (Lund, 1948), pp.191–207, Per Lindberg's "Några synpunkter på Pär Lagerkvists dramatik," *SLT*, III (1940), 155–86, A. Manfred's "Pär Lagerkvist och Heidenstam," *OoB*, L (1941), 233–36, Jöran Mjöberg's "Ekon av Pär Lagerkvist i samtida diktning," *OoB*, L (1941), 201–9, Victor Svanberg's "Heidenstam och Lagerkvist: en studie i diktens sociologi," *Tiden*, XXXIII (1941), 104–18, Stig Ahlgren's "Pär Lagerkvists lyriska mission" in *Obehagliga stycken* (1944), pp.59–65, Gunnar Castrén's "Pär Lagerkvists humanism," *Finska Vetenskapssocietetens Årsbok*, XXIII (1945), 3–13, Erik Hörnström's "Pär Lagerkvist och religionen," *Årsbok för kristen humanism*, VIII (1946), 40–56, Sven

Linnér's "Pär Lagerkvists barndomsmiljö," *S*, xxvIII n.f. (1947), 53–90, Brita Tiger-schiöld's "De vises sten," *BLM*, xvIII (1949), 283–90, Holger Ahlenius's "Barabbas vår like," *BLM*, xIx (1950), 519–23, Margit Abenius's "Mörkret som symbol i Barab-bas," *BLM*, xx (1951), 285–87, Erik Hörnström's "Klassikern Pär Lagerkvist," *OoB*, LX (1951), 516–20, Åke Janzon's "Samtida med Pär Lagerkvist," *BLM*, xx (1951), 737–41, Leif Åslund's "Pär Lagerkvists Ordkonst och bildkonst och det nya måler-iet," *OoB*, LxIv (1955), 35–49, and Gunnar Tideström's "Tankar kring Pär Lager-kvists *Sibyllan*," *S*, n.f. xxIx (1958), 80–96. In German there has recently appeared one of the more ambitious books on Lagerkvist, Otto Oberholzer's *Pär Lagerkvist: Studien zu seiner Prosa und seinen Dramen* (Heidelberg, 1958).

In English some notes on Lagerkvist's literary theory and practice have been provided by Walter W. Gustafson (*Edda*, 1954, and *SS*, 1955); aspects of the prose fiction have been analyzed by Richard B. Vowles (*The Norseman*, 1954, *Western Humanities Review*, 1954, and the Introduction to Lagerkvist's *The Eternal Smile and Other Stories*), by Alrik Gustafson (*The American Swedish Monthly*, Novem-ber 1951), and by Robert D. Spector (*Modern Language Notes*, 1956, and *Western Humanities Review*, 1958); the drama by Holger Ahlenius (*ASR*, 1940), by Rich-ard B. Vowles (*Saturday Review of Literature*, 1951), and by Alrik Gustafson (in *Scandinavian Plays of the Twentieth Century*, First and Third Series, 1944, 1951, and *A History of Modern Drama*, 1947). Robert D. Spector has also provided a few notes on what he calls "the limbo world" of Lagerkvist (*ASR*, 1955) and on Lager-kvist's use of human deformity (*Modern Language Notes*, 1955); Eric O. Johan-nesson has offered extensive notes on the rebellion motif in Lagerkvist's work (*SS*, 1958); and Adolph B. Benson (in *College English*, 1952), Johannes Edfelt (*The Norseman*, 1952), and Terence Hayward (*The Anglo-Swedish Review*, 1952) have offered sketchy surveys.

On Birger Sjöberg, the third of the portal figures in contemporary Swedish literature, nothing of any importance is available in English. The longer Sjöberg studies in Swedish are concerned largely with background detail and biographical matters, while the shorter critical essays and specialized studies deal more often with matters of idea and form, especially as these provide crucial points of depar-ture for a Swedish poetic "modernism." August Peterson has done much of the pioneer biographical investigation – in the lengthy monograph *Birger Sjöberg den okände* (1944) and in the two shorter works *Vänersborg i Birger Sjöbergs diktning* (Vänersborg, 1940), and *Birger Sjöberg, Frida och Lilla Paris* (Vänersborg, 1944). Two other books of considerable biographical value are Sjöberg's housekeeper Anna Rosdahl's *Mina minnen av Birger Sjöberg* (1956) and Hedvig af Petersens' *Om Birger Sjöberg* (Lund, 1956). A detailed stylistic study is provided in Gunnar Helén's dissertation *Birger Sjöbergs 'Kriser och kranser' i stilhistorisk belysning* (1946). Among the shorter studies and surveys that may be mentioned are John Landquist's "Birger Sjöberg," *Vår Tid*, xI (1930), 18–53, Ivar Harrie's "Birger Sjöberg," *OoB*, xLII (1933), 469–79, Artur Lundkvist's "Krisernas diktare," *BLM*, Ix (1940), 283–89, and Knut Jaensson's "Birger Sjöberg" in *Essayer* (1946), pp.137–63. Margit Abenius has in *Kontakter* (1944), pp.53–68, contributed three Sjöberg items, the last of which is on the posthumous work *Minnen från jorden*, which has also been treated in Ivar Harrie's "Birger Sjöbergs kvarlåtenskap" in *In i fyrtiotalet* (1944), pp.301–8. Gunnar Tideström has analyzed one of Sjöberg's most famous poems from two different points of view in "Birger Sjöbergs 'Konferensman'," *SLT*, vII (1944), 180–89, and in "Det dagsaktuella i Birger Sjöbergs 'Konferensman'," *Studier tillägnade Anton Blanck* (Uppsala, 1946), pp.351–63, while Gunnar Axberger

A HISTORY OF SWEDISH LITERATURE

has subjected two other key poems to similarly intensive study in "Drömbutiken och Industria colossale: en Birger Sjöberg-studie," *OoB*, LXV (1956), 38–48. August Brunius has contributed the perceptive early study "Något om naïvismen och Fridas bok," *Forum*, x (1923), 49–55 (reprinted in *Kätterier*, 1923). Three more recent items of interest in one context or other are Henry Villgrund's "Birger Sjöberg, Järnblåst och 'Pensionatskurken,' " *SLT*, II (1939), 157–66, Hedvig af Petersens' "Birger Sjöberg – fragment ur minnesanteckningar," *SLT*, XII (1949), 127–37, and Gunnar Axberger's "Lilla Paris' undergång: en Birger Sjöberg studie," *Studier tillägnade Henry Olsson* (1956), pp.277–95. Axberger's study has been expanded into a whole book, *Lilla Paris' undergång. En bok om Birger Sjöberg* (1960).

On the rise of the first significant working-class authors in the years before 1920, and their successors in the generation which followed, three collections of autobiographical sketches are of great importance – *Ansikten* (1932), *Mitt möte med boken* (1943), and *Avsikter* (1945). Of considerable documentary value also are Fredrik Ström's *Rebellerna* (1930), *Min ungdoms strider* (1940), and *Arbetardikt i kamptid* (1941), Ragnar Jändel's two articles "Folket och bildningen" and "Arbetardiktningen och den akademiska kritiken" in *Jag och vi* (*Samlade skrifter*, 1940, III, 213–35), and such autobiographical novels by authors of working-class origins to which I have referred at appropriate places above in the body of the present book. The chapter entitled "Proletärdiktningen" in Richard Steffen's *Sidor av en samtida* (1947) sketches the mixed critical reception accorded the term "proletär-författare" when first used by Steffen in the fifth volume of his anthology *Översikt av svenska litteraturen* (1921). Martin Koch, one of the few authors dubbed by Steffen a "proletärförfattare" who approved of the label, has contributed to the Verdandi series the little book *Proletärdiktning* (1929). Thorsten Jonsson's *Stor-Norrland och litteraturen* (1938) includes sections on Koch and Hedenvind-Eriksson and contains socioeconomic background materials on working-class conditions in Norrland. Excellent general surveys of working-class literature in our century are provided in Holger Ahlenius's *Arbetaren i svensk diktning* (1934) and Åke Runnquist's *Arbetarskildrare från Hedenvind till Fridell* (1952). Alf Ahlberg's *Brunnsviks folkhögskolas historia* (1952, 1956) deals with the folk high school which came to be most closely allied with the Swedish labor movement and which from time to time included among those who were enrolled for longer or shorter periods young authors of labor-class origins. An anthology *Svensk arbetardikt: poesi och prosa från femtio år* (1952) has been edited by Örjan Lindberger. Of great interest in these general contexts is Lennart Thorsell's lengthy study "Den svenska parnassens 'demokratisering' och de folkliga bildningsvägarna," *S*, n.f. XXXVIII (1957), 53–135. In English we have a scattering of articles on working-class authors and their backgrounds. Aside from the items listed under individual working-class authors below, a couple of sketchy articles may here be mentioned, Sven Stolpe's "Workingmen Who Write," *ASR*, xx (1932), 348–54, and Gurli Hertzman-Ericson's "Fabian Månsson," *ASR*, xx (1932), 212–15. Birgit Magnusdotter Hedström has given us a rather overenthusiastic but otherwise illuminating historical sketch of working-class educational ventures in "Studies for Working Men and Women," *ASR*, xxv (1937), 28–34. Other, somewhat more inclusive accounts of popular education in Sweden are F. Margaret Forster's *School for Life: A Study of the People's Colleges in Sweden* (London, 1944) and Per G. Stensland's two articles "Adult Education: A Force in Swedish Democracy," *ASR*, XXXIII (1945), 118–28, and "Adult Education" in *Scandinavia Between East and West* (Ithaca, N.Y., 1950), pp.226–53. On the part played by Brunnsvik in the education of the working classes see Ivar

Vennerström's "The Brunnsvik Folk High School," *ASR*, XIX (1931), 209–17, and Marquis W. Childs' chapter "Labor Goes to School" in *This Is Democracy* (New Haven, Conn., 1938), pp.102–15. *When I Was a Child* (New York, 1956), a sharply condensed English version of Vilhelm Moberg's autobiographical novel *Soldat med brutet gevär* (1944), reflects in various ways the struggle of the working classes on the Swedish countryside for better living conditions and educational opportunities. ¶ Though Martin Koch has not received as much critical attention as some of his fellows among those who have written about the working classes, he has been the subject of studies by a number of the more discriminating critics – by, for instance, Thorsten Jonsson in the excellent little book *Martin Koch* (1941) and, in passing, in Jonsson's *Stor-Norrland och litteraturen* (1938), by John Karlzén, "Martin Koch," *SLT*, II (1939), 49–64 (reprinted in Karlzén's *Modernister och omoderna*, 1952), and by Holger Ahlenius, "Martin Koch," *BLM* (1942), 24–32. Among the better early reviews of Koch's novels are those by Erik Hedén, reprinted in Hedén's *Litteraturkritik* (1927), II, 154–63. Hans O. Granlid has attained the doctorate at Göteborg in consequence of the dissertation *Martin Koch och arbetarskildringen* (1957), and Sven Cederblad has contributed a half dozen studies in various periodical publications, most recently "Den unge Martin Koch" and "Martin Kochs Ellen," *SLT*, XI (1948), 1–14, 61–70, and "Vattendroppen: Martin Koch och nykterhetsrörelsen," *SLT*, XIII (1950), 159–75. ¶ The only full-length study of Gustav Hedenvind-Eriksson and his work is Örjan Lindberger's *Gustav Hedenvind-Eriksson* (1945). See also Lindberger's "Om Gustav Hedenvind-Eriksson," *Tiden*, XXXIV (1942), 620–33, Thorsten Jonsson's *Stor-Norrland och litteraturen* (1938), pp.57–59, Eyvind Johnson's "Anteckningar vid läsning i Gustav Hedenvind-Erikssons verk," *SLT*, II (1939), 145–56, Frederik Ström's "Jag råkar Gustav Hedenvind-Eriksson" in *Min ungdoms strider* (1940), pp.302–5, and Ragnar Oldberg's "Gustav Hedenvind-Eriksson" in *Några moderna svenska författare* (1944), pp.230–40. ¶ Aside from a fairly large number of shorter studies and notes on Dan Andersson, critical, more or less scholarly activity on him has resulted in one lengthy interpretative essay, Torsten Fogelqvist's Introduction to the *Samlade skrifter* (1934), I, i–lxxvi, and three books, W. Bernhard's *En bok om Dan Andersson* (1941), A.-M. Odstedt's *Dan Andersson* (1941), and Eric Uhlin's dissertation *Dan Andersson före Svarta ballader: liv och diktning fram till 1916* (1950). Among the earlier general tributes to Andersson are Ragnar Jändel's "Dan Andersson" in *Vägvisare*, 1921 (reprinted in J's *Samlade skrifter*, 1940, II, 25–37), G. W. Silverstolpe's "Dan Andersson," *OoB*, XXXII (1923), 529–37, and Victor Svanberg's "En ursprunglig diktare," *Forum*, X (1923), 496–502. Other essays and studies of value are Erik Therman's "Dan Anderssons livsåskådning," *FT*, CVI (1929), 131–50, E. R. Gummerus's "Karl-Erik Forsslund och Dan Andersson," *OoB*, LVI (1947), 85–91, two articles by Eric Uhlin, "Dan Anderssons lyrik och de frireligiösa sångerna," *S*, XXII (1941), 53–79, and "Dan Andersson och litteratur-forskningen" in *Göteborgsstudier i litteraturhistoria tillägnade Sverker Ek* (Göteborg, 1954), pp.306–15, and the little memorial brochure *En spelman och en drömmare* (1945) with contributions by G. W. Silverstolpe, Gunnar Turesson, and Bernh. Greitz. In English we have two short appreciations, Per G. Stensland's "Dan Andersson, Pilgrim and poet," *ASR*, XXXI (1943), 249–52, and the sensitive translator of Andersson's verse Caroline Schleef's "Dan Andersson: Charcoal Burner and Poet," *ASR*, XLII (1954), 231–37.

Neither the group of young working-class authors who came temporarily into prominence around 1920 (Ivan Oljelund, Erik Lindorm, Ragnar Jändel, Harry Blomberg, and others) nor the group of poetic idyllicists of the 1920's (Karl Asplund, Gunnar Mascoll Silfverstolpe, and Sten Selander) has attracted much really serious critical attention beyond the years of their early literary activity. In the 1920's they aroused enthusiasm or aversion depending upon the critic's political loyalties or literary tastes, but since the 1920's they have only occasionally engendered strong feelings among the critics, most notably in Stig Ahlgren's Leftist-inspired animadversions on Sten Selander in *Obehagliga stycken* (1944), pp.74-83, 197-207, and in Axel Strindberg's devastating strictures on the whole poetic idyllicist group in *Människor mellan krig* (1941), pp.83ff., 96ff., 108ff., 115ff. Readers interested in a measured, more objective treatment of both the young workingmen authors and the idyllicist group should consult the appropriate chapters in Erik Hjalmar Linder's *Fyra decennier av nittonhundratalet* (1952). ¶ On the working-class group see otherwise the two little books by Holger Ahlenius and Åke Runnquist previously cited, and on individual authors in this group such items on Oljelund as Erik Blomberg's "En reaktionär författare," *Tiden*, XVI (1924), 209-20, G. Lindeberg's "Ivan Oljelunds ställning till kyrkan och religionen" in *Svenska diktarsilhuetter* (1924), II, 72-79, and Hans Larsson's "Platonism hos Ivan Oljelund" in *Gemenskap* (1932), pp.174-82; on Lindorm, Helge Åkerhielm's "Livstidsfången: ett motiv i Erik Lindorms lyrik," *BLM*, VIII (1939), 769-75, J. Viktor Johansson's, "Erik Lindorm," *SLT*, IV (1941), 49-80, Axel Uhlén's "Erik Lindorm under proletärdiktningens kamptid," *BLM*, XI (1943), 39-44, Olle Holmberg's "Från Erik Lindorms ungdom," *SLT*, XI (1948), 71-80, G. Valentin's *Min vän Erik Lindorm* (1945), and G. W. Silverstolpe, J. Viktor Johansson, and Axel Uhlén's *Vardagens skald: Tre vänner berättar om Erik Lindorm* (1946); on Jändel, Eric Hedén's "Ragnar Jändel" in *Litteraturkritik* (1927), II, 235-45, N. Johnson's "Ragnar Jändel" in *Profiler i svensk nutidsdiktning* (1936), pp.104-16, and S. Arnér's "Ragnar Jändel mystikern," *OoB*, LII (1943), 191-97; and on Harry Blomberg, J. Hemmer's "En ovanlig epigon," *Nya Argus*, XIII (1920), 127-29, Sven Stolpe's "Lyrikern Harry Blomberg," *FT*, CIX (1930), 49-73, and Stig Ahlgren's "Guds lilla guldfisk" in *Obehagliga stycken* (1944), pp.106-10. ¶ On the poetic idyllicists consult as a representative sampling of the available material Bo Bergman's "Karl Asplunds lyrik," *OoB*, LV (1944), 66-72, Ivar Harrie's "Gunnar Mascoll Silfverstolpe död" in *In i fyrtiotalet* (1944), pp.324-26, Gustaf Hellström's *Gunnar Mascoll Silfverstolpe: Inträdestal i Svenska Akademien* (1942), Stig Ahlgren's "Gunnar Mascoll Silfverstolpe" in *Obehagliga stycken* (1944), pp.177-96, Sten Selander's "Gunnar Mascoll Silfverstolpe," *BLM*, XII (1943), 293-304, Sven Kjersén's *Gunnar Mascoll Silfverstolpe* (1943), *En bok om Gunnar Mascoll Silfverstolpe af 14 författare* (Uppsala, 1944), Stig Ahlgren's "Borgerlig och radikal naturuppfattning i svensk 30-talslitteratur" in *Orfeus i folkhemmet* (1938), and "Kring Sten Selander" and "Sakrament i spårvagn" in *Obehagliga stycken* (1944), pp.74-83, 197-207, and Olle Hedberg's *Sten Selander: Inträdestal i Svenska Akademien* (1957).

Chapter 11. The Modernistic Ground Swell and Attendant Social Criticism

The "modernistic" renewal of poetry and prose fiction characteristic of Swedish literature in the late 1920's and in the 1930's developed out of a complex of conditions and ideas which is reflected most clearly in the so-called "cultural debate" of the early 1930's. Some of the more typical aspects of this "debate" have been sketched by Erik Hjalmar Linder in the chapter "Modernism och 'kulturdebatt': ideologiernas skede" in *Fyra decennier av nittonhundratalet* (1952), pp.623-35. An illuminating examination of the journal *Fronten*, one of the most sharply vocal of the half dozen more or less "radical," short-lived periodicals which appeared in the early 1930's, has been made in Birger Christofferson's "Frontens litteraturkritik," *OoB*, LXIII (1954), 232–56. Among the books which reflect most directly certain sides of the "cultural debate" are Sven Stolpe's *Två generationer* (1929), which with youthful aplomb attacks traditionalism in poetry and criticism and praises various manifestations of "the new literature," Artur Lundkvist's *Atlantvind* (1932), which provides an intelligent survey of the American literature of the day, discusses *avant garde* film, and provides a couple of essays on "Swedish modernism," and a work by a number of hands entitled *Dikten, diktaren och samhället* (1935), which, using as its point of reference a famous contemporary debate in Sweden on sex-in-literature, discusses from various points of view the rights and responsibilities of authorship. Other books of value on the literature of the 1920's and 1930's which are not directly involved in the "cultural debate" itself but reflect some of its ramifications while providing general "surveys" of one kind or other are Ivar Harrie's *Tjugutalet in memoriam* (1938), an analysis of characteristic idea trends from 1920 to 1933, Jöran Mjöberg's *Dikt och diktatur* (1944), a survey of Swedish antitotalitarian literature from 1933 to 1943, and Nils Ålenius's *Studier i trettiotalets svenska tidsdikt* I–II (1943) and Knut Jaensson's *Nio moderna svenska prosaförfattare* (1941), brief but penetrating studies in respectively the poetry and prose fiction of the period. Though Axel Strindberg's *Människor mellan krig: några kapitel ur mellankrigslitteraturen* (1941) is slanted toward the Left in its treatment of the between-the-wars literature of Sweden, it is always highly stimulating and in many ways essentially sound. For those readers who may wish to examine in more detail than I have in the text of the present book Swedo-Finnish modernism and its impact on Swedish poetry, the following surveys are recommended: Erik Kihlman, *Svensk nutidsdikt i Finland* (1928), John Landquist, *Modern svensk litteratur i Finland* (1929), Th. Warburton, *Finlandssvensk litteratur 1898–1948* (1951), and Bengt Holmqvist, *Modern finlandssvensk litteratur* (1951). To these may be added E. N. Tigerstedt's *Det religiösa problemet i modern finlandssvensk litteratur* (1939) and such other books and articles as Artur Lundkvist's "Profiler" in *Atlantvind* (1932), pp.191–216, Per Erik Wahlund, Introduction to the anthology *Finlandssvensk lyrik från Edith Södergran till nu* (1947), pp.9–52, Hans Ruin, "Findlandssvensk modernism," *SLT*, x (1947), 49–66 (with an attack by Walter Dickson and a reply by Hans Ruin, pp.138–42), Folke Isaksson, "Flykten till det personliga," *BLM*, xxi (1952), 274–78, Hagar Olsson, *Tidiga fanfarer och annan dagskritik* (Helsingfors, 1953), Anders Österling, "Edith Södergran" in *Dagens gärning: tredje samlingen* (1931), pp.247–56, Gunnar Tideström, *Edith Södergran* (1949), and *Diktonius: en bok på hans 60-årsdag*, ed. by Stig Carlson (1956). On the 1930's, as well as on the 1940's and 1950's, Åke Runnquist's *Moderna svenska författare* (1959) provides convenient, essentially sound thumbnail sketches on each of the decades together with individual portraits of practically every author of any importance of the time. Important journal articles and essays on particular authors from these years will be noted below, under the authors concerned.

Despite the fairly satisfactory accumulation of shorter studies in English on Swedish poets, novelists, and dramatists of the period, we have only one brief article in English (Ellen Lundberg Nyblom's "American Books and Swedish Critics," *ASR*, xx [1932], 97–103) devoted exclusively to a particular aspect of the "literary modernism" of the years around 1930. The incomparably most sensitive and penetrating articles in English on individual Swedish poets of modernistic leanings are those (see below under particular poets) by Richard B. Vowles, who has promised us a general book on these poets. There exists a sufficiency of popular articles and books in English on the drift toward functionalism in the non-literary Swedish arts culminating in the Stockholm Exposition of 1930, a counterpart in the applied arts of the rising literary modernism of the day. Readers who may wish to examine the early phases of what has been called "Swedish modern" in the applied arts may consult (in addition to some of the items listed above, pp.622-23) Erik Wettergren's *The Modern Decorative Arts in Sweden* (New York, 1926), Nils G. Wollin's "Swedish Interiors," *ASR*, xi (1923), 484-88, Mary Fenton Roberts' "A New Spirit in Decorative Art," *ASR*, xv (1927), 287-97, and Robert W. McLaughlin's "Modern Architecture in Sweden," *ASR*, xvii (1929), 90-100. Later developments are reflected in Sven Markelius's "Stockholm's First Collective House," *ASR*, xxvi (1938), 243-47, Åke Stavenow and others' *Swedish Modern: A Movement Toward Sanity in Design* (New York, 1939), and G. E. Kidder-Smith's *Sweden Builds* (New York and Stockholm, 1950). The Stockholm Exposition of 1930 as reflected in the critical commentary of American journals can be examined in G. W. Eggers' "Functionalism in the Stockholm Exhibition," *ASR*, xviii (1930), 428-32, C. A. Glassgold's "The Stockholm Exposition Reviewed," *ASR*, xviii (1930), 651-63, Frances Keally's "My Impressions of the Stockholm Exposition," *American Architect*, cxxxviii (December 1930), 35-41, and Alma Luise Olson's "Functionalism in Swedish Arts and Crafts," *American Magazine of Art*, xxii (March 1931), 197-206. Later developments in the Swedish arts and crafts, developments particularly of the 1950's, are covered in a number of recent items in English — in entire issues of periodical publications, *Design Quarterly*, nr. 34 (The Walker Art Center, Minneapolis, 1956), *Kontur* 7 (The Swedish Society of Industrial Design, Stockholm, 1958), and *Craft Horizons*, xviii (March/April 1958), and in two separate publications, *Swedish Design*, with an Introduction by Arthur Hald (The Swedish Institute, Stockholm, 1958), and *Contemporary Swedish Design. A Survey in Pictures* by Arthur Hald and Sven Eric Skawonius (Stockholm, 1958). I should emphasize here, of course, as I have in the text of the present book, that though Swedish *literary* modernism is related at some points to modernism in the applied arts, modernism in Swedish literature is on the whole a much more complex phenomenon.

On the contemporary drama and theater as represented by Rudolf Värnlund, Herbert Grevenius, Karl Ragnar Gierow, Ragnar Josephson, Lars Levi Laestadius, Ingmar Bergman, and others, see (in addition to the items listed above on p.624) Sven Stolpe, "Svensk arbetardikt [largely on Värnlund]" in *Två generationer* (1929), pp.157-77, T. Blom, *Rudolf Värnlund* (1946), Ragnar Oldberg, "Rudolf Värnlund" in *Några moderna svenska författare* (1944), pp.159-66, Åke Runnquist, "Den unge Rudolf Värnlund," *BLM*, xix (1950), 344-54, T. Nyblom, "Herbert Grevenius: Klarapojke, kulturkritiker och vardagsspråkets mästare" in *De nya herrarna* (1945), Bertil Malmberg, "Judisk genius [Ragnar Josephson]" in *Värderingar* (1937), pp.168-78, Alrik Gustafson (on Ragnar Josephson) in Introduction to *Scandinavian Plays of the Twentieth Century*, Series One (New York, 1944), pp.13-16, and the Enquête in *BLM*, xviii (1949), 196-206, with contributions by Karl Ragnar Gierow, Herbert Grevenius, Björn-Erik Höijer, Lars Levi Laestadius, Vilhelm Moberg, and Axel Strindberg.

On such poets of the 1920's as Bertil Malmberg, Erik Blomberg, and Harriet Löwenhjelm, who are neither to be counted among the proletarian authors nor the poetic idyllicists and who are scarcely "modernistic" in any pronounced way, the following works may be consulted. ¶ On Malmberg, see Alf Ahlberg, "Bertil Malmberg: en otidsenlig nutidsdiktare," *BLM*, III, nr. 9 (1934), 5–13, and *Bertil Malmberg* (1939), W. Aspenström, "Bertil Malmberg och religionen," *Tiden*, XXXV (1943), 617–25, Artur Lundkvist, "Bertil Malmberg," *BLM*, XV (1943), 455–64, Ivar Harrie, "Nel mezzo del cammin" in *In i fyrtiotalet* (1944), pp.309–14, and Ernst Alker, "A Swedish Play on Hofmannsthal's Belief," *Renascence*, VIII (1956), 146–47. ¶ On Erik Blomberg, see Sven Stolpe, "Den fångne guden" in *Två generationer* (1929), pp.59–119, Stig Ahlgren, "En konjunkturfiende" in *Obehagliga stycken* (1944), pp.44–52, Victor Svanberg, "Erik Blomberg, femtio år," *OoB*, LIII (1944), 355–63, and Bertil Malmberg, "Tankar om litteratur" in *Utan resolution* (1949), pp.264–69. ¶ On Harriet Löwenhjelm, see Olle Holmberg, "Harriet Löwenhjelm," *OoB*, XXXVI (1927), 413–24 (rewritten in *Madonnan och järnjungfrun*, 1927), Ragnar Jändel, "Harriet Löwenhjelm" in *Jag och vi* (*Samlade skrifter*, 1940, III, 257–64), and the book *Harriet Löwenhjelm* (1947), together with a number of articles (*SLT*, I [1938], 49–62, X [1947], 1–13, and XV [1952], 57–62, 63–86), all by Elsa Björkman-Goldschmidt.

Items of general importance particularly on the more "modernistic" trends in contemporary Swedish poetry are Artur Lundkvist's "Svensk modernism: profiler och perspektiv" in *Atlantvind* (1932), pp.191–234, and "Trettiotalets lyrik," *Tiden*, XXXIII (1941), 163–74, Margit Abenius's "Spiseln är kall och kantig: reflexioner om läsaren och den moderna dikten," *BLM*, II, nr. 2 (1933), 35–38, Gunnar Ekelöf's "Diktens medel och mål," *BLM*, II, nr. 5 (1933), 18–21, Johannes Edfelt's "Svensk lyrik 1837–1937," *BLM*, VI (1937), 593–99, Ragnar Oldberg's "Några poeter" in *Några moderna svenska författare* (1944), pp.182–95, and "Modernisterna" in *Nutidsförfattare* (1949), pp.82–87, Folke Isaksson's "Flykten till det personliga," *BLM*, XXI (1952), 274–78, Bertil Malmberg's "Nittiotalet och modernism" in *Förklädda memoarer* (1956), pp.221–27, the essay collection *Poeter om poesi*, ed. by Johannes Edfelt and Olof Lagercrantz (1947), and *Lyrisk tidsspegel: diktanalyser av Carl-Erik af Geijerstam, Erik Hörnström, Gunnar Svanfeldt och Gunnar Tideström* (Lund, 1947), the last being what has been called "an effort in Professor Richards' manner" of poetic analysis, largely concerned with the more advanced, "difficult" features of modern Swedish poetry.

On Hjalmar Gullberg and Johannes Edfelt, who take the first limited steps in the direction of a deliberate Swedish poetic modernism, consult, on Gullberg, Carl Fehrman's excellent study *Hjalmar Gullberg* (1958), Ivar Harrie's "Främlingen i staden" in *Orientering* (1932), pp.196–210, Olle Holmberg's "Hjalmar Gullberg," *OoB*, XLVII (1938), 313–17, Karl-Gustaf Hildebrand's section on Gullberg in *Bibeln i nutida svensk lyrik* (2nd ed. 1939), pp.153–83, Lennart Göthberg's *Hjalmar Gullberg och hans värld* (1943) and "Diktaren och hans instrument," *OoB*, LII (1943), 487–96, Stig Ahlgren's "Beredskapstanken hos Hjalmar Gullberg" in *Obehagliga stycken* (1944), pp.233–52, Erik Hj. Linder's *Hjalmar Gullberg* (1946), Carl Magnus von Seth's "Hjalmar Gullberg och Johannes Edfelt: en studie i parallellitet," *OoB*, LX (1951), 459–71, Richard B. Vowles's "Hjalmar Gullberg: An Ancient and a Modern," *SS*, XXIV (1952), 111–18, and the volume ed. by Stig Carlson and Axel Liffner *En bok om Hjalmar Gullberg* (Stockholm, 1955). ¶ On Edfelt, in addition to von Seth's study in Gullberg-Edfelt parallels and Edfelt's essay "Lyrisk stil" in *Poeter om poesi* (1947), pp.80–95, see Bertil Malmberg's "Johannes Edfelt" in *Värderingar* (1937), pp.101–13, and "Johannes Edfelt" in *Utan resolution* (1949), pp.241–57, Olof Lagercrantz's "Johannes Edfelt," *BLM*, VII (1938), 615–19, Gunnar Brandell's review of Edfelt's *Strövtåg* in *BLM*, X (1941), 391–93, Harry Martinson's "Johannes Edfelts lyrik," *BLM*, X (1941), 781–92, Artur Lundkvist's "Johannes Edfelt," *Tiden*, xxxv (1943), 551–61, and the volume issued in honor of Edfelt's fiftieth birthday, *En bok om Johannes Edfelt* (1954).

The basic book on Karin Boye is the sensitive full-length biography *Drabbad av renhet* (2nd ed. 1951) by Margit Abenius, who has also in the volume of essays *Kontakter* (1944), pp.207–33, published a lecture on Karin Boye's posthumous work *De sju dödssynderna*. Another work of considerable importance is *Karin Boye: minnen och studier* ed. by Margit Abenius and Olof Lagercrantz (1942), consisting of a dozen appreciative essays and sketches, among which two had previously appeared elsewhere, Victor Svanberg's "I rörelse," *OoB*, L (1941), 510–515, and Harry Martinson's "Karaktären Boye," *SLT*, IV (1941), 91–100. Eskil Bergen's *Clarté: poeter och politiker* (1945) [cf. Melker Johnsson's review "Första boken om Clarté" in *Ledmotiv 1939–1946*] contains material on the relations of Karin Boye and other young authors to the radical Clarté society's activities in Sweden in the years around 1930. An early Swedo-Finnish appreciation of Karin Boye's poetry is Hagar Olsson's "Ny ton i svensk poesi," first appearing in 1927, reprinted in the critic's *Tidiga fanfarer* (Helsingfors, 1953), pp.67–70. Later studies of value are Maja Bergstrand's "Med hednisk tendens," *BLM*, VII (1938), 112–19, Knut Jaensson's "Karin Boye" in *Nio moderna svenska prosaförfattare* (1941), pp.62–66, two items by Ivar Harrie in *In i fyrtiotalet* (1944), pp.332–43, Alf Kjellén's "Havssymbolik hos Karin Boye: en utvecklingslinje i hennes 20-talsdiktning" in *Studier tillägnade Henry Olsson* (1956), pp.296–313, and – in English – Richard B. Vowles's "Ripeness Is All: A Study in Karin Boye's Poetry," *Bulletin of the American-Swedish Institute* (Minneapolis, Spring 1952), pp.3–7.

Of the group who joined in issuing the challenging experimental poetry and prose of the little volume *fem unga* (1929) only two, Artur Lundkvist and Harry Martinson, have maintained a sufficiently high level of production to attract much critical attention, and of these two Lundkvist has continued to attract critical attention in considerable measure because of his own highly articulate participation in the literary debate of the last quarter century. On the "Five Young Men" as a whole see Stig Ahlgren's "De fem ungas estetik" in *Orpheus i folkhemmet* (1938), pp.82–107, and "De fem unga," *OoB*, XLVII (1939), 251–59, Åke Runnquist's "Fem unga" in *Arbetarskildrare* (1952), pp.145–61, and an editorial commentary in *BLM*, XVII (1948), 324–25, on the early reception of the group. ¶ Among Artur Lundkvist's many critical pronouncements are those provided in "Svensk modernism" in *Atlantvind* (1932) and in the two items "Protest och poesi" and "Panisk poesi" in the collective volumes *Avsikter* (1945) and *Poeter om poesi* (1947). On Lundkvist see Walter Dickson's "Stildrag i Artur Lundkvists Dikter mellan djur och gud," contributed to *Kritiskt 40-tal* (1948), pp.273–81, Ragnar Oldberg's "Artur Lundkvist" in *Nutidsförfattare* (1949), pp.267–78, two articles by Richard B. Vowles, "From Pan to Panic: The Poetry of Artur Lundkvist," *New Mexico Quarterly*, XXII (1952), 288–96, and "Sweden's Modern Muse: Exploded Sonnets and Panic Poetry," *Kentucky Foreign Language Quarterly*, II (1955), 134–38, and the appreciative volume by various hands *Artur Lundkvist 3 mars 1956* (1956), ed. by Stig Carlson. ¶ On Harry Martinson much has been written, including five book-length works and many shorter studies. Of broadly inclusive interest are the Danish poet-critic Tom Kristensen's *Harry Martinson, den fribaarne Fyrbøder* (Copenhagen, 1941) and two works by Lars Ulvenstam, *Harry Martinson* (1950) and *Den unge Harry Martinson* (1954). Tord Hall's *Vår tids stjärnsång* (1958) analyzes the scientific background of Martinson's space-cycle *Aniara*. On the same subject Tord Hall has published two articles in *BLM*, 1959. Among the representative shorter studies are the following:

Artur Lundkvist's notes in *Atlantvind* (1932), pp.211–16, two articles by Knut Jaensson, "Harry Martinson" in *Nio moderna svenska prosaförfattare* (1941), pp.48–55, and "Återblick på Harry Martinson" in *Essayer* (1946) [also in *BLM*, xv, 112–26], pp.167–206, Walter Dickson's "Stildrag i Harry Martinsons 'Natur'," *OoB*, LVI (1947), 408–12, Ingvar Holm's "Tankar och tendenser i Harry Martinsons diktning," *SLT*, xi (1948), 97–127, Lars Ulvenstam's "Li Kan talar under trädet: ett motiv hos Harry Martinson," *BLM*, xix (1950), 28–34, Sven A. Bergmann's "Harry Martinson och ordens leende" in *Göteborgsstudier i litteratur-historia tillägnade Sverker Ek* (Göteborg, 1954), pp.343–65, Ingalisa Munck's "Klockbojen och koltrampen: Harry Martinsons lyriska genombrott," *BLM*, xxi (1952), 102–9, Olle Holmberg's "Vägen till Klockrike" in *Lovtal över svenska romaner* (1957), and Richard B. Vowles's "Harry Martinson, Sweden's Seaman Poet," *Books Abroad*, xxv (1951), 332–35. ¶ The other figures in the "Five Young Men" group — Erik Asklund, Josef Kellgren, and Gustav Sandgren — have made interesting contributions to *Ansikten* (1932) and *Avsikter* (1945). Asklund has written with feeling and understanding about Josef Kellgren (*BLM*, xix [1950], 582–92), and Sandgren has reminisced delightfully about the early days of the group (*BLM*, xx [1951], 424–30).

Fortunately for those readers who may have difficulty in following the shifting patterns of modernity in the highly sophisticated verse of Gunnar Ekelöf, certain keys to these shifting poetic patterns have been provided by the poet himself in a long series of speculative essays and fragments on the nature of poetry as he sees it at various points in his poetic development; and in addition to the speculative essays of Ekelöf a number of finely perceptive critics have contributed interpretative studies on Ekelöf. Among Ekelöf's speculative essays and fragments are "Diktens medel och mål," *BLM*, II, nr. 5 (1933), 18–21, "Från dadaism till surrealism," *BLM*, III, nr. 1 (1934), 34–40, "Konsten och livet," *BLM*, III, nr. 8 (1934), 58–62, "En återblick," *BLM*, ix (1940), 771–73, "Självsyn" in *Poeter om poesi* (1947), pp.101–21, and various items in Ekelöf's *Blandade kort* (1957). Of the better critical items on Ekelöf, four in particular should be mentioned, one by the sensitive academic critic Carl Fehrman, "Teknik och tradition hos Gunnar Ekelöf," *SLT*, ix (1946), 97–117, and three by as many fellow-poet-critics, Olof Lagercrantz's "Två lyriker [Ekelöf and Karl Vennberg]," *OoB*, LV (1946), 148–51, Artur Lundkvist's "Gunnar Ekelöf" in *Den unga parnassen*, ed. by G. Näsström and M. Strömberg (1947), pp.68–72, and, of central importance, Erik Lindegren's "Gunnar Ekelöf — en modern mystiker" in *Kritiskt 40-tal*, ed. by Karl Vennberg and Werner Aspenström (1948), pp.282–304 (orig. publ. in the journal *Tiden*, 1943). Two recent items of considerable importance are a book by a fellow-poet, Bertil Malmberg's *Gunnar Ekelöf* (1958), and Kjell Espmark's comparative study "Ekelöf och Eliot: en studie kring Färjesång," *BLM*, xxviii (1959), 683–90. See also *En bok om Gunnar Ekelöf*, ed. by Stig Carlson and Axel Liffner (1956), and two American items, Richard B. Vowles's "Gunnar Ekelöf, Swedish Eclectic," *Western Humanities Review*, vi (1952), 53–58, and Grace Hunter's "Two Contemporary Swedish Poets [Ekelöf and Harry Martinson]," *Prairie Schooner*, xxvii (1955), 57–67.

On Nils Ferlin three books have appeared to date, one, Arne Häggqvist's *Ferlin: ungdomsåren* (1942), an uncritically enthusiastic biographical study of the years down to Ferlin's literary debut, another, *En bok om Nils Ferlin*, ed. by Stig Carlson and Axel Liffner (1954), a biographical and critical miscellany of some value, the third, Åke Runnquist's *Poeten Nils Ferlin* (1958), a competent, at times fascinating, biographical and critical sketch. Among the shorter items on Ferlin are Sven Stolpe's "Nils Ferlin" in *Kämpande dikt* (1938), pp.45–51, H. Åkerhielm's "Nils Ferlin," *OoB*,

XLVIII (1939), 91–94, Sven Ulric Johanson's "Faror för Nils Ferlin," *SLT*, IX (1946), 34–37 (cf. Martin Ivarsson's marginal notes in the same journal, pp.142–44), and Richard B. Vowles's "Nils Ferlin: The Poet as Clown and Scapegoat," *The Norseman*, XII (1954), 424–29.

A series of brief but brilliant essays on representative practitioners of prose fiction in the late 1920's and the 1930's is provided in Knut Jaensson's *Nio moderna svenska prosaförfattare* (1939). Other books such as Ragnar Oldberg's *Några moderna svenska författare* (1944), Åke Runnquist's *Arbetarskildrare* (1952), and Holger Ahlenius's "Svensk dikt och debatt: en bokkavalkad," *Den svenska boken under 50 år* (1943), provide material on a number of the novelists of the period or place particular novels of the day in their immediate social and literary contexts, while Staffan Björck's *Romanens formvärld* (4th ed. 1957) often uses the Swedish novel of the 1930's as illustrative material in analyzing various fictional forms. See also Margit Abenius's "Ansatser och segrar i svensk prosa 1934–1937," *Nordisk Tidskrift*, XIV (1938), 203–25, the closing paragraphs of Ivar Harrie's "Svensk roman 1837–1937," *BLM*, VI (1937), 600–5, and Örjan Lindberger's "Berättarteknikens utveckling från Hjalmar Söderberg till Eyvind Johnson," *MFÅ* (1939), 94–116.

The literature on Agnes von Krusenstjerna is extensive, in part because she has been such a controversial figure in contemporary Swedish literature. Two books of central importance are Stig Ahlgren's brilliant but somewhat uneven *Krusenstjernastudier* (1946) and Olof Lagercrantz's sensitive dissertation, *Agnes von Krusenstjerna* (1951). The collection of essays from various hands *Dikten, diktaren och samhället* (1935) discusses, more or less discreetly with Agnes von Krusenstjerna's case in mind, the problem of sex in literature together with the author's freedom and responsibility with regard to the problem, while David Sprengel's anything but discreet belaboring of publishers, authors, and critics in the Introduction to *Förläggarna, författarna, kritikerna om Agnes von Krusenstjerna och hennes senaste arbeten* (1935) created such a sensation that few critics wished to cross swords directly with its author (Agnes von Krusenstjerna's husband) and fewer publishers were prepared to print answers to his charges. On the occasion of Sprengel's death in 1941 Stig Ahlgren wrote a lively necrologue (reprinted in A's *Obehagliga stycken*, pp.66–73), and some years later Olof Lagercrantz published (in *BLM*, XVIII [1949], 773–83) a balanced final appraisal of Sprengel's work as a critic and his fate as a man. Of the articles and essays on Agnes von Krusenstjerna which are not hopelessly bogged down in the morass of contemporary controversy about her work the following may be listed: Erik Blomberg's "Kvinnospegel" in *Mosaik* (1940), pp.106–16, Niels Christian Brøgger's "En stor roman" in *Det moderne menneske og andre essays* (Oslo, 1937), pp.51–59, Hagar Olsson's "Agnes von Krusenstjerna," *BLM*, VI (1937), 515–26, Knut Jaensson's "Agnes von Krusenstjerna" in *Nio moderna svenska prosaförfattare* (1941), pp.5–12, H. Åkerhielm's "Drömmen om kvinnoriket," *Tiden*, XXXIV (1942), 493–501, Johannes Edfelt's "Agnes von Krusenstjernas ungdomsdiktning," *BLM*, XII (1943), 549–57, and Gerard Ordencrantz's commentary (in *SLT*, XVI [1952], 101–4) on Olof Lagercrantz's Krusenstjerna book.

Among Eyvind Johnson's more revealing autobiographical fragments and literary commentaries are "Personligt dokument" and "Romanfunderingar," contributed respectively to *Ansikten* (1932) and *Avsikter* (1945), and the lecture "Diktaren — samhället" published in *SLT*, VIII (1945), 145–56. With Eyvind Johnson's "Romanfunderingar" as a point of departure, Örjan Lindberger, whose book on Eyvind Johnson is about to go to press, has contributed a valuable lecture (see *Den 2. internasjonale studiekonferanse om nordisk litteratur*. Lillehammer 7.–12. juli 1958) on the Swedish novelist's search for fictional form. Jørgen Claudi's *Eyvind Johnson: en karakteristik* (Copenhagen, 1947) is popular and sketchy. Intelligent general surveys in article or essay form are Ivar Harrie's "Eyvind Johnson," *SLT*, 1 (1938), 185–98 (reprinted in *In i fyrtiotalet*, 1944, pp.349–65), Henning Söderhjelm's "Eyvind Johnson" in *Författareprofiler* (1938), pp.169–99, Knut Jaensson's "Eyvind Johnson" in *Nio moderna svenska prosaförfattare* (1941), Artur Lundkvist's "Eyvind Johnson," *Tiden*, xxxvi (1944), 289–304, and Jöran Mjöberg's "Eyvind Johnson," *Samtiden*, lvii (1948), 295–308. Thorsten Jonsson has an illuminating section on Eyvind Johnson and Norrland in *Stor-Norrland och litteraturen* (1938). More or less detailed examinations of three of Johnson's most arresting novels have been made – the so-called "Olof romanen" by Erik Blomberg, "Kollektiv jagroman" in *Mosaik* (1940), pp.127–46, (1940), pp.127–46, and by Olle Holmberg in *Lovtal över svenska romaner* (1957), pp.141–49, the "Krilon" series by Stig Ahlgren in *Obehagliga stycken* (1944), pp.111–27, and *Strändernas svall* (tr. *Return to Ithaca*) by Axel Strindberg, "En krigare drager hemåt" in *Stick och ståndpunkter* (1947), pp.129–34, and by J. Sundvall, "Homeros och Johnson," *FT*, cxli (1947), 164–75. Örjan Lindberger's very recent "Eyvind Johnsons möte med Proust och Joyce," *BLM*, xxix (1960), 554–63, traces the circumstances under which Eyvind Johnson "discovered" two modern novelists who were to have the greatest importance in his career as the first distinctly modernistic Swedish novelist.

A recurrent theme in Swedish prose fiction in the 1930's – the drift from the countryside to the city and its social consequences for the rural areas – has been examined, in representative works of Moberg, Lo-Johansson, and Fridegård, by Erik Blomberg in "Stad och land i några nyare svenska romaner," *Mosaik* (1940), pp. 147–70 (reprinted in EB's *Från Öst och Väst*, 1951, pp.137–57). The only book-length examination of the total work to date of Vilhelm Moberg is *Vilhelm Moberg: en biografi* (1956) by Sigvard Mårtensson, who has also written a popular book on Moberg's dramatic production entitled *En bok om Vilhelm Moberg* (1953). See also on Moberg's drama Gunnar Ollén's *Berömd nordisk dramatik*, 3 (1945), and on performances of his plays consult the volumes of reviews of performances listed above (p.621). Of general interest, particularly about Moberg's prose fiction, are Knut Jaensson's brief survey "Vilhelm Moberg" in *Nio moderna svenska prosaförfattare* (1941), pp.21–27, Stig Ahlgren's "Vilhelm Mobergs värld," *OoB*, xlvii (1938), 598–602, and "Rid i natt! och efteråt" in *Det kritiska uppdraget* (1946), pp.81–91, Henning Söderhjelm's "Vilhelm Moberg" in *Författareprofiler* (1938), pp.200–22, Artur Lundkvist's "Vilhelm Moberg," *Tiden*, xxxv (1943), 296–308, and Ragnar Oldberg's "Vilhelm Moberg" in *Några moderna svenska författare* (1944), pp.117–28. Folkloristic elements in Moberg's novels are analyzed in an article by Bror Olsson, *SLT*, 1 (1938), 63–71. Particular novels have been examined from one point of view or other in Ivar Harrie's "Budkavle går" in *In i fyrtiotalet* (1944), pp.334–48, Axel Strindberg's "Brunst och bråddöd" in *Stick och ståndpunkter* (1947), pp.124–28, and Alrik Gustafson's " 'A Dream Worth Dying for – ': The Price of Freedom in Vilhelm Moberg's Recent Novels," *ASR*, xxx (1942), 296–307. Moberg himself has thrown a great deal of light on his backgrounds and his literary program in the autobiographical novels *Knut Toring*, 1935–39 (tr. *The Earth Is Ours*) and *Soldat med brutet gevär*, 1944 (Eng. adaptation in much shorter form *When I Was a Child*), and in such items as "Brodd" in *Ansikten* (1932), pp.155–56, "Bonden och naturen," *BLM*, viii (1939), 22–26, and "Betraktelse om romanskrivning" in *Avsikter* (1945), pp. 157–67. ¶ None of the novelists of the 1930's has been so aggressively prolific in stating his literary program as Ivar Lo-Johansson, many of whose literary and social pronouncements originally appearing in various journals have been collected in the volume *Stridsskrifter* (1956). Three book-length studies and a rather large number of critical essays on Lo-Johansson have appeared. Of the three books, two are of importance, Mauritz Edström's little volume *Ivar Lo-Johansson* (1954) and Ragnar Oldberg's *Ivar Lo-Johansson: en monografi* (1957). Cf. also Oldberg's *Uteslutet om Lo-Jo: av utrymmesskäl utbrutna partier ur manuskriptet till Ivar Lo-Johansson, en monografi* (1957). Of the shorter items the following may be mentioned: Knut Jaensson's "Ivar Lo-Johansson" in *Nio moderna svenska prosaförfattare* (1941), pp. 28–35, Stig Ahlgren's "Statarepik" in *Det kritiska uppdraget* (1946), pp.138–43, Axel Strindberg's "Individ och kollektiv" and "Jordproletärerna" in *Stick och ståndpunkter* (1947), pp.75–80, 113–18, Ebbe Linde's "Lo-Johansson och onan," *BLM*, xvii (1948), 191–96, Elisabeth Tykesson's "Ivar Lo-Johansson och Atterboms äktenskap," *SLT*, xi (1948), 44–46, Ragnar Oldberg's "Bild och idé: en sida av Ivar Lo-Johanssons konstnärskap," *BLM*, xviii (1949), 537–43, and Mauritz Edström's "Ivar Lo-Johanssons samhällskritik," *BLM*, xxii (1953), 436–42. ¶ Among the more quietly modest of Swedish autobiographical fragments and literary observations are those by Jan Fridegård, examples of which are "De sju magra åren," *BLM*, x (1941), 449–53, "Om påverkan," *BLM*, xiv (1945), 290–93, and "Utan rubrik" in *Avsikter* (1945), pp.39–43. Of Fridegård's novels the Lars Hård series has created the greatest sensation and provided the subject for innumerable critical commentaries, of which Erik Blomberg's in *Mosaik* (1940), pp.164–70, Knut Jaensson's in *BLM*, xv (1946), 548–59 (reprinted in J's *Essayer*, 1946, pp.81–115), Hagar Olsson's in *Tidiga fanfarer* (1953), pp.105–8, Nils Johan Rud's in the Norwegian journal *Vinduet*, ii (1948), 571–76, and Axel Strindberg's in *Människor mellan krig* (1941), pp.300–5, are among the more perceptive and intelligent. Of the more general and inclusive studies the following may be consulted: Knut Jaensson's "Jan Fridegård" in *Nio moderna svenska prosaförfattare* (1941), pp.36–44, Artur Lundkvist's "Jan Fridegård," *Tiden*, xxxv (1943), 160–73, Ragnar Oldberg's "Jan Fridegård" in *Några moderna svenska författare* (1944), pp.47–55, and "Jan Fridegård" in *Nutidsförfattare* (1949), pp.195–207, and Jöran Mjöberg's "Jan Fridegård, en social diktare," *Samtiden*, lvii (1948), 588–99. Erik Gamby has written the little book *Jan Fridegård: introduktion till ett författarskap* (1956) and edited *En bok om Jan Fridegård: vänbok till F's 60-årsdag* (1957). ¶ "Vad jag vill med mina böcker" is the characteristically direct manner in which is formulated the title of a contribution to *Avsikter* (1945) by Moa Martinson, whose work has been relatively neglected by the serious critics. Among the items on her of some importance outside the general literary surveys are Marika Stiernstedt's "Om Moa Martinson," *BLM*, viii (1939), 511–21 (reprinted in the brochure *Marika Stiernstedt om Moa Martinson*, 1946), Knut Jaensson's "Moa Martinson" in *Nio moderna svenska prosaförfattare* (1941), pp.45–47, and Åke Runnquist's "Debuter i skymundan: Jan Fridegård och Moa Martinson," *BLM*, xxii (1953), 197–203.

Of the two most incisive probers into middle-class mentality in the Swedish novel of the 1930's and 1940's, Olle Hedberg and Arvid Brenner (pseud. of Helge Heerberger), the latter has received the less attention from critics, but what some of the critics have written about Brenner — such as Elisabeth Tykesson's "Arvid Brenner, barnen och kriget" in *Tolv essayer* (1945), pp.85–93, and Örjan Lindberger's "Stillsam sanningssökare," *Vi*, 1945, nr. 41 — is on a high critical level. ¶ Of the shorter general studies on Hedberg see Holger Ahlenius's "Olle Hedbergs författarskap," *BLM*, vi (1937), 452–60, Örjan Lindberger's "Olle Hedbergs romaner," *OoB*, xl (1937), 335–44, Henning Söderhjelm's "Olle Hedberg" in *Författareprofiler*

(1938), pp.223–55, Knut Jaensson's "Olle Hedberg" in *Nio moderna svenska prosa-författare* (1944), pp.56–61, and Elisabeth Tykesson's "Olle Hedbergs två världar," *SLT*, VII (1944), 1–17 (reprinted in ET's *Tolv essayer*, 1945, pp.95–122). Elis Andersson has written the brochure *Olle Hedberg* (1944) and Jacob Kulling has examined in detail the moral and religious problems in Hedberg's novels in *Olle Hedbergs romaner* (Stockholm, 1952). ¶ On the women novelists of the 1930's as a group consult Ragnar Oldberg's "Sju författarinnor" in *Några moderna svenska författare* (1944), pp.167–81; on Stina Aronson and Tora Dahl, Margit Abenius's "Två berätterskor," *BLM*, XXI (1952), 604–7; on Marika Stiernstedt, Ulf Wittrock's sensitive and candid biography *Marika Stiernstedt* (1959); on Irja Browallius, John Karlzén's "Irja Browallius," *SLT*, IV (1941), 81–90 (reprinted in K's *Modernister och omoderna*, 1952, pp.30–43), Erik Hj. Linder's "Irja Browallius och hennes närkingar" in *Stenarna där barn jag lekt* (1942), pp.161–76, and Ragnar Oldberg's "Irja Browallius" in *Nutidsförfattare* (1949), pp.153–62. ¶ Of the three prose writers deriving from the university circles at Lund, Frans G. Bengtsson, Fritiof Nilsson Piraten, and Sigfrid Lindström, the latter two have attracted only limited critical attention: Fritiof Nilsson Piraten in such studies as Erik Noreen's "Nutida svensk berättarstil: Fritiof Nilsson Piraten" in *Från Birgitta till Piraten* (1942), pp.167–89, and Elisabeth Tykesson's "Lek, lögn och lidande: Fritiof Nilsson Piratens romaner och noveller," *SLT*, VI (1943), 33–46 (reprinted in *Tolv essayer*, 1945, pp.123–50), and Sigfrid Lindström in Ingvar Andersson's "Sigfrid Lindström," *SLT*, II (1939), 1–17, Ivar Harrie's "Den obesegrade" in *Orientering* (1932), pp.179–86, and "Prosa-dikter" in *In i fyrtiotalet* (1944), pp.327–31, Algot Werin's "Tristran – de besegrades diktare" in *Den svenske Faust och andra essayer* (Lund, 1950), pp.208–16, and Olle Holmberg's *Sigfrid Lindström* (1951). ¶ Aside from the valuable miscellany *Frans G. Bengtsson: en minnesbok*, ed. by Germund Michanek (Uppsala, 1955), mention can be made here as representative of the literature on Bengtsson such surveys, essays, reminiscences, and special studies as Ivar Harrie's "En herre yttrar sig" in *Orientering* (1932), pp.187–95, Artur Lundkvist's "Frans G. Bengtsson, Essayist," *Tiden*, XXXIII (1941), 612–21, Karl Ragnar Gierow's "Frans G. Bengtsson," *SLT*, V (1942), 81–93, Elof Ehnmark's *Frans G. Bengtsson* (1946), Olle Holmberg's "Något om Frans G. Bengtsson," *SLT*, XVIII (1955), 75–104, and Algot Werin's "Frans G. Bengtssons poetiska år," *SLT* (1955), 39–74. In English consult Bengtsson's half-waggish autobiographical fragments "How I Became a Writer" in *A Walk to an Ant Hill and Other Essays* (New York, 1950), Gurli Hertzman-Ericson's "A New Biography of Charles XII," *ASR*, XXV (1937), 354–55, and Lawrence S. Thompson's survey-necrologue "Frans G. Bengtsson, 1894–1954," *Kentucky Foreign Language Quarterly*, II (1955), 75–79. ¶ The three markedly experimental novelists and short story writers from the middle and late 1930's Walter Ljungquist, Tage Aurell, and Thorsten Jonsson have particularly in the 1940's and later come to be admired by the more advanced critics. On Ljungquist and Jonsson see items by Artur Lundkvist and Tore Zetterholm in *Den unga parnassen*, ed. by G. Näsström and M. Strömberg (1947). On Ljungquist consult also F. Vetterlund, "Walter Ljungquist, en modern novellist," *OoB*, LI (1942), 269–75, Carl-Eric Nordberg, "Walter Ljungquist – den intime visionären," *BLM*, XIX (1950), 749–58, John Karlzén, "Walter Ljungquists Azalea" in *Modernister och omoderna* (1952), pp.79–99, Bengt Nerman, "När Walter Ljungquist mötte Hemingway" in *Studier tillägnade Henry Olsson* (1956), pp.314–41, and Lars Bäckström, "Väntan och klarsyn: en Walter-Ljungquist-översikt," *SLT*, XIX (1956), 49–72. ¶ On Thorsten Jonsson see, in addition to the Zetterholm item above, Stig Ahlgren's "Allvar inför brottet" in *Obehagliga stycken* (1944), pp.84–92, and the brief obituary notice in *BLM*, xix (1950), 483–85. ¶ On Tage Aurell consult Knut Jaensson's "Tage Aurell egenartad berättare," *BLM*, xii (1943), 491–94 (reprinted in *Essayer*, 1946, pp.119–33), Elisabeth Tykesson's "Tage Aurell, författare," *SLT*, viii (1945), 183–90 (reprinted in *Tolv essayer*, 1945, pp.19–32), John Karlzén's "Hos Tage Aurell," *SLT*, x (1947), 97–103, and Karl Vennberg's "Provinsen Aurell," *Vi*, 1950, nr. 13.

Chapter 12. Modernism Triumphant and Its Aftermath

The student who wishes to gain a reasonably inclusive understanding of the complex patterns of development in the last two decades of Swedish literary production should, as minimal reading, immerse himself in such representative anthologies as *40-talslyrik*, ed. by Erik Lindegren and Karl Vennberg (1947), *Kritiskt 40-tal*, ed. by Karl Vennberg and Werner Aspenström (1948), and *50-talslyrik*, ed. by Bengt Holmqvist and Folke Isaksson (1955; new augmented ed. under same title, 1959, ed. by Folke Isaksson and Göran Palm), and should consult as occasion demands the brief but often illuminating critical portraits in such collective works as *Den unga parnassen*, ed. by G. Näsström and M. Strömberg (1947) and *Den nya parnassen*, ed. by Birger Christofferson (1956). Two books of special value on literary developments of our day are Bengt Holmqvist's *Svensk 40-talslyrik* (1951), which provides a general introduction to the poetry of the 1940's, and Åke Runnquist's *Moderna svenska författare* (1959), which includes – in addition to brief sketches on individual authors – some general observations on the 1940's and 1950's. For those who may wish to follow contemporary literary developments from month to month *Bonniers Litterära Magasin* is an indispensable source, which may be supplemented by other Swedish journals of cultural leanings and the often excellent pages devoted to literature in the leading Swedish newspapers.

Brief contemporary surveys of current literary production in each of the Scandinavian countries are to be had in *Ny litteratur i Norden* (Stockholm, 1949ff.), whose first issue covers the period 1945–49, with later issues at three-year intervals. Of more or less general interest also are: Jöran Mjöberg's *Dikt och diktatur* (1944), which examines in considerable detail the "humanistic" reaction against Continental totalitarianism before and after the outbreak of the Second World War; Stig Ahlgren's "Varning för efterkrigspessimism" in *Det kritiska uppdraget* (1946), pp.158–64, which introduced in the April 1946 issue of the popular weekly *Vi* a round of contributions on postwar "pessimism" in literature; Karl Ragnar Gierow and other dramatists' contributions to an *enquête* on Swedish drama today, in *BLM*, xviii (1949), 196–206; Ragnar Oldberg's "De unga författarna" in *Nutidsförfattare* (1949), pp.96–114, which sketches in some detail the background and characteristic moods and forms of expression of the 1940's; Axel Strindberg's "Ny prosa" in *Stick och ståndpunkter* (1946), pp.136–54, which deals with a number of the representative novels of the period; Ivar Harrie's "Född 1919" in *In i fyrtiotalet* (1944), pp.372–76, which contrasts the moods and attitudes of the generation of the 1940's with the authors of two decades earlier; Karl Vennberg's Introduction to the anthology *Sex unga lyriker* (1954), which analyzes sensitively and with genuine understanding a group of the youngest generation of Swedish poets; also the little volume edited by Lasse Bergström *Varför skriver vi?* (1953), whose candid contributions by fourteen youthful authors reflect among other things the diversity of points of view represented in the youngest generation of Swedish authors; and two recent items, Lars Bäckström's *Under välfärdens yta: litterärt under femtitalet* (1959) and

Ingemar Wizelius's "Svensk skönlitteratur 1956–58," *Nordisk Tidskrift*, xxxv (1959), 232–50, which are of considerable importance on the literature of the 1950's. Various problems of special concern to the fraternity of authors of our day are subjected to frank and sometimes searching analysis in *Nordiske diktare debatterar* (1953), the published record of discussions held at the Nordic Authors' Congress in Sweden, November 24–30, 1946.

To these items of general interest on Swedish literature of the last two decades may be added a sampling of essays and articles on individual authors who have during this period come to occupy places of central importance. Brief but excellent items on Stig Dagerman, Erik Lindegren, Karl Vennberg, Lars Ahlin, Sivar Arnér, and other less important figures are included in *Den unga parnassen* (1947) and on Sara Lidman and more than a score of others in *Den nya parnassen* (Stockholm, 1956). Ragnar Oldberg's *Nutidsförfattare* (1949) provides some notes on Erik Lindegren, Karl Vennberg, and Sivar Arnér, as well as a fairly full treatment of Stig Dagerman and Lars Ahlin. ¶ On Stig Dagerman otherwise see A. Gunnar Bergman's "Stig Dagerman: en första presentation," *Vinduet*, ii (1948), 59–64, Ragnar Svanström's *Stig Dagerman: några minnesbilder* (1954), the poet-critic Olof Lagercrantz's *Stig Dagerman* (1958), and reviews of Dagerman's plays in production in the collections of such material listed above on p.621. In English see Alrik Gustafson's Introduction to *Scandinavian Plays of the Twentieth Century*, Third Series (Princeton and New York, 1951). ¶ On Erik Lindegren consult Stig Ahlgren's "Erik Lindegren" in *Obehagliga stycken* (1944), pp.216–26, Lars Bäckström's "Alltet och den stelnade: några ledtrådar genom Lindegren," *OoB*, lxiv (1955), 227–84, and Göran Printz-Påhlson's "Om Lindegrens statyer," *SLT*, xix (1956), 162–65. ¶ On Karl Vennberg see Olof Lagercrantz's "Två lyriker Ekelöf och Vennberg," *OoB*, lv (1946), 148–51, Walter Dickson's "Smärtan och dess rening hos Karl Vennberg," *BLM*, xxi (1952), 262–68, and Karl Erik Lagerlöf's "Det religiösa problemet hos Karl Vennberg," *OoB*, lxv (1956), 484–90. ¶ On Lars Ahlin see Ulf Linde's brilliant study "Det Ahlinska alternativet," *BLM*, xxix (1960), 464–75, followed in the same journal (pp.476–77) by some paragraphs from a letter by Ahlin which may be considered a commentary on Linde's essay. ¶ On Sivar Arnér see Elisabeth Tykesson's "Sivar Arnér, nåden och domen" in *Tolv essayer* (1945), pp.11–18, Jöran Mjöberg's "Den fjärran verkligheten: psykologiska synpunkter på Sivar Arnérs författarskap," *BLM*, xvii (1948), 178–83, and Carl-Erik Nordberg's "Teater för slutna ögon: Sivar Arnér som radiodramatiker," *BLM*, xxviii (1959), 693–99. ¶ On Sara Lidman see the reviews of *Tjärdalen* and *Hjortronlandet* by Elisabeth Tykesson and Margit Abenius respectively, *BLM*, xxii (1953), 295–96, xxiv (1955), 545–47, Birger Vikström's "Om Sara Lidmans dialekt," *BLM*, xxv (1956), 213–17, and Erna Ofstad's "Sara Lidman," *Samtiden*, lxviii (1959), 467–75.

Very little has appeared in English on the most recent developments in Swedish literature. Aside from two items by Swedish critics on Swedish literature during the Second World War – Georg Svensson's chapter in *Sweden: A Wartime Survey* (New York, 1944), pp.217–26, and Örjan Lindberger's article in *The Norseman*, v (1947), 133–37 – another Swede, Jöran Mjöberg, writes on "Swedish Postwar Literature," *The Norseman*, viii (1950), 132–40, and Richard B. Vowles has contributed two items, "Sweden's Modern Muse: Exploded Sonnets and Panic Poetry," *Kentucky Foreign Language Quarterly*, ii (1955), 134–38, which is an article concerned with Erik Lindegren and Artur Lundkvist, and "Six Modern Swedish Poets" appearing in the Mentor Book *New World Writing*, nr. 11 (New York, 1957), which includes – in addition to some stimulating notes on recent Swedish poetry as represented in Harry Martinson, Artur Lundkvist, Gunnar Ekelöf, Stig Dagerman, Erik Lindegren, and Karl Vennberg — a competent translation of a poem by each of them. Some notes on Swedish literature today are available also in the January 1959 issue of *The American-Swedish Monthly*, which in its Editor's Corner quotes liberally from a paper by the Swedish critic Lars Ulvenstam, who provides revealing glimpses into the frames of reference and search for values among Swedish authors today. Ulvenstam's paper was delivered at the Harvard International Seminar in the summer of 1958.

Ingemar Wizelius's excellent short survey *Swedish Literature 1956–1960* was issued by the Swedish Institute, Stockholm, just as this book went to press.

Grateful acknowledgment is here made to fil. lic. Bure Holmbäck of the Royal Library, Stockholm, for his careful reading of the galley proofs of this bibliographical guide and for suggesting the inclusion of a few titles missing in the original manuscript.

A List of Translations into English

WITH SOME CRITICAL AND EXPLANATORY NOTES

THE following list of translations is quite full without being exhaustive; a few authors of no importance have been excluded entirely while certain others are represented only by such translations as are, in their cases, of chief importance. Those readers who may be interested in a somewhat fuller listing of translations into English than is here provided are referred to the section entitled "Literary Works" in Nils Afzelius's *Books in English on Sweden* (Stockholm, 3rd enlarged and revised ed. 1951), which in its attempt to be as complete as possible includes translations of authors of little if any importance and lists all translations of any given author regardless of the relative significance of the works listed. Of some interest also, particularly in matters of bibliographical detail and commentary on certain translations and translators, is Adolph B. Benson's "Translations of Swedish Literature" in *Swedes in America*, ed. by Adolph B. Benson and Naboth Hedin (New Haven, 1938), pp.237-52.

Among the more inclusive anthologies (that is, those which range broadly over two or more periods of Swedish literature) the most useful and on the whole most sound are *Anthology of Swedish Lyrics from 1750 to 1925*, tr. with an Introduction by C. W. Stork (New York, 1917; slightly augmented edition 1930), *A Selection from Modern Swedish Poetry*, tr. by C. D. Locock (London and New York, 1929), *Modern Swedish Masterpieces: Short Stories Selected and Translated* by C. W. Stork (New York, 1923), *Sweden's Best Stories*, tr. by C. W. Stork with in Introduction by Hanna Astrup Larsen (New York, 1928), and *Modern Swedish Short Stories*, published under the auspices of the Anglo-Swedish Literary Foundation (London, 1934). Of considerably less importance but of some general value are such items as *Swedish Songs and Ballads*, tr. by M. S. Alwood, Helen Asbury, Lars Forsell, and others (New York and Mullsjö, Sweden, 1950) and *Scandinavian Short Stories*, ed. by Estrid Bannister (London, 1943). English versions of Swedish verse and prose, particularly from the last century or so, appear regularly in the columns of two periodicals, *The American-Scandinavian Review* (1913ff.) and, until recently, *The Norseman* (1943ff.).

Such collections of poetry or prose fiction or drama as limit their coverage more strictly to a given period in Swedish literature (e.g. *Scandinavian Plays of the Twentieth Century*, First and Third Series) will be listed in their appropriate places below.

Inasmuch as considerations of space permit me to list under each author only book-length works (novels, plays, longer poems, etc.), I can here but assure the reader that most of the more important poets and short story writers of the last two centuries are represented (if not in all cases well, at least *represented*) in the general collections of verse and prose listed here and in the preceding bibliography. Only for the earlier periods (that is to say down roughly to the middle of the eighteenth century) are reasonably representative specimens of Swedish literature in English garb hard to come upon; but one need not be unduly disturbed by this, for in only a limited number of cases does Swedish literature in these earlier periods take on such really memorable form — as in such instances as the Swedish provincial laws, in certain of Saint Birgitta's visions, and in the best verse of Stiernhielm and Lucidor, Wivallius and Olof von Dalin — that it calls for translation into foreign tongues.

FROM THE ORIGINS THROUGH THE PERIOD OF THE ENLIGHTENMENT

Works of broadly Scandinavian as distinguished from exclusively Swedish interest:

A Pageant of Old Scandinavia, ed. by Henry Goddard Leach (Princeton and New York, 1946; reprinted, 1955).
The Poetic Edda, tr. by Henry Adams Bellows (New York, 1923).
The Poetic Edda, tr. by Lee M. Hollander (Austin, Texas, 1928).
The Prose Edda, tr. by Arthur G. Brodeur (New York, 1916).
The Prose Edda, tr. by Jean I. Young with an Introduction by Sigurður Nordal (Cambridge, 1954).
The Heimskringla, tr. by Samuel Laing (London, 1844). Also available in Everyman's Library, nrs. 717, 847.
Heimskringla, tr. by Erling Monsen and A. H. Smith (Cambridge and New York, 1932).
The Stories of the Kings of Norway [*Heimskringla*], tr. by William Morris and E. Magnússon (London, 1893–1905).
The Saga of the Volsungs and the Saga of Ragnar Lodbrok, tr. by Margaret Schlauch (New York, 1930).
Four Icelandic Sagas, tr. by Gwyn Jones (New York, 1935).
Voyages to Vinland, tr. and interpreted by Einar Haugen (New York, 1942).
The Vatnsdalers' Saga, tr. by Gwyn Jones (New York, 1944).
The Sagas of Kormak and The Sworn Brothers, tr. by Lee M. Hollander (Princeton and New York, 1949).
Three Icelandic Sagas, tr. by M. H. Scargill and Margaret Schlauch (Princeton and New York, 1950).
Njál's Saga, tr. with an Introduction and Notes by Carl F. Bayerschmidt and Lee M. Hollander (New York, 1955).
Old Norse Poems, tr. by Lee M. Hollander (New York, 1936).
The Skalds. A Selection of Their Poems with Introductions and Notes by Lee M. Hollander (Princeton and New York, 1945).
The First Nine Books of the Danish History of Saxo Grammaticus, tr. by Oliver Elton (London, 1894). Reprinted New York, 1905.
A Book of Danish Ballads, tr. by E. M. Smith-Dampier with an Introduction by Axel Olrik (New York, 1939).

Of the numerous translations of *Beowulf* into modern English the following are especially recommended: *Beowulf and the Finnesburg Fragment*, a translation in modern English prose by John R. Clark Hall. New and rev. ed. by C. L. Wrenn and Prefatory Remarks by J. R. R. Tolkien (London, 1940); *Beowulf*, a Metrical Translation into Modern English by John R. Clark Hall (Cambridge, 1914); *Beowulf: The Oldest English Epic*. Translated into Alliterative Verse with a Critical Introduction by Charles W. Kennedy (Oxford, 1940). A convenient and inexpensive version, competent but somewhat stilted, is David Wright's *Beowulf: A New Translation* (Penguin Books, 1957).

Of the above works only *A Pageant of Old Scandinavia* provides us with English versions of a number of brief early Swedish texts. The *Ynglinga Saga* (which opens Snorre Sturlasson's *Heimskringla* sagas of the Norwegian kings) has a great deal to relate, however, about the ancient Swedish-Uppsala dynasties, and much can be claimed for a Swedish provenance of large parts of the material in *Beowulf*.

Works of specifically Swedish authorship:

Olaus Magnus, *A Compendious History of the Goths, Swedes & Vandals, and Other Northern Nations* (London, 1658).

Queen Christina, *Maxims of a Queen*. Selected and translated by Una Birch (London, 1906).
   Works. Containing Maxims and Sentences . . . Now first translated from the Original French . . . (London, 1753).

Swedish Poets of the Seventeenth Century: Some Gleanings from the Swedish Parnassus. Translations from the Swedish and Biographical Notes by Reinhold Ahléen (San Francisco, 1932). The only attempt (an unhappy amateurish one) to provide English versions of seventeenth-century Swedish verse, both lyrics and excerpts from longer poetic genres.

Olof von Dalin, *Envy, a Drama in Three Acts*, tr. by Edith Swanson (St. Louis, Mo., 1876).

So numerous are the English versions of works by Swedenborg and Linné (Linnaeus), and so predominantly scientific (in the case of Swedenborg also religious-visionary or religious-dogmatic) in character, that a literary history is scarcely the place in which to list them in detail. But for those readers who may be interested in sampling a representative number of these works in translation the following titles (with an indication of at least one date of English or American publication for each) may be listed:

Emanuel Swedenborg

The Apocalypse Explained According to the Spiritual Sense . . . , tr. by J. C. Ager (New York, 1892–1900), 6 vols. Other earlier English versions exist.

Arcana Cœlestia, the Heavenly Arcana contained in the Holy Scriptures . . . (New York, 1870–1873).

Conjugal Love and Its Chaste Delights: also Adulterous Love and Its Sinful Pleasures (New York, 1871). Another version entitled *The Delights of Wisdom Pertaining to Conjugal Love*, tr. by S. Warren (New York, 1928).

The Earths in Our Solar System . . . and the Earths in the Starry Heavens, Their Inhabitants and Spirits and Angels (Boston, 1928).

The Economy of the Animal Kingdom, considered anatomically, physically, and philosophically, tr. by A. Clissold (London and Boston, 1845–1868), 2 vols.

The Four Doctrines, tr. and ed. by J. F. Potts (New York, 1923). Includes *The Doctrine of the New Jerusalem concerning the Lord, The Doctrine of the New Jerusalem concerning the Holy Scripture, The Doctrine for the New Jerusalem from the Ten Commandments*, and *The Doctrine of the New Jerusalem concerning Faith*.

Rational Psychology, tr. by Norbert H. Rogers and Alfred Acton (Philadelphia, 1950).

Three Transactions on the Cerebrum, tr. and ed. by Alfred Acton (Philadelphia, 1938, 1940), 2 vols.

Available in Everyman's Library (as well as in many other English and American editions) are *Divine Love and Wisdom*, EL 635; *Divine Providence*, EL 658; *Heaven and Its Wonders, and Hell: From Things Heard & Seen,* EL 379; *The True Christian Religion,* EL 893.

Carl von Linné

Of the following, all except the last item are highly technical and of little if any literary interest:

The Families of Plants . . . (Lichfield, 1787).
The Genera Insectorum of Linnaeus, exemplified by various specimens of English Insects drawn from Nature by James Barbut (London, 1781). English and French texts.
A Generic and Specific Description of British Plants (London, 1775).
A Genuine and Universal System of Natural History; comprising the three Kingdoms of Animals, Vegetables, and Minerals. . . . (London, 1794–1810).
Institutions of Entomology. . . . , tr. by T. P. Yeats (London, 1773).
Miscellaneous Tracts Relating to Natural History, Husbandry, and Physick, tr. and ed. by B. Stillingfleet (London, 1759).
A System of Vegetables According to Their Classes, Orders, Genera, Species. . . . (Lichfield, 1783).
Lachesis Lapponica, or a Tour to Lappland. Now first published from the Original Manuscript Journal of the celebrated Linnaeus, by James Edward Smith (London, 1811), 2 vols.

Neither *The Letters and Memorials of Emanuel Swedenborg,* tr. and ed. by Alfred Acton (Bryn Athyn, Pa., 1948) nor *A Selection of the Correspondence of Linnaeus, and Other Naturalists* (London, 1821) is of any literary interest.

Scientific travel books of at least three of Linné's Swedish disciples have appeared in English, Fr. Hasselquist's *Voyages and Travels in the Levant, in the years 1749–1752* (London, 1766), A. Sparrman's *A Voyage to the Cape of Good Hope, towards the Antarctic Polar Circle, and Round the World* . . . *from the years 1772 to 1776,* tr. from the Swedish original [by George Forster] (London, 1785), and Peter Kalm's *America of 1750: Peter Kalm's Travels in North America,* tr., rev., and ed. by A. B. Benson (Elmira, N.Y., 1937).

Carl Michael Bellman

The Last of the Troubadours: The Life and Music of Carl Michael Bellman. By Hendrik Willem van Loon and Grace Castagnetta (New York, 1939). Includes English texts together with music for twenty of Bellman's songs from *Fredmans epistlar* and *Fredmans sånger.* Popular.

The only other readily available source of a goodly number of Bellman's poems in English is C. W. Stork's *Anthology of Swedish Lyrics from 1750 to 1925* (New York, 1917; rev. and slightly augmented ed. 1930), which also contains a poem or two from each of a number of Bellman's contemporaries (Kellgren, Anna Maria Lenngren, Leopold, Lidner, and Franzén).

ROMANTICISM

Poetry of the Romantics generally is reasonably well represented in C. W. Stork's *Anthology of Swedish Lyrics from 1750 to 1925.*

Erik Gustaf Geijer

The History of the Swedes, tr. with an Introduction and Notes by J. H. Turner (London, [1845]).
Impressions of England. Compiled from Geijer's letters and diaries with an Intro-

duction by Anton Blank. Tr. by Elizabeth Sprigge and C. Napier (London, 1932).

The Poor Laws and Their Bearing on Society. A Series of Political and Historical Essays (Stockholm, 1840).

Esaias Tegnér

Aside from C. W. Stork's *Anthology of Swedish Lyrics* see *Specimens of Swedish and German Poetry*, Part 1, tr. by J. E. D. Bethune (London, 1948), for English versions of Tegnér's shorter poems. Of his longer poems, two, *Axel* and *Fritiofs Saga*, have frequently been translated into English. For complete listings of these translations see Gustaf N. Swan, "The English Versions of Tegnér's *Axel*," *Scandinavian Studies*, 1 (1911–14), 179–84, and Adolph B. Benson, "A List of Translations of the 'Frithiofs Saga,' " *Germanic Review* (1926), 142–67 (reprinted in the author's *American Scandinavian Studies* [New York, 1952], pp.277–98). Here I shall but list a limited number of the dozen or more generally undistinguished English renderings of *Axel* together with the more competently translated of the fifteen English versions of *Fritiofs Saga*.

Axel, tr. by J. E. D. Bethune in *Specimens of Swedish and German Poetry* (London, 1948). Other translations of *Axel* are those by A. Dobrée (Gothenburg, 1866); L. A. Sherman in *The Chatauquan* (Meadville, Pa., March and April, 1883); Frederick Peterson in *Poems and Swedish Translations* (Buffalo, N.Y., 1883); and M. Bernhard (New York, 1910), rev. ed. under the title *His Majesty's Courier* (Manila, 1912; Buffalo, N.Y., 1915).

The Children of the Lord's Supper, tr. by Henry Wadsworth Longfellow in *Poems by Tegnér* (New York, 1914).

Fridthiof's Saga. . . . A Legend of the North, tr. by George Stephens (Stockholm and London, 1839). Several later editions.

Fridthiof's Saga, A Norse Romance, tr. by Thomas A. E. Holcomb and Martha A. Lyon Holcomb (Chicago, 1877), 7th ed. 1912.

The Frithiof Saga, or Lay of Frithiof, tr. in the original meters by W. Lewery Blackley (Dublin, 1857). Several later editions, the most recent of which is included in *Poems by Tegnér: The Children of the Lord's Supper and Frithiof's Saga*, tr. by Henry Wadsworth Longfellow and W. Lewery Blackley, with an Introduction by Paul R. Lieder (New York, 1914).

Frithiof's Saga, A Legend of Ancient Norway, tr. by L. A. Sherman, with illustrations (Boston, 1878).

Frithiof's Saga, A Legend of Ancient Norway, tr. in the original meters by Clement B. Shaw (Chicago, 1908; rev. ed. 1911, 1921). Richly illustrated and with a great deal of explanatory material.

Frithiof's Saga, tr. in the original meters by C. D. Locock (London and New York, 1924). Centenary edition.

Johan Olof Wallin

"The Angel of Death" has been translated by O. T. Richmond (Chicago, 1868), by A. W. Almqvist (London and New York, 1884), by C. B. Shaw (Chicago, 1910), by H. F. Rosing (Minneapolis, 1920), and in part by C. W. Stork in *Anthology of Swedish Lyrics from 1750 to 1925*.

MID-CENTURY FERMENT

C. J. L. Almqvist

Gabriele Mimanso, the Niece of Abd-el-Kader, or An Attempt to Assassinate Louis Philippe, King of France, tr. by G. C. Hebbe (New York, 1846).

Sara Videbeck [and] *The Chapel*, tr. by Adolph B. Benson (New York and Oxford, 1919).

Fredrika Bremer

Of the nearly fifty works (some in several editions and reprintings) by Fredrika Bremer which have appeared in English, the following are representative:

GENERAL COLLECTIONS AND MULTIPLE-TITLE SINGLE VOLUMES

A Diary. The H— Family. Axel and Anna and Other Tales, tr. by Mary Howitt (London, 1853).

The H— Family. Trälinnan, Axel and Anna, and Other Tales, tr. by Mary Howitt (London, 1844), 2 vols.

The Home, or Life in Sweden [and] *Strife and Peace*, tr. by Mary Howitt (London, 1853).

Life, Letters, and Posthumous Works. Ed. by Charlotte Bremer. Tr. by Fredr. Milow (London and New York, 1868).

New Sketches of Everyday Life. A Diary, together with Strife and Peace, tr. by Mary Howitt (London and New York, 1844), 2 vols.

Novels [includes *The H. Family, The President's Daughters, The Neighbours*, etc.] (London, 1844).

The President's Daughters [including] *Nina*, tr. by Mary Howitt (London, 1843), 3 vols.

Works. Tr. by Mary Howitt (London, 1853; London and New York, 1892–1909), 4 vols.

INDIVIDUAL NOVELS AND TALES

The Bondmaid, tr. by M. L. Putnam (Boston and London, 1844).

Brothers and Sisters, tr. by Mary Howitt (London and New York, 1848).

The H— Family. Translated from the Swedish (Boston, 1843).

Hertha, tr. by Mary Howitt (London and New York, 1856).

The Home, or Family Cares and Family Joys, tr. by Mary Howitt (London, 1843). Also translated under same title by E. A. Friedlaender (London, 1844).

The Neighbours, tr. by Mary Howitt (London, 1842), 2 vols. Also translated by E. A. Friedlaender (London, 1844), 2 vols.

The Three Sisters, tr. by Mary Howitt (Philadelphia, [1860?]).

TRAVEL WORKS

America of the Fifties. Letters of Fredrika Bremer. Selected and edited by Adolph B. Benson (New York, 1924).

England in 1851, or Sketches of a Tour in England, tr. by L. A. H. Boulogne (London, 1853).

Greece and the Greeks, tr. by Mary Howitt (London, 1863), 2 vols.

The Homes of the New World: Impressions of America, tr. by Mary Howitt (New York, 1854), 2 vols.

Travels in the Holy Land, tr. by Mary Howitt (London, 1862), 2 vols.

Two Years in Switzerland and Italy, tr. by Mary Howitt (London, 1861), 2 vols. American edition bears title *Life in the Old World* (Philadelphia, [1861]).

Other Mid-Century Novelists

Of the Swedish practitioners of prose fiction contemporaneous with Fredrika Bremer only one, Émilie Flygare-Carlén, has been extensively translated, nearly thirty of her novels having appeared in English, one of her best and most popular, *Rosen på Tistelön* (1842), being published two years after the Swedish original in both English and American versions: *The Rose of Tistelön. A Tale of the Swedish Coast*, tr. by Mary Howitt (London) and *The Smugglers of the Swedish Coast, or The Rose of Thistle Island*, tr. by G. C. Hebbe and H. C. Deming (New York).

Three other novelists of the mid-century have appeared only in an occasional English version, Sophie von Knorring with *The Peasant and His Landlord*, tr. by Mary Howitt (London and New York, 1848), Carl Anton Wetterbergh [Onkel Adam] with *Revenge and Reconciliation*, [translator unknown] (New York, 1845), and August Blanche with *The Bandit*, tr. and ed. by Selma Borg and Marie A. Brown (New York, 1872) and *Master of His Fate*, tr. by M. R. Barnard (London, 1886).

Johan Ludvig Runeberg

Christmas Eve, or the Angel Guest. From the Swedish [by Mrs. Eric Baker] (New York, [1887]).
King Fialar: A Poem in Five Songs, tr. by E. Magnússon (London, 1912).
King Fjalar: A Poem in Five Songs, rendered into English by Anna Bahnhof, with an Introduction by B. Estlander (Helsingfors, 1904).
Lyrical Songs, Idylls, and Epigrams, done into English by E. Magnússon and E. H. Palmer (London, 1878).
Nadeschda: A Poem in Nine Cantos, tr. by Marie A. Brown (Boston, 1879). Also New York, 1890, and London, 1891.
A Selection from the Series of Poems Entitled Ensign Stål's Songs, rendered into English by Isabel Donner (Helsingfors, 1907).
The Songs of Ensign Stål, tr. by Clement B. Shaw (New York, 1925).
The Tales of Ensign Stål, selected and translated by C. W. Stork, with an Introduction by Y. Hirn (Princeton and New York, 1938).

Viktor Rydberg

Both Runeberg and Rydberg are rather liberally represented in C. W. Stork's *Anthology of Swedish Lyrics from 1750 to 1925*. Of Rydberg's prose we have in English three novels and four works of criticism and scholarship:

The Freebooter of the Baltic, tr. by Caroline L. Broomall (Media, Pa., 1891).
The Last Athenian, tr. by William W. Thomas, Jr. (Philadelphia, 1869; 2nd ed. 1879).
Singoalla, tr. by Aksel Josephson. Illustrated by Carl Larsson (New York, 1903). Also under the same title a translation by Josef Fredbärj (London, 1904).
The Magic of the Middle Ages, tr. by Hj. Edgren (New York, 1879).
Roman Days, tr. by Alfred C. Clark (New York and London, 1879).
Roman Legends about the Apostles Paul and Peter, tr. by Ottilia von Düben (London, 1898). Another translation under virtually the same title by Josef Fredbärj (Milwaukee, 1911).
Teutonic Mythology, tr. by R. B. Anderson (London, 1889). New ed. London, Stockholm, and New York, 1906. First volume only of Rydberg's *Undersökningar i germanisk mytologi*.

Carl Snoilsky

An excellent and generous selection from the verse of Carl Snoilsky has been sensitively rendered into English by C. W. Stork in his *Anthology of Swedish Lyrics from 1750 to 1925*.

STRINDBERG AND THE REALISTIC BREAKTHROUGH

August Strindberg

COLLECTED PLAYS

Plays by August Strindberg, Five Series, tr. with Introductions by Edwin Björkman (New York, 1912–16). First Series: *The Dream Play, The Link, The Dance of*

Death, I, II; Second Series: *There Are Crimes and Crimes, Miss Julia, The Stronger, Creditors, Pariah*; Third Series: *Swanwhite, Simoon, Debit and Credit, Advent, The Thunderstorm, After the Fire*; Fourth Series: *The Bridal Crown, The Spook Sonata, The First Warning, Gustavus Vasa*; Fifth Series: *The Father, The Black Glove, The Pelican, Moses*.

Plays, tr. by Edith and Warner Oland (Boston, 1912–14), 3 vols. I. *The Father, Countess Julie, The Outlaw, The Stronger*; II. *Comrades, Facing Death, Pariah, Easter*; III. *Swanwhite, Advent, The Storm*.

Eight Famous Plays by Strindberg [*The Link, The Father, Miss Julia, The Stronger, There Are Crimes and Crimes, Gustavus Vasa, The Dance of Death, The Spook Sonata*], tr. by Edwin Björkman and N. Erichsen (New York and London, 1949).

Six Plays of Strindberg [*The Father, Miss Julie, The Stronger, Easter, A Dream Play, The Ghost Sonata*], tr. by Elizabeth Sprigge (Garden City, N.Y., 1955).

Five Plays of Strindberg [*Creditors, Crime and Crime, The Dance of Death, Swanwhite, The Great Highway*], tr. by Elizabeth Sprigge (Garden City, N.Y., 1960).

Three Plays by August Strindberg [*The Father, Miss Julia, Easter*], tr. by Peter Watts (Penguin Books, London, 1958).

Seven Plays by August Strindberg [*The Father, Miss Julie, Comrades, The Stronger, The Bond, Crimes and Crimes, Easter*], tr. by Arvid Paulson with an Introduction by John Gassner (New York, 1960).

Miss Julie and Other Plays [*Miss Julie, The Creditor, The Stronger, Woman, Motherly Love, Pariah, Simoon*], no translator indicated (New York, Modern Library Series, [1918]).

Pariah, Simoon: Two Plays by August Strindberg, tr. by H. B. Samuel (London, 1914).

The Anglo-Swedish Literary Foundation's edition of Strindberg's plays includes:
Easter and Other Plays [*Easter, The Dance of Death, The Ghost Sonata*, and *A Dream Play*], tr. by E. Classen, C. D. Locock, and Erik Palmstierna and James Bernard Fagan (London, 1929).

Lucky Peter's Travels and Other Plays [*Lucky Peter's Travels, The Father, Lady Julie, Playing with Fire*, and *The Bond*], tr. by E. Classen, C. D. Locock, Elizabeth Sprigge, and Claude Napier (London, 1930).

Master Olof and Other Plays [*Master Olof, Gustav Vasa, Erik XIV*, and *The Saga of the Folkungs*], tr. by C. D. Locock and Joan Bulman (London, 1931).

To Damascus. A Trilogy. English version by Graham Rawson (London, 1939).

Selected historical plays, tr. with Introductions by Walter Johnson:
Queen Christina, Charles XII, Gustaf III (Seattle and New York, 1955).
The Last of the Knights, The Regent, Earl Birger of Bjälbo (Seattle, 1956).
Gustav Adolf (Seattle and New York, 1957).
The Vasa Trilogy [*Master Olof, Gustav Vasa*, and *Erik XIV*] (Seattle, 1959).
The Saga of the Folkungs [and] *Engelbrekt* (Seattle, 1959).

PLAYS SEPARATELY ISSUED OR APPEARING IN ANTHOLOGIES
AND PERIODICALS

Advent, tr. by C. Field (London, 1913; Boston, 1914).
Comrades, tr. by H. B. Samuel (London, 1914).
Countess Julia, tr. by C. Recht (Philadelphia, 1912).
The Creditor, tr. by H. B. Samuel (London, 1914).
The Creditor, tr. by F. J. Ziegler (Philadelphia, 1910).
The Dream Play, tr. by Edwin Björkman in *Contemporary Drama: European Plays*, III. Selected with Introductory Notes by E. Bradlee Watson and Benfield Pressey (New York, 1933).
Easter, and Stories, tr. by Velma S. Howard (Cincinnati, 1912).

Easter. A new translation for the theatre and an Introduction by Elizabeth Sprigge (London, 1949).

Facing Death, tr. by O. M. Johnson ([Easton, Pa., 1911]).

The Father, tr. by N. Erichsen (London, 1899, 1911; Boston, 1907).

The Father, tr. by N. Erichsen in *Chief Contemporary Dramatists,* selected and edited by Thomas H. Dickinson (Boston, 1915).

The Ghost Sonata, tr. by Elizabeth Sprigge in *The Play: A Critical Anthology,* ed. by Eric Bentley (New York, 1951).

The Great Highway, tr. by Arvid Paulson in *Modern Scandinavian Plays* (New York, 1954).

Lucky Pehr, tr. by Velma S. Howard (Cincinnati, 1912).

Master Olof, tr. with an Introduction by Edwin Björkman (New York, 1915).

Motherlove, tr. by F. J. Ziegler (Philadelphia, 1910, 1916).

The Pelican, tr. by Evert Sprinchorn. In *The Tulane Drama Review,* iv (March, 1960), 117–43.

Swanwhite, tr. by F. J. Ziegler (Philadelphia, 1909).

There Are Crimes and Crimes, tr. by Edwin Björkman (New York, 1912).

To Damascus. A Dream Trilogy in Three Parts, tr. by Sam E. Davidson (Boston, 1913). In *Poet Lore* [Boston], xlii (Spring, Autumn 1933; Winter 1935) 1–70, 99–155, 195–264.

To Damascus. Paperback reissue of the Anglo-Swedish Literary Foundation's edition (New York, 1960).

Three One-Act Plays [*The Outcast, Simoon, Debit and Credit*], tr. from the German of Emil Schering by Mary Harned, in *Poet Lore,* xvii (Autumn 1906), 1–37.

PROSE FICTION

By the Open Sea, tr. by Ellie Schleussner (London and New York, 1913).

Easter, and Stories [the "stories" consist of a selection from *Sagor*], tr. by Velma S. Howard (Cincinnati, 1912).

Fair Haven and Foul Strand, [no translator indicated] (London, [1914]). Though the title of this volume is taken from Strindberg's *Fagervik och Skamsund,* a miscellany of prose and poetry, only the two so-called Doctor's Stories (the second of which is autobiographical) are included in this English translation.

The German Lieutenant and Other Stories, tr. by C. Field (London and Chicago, 1915).

Married: Twenty Stories of Married Life, tr. by Ellie Schleussner (London, 1913, 1915; New York, 1917).

Married [and] *Miss Julie,* Modern Library series (New York, 1925).

The Martyr of Stockholm [orig. *På godt och ondt*], tr. by C. Field (London, 1914).

On the Seaboard, tr. by Elizabeth Clarke Westergren (New York, 1913). Same novel as the Schleussner translation *By the Open Sea.*

"Paul and Per" and "The Votive Offering," two short stories, tr. by C. D. Locock in *Modern Swedish Short Stories* (London, 1934).

The People of Hemsö, tr. by Elspeth Harley Schubert (London, 1959).

The Red Room, tr. by Ellie Schleussner (London and New York, 1913).

Tales, tr. by L. J. Potts (London, 1930).

AUTOBIOGRAPHICAL WORKS (IN THE ORDER OF THEIR APPEARANCE IN SWEDISH)

The Son of a Servant and *The Growth of a Soul,* both tr. by C. Field (New York and London, 1913, 1914), include the first two volumes and a couple of chapters from the third of the autobiographical tetralogy *Tjänstkvinnans son,* completed in 1886.

The Confession of a Fool, tr. by Ellie Schleussner (London, 1912, 1913). Reissued, with a Preface by Ernest Boyd (New York, 1925).
"The Doctor's Second Story" in *Fair Haven and Foul Strand* (London, [1914]).
The Inferno, tr. by C. Field (London, 1912; London and New York, 1913).
Legends: Autobiographical Sketches, [no translator indicated] (London, 1912). A continuation of *The Inferno.*
"The Return Home" [first chapter of *Ensam,* 1903], tr. by Aksel G. S. Josephson, *The American-Scandinavian Review,* 1 (July 1913), 9–13.

MISCELLANEOUS PROSE

Historical Miniatures, tr. by C. Field (London, 1913).
Letters of Strindberg to Harriet Bosse, ed. and tr. by Arvid Paulson (New York, 1959).
Zones of the Spirit: A Book of Thoughts, tr. by C. Field with an Introduction by Arthur Babillotte (New York and London, 1913). Selections from Strindberg's so-called *Blå böcker.*

Gustaf af Geijerstam

Big and Little Brother, tr. by B. B. Lifschultz (Chicago, 1930).
The Book about Little Brother: A Story of Married Life, tr. by Edwin Björkman (New York, 1921).
My Boys: A Holiday Book for Big and Little, tr. by Alfhild Huebsch (New York, 1933).
Woman Power, tr. by Esther Rapp (New York, 1927).

Tor Hedberg

Borga Gård. A Play in Four Acts, tr. by Helga Colquist, *Poet Lore,* XXXII (1921), 317–74.
Johan Ulfstjerna. A Drama in Five Acts, tr. by Helga Colquist, *Poet Lore,* XXXII (1921), 1–63.

Other Authors of the 1880's

Victoria Benedictsson, *Truls Jonasson,* tr. by K. Ählström (London, 1895).
Ola Hansson, *Young Ofeg's Ditties,* tr., with an Introductory Note, by George Egerton [Mary Chavelita Bright] (London and Boston, 1895).
Anne-Charlotte Leffler, *True Women. A Play in Three Acts,* tr. by H. L. Brækstad (London, [1885?]).
Axel Lundegård, *The Storm Bird. A Historical Silhouette with Background and Frame,* tr. by Agnes Kilgour (London, 1895).

THE POETIC RENAISSANCE OF THE 1890's

Verner von Heidenstam

The Birth of God, tr. by Karoline M. Knudsen (Boston, 1920).
The Charles Men, tr. by C. W. Stork, with an Introduction by Fredrik Böök (New York, 1920; London, 1933), 2 vols. A translation of *Karolinerna,* earlier rendered into English by A. Tegnier under the title *A King and His Campaigners* (London, 1902).
Christmas Eve at Finnstad, tr. by Margareth Sperry (Stockholm, 1950).
Fem berättelser hämtade från "Karolinerna." Five Stories Selected from the "Karolines," tr. by Agnes A. Allnutt (London and New York, 1922). Bilingual Series, Swedish and English texts.
The Soothsayer, tr. by Karoline M. Knudsen (Boston, 1919).

Sweden's Laureate. Selected Poems of Verner von Heidenstam, tr., with an Introduction, by C. W. Stork (New Haven, 1919).

The Swedes and Their Chieftains, tr. by C. W. Stork (New York, 1925). Tales illustrative of Swedish history for school children.

The Tree of the Folkungs, [no translator indicated] (London and Copenhagen, 1925). American ed. of same work tr. by A. G. Chater (New York, 1925).

Selma Lagerlöf

PROSE FICTION

Charlotte Löwensköld, tr. by Velma S. Howard (New York, 1927).

Christ Legends, tr. by Velma S. Howard (New York, 1908). Later illus. American and English editions.

The Emperor of Portugallia, tr. by Velma S. Howard (New York and London, 1917, 1926).

From a Swedish Homestead, tr. by Jessie Bröchner (New York and London, 1901; New York, 1923).

The General's Ring, tr. by Francesca Martin (New York and London, 1928).

The Girl from the Marshcroft, tr. by Velma S. Howard (Boston, 1910; Garden City, N.Y., 1916, 1924).

Gösta Berling's Saga, tr. by Lillie Tudeer (London, 1898; New York, 1918). New eds. tr. by Lillie Tudeer and Velma S. Howard (New York, 1928, 1960). New ed. London, 1933.

The Story of Gösta Berling, tr. by Pauline B. Flach (London and Boston, 1898; many later editions).

Herr Arne's Hoard, tr. by A. G. Chater (London, 1923). American ed., with title *The Treasure* (New York, 1925).

Invisible Links, tr. by Pauline B. Flach (Boston, 1899; later eds. 1909, 1912, 1918).

Jerusalem, tr. by Velma S. Howard (New York, 1915; frequently reprinted). *The Holy City: Jerusalem II*, tr. by Velma S. Howard (New York, 1918; frequently reprinted).

The Legend of the Sacred Image, tr. by Velma S. Howard (New York, 1914).

Liliecrona's Home, tr. by Anna Barwell (London, 1913; New York, 1914).

The Miracles of Antichrist, tr. by Pauline B. Flach (London and Boston, 1899; Boston, 1910). Another English rendering of this novel by Selma Ahlström Trotz (New York, 1899).

The Outcast, tr. by W. Worster (London, [1920]; New York, 1922, 1927).

The Queens of Kungahälla and Other Sketches, tr. by C. Field (London, [1917]).

The Ring of the Löwenskölds. A Trilogy including *The General's Ring, Charlotte Löwensköld*, and *Anna Svärd* tr. by Francesca Martin and Velma S. Howard (New York, 1931).

The Tale of a Manor and Other Sketches, tr. by C. Field (London, 1923).

The Treasure, tr. by A. G. Chater (New York, 1925). American ed. of *Herr Arne's Hoard* (London, 1923).

Thy Soul Shall Bear Witness! tr. by W. F. Harvey (London, 1921). Swedish original: *Körkarlen*.

AUTOBIOGRAPHY, PEDAGOGICAL FANTASY, AND ADDRESSES

Mårbacka, tr. by Velma S. Howard (New York and London, 1921; New York, 1924, 1931).

Memories of My Childhood: Further Years at Mårbacka, tr. by Velma S. Howard (New York and London, 1934).

The Diary of Selma Lagerlöf, tr. by Velma S. Howard (New York and London, 1936).

The Wonderful Adventures of Nils, tr. by Velma S. Howard (New York, 1907). Frequently reissued, often in illustrated editions.
Further Adventures of Nils, tr. by Velma S. Howard (New York and London, 1911). Other eds.
Harvest, tr. by Florence and Naboth Hedin (New York and London, 1935).

Gustaf Fröding

Gustaf Fröding, Selected Poems. Tr. with an Introduction by C. W. Stork (New York, 1916).
Guitar and Concertina. A Century of Poems by Gustaf Fröding. Tr. in the Original Metres by C. D. Locock (London, 1925).

Erik Axel Karlfeldt

Arcadia Borealis: Selected Poems of Erik Axel Karlfeldt. Tr. with an Introduction by C. W. Stork (Minneapolis, 1938).

Ellen Key

Love and Marriage, tr. by A. G. Chater. With a Critical and Biographical Introduction by Havelock Ellis (New York and London, 1911).
The Morality of Woman and Other Essays, tr. by Mamah B. Borthwick (Chicago, 1911).
Rahel Varnhagen, tr. by A. G. Chater. With an Introduction by Havelock Ellis (New York and London, 1913).
The Renaissance of Motherhood, tr. by Anna E. B. Fries (New York and London, 1914).
Torpedo Under the Ark: Ibsen and Women, tr. by Mamah B. Borthwick (Chicago, 1912).
The Woman Movement, tr. by Mamah B. Borthwick. With an Introduction by Havelock Ellis (New York and London, 1912).
The Younger Generation, tr. by A. G. Chater (New York and London, 1914).

Albert Engström

Twelve Tales by Albert Engström, tr. by H. Borland. With a Foreword by R. Ekblom (London, 1949). Bilingual Series, text in both Swedish and English.

Per Hallström

Selected Short Stories, tr. with an Introduction by F. J. Fielden (New York, 1922).
Short Stories. Selected and translated by F. J. Fielden (London, 1933).

In addition to the titles listed above under each author of the 1890's, the reader is referred to the prose collections *Modern Swedish Masterpieces*, *Sweden's Best Stories*, and *Modern Swedish Short Stories*, in which three volumes Heidenstam is represented with seven stories, Selma Lagerlöf with two, Hallström with three, and Engström with five, and to the poetic anthologies *Modern Swedish Poetry* and *Anthology of Swedish Lyrics from 1750 to 1925*, in which two volumes Heidenstam is represented with twenty-seven translations, Fröding with eighteen, Karlfeldt with thirty-five, and Levertin with ten.

REALISM RENEWED AND CHALLENGED. THE MODERNISTIC GROUND SWELL AND ATTENDANT SOCIAL CRITICISM. MODERNISM TRIUMPHANT AND ITS AFTERMATH

Because of the complex patterns of development and the diverse literary personalities in Swedish literature of the last half century, I have here felt it best (after briefly calling attention to certain collective works) simply to list in alphabetical order representative translated authors of our century, followed in each instance by the book-length titles in which their work has appeared under their names in English. In listing translated authors I have deliberately included some who are acceptable rather than distinguished or even distinctive. I have ignored only those translated authors who in my judgment are quite negligible.

Though Swedish poetry of our century has been rather extensively translated, the quality of the translations not infrequently leaves much to be desired, particularly in the two volumes edited by M. S. Allwood, *20th Century Scandinavian Poetry* (Mullsjö, Sweden, 1950) and *Swedish Songs and Ballads* (Mullsjö, Sweden, 1950), in which the English renderings range from excellent to atrocious. Locock's translations in *Modern Swedish Poetry* (London, 1929) are, on the other hand, uniformly competent and at times inspired. The most distinguished English renderings of strictly "modernistic" contemporary Swedish verse are those by Richard B. Vowles, whose translations are unfortunately, however, scattered in numerous places, some of them appearing in *20th Century Scandinavian Poetry*, others in *New World Writing*, nr. 11 (New York, 1957), and still others in various American journals, usually as accessory to critical essays on the poets concerned. Of interest also is the little bilingual volume *modern swedish poems* (Rock Island, 1948), which includes, besides two excellent translations by Richard B. Vowles, twenty-six not always satisfactory renderings by other hands into English of contemporary Swedish poetry.

In prose fiction the two volumes *Modern Swedish Masterpieces*, tr. by C. W. Stork (New York, 1923) and *Modern Swedish Short Stories*, tr. by various hands (London, 1934) are devoted largely to the twentieth century, while *Sweden's Best Stories*, tr. by C. W. Stork (New York, 1928), includes substantially more short stories from the nineteenth century than from the twentieth century. Of these three works, those selected and translated by Stork are relatively conservative in the choice of stories included, while the volume entitled *Modern Swedish Short Stories* ranges much more imaginatively in choice of material, including in its English renderings such central figures in recent Swedish literature as Hjalmar Bergman and Pär Lagerkvist, Agnes von Krusenstjerna and Eyvind Johnson.

The Swedish drama of our day is represented in *Scandinavian Plays of the Twentieth Century*: First and Third Series, tr. by various hands and with Introductions by Alrik Gustafson (Princeton and New York, 1944, 1951).

Of general interest are the English versions of both verse and prose from a cross section of contemporary Swedish authors (Tage Aurell, Frans G. Bengtsson, Hjalmar Bergman, Karin Boye, Stig Dagerman, Pär Lagerkvist, Artur Lundkvist, and Harry Martinson) available in the October 1949 issue of *Life and Letters, continuing The London Mercury*.

Aside from the material from various authors of the twentieth century included in the works mentioned above, the following individual authors are represented in English by book-length works (or works originally of book length) as indicated.

Dan Andersson

Charcoal-Burner's Ballad & Other Poems, tr. by Caroline Schleef (New York, 1943).

Frans G. Bengtsson

The Long Ships. A Saga of the Viking Age, tr. by Michael Meyer (New York and London, 1954). Reissued (New York, 1957) in an inexpensive paperback edition.
Red Orm, tr. by Barrows Mussey (New York, 1943). Translation of the first volume of the Swedish original *Röde Orm*, both volumes of which are translated by Michael Meyer in *The Long Ships*.
A Walk to an Ant Hill and Other Essays, tr. by Michael Roberts and Elspeth Schubert (New York, 1951).

Hjalmar Bergman

God's Orchid [*Markurells i Wadköping*], tr. by E. Classen (New York, 1924).
The Head of the Firm, tr. by Elizabeth Sprigge and C. Napier, with an Introduction by R. G:son Berg (London, 1936).
Thy Rod and Thy Staff [*Farmor och Vår Herre*], tr. by C. Napier (London, 1937).
Mr. Sleeman Is Coming, tr. by Henry Alexander in *Scandinavian Plays of the Twentieth Century*, First Series, (Princeton and New York, 1944).
The Swedenhielms, tr. by Henry Alexander and Llewellyn Jones in *Scandinavian Plays of the Twentieth Century*, Third Series (Princeton and New York, 1951).

Stig Dagerman

A Burnt Child: A Novel, tr. by Alan Blair (London, 1950).
The Condemned, tr. by Henry Alexander and Llewellyn Jones in *Scandinavian Plays of the Twentieth Century*, Third Series (Princeton and New York, 1951).
The Games of Night, tr. by Naomi Walford (London, 1960).

Dagmar Edqvist

The Marriage of Ebba Garland, tr. by Elizabeth Sprigge and C. Napier (London, 1933).
Brave Fugitive, tr. by Paula Wiking (London and Toronto, 1935).

Gösta Gustaf-Janson

The Old Man's Coming, tr. by C. Napier (New York, 1936).

Olle Hedberg

Prisoner's Base (London, 1932).

Gustaf Hellström

Lacemaker Lekholm Has an Idea, tr. by F. H. Lyon (London, 1930).

Eyvind Johnson

Return to Ithaca: The Odyssey Retold as a Modern Novel, tr. by A. M. Michael (London and New York, 1952).

Ragnar Josephson

Perhaps a Poet, tr. by Holger Lundbergh in *Scandinavian Plays of the Twentieth Century*, First Series (Princeton and New York, 1944).

Pär Lagerkvist

Barabbas, tr. by Alan Blair, with a Preface by Lucien Maury and a letter by André Gide (New York, 1951). Reissued as a Modern Library Series paperback (New York, 1951).
The Dwarf, tr. by Alexandra Dick (New York, 1945). Reissued in paperback edition (New York, n.d.).
The Eternal Smile and Other Stories, translations by Alan Blair, Erik Mesterton, Denys W. Harding, and Carl Eric Lindin. With an Introduction by Richard B. Vowles (New York, 1954).
The Eternal Smile, tr. by Denys W. Harding and Erik Mesterton (Cambridge, 1934).

Guest of Reality, tr. by Erik Mesterton and Denys W. Harding (London, 1936).
Includes — besides *Guest of Reality* — *The Eternal Smile* and *The Hangman.*
The Marriage Feast, tr. by Alan Blair (London, 1955).
The Sybil, tr. by Naomi Walford (New York, 1958).
Let Man Live, tr. by Henry Alexander and Llewellyn Jones in *Scandinavian Plays of the Twentieth Century*, Third Series (Princeton and New York, 1951). Reprinted in *Religious Drama 3*, selected and introduced by Marvin Halverson (New York, 1959).
The Man without a Soul, tr. by Helge Kökeritz in *Scandinavian Plays of the Twentieth Century*, First Series (Princeton and New York, 1944).
Midsummer Dream in the Workhouse. A Play in Three Acts, tr. by Alan Blair (London, 1953).

Rune Lindström

A Play Which Tells of a Road That Leads to Heaven (Stockholm, 1941).

Bertil Malmberg

Åke and His World, tr. by Marguerite Wenner-Gren (New York and Toronto, 1940).

Harry Martinson

Cape Farewell, tr. by Naomi Walford (London and New York, 1934).
Flowering Nettle, tr. by Naomi Walford (London, 1936).
The Road [*Vägen till Klockrike*], tr. by M. A. Michael, with an Introduction by P. F. D. Tennant (London, 1955).

Vilhelm Moberg

The Earth Is Ours [*Knut Toring*], tr. by Edwin Björkman (New York, 1940).
The Emigrants, tr. by Gustaf Lannestock (New York, 1951).
Memory of Youth, tr. by Edwin Björkman (New York, 1938). The first volume of the original Swedish trilogy *Knut Toring* translated entire under the title *The Earth Is Ours.*
Ride This Night!, tr. by Henry Alexander (New York, 1943).
Unto a Good Land, tr. by Gustaf Lannestock (New York, 1954). *The Emigrants* and *Unto a Good Land* are English versions of *Utvandrarna* and *Invandrarna*, the first two volumes of Moberg's monumental tetralogy on Swedish immigration to the United States. The last two volumes, *Nybyggarna* and *Sista brevet till Sverige*, will appear in English in a single volume early in 1961.
When I Was a Child, tr. by Gustaf Lannestock (New York, 1956). A sharply condensed English version of Moberg's autobiographical novel *Soldat med brutet gevär.*
Fulfillment. A Play in Five Acts, tr. by M. Heron (London, 1953). A dramatization of the short novel *Mans kvinna.*

Peter Nisser

The Red Marten, tr. by Naomi Walford (New York, 1957).

Fritiof Nilsson Piraten

Bombi Bitt. The Story of a Swedish Huckleberry Finn, tr. by Paula Wiking (London, 1933).

Sigfrid Siwertz

Downstream [Selambs], tr. by E. Classen (London and Copenhagen, 1922).
Goldman's [Det stora varuhuset], tr. by E. Gee Nash (London, 1929).

Hjalmar Söderberg

Martin Birck's Youth, tr. by C. W. Stork (New York and London, 1930).
Selected Short Stories by Hjalmar Söderberg, tr. by C. W. Stork (Princeton and New York, 1935).

Sven Stolpe

The Maid of Orleans, tr. by Eric Lewenhaupt (New York, 1956).
Sound of the Distant Horn. A Novel, tr. by George Lamb (New York, 1957).

Mention may finally be made in these twentieth-century contexts of the little collection of contemporary Swedish poems issued by The Swedish Institute, Stockholm, and tr. by Carolyn Hannay and J. M. Nosworthy entitled *Some Swedish Poems* (1958) and of C. D. Locock's happy rendering especially of the verse of Bo Bergman, Anders Österling, and Harriet Löwenhjelm in Locock's *Modern Swedish Poetry*.

The Pronunciation of Swedish Names

The ACCENT in Swedish normally falls on the first syllable, even in words with a double accent, in which latter case, however, the second accent is the stronger of the two. Many words of foreign derivation, especially those from the French, place the accent usually on the final syllable.

VOWEL sounds in Swedish differ not infrequently from their English equivalents:

a, which has no equivalent to the long *a* in English (as in *hate*), is pronounced usually in Swedish like the *a* in *tall* or the first *a* in *aha*: Lagerkvist, Bellman

i likewise has no equivalent to the long *i* in English (*high*), but is pronounced rather like the *i* in *machine*: Lidner, Lidman

e falls roughly between the sound of *e* in *they* and the *i* in *pit*, or the *e* in *them* and the *i* in *swim*: Lenngren, Tegnér

o is similar to the *oo* in *stool* or like the *o* in *hope*: Atterbom, Leopold

u is pronounced roughly like the *u* in *yule*, but with rounded, almost closed lips: Rudbeck

y, similar to the French *u* in *une*; like the Swedish *i* pronounced with rounded lips: Rydberg, Snoilsky

å, like the *o* in *lore*: Bååth, Fridegård

ä, roughly like the *a* in *care*: Värnlund

ö, like the French *eu* or German *ö* (*œ*) as in *böse*: Fröding, Lagerlöf, Söderberg

The vowels generally are pronounced long (in *duration*) before a single consonant, short before double consonants.

The DIPHTHONG *ei* is sounded like the *ay* in *hay*: Geïjer, Heidenstam

It is usually safe to pronounce Swedish CONSONANTS like their English equivalents, except in the following instances:

d, *g*, *h*, and *l* are silent before *j*: Gjörwell, Ljungquist

g, *k*, and *sk* are pronounced hard before *a*, *o*, *u*, and *å*; soft before *e*, *i*, *y*, *ä*, and *ö*: Gullberg, Gierow, Karlfeldt, Kellgren

g after *r* is nearly always pronounced soft: Strindberg, Moberg

j, like *y*, except in words of French origin, where it is like a thick *sh*: Jonsson, Jändel *ng*, always like the *ng* in English *singer*, never like *finger*: E*ng*ström, I*ng*elgren

gn within a word is pronounced like the Swedish *ng*: Teg*n*ér, Stag*n*elius

sj, *skj*, *sti*, and *stj* are, like the soft Swedish *sk*, pronounced somewhat like the English *sh*, but with a rather rougher texture: *Sti*ernhielm, *Sj*öberg, Krusen*stj*erna

th, like *t*: *Th*omas, *Th*orild

w, like *v*: S*w*edenborg, *W*allin, Si*w*ertz

Index

THIS is an index of names, places, titles, and subject matter extracted from the body of the present book and, less exhaustively, from its Bibliographical Guide. It does not cover the data and commentary provided in the section entitled "A List of Translations into English." The page numbers *in italics* under a given author refer to the main entry, while all page numbers *within parentheses* indicate the bibliographical entry or entries for the author or subject concerned. Titles are listed alphabetically in their original Swedish forms, followed immediately within parentheses by their English equivalents whether or not they have been translated into English. In those cases where they have been translated the abbreviation "tr." has been placed before the translated title, which in the case of full-length books (novels, plays, longer poems, etc.) is italicized. The English titles of translated works have also been listed separately, followed immediately in each instance by the abbreviation "tr." Titles of newspapers, magazines, and journals are in all cases cited only in their original Swedish forms. Subentries are in most cases listed in alphabetical order. Entries beginning with the Swedish letters å, ä, and ö are placed, as in Swedish usage, at the close of the alphabetical listing.

674

hero, 415, 477; monologue, inner monologue, 396, 404, 494, 498, 539; multiple planes, 499; multiple point of view, 495; "narrative frame" device, 498; objectivity, 537; pace, 511; panoramic manner, 516; patterns, 519, 536; scene, 404, 418, 558; stories within stories, 494; stream-of-consciousness techniques, 441, 524; structure, point of view, 389, 404, 494, 506, 510, 556, 561; symbolical usages, 397, 403, 419–20, 516, 545; variety of forms, 556; visionary scenes and episodic sequences, 403, 404. *See also* Style, prose

Prosody: practices and developmental changes, 35–36, 45, 46, 83, 88, 109, 147, 149, 150, 151, 158, 160, 164, 224, 228, 261, 283, 317, 334, 360–61, 362, 365, 402, 409, 411, 424, 428, 429, 433, 443, 460, 468, 471, 478, 481, 482, (569, 579, 580, 589); alexandrine, 36, 83, 149, 158; alliterative patterns, 35, 168; "bardic" verse, 150; blank verse, 36, 158, 411; canzone, 158; cadences, broken, 409; couplet rhyming on runic inscriptions, 35; dactyls, 109, 151, 283; dithyrambs, 160; doggerel verse (*knittelvers*), 35–36, 83; free, flexible verse, 150, 283, 362, 365, 471; hexameter, 36, 83, 88, 147, 158, 224, 228; ottava rima stanza, 158; refrain, in ballad, 45, 46; rhymed and unrhymed verse, 36, 147, 334, 365, 402, 478, 482; rhythms, 334, 365, 409, 424, 428, 429, 433, 443, 468, 481, 482; terza rima, 460

Proust, Marcel, 355, 441, 492, 494, 542, (639)

Proverbs, 23, 50, (575)

Provincetown Players, 272

Provincial laws, of Middle Ages, 3, 12, 19, 21–23, 25, 37, 38, 42, 395, (574)

Psalm Book, of 1819, 187

Psalms. *See* Poetry, poetic genres

Publicity, and American business procedures, Hj. Bergman's commentary on, 386

Publishers: Bonniers, 265, 490–91; Spektrum, 490

Purism, stylistic: Rydberg's championing of, 234, (600)

Purpur (Purple), 343–44

På marsch (On the March), 428–29

På Torpa gård (On Torpa Farm), 278

Påsk (tr. *Easter*), 271, 273

"Pälsen" (tr. The Fur Coat), 358

Quakers, 369–70, 378, 430

Quarterly Review, The, 202

Queen Christina, tr., 271

Queens of Kungahälla, The, tr., 308, 310

Quillfeldt, Ch. de, 284

Rabelais, François, 374

Racine, Jean, 108, 137, 457

Radicalism: in mid-19th century, 211, 230–31; in 1880's and late 19th century, 230, 240, 250, 251, 292, 317–19, 345; around 1920, 427ff., 430; around 1930, 466–67, 478. *See also* Labor movement; Leftist literary predilections; Modernism; Politics; Socialism

Ragvaldi, Phillipus, 37

Rallare (construction worker), in work of Hedenvind-Eriksson, 417–20

Ramido Marinesco, 208

Ramsundsberg rock carving, 8

Raskens, 501, 502

Rationalism, of 18th century, Romantics' disapproval of, 168, 180, 187

Reading public: expansion of, 78, 113, 201, 218, 248, 347–48; bitter commentary on, 384–85; difficulty of adjustment to Hj. Bergman, 384, to Lagerkvist, 404, to modernistic poetry and prose generally, 466; enlightenment provided by journals and newspapers, 442

Realism

Development of: latent in Gustavian era, 143; in mid-19th century, 203, 245; beginnings of modern, 201–4, (595); sharp breakthrough of in 1880's, 244–54, 258–59, 260–67, 275–78, 280, 284–87, (601ff.); persistence of in 20th century, 345ff., 351–56, 367, 368–83, 412–24, 426–31, 445–46, 469–72, 477, 486–88, 495–97, 500–29, 544, 547, 557, 558

Types of: documentary, 392–93, 534; everyday, 216, 221, 332, 428, 436, 512, 523; folkloristic, 286; "healthy" (*sund realism*), 243; idealistic, 177; idyllic, 428, 430; impressionistic, 133, 215; middle-class, 220–21; mixed, with fantasy, symbol, etc., 399, 516, 521, 533, 556; photographic, 290; poetic, 224, 237, 280–81, 289, 294, 367, 428; racy, 298–99

Reality: attitude of authors of 1950's toward world of, 563; in Ekelöf's work, 479–80; Fröding and world of, 317; precarious balance between "real" and "imagined" worlds in Strindberg, 271, 273

Reconvalescentia, 318

Red Room, The, tr., 213, 240, 244, 246, 255, 257, 258–59, 260, 269, 270, 276, 357, (606)

16; influence on 20th-century literature, 443, 479, 480, 562, 563; and naturalistic convictions, 317; and radicalism, 190, 205–8. *See also* Romanticism

Romanticism, Swedish: general characteristics, 153–60; chief poets, 160–97; persistence of and reactions against, 199, 201, 202–3, 205–13, 221, 223, 226, 231, 242, 294–95, 562. *See also* New Romantics, Pre-Romantic literature

Rome, 29, 77, 128

Rondeletius, Jacobus Petri, 69

Rosa rorans, 25–26

"Rosen i världsfurstens park" (The Rose in the Prince of the World's Park), 194

Rosen på Tistelön (tr. *The Rose of Tistelön*), 219–20

Rosenkransen (The Crown of Roses), 558–59

Rosenstein, Nils Rosén von, 118

Rosimunda, 108–9

Roslagen, 335

Rosmersholm, 242

Rossetti, Dante Gabriel, 293

Rougon-Macquart series, 386

Rousseauism, 111, 126, 128, 146, 177, 206, 209–10, 262

Rovdjuret (The Beast of Prey), 447–48

Royal Dramatic Theater, 136, 256, 279, 447, 448

Royal Guards Prison, 129

Royal Library, Stockholm, 242, 257, 327

Royal Opera, founding of, 136

Royal Society (English), 109

Rudbeck, Olaus, 78, 79, 80, 82, 84, 90–95, 116, 119, 171–72, 241, (579–80)

Rudbeckius, Johannes, 71, 79

Rum för ensam dam (Room to Let for Single Lady), 527

Runa Förbundet, 256

Runeberg, Johan Ludvig, 202, 204, 221–29, 230, 236, 240, 280, 304, 311, 316, 317, 361, 432, (598–99)

Runes, runic inscriptions, and runology, 4–10, 12–13, 35, 80, (572)

Runius, Johan, 83, 102, 103, 105–6, 131, (580)

Rural conditions, 375, 439, *et passim*

Rural society: communal culture of, 324–27, 329–35, 379, 503–6; in Dalarna, 310–12, 324–27, 329–35, 420–22, 423–24; least-favored class, 514–23; in Norrland, 373–75, 415–16, 417–20; in Närke, 528–29; in Skåne, 280–81, 284–87, 365–68; in Småland, 335, 377–79, 499–514; in Värmland, 309–15, 319–20, 536; in Västerbotten,

550–51; in Östergotland, 523. *See also* Countryside, Peasants and peasantry

Russia, 156, 179, 239, 426, 429, 431, 475; literary influence of, 249, 275, 464, 515

Rustgården, 282

Rydberg, Viktor, 202, 203, 204, *230–36*, 243, 250, 361, (599–600)

Rymmare och fasttagare (Runaways and Captors), 524–25

Ryttaren (The Equestrian), 563

Rågvakt (Rye Watch), 523

"Räddningsbåten" (The Life Boat), 371

Rättfärdiggörelsen genom tron (Justification by Faith), 431

Rääf, L. F., 170

Röda rummet (tr. *The Red Room*), 212, 240, 244, 246, 255, 257, 258–59, 260, 269, 270, 276, 357, (606)

Röde Orm (tr. *The Long Ships*), 530, 532

Röde prinsen (The Red Prince), 284

Rök stone, runic, 8

Rølvaag, O. E., 510, 513

Saarijärvi, 223, 227

Sacco and Vanzetti, 430

Saga of the Folkungs, The, tr., 32, 269, 271

Saga om en saga och andra sagor, En (tr. *A Saga About a Saga and Other Sagas*), 313

"Sagan om dimman och lungsoten" (The Saga About the Fog and Tuberculosis), 496

"Sagan om gral" (tr. The Story of the Grail), 323

"Sagan om hästen" (The Tale About the Horse), 116

Sagas and saga material, 13, 93, 162, 167, 170; Selma Lagerlöf's indebtedness to, 308; Tegnér's "modernizing" of, 182–83. See also *Fornaldarsaga*, Icelandic sagas

Sagofolket som kom bort (Saga Folk Who Disappeared), 420

St. Paul, the Apostle, 192

Saint Simonism, 175

Saints' legends, 22, 25, 26. *See also* Petrus de Dacia

"Sakrament" (Sacrament), 462, 463

"Salomos insegel" (tr. Solomon's Seal), 319

Salvation Army, 482

Samlade dikter (Collected Poems; by Atterbom), 164, 168

Samlade skrifter (Collected Works; by Stagnelius), 165–66, 190

Sand, Arne, 562